David McNeill

Processing of
Visible Language

Volume 1

Processing of
Visible Language

Volume 1

Edited by

Paul A. Kolers

University of Toronto
Toronto, Ontario, Canada

Merald E. Wrolstad

Visible Language Journal
Cleveland, Ohio

and

Herman Bouma

Institute for Perception Research
Eindhoven, The Netherlands

PLENUM PRESS · NEW YORK AND LONDON

Library of Congress Cataloging in Publication Data

Main entry under title:

Processing of visible language.
  "Proceedings of the conference held at the Institute for Perception Research, IPO,
Eindhoven, the Netherlands, September 4–8, 1977."
  Includes indexes.
  1. Reading, Psychology of – Congresses. I. Kolers, Paul A. II. Wrolstad, Merald
Ernest. III. Bouma, H.
BF456.R2P79   153   79-13530
ISBN 0-306-40186-X

Proceedings of the conference held at the Institute for Perception Research,
IPO, Eindhoven, the Netherlands, September 5–8, 1977

©1979 Plenum Press, New York
A Division of Plenum Publishing Corporation
227 West 17th Street, New York, N.Y. 10011

Printed in the United States of America

Introduction

The organization of the page as a technological device and our acquisition
of information from it were subjects of keen interest to psychologists and
designers a century ago. Research on the topics proceeded briskly for more
than a quarter of a century then, and was brought together in the still useful
survey and analysis of them all that E.B. Huey published in 1908 as "The
psychology and pedagogy of reading, with a review of the history of reading
and writing and of methods, texts, and hygiene in reading."

Research on the psychological aspects of literacy tended to diminish after
that peak, but research on design and on the technology of presenting information has flourished apace meanwhile. Perhaps somewhat stimulated by
the reissue of Huey's book by MIT Press in 1968, psychologists have returned
to the study of literacy. The symposium that the present volume reports
was an effort to bring together again psychologists interested in literacy
and related forms of information acquisition, graphics designers, and engineers
actively involved in the development and deployment of the newer technology.

During this century, psychologists, graphics designers, and engineers have
lost much of the mutual communication that their joint enterprise should
encourage. The design of machines has often followed the convenience of
packaging, the design of displays has often followed the designer's personal
esthetic. Perhaps psychologists have been remiss in allowing the study of
literacy and related forms of symbol manipulation to escape from their field
of study; had they retained their interest, perhaps now there would be greater
cooperation among the three disciplines. The point here is that the machine
is designed for human use; at the same time the machine elicits forms of
human function not otherwise seen. The psychologist can inform the designer
and the engineer about the characteristics of human performance; the
designer and the engineer can create circumstances that extend its range.
By coming together and sharing knowledge, specialists in the various fields
may provide useful insights for each other.

The research reported in the present volume spans the range of interest in literacy as a process: for the psychologist, from the acquisition of skills in identifying or recognizing alphabetic elements and the rules that govern their combination, through models characterizing the recognition of individual words, to the interpretation of texts and the use of libraries; for the designer of displays, from the design of pictographic elements for international signs, through maps as display devices, to the organization of texts; and for the engineer, the research reported ranges from interaction with a computer-based television set to find out what movies are at the local cinema to a description of one form of office of the future.

The development of interest in communication processes has been remarkably rapid in the past few decades; it has been stimulated by the rise of the computer and technology associated with it, by developments in the formal representation of language, and by a return by psychologists to an interest in cognitive processes. If a decade or two ago could be denoted "The age of anxiety," we may well be into the age of information or the age of communication. Electronics as the means of routing information--in cables, microwaves, or laser beams--has been one of the major humanistic contributions of the last hundred years and will continue to change our relation to each other and to the world's resources of information and knowledge.

It seems likely that over the near term we will witness a major change in the way we access stored information. A reasonable assumption is that the professional user of information--scientist, engineer, physician, student--will spend his hours not among his books, journals, or the shelves of a library, but will sit at a keyboard to call up much of the wanted information, which will appear immediately on a screen or be printed out at his desk. This is not to say, as some do, that the day of the printed page is past; such a day is not foreseeable, for books will remain portable objects of pleasure and affection, even of instruction, for still some time. It is to say that the way we gain access to information of immediate need is likely to change. The present symposium would have been timely and useful even if such changes were not imminent; the likelihood of change makes it even more so.

Psychologists and educators know a great deal about some of the constituents of the human reader's performance. Designers of graphics know a great deal about the appearance of pages and of type. Engineers are informed in the techniques required to get electrons to do wonders. The difficulty for synthesis is that the practitioners have gone their separate ways, so psychologists know little about typography or technology, designers know little about human performance, and engineers sometimes have been indifferent to both. A symposium designed to enhance interaction among practitioners of the three disciplines can be only a good thing therefore.

Pages still form an important part of our commerce with stored information. How should they best be laid out, how should text and illustration be paired, what sorts of information require what sorts of display? Some of the present symposium is concerned with practical questions of presenting information in printed form; some of it is concerned with theoretical issues of the representation of information in the reader's mind. Aspects of design and a schema for classifying designs form a substantial contribution; and engineers discuss some promises of technology and characteristic uses for the future. The intention of the organizers of the symposium was that the three disciplines would receive equal weight in the whole; but as events developed, psychological aspects of literacy were given a heavier weighting than the other two. We offer no apology for this imbalance; indeed, it reflects something of the vigor and excitement psychologists seem to be experiencing as they rediscover the printed word as a worthwhile stimulus for manipulation. Moreover, the renewed interest of psychologists in this topic may be timely in an additional sense: the opportunity to provide input to designer and engineer as we all learn new techniques and new strategies of literacy directed at the electronic page.

The symposium was held at Geldrop, The Netherlands, from September 4-8, 1977, sponsored by the Institute for Perception Research of Eindhoven. It was funded by generous grants from Philips Research Laboratories, Technological University of Eindhoven, Netherlands Ministry of Education and Sciences, and the International Reading Association. The symposium was conducted on an interactive basis, people talking about rather than reading their papers, and revisions of initial drafts were aided by notes taken by members of the Institute for Perception Research, particularly D. Bouwhuis, B. Breimer, V. van Heuven, S. Marcus, and H. Timmers. Manuscripts were edited by Charlotte Stevenson, and set by Barbara Wright and Joan Cherry. (Consistent with the international attendance at the conference, spelling and related orthographic conventions were not forced into a single format but preserved the conventions of the writer's national style.) Many of the arrangements for the conference were handled by Mieke Boerrigter, Rosalind Smith, and other members of the Institute's staff. To all of these, the editors and participants extend their thanks. We hope that future symposia will result in the same warm interaction that this one did.

P.A. Kolers
M.E. Wrolstad
H. Bouma

Contributors

Alan Allport

Department of Psychology
University of Reading
Reading RG6 2AL, England

A.D. Baddeley

MRC Applied Psychology Unit
15 Chaucer Road
Cambridge CB2 2EF, England

Philip Barnard

MRC Applied Psychology Unit
15 Chaucer Road
Cambridge CB2 2EF, England

H. Bouma

Institute for Perception Research
Box 513
5600 MB Eindhoven
The Netherlands

Don G. Bouwhuis

Institute for Perception Research
Box 513
5600 MB Eindhoven
The Netherlands

Lee Brooks

Department of Psychology
McMaster University
Hamilton, Ontario, Canada L8S 4K1

Thomas H. Carr

Department of Psychology
Michigan State University
East Lansing, Michigan 48824, U.S.A.

L.J. Chapman   Faculty of Educational Studies
                                The Open University
                                Milton Keynes MK7 6AA, England

Colin Cherry   Imperial College of Science and Technology
                                University of London
                                London SW7 2BT, England

Wim Crouwel   Association for Total Design N.V.
                                Herengracht 567
                                Amsterdam, The Netherlands

Arthur O. Eger   S.A.R.A.
                                De Boelelaan 4101
                                Amsterdam-Buitenveldert
                                The Netherlands

Dennis F. Fisher   U.S. Army Human Engineering Laboratories
                                Aberdeen Proving Ground
                                Maryland 21005, U.S.A.

Jeremy J. Foster   Department of Social Science
                                Manchester Polytechnic
                                Manchester 15, England

Uta Frith   MRC Developmental Psychology Unit
                                Drayton House, Gordon Street
                                London WC1H 0AN, England

Anne Groat   Department of Psychology
                                University of Stirling
                                Stirling FK9 4LA, Scotland

H. Hoekstra   Philips Data Systems
                                Apeldoorn, The Netherlands

Richard Jackson   Philips Research Laboratories
                                Salfords, Nr. Redhill
                                Surrey, England

Mogens Jansen   The Danish Institute for Educational Research
                                28, Hermodsgade
                                CK2200 Copenhagen, Denmark

P.A. Kolers   Department of Psychology
                                University of Toronto
                                Toronto, Ontario, Canada M5S 1A1

Lester A. Lefton   Department of Psychology
                                    University of South Carolina
                                    Columbia, South Carolina 29208, U.S.A.

Ariane Levy-Schoen   Laboratoire de Psychologie Expérimentale
                                        et Comparée
                                    28, Rue Serpente
                                    75006 Paris, France

C.A. Linden   Computer Laboratory
                                    University of Cambridge
                                    Cambridge CB2 3QG, England

Tony Marcel   MRC Applied Psychology Unit
                                    15 Chaucer Road
                                    Cambridge CB2 2EF, England

Dominic W. Massaro   Department of Psychology
                                    University of Wisconsin
                                    Madison, Wisconsin 53706, U.S.A.

George W. McConkie   Children's Research Center
                                    University of Illinois
                                    Champaign, Illinois 61820, U.S.A.

Amina Miller   Department of Psychology
                                    McMaster University
                                    Hamilton, Ontario, Canada L8S 4K1

John Morton   MRC Applied Psychology Unit
                                    15 Chaucer Road
                                    Cambridge CB2 2EF, England

Kevin O'Regan   CNRS, Laboratoire de Psychologie
                                    54, Boulevard Raspail
                                    75006 Paris, France

Richard J. Phillips   Department of Psychology
                                    University College London
                                    London WC1E 6BT, England

Alexander Pollatsek   Department of Psychology
                                    University of Massachusetts
                                    Amherst, Massachusetts 01002, U.S.A.

A.K. Pugh   The Open University
                                    Yorkshire Region
                                    Leeds LS2 8JU, England

Keith Rayner   Department of Psychology
                                  University of Massachusetts
                                  Amherst, Massachusetts 01002, U.S.A.

Shulamit S. Reich   Academic Department of Psychiatry
                                  Middlesex Hospital Medical School
                                  London W1P 8AA, England

Robert I. Rosenthal   Bell Laboratories
                                  Holmdel, New Jersey 07733, U.S.A.

Wayne L. Shebilske   Department of Psychology
                                  University of Virginia
                                  Charlottesville, Virginia 22901, U.S.A.

Philip T. Smith   Department of Psychology
                                  University of Stirling
                                  Stirling FK9 4LA, Scotland

Michael Twyman   Department of Typography and
                                        Graphic Communication
                                  University of Reading
                                  Reading RG6 2AU, England

Richard L. Venezky   Department of Educational Foundations
                                  University of Delaware
                                  Newark, Delaware 19711, U.S.A.

Robert H.W. Waller   Institute of Educational Technology
                                  The Open University
                                  Milton Keynes MK7 6AA, England

P. Wilcox   MRC Applied Psychology Unit
                                  15 Chaucer Road
                                  Cambridge CB2 2EF, England

N. E. Wiseman   Computer Laboratory
                                  University of Cambridge
                                  Cambridge CB2 3QG, England

P. Wright   MRC Applied Psychology Unit
                                  15 Chaucer Road
                                  Cambridge CB2 2EF, England

M.E. Wrolstad   Visible Language
                                  Box 1972, CMA
                                  Cleveland, Ohio 44106, U.S.A.

Contents

Eye Movements in Search and Reading

Introduction

P.A. Kolers

Measurement of the eyes' movements was one of the first interests of the early investigators of reading; indeed, onset of the empirical study of reading and discovery that the eyes move saccadically have approximately similar dates. The French ophthalmologist Emile Javal published a series of articles in 1878-1879 that seem to be the first documentation of the eyes' errant behavior. His observations both startled the scientific community of the time and, incidentally, set a limit to the uses of introspection as the source of data regarding cognitive processes. From introspection alone one would be unlikely to guess that the eyes moved in jumps; the compelling introspective experience seems to be that the eyes move smoothly and continuously along a line of print when one is reading. That this is not a correct interpretation can be gathered from a moment's observation of someone else's eyes while he or she reads. The saltatory nature of the movements is quite visible and, indeed, somewhat unnerving.

The counter-intuitive nature of the discovery of the eyes' searching movements induced a number of investigators to measure the event, and heroic measures they were, in both senses of the word. After-images of bright lights, observed while one read a line; ink or dye or other markers placed on the surface of the eye; plaster cups to which string galvanometers or other, related, marking systems were attached, were placed on or over the eye--these were just a few of the techniques used. Their very cumbersomeness, the imprecision of the resulting measurements, and the large cost/benefit ratio that related difficulty in making the measurements to their worth, allowed interest in the subject to wane for a while.

Using photographic methods in the 1920's and 1930's, Buswell and Tinker revived the subject somewhat, but these methods too proved unwieldy, generating large amounts of data (photographic film) in small amounts of time. Recent developments in electronics have enabled psychologists and engineers to undertake a new approach.

3

Two different sorts of question have been asked. The biophysically-oriented investigator has been most interested in control of the eyes' movements -- the action of the neuromuscular system, its commands, the feedback loops, the velocity of movement, and related parameters that characterize the movement as a physical event. Several models have been developed and, indeed, several volumes have been devoted to discussion of them. The psychologically oriented investigator has been interested more in models of information processing that sampling eye movements implicate. The biophysical experiment characteristically studies the eye making one or two movements in response to signals that the investigator provides. The psychological experiment characteristically studies the sampling movements across time, a few seconds' worth at least, and more if possible. (Even with contemporary technology investigators have not been able to track the eye for more than a few seconds at a time. We are in fact almost wholly ignorant of the statistics that would describe the eyes' movements over extended intervals. There is no telling what will happen to current controversies and the models associated with them when technology permits measurements to extend over longer periods of time -- say 20 min or 40 min of continuous reading.)

Much of what is known regarding characteristics of the reader is surveyed in the paper by Levy-Schoen and O'Regan, who provide both an historical and an intellectual introduction to the subject. After surveying a number of conditions that have been found to affect the measured movements, characteristics of the reader and characteristics of the text, they confront one of the key controversies among contemporary students of eye movements during reading -- the nature and degree of control of individual movements. Indeed, this question is dealt with by all of the papers on eye movements. On one side are the views of McConkie, for example, who argues for absolute control of every saccade, the control system computing on the basis of each fixation where the eye is to go next. Apparently supportive data are provided by O'Regan in his report on THE-skipping (the fact that the eye tended to skip over the word THE in the displays O'Regan used). Set in opposition to the direct control view is the notion of autonomy -- that the eyes move to their own rhythm, more or less inflexibly, and with little concern for local variation in the nature of the text. It is not clear, however, who holds this view at the present time. Even those who argue for absence of rigid control allow for the fact that the control system clearly is sensitive to the nature of the information acquired in a fixation; Buswell's data collected almost. sixty years ago showed the eye maintaining fixation on approximately the same place while the reader struggled with an unfamiliar or difficult word. Hence, rather than as a controversy between rigid control and no control, the issue might better be put as one of deciding the conditions under which the control system participates either closely or loosely in the information acquisition process. What, for example, would a proponent of rigid control claim is the case when the reader has drifted off into that state in which his own internal drama dominates his reading, discovering many pages later that he has only a remote notion (if any notion at all) of what he has been "reading"? A model that holds that the eyes move more or less autonomously accounts for this perfectly. But what, for a counter example, would the proponent of autonomy claim about the prolonged fixations that Buswell discovered? A closely controlled system more readily accounts for that.

The experiments by Rayner seem to argue for modest control at the level of recognition of words and sentences. Other aspects of the perceptuo-motor processing are developed in the studies by Fisher and by Lefton, both of whom demonstrate that habits and skills dominate much of the processing of text. Adults are particularly hampered by unfamiliar word forms. A right-to-left word order with normal word form gave less difficulty. Thus, perceptually, it appears that text is a succession of words, but a word is not a succession of letters. Capping this line of argument is the paper by Shebilske and Reid, whose implication might be taken as the notion that too fine a look at details can limit understanding of the processes of understanding itself.

Hence, the consensus seems to be that there is some control of eye movements, but exactly how much and under what conditions and to what purpose are questions remaining to be answered. Meanwhile, the ingenuity underlying the way the questions are operationalized in experiment, and the technology that provides the answers, are themselves full of pleasure and delight.

The Control of Eye Movements in Reading (Tutorial Paper)

Ariane Levy-Schoen and Kevin O'Regan

The first part of this paper reviews recent data on how the characteristics of eye movements in reading depend on three classes of experimental variables: those related to the reader (age, reading skill); those related to the material being read (overall appearance, difficulty, word length); and a third class, the attitude of the reader toward the text (search versus comprehension).

In the second part, a distinction is made between global eye movement measures (average over a number of lines of text), and local ones (measures made for a single position on text). Local measures are of interest because of the psycholinguist's hope that they will reflect ongoing sentence processing. For this hope to be realistic, it must be shown that the eye movement control mechanisms are sufficiently rapid to allow the eye's course to be adjusted immediately on the basis of the information being gathered at every instant. The evidence presently available shows the possibility of immediate control of fixation duration, and "almost immediate" control of saccade size.

Reading is a basic and constant occupation for most people. We are bombarded by written material, words pop out of posters and signs and, even if we try to avoid them, our eyes seem driven to read them.

For a good definition of the mechanisms at work in reading, let us cite Carmichael and Dearborn (1947): "Reading involves patterned movements of the eyes and adjustments of the eyes themselves to bring into appropriate view, in a suitable temporal order, symbols which are to be perceived as words or phrases. These words and the processes which are related to them then evoke images, ideas and action and lead to states called by such names as comprehension and enjoyment." If Carmichael and Dearborn do not define the output of reading activity very clearly, they do emphasize the sensory-motor adjustments necessary to maintain suitable visual input. These will be our concern.

In reading, the serial temporal order of language is recreated from written text by the eyes' scanning movements. What kind of control is exerted over eye movements so that they are adequate for the decoding operations involved? The visual input is provided through the combined functioning of both eyes whose sensory field is often considered to be divided into a central fovea and a peripheral region. The foveal part of the binocular field of vision (about 2 deg wide) permits fine form discrimination and a feeling of high certainty, usually corresponding to what the observer is "focussing his attention" on. The peripheral part (more than 180 deg of aperture) provides "ambiant vision" giving global localization of elements within the field, with lower resolution and a low level of certainty, but equal sensitivity to motion.

Psychophysiologists have provided much data concerning the possibilities and limits of the oculomotor system. For good reviews of the present state of this research, see Jung, 1972; Ditchburn, 1973; or the symposium edited by Lennerstrand and Bach-y-Rita, 1975. The human oculomotor system is an elaborate machine working in several different modes adapted to several different vital functions. In locomotion (and body movements) an automatic compensation mechanism guarantees precise compensation of body movements, allowing the gaze to maintain fixation on stable targets. In the observation of mobile objects or scenes, a tracking mechanism also allows the gaze to follow a target in a "smooth pursuit" motion, thereby maintaining fixation upon it. A different system, the saccadic, effects high speed displacements of fixation from one target to another. This system, usually in operation in the observation of stationary scenes, produces discontinuous scanning behaviour of alternating saccades and fixations. Reading eye movements are a particular instance of such scanning behaviour. In fact, the three systems are always in constant interaction: while reading, for instance, the head may move quite freely without destroying the organization of scanning.

The oculomotor mechanisms just described move both eyes in conjunction. The disjunctive mechanism of convergence, associated with accommodation, enables the distance of the gaze to be adjusted. It is not clear whether the associated drifts or glissades sometimes observed during fixation pauses are controlled and adaptive, or instabilities of the system. (For details, see Weber & Daroff, 1972; Steinman, Haddad, Skavenski, & Wyman, 1973; Ditchburn, 1973.)

Another question concerns the distinction between fixations and saccades. The simplified, generally accepted view is that fixations and saccades are easily distinguishable states and that visual perception is efficient only during the pauses. However, psychophysiological experiments leave several points unclear. Is there a limit between what are usually called saccades (corresponding to a change in target) and microsaccades (corresponding to readjustments or slight drifts occurring during fixation)? Is vision ineffective or is it only modified during high speed saccadic jumps, and is there a "clearing up period" following a saccade?

While these psychophysiological questions are relevant in defining the low-level limits constraining oculomotor scanning activity, they do not

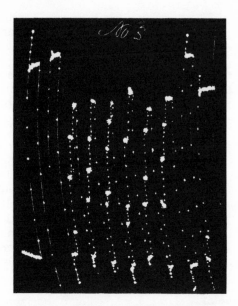

Figure 1. "Spark" record made by Huey, 1900. This record was obtained
on a smoked drum by the motion of a light stylus attached to the eye with
a plaster cup. Time was marked by rhythmical electrical sparks through
the stylus.

necessarily bear on higher level eye movement control involving, for example,
the choice of target or the kind of scanning strategy adopted.

In order to understand how reading may work, one has to understand how
text is explored. Conversely, to know how the gaze scans a text may help
us to know how this text is processed. For both these reasons, we will consider how eye movements are controlled during reading. First, we will briefly
recall the techniques currently used in recording these types of eye movements.
We will then review currently relevant data concerning eye movements in
reading: What are their characteristics? What makes them change? Finally,
we will try to answer a question critical to the formulation of models of eye
movement guidance: What is the time-scale over which eye movement control
is effective?

Before beginning, a note of warning is necessary. An understanding of
eye movement control is only one step toward an understanding of reading,
indeed, it is a step that is useless by itself. The problems of the prerequisites
for reading and learning to read, on a cognitive, perceptual, and social level,
constitute a large and important domain which must be pursued simultaneously,
but which must remain untouched by this review.

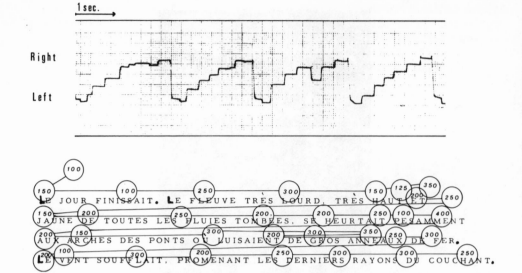

Figure 2. An example of a classical recording of horizontal eye movements in reading. This kind of record can be obtained by electro-oculography as well as by photo-electric techniques. The fixation locations on successive lines and their durations have been subsequently marked upon the text being read.

CURRENT DATA CONCERNING EYE MOVEMENTS IN READING

Current Recording Techniques

To an acceptable degree of approximation (for details see Ditchburn, 1973), visual centering upon a plane stationary display, such as a page of text, corresponds to the virtual crossing of the two ocular globe axes with this plane. Technically, determining the position centered upon is difficult because of problems of interference with the ocular activity itself, of calibration, of elimination of artefacts associated with periocular muscular activity, blinks and lid movements, ambiant illumination, and so on.

Starting a century ago, inventive and dynamic pioneer researchers discovered and analysed the saccadic movements during reading (Lamare, 1893; Huey, 1900; Dodge, 1907; Buswell, 1920; Kolers, 1976, has described some of Buswell's reading data; and Carmichael & Dearborn, 1947). Using corneal plaster cups or sunshine reflection, they had sufficiently solved the technical problems to enable them to study most aspects of reading eye movements. Today, even with more sophisticated instruments, the main characteristics of eye movements during reading still remain those defined by Dodge and Buswell.

Nevertheless, modern computerized techniques (Mason, 1976; O'Regan, 1978) open the way to better knowledge in two ways: first, quantitatively, they provide more observations in less tedious experimental situations. Second, qualitatively, the experimental conditions can be better controlled, thus giving better data: through "real time" control, "contingent" experimental paradigms can be set up where the situation (visual stimulus for instance) can be made dependent on the subject's ocular response.

Among the criteria making eye movement apparatus suitable for work in reading, the most difficult to obtain is enough absolute precision in a horizontal visual field subtending about 20 deg to permit reliable distinction of about 60 letter positions. (Usually, printed matter is read from a distance of about 30 cm. Lines 12 to 15 cm long (= 20 to 25 deg) contain from 50 to 80 Characters, of width ¼ to ½ deg. Another criterion is sampling rate: fixation durations often differ by only a few tens of milliseconds, so a 20 msec sampling rate is about the slowest acceptable. Finally, it is very useful to have eye position sampled directly by a computer.

Young and Sheena (1975) give an exhaustive review of current eye movement recording methods. It is worth noting that most methods take recordings from only one eye, making the implicit, but perhaps unjustified, assumption that the eyes are perfectly conjugate. Carmichael and Dearborn (1947) have noted that in reading, some systematic de- and re-convergence may occur from fixation to fixation. This may give rise to artefacts in monocular recordings.

General Characteristics of Ocular Activity during Reading

Although one has the impression during reading of sweeping one's gaze smoothly over the print, the actual motor activity is essentially discontinuous. The succession of pauses and saccadic jumps which occurs is similar to what happens in ordinary visual exploration of a motionless scene. Figures 1, 2, and 3 show records typically obtained during reading. Three types of movement

Figure 3. An automatically calibrated record displayed on a computer screen, showing the text read and the eye positions, sampled every 10 msec, correctly placed with respect to the text. Time is on the ordinate. (O'Regan, 1975).

can be discerned:

Progressive Movements.(in the forward reading direction). The amplitude
of these movements or saccades depends on the dimensions of the text, not
on the visual angle. The eyes stop on every one or two words, independent
of the distance at which the text is read.

Regressive Movements.(backwards). These movements are rare relative to
progressions (about once per line in general). They are also smaller in amplitude, approximately half the length of progression saccades.

Return Sweeps.(bringing the eye from the end of each line to the beginning
of the next). Undershoots often occur, that is, the eye makes a large leftward
movement to near the beginning of the line, followed by what may be interpreted as a small (1 to 2 deg) corrective movement, also leftward.
    The standard saccade rate is 3 to 5 per sec. Since one reading eye move-
ment takes about 20 msec to execute (50 to 100 msec for the return sweeps),
the eye is stationary during nine-tenths of the total reading time.
    Figure 1 shows an engraving of one of Huey's (1900) "spark recordings"
made using direct attachment of a plaster cup to the eye. Figure 2 gives
an example of the typical "step like" record currently obtained by a pen recorder, which shows the horizontal displacement of the eyes as related to time.
Figure 3 is a record from modern computerized apparatus, by which eye position is sampled every 10 msec and automatically localized in relation to letter position in the line of text (O'Regan, 1975).
    Figure 4 shows distribution of eye movement characteristics as given
by Andriessen and de Voogd (1973). Large samples such as this provide grossly
consistent estimations. In silent reading of an easy text, fixation durations
average around 200 msec with an overall standard deviation of about 60 msec
(Andriessen & de Voogd, 1973). In another study, they center around 260
msec, with a standard deviation of around 100 msec (Levy-Schoen, unpublished
data). Massé (1976) found 80% of the fixation durations included between
150 and 300 msec. Lesèvre (1964) found a mean for progression fixations
around 225 msec, with an intra-individual standard deviation of around 40
msec. All of these studies obtained saccade amplitudes, centering around
8 character spaces for progression movements, and about 4 or 5 characters
for regressions.

Sequential Correlations.   In order to discover the regularities of the oculomotor reading behaviour, the relation between successive saccades or pause
durations has been investigated. Lesèvre (1964) observed that the last fixation
on a line has a significantly shorter duration than other fixations (also Abrams
& Zuber, 1972). Dearborn's finding (cf. Carmichael & Dearborn, 1947) that
the first fixation in the line is longer than the others does not seem to be
confirmed. Lesèvre (1964) concluded in favour of a stable "oculomotor pattern"
in reading, showing for instance that, when followed by a regression saccade,
progression movements are wider and pauses briefer than when followed by
another progression. Andriessen and de Voogd (1973) looked for sequential
correlations between durations of successive fixations, successive saccade
extents, and durations and extent of successive fixations and saccades. They

also showed that after a large forward saccade, the relative frequency of regressions increases, and that, after small progressions or return sweeps, fixation durations are somewhat shorter. But they concluded that these effects are slight and that only in a few cases might some correlation exist. Rayner and McConkie (1976) also concluded that sequential relations between successive saccade lengths or fixation durations are very low.

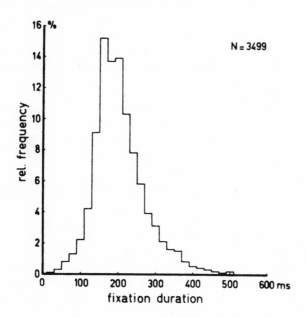

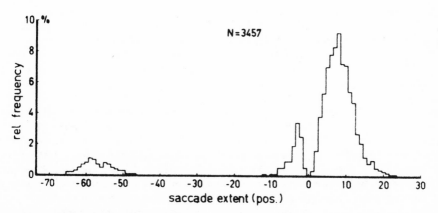

Figure 4. The distribution of fixation durations (a) and of saccade extents (b) during silent reading. Fixation durations are measured in msec and saccade extents in character spaces, either rightwards (positive) or leftwards (negative). Reproduced from Andriessen and de Voogd, 1973.

Cunitz and Steinman (1969) compared the characteristics of eye movements in reading a text to those while examining a capital letter T. They
found that inter-saccadic time intervals had similar distributions, suggesting
that the same control mechanisms could be at work in both activities.

Variables Known to Influence Reading Eye Movements
The variables whose influence on reading eye movements have been studied
can be classified into three categories: those related to the reader (development, individual differences, disabilities); those related to the text (graphic
layout, linguistic structure, content); and a third class, the attitude of the
reader toward the reading task, which may vary from great concentration
on meaning or graphic details, to "automatic" line scanning.

Variables Related to the Reader
Development. How is the transition from the early "deciphering" to later
fluent reading reflected in eye movements? Surprisingly, there is little
change in the essential characteristics of eye movements in the course of
learning to read. The underlying succession of saccades exists from the
beginning, although the fact that the finger is often used to guide the eye
suggests that some help is needed in developing the efficiency of this motor
activity.

Several experimental investigations of eye movements in school children
generally agree about the aspects that change with age (Taylor, 1960, cited
by Shebilske, 1975; Lesèvre, 1964; Spragins, Lefton, & Fisher, 1976). Reading
speed increases from less than 100 words per minute in first or second grade
to more than 250 words per minute in adults. Silent reading seems to increase
speed with respect to oral reading only when a certain degree of skill has
been attained. The number of forward movements per line decreases, each
movement becoming bigger: from about 3 character spaces in second grade
to 6 to 8 in adults (Lesèvre, 1964; Spragins et al., 1976). This increase in
saccade size suggests that more material is encompassed by each fixation:
from about half a word in the earlier grades to around 1.2 words later. The
number of regressions decreases from 40 per 100 words in first grade to 15
per 100 in college (Taylor) or, from 70 to 6 per 100 words (Lesèvre).

Data on the evolution of fixation durations are not wholly agreed upon.
While classical data claim a decrease in mean fixation duration from elementary classes to adults (Taylor: 330 to 240 msec; Spragins: 400 to 230
msec), Lesèvre observes a different pattern, 205 msec in first grade, 215
msec for adults, passing through a maximum of 240 msec around 10 years
of age (see Figure 5). It appeared that, in this latter study, what decreased
through the first age groups was the number of very brief pauses, interpreted
as corrected fixations. This bimodal distribution of reading eye movement
durations diminishes with age. It is interpreted by the author as an aspect
of progressively better "oculomotor praxis" and "ocular stability," appearing
also in a non-reading task (scanning rows of crosses).

These effects may be compared to developmental characteristics of eye
movements in picture inspection. An evolution appears more in the progressive
concentration of the fixation durations around an overall mean value than
in the reduction of this value: very short and very long pauses are more frequent in the scanning behaviour of young children (Moal, 1978). In a study

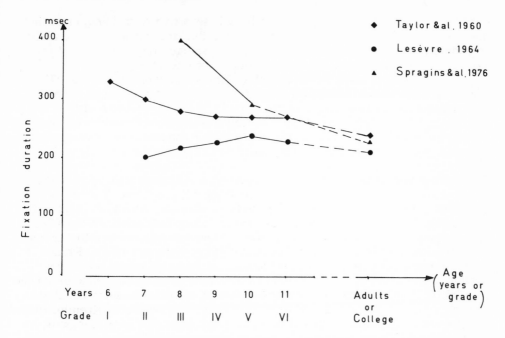

Figure 5. The evolution with age of the mean duration of reading fixations in children, plotted from data given by three authors.

by Mackworth and Bruner (1970), 6-year-old children inspect or recognize blurred or clear pictures. Their eye movements, compared to those of adults in the same situation, show shorter fixation durations, together with a tendency to make many very small movements instead of "leaps." They distribute their fixations over a restricted area "placing them less skillfully over informative areas" and seeming "hooked by the details." This is consistent with a combined progress in sensory-motor ocular skill and in the ability to select and process significant material.

In summary, increased reading proficiency in growing children appears, in oculomotor behaviour, essentially as a reduction of the number of movements and pauses necessary to scan the text. This trend disappears at approximately age 10 when ocular behaviour seems to become stable (Tinker, 1965).

Training for Fast Reading. It is tempting to conclude that efficient reading can be achieved by merely training the eye to make larger, more rhythmical movements. This notion has been at the basis of a plethora of speed reading programs. Serious investigations of what really happens in these conditions (most recently Lee, 1973; Stoll, 1974; see Gibson & Levin, 1975, for some older references) have shown that ocular behaviour is indeed sensitive to training. The changes that may occur are: reduced number of eye movements and fixations, reduced proportion of regressions, and even slightly shorter fixation durations. But ocular rhythm may become more irregular and, most important, comprehension does not necessarily improve. Stoll's (1974) experiment shows that oculomotor activity is sensitive to training, or to mere non-specific encouragement. "What is true is that those who have the ability to understand quickly and to memorize well also have the possibility of reading fast. This ability is not always spontaneously utilized."

In fact, we have come no further than Tinker's conclusion in 1958: "The improvement obtained by such training (eye movement training or training to provide improved eye movements in reading), with or without elaborate apparatus, is no greater than that resulting from well-motivated reading practice alone." Morton (1966), in his "Two-hour reading course" has given a convincing demonstration of this point.

Eye Movements of Disabled Readers: Dyslexias. Children with reading disabilities are not rare, and pose serious pedagogical problems. They have been shown to produce more fixations with smaller saccades than those with no reading difficulties (Lesèvre, 1964, 1968; Rubino & Minden, 1973). Fixation durations do not differ significantly. A kind of ocular instability or hyperactivity, detected by Lesèvre in dyslexic children, is also found by Roland (1972) in stutterers. Again, the problem of cause and effect is not solved: oculomotor behaviour and its anomalies may be a mere consequence of slowed information intake caused by comprehension problems. The same conclusion seems to hold for alexia related to brain damage (cf. review by Kremin, 1976; Hartze, 1972; Stennett, Smythe, Pinkney, & Fairbairn, 1972-73; Zangwill & Blakemore, 1972).

There is consensus among psychologists that reading disability is not usually caused by oculomotor dysfunction. However, this has not prevented a large number of workers, principally educational, from interpreting eye movements correlated with slow reading as "inefficient" eye movements (Grossman & Philips, 1973; Friedman, 1974a, b; Griffin, Walton, & Ives, 1974; Heiman & Ross, 1974; Walsh, 1974; Dossetor & Papaioannou, 1975).

Effects of Fatigue and Drugs. No more recent study of the effect of fatigue on eye movements in reading has come to our notice than the famous reading marathons of Carmichael and Dearborn (1947) (12 hours in all). Despite complaints from the subjects, no significant changes in global oculomotor parameters (fixation duration, number of fixations, and regressions) were found. The effect of drugs on reading behaviour has not been studied thoroughly, although Stern, Bremer, and McClure (1974) found that administration of Valium slowed reading, long fixations becoming more frequent, and the velocity of return sweeps decreasing. This last effect may be due to general interference with oculomotor characteristics.

In summary, oculomotor behaviour in reading consists of a stable scanning program which is set up almost as soon as children start to read. The parameters of the program that differ most between individuals are the spatial distribution of the pauses along the line: length of forward displacements and number of regressions. The rhythm of fixation pauses seems to vary little, so that when a person can only read slowly, he does so by making shorter saccades and more regressions, rather than by significantly altering the basic three or four per second fixation rate. From these facts it follows that apart from an (apparent) gain in "scientificity" through the use of complicated technology, measuring global eye movement differences amounts to no more than measuring differences in mean saccade size. But this is just another measure of reading speed. It tells us how people read faster but it will not tell us why some read faster than others. Sociocultural factors concerning, for example, the necessity for children to know the difference between pictorial and written material (Ferreiro, 1978), perceptual or cognitive variables involving, for example, the "perceptual span" for letters vs. letter strings (Jackson & McClelland, 1975; Willows, 1974), or for words in sentences (Marcel, 1974), all represent areas where research on individual differences may help more in understanding reading than work on global eye movement measurement. We believe that eye movement research will help to understand reading when small local variations in eye movement parameters are studied, since these may reflect the moment-to-moment mechanisms involved in reading.

Variables Related to Text.
If one supposes that a reader is engaged in an iterative decoding activity in order to comprehend the written signs he is reading, one can consider the succession of fixations as an interface which must be paced in time and space so as to collect the visual information in an optimal manner. Therefore one can expect the oculomotor parameters to vary according to those characteristics of the text which are critical for this decoding process.

Graphic Features.   Sensory constraints such as limitations in visual resolution, and lateral masking effects when graphical elements are in close proximity (Bouma, 1978), suggest that certain text layouts and type faces might hamper reading. Numerous investigations by Tinker and Paterson in the 1930s and 1940s (Tinker, 1965) provide data about the influence of graphic features, print case, colour, etc. upon eye movements, thus measuring "legibility." They show, for instance, that in contrast with lower case print, capital print is read with more fixations, a decrease in pause duration, and no change in regression frequency. On the other hand, when the size of letters and spaces is changed, fixation duration remains the same, and average saccade length adjusts so that about the same number of characters is covered in each fixation (Gilliland, 1923; Javal, 1879; Huey, 1900).

Such studies were motivated by the practical considerations of finding out what kind of print was most legible. Lately, however, of interest are more theoretical issues concerning the roles of character shape, spacing, and word length in the process of identifying words. Fisher (1976) and Spragins et al. (1976), found that alternating capital and lower case letters slows down both reading and search, more than all capital letters do. Filling or suppressing inter-word spaces reduces scanning speed by one half or one third. This is related to a reduction of saccade size rather than to the slight increase in fixation duration.

The above studies do not distinguish whether letter shape and spacing have their effects by acting through the foveal or peripheral visual field. This can be done by using experimental paradigms where computerized real-time analysis of gaze position allows the text display to be altered as a function of where the subject is looking. In a study by O'Regan (1975), the text to be read, presented on a computer display screen, was seen by the subject through a kind of moving "window" 15 character positions wide, whose centre the computer always maintained at the subject's point of fixation. The text outside the window was mutilated by the computer so that only word length information remained available. This was done by replacing all letters outside the window by X's, but leaving spaces untouched. Subjects could read quite normally and were unable to see the X's, even when informed of their presence. And yet oculomotor parameters were affected: the longest saccades were shortened, and average fixation durations decreased.

A more sophisticated experiment by McConkie and Rayner (1975) attempted to distinguish the relative importance of individual letter and overall word shape information in peripheral vision. They also used a moving window, except instead of merely having X's displayed outside the window, they used more subtle mutilations. In one condition, letters outside the window were replaced by similar letters, but overall word shape was preserved. In this condition fixation durations increased, but less than when word shape was not preserved.

Although the exact changes involved were different in the two studies, O'Regan, and McConkie and Rayner agreed that fixation durations can be altered by modifying the information about letter and word shape available in peripheral vision. However, while O'Regan found an effect of word shape on saccade length, McConkie and Rayner did not. The difference may have something to do with differences in the speed at which the computer made the display changes. In the McConkie and Rayner study, a condition was included in which word length information was destroyed outside the moving window by filling the spaces between words. The authors found that this significantly decreased the size of saccades while fixation durations were unaltered.

Other studies showing the sensitivity of saccade size to word length and spacing information will be described in the section on eye movement control models. Here, it is worth noting that while there is a consensus that spacing and word length affect saccade size, this does not necessarily mean that the eye is "aiming" for a particular point in a word. This is suggested by a pilot study by O'Regan where the text was slipped slightly forward or backward every time the subject made a saccade. If the movement of the text is no larger than about ¼ of the size of the saccade in which it occurs, then, under certain conditions, subjects are not only unable to discern anything odd occurring, but they make no correction saccades. If the phenomenon is confirmed by further work (McConkie, this volume) then it would appear that the precise position at which the eye arrives in a word is immaterial.

In summary, oculomotor patterns are sensitive to graphic cues, such as the spaces between words, word length, and word shape, which may permit peripheral pre-coding and adjustment of the eye movements both in time and space. These same variables are of course the ones that influence performance in a static perceptual task such as identification of words briefly presented in the peripheral field (Bouma, 1973, 1978; Schiepers, 1976), or discovery of targets in conditions of visual noise (Engel, 1976, 1977). It is tempting to speculate that the cues involved are utilized by the oculomotor control mechanisms before they come into the observer's awareness.

Text Content and Organization   If eye movement adjustments depend on graphic features, are they also sensitive to language structure or content?

It is common sense to say that one can read easy texts more quickly than difficult texts. What makes a text "easily" readable? And which characteristics of ocular scanning are modified?

Words. As will be mentioned in the section on eye movement control mechanisms, studies by Rayner and McConkie (1976) and O'Regan (1975) show that the probability of a fixation falling on a word depends on its length. Concerning fixation duration, at least in reading or pronouncing a single word, an effect of implicit speech (Klapp's 1971 syllable effect) can be found, related to the fact that a word takes longer to identify when it requires more time to pronounce. Thus, when subjects scanned a sequence of small drawings in order to report on them later, longer durations were found by Pynte (1976) in looking at a drawing labelled by a long word (French "helicoptère") than a short word ("pont"), word frequency being constant. In 1974, Pynte had found a similar effect when subjects were silently reading a series of numbers. A 2-digit number pronounced with 4 syllables (82 = "quatre-vingt deux") is fixated longer than the reversed number having 2 syllables (28 = "vingt huit").

The experiment has not been done in a normal text-reading situation, so no conclusions should be drawn about the necessary existence of implicit speech in reading. Nevertheless, the fact that an effect is observed on the duration of an individual fixation and not as a global effect on the whole sequence of fixations is evidence for the possible existence of a moment-to-moment regulation in the timing of eye movements. This will be important in the analysis of the control mechanisms.

Word Sequence (Context, Redundancy). The role of context in guiding eye movements (and on the eye-voice span) has been known since Morton's (1964) basic experimental study. Real texts and statistical approximations to English of zero to 8th order were read aloud "as quickly as possible, minimizing errors." Global reading speed increased up to 5th or 6th order of approximation, but not for higher orders. While no variation in the mean duration of the fixations appeared (always around 240 msec for approximations as well as for coherent text), the number of forward and regressive eye movements decreased for approximations up to 5th order and then remained stable. Fast readers remained faster than slow readers (fewer eye movements, but of about same fixation duration) on all the levels of approximation. In addition, Morton claimed that fast readers were helped by order of approximation up to a higher level than slow readers.

Vanacek (1972), however, notes that the changes in fixation frequency observed by Morton might have been due to a seldom noticed artifact about approximations to English constructed by the Miller and Selfridge (1950) method: higher order approximations tend to contain high frequency words and lower order approximations contain low frequency words (Morawetz, 1961). Vanacek, therefore, repeated Morton's experiment, for silent reading, using in addition a series of control conditions where the words in each text approximation were scrambled and their average frequency measured. Vanacek was able to confirm Morton's idea that it is the contextual constraints that diminish the number of fixations: the effect of word frequency only had a significant effect when the words were very rare. Vanacek found a small but significant increase in fixation duration for the lowest orders of text approximation.

Grammatical Structure. Is ocular scanning tuned to the linguistic structure of the text being read? It seems plausible that decoding a sentence would be efficiently done by giving more attention to crucial words than less important ones (compare Mackworth & Morandi's (1967) "information areas"; see also Antes, 1974; and Loftus, 1972).

If this principle of economy did work, one should find a distribution of eye fixation locations reproducing the grammatical "relief" of the sentences. In fact no such "reliefs" emerge from contemplating fixation positions of individual readers. Records from many readers reading the same text must be accumulated before a pattern emerges, and even then the exact nature of the pattern may be unclear (O'Regan, this volume). Still, though we lack precise hypotheses about what this "relief" should look like, it is possible to compare ocular behaviour across sentences whose particular grammatical structure is varied systematically.

Such structure as active vs. passive forms, right-embedding (The cat saw the rat that ate the cheese) vs. left-embedding (The rat that the cat saw ate the cheese) are known to differ in comprehension and manipulation tasks — in particular for children. Wanat (1976) as well as Klein and Kurkowski (1974) looked for corresponding changes in the way the eyes are guided in reading such sentences. They found that a sentence's constituent structure affected the way the reader's fixations were distributed across it. Wanat found that forward eye fixation patterning seemed to be related to right- or left-embedded structure differences, while the number of regression eye movements differed between active and passive sentences. These effects were more apparent in oral than in silent reading, and Klein and Kurkowski found more movements and higher contrasts when the task was enhanced by questions about the text.

Mehler, Bever, and Carey (1967) tried to give a precise rule that would predict the distribution of fixations in sentences, purely as a function of their surface syntactic structure. For their own data the rule was successful, but an exact replication of their experiment by O'Regan (1975) gave quite different results. Both Comunale (1973) and Rayner (1975) found no evidence that the eye positioned itself differently in the area occupied by the main verb of a sentence, an area which might be considered to be particularly informative.

In summary, one has the impression from the data concerning effects of linguistic structure that some relation with eye fixation patterns exists, although the precise nature of this relation remains unclear. It is possible that saccade size and fixation duration depend at each moment on the predictability of the text. Although this idea has not been seriously investigated, a start has been made by O'Regan (1975, and this volume).

Variables Related to Attitudes of Reader Toward Text
The same text may be read in quite different manners: looking for general meaning or merely to get an idea of what it is about, looking for exhaustive comprehension, examining the form in which the ideas are expressed, analysing the words used, verifying the spelling or the layout. The different

approaches to a text may be classified between two extremes. At one end the text is an intermediary, bearing a representation of the author's "mental operations" to be understood. The text itself should be as transparent as possible, so the reader can ignore the particular words and sentences used, and concentrate on the concepts. At the other end: proof reading, in which the text must be as untransparent as possible — a proof reader or typist can ignore content.

Since ocular scanning is an intermediary between the reader's mind and the text, it will depend on the reader's approach to the text. This is an interfering variable, often assumed secondary in reading experiments, but which may significantly influence the data.

Hochberg (1976) defines four types of reading which involve different processes:

Type I: word decoding by analysis of the word, determining each letter's location within each word.

Type II: careful reading; words picked up out to 4 or 6 letter-spaces per fixation (about 200 words per minute).

Type III: some information is taken from every word, but partly in peripheral vision (about 500 words per minute). Upper limit of what is usually called reading.

Type IV: skimming, i.e., picking up information only out of every 8th, 10th or 15th word (about 1500 wpm).

We propose to add a fifth condition: reading without consciously extracting any information. This happens when one's thoughts wander while reading a book. The eyes continue to scan the lines and one may even turn the pages while thinking about something else. How is the gaze guided in these conditions of automatic functioning of the "reading system?" What becomes of the control mechanisms that would normally involve higher order information processing and comprehension? Do the oculomotor parameters approach what they are when one scans a picture made of non-significant signs aligned in rows? Are regressions suppressed or not?

Usually, in the experiments previously mentioned, the reading task is only approximately defined through instructions and comprehension tests. At least when oral reading is required, one may think that the rhythm is partly determined by constraints associated with verbal output. What meaning processing is done remains unclear. When the instructions are merely to read silently, the task is even less clear: the reader may move his eyes without extracting any information. The dependence of eye movement behaviour upon these conditions has not been seriously examined (Just & Carpenter, 1976).

MODELS OF EYE MOVEMENT CONTROL IN READING

Several investigators have reviewed models of eye movement control in reading (Hochberg & Brooks, 1970; Bouma & de Voogd, 1974; Shebilske, 1975; Haber, 1976; Rayner & McConkie, 1976). Finally, the recent study by Bouma (1978) contains some very interesting new ideas.

Local Versus Global Eye Movement Measures
There is an important distinction in eye movement research which has never
been clearly expressed: the distinction between local and global measures
of eye movement behaviour. Local measures are made over a short time
span and taken in the vicinity of particular words of a text: duration of individual fixations and length of individual saccades. Global measures, on the
other hand, are essentially combinations of these local measures taken over
a longer time span, usually of the order of seconds: average fixation duration
per line, average saccade size, number of fixations, number of regressions,
total time spent on certain regions.

What is the relevance of this distinction? It is that since local measures
are taken over a short time span, we expect them predominantly to reflect
underlying processes that function over a short time span, namely processes
that concern the fine organization or microstructure of cognitive events,
for example, perception of cognitively significant symbols like words. We
will call these processes low-level cognitive processes. Global measures,
functioning over a longer time span, would be expected to reflect higher
level cognitive processes, relying upon information gathered over a longer
period of time.

Whether a researcher will study high or low level processes is a matter
of taste. But what is clear is that one needs considerably better theories
about sentence processing to launch into a description of the elementary
local processes involved. It would appear that during the last fifty or so years
psychologists have been gathering up their courage for this attack. Thus,
since it was often concerned with reading efficiency and educational applications, classical research on reading eye movements concentrated mainly
on global parameters (reviews by Tinker). Though data about individual fixation positions and durations were available to careful researchers, in particular Dodge, Huey, Buswell, and Dearborn, they were not usually the subject
of controlled experimentation (Dodge is an exception to this).

Recently, interest in information processing models of cognitive tasks
has generated the hope that more local eye movement measures might reflect
moment-to-moment mental events. A Russian research impulse showing
how the scanning of a scene depends on the task, is perhaps what pioneered
this approach (Tikhomirov & Poznanskaya, 1966; Yarbus, 1967; also Pailhous,
1970, for a review). Many workers are now using eye fixation data in an
effort to elucidate problem-solving and memory processes (Vurpillot & Baudonnière, 1976; Groner, 1976; Just & Carpenter, 1976; Russo & Rosen, 1975;
Tversky, 1974), and visual search (Gould & Carn, 1973; Mackworth & Bruner,
1970; Luria & Strauss, 1975). Of interest to reading research is a study by
Carpenter (1978) which demonstrates that when subjects read a sentence
with an ambiguous referent, they will go back a few lines to disambiguate
it. The interpretation they choose will correlate with where they regress
to. It is noteworthy in this study that the measures used are not the most
local ones possible. In fact, Just and Carpenter (1976) expressly reject the
idea that individual fixation durations and the small changes of fixation position within one picture region are of any interest to their level of theorizing.
They propose their own unit of eye movement measurement, the gaze, which
unites several fixations occurring within the same region of a picture.

The "gaze" is still too global a measure for the most recent trend in reading eye movement studies. Ever since Cherry (1956) suggested that eye saccades might be controlled as a function of predictions the reader is making about the text, the notion that moment-to-moment processing of sentences might be reflected "on-line" in fixation durations and saccade lengths, has been gaining ground. The idea is currently pleasing because of the advent of psycholinguistics, which gives some indications of where in sentences one might look for evidence of this on-line processing.

Several authors have made first steps towards working out this notion by either proposing particular eye movement control models, or by making classifications of possible models. Rayner and McConkie (1976) define two dimensions with which to classify models: level of processing (high or low) that affects eye movement behaviour, and another dimension they call "process-monitoring" as distinct from "language processing" itself. In a process-monitoring model, instead of being "directly controlled by information in lower or higher-level codes, [the eyes] are controlled by a mechanism which monitors some aspect of the processes involved in generating these codes." Using these distinctions, McConkie and Rayner (1975) were able to classify models of eye guidance into five classes: minimal control, low-level control, high-level control, process-monitoring, and mixed models.

Two different dimensions appear to us to allow a more natural classification. The two dimensions correspond to two crucial questions underlying all eye movement control models. The first question is: Where does the information come from that is used to guide the eye? Is it from the region of text currently being fixated, from the peripheral visual field, or from inferences made on the basis of what has already been read? The second question is: How quickly does this information influence the eye's motion? Does the information (wherever it comes from) immediately determine the size of the next saccade or the duration of the current fixation, or is it only one or several fixations after the information first became available that changes occur in oculomotor parameters? The models proposed by various authors have treated these two questions differently.

Hochberg's (1970) proposal revolves around the question of where the information guiding the eye comes from. He suggests two sources. The first is cognitive: knowledge about what has already been read together with knowledge about language and grammar, might enable the reader to make predictions about what words are likely to follow. The eye might therefore be able to skip over them. Hochberg calls this "cognitive search guidance." The second source of information that might guide the eye is peripheral vision. If, at the current fixation point, there is a little information about what is coming (say, for example, that the next word is short and begins with a T), then, with added cognitive predictions it might be possible to guess that the next word is THE, and the eye would be able to skip over it. Hochberg calls this "peripheral search guidance." Note that Hochberg's model assumes that the information, peripheral or cognitive, acts immediately on the next saccade. In this sense he only looks at one answer to our question of "How fast does the eye react?"

Shebilske (1975) makes the various answers to this question the center of a distinction between indirectly regulated scanning and directly regulated scanning. To describe the former, he quotes Bouma and de Voogd (1974):

"For efficient reading the point of fixation should proceed on the average just as fast as recognition, and for bridging momentary differences between the eye and the brain, a buffer function has to be assumed. For efficient operation, the proceeding of the eyes over the text should then be under control of the content of the buffer: an empty buffer should lead to increase of eye speed whereas a filled buffer should slow down the eyes." So here, because of the buffer, eye movements will only be loosely related to, and change slowly with, parameters of the text. Shebilske suggests that periodically, however, this autonomous process may be interrupted to give way to a more direct kind of control (directly regulated scanning), where the buffer is momentarily by-passed. An example he gives is for the eye to skip over a very long name that occurs frequently.

Another instance when the buffer would be by-passed might be when comprehension fails and regressions have to be made. Geyer (1970) relates regressions to overload in a kind of "pipeline" between visual input and derived meaning output. Shebilske also proposes that in cases of directly regulated scanning, if information from peripheral vision plays a role, it can only be by extracting gross physical cues (such as a blank space) and not cues involving "meaning-extraction processes." In an information processing approach this seems plausible since gross visual cues presumably require less processing time than higher level predictions about the identity of a word.

Haber (1976), while not affirming that it takes more time to extract higher level information, nevertheless makes this the basis of his classification of eye movement guidance models. His "stimulus control" involves peripheral and cognitive sources of information, and immediate action upon the eyes. It is broadly equivalent to a combination of Hochberg's "peripheral" and "cognitive search guidance." Haber's "internal control" involves only cognitive information and has slightly slower control: "The next landing place for the eye is determined not by any characteristic of the landing site but only by the amount of new information the reader thinks he will be able to process next." Haber's "random control" uses no cognitive or peripheral information, and has extremely slow action on the eye movements — a sort of "gain control" determining average eye movement parameters is set when the reader starts to read.

We see that in Haber's classification the dimension of source or kind of information covaries with the dimension concerning the speed with which this information affects eye movements. This covariance is a natural reflection of the notion that it takes more time to extract higher level than lower level information. The essential question that must therefore be answered to distinguish between models of eye movement guidance in reading is, "How quickly can information influence the eye's behaviour?" This question will be examined in the next section.

Finally, let us mention another model of oculomotor regulation in reading, proposed from an engineering point of view by Massé (1976). A hierarchy of three control systems with different time periods is at work: a general pacing system, a local saccadic motor execution system, and, in between, another rapid system concerned with "logical operations" which would only temporarily take priority over the first one. Here again is the idea of switching from indirectly regulated scanning (adapting slowly) to direct control (adapting quickly).

Can the Eye React Immediately to What it Sees?

The question of how fast the eye can react to incoming information aids in differentiating possible models of eye guidance. If it is found that the eye cannot change its course on the basis of information gathered in the present fixation, then we will know, for example, that very local measures of eye movement behaviour, such as individual fixation duration and saccade size, are probably not useful places to look for reflections of sentence processing during reading. If, on the other hand, we find that the eye can react very quickly, then it is possible that these local measures have something to do with local sentence processing, and we will be justified in trying to find out just how they reflect these processes. There is, of course, no guarantee that if rapid adjustments can be made, they usually are made. This is a question which subsequent experimentation will answer.

Supposed Theoretical Arguments Against Immediate Control

One of the most frequent theoretical arguments against the idea that eye saccades could be immediately controlled as a function of incoming information is to say that there is no time during the fixation to do all the things that would have to be done, viz., gather the information, decide what to do, and program the saccade. Such arguments have been given by Morton (1964), Kolers and Lewis (1972), and Bouma and de Voogd (1974); they have been questioned by, among others, Haber (1976), and Just and Carpenter (1976).

The sampled data model of Young and Stark (1963) suggested that after the onset of a 150 msec latency period preceding each saccade, the course of the saccade could no longer be modified by incoming information. If this were true, little time (at most 100 msec) would be left in a typical 250 msec fixation to take into account cognitive calculations made on the basis of the information coming from the current fixation. If there is control of saccades, it could only depend on information already present before the current fixation. However, in a review of recent work, Fuchs (1971) notes that the sampled data model cannot account for what is now an increasing body of evidence suggesting that the oculomotor system is more flexible than originally thought. Conditions are now systematically found under which the eye can adjust the course of the saccade for about 80 msec from its onset (Levy-Schoen & Blanc-Garin, 1974; Becker & Jurgens, 1975). This weakens the argument made on the basis of the sampled data model. In any case, as pointed out by Haber (1976) and Just and Carpenter (1976), the predictions of the sampled data model, which was constructed to explain eye movements in response to unpredictable stimuli, cannot necessarily be extended to reading, where the material is meaningful and partly predictable.

A psychological argument often given to strengthen the sampled data type of argument originated with Dodge (1907). He thought that after each saccade there was a "clearing up period" of about 100 msec, during which little information could be extracted from the visual field. There is no doubt that a disturbance in perception occurs during saccades, even if the causes are not agreed upon (review by E. Matin, 1974). There may also be perhaps related effects associated with lateral masking, and with correlating retinal and real-world coordinate systems (cf. important work of Bischof & Kramer, 1968; Matin, Clymer & Matin, 1972). No one, however, has expressly studied how such perturbations might relate to reading.

A philosophical reason that might be invoked against immediate control of eye movements in reading is that there would be little point in guiding the eye very precisely from moment to moment: a word can be easily read when the eye is fixating anywhere within it. As suggested by Woodworth (1938), it would suffice to keep moving the eyes at such a rate that there is always some information to be processed. Geyer (1970) has proposed a similar view, and Bouma and de Voogd (1974) have shown that it is indeed possible to read by looking at successive clusters of words shown for equal times of about 250 msec each. However, as Bouma and de Voogd themselves point out (also Hochberg, 1975), this is no proof that in ordinary reading no control of fixation duration occurs. It is also worth noting that these authors did not test their subjects' comprehension. Nevertheless, this study shows that at least some kinds of reading are possible without precise oculomotor control.

A more troubling fact that the believer in immediate control must account for is the strong similarity found by Cunitz and Steinman (1969) between the distribution of fixation durations in reading and in the prolonged examination of a single, slightly enlarged letter. Surely, if fixation durations are controlled from moment to moment, one would expect greater variability in reading than in the exploration of such a simple stimulus. Cunitz and Steinman argue that fixation durations in looking at a single letter are voluntarily controlled as much as reading eye movements are. But it is possible to make the opposite argument and say that both are equally random. While the identity of the two sets of distributions is not necessarily harmful to the immediate control notion's supporters, it leaves them with some explaining to do.

Finally, we come to one of the classic predictions made under the hypothesis that eye movements can be guided on the basis of immediate deductions made from peripheral vision, namely that short function words might be less often fixated than chance would predict. Shebilske (1975), in a reanalysis of 17 plates of eye movement records from the work of Judd and Buswell (1922), found no evidence for this hypothesis. This finding, of course, only goes against the idea of immediate eye movement control if it can be proven that function words really must be less often fixated in order to process sentences correctly. And that would naturally be difficult to show.

Direct Experimental Evidence for Immediate Control
The preceding arguments against immediate control are essentially theoretical, consisting of extrapolations from situations which are not real reading situations, for example, tracking simple dot targets or reading isolated words. However research which addresses itself more directly to the question, generally supports immediate control.

Saccade Size Control. In an important experiment that awaits confirmation using statistical tests, Abrams and Zuber (1972) noticed that while reading a text, the eye avoided random positions where the spaces between words were normally large. To do this, information from peripheral vision must act sufficiently rapidly to allow the next saccade to be lengthened: evidence for immediate control. But note that the spaces might have been seen, not on the fixation preceding the space, but on some earlier fixation. Abrams and Zuber's data therefore at least argues for "almost immediate" control.

Still more evidence comes from the analysis done by Rayner and McConkie (1976) of the probability of fixating letters in words as a function of their length. The authors found that letters in short and long words have slightly smaller probability of being fixated than letters in medium length words, the greatest probabilities being for six-letter words. This shows that the eye must adjust its course as a function of word length, otherwise letters would be fixated with equal probability independently of word length. Again, although it seems likely that this should happen because of information coming from the periphery on the current fixation, one cannot logically exclude the possiblity that earlier fixations might play some role.

Another experiment showing almost immediate control is that by O'Regan (1975), who found that the eye tended to jump further into and out of long words than short words. As before, we cannot exclude preprogramming from previous fixations. O'Regan (1975) also found that in certain sentences, a short three-letter verb attracted more fixations than the article THE which followed it. This may be evidence that the word THE can be skipped on the basis of partial information from peripheral vision. However, the phenomenon may be due to the sentence positions occupied by the verb and the THE. This was controlled in an experiment reported by O'Regan (this volume), where it was shown that, following an identical sentence context, THE elicited longer saccades than a three-letter verb.

Control of Fixation Durations. In their "spaced text" experiment cited above, Abrams and Zuber (1972) observed that fixation durations preceding a jump across a randomly spaced blank in the text were shortened by about 50 msec with respect to the average fixation duration. However, the standard deviation of the distributions were of this order, so the data need statistical confirmation.

Pynte's experiments (1974, 1978) provide individual measures of the duration of eye fixations upon numbers or syllables which are scanned for subsequent identification. These durations are longer for numbers having more syllables, suggesting that oculomotor programming seems to occur at each fixation. In a similar task, Verschueren and Levy-Schoen (1973) noted that a longer pause can be elicited when an unexpected missing element in an anagram is encountered (Figure 6).

Rayner (1975a) made the text display contingent on the eye's position in such a way that only when the eye made a saccade toward a critical position in a sentence did the letters at that position change into a different set of letters. He found that the duration of the fixation at the critical location increased, depending on what was there before the change, and on the distance the eye travelled. Even if the "trick" displays are unnatural, the data show that fixation duration can be affected immediately by the relationship between information gathered by peripheral vision in the preceding fixation, and information gathered centrally at the current fixation.

Rayner's experiment is a more subtle version of a clever experiment performed by Dodge in 1907. Dodge found that the time the eye fixates the stimulus before oral response to a peripherally presented word is less than for a centrally presented word, the peripheral advantage disappearing around 10 deg. Using an eye-position-contingent control condition in which the peripheral stimulus only became informative when the eye landed on it, Levy-Schoen

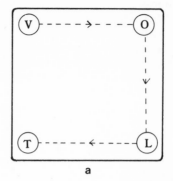

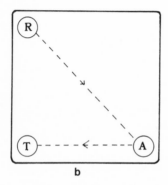 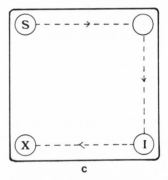

Figure 6. Anagram displays like (a) are repeatedly presented: they are scanned in the way shown by the arrows. When one like (b) is shown, the blank location is generally omitted. For one like (c), the empty circle is usually fixated longer than if a letter had been present. (From Verschueren & Levy-Schoen, 1973).

(in press) has shown that the time saving in Dodge's experiment cannot be explained by some general activation or foreperiod effect produced by the saccade itself. That foreperiod effects can be important, however, has been shown by Vaughan and Graefe (1977), who delayed stimulus onset while the eye oscillated between two points in search of a target letter. They found evidence for some pre-programming of fixation durations, but the task may be too simple to allow extrapolation to reading.

Which Kinds of Information are Active?
The above discussion has shown that in reading there are instances when the eyes make very rapid adjustments as a function of incoming information. We will now look more closely at the question of exactly what kinds of information are involved, both for saccade size control and for fixation duration controls. As already noted, an undemonstrated though natural supposition

is that the most rapid adjustments should reflect "sensory" processes. Higher level cognitive processes should influence more global, that is, slower-changing eye movement parameters. At what cognitive level, if any, does immediate control no longer become possible? If we are interested in finding reflections of sentence processing in eye movement parameters, we must know what level of processing is likely to be reflected. It would be useless to look for the effects of linguistic variables in isolated fixation durations or saccade sizes, if these are affected only by gross visual cues like brightness, blurring, or spacing.

We will look first at the variables that affect saccade size changes. The instances mentioned above of almost immediate control were due to low level, easy-to-see characteristics in peripheral vision -- word length or spacing. Can we get immediate control of saccades from higher level variables? O'Regan's THE-skipping experiment (this volume) claims the answer is affirmative: the eye makes a bigger saccade if the next word is THE than if it is a verb.

This is contrary to Shebilske's (1975) finding that the only peripheral cues which could guide the eye would be the physical aspect of the peripheral word, not higher level information concerned with meaning or syntactic category. To reconcile Shebilske's view with the data, it is possible to make the hypothesis that in situations where good predictions about the peripheral words can be made, gross physical cues such as word length and end letters become cues to meaning, since in principle they narrow down the possible choices in the identification of the peripheral words. The idea is expressed more fully in O'Regan (1975) and is related to Marcel's (1974) finding that when someone reads well, "increased contextual effectiveness aids visual processing as well as effecting response bias in word identification, and also appears in so doing to free visual information processing capacity for use at more peripheral locations of the visual field."

What Variables Immediately Affect Fixation Duration?   Rayner's (1975a, 1978) experiments are consistent with an interpretation according to which immediate control of fixation duration depends on word length, end letters, and shape; this is also an appealing notion, since these three kinds of information available in peripheral vision could help to reduce the number of choices in the identification of the word in the periphery. Unfortunately, it may be that the display changes occurring in Rayner's experiments gave rise to flicker and brightness changes, and that these disturbances artifactually caused the increase in fixation duration. One aspect of the Rayner data does go against the flicker explanation however. It is that there is a small but significant difference between the effects on fixation durations produced by changing the critical word from a different word to the correct word, as compared with changing it from a nonword to the correct word. Since the amount of flicker produced should have been about the same, he is probably justified in concluding that it is truly information about wordness which has given rise to the fixation duration change.

Whereas Rayner's experiment addresses the question of fixation durations as a function of variables in peripheral vision, one could also look for effects caused by material in central vision. The most obvious candidate is stimulus clarity. However, nothing has been done to find out if the eye, when it encounters an unclear word, makes a longer fixation. Word frequency is another, though higher level, candidate. Again no direct work has been done on the question of its influence on individual fixation durations, although a few points we have plotted on the basis of Vanacek's (1972) data for silent reading of scrambled texts hint that fixation duration may increase with word frequency. Only careful experimentation in a true reading situation will clarify this matter.

In Pynte's (1978) and Verschueren and Levy-Schoen's (1973) experiments involving non-reading tasks, it was shown that fixation can be prolonged by peculiarities of the element fixated: number of syllables or unexpectedness of content.

SUMMARY AND GENERAL CONCLUSIONS

A global analysis of reading eye movements reveals a general reading pattern consisting of a series of step-like rightwards saccades sometimes interrupted by shorter leftwards regressions. Long leftwards return sweeps occur at the right hand boundary of the text. Constant features of this pattern are the distribution of fixation duration around a mean value of between 200 and 300 msec, and the distribution of saccade extent, which typically has three peaks corresponding to forward saccades, regressions, and return sweeps. Over a given text, systematic relations between successive saccade lengths or fixation durations do not seem to exist. The variable feature of the general reading pattern across different readers or different texts is mainly the number of regressions. Mean saccade size is found to vary less, and mean fixation duration still less. Like reading of easy material, efficient and mature reading appears free from regression movements, progresses with larger saccades, and sometimes involves shorter fixation durations.

Recent work in reading eye movements has been characterized by interest in the moment-to-moment details of ocular behaviour: these details are assumed to be an "on line" reflection of language processing. A number of researchers are asking: How fast can eye movements be influenced by situational variables (direct or indirect control, buffer or no buffer, pipeline, rapid rhythm system)? What kinds of information are active (high or low level, cognitive or sensory, cognitive or peripheral, semantic, linguistic, graphic, etc.)? Both questions may concern the modulations of either saccade size or fixation duration. The occurrence of regressions has not been studied in this way.

Present conclusions are that eye movements can be "immediately" controlled: some kind of on-line regulator does increase or decrease the time spent on an item, and also the extent of the jump bringing the eyes to the next stop. The question about what kinds of information can give rise to such moment-to-moment regulations has not been clearly answered, nor is it known under what conditions local control is active or worthwhile.

REFERENCES

Abrams, S.G., & Zuber, B.L. Some characteristics of information processing
    during reading. Reading Research Quarterly, 1972, 8, 40-51.
Andriessen, J.J., & de Voogd, A.H. Analysis of eye movement patterns in silent
    reading, I.P.O. Annual Progress Report, 1973, 8, 29-34.
Antes, J.R. The time-course of picture viewing. Journal of Experimental
    Psychology, 1974, 103, 62-70.
Bahill, A.T., & Stark, L. Overlapping saccades and glissades are produced by
    fatigue in the saccadic eye movement system. Experimental Neurology,
    1975, 48, 95-106.
Becker, W., & Jurgens, R. Saccadic reactions to double step stimuli. In
    G. Lennerstrand & P. Bach-y-Rita (Eds.), Basic mechanisms of ocular
    motility and their clinical applications. Oxford: Pergamon, 1975.
Bischof, N., & Kramer, E. Untersuchungen und Überlegungen zur Richtungs-
    wahrnehmung bei willkürlichen sakkadischen Augenbewegungen.
    Psychologische Forschung, 1968, 32, 185-218.
Bouma, H. Visual interference in the parafoveal recognition of initial and
    final letters of words. Vision Research, 1973, 13, 767-782.
Bouma, H. Visual search and reading: Eye movements and functional visual
    field. In J. Réquin (Ed.), Attention and performance VII. Hillsdale, NJ:
    Erlbaum, 1978.
Bouma, H., & de Voogd, A.H. On the control of eye saccades in reading.
    Vision Research, 1974, 14, 273-284.
Bouma, H., & Legein, C.P. Foveal and parafoveal recognition of letters and
    words by dyslexics and by average readers. Neuropsychologia, 1977,
    15, 69-80.
Buswell, G.T. An experimental study of the eye-voice span in reading.
    Supplementary Educational Monographs, No. 17. Chicago: University of
    Chicago, 1920.
Carmichael, L., & Dearborn, W.F. Reading and visual fatigue. Boston:
    Houghton Mifflin Co., 1947.
Carpenter, P.A. Inference processes during reading: Reflections from eye
    fixations. In J.W. Senders, D.F. Fisher, & R.A. Monty (Eds.), Eye move-
    ments and psychological processes II. Hillsdale, NJ: Erlbaum, 1978.
Cherry, C. On human communication. New York: Wiley, 1956.
Comunale, A.S. Visual selectivity in reading: A study of the relationship
    between eye movements and linguistic structure. Dissertation Abstracts
    International, 1973, 34, 1692-1693.
Cunitz, R.J., & Steinman, R.M. Comparison of saccadic eye movements
    during fixation and reading. Vision Research, 1969, 9, 683-693.
Ditchburn, R.W. Eye movements and visual perception. Oxford: Clarendon
    Press, 1973.
Dodge, R. An experimental study of visual fixation. Psychological
    Review Monograph Supplement, 1907, 35, 1-95.
Dossetor, D.R., & Papaioannou, J. Dyslexia and eye movements. Language &
    Speech, 1975, 18, 312-317.
Engel, F.L. Visual conspicuity as an external determinant of eye movements
    and selective attention. Ph.D. Thesis, Eindhoven, 1976.

Engel, F.L. Visual conspicuity: Visual search and fixation tendencies of the eye. Vision Research, 1977, 17, 95-108.

Ferreiro, E. What is written in a written sentence? A developmental answer. Journal of Education, 1978, 160, 25-39.

Fisher, D. Spatial factors in reading and search. The case for space. In R.A. Monty & J.W. Senders (Eds.), Eye movements and psychological processes. Hillsdale, NJ: Erlbaum, 1976.

Friedman, N. Is reading disability a fusional dysfunction? Journal of the American Optometric Association, 1974, 45, 619-622, Part I (a); 727-732, Part II (b).

Fuchs, A.F. The saccadic system. In P. Bach-y-Rita, C.C. Collins, & J.E. Hyde (Eds.), The control of eye movements. New York: Academic Press, 1971.

Geyer, J.J. Models of perceptual processes in reading. In H. Singer & R.B. Ruddell (Eds.), Theoretical models and processes of reading. Newark, DEL: International Reading Association, 1970.

Gibson, E.J., & Levin, H . The psychology of reading. Cambridge, MA: MIT Press, 1975.

Gilliland, A.R. The effect on reading of changes in the size of type. Elementary School Journal, 1923, 24, 138-146.

Gould, J.D., & Carn, R. Visual search, complex backgrounds, mental counters and eye movements. Perception & Psychophysics, 1973, 14, 125-132.

Griffin, D.C., Walton, H.N., & Ives, V. Saccades as related to reading disorders. Journal of Learning Disabilities, 1974, 7, 310-316.

Groner, R. Eye movements and hypothesis testing behavior. Paper presented at XXIst International Congress of Psychology, Paris, 1976.

Grossman, M., & Philips, M. Ocular motility and reading skills. Child Study Journal, 1973, 3, 39-42.

Haber, R.N. Control of eye movements during reading. In R.A. Monty & J.W. Senders (Eds.), Eye movements and psychological processes. Hillsdale, NJ: Erlbaum, 1976.

Hartze, W. Reading disturbances in the presence of oculomotor disorders. European Neurology, 1972, 7, 249-264.

Heiman, J.R., & Ross, A.O. Saccadic eye movements and reading difficulties. Journal of Abnormal Child Psychology, 1974, 2, 53-61.

Hochberg, J. Components of literacy: Speculations and exploration research. In H. Levin & J.P. Williams (Eds.), Basic studies on reading. New York: Basic Books, 1970.

Hochberg, J. On the control of saccades in reading. Vision Research, 1975, 15, 620.

Hochberg, J. Toward a speech-plan eye movement model of reading. In R.A. Monty & J.W. Senders (Eds.), Eye movements and psychological processes. Hillsdale, NJ: Erlbaum, 1976.

Hochberg, J., & Brooks, V. Reading as an intentional behavior. In H. Singer & R.B. Ruddell (Eds.), Theoretical models and processes of reading. Newark, DEL: International Reading Association, 1970.

Huey, E.B. On the psychology and physiology of reading. I. American Journal of Psychology, 1900, 11, 283-302.

Jackson, M.D., & McClelland, J.L. Sensory and cognitive determinants of reading speed. Journal of Verbal Learning and Verbal Behavior, 1975, 14, 565-574.

Javal, K.E. Essai sur la physiologie de la lecture. Annales d'Oculistique, 1879, 82, 242-253.

Judd, C.H., & Buswell, G.T. Silent reading: A study of the various types. Elementary Educational Monographs, 1922, 27, 23.

Jung, R. How do we see with moving eyes? In J. Dichgans & E. Bizzi (Eds.), Cerebral control of eye movements and motion perception. Basel: Karger, 1972. Also: Bibliotheca Ophthalmologica, 1972, 82, 377-395.

Just, M.A., & Carpenter, P.A. Eye fixations and cognitive processes. Cognitive Psychology, 1976, 8, 441-480.

Kavanagh, J.F., & Mattingly, I.G. Language by ear and by eye. Cambridge, MA: MIT Press, 1972.

Klapp, S.T. Implicit speech inferred from response latencies in same-different decisions. Journal of Experimental Psychology, 1971, 91, 261-267.

Klein, G.A., & Kurkowski, F. Effect of task demands on relationship between eye movements and sentence complexity. Perceptual and Motor Skills, 1974, 39, 463-466.

Kolers, P.A. Buswell's discoveries. In R.A. Monty & J.W. Senders (Eds.), Eye movements and psychological processes. Hillsdale, NJ: Erlbaum, 1976.

Kolers, P.A., & Lewis, C. Bounding of letter sequences and the integration of visually presented words. Acta Psychologica, 1972, 36, 112-124.

Kremin, H. L'approche neurolinguistique des alexies: 1969-1976. Langages, No. special "Les troubles de la lecture — l'alexie", 1976, 44, 63-81.

Lamare, A. Des mouvements des yeux dans la lecture. Comptes- rendus de la Société Francaise d'Ophtalmologie, 1893, cité par Javal, E.: Physiologie de la lecture et de l'écriture. Paris, Alcan, 1905.

Lee, J.C. The effectiveness of two types of visual aid treatments on eye movement performance of educationally handicapped pupils in the elementary school. Dissertation Abstracts International, 1973, 34(3-A), 1084.

Lennerstrand, G., & Bach-y-Rita, P. (Eds.). Basic mechanisms of ocular motility and their clinical implications. London: Pergamon Press, 1975.

Lesèvre, N. Les mouvements oculaires d'exploration. Etude électro-oculographique comparée d'enfants normaux et d'enfants dyslexiques. Thèse, Paris, 1964.

Lesèvre, N. L'organisation du regard chez des enfants d'âge scolaire, lecteurs normaux et dyslexiques (étude électro-oculographique). Revue de Neuropsychiatrie Infantile, 1968, 16, 323-349.

Levy-Schoen, A., & Blanc-Garin, J. On oculomotor programming and perception. Brain Research, 1974, 71, 443-450.

Levy-Schoen, A., & Rigaut-Renard, C. Préperception ou activation motrice au cours du TR oculomoteur? In J. Réquin (Ed.), Fonctions anticipatrices du système nerveux et processus psychologique (in press).

Loftus, G.R. Eye fixations and recognition memory for pictures. Cognitive Psychology, 1972, 3, 525-551.

Luria, S.M., & Strauss, M.S. Eye movements during search for coded and uncoded targets. Perception & Psychophysics, 1975, 17, 303-308.

McConkie, G.W. On the role and control of eye movements in reading. (This volume.)

McConkie, G.W., & Rayner, K. The span of the effective stimulus during a fixation in reading. Perception & Psychophysics, 1975, 17, 578-586.

Mackworth, N.H., & Bruner, J.S. How adults and children search and recognize pictures. Human Development, 1970, 13, 149-177.

Mackworth, N.H., & Morandi, A. The gaze selects informative details within pictures. Perception & Psychophysics, 1967, 2, 547-552.

Marcel, T. The effective visual field and the use of context in fast and slow readers of two ages. British Journal of Psychology, 1974, 65, 479-492.

Mason, R.L. Digital computer estimation of eye fixations. Behavior Research Methods and Instrumentation, 1976, 8, 185-188.

Massé, D. Le contrôle des mouvements oculaires. Thèse, Universite de Grenoble, 1976.

Matin, E. Saccadic suppression: A review and an analysis. Psychological Bulletin, 1974, 81, 899-917.

Matin, E., Clymer, A., & Matin, L. Metacontrast and saccadic suppression. Science, 1972, 178, 179-182.

Mehler, J., Bever, T.G., & Carey, P. What we look at when we read. Perception & Psychophysics, 1967, 2, 213-218.

Miller, G.A., & Selfridge, J.A. Verbal context and recall of meaningful material. American Journal of Psychology, 1950, 63, 176-185.

Moal, A. L'activité d'exploration oculaire. Sa mise en relation avec l'activité cognitive chez l'enfant d'âge préscolaire. Thèse, Université Paris V, 1978).

Morawetz, E. Informations-theoretische Analyse des Lernens von Material mit verschieden hohem Sinngehalt. Unpublished dissertation, Psychologisches Institut, Wien Universität, 1961.

Morton, J. The effects of context upon speed of reading, eye movements and eye voice span. Quarterly Journal of Experimental Psychology, 1964, 16, 340-354.

Morton, J. A two hours reading course. Nature, 1966, 211, 323-324.

O'Regan, J.K. Structural and contextual constraints on eye movements in reading. Unpublished doctoral thesis. University of Cambridge, 1975.

O'Regan, J.K. A better horizontal eye movement calibration method: Smooth pursuit and zero drift. Behavior Research Methods and Instrumentation, 1978, 10, 393-397.

O'Regan, J.K. Moment-to-moment control of eye saccades as a function of textual parameters in reading. (This volume.)

Pailhous, J. L'analyse des tâches complexes par les mouvements oculaires. L'Année Psychologique, 1970, 2, 487-504.

Pynte, J. Readiness for pronunciation during the reading process. Perception & Psychophysics, 1974, 16, 110-112.

Pynte, J. Implicit labelling and readiness for pronunciation during the perceptual process. Perception, 1976, 5, 217-223.

Pynte, J. Implicit speech in the reading of numbers and meaningless syllables. In J. Réquin (Ed.), Attention and Performance VII. Hillsdale, NJ: Erlbaum, 1978.

Rayner, K. The perceptual span and peripheral cues in reading. Cognitive Psychology, 1975, 7, 65-81. (a)

Rayner, K. Parafoveal identification during a fixation in reading. Acta Psychologica, 1975, 39, 271-282. (b)

Rayner, K. Foveal and parafoveal cues in reading. In J. Réquin (Ed.), Attention and performance VII. Hillsdale, NJ: Erlbaum, 1978.

Rayner, K., & McConkie, G.W. What guides a reader's eye movements? Vision Research, 1976, 16, 829-837.

Roland, B.C. Eye movements of stutterers and non-stutterers during silent, oral and choral reading. Perceptual and Motor Skills, 1972, 35, 297-298.

Rubino, C.A., & Minden, H.A. An analysis of eye movements in children with a reading disability. Cortex, 1973, 9, 217-220.

Russo, J.E., & Rosen, L.D. An eye fixation analysis of multialternative choice. Memory & Cognition, 1975, 3, 267-276.

Schiepers, C.W.J. Global attributes in visual word recognition. Part 1. Length perception of letter strings. Vision Research, 1976, 16, 1343-1349.

Shebilske, W. Reading eye movements from an information-processing point of view. In D. Massaro (Ed.), Understanding language. NY: Academic Press, 1975.

Spragins, A.B., Lefton, L.A., & Fisher, D.F. Eye movements while reading and searching spatially transformed text: A developmental examination. Memory & Cognition, 1976, 4, 36-42.

Steinman, R.M., Haddad, G.M., Skavenski, A.A., & Wyman, D. Miniature eye movements. Science, 1973, 181, 810-819.

Stennett, R.G., Smythe, P.C., Pinkney, J., & Fairbairn, A. The relationship of eye movement measures to psychomotor skills and other elemental skills involved in learning to read. Journal of Reading Behavior, 1972-1973, 5, 1-13.

Stern, J.A., Bremer, D.A., & McClure, J. Analysis of eye movements and blinks during reading: Effects of Valium. Psychopharmacologia, 1974, 40, 171-175.

Stoll, F. Evaluation de trois types d'exercice de lecture rapide. Travail Humain, 1974, 37, 249-262.

Tikhomirov, O.K., & Poznanskaya, E.D. An investigation of visual search as a means of analysing heuristics. Soviet Psychology, 1966-67, 5, 2-15.

Tinker, M.A. Recent studies of eye movements in reading. Psychological Bulletin, 1958, 55, 215-231.

Tinker, M.A. Bases for effective reading. Minneapolis: University of Minnesota Press, 1965.

Tversky, B. Eye fixations in prediction of recognition and recall. Memory & Cognition, 1974, 2, 275-278.

Vanacek, E. Fixationsdauer und Fixationsfrequenz beim stillen Lesen von Sprachapproximationen. Zeitschrift für Experimentelle und Angewandte Psychologie, 1972, 19, 671-689.

Vaughan, J., & Graefe, T.M. Delay of stimulus presentation after the saccade in visual search. Perception & Psychophysics, 1977, 22, 201-205.

Verschueren, M., & Levy-Schoen, A. Information inattendue et stratégies d'exploration oculaire. L'Année Psychologique, 1973, 73, 51-65.

Vurpillot, E., & Baudonnière, P.M. Etude génétique des stratégies d'exploration en fonction du vecteur vertical ou horizontal de comparaison. Le Travail Humain, 1976, 39, 155-166.

Walsh, L.E. Measuring ocular motor performance of cerebral-palsied children. American Journal of Occupational Therapy, 1974, 28, 265-271.

Wanat, S.F. Language behind the eye: Some findings, speculations, and research strategies. In R.A. Monty & J.W. Senders (Eds.), Eye movements and psychological processes. Hillsdale, NJ: Erlbaum, 1976.

Weber, R.B., & Daroff, R.B. Corrective movements following fixation saccades: Types and control system analysis. Vision Research, 1972, 12, 467-475.

Willows, D.M. Reading between the lines: Selective attention in good and poor readers. Child Development, 1974, 45, 408-415.

Woodworth, R.S. Experimental psychology. New York: Holt, 1938.

Yarbus, A.L. Eye movements and vision. New York: Plenum Press, 1967.

Young, L.R., & Sheena, D. Survey of eye movement recording methods. Behavior Research Methods and Instrumentation, 1975, 7, 394-429.

Young, L.R., & Stark, L. A discrete model for eye-tracking movements. IEEE Transactions on military electronics, 1963, Vol. MIL 7, 2-3.

Zangwill, O.L., & Blakemore, C. Dyslexia: Reversal of eye movements during reading. Neuropsychologia, 1972, 10, 371-373.

On the Role and Control of Eye Movements in Reading

George W. McConkie

Three issues concerning reading are considered: the integration of visual information across fixations, the asymmetry of the perceptual span, and the control of eye movements. A model of eye movement control is described which is compatible with present data on these issues, and which may clarify the relationship between language and eye behavior in reading.

For nearly a century psychologists have examined eye movement records in order to discover the mental activities occurring during reading. Although decades of research have produced many summary statistics about eye movement patterns, few conclusions about the perceptual and comprehension processes taking place during reading have been reached. Most of the studies have provided information about eye movements, not about reading.

Why has it been so difficult to learn from eye movement data about the mental operations involved in reading? I believe it is because there are two prior problems that must be solved before eye movement data can effectively be used in this way. First, when the data indicate that the eye is centered at a particular position, it is still unknown what region of the text is actually being used in language processing. This is the question of the perceptual span, which Rayner and I have studied in the past (Rayner, 1975; McConkie & Rayner, 1976). Second, when we observe that a reader's eye stopped at one location then jumped to another for the next fixation, we still do not know the mental activities which resulted in this pattern. That is, we do not know the nature of the relationship between a given eye movement pattern and the cognitive processes occurring, so we are unable to take one and from it infer the other. This is the problem of the control of eye movements. Until there is better information about what is being seen during a fixation, and how the mind decides when and where to send the eye, it will be difficult to use eye movement data to test theories of reading.

A fundamental question in the study of reading is whether or not a tight relationship exists between readers' cognitive processes and their eye movements. Bouma and deVoogd (1974), Shebilske (1975), and Kolers (1976) argue against such a close relationship; Rayner and McConkie (1976) attempted to summarize various positions taken on eye movement control, together with the present evidence, and they argued for a tight control position. The papers in this conference (Levy-Schoen & O'Regan; O'Regan; and Rayner) also argue for relatively tight control. For now, I will assume on the basis of the data available in these sources, that the locations and durations of fixations are under the rather precise control of the ongoing cognitive processes. However, even if everyone were convinced that such control exists, there would still be the problem of identifying the nature of this control. This paper suggests a way of thinking about the relationship between the cognitive processes and eye movement control in reading that may be useful for future research.

A Common View of Reading

A common way of thinking about the cognitive and perceptual process involved in reading seems to underlie much of the writing in the field. It is assumed that since reading takes place only during fixations, each fixation (with the eye now in a new location) provides a new view of the text. During each fixation, the reader has a clear view of only a part of the page, a region extending relatively short distances from the center of vision. On each fixation, then, this is the region within which reading occurs. Smith (1971) argues that since the same word will likely be present within this reading span on more than one fixation, the accuracy of its identification is increased. Kolers (1976) has reviewed Buswell's arguments that one of the problems a poor reader has is that he encounters the words in non-normal sequences through frequent regressive movements which give views of text previously seen. It is assumed, then, that what is included within the perceptual span region during a fixation is seen.

Fixations occur at the rate of about four per sec, each giving a new view of the text, and yet the person has no sense of receiving such rapid succession of discrete images. There must be some means by which these are integrated into a single coherent image of the text. The problem will be discussed in more detail later.

Finally, if it is accepted that there is rather precise control of eye movements, the mind must be calculating during each fixation where the eye should be sent for the next fixation to provide the most information. This calculation is assumed to require information obtained from the peripheral visual areas where only grosser textual detail is available (word length, patterns, etc.), knowledge about what the passage has said up to this point and what is likely to be said next, and knowledge of the rules and regularities of language.

A number of questions naturally follow from this view of reading How large is the region we see on each fixation? How is information integrated across fixations? What is the nature of the complex calculation which the mind must make in deciding where to place the eye for each fixation? The following sections of the paper will review data on each of these topics which suggest the need for some reinterpretation of the views described above. Finally, a model of eye movement control in reading, compatible with the data to be reviewed, will be described and some implications of this model will be developed.

The Perceptual Span

Bouma (1973) and others have tested how far into the peripheral retinal areas letters and words can be identified. In general, for these stimuli, such identification can be carried out further to the right of the fixation point than to the left. However, McConkie and Rayner (1976b) failed to find any evidence that readers were obtaining visual information more than four letter positions (1 deg of visual angle) to the left of the fixation point. Thus their subjects were apparently not using visual information from a region Bouma found to be well within the area where letters and words can be identified. It does not seem to be true that all text lying within the region of clear visual detail will in fact be read during a fixation.

In another study which provides more evidence for this, Rayner (1975) found that if a person 1) fixates immediately in front of a short common word, close enough that the word can be identified, and 2) the next fixation is directly on that word (probably on the latter part), and 3) if during the saccade the word in that location has been changed to a different word with similar visual characteristics, then there is no evidence that the changed word is detected on the second fixation. The eye movement pattern manifests no disruption. It appears that the subjects, having read the word on the fixation preceding the change, ignored the word in that location on the second fixation and thus failed to detect the change. If this is so, and we will analyze this more precisely later, it indicates that readers fail to identify a word lying directly in the foveal region if it was identified on a prior fixation. Thus, it may be that during a fixation the words identified on previous fixations are ignored unless some difficulty forces the reader to return to an earlier point in the text. This may be why readers seem to use so little visual information to the left of the center of vision. This contrasts sharply with Smith's (1971) suggestion that each word is probably identified on several fixations.

The notion that text lying directly in the fovea can be ignored during a fixation suggests that people can shift attention during fixation to pick up visual information from different regions. Attending to one region increases the likelihood of detecting a target there, while reducing target detection in other areas (demonstrated by Engel, 1976). Also, Rayner, McConkie, and Ehrlich (in press), in harmony with Cunitz and Steinman (1969), found that subjects, while maintaining fixation on a dot, derive more information from the word to which a saccade would next be sent than from another in the visual field.

If, during a fixation, readers do shift the region from which they take visual information, then the concept of perceptual span changes. The perceptual span mapped by Bouma (1973) is the region within which sufficient visual information is available for the identification of isolated letters and words. However, the region within which visual information is taken during a fixation may depend upon what information is needed to support the language process taking place at the time. In fact, it is suggested that this region may change frequently during the fixation as different information is needed. While this seems similar to Geyer's (1970) and Gough's (1972) serial "read-in" of visual data at the beginning of a fixation, it is in fact quite different. There is no need for a serial input to make the visual data available; it is present on the retina and within the system as a result, and hence can be accessed as needed. However, the time at which aspects of this information are accessed and used for reading depends on when they are needed for language processing. It is not clear what units are accessed, whether features, letters, letter groups, syllables, words, etc. The important point seems to be that there is probably no constant perceptual span within which all text is read during each fixation, but information is accessed as it is needed (Miller & Johnson-Laird, 1976).

Integrating Information across Fixations

A series of studies investigating the question of what information is carried across from one fixation to the next has also suggested the need for some reconceptualization of the common view of reading described earlier. The first of these studies was conducted by Rayner (1975), in which he changed the contents of a particular word position in the text displayed on a CRT as the reader's eye was making a saccade. Thus, the word at that location on one fixation was different on the next fixation. Under certain conditions this resulted in a longer fixation, indicating that the disparity between the displays on the two fixations had caused a slight disruption in reading. Also, Rayner (this volume) reviews studies indicating that information obtained parafoveally on one fixation can reduce the time it takes to name a word on the next fixation. Thus, information can be carried over from one fixation to the next. Rayner (1975) and McConkie and Rayner (1976a) suggested that this was accomplished through an Integrative Visual Buffer. The visual information obtained on one fixation, it was thought, was spatially justified with the information still available from the prior fixation, and integrated into a single set of visual data from which the language processes could draw as needed. It was further suggested that this process of justifying the two sets of visual information was accomplished on the basis of pattern similarity rather than on the basis of knowing how far the eye had been sent (see Cumming, in press, for a brief description of this distinction) since the text could be shifted short distances during a saccade without the movement being consciously detected (McConkie & Rayner, 1976a). If aspects of the two visual patterns did not agree, it was assumed that this integration process would be disrupted, thus producing a longer fixation. If the information coincided, as is normally the case, then any processing of the visual information that had been initiated on one fixation could be continued on the next, producing the reduced naming times obtained by Rayner (this volume). The visual integrative buffer was assumed to hold strictly visual patterns, the data necessary for higher level identification, and language processes.

In order to test the notion that strictly visual information is integrated across fixations, McConkie and Zola (in press) conducted a study in which characteristics of the text were changed from one fixation to the next without changing the language. In this study, subjects read text from a CRT in which successive letters AlTeRnAtEd BeTwEeN uPpEr aNd lOwEr CaSe.

The subjects first read a passage of this type to get used to the style. They then read a second passage during which display changes occurred. During three of the saccades on every other line, the display switched between the two forms of the line shown in Figure 1; each letter that was in upper case on one of these fixations was in lower case on the next, and vice-versa. Thus, there were three fixations on certain lines in which the shape of every letter was different from its shape during the previous fixation. We assumed that if visual patterns or features were being integrated from one fixation to the next, this type of display change should be highly disruptive, thus producing eye movement irregularities.

In fact, this manipulation created no difficulty for the reader. There was no effect on the eye movement pattern. Our subjects were not even aware that any change had taken place; even when a person knew the nature of the change that was occurring, he was unable to detect any change as he read. This manipulation was obvious to an onlooker watching the display, since the changes were not synchronized with his eye movements.

If changing the shapes of the letters from one fixation to the next has no effect, this seems to be good evidence that the visual features or shapes are not maintained or integrated across fixations. What was it, then, that was maintained from one fixation to the next in Rayner's (1975) study? It was not just visual pattern or features; nor does it seem to have been semantic information, since Rayner found evidence that disruptions were occurring when semantic information was not yet being obtained. It must have been some intermediary coding existing between the visual and the semantic levels; possibilities include identified letters or letter groupings, or some type of phonetic encoding.

These results raise the question of whether any visual pattern information persists from fixation to fixation. David Zola and I wondered if changing more gross figural characteristics of the text from one fixation to the next would be noticed. Using ourselves as subjects, and our introspections as our only data, we read passages on which, after several saccades on a given line, the first 5, 10, or 15 letters of the line (by now some distance to the left of the fixation) disappeared and reappeared on successive fixations. Our experience was that, unlike the changes in case of individual letters, these changes were quite noticeable. They did not seem to interfere with reading, however. Thus, a general image of the grosser characteristics of the scene of the text seems to be maintained across fixations, since changes of this sort are noticed. We also found that if the entire line were presented in upper case, and switched to lower case during a particular saccade, this was noticed. Although the

---

I.   dIsTrIbUtEd. It ApPeArS tHaT pItCh-NaMiNg AbIlItY cAn Be

II.   DiStRiBuTeD. iT aPpEaRs ThAt PiTcH-nAmInG aBiLiTy CaN bE

Figure 1. Two versions of a line of text printed in alternating case. Changing a line from one version to the other changes visual features of all the letters.

changes made in individual letters were identical to those made in the alternating case study (where the switch was not noticed), the change from all
upper to all lower case and vice versa produces a line having very different
gross figural properties than does the change from one version of an alternating case line to another. It may be necessary to make a distinction between
the aspects of a text that are seen as a picture, the "scene" of the text, and
those that are actually used in support of language processing. The former
may be carried from one fixation to the next, whereas the latter may not
be. In any case, the fact that the visual features of letters can be changed
from one fixation to the next with no apparent effect on reading, and without
being detected by the reader, is clearly contradictory to the notion of an
Integrative Visual Buffer.

It may be that the concept of integration is the wrong way to think about
what is taking place in reading. Perhaps the reader simply accesses the
visual detail available at the time from the retina as it is needed to carry
out the language processing in reading. When a stimulus change occurs during
a saccade, the change will be disruptive if the new information sought is
not in harmony with the previous processing. If the changed information
is not accessed, or if the nature of the changes are such that no disharmony
results, then the change will not disrupt the reading and may not even be
noticed.

Control of Eye Behavior in Reading

Papers in this volume by Levy-Schoen and O'Regan, Rayner, O'Regan, and
Fisher indicate a great interest in identifying the rules used by the mind to
control where the eye will be sent. It is suggested that on the basis of knowledge of the language, the topic being discussed (Fisher refers to Hochberg's
Cognitive Search Guidance), and of visual patterns in the peripheral regions
(Hochberg's Peripheral Search Guidance), the mind calculates where it should
send the eye next. The nature of this calculation is of great interest, since
it is here that the answer to the question asked earlier should be found: What
is the relation between the language processes and eye movement pattern?
Involved are factors such as word length (O'Regan, 1975; McConkie & Rayner,
1975; Rayner & McConkie, 1976), grammatical structure (Wanat, 1976), location of blanks (Abrams & Zuber, 1972), and which particular words lie in the
periphery (O'Regan, this volume). The brain must make this complicated
calculation about four times a second. However, the view of attentional
activity during fixation described earlier raises an interesting possible view
of eye movement control which does not require these complex calculations.
This view will be presented as a series of assumptions.

A Proposed Model of Eye Movement Control in Reading

1   Assume that the region from which information is sought from the retina
to support language processing shifts during fixation, while the eye remains
relatively still. Assume further that under normal circumstances, when language processing is proceeding without problem, this region moves from left
to right along the line of text. To facilitate communication, the region within
which visual detail is being considered at a given moment will be referred
to as the attended region. It is not presently known whether this attended
region is related to specific letters, letter groups, words, etcetera; whether

the size of the region varies from moment to moment; or whether there is some normal sequence of information access within the region (see Brown's (1970) noticing order).

2   Assume that identification in reading is accomplished by using visual information and knowledge of language and of the world (Tulving & Gold, 1963). If this is the case, then the more the text is constrained by other information, the less visual information will be required for identification to be complete.

3   Assume that at some point during a fixation, as the attended region is shifted along the line of text, visual information is sought from a retinal region too far from central vision to readily supply the visual detail needed for identification. The point at which this occurs varies depending on what level of visual detail is needed from this retinal location for text identification.

4   Assume that seeking visual detail from a retinal region which is not readily available causes the saccadic system to initiate a saccadic eye movement. The eye is sent a distance and direction corresponding to the distance and direction that this attended retinal region lies from the center of vision. That is, the eye is simply rotated so the attended region is brought to central vision. This is assumed to be the primary basis for saccadic eye movement control in reading. A secondary basis will be described later.

5   Assume that this sequence continues along the line of text. The language processes call for visual data from text locations usually shifting rightward along the line. Whenever insufficient visual information is available, the eye is moved and centered on the location from which visual detail is presently sought. Thus, the needed visual detail is then available and reading proceeds along the line.

6   Assume that, occasionally, visual information is needed from a region previously read. When this information is sought some distance to the left of the center of vision, far enough out that insufficient visual detail is available, the eye makes a regressive movement and is centered on the new text location.

These assumptions describe a very simple mechanism for controlling eye movements. All that is required is information about how far from the center of vision, and in what direction, visual information, not readily available, is being sought. The eye is then sent that distance in that direction. There is no complex calculation of where to send the eye; no prediction of what region is likely to be most informative or of what might lie in the next region; there is no distinction between the use of visual information from central versus peripheral vision and thus no Cognitive Search Guidance -- Peripheral Search Guidance distinction; there is no integration of visual features from one fixation to the next. Yet this simple mechanism seems capable of accounting for all the phenomena which more complex models have been developed to handle. Let us consider a series of questions, with answers based on the above assumptions.

Some Questions about Eye Movement Control
Why does the length of saccades vary? The level of visual detail needed for identification varies due to differences in language redundancy and in the specific features needed to select among alternative possible words. Therefore, the distance which reading will proceed into the periphery before the

needed visual detail is unavailable will vary. A saccade is only initiated when the level of detail available from the retina is insufficient to make the decisions required in language processing at that point. Where this occurs is likely to be influenced by factors such as word length, grammatical patterns, the number of words having common gross characteristics that could occupy that point in the text, etcetera. For example, in certain locations the presence of the word "the" may be quite probable, so that it can be identified from rather gross visual detail, and will not usually be the locus of the next fixation. If another word were placed in the same location, it might require greater visual detail for identification, thus being a good candidate for fixation when it lies some distance from the fovea. In other locations, where the word "the" is not so highly constrained, it would require an amount of visual detail similar to other words and would thus possess the same likelihood of being fixated. This seems to be the pattern obtained by O'Regan (this volume). The location of a fixation indicates the text region from which visual information was being sought at the end of the prior fixation, and from which greater visual detail is taken at the beginning of the new fixation.

Why do the durations of fixation vary? Since it is assumed that the language processes only seek visual information when needed, and since at different points in the text the cognitive operations initiated vary in the time required, the amount of time that passes before unavailable visual detail is sought varies. In fact, then, under most conditions, the fixation time indicates the time required to carry out language processing of the text between the location of the present fixation and that of the next. This is most likely to be the case when the eye is executing a series of sizeable forward movements in reading. The problem becomes more complex in regressive movements, and perhaps in very short saccades, which will be discussed later.

Why, as people improve their reading skills, do the length of saccades increase? It is because the amount of visual detail needed depends on the reader's knowledge of the language; and as this knowledge increases, less detail is required and reading can proceed further into the periphery before the needed visual data become unavailable. This, of course, leads to longer saccades.

Why is there an extreme asymmetry to the perceptual span in reading? As explained previously, it is assumed that a saccade centers the eye on the region from which visual information is being sought. Regions lying to the left of the center of vision will normally contain text already identified. Further information from this region will be sought only on the first fixation of a line, and on fixations in which, for some reason, additional information is needed from a previously read region. This would presumably be due to some sort of error-correction procedure.

Why did Rayner, McConkie, and Ehrlich (described by Rayner, this volume) find that, without an eye movement, two prior letter strings both influence the naming time of a foveally-presented word, whereas when the subjects were instructed to move their eyes to look at one of the words, the string to which the eye was moved primarily affected naming times? If saccadic movements are made only to seek information from an attended region, then the instruction to move the eye to one of the letter strings is essentially an instruction to seek information from that string. When subjects were instructed not to make an eye movement, there were fewer constraints on the region from which visual information could be taken.

Why do readers have the feeling that they are passing continuously along the line of text when, in reality, their eyes are making discrete jumps? Readers have this impression because, in fact, they are passing continuously along a line. The region attended normally proceeds along the line as language processing progresses through the text. It is this pattern that is psychologically real. The saccadic movement pattern is automatically produced according to a simple, almost reflexive, procedure which simply brings an attended region to the fovea when greater detail is required, thus allowing the cognitive processes to continue to obtain needed visual information. It may be that the emphasis on saccadic movement and discrete images of the text, which have been taken as a primary psychological fact about reading, will suffer the same fate as the Structuralists' fundamental psychological fact of simple primary sensations in perception.

Implications of the Model
If the model of eye movement control just described turns out to have some validity, it suggests that in our attempts to understand eye movement control we have confused the mind's problem with the experimenter's problem. The mind's problem is very simple: when the visual information available leaves an ambiguity that should be visually resolvable, orient the fovea to the region from which this information is sought. The experimenter's problem is much more difficult. In order to predict where the eye will be sent, the experimenter must have information about the degree of visual detail obtainable at different distances into the periphery for each subject, the amount of constraint in the language at given points in the text, the visual features which distinguish between alternative words which might lie at specific regions of the text, and the nature of the subject's reading skill. All these become implicated in determining how far into the periphery reading can proceed before the needed visual detail becomes unavailable. Accurately predicting where the eye will go next may be a formidable problem for the experimenter, though the effects of certain variables can be tested.

While the view of eye movement control that has been described here tends to reduce the psychological importance of the saccade itself, it also indicates that eye movement data may have an important role in the study of language processes in reading. If the model is correct, it clarifies the nature of the information which can be gained from eye movement records. While knowing where the eye is centered for a fixation may not indicate the region from which visual information is being taken at different times during the fixation, it may specify the region being attended at the beginning of the fixation. Knowing when certain regions are being attended, and the amount of time intervening between these bench-marks, provides us with a measure of the time required to process the text in the area thus bounded. This information can be useful for testing models which suggest that the amount of cognitive activity carried out at different locations in the text varies, and which predict where more and less cognitive work should need to be done. Eye movement data also provide information about where the reader seeks visual information from text previously read, an aspect of the data capitalized upon by Just and Carpenter (1976). While we may wish that eye movement data would provide even more detail, this is still considerably more information than would be suggested by the prominent buffer models of eye movement control (Rayner & McConkie, 1976). It provides information without first having to solve the problem of predicting where the eye will go next. Thus, if accurate, this model avoids the problems involved in predicting where the person will look in reading, while still being able to utilize the eye movement data in the study of reading.

The Control of Short Saccades
There is one aspect of eye movement data for which the approach described above fails to give a satisfactory explanation. Why do small saccades occur in reading? In data from six college students, 7% of the saccades were 40 minutes of arc or less in extent (two letter positions or less, in the display used). When a saccade of this length is executed, the eye is moved such a short distance that the region lying at the center of vision following the saccade was actually within the fovea on the prior fixation. It seems unlikely that insufficient visual detail was available from that region on the prior fixation, so the explanation of saccadic movement given above seems to fail in this case. However, it has been suggested by several researchers (Cunitz & Steinman, 1969; Engel, 1976) that a small saccade will often occur when the person makes a discrete shift of attention. Thus, while the attended region normally proceeds smoothly from unit to unit, there may be times when difficulty is encountered and a discrete shift of attention is made to a region from which specific information is needed. If the shift were large, a normal saccade would result. However, the new place attended may be within the region where adequate visual detail is available without moving the eye. If so, a normal saccade would not be triggered. However, there may be a sufficiently tight link between the attentional system and the saccadic control system that a discrete attention shift would cause a discharge in the saccadic system, resulting in a short, unneeded saccade in the direction of the attention shift. If this is supported by further research, small saccades may turn out to be useful indicators of yet another aspect of the cognitive processing occurring in reading.

In summary, the concepts of perceptual span and integration across fixations, as they are often used in theories of reading, have been questioned. An attempt has been made to develop a way of thinking about the control of eye movements in reading which is in harmony with the facts and suggestions presented.

The preparation of this paper was supported in part by Grant No. MH24241 from National Institutes of Mental Health.

REFERENCES

Abrams, S.G., & Zuber, B.L. Some temporal characteristics of information processing during reading. Reading Research Quarterly, 1972, 8, 40-51.
Bouma, H. Visual interference in the parafoveal recognition of initial and final letters of words. Vision Research, 1973, 13, 767-782.

Bouma, H., & deVoogd, A.H. On the control of eye saccades in reading. Vision Research, 1974, 14, 273-284.

Brown, R. Psychology and reading. In H. Levin & J.P. Williams (Eds.), Basic studies on reading. New York: Basic Books, 1970.

Cumming, G.D. Eye movements and visual perception. In E.C. Carterette and M. Friedman (Eds.), Handbook of perception, Vol. VIII. New York: Academic Press, in press.

Cunitz, R.J., & Steinman, R.M. Comparison of saccadic eye movements during fixation and reading. Vision Research, 1969, 9, 683-693.

Engel, F.L. Visual conspicuity as an external determinant of eye movements and selective attention. Thesis, Eindhoven, The Netherlands, 1976.

Fisher, D.F. Understanding the reading process through the use of transformed typography: PSG, CSG, and automaticity. (This volume.)

Geyer, J.J. Models of perceptual processes in reading. In H. Singer and R.B. Ruddell (Eds.), Theoretical models and processes of reading. Newark, DE: International Reading Association, 1970.

Gough, P.B. One second of reading. In J.F. Kavanagh and I.G. Mattingly (Eds.), Language by ear and by eye. Cambridge, MA: MIT, 1972.

Just, M.A., & Carpenter, P.A. Eye fixation and cognitive processes. Cognitive Psychology, 1976, 8, 441-480.

Kolers, P.A. Buswell's discoveries. In R.A. Monty & J.W. Senders (Eds.), Eye movements and psychological processes. Hillsdale, NJ: Erlbaum, 1976.

Levy-Schoen, A., & O'Regan, K. The control of eye movements in reading. (This volume.)

McConkie, G.W. & Rayner, K. The span of the effective stimulus during a fixation in reading. Perception & Psychophysics, 1975, 17, 578-586.

McConkie, G.W., & Rayner, K. Identifying the span of the effective stimulus in reading: Literature review and theories of reading. In H. Singer and R.B. Ruddell (Eds.), Theoretical models and processes of reading (2nd ed.). Newark, DE: International Reading Association, 1976. (a)

McConkie, G.W., & Rayner, K. Asymmetry of the perceptual span in reading. Bulletin of the Psychonomic Society, 1976, 8, 365-368. (b)

Miller, G.A., & Johnson-Laird, P.N. Language and perception. Cambridge, MA: Harvard University Press, 1976.

O'Regan, J.K. Structural and contextual constraints on eye movements in reading. Doctoral dissertation, University of Cambridge, 1975.

O'Regan, J.K. Moment-to-moment control of eye saccades as a function of textual parameters in reading. (This volume.)

Rayner, K. The perceptual span and peripheral cues in reading. Cognitive Psychology, 1975, 7, 65-81.

Rayner, K. Eye movements in reading: Eye guidance in integration. (This volume.)

Rayner, K., & McConkie, G.W. What guides a reader's eye movements? Vision Research, 1976, 16, 829-837.

Rayner, K., McConkie, G.W., & Ehrlich, S. Eye movements and integrating information over fixations. Journal of Experimental Psychology: Human Perception and Performance, in press.

Shebilske, W. Reading eye movements from an information-processing point of view. In D. Massaro (Ed.), Understanding language. New York: Academic Press, 1975.

Smith, F. Understanding reading. New York: Holt, Rinehart & Winston, 1971.

Tulving, E., & Gold, C. Stimulus information and contextual information as determinants of tachistoscopic recognition of words. Journal of Experimental Psychology, 1963, 66, 319-327.

Wanat, S.F. Language behind the eye: Some findings, speculations, and research strategies. In R.A. Monty & J.W. Senders (Eds.), Eye movements and psychological processes. Hillsdale, NJ: Erlbaum, 1976.

Moment to Moment Control of Eye Saccades as a Function of Textual Parameters in Reading

Kevin O'Regan

Until recently, it has been assumed that saccade size during reading only changes slowly as a function of the global parameters of the text being read. Evidence from two series of experiments demonstrates, on the contrary, that at each instant during reading the size of the next saccade is determined by the nature of the material in the near periphery. First, purely physical parameters are active: the saccade will be longer if the next word is long, shorter if it is short. Second, purely lexical parameters are at work: in the identical preceding context, where no differences in syntactic predictions are possible, a three-letter verb will attract more fixations than the article THE. The decision to make a large or small saccade is therefore taken on the basis of a partial decoding of the word in peripheral vision. Finally, the strength of the effect is dependent on preceding sentence structure, suggesting that this is a third factor in determining saccade sizes from moment to moment.

In previous work (O'Regan, 1975), I presented evidence that when someone reads, his eyes make moment to moment adjustments in saccade size which are related to local characteristics of the text being read. What information is being used to control such adjustments? Would gross visual features like character size and word length suffice to control the process of adapting the rate of information intake by the eyes to the rate of cognitive processing? Or, are the moment to moment adjustments a reflection of the perceptual or the linguistic processing occurring at each position in the text? Before making this distinction more precise and trying to answer the questions posed, I will briefly describe my earlier evidence for moment to moment saccade size adjustments.

Table 1. Median Landing Positions as a Function of the Length of the Word in Periphery. (Median Tests Were Used for Statistics).

Leaving Subject of Sentence

Departure Zone		Landing Zone	Median Landing Position in Landing Zone	
SHORT	–	SHORT	3	$p < .001$
SHORT	–	LONG	6	
LONG	–	SHORT	4	$p < .01$
LONG	–	LONG	7.5	

Leaving Verb of Sentence

Departure Zone		Landing Zone	Median Landing Position in Landing Zone	
SHORT	–	THE SHORT	7	n.s.
SHORT	–	THE LONG	7	
LONG	–	THE SHORT	4	$p < .01$
LONG	–	THE LONG	6.5	

Table 2. Median Saccade Size as a Function of the Length of the Word Fixated. (Median Tests Were Used for Statistics).

Leaving Subject of Sentence

Departure Zone	Landing Zone	Median Saccade Size Leaving Departure Zone	
SHORT	- SHORT	4	p < .001
LONG	- SHORT	8	
SHORT	- LONG	7.5	p < .025
LONG	- LONG	12	

Leaving Verb of Sentence

Departure Zone	Landing Zone	Median Saccade Size Leaving Departure Zone	
SHORT	- THE SHORT	8	n.s.
LONG	- THE SHORT	10	
SHORT	- THE LONG	8	p < .01
LONG	- THE LONG	12	

In one experiment, people read sentences of the form: THE (noun 1) (verb) THE (noun 2) (prepositional phrase), where noun 1, noun 2, and verb were either long words (10 to 14 letters) or short words (3 letters). There were eight sentences, one corresponding to each of the possible combinations of long and short words. For example, the sentence for the combination SHORT SHORT SHORT was THE CAT SAW THE RAT IN THE BARN, and for SHORT LONG LONG it was THE MAN ACKNOWLEDGED THE INTELLIGENCE OF HIS BOSS. The eight sentences were inserted randomly in a list of 36 filler sentences of diverse structure. Twenty subjects, whose eye movements were being recorded, read the sentences as they appeared in capital letters, one sentence at a time, on the computer display screen.

The subjects' eye movements in relation to the length of the word in peripheral vision were scrutinized. When the eye is faced with the transition from a short word like MAN or CAT to another short word like RAN or SAW, it moves to a median landing position at the third letter of the landing zone (since the landing zone contains the space preceding the word, this is the second letter of RAN or SAW). But when the eye goes from a short word to a long one (e.g., from MAN to ACKNOWLEDGED or from MAN to CONGRATULATED), the eye goes to a median landing position 6 letters into the landing zone (cf. Table 1).

Just as the length of the word in peripheral vision influences saccade size, so also does the length of the word currently being fixated. The data in Table 2 show that for a given length of word in the periphery, the eye makes significantly bigger saccades if it starts from a long rather than a short word. Approaching a short verb, the median saccade size was 4 letters if the previous noun was short, and 8 letters if it was long. Similarly, going towards a long verb, the eye made a median saccade of 7.5 letters leaving a short noun, and 12 letters leaving a long one. For reasons to do with "THE-skipping" (see later), the effect is slightly weaker when we are looking at transitions out of the verb.

These two results are consistent with an analysis by Rayner and McConkie (1976) of the probability of fixating the letters of a word as a function of the word's length: letters in words of length 7 to 12 are less likely to be fixated than those in 6-letter words. This means that the eye must make longer saccades near long words, which accommodates the results I have just described.

It seems natural that we should find the eye making bigger saccades in regions with long words; after all, a single tachistoscopic view suffices to identify words of any length. But is this adaptation a general "length control" strategy that the reader learns for efficient reading, or is it a consequence of momentary variations in processing as he encounters long or short words ("cognitive control")?

Under the length control hypothesis, the adjustments are part of a general reading pattern that leads to a satisfactory rate of information intake, and which involves a simple overall strategy like "Fixate each word once near the middle." Since each word can best be encoded from a position near its middle, this appears to be a good strategy. It also makes few demands on the oculomotor control system, since the middle of the next word is easily definable in terms of simple sensory factors like spaces in the text (filling or removing the spaces strongly perturbs reading).

Under the cognitive control hypothesis, the eye makes instantaneous adjustments as a function of ongoing cognitive processing. This is what Shebilske (1975) calls the "classic span of perception" model. It is assumed that the distance into the periphery that visual encoding can take place--the distance the eye can "see" into the periphery--is determined by cognitive factors such as grammatical predictability, transition probability, word frequency, as well as visual factors involving partial clues from peripheral vision. It is also assumed that the eye moves to the nearest region which it cannot "see" clearly, just beyond the current perceptual span. Since words, independent of length, are equally visible, the perceptual span will be wider for long words and the eye will tend to jump further.

To distinguish between length control and cognitive control, it suffices to note that the strategy depending purely on length information should be unaffected by the identity of particular words. So, if the word in peripheral vision is a very predictable one, like THE in the sentences used here, the eye should behave the same as when approaching any other three-letter word. The data in Table 1 show that this is not the case. If we compare transitions from SHORT to SHORT with SHORT to THE SHORT, it is clear that the eye is skipping the THE (p < .0001). Again, in the transition SHORT THE LONG, the eye jumps further than in the transition SHORT SHORT (p < .001). When the eye is leaving a long word, one comparison gives significant THE-skipping (LONG SHORT versus LONG THE LONG, p < .0001), and the other does not (LONG SHORT versus LONG THE SHORT).

The foregoing results enable one to firmly reject a simple length control eye movement strategy, where the subject uses the spaces in the text to guide him to the middle of each new word. To explain the above results, the subjects must have been doing one or both of the following: using their syntactic knowledge of English to predict a THE after the verb, thus programming a larger saccade; or using partial visual clues about the word in peripheral vision (length, first and last letters, general shape such as the density of letters and position of ascenders and descenders) to reduce the choices. Using their knowledge of English, the subjects would then be able to guess that the next word was THE and program a larger saccade.

This second alternative makes more demands on the oculomotor control system than the first, since poor quality peripheral information from the current fixation must have time to be processed and compared to lexical knowledge. In the following experiment the THE-skipping result could only be accounted for by this more demanding processing of instantaneous lexical and peripheral visual information, not by grammatical predictions.

Experiment
Pairs of sentences were constructed in such a way that the members of a pair began with the same words, but ended differently; one ending started with THE, the other started with one of six 3-letter verbs (HAD WAS ARE ATE RAN MET)--see Table 3. (Three of the VRBs were high frequency auxiliaries, three were not. Half of the GRUNTED and LOVERS type sentences were therefore "auxiliary," and half "non-auxiliary." This extra factor in the structure of the experiment will not be discussed here. All tabulated values (and Figures) in this paper have been obtained by taking the mean of the two values calculated for the two types of verb.)

Table 3. Structure of Experiment.

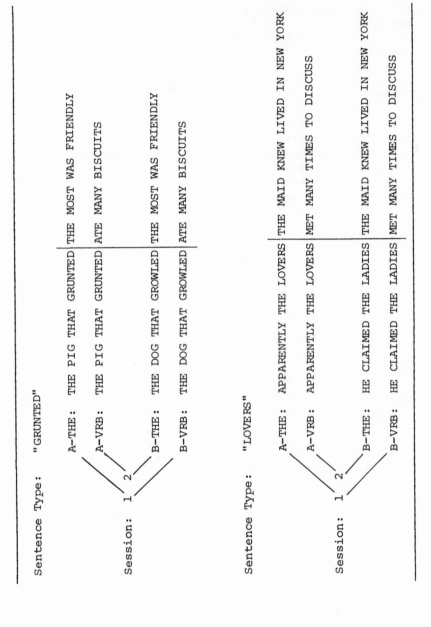

Sentence Type: "GRUNTED"

A-THE: THE PIG THAT GRUNTED THE MOST WAS FRIENDLY

A-VRB: THE PIG THAT GRUNTED ATE MANY BISCUITS

B-THE: THE DOG THAT GROWLED THE MOST WAS FRIENDLY

B-VRB: THE DOG THAT GROWLED ATE MANY BISCUITS

Session: 1   2

Sentence Type: "LOVERS"

A-THE: APPARENTLY THE LOVERS THE MAID KNEW LIVED IN NEW YORK

A-VRB: APPARENTLY THE LOVERS MET MANY TIMES TO DISCUSS

B-THE: HE CLAIMED THE LADIES THE MAID KNEW LIVED IN NEW YORK

B-VRB: HE CLAIMED THE LADIES MET MANY TIMES TO DISCUSS

Session: 1   2

I wanted to compare eye movement behaviour just before the critical position where there was either a THE or a VRB. My hypothesis was that partial visual information would enable the eye to move further in the case of THE than in the case of VRB; since THE is extremely common, it might be easier to see.

I couldn't ask the same subjects to read both sentences of a pair in the same experimental session, since they might remember the beginnings and be bored on the second encounter. So, for each sentence pair (Pair A), I constructed another sentence pair (Pair B), very similar in visual and grammatical structure, corresponding to the first pair. Elements kept constant were the position in the sentence of the critical THE or VRB; the number of letters in at least the two preceding words; the end letters of the words preceding; and the first letter of the word following the critical THE or VERB. Having taken these precautions, I felt I could make my comparisons across pairs A and B instead of within each pair. Table 3 shows this.

To further decrease the variability of the data, each subject did the experiment twice, at several days' interval. In one session a subject would see the THE sentence of Pair A and the VRB sentence of Pair B. In the other session he would see the opposite combination (cf. Table 3).

In each session there were 48 test sentences and 96 filler sentences. All the filler sentences and the 48 endings of the test sentences changed between sessions.

Because I could not find enough test sentences of a single type, I used a variety of grammatical structures; these can be divided into two broad categories according to whether the word preceding the critical THE or VRB was a noun or a verb. The GRUNTED and GROWLED sentences in Table 3 are examples of the verb-type structure, and the LOVERS and LADIES of noun-type structure. I will refer to the prototypical sentence types GRUNTED and LOVERS for any sentence of the verb or noun type, respectively.

In each session, the subjects read the appropriate list of 144 sentences as they appeared, singly, in random order on the computer display screen. Only capital letters were used. Every 6 or 7 sentences the computer interrupted the sequence and displayed a question to see if the subject was paying attention. The task was to decide if the question sentence had already appeared in the preceding group of 5 or 6 sentences. The computer recorded the subjects' eye movements, and by means of a 15-sec "smooth pursuit" calibration procedure (O'Regan, 1978), maintained an accuracy of one or two letters throughout the experiment.

For the results, I tabulated the median positions subjects fixated upon when first leaving the departure zone consisting of the word preceding the critical THE or VRB. For example, in the sentence THE MAN WHO BOUGHT LABELS HAD CASES FULL OF THEM, the computer searched for the first occurrence of a saccade leaving the departure zone LABELS, and noted the arrival point. There were of course instances where the subject might have already received information about whether there was a THE or a VRB in the critical position before he arrived at LABELS. For example, if someone started by looking at THE MAN, moved by a large saccade to CASES, and then arrived at LABELS, he would have had a glimpse of the critical word HAD. The computer therefore excluded all records where the eye moved beyond the beginning of the departure zone before actually fixating inside it. That is, once a regression was found at or beyond the first letter of LABELS, the record was excluded.

Table 4 shows the mean landing positions for THE and VRB conditions of the GRUNTED and LOVERS sentence types. Each entry in the table corresponds to data for 24 sentences, 12 from each of the two sessions. A clear THE-skipping effect can be seen: the landing positions for THE sentences are larger numbers than for VRB sentences in five out of seven subjects, implying that the eye tended to jump further to the right on leaving the departure zone if the next word was THE than if it was a VRB (main effect of ANOVA, p < .01). For GRUNTED sentences, the mean landing position is 1.5 letters further to the right when the eye is going towards a THE than when it is going towards a VRB. The difference is much smaller for the LOVERS sentences, but still systematic in five subjects out of seven. Notice also that in all cases the differences here are smaller than those found for THE-skipping in Table 1, where preceding context was different for the THE and VRB cases.

Why is the effect smaller in the case of the LOVERS sentence type? One possibility is the difference in the distribution of fixations prior to the critical VRB or THE. Suppose, for example, that because of syntatic differences in the beginnings of GRUNTED-type sentences, the eyes tended to arrive further to the right in the departure zone GRUNTED than in the departure zone LOVERS. Then they would tend to be closer to the critical THE or VRB, and have a better view: it would be easier to take account of the differences between THE and VRB.

A way of avoiding this problem is to tabulate, not landing positions in the critical THE/VRB region, but the size of saccades made when leaving the departure zone. This has been done in Figure 1A where each point of the graphs represents a mean, over the seven subjects, of the median forward-going saccade size made starting from the 3-letter zone over which the point is placed. For example, in the left-hand graph, starting from the 3-letter zone centred on the letter T of GRUNTED, the subjects made a mean saccade of size 7.3 when the next word was THE, and 6.5 letters when the next word was a VRB, such as ATE. Regressions were excluded in the same way as for the landing point data.

What behaviour do we expect from these graphs? Since solid and dotted lines correspond to pairs of sentences with exactly the same beginnings, the curves should follow each other closely over the beginnings of the sentences. Only when the effect of the different sentence endings begins to appear, that is, near the critical THE/VRB region, should the curves start to separate, saccade size becoming bigger when approaching THE than when approaching a VRB. As can be seen from the figure, this is what happens. Only when we get close to the critical THE/VRB, does the dotted THE condition line properly rise above the solid VRB line. Note, also, that in the GRUNTED sentences the dotted THE curve is slightly above the solid VRB curve at almost every position of GRUNTED, whereas for LOVERS there is some indecision before final separation at the letter R. This means that eye saccades are being influenced much earlier in the GRUNTED case, a fact which may be related to the stronger THE-skipping effect found in the landing point data for this sentence type (Table 4).

Table 4. Median Landing Points for Each Subject.

Departure Zone	Going Towards	Subjects							Mean
		I	M	U	A	C	K	R	
GRUNTED	VRB	6	3	6	5	4	4	1.5	4.2
	THE	5.5	5	7.5	6.3	6.8	5	5	5.9
LOVERS	VRB	7.3	3.8	5.5	5	6	4	8	5.7
	THE	6.5	4.5	6.8	5.8	7	4.8	4.5	5.7

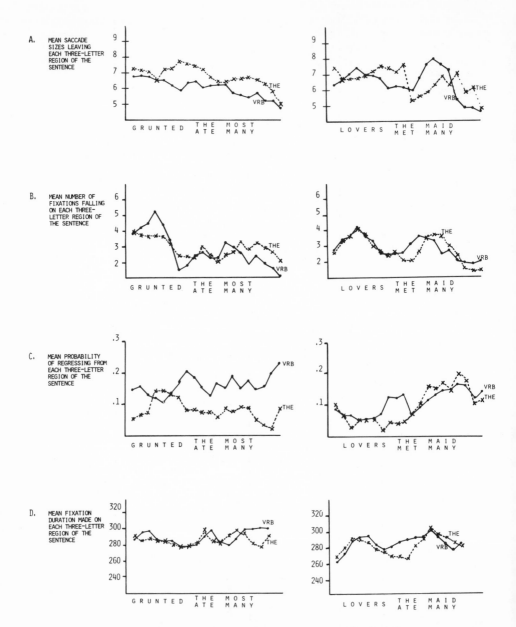

Figure 1. Instantaneous eye movement parameters. Each point represents a mean of the medians, for seven subjects of the values cumulated over the 3-letter region above which the point is centred, and cumulated over sentence types and over the two sessions.

Figure lB shows the mean number of fixations at each sentence position. For the righthand LOVERS graph, the dotted and solid curves follow each other perfectly until the critical region. The hills and valleys of the curve are therefore not random perturbations, but the systematic result of eye movement control. Note that the basic THE-skipping effect is visible, slightly fewer fixations occuring on the THE than on the VRB. A better way of looking at the THE-skipping effect is to observe the global form of the dotted and solid curves. For the THE condition, there is a large hump in the (dotted) curve above MAID; for the VRB condition the hump is shifted to the left by two letter positions.

The left-hand GRUNTED graph of Figure lB tells a different story. To start with, slightly more fixations occur on THE than on VRB, despite the fact that the saccade size and landing position data show GRUNTED to be the case where THE-skipping is strongest. The problem resolves itself when one looks at the humps. The dotted curve's hump is shifted to the right (to the end of MOST), while the solid VRB condition curve is centred on the M of MANY. The fixation duration curve will suggest that the dotted hump on THE has a special status.

Another aspect of the GRUNTED graph is that solid and dotted lines separate from the beginning. Given the consistency of the LOVERS graph, it would be surprising if this were a random fluctuation. Further, the effect is coherent with the early separation of the curves of the saccade size graph (lefthand, Figure lA), both agreeing that the critical THE or VRB made itself felt much earlier than in the LOVERS case. Further confirmation of this comes from the graphs of regression probability (Figure lC). Again LOVERS curves follow each other perfectly until they get to the critical region, but GRUNTED curves are separate from the beginning. As expected, in both cases the THE sentences contain fewer regressions than the VRB ones.

Whereas number of fixations, saccade size, and regression probability show the same basic effect of THE-skipping, with the difference apparent earlier for GRUNTED sentences, an interesting break in this pattern occurs for fixation durations (Figure lD). The LOVERS curves behave as usual, separating only near the critical region. As expected, THE receives fixations of shorter duration than VRB. But the GRUNTED fixation duration curves (left-hand graph) hardly separate at all. Possibly since THE was skipped more often in the GRUNTED curves, when it was not skipped, this happened for peculiar reasons that increased the fixation duration. An analysis of fixation durations as a function of whether THE was skipped has not yet been done.

The conclusions to be drawn from this experiment are first, that local eye movement parameters (saccade size, regression probability, number of fixations, and perhaps fixation duration), are controlled sufficiently rapidly to be influenced from moment to moment by information concerning the lexical category of a word in peripheral vision. In particular, the word THE tended to be skipped more often and gave rise to fewer and shorter fixations in certain regions, and fewer regressions, than one of six 3-letter verbs occurring in the same context. Second, differences in preceding context interact with the THE-skipping effect making it on occasion either stronger or weaker. The variety of sentence structures used in this experiment was too large to warrant any guess about the nature of the interaction, but it is clear that some systematic influence of sentence structure exists.

Finally, the high consistency of the moment to moment measures of eye movement behaviour presented in Figure 1 shows that when elementary factors like word length and context are controlled, local eye movement measures are highly sensitive to the mechanisms underlying sentence processing. Far from being erratic or random, instantaneous saccade size, fixation duration, regression probability, and fixation density appear to be controlled from moment to moment in a coherent way.

I thank John Morton for his help with the first experiment. The second experiment was done while I was at the LNR research group at UCSD in 1976. I greatly appreciated their hospitality, and thank in particular Jay McClelland, Dave Rumelhart, and Don Norman. For other types of support, I thank Vincent Morlighem, Aline Mizrahi, and Heidi Feldman.

REFERENCES

O'Regan, J.K. Structural and contextual constraints on eye movements in reading. Unpublished doctoral thesis, University of Cambridge, 1975; available in mimeo from author.

O'Regan, J.K. A new horizontal eye movement calibration method: Subject controlled "smooth pursuit" and "zero drift." Behavior Research Methods and Instrumentation, 1978, 10, 393-397.

Rayner, J. Parafoveal identification during a fixation in reading. Acta Psychologica, 1975, 39, 271-282.

Rayner, K. & McConkie, G. W. What guides a reader's eye movements? Vision Research, 1976, 16, 829-837.

Shebilske, W. Reading eye movements from an information-processing point of view. In D. Massaro (Ed.), Understanding language. New York: Academic Press, 1975.

Eye Movements in Reading: Eye Guidance and Integration

Keith Rayner

*Eye guidance in reading and control of fixation durations
are discussed and relevant data reviewed. It is concluded
that the location of fixations in reading is determined in
a nonrandom manner and that fixation durations are affected
by cognitive activities occurring during the fixation. Recent
experiments on the integration of information across successive saccades are described. These experiments suggest
that l) eye movements per se are not necessary for integration since similar patterns of results were obtained when
subjects made eye movements and when the saccade was
simulated; 2) attentional allocation is tied to the direction
of an eye movement; and 3) purely visual information
obtained from parafoveal vision is not overlapped with visual
information in foveal vision after the saccade. On the basis
of the data and experiments reviewed, a tentative process-
monitoring view of eye movements in reading is proposed.*

Saccadic eye movements during reading generally extend about 8 character
spaces (or 2 deg of visual angle), while the mean duration of the fixational
pauses separating each saccade is 200-250 msec. However, there is a great
deal of variability in both these eye movement characteristics so that the
range of saccades is often l to 20 character spaces and the mean fixation
duration is from 100 to over 500 msec (Rayner & McConkie, 1976). Recently,
there have been a large number of studies utilizing eye movement data as
dependent variables in attempts to understand the reading process (see Rayner,
1978a, for a review.)

The extent to which nonfoveal vision is important in reading has received
considerable attention in these studies. A line of text which falls on the
retina during reading, can be divided into three regions: the foveal, the

parafoveal, and the peripheral. The foveal area subtends 1 to 2 deg of visual angle around the reader's fixation point and is the area of clear visual acuity. Thus, a typical saccade (8 character spaces) would bring a given region of text into the fovea. Beyond the fovea, acuity drops markedly and a reader's ability to identify a word is diminished. The parafoveal region subtends about 10 deg of visual angle around the reader's fixation point (Ditchburn, 1973) and the peripheral region includes everything on the line of text beyond the parafoveal region. There are two major ways in which information from parafoveal and peripheral vision may be useful to a reader. Such information may be important in guiding a reader's eye movements, and information from these nonfoveal areas may enable a reader to integrate information obtained from parafoveal vision on one fixation with more detailed information obtained from foveal vision on the next fixation. I will first discuss eye guidance, arguing that the eyes move in a nonrandom manner in reading   Second, I will discuss fixation durations, arguing that cognitive events determine how long the eyes remain fixated at any position. Then some recent experiments dealing with integration of information across successive saccades will be examined. Finally, I will conclude by proposing a tentative view of eye movements in reading, based on a process-monitoring model of reading.

Eye Guidance in Reading
Recently a number of models of the control mechanisms that guide the eye during reading have been proposed (Bouma & deVoogd, 1974; Haber, 1976; Kolers, 1976; O'Regan, 1975; Rayner, 1974, 1978a; Rayner & McConkie, 1976; and Shebilske, 1975). Although they were arrived at independently, most of these models are remarkably similar. As indicated elsewhere (Rayner, 1978a), models which suggest that eye movements are not under cognitive control are unsupported by available data. Such models assume that on each saccade the eyes move a certain distance and remain fixed for a set period of time. However, the great variability in eye movement data seems to rule out such a possibility. On the other hand, most of the other models can accommodate much of the available data. The evidence seems to indicate that the location of fixations in reading is determined in some nonrandom manner, the rules of which have not yet been established.

Data supporting the notion that eye movements are made in a nonrandom manner include the following: 1) words with the intervening spaces filled in produce shorter saccades than when the spaces are not filled (McConkie & Rayner, 1975; Spragins, Lefton, & Fisher, 1976); 2) readers tend not to fixate on blank areas inserted in text (Abrams & Zuber, 1972) or in the region marking the end of one sentence and the beginning of the next (Rayner, 1975a); 3) the length of the word to the right of fixation influences the length of the next saccade--if that word is longer, the eye tends to jump further (O'Regan, 1975); and 4) the function word "the" tends to be skipped more frequently than other three-letter words (O'Regan, 1975), particularly when it begins a sentence (Rayner, 1975a). In addition, Rayner and McConkie (1976) computed the probability of a fixation landing on words of different lengths and the probability of fixating on a letter within a word of a given length. In the first case they found a linear trend: as word length increased, the probability of fixating the word increased. However, a curvilinear trend was found for the probability of fixating a letter within a word of a given length, so that a letter in a word four to seven letters long was more likely to be fixated than one in either a shorter or longer word. Thus, where the eye was sent for a fixation was related to word length.

Finally, Rayner and McConkie (1976) found that there was no correlation between the length of a saccade and the resulting fixation duration, no correlation between the duration of a fixation and the following saccade, no correlation between successive saccades, and no correlation between successive fixation durations. Thus, we concluded that saccade length and fixation duration seem to represent independent aspects of eye behavior, each of which must be accounted for separately.

Fixation Durations in Reading

Two major positions have traditionally been taken with regard to fixation periods during reading (Rayner, 1977). The first position, referred to as the cognitive lag hypothesis, suggests that eye movements are so rapid and the duration of the fixations so short that semantic processing must necessarily lag behind the perceptual input. The second position, the process monitoring hypothesis, suggests that fixation durations are affected by the cognitive processes occurring during the fixation. Thus, more difficult words and passages should lead to longer fixation durations.

It has been demonstrated that both difficult passages (Tinker, 1965) and embedded sentences (Klein & Kurkowski, 1974) lead to more and longer fixations. However, both demonstrations rely on global aspects of eye movements and do not deal with moment-to-moment changes as a function of difficulty. Data which more directly support the process monitoring position include these facts: 1) fixation duration is affected by the number of syllables necessary to pronounce the stimulus (Pynte, 1974); 2) nonwords inserted in text result in significantly increased fixation durations (Rayner, 1975b); 3) unusual and infrequent words receive lengthened fixation times (Rayner, 1977; Kolers, 1976; Dearborn, 1906; Buswell, 1922); 4) if visual information is made inconsistent from one fixation to the next, the fixation duration is longer (Rayner, 1975b); and 5) certain grammatical elements in text yield longer fixation durations than other elements (Wanat, 1976; Rayner, 1977). Thus, it would appear that on many occasions fixation durations are determined by the visual, syntatic, and semantic characteristics of the region being fixated. It should also be pointed out that there are differences in fixation duration purely as a function of location on the line. For example, the first fixation on a line of text is longer than fixations in the middle of the line and the last fixation is shorter than all others (Rayner, 1977). This observation could also be used as evidence for the process monitoring hypothesis. In essence, the argument is that the difference between the first and last fixation on a line could be attributed to parafoveal processing. That is, with the first fixation on a line, the reader has not had the opportunity to preprocess any of that area. Conversely, with the last fixation there is no need to engage in parafoveal processing to the right of the fixation point. All the reader must do is program a return sweep since the next line is too far away to obtain any useful information from. While such an argument is consistent with the process monitoring hypothesis, an interpretation of fixation durations as a function of location on the line is somewhat ambiguous. For example, the longer fixation at the beginning could be due to purely visual factors such

Table 1. Examples of the Base Word and Different Alternatives.

Base-Word	W-Ident	W-SL	N-SL	N-L	N-S
chest	chest	chart	chovt	chfbt	ekovf
phone	phone	plane	ptcne	psfne	qtcuc
author	author	antler	amttcr	abtsir	omttcv
palace	palace	police	pcluce	pyltce	qcluec
crossed	crossed	cruised	crmesed	crkhsed	evmercb
granted	granted	guarded	gmavbed	gkabned	pmavbcb

W = word.
N = nonword.
W-Ident = identical to the base word
W-SL = a word with the same shape and end-letters as the base word.
N-SL = a nonword with the same shape and end-letters as the base word.
N-L = a nonword with the same end-letters as the base word.
N-S = a nonword with the same shape as the base word.

Note.   In the experiments, a word (W-Ident or W-SL conditions) or nonword
        (N conditions) was initially presented in parafoveal vision and
        replaced by the base word during the saccade.

as the possibility that monocular accommodation is detuned during the return sweep; thus, focus is imperfect at the outset of the initial fixation and information processing is slowed.

Integration Across Saccades in Reading

When the eyes move from one position on a line to another, there may be backward and forward masking as the retinal image from one fixation overrides the image from the other. This masking or interference effect occurs at low levels in the perceptual system. However, at higher levels, information from the two fixations may be integrated. On the basis of some experiments dealing with the perceptual span in reading McConkie & Rayner (1976) proposed that integration occurs as information from two fixations is brought together into a single representation of the stimulus. During an eye fixation, readers obtain visual information from parafoveal and peripheral vision, storing it in a temporary visual buffer called the Integrative Visual Buffer. The information stored there is then used as a base to which new information is added when the next region is fixated. The justification of the information from the two fixations could be based on 1) knowledge about how far the eye moved, and 2) the commonality of the visual patterns from the two fixations.

In an attempt to understand how information is integrated across successive saccades, we have recently conducted some experiments in which we were able to study the integration process independently of semantic and syntactic constraints. In these experiments (Rayner, 1978b; Rayner, McConkie, & Ehrlich, 1978), subjects' eye movements were monitored by a computer-based, eye movement recording system as they looked at a Cathode Ray Tube (CRT). Subjects were instructed to fixate on a target dot and push a button as they did so. The button push resulted in the appearance of a word or nonword letter string in parafoveal vision. Subjects were instructed to move their eyes to the location of the stimulus when it appeared on the CRT. As soon as the subject began a saccade, the computer replaced the initially presented stimulus with another word (called the base word) which the subjects were to name. Table 1 shows the characteristics of the stimuli used in these experiments.

Figure 1 shows a pattern of results typical of these experiments. The data in Figure 1 show the naming latency after the eyes arrived at the target, but the addition of saccadic latencies did not change the pattern of results. Figure 1 clearly indicates that prior parafoveal information of the type studied can facilitate the naming of a word in the fovea after the saccade since all conditions resulted in faster naming times than the control condition in which an asterisk was presented in parafoveal vision and was replaced by the base word during the saccade. The greater the consistency between the initially displayed alternative and base word, the greater was the facilitation. When the stimuli were presented 5 deg from fixation, there were minimal differences between the experimental conditions. However, when the initially displayed alternative was presented closer to the fovea, there were consistent differences. If the initially displayed alternative had the same terminal letters and word shape as the base word, naming times were faster at 3 deg than when those characteristics were dissimilar. At 1 deg, the same pattern was found, but there was also evidence that lexical or semantic information affected naming time (i.e., the difference between the W-SL and N-SL

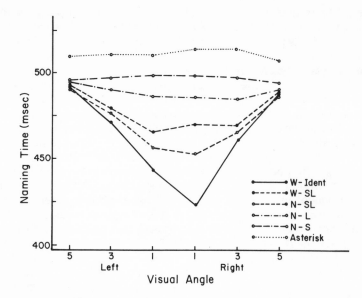

Figure 1. Mean naming times as a function of initially displayed alternative and visual angle.

condition). These results are consistent with the earlier finding (Rayner, 1975b) that different types of information are obtained from different regions of a reader's perceptual span.

The results of these studies indicated that subjects were able to use certain types of information from parafoveal vision to facilitate their responses. An interesting question is whether the sort of facilitation observed actually occurs during reading. While it seems possible and likely, the data are not perfectly clear on this point. Earlier I found that when the contents of a particular word position in the text (called the critical word location) were changed during an eye movement such that the contents of that word position when it was in parafoveal vision were different from the contents on the next fixation when it was directly fixated, the duration of the fixation on that word was affected (Rayner, 1975b). In fact, the conditions which produced longer response times in the present studies were the same conditions which produced longer fixations in the earlier study. However, the data from the earlier study were interpreted as showing interference effects during reading when stimulus patterns are changed, and the present studies provided evidence for facilitation effects in word identification when the stimulus pattern is not changed. Nevertheless, the pattern of results in the reading study and those in the present naming study are quite consistent.

Another interesting question is whether the saccade per se is important to the integration process and to the facilitation effect we obtained. Some theories of visual perception (cf., Gould, 1976) assume that eye movements are critical for perception and cognition. In order to investigate this question, we (Rayner et al., 1978) replicated the naming experiment. One condition was identical to the previous experiment. However, in another condition subjects maintained fixation as the initially displayed alternative was presented in parafoveal vision. After a period of time approximating the latency of the saccade, the base word appeared in the fovea. Thus, in both conditions the sequence of events on the retina was the same: the initially displayed alternative impinged on the parafoveal retina and the base word impinged on the fovea. In one condition an eye movement occurred, in the other condition, the eye movement was simulated.

The results of the experiment yielded no differences between the eye movement condition and the simulation condition; the data pattern was similar to that shown in Figure 1 for both conditions. Thus, we concluded that integration and facilitation were not dependent upon the saccade per se. The saccade is functional in that it serves to bring a portion of text into the fovea for detailed analysis, but integration can occur in the absence of eye movements. While this result may seem surprising, it is consistent with a great deal of data about shifts of the visual world during saccades. A number of experiments (cf. Bridgeman, Hendry, & Stark, 1975) have demonstrated that subjects have difficulty telling when a stimulus has been displaced during a saccade. That the saccade per se is not necessary for the integration process is also consistent with an informal observation made a few years ago by McConkie and me that readers apparently failed to detect small shifts of text during saccades. If the text was shifted to the right (during a left-to-right saccade), the shift was noticeable; if the shift was to the left, it was difficult to detect. This observation is consistent with Yarbus's (1967) finding that if the direction of the retinal image shift in step with the saccade were not directly opposite to the direction of the movement of the retina, the visual object also appeared to be moving jerkily. Also, Bouma and deVoogd (1974) demonstrated that subjects can read text when it is presented to them with the saccades simulated.

Do the results of our experiment mean that eye movements only bring information into the fovea for detailed analysis and that they are not important in reading and in our naming task? Hochberg (1975) has argued convincingly that the fact that people can read when they have little control over visual exposure (as in Bouma and deVoogd's task) does not mean that they do not exercise such control when they have the opportunity to do so. Earlier in this paper and elsewhere (Rayner, 1978a) I have argued that there is good evidence that eye movements are under cognitive control. Two subsequent experiments with our naming task have further clarified the role of eye movements and have, I believe, definite implications for reading.

In this next set of experiments we (Rayner et al., 1978) investigated whether the simplicity of the visual display accounted in part for our pattern of results; that is, we always presented a single word on the CRT. Suppose the display were made complex by presenting stimuli simultaneously left and right of the fixation point; would the same pattern of results hold? In the first experiment, using the simulation technique, there were two conditions. In both conditions the subject fixated on the fixation dot as his eye movements were monitored. When the subject pushed the fixation button, stimuli appeared symmetrically left and right of fixation (i.e., the stimulus on the right began 3 deg from fixation and the stimulus on the left ended 3 deg from fixation). After a period of time approximating the latency for a saccade, the base word appeared in the fovea. In one condition the same initially displayed stimulus appeared on both sides of fixation. In the other condition, an initially displayed stimulus appeared on one side of the fixation and a random letter string bearing no relationship to the base word appeared on the opposite side. When the initially displayed alternative was presented on both sides of the fixation, the data pattern was identical to that shown in Figure 1. However, when a random letter string was presented on one side of the fixation, mean naming times were increased by about 30-80 msec, and the overall data pattern was compressed. Our initial intuition was that selective attention mechanisms could account for the compression of the pattern. That is, we assumed that the subject could only allocate attention to one side of the display or the other. Since the letter string appeared randomly to each side of fixation, any strategy (such as always attending to the right of fixation or alternating attention) would result in the subject getting useless information 50% of the time. Thus, the useful information obtained on half of the trials would yield means which, when combined with the means for cases when attention was directed to the useless information, would result in the compressed pattern. However, a more detailed analysis of the data showed convincingly that subjects' responses were affected by both sides of the display.

This led us to consider again the potential role of eye movements in the task. Some time ago Bryden (1961) and Crovitz and Daves (1962) independently reported that in studies in which a letter string was presented tachistoscopically across fixation, subjects were more accurate in reporting letters from the side of the array toward which they made an eye movement. Since the display only lasted for 100 msec, there would be no visible information present by the time the eye movement was completed. One explanation is that subjects were reading information out of iconic memory. Although such an explanation is possible, it is questionable since there is evidence that the iconic representation moves with the eye movement (Davidson, Fox & Dick, 1973). Another explanation is that programing an eye movement to a particular location is associated with giving greater attention to that area. The results of our next experiment were consistent with this latter explanation regarding the tendency to eye movement phenomenon reported by Bryden and by Crovitz and Daves.

In this experiment, two of the initially displayed alternatives (W-Ident and N-S) used previously were used again. One of these alternatives initially appeared on the left or right of fixation, and on the other side a random string of letters (N-RS) appeared. Initially, the experiment was set up so that the subject made a saccade either to the right or the left on each trial, the display change then occurred, and the subject named the base word. However, we found that subjects had a very strong bias to move their eyes to the right. Since we also wanted data from the left of fixation, subjects were instructed to make a saccade on a particular block of trials either to the left or right for the entire block. Figure 2 shows the main results of the experiment. Although there was some indication that information on the side of the display opposite to which the saccade was made influenced naming time, the major result shown in Figure 2 was clearly that subjects were directing attention to the location to which they were to move their eyes.

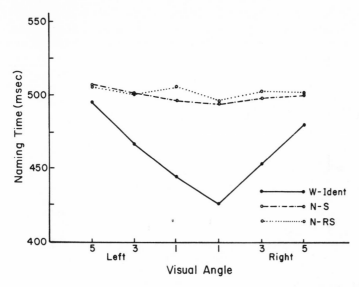

Figure 2. Mean naming times as a function of initially displayed alternative and visual angle. In the N-RS condition, the subject made an eye movement toward the random letter string which was replaced by the base word during the saccade.

Thus, we have concluded that eye movements have two very important roles in tasks such as reading. First, as indicated previously, they are functional in that they bring a region of text into the fovea for detailed analysis. Second, attentional allocation seems to be tied to the direction of the eye movement.

Returning to the issue of integrating information across saccades, our finding that the same facilitation effect in the naming task occurred when the saccade was simulated, presents a problem for the notion of an Integrative Visual Buffer, as does the observation that readers had difficulty recognizing a text shift during a saccade. Such findings are problematic for the Integrative Visual Buffer interpretation unless it is assumed that the buffer is flexible enough that information about the distance the eye has moved is not important for integration. Thus, integration would occur only on the basis of visual similarity of patterns from one fixation to the next. In a task such as reading, the complexity of the textual pattern might make such justification difficult. A experiment by McConkie (described in this volume) casts even more serious doubt on the notion that the integration occurs from the overlap of purely visual information. In McConkie's study, subjects read text in which the characters alternated between upper and lower case. At certain points in the text the display was changed so that if a word appeared as "cHeSt" prior to the saccade, after the saccade it would appear as "ChEsT." Now, if readers are storing visual information obtained from the parafovea on one

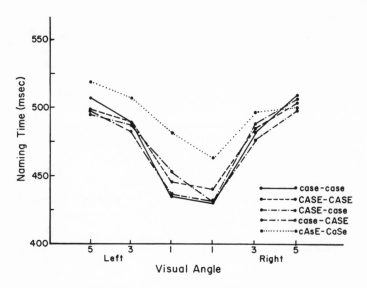

Figure 3. Mean naming times as a function of initially displayed alternative and visual angle. The legend shows the types of change which occurred.

fixation and overlapping it with information in the fovea on the next, there should be considerable disruption in reading under these conditions. However, McConkie found no differences between conditions in which there was a display change and conditions in which there was no display change.

McConkie and I have done a similar study using the naming task described previously. In this experiment, as the subject made an eye movement a word which appeared initially in lower-case was replaced by the same word in upper-case. Once again, if visual information is stored and integrated across fixations, there should be considerable disruption since the characteristics of upper- and lower-case letters are different. Figure 3 shows the results of the experiment. There was no difference between the two conditions in which there was a change in case during the saccade and the two control conditions in which there was no change. The fifth condition, identical to the characteristics of the display change in McConkie's study, did result in somewhat longer naming times. However, this is probably due to the fact that words presented in alternating case are more difficult to read; the shape of the curve for that condition is basically the same as for the other conditions.

One problem with the experiment just described is that it is possible to argue that the subject identified the base word on the first fixation, and the case change was irrelevant because the word was identified. On one count this interpretation is unlikely since the latencies for the eye movement in the experiment were no longer than in our other experiements. However, in another experiment both the case of the word and the word itself were varied. The stimuli were as follows (the first member of each pair was

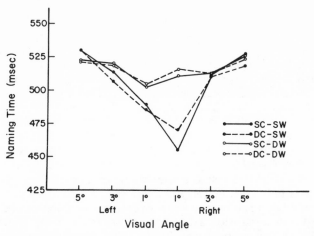

Figure 4. Mean naming times as a function of initially displayed alternative and visual angle. SC-SW = same case-same word; DC-SW = different case-same word; SC-DW = same case-different word; and DC-DW = different case-different word.

presented in parafoveal vision and replaced by the second during the saccade): chest-chest (same case--same word), chest-CHEST (different case--same word), chest-chart (different word--same case), and chest-CHART (different case--different word). In the different-case conditions, words could initially appear in either upper- or lower-case. Half of the word pairs began with the same letter and the same phoneme (brand-beard) while the other half began with the same letter but a different phoneme (phone-plane). Figure 4 shows the results of that experiment. As seen in Figure 4, the information obtained from parafoveal vision which was facilitative of naming the word in the fovea was again independent of case considerations. The SC-DW condition is the same as the W-SL condition in our earlier experiments. The pattern for that condition in this case change experiment is similar to the pattern obtained earlier where case changes did not occur. The fact that there was no difference between the SC-SW and the DC-SW replicates the results shown in Figure 3.

(One difference between the experiments in which there was no case change and the case change experiments should be noted. In the former experiments, subjects were not aware that a display change occurred if the change were made during the saccade. Drifts of the eyes resulted in display changes which were quite noticeable and these trials were repeated. In the case change experiments, subjects were much more aware that a display change had occurred. In fact, the subjective experience was that the word "shrank" or "moved away" when the change was from upper- to lower-case and the word seemed to "jump forward" when the case change reversed.)

These results are consistent with McConkie's changing case reading experiment and seem to indicate that visual information is not being stored on one

fixation and overlapped with visual information on the next fixation. If it
is not purely visual information that is being integrated from one fixation
to the next, what is being integrated? We have data which clearly show that
there is a strong faciliation effect. In Figure 1, all of the conditions are
facilitative with respect to the condition in which an asterisk was initially
displayed and the base word was presented in the area of the asterisk during
the saccade. The most obvious alternatives, other than that visual information
is being integrated, are phonemic, lexical, and semantic information. Unfortunately, our data do not support any of the alternatives. First, we found in
the data shown in Figure 4 that word pairs like phone-plane, which have the
same initial letter but different initial phonemes, did not result in longer
naming times at any of the visual angles than word pairs like brand-beard,
which have the same initial letter and phoneme. Furthermore, the naming
experiments have been replicated when overt vocalizations were not required
(same-different and semantic categorization tasks--an experiment carried
out by David Zola) and we have obtained results which are consistent with
the data in Figure 1. Second, if lexical information were the crucial factor,
one would expect that all of the NW conditions in Figure 1 should result in
longer naming times than the W conditions. Clearly, this was not the case
since the NW-SL condition yielded shorter naming times than the W-SL condition. Finally, there is some evidence that semantic or lexical information
affects naming time, particularly for stimuli presented 1 deg from fixation,
since naming times for the W-SL and N-SL conditions were significantly different from those of the W-Ident condition. As Figure 1 clearly shows, both
conditions were facilitative for naming the base word. If semantic or lexical
information were being identified from the initially displayed alternative
prior to the eye movement, it would seem that such processing would interfere rather than facilitate naming. I should also note that we have presented
as the initially displayed alternative semantic associates of the base word
(of the same length) and found no evidence of facilitation.

   If it is not purely visual, phonemic, lexical, or semantic information that
is being integrated across fixations, what is? One thing that is clear is that
some type of processing must be done with the purely visual information
with which the reader starts. McConkie suggests, as one alternative, that
perhaps letters or letter groups as a higher-level code are being integrated
across fixations. Thus the reader codes certain features into some abstract
code, such as the letter c in the first position of a five-letter word and h
in the second, then after the saccade he processes the last three letters and
identifies the word chest. Another possibility is that some very complex
type of interaction between the visual, phonemic, lexical, and semantic information may account for the results obtained so far. It is, however, difficult
to specify the nature of this interaction. All that can be said now is that
the reader somehow processes the visual parafoveal information and the
product of this processing is integrated with the information after the saccade.

A Process-Monitoring View of Reading
On the basis of the experiments carried out, I would like to propose a tentative
view of eye movements in reading, regarding eye guidance and integration.
According to the process-monitoring view (see Rayner & McConkie, 1976),
semantic identification occurs very rapidly. Central cognitive activities

affect the duration of fixation and the distance the eyes move. The processed parafoveal information, together with the context effects, make it possible for a reader to abstract the meaning of fixated words more rapidly than if both of these sources of information were not available. As an example of the process-monitoring view, suppose the reader is fixated on the second letter of a 7-letter word and to the right of that word is an 11-letter space region. Assume that in one instance the 11 letter spaces are occupied by two 5-letter words with a space between, and in another instance by a single 11-letter word. In both cases, the reader identifies the meaning of the 7-letter word, but because of visual characteristics cannot identify the next word. In the first instance, his eye movement will not be quite as long as in the second instance, so that his eyes land on the second letter of the first 5-letter word. He identifies the first 5-letter word, but again cannot identify the second word, so makes an eye movement into that word. In the second instance (the 11-letter word), the saccade is longer, his eyes land on the fourth letter of the 11-letter word, and although he is unable to see all of the word, the redundancy of the language makes it possible for him to identify it without another eye movement. Eye movements then are very important to processing because they bring a region of text into the fovea so semantic identification can occur, but they are also important because the intended direction and location of the next eye movement is tied to attentional allocation used for preprocessing parafoveal information. Our research effort in the next few years will be aimed at specifying more precisely the nature of the preprocessing and determining what is integrated across saccades.

Preparation of this paper and much of the research described was supported by grant BNS76-05017 from the National Science Foundation. I thank Carla Posnansky, Susan Ehrlich, and Emily Ellsworth for their comments on an earlier version of the paper, and George McConkie and Susan Ehrlich for many interesting discussions regarding some of the experiments described here.

REFERENCES

Abrams, S.G., & Zuber, B.L. Some temporal characteristics of information processing during reading. Reading Research Quarterly, 1972, 12, 41-51.

Bouma, H., & deVoogd, A.H. On the control of eye saccades in reading. Vision Research, 1974, 14, 273-284.

Bridgeman, B., Hendry, D., & Stark, L. Failure to detect displacement of the visual world during saccadic eye movements. Vision Research, 1975, 15, 719-722.

Bryden, M.P. The role of post-exposural eye movements in tachistoscopic presentations. Canadian Journal of Psychology, 1961, 15, 220-225.

Buswell, G.T. Fundamental reading habits: A study of their development. Chicago: Chicago University Press, 1922.

Crovitz, H.F., & Daves, W. Tendencies to eye movements and perceptual accuracy. Journal of Experimental Psychology, 1962, 63, 495-498.

Davidson, M.L., Fox, M.J., & Dick, A.O. The effect of eye movements and backward masking on perceptual location. Perception & Psychophysics, 1973, 14, 11-116.

Dearborn, W.F. The psychology of reading. Archives of Philosophy, Psychology and Scientific Methods, Columbia University Contributions to Philosophy & Psychology 14:1, 1906.

Ditchburn, R.W. Eye-movements and visual perception. London: Oxford University Press, 1973.

Gould, J.D. Looking at pictures. In R.A. Monty & J.W. Senders (Eds.), Eye movements and psychological processes. Hillsdale, NJ: Erlbaum, 1976.

Haber, R.N. Control of eye movements during reading. In R.A. Monty & J.W. Senders (Eds.), Eye movements and psychological processes. Hillsdale, NJ: Erlbaum, 1976.

Hochberg, J. On the control of eye saccades in reading. Vision Research, 1975, 15, 620.

Klein, G.A., & Kurkowski, F. Effect of task demands on relationships between eye movements and sentence complexity. Perceptual and Motor Skills, 1974, 39, 463-466.

Kolers, P.A. Buswell's discoveries. In R.A. Monty & J.W. Senders (Eds.), Eye movements and psychological processes. Hillsdale, NJ: Erlbaum, 1976.

McConkie, G.W. On the role and control of eye movements in reading. (This volume)

McConkie, G.W., & Rayner, K. The span of the effective stimulus during a fixation in reading. Perception & Psychophysics, 1975, 17, 578-586.

McConkie, G.W. & Rayner, K. Identifying the span of the effective stimulus in reading: Literature review and theories of reading. In H. Singer & R.B. Ruddell (Eds), Theoretical models and processes of reading. Newark, DEL: International Reading Association, 1976.

O'Regan, J.K. Structural and contextual constraints on eye movements in reading. Unpublished doctoral dissertation, University of Cambridge, 1975.

Pynte, J. Readiness for pronunciation during the reading process. Perception & Psychophysics, 1974, 16, 110-112.

Rayner, K. The perceptual span and peripheral cues in reading. Unpublished doctoral dissertation, Cornell University, 1974.

Rayner, K. Parafoveal identification during a fixation in reading. Acta Psychologica 1975, 39, 271-282. (a)

Rayner, K. The perceptual span and peripheral cues in reading. Cognitive Psychology, 1975, 7, 65-81. (b)

Rayner, K. Visual attention in reading: Eye movements reflect cognitive processes. Memory & Cognition, 1977, 5, 443-448.

Rayner, K. Eye movements in reading and information processing. Psychological Bulletin, 1978, 85, 618-660. (a)

Rayner, K. Foveal and parafoveal cues in reading. In J. Requin (Ed.), Attention and performance VII. Hillsdale, NJ: Erlbaum, 1978. (b)

Rayner, K., & McConkie, G.W. What guides a reader's eye movements? Vision Research, 1976, 16, 829-837.

Rayner, K., McConkie, G.W., & Ehrlich, S. Eye movements and integrating information across fixations. Journal of Experimental Psychology: Human Perception and Performance, 1978, 4, 529-544.

Shebilske, W. Reading eye movements from an information-processing point of view. In D. Massaro (Ed.), Understanding language. New York: Academic Press, 1975.

Spragins, A.B. Lefton, L.A., & Fisher, D.F. Eye movements while reading spatially transformed text: A developmental study. Memory & Cognition, 1976, 4, 36-42.

Tinker, M.A. Bases for effective reading. Minneapolis: University of Minnesota Press, 1965.

Wanat, S.F. Language behind the eye: Some findings, speculations, and research strategies. In R.A. Monty & J.W. Senders (Eds.), Eye movements and psychological processes. Hillsdale, NJ: Erlbaum, 1976.

Yarbus, A. Eye movements and vision. New York: Plenum Press, 1967.

Understanding the Reading Process through the Use of Transformed Typography: PSG, CSG and Automaticity

Dennis F. Fisher

This paper examines the developmental progression of peri-
pheral retinal processing (prescreening) of text. Altering
textual density by removing spaces between words, altering
word shape by alternating upper and lower case letters, and
altering text orientation through geometrical transformations
were some of the techniques used to characterize peripheral
retinal involvement during reading. All of these techniques
attempted to impose a "tunnel vision effect," reduce word
recognition, and modify ocular motility. Dependent measures
such as speed, accuracy, and eye movement dynamics (fixa-
tion duration, frequency of fixation, perceptual span esti-
mates, etc.) are compared between conditions of low (search)
and high (reading) contextual constraint. Finally, a model
is described which attempts to complement Hochberg's notion
of peripheral to cognitive search guidance with the automa-
ticity notion of LaBerge and Samuels .

My primary concern in this paper is with decoding or pattern analysis of visible
language and its contribution to the development of fluent reading. Decoding
activities, though seemingly separate from meaning extraction and memory,
are related through rather complex and complementary interactions.

Three series of experiments dealing with word shape, spacing, and orientation provided the impetus for our efforts. These are:

a) Smith and his colleagues (Smith, 1969; Smith, Lott, & Cronnell (1969)
examined reading and search performance with text that had been typographically mutilated to alter word shape in several ways, the most dramatic being
alternating case and letter size. This manipulation reduced reading speed
by 20% and search efficiency by 10%.

b) Hochberg (1970) reported an experiment by Hochberg, Levin, and Frail (1966) in which oral reading errors (efficiency) and reading speeds were measured for good and poor second and fifth graders who read text that had the spaces between words filled with ampersands. He reported that performance of the second graders changed slightly, whereas fifth graders performed more poorly when spaces between the words were filled.

c) Kolers (1968) and Kolers and Perkins (1969a, b) geometrically transformed typography so that it was normal, rotated, inverted, turned inside out, and presented in mirror views while the readers read letter string and 310-word paragraphs left to right and right to left. The most difficult paragraphs, rR (words inverted and rotated 180 deg and letters rotated 180 deg), took nearly six times as long to read as normal paragraphs. Eight practice paragraphs later the readers had improved by only a factor of two.

From these roots has developed a series of experiments aimed at gaining insight into the progression of decoding characteristics from early exposure to text to fluency.

Some Experiments: A Review

Word Shape and Spacing

Fisher (1975) chose three variations of type — normal, capitals, and alternating upper and lower case, each of different size — and three variations of spacing — normal, spaces filled, and spacing absent as stimuli and combined them factorially. When case was changed from normal to alternating type, changing word shape, reductions of 10 to 15% in reading and search speeds resulted, agreeing with the findings of Smith. Reductions of 50% in reading and search speeds were found when spacing was varied from normal to absent. However, reading speed decreased from 220 wmp to 70 wmp between conditions of normal typography and the most contrived manipulation where case was altered and spaces between words were absent. Although similar effects were found during search, search speeds were consistently about three times faster than reading.

Fisher and Lefton (1976) adapted these same manipulations with graded material for third, fourth, and sixth graders as well as adults, and identified a developmental progression in the proficiency with which the typographical mutilations were decoded. Reading speed increased directly with experience when space and case were varied independently; however, when they were combined, as in the most extreme conditions, all subjects performed at precisely the same speed. Of particular importance was the fact that adult readers retained the capacity to fall back on some previously used elemental reading strategy (reading word by word), when the typographical constraints demanded it, indicating that a repertoire of strategies is maintained representative of successive approximations toward fluency.

Spragins, Lefton and Fisher (1976) examined these decoding characteristics of subjects who read and searched through typographically mutilated texts, while eye movements were recorded. Here, developmental progressions that agreed with Taylor's (1965) findings were witnessed for normally typed paragraphs on all measures of reading speed, such as words per fixation (perceptual

Table 1. Reading Rate by Condition in Words Per Minute.

Grade	Paragraph Grade Level and Type			
	2 Normal	2 Filled	5 Normal	5 Filled
2	101.3	58.0	58.6	42.1
5	197.9	164.0	164.0	115.8

span), fixation duration, and number of regressions. Again, in the most con-trived situation — alternating type, no space — adults' and early readers' performance measures were equivalent. Speeds were faster, spans larger, fixation durations shorter, regressions fewer, for search than for reading.

The primary changes in reading speed thus far discussed can be attributed to decoding, but other evidence indicates that the cause is more complex. As described above, Hochberg et al. (1966), as reported by Hochberg (1970), examined reading efficiency with normally typed text and text that had the spaces between words filled. However, a discrepancy is found between the description of those data and the data themselves. The task did compare oral reading efficiency and later reading speed between fast and slow reading second and fifth graders. However, all of the children read second-grade level paragraphs. All of the groups were found to have reduced oral reading fluency when word boundary cues were minimized by filling the spaces, but no differences were found between grades. The greatest decrements occurred for the older slow reading and the younger fast reading children, contrary to expectation based on the theory. What influence did the second grade paragraphs have on fifth-grade reader performance?

In an attempt to answer this question and to resolve the discrepancy be-tween the report and the data, Fisher and Montanary (1977) gave one set of second and fifth graders, second and fifth-grade paragraphs to read, respec-tively. Here, fifth graders read faster than second graders and normal type was read faster than filled type, but no interaction was found. In a second task, second and fifth graders were both presented with second and fifth-grade paragraphs that were normal or had spaces filled. The results are shown in Table 1.

The data in the left two columns of the table reflect Hochberg's conditions, but the data show the greatest decrement in performance occurring for the second graders. The center two columns are viewed as more important to the theory for they reflect tradeoffs between typographical and contextual change. It can be seen that although the fifth graders read nearly three times as fast as second graders, a change from the filled second-grade paragraph to a normal fifth-grade paragraph has the same effect on both grades. That is, increased difficulty of the text leads to changes in reading dynamics (eye movements, perceptual span) similar to those found when typography changes. Tinker (1951) varied typography and contextual level independently, while Kolers (1974, 1976) demonstrated that typographical "tags" aided contextual memory, but here, both perceptual and cognitive processes seem to share or act as complements within the confines of processing capacity. The more difficult paragraphs (N5) were made difficult for the second graders by filling the spaces (F5) but effected only slight additional reductions in speed. A more dramatic speed reduction occurs for fifth graders. Had Fisher and Montanary (1977) increased the paragraph difficulty to eighth-grade level, further speed reductions may well have been witnessed for the fifth graders, equal to the speed of second graders reading fifth-grade paragraphs.

Developmentally, quantitative differences in reading fluency can be found as well as qualitative differences in eye movement dynamics and perceptual span, consonant with increasing language awareness (Taylor, 1965; Lefton & Fisher, 1976). Fisher and Lefton (1976) specifically addressed the possibility that developmental differences are present in processing retinally eccentric stimuli. Second, third, fifth graders and adults were given a "context free" tachistoscopic same-different reaction time task where stimuli could appear 0-4 deg from fixation. Here, a significant developmental progression was found indicating that younger children reacted more slowly as a function of retinal eccentricity, and had slower overall reaction times. To us this indicated that although acuity, at least to 4 deg, was equivalent for children and adults, indicated by equivalent error rates, the early grade children did not have the facility to utilize the information as efficiently as older readers and adults. More dramatic differences could be expected with more eccentric stimuli, but more importantly these data were interpreted as providing an important clue to understanding the role of the visual periphery to processing visible language.

Geometric Transformations

Requiring subjects to rectify all sorts of geometric transformations, as Kolers and his associates have done, can be considered a means of extending decoding requirements beyond normal limits because many steps must be successfully completed prior to decoding and subsequent meaning extraction. Concern for an understanding of the developmental progression toward fluency led Fisher, Lefton and Moss (1978) to examine selected types of transformations, specifically, sentences left to right and right to left and words within sentences left to right and right to left. Of interest was the possibility that a progression existed in the ease with which these transformations were rectified as a function of experience. A summary of these data is shown in Table 2.

Briefly, these data indicate that regardless of sentence orientation, reading progresses rapidly if word orientation is left to right. That is, right-to-left reading speed remains high as long as words are oriented left to right, the familiar pattern. This trend was consistent for all age groups. Again, as described above, adults seem able to fall back on an elementary word-by-word processing strategy to satisfy task demands. In addition, reading right to left forces the reader to perform successive "regressions" with only minor interference. This finding proved intriguing in that it could provide insight

TABLE 2. Mean Number of Words Read per Minute.

Sentence	WORD L→R (N)		WORD R→L (R)	
	L→R (N)	R→L (R)	L→R (N)	R→L (R)
Grade 3	135	99	38	38
5	200	97	31	30
Adult	215	123	32	36

into the ways in which normal regressions, and their accompanying fixations, can be so precise yet frequently extend beyond the normal 1-2 deg high acuity extent over which forward saccades operate during reading.

Eye movements were monitored as an adult read adult-level paragraphs where the typography appeared as normal right-going sentences and words (NN), left-going sentences with right-going words (RN), right-going sentences and words with left-going words (NR), and left-going sentences with left-going words (RR). The subject read 350 words in each transformation prior to the recording of the scanpaths, which may be viewed in Figures 1 NN, NR, RN, and RR, respectively. Here, line discontinuities represent fixations and lines show probable paths of the associated saccades.

Comparing Figures 1NN and 1RN: both are left-to-right-going sentences, but saccadic extent is much more constricted and eye movements are more frequent and at times resemble triangulated loops, during reading of the RN paragraph when words are oriented right to left. This characteristic may be directly related to a point emphasized by Kolers that the transform occurs prior to recognition, for it may well be that the eye movement assists in the transforming, and a rectification is not entirely "in the brain." Even though the paragraph had to be read from right to left, Figure 1RN in many ways is closely aligned to Figure 1RR; however, the words were again in the unfamiliar right-to-left orientation. Figure 1NR represents the eye movement sequence for the subject while reading paragraphs from right to left with words oriented left to right, and except for a few erratic patterns the left going saccades are quite comparable and as accurate on the return sweep as those shown in Figure 1NN. Accompanying data are shown in Table 3.

TABLE 3. Values of Data Shown in Figure 2.

	WORD L→R (N)		WORD R→L (R)	
Sentence	L→R (N)	R→L (R)	L→R (N)	R→L (R)
Fixations	110	233	919	558
Duration (msec)	229	177	262	185
Speed (wpm)	281.3	171.8	29.4	68.7
Span (x/fix)	1.07	.53	.13	.21

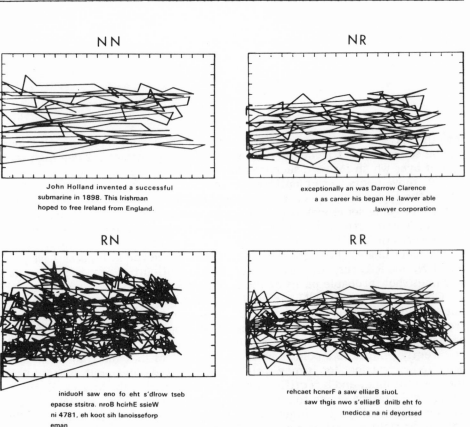

NN

John Holland invented a successful
submarine in 1898. This Irishman
hoped to free Ireland from England.

NR

exceptionally an was Darrow Clarence
a as career his began He .lawyer able
.lawyer corporation

RN

iniduoH saw eno fo eht s'dlrow tseb
epacse stsitra. nroB hcirhE ssieW
ni 4781, eh koot sih lanoisseforp
eman

RR

rehcaet hcnerF a saw elliarB siuoL
saw thgis nwo s'elliarB dnilb eht fo
tnedicca na ni deyortsed

Figure 1. Reading scanpaths. All paragraphs were 118 words in length and records were made after subject completed three practice paragraphs in each typography. Line discontinuities represent fixations, while straight lines represent saccades.

Complements: A Theory and Extension

There are many models of reading (Kavanagh & Mattingly, 1972; Levin & Williams, 1970; Singer & Ruddell, 1970, 1975) and the need for more is not very great since it is reasonable to assume that all of the processes operating during reading have been adequately defined, refined, and described. However, I have taken two existing theories and combined them to provide a more complete synthesis. The first of these (Hochberg, 1970) involves the notion of a functional peripheral visual system for prescreening, and the other (LaBerge & Samuels, 1974) concerns experiential and attentional contributions to reading fluency.

Hochberg (1970) interpreted the data of Hochberg et al. (1966) as indicating that fifth graders had become dependent upon peripheral retinal input, and consequently read faster than second graders on normal paragraphs, but when the spaces between the words were filled they could no longer rely on the periphery and reading slowed down. Second graders, on the other hand, were claimed to have minimal access to peripheral retinal processing, and consequently were limited to word-by-word reading irrespective of the typography experienced.

His model included an initial peripheral search guidance (PSG) stage in which gross physical cues like word boundary and word shape are detected in the visual periphery and screened for subsequent analysis. Saccadic eye movements are initiated to bring the relevant cues and features to the fovea for higher order, cognitive search guidance (CSG) processing. The input receptive sequence is cyclic. That is, CSG provides PSG with global information about what cues are to be expected, PSG is then sensitized to those cues, they are then located/detected, and eye movements bring the cues into higher acuity regions for more in-depth analyses and perhaps integration across a number of fixations, which leads to the development of more global information.

It should be understood that word identification and minute stimulus discriminations are limited by the boundaries described by Bouma (1978), Rayner (1975), and McConkie and Rayner (1975), not in the periphery, but foveally and parafoveally (i.e., less than 4 deg visual angle). Beyond 4 deg acuity is less than 25% that of the fovea — too poor to identify words. However, Poulton (1962) showed that when the width of a movable window was changed from 14 words (about 70 letter spaces or 17 deg) to 5 words, reading speed slowed dramatically. Such a finding would not be expected on the basis of the resolving capability of the visual system at such an eccentric field of view, but a notion of functional acuity, based upon the peripheral retina's role in locating gross cues like word shapes and boundaries, can account for such findings.

The data described above from Fisher (1975), Fisher and Lefton (1976), Lefton and Fisher (1976), and Spragins et al. (1976) were interpreted as supporting Hochberg's notions. In essence, the periphery was relied upon to provide cues to the cognitive processes increasingly up to fifth grade, a time when children become as efficient at decoding as adults. Reading always progressed slower than search indicating that both cognitive factors (meaning extraction) and perceptual factors (typography) slow down processing of visible language. It was noted that as adults become fluent, successive decoding strategies are supplanted rather than replaced so that if text or typography demands require word-by-word processing it can be implemented. (Woodworth (1938) had described the perceptual effects of viewing a dense stimulus array, exemplified with the familiar letter pyramid. Here, as the viewer fixated the center letters of successive rows of letters from peak to base, fewer letters are seen. This phenomenon, known as lateral inhibition or masking by spatially contiguous letters, has also been the concern of Mackworth (1965) and others (cf. Bouma, 1978). One way we have attempted to assess whether lateral inhibitory effects were accounting for speed reduction or whether these were attributable to constriction of functional field of view was to compare the visual processing differences between reading and search. Saccadic extent and perceptual spans are always larger and speed always faster during search, reflecting differences in peripheral retinal processing as a function of cognitive load, not lateral inhibition.)

An analysis of reading based solely on decoding might be accounted for with notions of PSG and CSG, but there is much more to reading than decoding. For example, Singer (1972) contended that by the time children reach fifth or sixth grade, their decoding skills are approximately those of adults. During this five-year period, letter and word recognition skills advance from a nonexistent or low level to a highly proficient level. It is as though at an early stage, the greatest concentration of effort must be dedicated to decoding, and only a modicum of effort dedicated to comprehension skills, while the ratio of effort changes with development — 95% decoding and 5% comprehension in first grade, and 5% decoding and 95% comprehension in fifth and sixth grades. Consequently, a correspondence can be noted between increased priority to cognitive aspects of text, reduced priority to decoding, and an increasing dependency on peripheral retinal processing.

As complements, PSG, CSG, and automaticity notions allow us to better describe the components of reading that range from elementary decoding strategies to fluent high-speed recognition. Hochberg's notions include peripheral prescreening and eye movements in cue acquisition sequences without specifying detail of higher order processing lumped into CSG. On the other hand, LaBerge and Samuels specify information processing in feature acquisition, extraction, consolidation, and the process whereby these features are integrated into phonological, episodic, and semantic memories, but omit contributions to automaticity stemming from peripheral prescreening and eye movements. While Hochberg's developmental considerations pertain to PSG function, the key contribution of LaBerge and Samuels is that with experience, less effort (attention) needs to be directed to formative processes, and that is the essence of automaticity. Both of these theories, while remaining vague about the evolution of comprehension, depend heavily upon development or experience as a means of affecting efficient reading strategies.

While I am hesitant about presenting a flow diagram because of the poor analogy blocks and lines represent about what goes on in the head, I also feel that occasional benefits may be derived for the "visual" reader and therefore the complementary model of Hochberg and LaBerge and Samuels as interpreted by me (Fisher, 1978, in press; Fisher & Montanary, 1977) is shown in Figure 2.

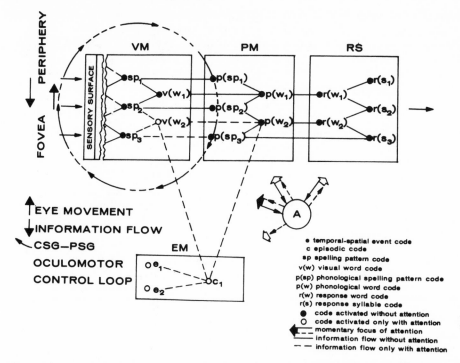

Figure 2. Complementary attentional model of information processing during reading. Model incorporates eye movement sequencing PSG and CSG onto an automatic information processing sequence. Here, information passes through the receptors, visual, primary and episodic memories, and response system. Attention is directed as needed. See text and original sources for more detail.

Geometric Transformations and the Complementary Model
Although Kolers's interests were global, evolving into a general theory of pattern analysis addressing rectification of variance in the "real world" and I remain specifically concerned with decoding contributions to fluent reading, the similarity between our views is considerable. Kolers's components model prescribes that prior to recognition the transformation is "undone." The undoing is accomplished for Kolers without the necessity of peripheral pre-screening, but I contend that it could not hurt to include it. Kolers (1975c) has concluded that his "results favor a theory that emphasizes recognition

in terms of pattern analyzing operations that are directed at surface lexical representations," and "pattern analysis at the graphemic level is part and parcel of representation of a sentence, not the means by which some deep semantic pearl is extracted from its superficial shell." I am convinced that both peripheral retinal involvement and eye movements actively aid this rectification process (see Figure 1).

Kolers and Perkins (1975) justifiably criticize the classical preprocessing notions, partly because preprocessing is usually described as an entity in itself and partially because the output of the preprocessing stage becomes the input for the recognition procedure while little or no feedback from the recognition stage returns to the preprocessing stage. Feedback may not be designed into the mechanical photointerpreters and pattern analyzers, but data are beginning to accumulate indicating that feedback is present in the human operator. Circular feedback is a necessity and the functional mechanism is there; unfortunately the anatomical mechanism remains elusive. That functional mechanism is oculomotor sequencing.

The first fixation on a line of text is usually longer than subsequent fixations (Stern, 1978). The added time is certainly not needed for recognition, but it is possible that the time is spent in consolidation and general contextual organization. During this time, meaning that has been developing out of previously read text can aid the reader in determining which words might be expected in subsequent text. I hypothesize that PSG and CSG communicate, and that this communication continues to facilitate reading across the line: PSG/CSG working as complements. The more that is known about the text, the wider the range or number of items over which PSG operates, and the more fluent the reading, ultimately approaching automaticity. The more complex the text and/or typography, the smaller the area over which PSG is operative. Kolers and Perkins (1975) state that "preprocessing is an intimate and fundamental aspect of recognition; preprocessing in humans is processing, and recognition is continuous and accretive, not stagewise and discrete." In essence, a conception of pattern analysis in which rectification is wedded intimately to recognition and active prescreening is common to both views. That is, prescreening is not a simple preliminary process.

It is possible to account for the differences in Kolers's (1968) various curves in terms of differing degrees of functional tunnel vision caused by inversions and rotations. The curves themselves can be viewed as representing the utility with which effort must be expended with experience, much as has been traced above for the beginning reader who advances to fluency. In all of Kolers's conditions, one of the primary peripheral cues was still there, that of spacing, and the data may be interpreted as indicating differing facilities by which readers are able to use spacing to aid their reading and upon the amount of necessary oculomotor compensatory activity, e.g., triangulated loops. When compared to normally oriented text, the various geometrical transformations caused varying reductions in reading speed, athough performance improved with practice. These increases are predicted by the complementary model. Kolers and Perkins (1975) point out that the main feature of the pattern analyzing components model is interaction between ongoing problem solving processes and the visual rectification of the sample being recognized. Again, little disagreement between the two notions can be found except to extend

Kolers's slightly so that the ongoing problem solving processes operate as effectively as they do because of the input from at least the parafoveal or near peripheral areas of the retina and limits on the efficiency of rectifying the transforms are probably determined by ability of the oculomotor system to efficiently undo the transform.

I have discussed the trade-offs between undoing typographical mutilations and meaning extraction when contextual level becomes more difficult, along with demonstrating (cf. Figure 1) the importance of eye movements in rectifying geometric transformations. Recently, Kolers (1975a, 1976) and Kolers and Ostry (1974) have identified a memorial component in visible language processing by showing that subjects recognize textual materials better if those materials are again presented in the same geometric transformation as they had originally been read. This facilitation lasts as long as one year. Finding a memorial component to what had historically been considered an insignificant physical aspect of text, is certainly intriguing.

In our complementary model, episodic memory would be a likely candidate for the role of typography tagging. The treatment of such tags would probably be analogous to color or category labelling and may well be represented in multiple addresses. Typography is probably encoded onto semantic tone rather than specific words, so that the undoing precedes recognition but surface structure is supplanted by deep structure. Such notions could be tested by presenting subjects with stories having the same meaning but varied typography and wording from a previously presented story, then testing recognition and reading speed. If reading of the subsequent paragraph is enhanced by knowing the meaning and experiencing the same typography, we would have a better understanidng of the ways typographical encoding interacts with expectancy and word predictability. Evidence for other memory representations or addresses (e.g., semantic/syntactic memory), can be hypothesized because when errors are made while reading transformed typography, words are frequently replaced by others of the same form-class.

The combined model for PSG, CSG and automaticity is not the ultimate answer to all of our questions about reading, but through it we can attempt to account for developmental progressions of reading from basic decoding to fluency. Data were reviewed showing that increased emphasis on meaning extraction runs concurrent to the expansion of the functional field of view and reduced effort in decoding. Also, a repertoire of reading strategies was identified in the fluent reader that allows him to cope with textual and typographical demands. Scanpaths were shown of fixations accumulated while a reader read text in various geometric transformations to provide indications of eye movement contributions, e.g., triangulated loop, to rectifying the transformation. Other important aspects of the model were described — cyclic (feedback) dialogue between CSG and PSG; experiential transfer of effort or attention from initial priority of decoding to the subsequent priority of comprehending at about fifth grade; directed attention dictated by task demands; and acknowledging that typography, syntax, and semantics are interactive textual characteristics which are tagged onto multiple addresses in memory. Implications of the model for reading disability are discussed elsewhere (Fisher, 1978, in press).

REFERENCES

Bouma, H. Visual search and reading: Eye movements and functional, visual
    field. In J. Réquin (Ed.), Attention and performance, VII. Hillsdale, NJ:
    Erlbaum, 1978.
Fisher, D.F. Reading and visual search. Memory & Cognition, 1975, 3,
    188-196.
Fisher, D. F. Dysfunctions in reading disability: There's more than meets
    the eye. In L. Resnick & P. Weaver (Eds.), Theory and practice of early
    reading (Vol 1). Hillsdale, NJ: Erlbaum, in press.
Fisher, D.F., & Lefton, L.A. Peripheral information extraction: A development
    examination of reading processes. Journal of Experimental Child Psychology,
    1976, 21, 77-93.
Fisher, D.F., Lefton, L.A., & Moss, J. Reading geometrically transformed
    text: A developmental approach. Bulletin of the Psychonomic Society,
    1978, 11, 157-160.
Fisher, D.F., & Montanary, W.E. Spatial and contextual factors in beginning
    reading: Evidence for PSG-CSG complements to developing automaticity.
    Memory & Cognition, 1977, 5, 247-251.
Hochberg, J. Components of literacy: Speculation and exploratory research.
    In H. Levin & J.P. Williams (Eds.), Basic studies on reading. New York:
    Basic Books, 1970.
Hochberg, J., Levin, H., & Frail, C. Studies of oral reading: VII. How interword
    spaces affect reading. Unpublished report, Cornell University, 1966.
Kavanagh, J.F., & Mattingly, I.G. Language by ear and by eye. Cambridge,
    MA: MIT Press, 1972.
Kolers, P.A. The recognition of geometrically transformed text. Perception
    & Psychophysics, 1968, 3, 57-64.
Kolers, P.A. Remembering trivia. Language and Speech, 1974, 17, 324-336.
Kolers, P.A. Memorial consequences of automatized encoding. Journal of
    Experimental Psychology: Human Learning and Memory, 1975, 1, 689-701. (a)
Kolers, P.A. Pattern-analyzing disability in poor readers. Developmental
    Psychology, 1975, 11, 282-290. (b)
Kolers, P.A. Specificity of operations in sentence recognition. Cognitive
    Psychology, 1975, 7, 289-306. (c)
Kolers P.A. Reading a year later. Journal of Experimental Psychology:
    Human Learning and Memory, 1976, 2, 554-565.
Kolers, P.A., & Ostry, D.J. Time course of loss of information regarding
    pattern analyzing operations. Journal of Verbal Learning and Verbal Behavior,
    1974, 13, 599-612.
Kolers, P.A., & Perkins, D.N. Orientation of letters and errors in their
    recognition. Perception & Psychophysics, 1969, 5, 265-269. (a)
Kolers, P.A., & Perkins, D.N. Orientation of letters and their speed of recognition.
    Perception & Psychophysics, 1969, 5, 275-280. (b)
Kolers, P.A., & Perkins, D.N. Spatial and ordinal components of form perception
    and literacy. Cognitive Psychology, 1975, 7, 228-267.
LaBerge, D. & Samuels, S.J. Toward a theory of automatic information processing
    in reading. Cognitive Psychology, 1974, 6, 293-323.

Lefton, L.A. & Fisher, D.F. Information extraction during visual search: A developmental progression. Journal of Experimental Child Psychology, 1976, 22, 346-361.

Mackworth, N.H. Visual noise causes tunnel vision. Psychonomic Science, 1965, 3, 67-68.

McConkie, G.W., & Rayner, K. The span of the effective stimulus during a fixation in reading. Perception & Psychophysics, 1975, 17, 578-586.

Poulton, E.C. Peripheral vision, refractoriness, and eye movements in fast oral reading. British Journal of Psychology, 1962, 53, 409-419.

Rayner, K. The perceptual span and peripheral cues in reading. Cognitive Psychology, 1975, 7, 65-81.

Singer, H. IQ is and is not related to reading. Paper presented at the Preconvention Institute on Intelligence and Reading, International Reading Association, 1972.

Singer, H., & Ruddell, R.B. Theoretical models and processes of reading. Newark, DE: International Reading Association, 1970; 2nd ed., 1975.

Smith, F. Use of featural dependencies across letters in the visual identification of words. Journal of Verbal Learning and Verbal Behavior, 1969, 8, 215-218.

Smith, F., Lott, D., & Cronnell, B. The effect of type size and case alternation of word identification. American Journal of Psychology, 1969, 82, 248-253.

Spragins, H.B., Lefton, L.A., & Fisher, D.F. Eye movements while reading and searching spatially transformed text: A developmental examination. Memory & Cognition, 1976, 4, 36-42.

Stern, J.A. Eye movements, reading and cognition. In J.W. Senders, D.F. Fisher, & R.A. Monty (Eds.), Eye movements and the higher psychological functions. Hillsdale, NJ: Erlbaum, 1978.

Taylor, S. E. Eye movements in reading: Facts and fallacies. American Educational Research Journal, 1965, 2, 187-202.

Tinker, M.A. Fixation pause during reading. Journal of Educational Research, 1951, 44, 471-479.

Woodworth, R.S. Experimental psychology. New York: Holt, 1938.

Reading and Searching through Geometrically Transformed Text

Lester A. Lefton

*An experiment is described in which third and fifth graders
and adults either read or searched through paragraphs of
text that varied the orientation of the sentence or word.
Individual words or sentences were printed from left to right
or right to left. Results show that the main factor that
determined reading and search speed was the orientation
of the word, regardless of the orientation of the sentence.
Further, a developmental progression in reading proficiency
was found; yet, when word orientation was reversed all subjects performed at essentially the same slow rates. The data
support the peripheral to cognitive search guidance system
proposed by Hochberg (1970) and the automaticity notion
of LaBerge and Samuels (1974).*

The role of visual periphery and textual cues in reading has recently been
under experimental scrutiny. The aim has been to assess how orientation
of textual material affects reading, particularly orientation of text not in
the fovea. Some of these studies have been psychophysical ones in which
textual material has been manipulated by degrading it (Fisher & Lefton, 1976;
Lefton & Fisher, 1976); others have been eye movement studies (Spragins,
Lefton, & Fisher, 1976); and still others have varied the amount of text presented in the periphery (McConkie & Rayner, 1975). Generally, these studies
support the notion that textual cues are important and that peripheral information is critical for normal reading.

Textual cues have been of importance in a model described by Hochberg
(1970) and Hochberg and Brooks (1970). Their reading model involves two
stages, peripheral search guidance and cognitive search guidance. The initial
stage allows a reader to scan the text by means of a small number of fixations where physical cues are picked up in the periphery. In the second stage

the reader formulates hypotheses about meaning and where to search the array for further information. The two systems are complementary since peripheral search guidance directs a reader's eye movements toward the periphery so that more cognitive decisions are made about meaning. As meaning is extracted from text, the peripheral mechanism is provided with new information and directs its peripheral search guidance.

According to the Hochberg model the disruption of normal textual cues should modulate reading speed. When a sentence is presented from right to left rather than normally, a subject's ability to extract information from the periphery should be degraded. Since the eye instead of moving in a forward direction from left to right now moves in the opposite direction, it might be expected that reading speed would decrease. Indeed, Kolers (1968; Kolers & Ostry, 1974; Kolers & Perkins, 1969a and 1969b) showed that this was the case; however, it was also shown that with practice subjects could increase their speed and make fewer errors.

The purpose of the present report is to further assess the effects of left-to-right and right-to-left reading and searching. In the experimental situations to be described, the direction in which a subject scanned was manipulated. Sentences were presented either normally from left to right or reversed from right to left (e.g., little a had Mary). In addition, the orientation of words was manipulated so that they were read either normally from left to right, or reversed and read from right to left (e.g., stcejbus). The experiment factorially combined these two conditions of word and sentence orientation. It also examined the effects of word and sentence orientation developmentally. Two tasks, search and reading, were used. Both involve information extraction, but in search comprehension demands are minimal whereas in reading they are the focus of the task.

The subjects for this study were children from grades three and five in public schools in Columbia, South Carolina, and students enrolled in courses at the University of South Carolina. There were 112 subjects at each grade level and all read at or above grade level, as assessed by standardized tests and evaluations. Chronological ages for the three grades were eight years, six months; ten years, five months; and twenty years, nine months.

The stimuli were typed paragraphs varying in length from 60 to 120 words. Six different paragraphs were used for each grade level and the same paragraphs were used for both reading and search tasks.

The paragraphs for each level were typed with variations in the direction of the individual words and sentences. For example, in the normal word orientation, individual words were typed in the normal left-to-right manner; whereas in the reverse word orientation, individual words were typed right-to-left, so that "subject" appeared as "tcejbus"; thus, word orientation referred to the direction in which the word was typed. Sentence orientation refers to the direction in which individual sentences were typed. Normal sentence orientation indicated that sentences were typed to be read from left to right while reverse sentence orientation indicated the opposite. Examples of these variations are shown in Figure 1. Word and sentence orientations were factorially combined yielding four experimental conditions.

Subjects were tested in either reading or search and appropriate booklets were prepared for each subject. In the reading task, subjects saw six para-

Orientation		Example
Word	**Sentence**	
Normal	Normal	John Holland invented a successful submarine in 1898. This Irishman hoped to free Ireland from England.
Normal	Reversed	exceptionally an was Darrow Clarence a as career his began He .lawyer able .lawyer corporation
Reversed	Normal	iniduoH saw eno fo eht s'dlrow tseb epacse stsitra. nroB hcirhE ssieW ni 4781, eh koot sih lanoisseforp eman
Reversed	Reversed	rehcaet hcnerF a saw elliarB siuoL saw thgis nwo s'elliarB .dnilb eht fo .tnedicca na ni deyortsed

Figure 1. Examples of the four experimental conditions.

graphs in the same word-sentence orientation condition. The first two paragraphs were considered practice and not included in data analysis, but for
the remaining four, ten "yes-no" comprehension questions were presented
following each paragraph. Reading times were measured to the nearest tenth
of a second.

In the search task the same booklets were used again but the comprehension questions were removed and in their place target words were chosen
for the paragraph to follow. A word that appeared only once in a paragraph
but not in the first or last sentence was selected and the subject's task was
to find that word. The word was always typed in normal orientation and
appeared preceding its corresponding paragraph. The time from beginning
the search to finding the target was measured using the same counters as
in the reading task.

At each grade level the subjects were divided into either reading or search
groups, with fifty-six participants in each. These were then randomly assigned
to one of four orientation conditions, thus yielding fourteen subjects per grade
in each orientation condition. There was appropriate counterbalancing of
subjects, paragraphs, targets, and order of paragraphs.

Times taken to read and search were converted into speed scores of words
per minute. The scores for each subject were averaged over test paragraphs
and the mean number of words read per minute or searched was entered into
separate analyses of variance. In reading, the analyses showed that reading
speed increased with grade level. Reversing the direction of a word or sen-

tence brought significant decreases in reading speed. As shown in Figure 2, reversing the direction of sentences eliminated differences between the third and fifth graders. Similarly, the adults were reduced to the same level of reading as the third and fifth graders in the two word-reversal conditions. While reversing sentence orientation slowed subjects down, it did not impair their reading to the same extent that reversing word orientation did.

When sentence orientation was reversed for adults, reading speed was decreased from 215 words per minute to 123; when word orientation was reversed, regardless of sentence orientation, reading speed was reduced to less than thirty-six words per minute. The comprehension data generally showed that all subjects were comprehending the material and there were no important differences as a function of condition.

The search data presented the same general pattern of results. The error rate was low, under 6%. Again, search speed was measured in words per minute and the analysis of variance showed that all main effects and interactions were signficant. Search speed increased with grade but decreased with variations in word-sentence orientation. The interaction of Grade X Treatment showed that although all three grades exhibited a reduction in search speed as a function of the distortion of the specific word-sentence orientation, this reduction proved greater for adults than third graders.

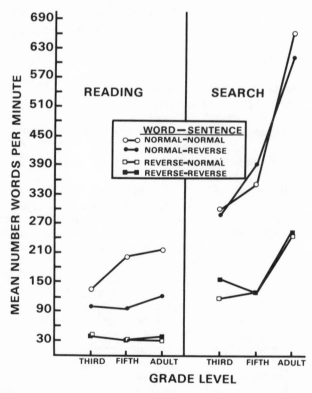

Figure 2. Mean number of words per minute per reading and search for the different grade levels.

There were some important differences between the two tasks. An analysis of variance comparing the tasks showed that all the main effects and interactions were significant. Search is faster than reading. The adults read normal text at the rate of 215 words per minute but searched at a rate of 666 per minute. A relatively small reduction in search speed was found when sentence orientation was reversed. However, when word orientation was reversed, search speed was reduced dramatically -- the adults' search speed dropped from 666 words per minute to approximately 250. In reading, subjects were reduced to a nearly letter-by-letter reading strategy such that they were reading fewer than 40 words per minute. In search, even the third graders were never reduced to a reading rate less than 118 words per minutes.

An important difference between reading and search lies in the comprehension demands involved. In reading, subjects are required to extract meaning; however, in search they need only extract physical features. Adults searched at a rate of 251 words per minute compared with the reading rate in the same condition of 36 words per minute. Since the stimuli were exactly the same, the only obvious difference between these two conditions was the task.

Subjects are able to screen the periphery for information in both reading and search. Whether a subject is moving his eyes from left to right or from right to left, peripheral information extraction can take place and subjects can read and search at fairly rapid rates. When the letters were presented from right to left, the ability of subjects to pre-screen was lessened.

An important aspect of these data are the developmental trends that were found. It appears that adults use the periphery more than children do and that increased experience with reading and the use of the periphery makes the process of reading and peripheral information extraction more automatic.

No single rule, theory, or model of reading will describe how the reader behaves in all situations. However, the model proposed by Hochberg (1970), in combination with the notions of automaticity put forth by LaBerge and Samuels (1974), can account for an amazing amount of data, in particular, the differences between children and adults and the increasing role of the periphery. As described by Fisher and Montanary (1977), Lefton and Fisher (1976), and Fisher and Lefton (1976), these two models suggest that peripheral information, context, and reading experience play a critical role in reading and search.

This research was supported by grants from the National Institute of Education (NE-G-00-3-0017) and from the US Army Human Engineering Laboratory and Army Research Offices (DAAG 29-77-G-0035). No official endorsement of NIE or ARO should be inferred. This paper may be reproduced in full or in part for any purpose of the United States Government.

REFERENCES

Fisher, D.F., & Lefton, L.A. Peripheral information extraction: A developmental examination of reading processes. Journal of Experimental Child Psychology, 1976, 21, 77-93.

Fisher, D.F., & Montanary, W.E. Spatial and contextual factors in beginning reading: Evidence for PSG-CSG complements to developing automaticity? Memory & Cognition, 1977, 5, 247-251.

Hochberg, J. Components of literacy: Speculation and exploratory research. In H. Levin and J.P. Williams (Eds.), Basic studies on reading. New York: Basic Books, 1970, 74-89.

Hochberg, J., & Brooks, V. Reading as an intentional behavior. In H. Singer and R.B. Ruddell (Eds.), Theoretical models and processes of reading. Newark, DE: International Reading Association, 1970, 304-314.

Kolers, P.A. The recognition of geometrically transformed text. Perception & Psychophysics, 1968, 3, 57-64.

Kolers, P.A., & Ostry, D.J. Time course of loss of information regarding pattern analyzing operations. Journal of Verbal Learning and Verbal Behavior, 1974, 13, 599-612.

Kolers, P.A., & Perkins, D.N. Orientation of letters and errors in their recognition. Perception & Psychophysics, 1969, 5, 265-270. (a)

Kolers, P.A., & Perkins, D.N. Orientation of letters and their speed of recognition. Perception & Psychophysics, 1969, 5, 275-280. (b)

LaBerge, D., & Samuels, S.J. Toward a theory of automatic information processing in reading. Cognitive Psychology, 1974, 6, 293-323.

Lefton, L.A., & Fisher, D.F. Information extraction during visual search: A developmental progression. Journal of Experimental Child Psychology, 1976, 22, 346-361.

McConkie, G.W., & Rayner, K. The span of the effective stimulus during a fixation in reading. Perception & Psychophysics, 1975, 17, 578-586.

Spragins, A.B., Lefton, L.A., & Fisher, D.F. Eye movements while reading and searching spatially transformed text: A developmental examination. Memory & Cognition, 1976, 4, 36-42.

Reading Eye Movements, Macro-structure and Comprehension
  Processes

Wayne L. Shebilske and L. Starling Reid

*Sentences usually are not read in isolation. They must be
related to the ideas expressed in other sentences in order
for a reader to comprehend the passage as a whole. These
comprehension processes were analyzed by measuring eye
movements while subjects read an 1888 word narrative text.
Measures of reading rate per sentence supported the idea
that reading eye movements are influenced by comprehension
processes that link sentential conceptual units together to
form higher-order conceptual units (macro-propositions).
On the strength of this finding, the present more global measure of reading eye movements was offered as an alternative
to the currently popular fine-grain analysis. According to
the procedures outlined in this paper, a strict moment-to-
moment link between language processes and eye movements
is not required for eye movements to be a useful tool for
analyzing comprehension processes during reading. One of
the practical applications of this approach is the possibility
that the analysis of comprehension processes during reading
will shed new light on the differences between average and
superior readers. Results were presented to support this
possibility, especially for those differences that relate to
active, flexible reading.*

*Professor Reid died on April 19, 1978. He shaped not only the model and
research presented in this paper, but also the personal and professional
goals of the first author, who here expresses his gratitude.*

Despite rapid developments in other areas of communication, skillful reading remains essential in education and is highly rewarded in modern society. Consequently, many people possessing only average reading ability are turning to "speed reading" courses that promise both an increased reading rate and an improved comprehension. Unfortunately, the success of these courses is dubious (cf. Gibson & Levin, 1975). Superior readers do exist, but most of them develop without special instruction. It is unlikely that teaching at this advanced level will improve until more is learned about how superior readers function. This is unlikely to happen until the emphasis of reading research is shifted from the processes of recognition to the processes of comprehension. To date, the majority of research on reading has focused on the processes of recognition. Thus, we know a good deal about how children and adults learn to recognize letters, syllables, words, and even sentences. Some of the knowledge gained through this research has been of practical value in the teaching of reading and the correction of various reading deficiencies. However, since this research has not dealt with reading as a whole, it has told us very little about the differences between average and highly skilled readers. While it is true that readers must recognize symbols, the central objective in reading is to comprehend the writer's message. Therefore, research on the comprehension processes may shed light on some aspects of reading which are not understood.

It has long been realized that the local processes in reading -- word recognition and eye movements -- depend upon and interact with the higher order processes of comprehension (e.g., Buswell, 1920; Huey, 1908). But it is only recently that the nature of these processes has been studied experimentally (cf. Carroll & Freedle, 1972; Gibson & Levin, 1975, Chapter 11; Kintsch, 1974). Macro-structural theory has been central in this research but, to date, has been applied mostly in memory research. This paper attempts to apply it to the analysis of comprehension processes that operate during reading. More specifically, this paper argues that a central process in reading comprehension is the construction by the reader of an effective macro-structure for the organization of the material being read. Comprehension processes not only link textual surface structure with its underlying conceptual structure, but also link the conceptual relationships that are specified by sentences to form a macro-structure which defines the global meaning of the material being read. A model will be presented which implies that when people read for comprehension, the comprehension processes influence reading rate. For example, the model predicts that when lower-order conceptual units are directly related to the underlying structure, fewer processing resources will be required for comprehension and reading will progress faster. Since changes in rate must be reflected in the parameters of reading eye movements, it follows that measures of eye movements could reveal the cognitive processes that underlie comprehension. Although far from being complete, the experimental work required to defend this premise is encouraging. Carpenter and Just (1977) and Scinto (1977) have shown that eye movements are related to comprehension processes that link pairs of sentences; this paper will present evidence that eye movements are related to comprehension processes that integrate sentences to form macro-propositions. Before experiments are discussed, however, it will be useful to consider how eye movements are related to other processes in reading.

A Model of Reading and Recall of Text
In the model shown in Figure 1, the processes that control eye movements during reading are related to the processes that build and retrieve macro-structure. The model will be described with an emphasis on how the comprehension processes influence eye movements during reading and how eye movements are related to recall of the material read.

Overview of the Model
According to the model, recognition and comprehension processes influence the oculomotor control system, which determines the direction and length of saccadic eye movements and the duration of fixations. The recognition processes receive their input from the eyes, which transform light patterns into a code that can be mapped onto recognition units. The recognition processes are operations that map the input from the eyes onto surface structural units that correspond to letters, syllables, sentences, and even paragraphs. The recognition processes draw upon the knowledge base for information about orthography, syntax, and semantics. Here, semantics refers to a knowledge of minimal or dictionary-like definitions of the words that constitute a sentence, that is, the meaning of those words independent of any specific context (Miller, 1972).

The comprehension processes: (1) link surface structural representations with the conceptual relationships represented by clauses and sentences, and (2) map these lower-order macro-structural units onto higher-order macro-structural units. For narratives, the higher-order macro-structural units correspond to categories like introduction, moral, episode, etc. (cf. Rumelhart, 1975; Van Dijk, 1975). The comprehension processes draw upon the knowledge base for background knowledge about what is being read and for rules for producing macro-structure.

The product of comprehension processes, a macro-structural representation of the reading material, is stored in, and retrieved from, episodic memory. A sketchy macro-structural framework is often entered into episodic memory by advance information about the text (e.g., advance learning goals) and is continually modified during and even after reading. Hence, even though macro-structure influences both eye movements and retrieval, retrieval may be influenced by a modified version of the structure that influenced eye movements.

The Influence of the Comprehension Processes
on Eye Movements During Reading
The comprehension processes could increase or decrease the rate of eye movements via two scanning control mechanisms (cf. Shebilske, 1975): an indirectly regulated scanning (IRS) mechanism (Bouma & de Voogd, 1974); and a directly regulated scanning (DRS) mechanism (Hochberg, 1975; Kolers, 1976; McConkie, 1976; Rayner & McConkie, 1976). The IRS mechanism monitors the amount of information in an input buffer, which holds visual information from two or three fixations, and, depending upon whether the buffer is empty or full, increases or decreases the rate of eye movements. The comprehension processes influence the rate of readout from the buffer and therefore indirectly influence eye movements. Rayner and McConkie (1976) ruled

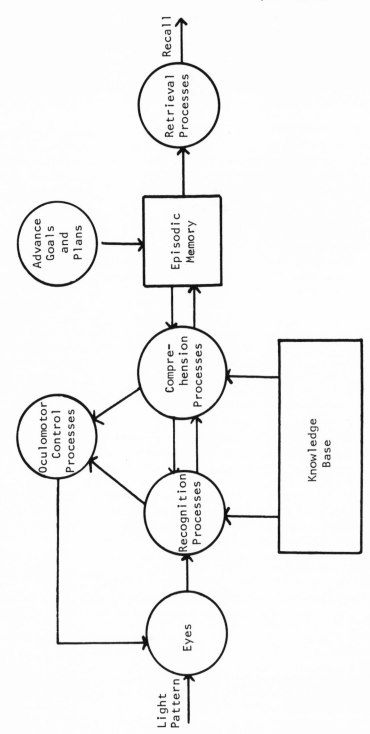

Figure 1. A model of reading and recall of text.

out some versions of IRS control, but feasible possibilities remain. Although
the existence of IRS control is not proven (cf. Hochberg, 1976), it is a viable
possibility in light of the experiments by Bouma and de Voogd (1974). It is
therefore important to show that a strict moment-to-moment link between
language processes and eye movements is not required for eye movements
to be a useful tool for analyzing comprehension processes during reading.

It is equally important to realize that readers are not slaves to an IRS
mechanism. Sometimes the eyes come under the command of the DRS mechanism through which eye movements are regulated directly by recognition
processes (O'Regan, this volume) or by comprehension processes. For example, when comprehension fails, parts may be reread or, when comprehension is assured, parts may be skipped. These intrusions of the DRS system
provide another opportunity to study the comprehension processes during
reading.

Experimental Analysis of the Comprehension Processes During Reading

A study of comprehension processes during reading is now feasible due to
advances in research on memory which have produced the means of quantifying
the relevant aspects of text. Data can be captured as never before by comparing a macro-structural representation of a text with a macro-structural
representation of a subject's recall of the text. Structural representations
have been determined by powerful formalisms (Frederiksen, 1975a; Norman
& Rumelhart, 1975; Anderson & Bower, 1973; Kintsch, 1974; Schank, 1973;
Grimes, 1972); or by empirical methods such as marking acceptable pause
locations (Brown & Smiley, 1977; Johnson, 1970). Although these methods
were developed for memory research, both the formal and empirical methods
for determining macro-structure are potentially useful for relating eye movements to comprehension. However, methodological barriers must first be
overcome as follows:

1) The methods that are available for studying the macro-structure of a
   reader's memory of complex materials measure final macro-structure,
   which is determined after the whole text is read. Eye movements, on
   the other hand, must be influenced by tentative macro-structure (the
   tentative assignment of micro-units to macro-categories), which is determined while the text is being read. Therefore, methods must be developed to study tentative macro-structure.
2) Eye movements are influenced by local recognition processes in addition
   to comprehension processes. Therefore, new derived measures will have
   to overpass the local influences of the recognition processes.
3) Individual differences in reading are considerable. Therefore, methods
   must be developed to quantify and analyze the relevant differences.

Experiments addressing these barriers will be described briefly in the remainder of this paper.

Tentative Macro-Structure
It is established that people appreciate macro-structure after they have read
a passage. But, can people predict macro-structure at any given moment

during reading on the basis of the preceding parts of the passage? So far
three experiments have been performed to answer this question. In all of
them, phrases and sentences were presented one at a time and subjects were
given one of two tasks: (1) rate the importance of the phrase or sentence
with respect to the structure of the whole passage (tentative importance
rating task); or (2) indicate which sentences "go together" by saying whether
each new sentence belongs to the same group as the preceding sentence or
whether it starts a new group (tentative grouping task).

These procedures measure tentative macro-structure rather than final
macro-structure because subjects have to use only prior phrases and sentences
to predict how each sentence fits into the structure of the whole passage.
However, these procedures measure explicit knowledge about tentative macro-
structure which may be different from the tacit knowledge that influences
eye movements (cf. Coltheart, 1977). In addition, the rate of presentation
is much slower than in normal reading and the responses may be distracting.
Therefore, the experiments attempted to add construct validity by showing:
1) that the measures varied as expected with independent variables that are
known to affect macro-structure; or 2) that the measures covaried as expected with other dependent measures that are known to be affected by macro-
structure. The results can be summarized as follows:

1)   Higher importance ratings were given to sentences that were salient
     in the macro-structure of various passages according to Van Dijk's (1975)
     recall data, and Thorndyke's (1977) recall data.
2)   Tentative groupings were consistent with the macro-structure that was
     derived from Van Dijk's (1975) recall data.

These experiments suggest that readers can use prior phrases and sentences to predict how each sentence of a narrative fits into the macro-structure of the whole passage. Thus, the results of these preliminary experiments
encouraged us to take eye movement records while subjects read a narrative.

Reading Rate Per Sentence and the Construction of
Macro-Structure During Reading

Clever manipulations have been used to infer from recall data that macro-
structure is constructed during acquisition as opposed to being constructed
during later stages of processing (Frederiksen, 1975a, 1975b, 1975c). According to this account, sentences express simple conceptual units which are
merged with simple conceptual units from other sentences to produce higher-
order conceptual units called macro-propositions. These are then related
to other macro-propositions to form still higher-order units such as episodes.
The simple units are maintained until they are merged, thus losing their identity. In contrast, the macro-propositions are grouped but do not lose their
identity and are thus recalled far better than simple conceptual units.

An even better case could be made for this model if it were tested by
a response measure taken during reading. The advantage of a method which
uses simultaneous measures over one taking measures after reading is that
only simultaneous measures can rule out the possibility that the results were
codetermined by later reconstruction activities such as recall. Therefore,
further tests of the above model were made by taking response measures

during reading.

In our main experiment, we measured eye movements while subjects read a story from Boccaccio's Decameron. The story had about 1900 words in 68 sentences. It was chosen because Van Dijk (1975) had derived a macro-structure for it based on his recall data and this structure was consistent with the above-mentioned tentative sort data. The eye movement records yield a response measure -- reading rate per sentence -- which allowed us to test the hypothesis that this structure was constructed during reading.

The rationale of the test was based on the observation that sentences in this passage differ in how directly they are related to the macro-structure. Van Dijk (1975) listed 25 macro-propositions which were included in over 75 of the recall protocols. As is sometimes the case in short stories, some macro-propositions superposed only one or two sentences. Other macro-propositions superposed from 3 to 7 sentences. For example, Figure 2 shows a page of text containing sentences 15 to 23. Sentence 17 directly corresponds to the macro-proposition "He took shelter in a bay," while sentences 18 to 22 must be integrated to derive the macro-proposition "There he was raided by merchants." We reasoned that reading rate should be slower when extra processing resources were required to maintain and integrate sentences into macro-propositions. Thus, we predicted that sentences which were indirectly related to macro-propositions (3 or more sentences per macro-proposition) would be read slower than sentences that directly expressed a macro-proposition (1 or 2 sentences per macro-proposition).

This is a straightforward prediction but several extraneous factors made it challenging to test. Three extraneous factors were controlled by choosing matched pairs of sentences. There were 24 sentences out of the total 68 sentences in Boccaccio's passage that were directly related to macro-propositions. These were paired with 24 other sentences in the passage which were matched for (1) serial position, (2) word length, and (3) number of simple propositions, which was a critical control, since Kintsch (1974) has shown that reading rate is faster for sentences with fewer simple propositions. Other extraneous factors that might have caused different reading rates were assessed in a control condition run for a separate group of subjects.

In order to measure reading rate for each sentence, an EDL/Biometrics Reading Eye II was used to measure horizontal eye movements in the left eye and vertical eye movements in the right. Subjects sat at a chin and forehead rest about 14 inches from the text, which was typed on 5" x 8" cards in Elite type with 35 single-spaced lines per card. Figure 2 shows one of the stimulus cards. Calibrations were rarely required between pages so that subjects read the whole passage with minimal interruptions. Eye movement records were taken from 12 third and fourth year college students at the University of Virginia, who were told to read as they normally read for recreation.

The records were analyzed by recording total looking time per sentence and then converting to words per minute for each sentence. (Notice that the line lengths were manipulated so that each sentence started at the beginning of a line and ended at the end of a line. Consequently, reading rate per sentence could be measured simply by recording the time between the appropriate return sweeps. Each card began at the beginning of a sentence and ended at the end of a sentence. The numbers "1, 2, and 3" were typed across the top and bottom of each card and subjects were instructed to look at each number at the start and finish. This created a distinctive eye pattern and a return sweep to mark the beginning and end. Subjects closed their eyes after reading the last number, then the experimenter "turned the page" and told the subjects to continue.) The results supported our prediction. Sentences that were directly related to macro-propositions were read at an average rate of 302 words per minute, while sentences that had to be integrated with others before they could be mapped onto macro-propositions were read at an average rate of 286 words per minute. This difference was statistically significant, $F(1, 11) = 13.78$, $p < .01$. An item analysis was done by averaging reading rates over the 12 subjects for each of the pairs of matched sentences. The results were fairly consistent over the 24 pairs: 17 went in the predicted direction, 2 were the same, and 4 went in the opposite direction. A matched pairs t-test using sentences as the random factor showed a significant difference in the predicted direction, $t(23) = 2.49$, $p < .05$. Similarly, an analysis of differences between individual readers showed that the predicted result was obtained consistently: 11 out of 12 subjects went in the predicted direction. Hence, although the obtained difference was small (5%) it seemed to be reliable.

According to the above hypothesis, this difference arose because subjects were integrating sentences into macro-propositions. Before this result could be offered in support of that hypothesis, however, an alternative explanation had to be ruled out since one could argue that the difference in reading rates was owing to intra-sentence differences in word difficulty, elliptical constructions, and ambiguous pronominalization. If that were the case, different reading rates would occur even if subjects were not trying to integrate sentences into macro-propositions. To check this we had another group of subjects read the sentences in isolation. Since the sentences should not be integrated into macro-propositions in this control condition, the difference in reading rate should vanish according to the macro-structural explanation, but it should remain according to the alternative explanation.

This control was simple in principle but, in fact, it was difficult to achieve. In our first attempt we had different groups of subjects read several random permutations of the sentences from the original story. To our surprise, subjects recalled most of the macro-propositions under these conditions; in fact, their recall protocols looked very similar to those of subjects who read the story in its correct order. Our next attempt was much more successful. To minimize the possibility of integration, we selected only eight pairs of sentences from the original. These 16 sentences were read in the context of 64 other sentences drawn from about 60 other stories. It was hoped that subjects would not try to integrate sentences on so many different topics, and, indeed, afterwards subjects said that they did not. The instructions also promoted reading the sentences in isolation. Subjects were told to read each sentence so that they could recall its main ideas immediately after they finished it. No more than one sentence was tested per page and subjects were told that they could forget the other sentence because they would not be tested. This procedure also gave us a way to be sure that subjects read the sentences. The results showed that they could recall about 80% of the propositions from the tested sentences.

1 2 3

15 He had had enough of commerce to be
shy of it, so he did not bother to
invest his money, but simply plying
his oars, he set out on the same little
bark with which he had earned it.

16 He had just entered the Archipelago,
when a mighty wind rushed up from
the south-east, which was not only
unfavorable to his course, but churned
up such terrible waves that his
tiny vessel could not weather them.

17 He pulled into the gulf made by the
projection of a small island, and there,
protected from the wind, resigned
himself to await more propitious weather.

18 Not long afterwards, however, two
large Genoese galleys coming from
Constantinople, made their way arduously
to the little haven, escaping from the
very thing Landolfo had avoided.

19 As soon as the captains caught sight
of the little vessel and learned it
belonged to Landolfo whom they knew to
be so wealthy, they made ready to seize
him, in their desire for rapine and gain.

20 Accordingly, they blocked his escape,
landed part of their armored men, wielding
crossbows, and stationed them in such
a way that it was impossible for anyone
to leave the bark without being shot.

21 The rest of the crew got out in
small crafts and with the help of the
current, neared Landolfo's ship.

22 It cost them little time and trouble to
seize it, crew and all, to the last man.

23 As for Landolfo, they took him
aboard one of their galleys, leaving
him nothing but a worn coat.

1 2 3

Figure 2. Page of stimulus materials. The brackets and numbers in the left margin were not on the cards that subjects read.

The 24 pairs from the original experiment were divided into three sets in such a way that the first set showed a large difference between the directly and indirectly related sentences and the next two sets showed a medium and a small difference. So far only the first set has been completed by a group of 12 subjects, who were matched to the experimental group in reading ability. In the original experiment where sentences were read in context, the reading rate was 314 for the directly related sentences and 287 for the indirectly related. In the control condition where the same sentences were read out of context, the comparable rates were 209 and 213. An analysis of variance was done on two factors, Context vs. No Context (between-Subjects) and Directly related vs. Indirectly related (within-Subjects). It showed a significant main effect of the context factor, $F(1, 22) = 10.97$, $p < .01$ and a significant interaction between the factors, $F(1, 22) = 8.99$, $p < .01$. A follow-up planned comparison showed that the difference between directly and indirectly related sentences was significant in context, $F(1, 11) = 10.71$, $p < .01$, but not out of context, $F(1, 11) < 1$. These findings support the idea that a central process in the comprehension of reading is the construction, on the part of the reader, of a macro-structure for the organization of the material being read and that eye movements are consequently influenced by relationships that exist beyond sentences or pairs of sentences.

Individual Differences and Flexible Reading
The difference in reading rates for our two types of sentences can be viewed as a measure of intra-passage flexibility. Flexible reading was defined by Weintraub (1967) as "...the ability to adjust one's rate and approach to reading with the purpose for reading, with the difficulty of material, and with one's background or knowledge of the particular subject matter." Educators generally recognize flexibility as an important component of superior reading (Harris & Sipay, 1975). Many have discussed the importance of intra-passage flexibility and its relationship to inter-passage flexibility (McDonald, 1963), but few have measured intra-passage flexibility (cf. Rankin & Hess, 1971; Rankin, 1974) and no one has related it empirically to inter-passage flexibility. Therefore, we compared our measure of intra-passage flexibility with a separate measure of inter-passage flexibility for each subject.

Inter-passage flexibility was measured five minutes after subjects finished reading the Decameron story. Each subject read two additional stories, "The Dragon's Tears" and "How to Fool a Cat," which were provided by Ann Brown, who had used them in her research on marking acceptable pause locations (Brown & Smiley, 1977). These stories have comparable readability levels (Dale-Chall readability scores of 5.2287 and 5.3682 respectively, and are approximately the same length, 432 and 393 words). The order of reading the stories was counterbalanced across subjects. The first story was read with the same instructional set that was given for the Decameron story, that is, subjects were told to read as they normally do for recreation since they would not be tested on this reading. In contrast, the second story was to be read rigorously, and subjects were told that they would be given a short - answer test on the story's details. The ratio of recreational reading rate over rigorous reading rate provided our measure of inter-passage flexibility.

Two tests showed a significant relationship between our measures of intra-passage flexibility and inter-passage flexibility. A Spearman rank-order correlation showed rho = +0.63, t = 2.57, p <.05, and a Pearson product-moment correlation showed r = +0.60, t = 2.37, p <.05. If our measure of intra-passage flexibility is taken as an indication of the construction of macro-structure, as argued above, then the correlation with inter-passage flexibility suggests that both intra-passage flexibility and inter-passage flexibility may be the by-product of the active construction of macro-structure during reading.

In order to mark our sample with respect to other studies in the literature, we gave our subjects a standardized reading test, McGraw-Hill Basic Skills System: Reading (Raygor, 1970). One interesting relationship is the correlation between reading rate on our test of rigorous reading of easy material and the standard test of rigorous reading of easy material, rho = +0.83, t = - 4.73, p <.001. Since the standard test was taken without the eye movement monitor, subjects' normal reading habits were not greatly disrupted by the eye movement monitor. An interesting comparison exists between the standard test's measure of inter-passage flexibility and our measure of inter-passage flexibility. Here, no correlation was found, rho = -0.16, p >.05. This may be because Raygor's test of flexibility held instructional set constant for rigorous reading (to-be-tested reading) and manipulated passage difficulty, while the present test of flexibility did the opposite. The lack of a relationship emphasizes a point stressed by Rankin (1974), that the measurement of reading flexibility has many problems that remain to be solved.

Macro-structural theory could provide a rationale for developing better tests and increased understanding of flexible reading. The model in Figure 1 shows that macro-structural theory can be related to the relevant dimensions of flexible reading since the construction of macro-structure is influenced by the purpose for reading (advanced learning goals), the structural difficulty of the material, and the reader's background knowledge. This, along with the present experimental results, suggests that an extension of this line of research may shed new light on flexible reading.

Summary and Conclusions

This paper has focused on comprehension processes as opposed to recognition processes. It began by trying to specify the nature of the control of reading eye movements in such a way as to be able to use eye movement records to analyze comprehension processes during reading. The model presented in Figure 1 suggested an alternative to fine-grain analyses of eye movement records. One rationale for this currently popular approach was expressed by McConkie (this volume). He claims that to gain information about language processing from eye movements we must understand: (1) what is "seen" during a fixation; and (2) the basic nature of the moment-to-moment relationship between eye movements and the cognitive processes. In contrast, a procedure based on the present model yielded results which suggest that more global measure of eye movements can reflect the nature of language processing without knowing (1) and (2) above. Specifically, measures of reading rate per sentence added evidence favoring the idea that reading eye movements are influenced by comprehension processes that link sentential conceptual units together to form macro-structural units. While progress is being made toward answering (1) and (2), much remains to be done according to the present model which emphasizes that reading eye movements are controlled at various levels by oculomotor processes, recognition processes, and comprehension processes. In the meantime, while these multi-level influences are being disentangled, this approach gives an alternative way to use eye movement records as a tool for analyzing comprehension processes during the reading of normal text. The practical value of this approach is based on the premise that the comprehension processes harbor important differences between average and highly skilled readers. The encouraging results obtained so far suggest that the cognitive processes that underlie comprehension can be analyzed during reading and this analysis may shed new light on the differences between average and superior readers, especially on those differences related to active, flexible reading.

We thank James Deese and John Rotondo for valuable input into all stages of this project; Cassandra B. Wright, Clifford M. Karmiol, Charles Massey, Cheryl D. Miles, and Ella Harbour for their help with data collection and analysis; and Edmund Henderson for providing the McGraw-Hill reading test and for critically reading a draft of this paper.

REFERENCES

Anderson, J.R., & Bower, G.H. Human associative memory. Washington, DC: V.H. Winston, 1963.
Bouma, H., & de Voogd, A.H. On the control of eye saccades in reading. Vision Research, 1974, 14, 273-284.
Brown, A.L., & Smiley, S.S. Rating the importance of structural units of prose passages: A problem of metacognitive development. Child Development, 1977, 48, 1-8.
Buswell, G.T. An experimental study of eye-voice span in reading. Supplementary Education Monographs, 1920, 17.
Carpenter, P.A., & Just, M.A. Reading comprehension as eyes see it. In M. Just and P. Carpenter (Eds.), Cognitive processes in comprehension. Hillsdale, NJ: Erlbaum, 1977.
Carroll, J.B., & Freedle, R. (Eds.), Language comprehension and the acquisition of knowledge. New York: Wiley, 1972.
Coltheart, M. Critical notice. Quarterly Journal of Experimental Psychology, 1977, 29, 157-167.
Frederiksen, C.H. Representing logical and semantic structures of knowledge acquired from discourse. Cognitive Psychology, 1975, 1, 371-458. (a)
Frederiksen, C.H. Acquisition of semantic information from discourse: Effects of repeated exposures. Journal of Verbal Learning and Verbal Behavior, 1975, 14, 158-169. (b)
Frederiksen, C.H. Effects of context-induced processing operations on semantic information acquired from discourse. Cognitive Psychology, 1975, 1, 139-166. (c)

Gibson, E.J., & Levin, H. The psychology of reading. Cambridge, MA: MIT Press, 1975.

Grimes, J.F. The thread of discourse. The Hague: Mouton, 1972.

Harris, A.J., & Sipay, E.R. How to increase reading ability: A guide to developmental and remedial methods (6th ed.). New York: David McKay Company Inc., 1975.

Hochberg, J. On the control of saccades in reading. Vision Research, 1975, 15, 620.

Hochberg, J. Toward a speech-plan eye-movement model of reading. In R.A. Monty and J.W. Senders (Eds.), Eye movements and psychological processes. Hillsdale, NJ: Erlbaum, 1976.

Huey, E.B. The psychology and pedagogy of reading. Cambridge, MA: MIT Press, 1968 (originally published in 1908).

Johnson, R.E. Recall of prose as a function of the structural importance of the linguistic units. Journal of Verbal Learning and Verbal Behavior, 1970, 9, 12-20.

Kintsch, W. The representation of meaning in memory. New York: Wiley, 1974.

Kolers, P.A. Buswell's discoveries. In R.A. Monty and J.W. Senders (Eds.), Eye movements and psychological processes. Hillsdale, NJ: Erlbaum, 1976.

McConkie, G.W. The use of eye-movement data in determining the perceptual span in reading. In R.A. Monty and J.W. Senders (Eds.), Eye movements and psychological processes. Hillsdale, NJ: Erlbaum, 1976.

McDonald, A.S. Flexibility in reading. International Reading Association Conference Proceedings, 1963, 8, 81-85.

Miller, G.A. English verbs of motion: A case study in semantics and lexical memory. In A.W. Melton and E. Martin (Eds.), Coding processes in human memory. Washington, DC: Winston, 1972.

Norman, D.A., & Rumelhart, D.E. Exploration in cognition. San Francisco: W.H. Freeman, 1975.

Rankin, E.F. The measurement of reading flexibility: Problems and perspectives. Reading Information Series: Where Do We Go? International Reading Association, 1974.

Rankin, E.F., & Hess, A.K. The measurement of internal (intra-article reading flexibility. Nineteenth Yearbook (Vol. 1). National Reading Conference Milwaukee. The National Reading Conference, 1971, 254-262.

Raygor, A.L. McGraw-Hill basic skills system: Reading test (Manual). New York: McGraw-Hill, 1970.

Rayner, K., & McConkie, G.W. What guides a reader's eye movements? Vision Research, 1976, 16, 829-837.

Rumelhart, D. Notes on a schema for stories. In D. Bobrow and A. Collins (Eds.), Representing and understanding: Studies in cognitive science. New York: Academic Press, 1975.

Schank, R. Identification of conceptualizations underlying natural language. In R. Schank and K. Colby (Eds.), Computer models of thought and language. San Francisco: W.H. Freeman, 1973.

Shebilske, W.L. Reading eye movements from an information-processing point of view. In D.W. Massaro (Eds.), Understanding language: An information-processing analysis of speech perception, reading and psycholinguistics. New York: Academic Press, 1975.

Scinto, L.F. Relation of eye fixations to old - new information of texts.
    Paper presented at the Conference of Psychological Processes and Eye
    Movements, Monterey, CA, February 1977.
Thorndyke, P.W. Cognitive structures in comprehension and memory of nar-
    rative discourse. Cognitive Psychology, 1977, 9, 77-110.
Van Dijk, T.A. Recalling and summarizing complex discourse. University of
    Amsterdam, 1975.
Weintraub, S. Research. The Reading Teacher, 1967, 21, 169-173.

Design of Graphic Language

Introduction

M.E. Wrolstad

As I sit here producing visible language and you sit there processing it, our meeting point across time and space is this page of print. But at best this is an uncertain meeting. In the translation of my thinking into written language and the graphic page, I can only hope to approximate what I actually mean. And you, in turn, are making your own approximation of what I manage to express!

Every contributor to this volume is concerned about this approximation process. On the reader's side of our meeting point, questions are raised about neurophysical processing of this package of information you hold. Just what are we doing when we read? How do we make best use of our visual equipment and our neurological wiring? What strategies do we devise, what shortcuts do we make, what accommodations do we arrange? Can we speed up the processing; can we make it more efficient?

Those of us concerned with the production of visible language are no less concerned with understanding and improving this approximation process. We have only to consider the enormous research effort being expended by mass media in attempting to perfect the generation of written language. But we lack perspective on this research effort because of its size and its complexity. Basic issues here are more elusive and their consideration lacks organizational structure; while reading remains essentially a personal activity, writing has become an industry. And in many important respects, the two areas are worlds apart. This page of print may be our meeting point, but for visible language research it traditionally has represented an operational chasm.

Could we agree, however, that our joint concern is understanding all that is involved in being literate? If so, it then follows that our interests in reading and in writing become interlocked -- if only at this initial stage in visible language theory. A major contribution of this conference was providing this larger umbrella under which representatives of both research areas could sit down and reason together. While it was a unique experience, we

realize that the exchange can only serve as an introduction to the the range
of issues that requires examination. It may be helpful to identify a few of
these issues in relation to ideas discussed by contributors to this section
on graphic languages.

Twyman reminds us that every piece of graphic communication -- from
the simplest handwritten note to the most sophisticated ten-volume ency-
clopedia -- has to be planned by someone. His schema for the study of
graphic languages organizes the planning options open to all of us, and in
so doing provides a much needed over-view of all graphic communication,
for the researcher as well as for the designer.

We all have a fairly restricted concept of the elements that go into the
planning of graphic communication. Researchers dealing with processing,
for example, tend to think in terms of simple linear text consisting of letters,
words, sentences, paragraphs.... Analysis of Twyman's schema, in fact,
reveals resulting inequities in research priorities. Only when we are called
upon to devise a visual description of an especially complicated concept do
we abandon pure linearity and begin to explore the range of design options
open to us.

Twyman's discussion suggests two general reasons why we turn to graphic
language to work out the presentation of complex ideas. In the first place,
we have time for planning. And related to this is the fact that visible language provides, as George Miller has pointed out, "the tangible representation
of our act of thought" -- our ideas become something we can work with and
react to. We have, therefore, both the time and the equipment to make proper use of language as well as to exercise control over its graphic presentation. In the second place, we are able to make use of the unique spatial
qualities inherent in our visual world. Imagine trying to explain all of the
intricate and subtle patterns involved in Twyman's schema over the telephone!

Twyman's main point, however, is that as communicators we are not
adequately aware of the graphic dimensions available to us. We fail to use
graphic language to its full potential, and we have not studied the interaction
of verbal and non-verbal visual information within an over-all concept of
graphic languages. We should, however, be slightly reassured to have his dis-
cernment of a general trend (over several centuries) towards non-linear pictorial and schematic modes in the presentation of our visual communication.

Crouwel addresses the question: what is the contribution of the designer
to the over-all communication of graphic language? His response: a creative
intuition. Involved, Crouwel suggests, is an element of exploration roughly
parallel to scientific inquiry, based not on experimental research, however,
but on a personal vision.

It has been the scribes who have shaped our visible language; it is the
graphic designer today who works at the leading edge of graphic language
evolution. But the graphic designer is practicing a "bound" art, as the Dutch
say, which must answer first to content, function, and the spirit of the times.
However, his personal search for more effective ways to develop and express
ideas is very strong. A leading graphic designer, Crouwel discusses and
illustrates the development over several years of his own experimentation
utilizing a three-dimensional graphic design theory.

Creative intuition is an elusive contribution, but it pushes continually
at the frontiers of graphic language expression. The graphic designer's

personal vision (which is his particular genius) is a continual reminder that his development of expressive form -- as a creative action -- is no less important to our understanding of literacy than is our scientific reaction.

If proof is required that the producers are concerned about understanding the approximation process that confronts us in visible language, consider the papers of Phillips, Foster, and Waller.

Phillips suggests a basic theme in reporting two conflicting schools of thought in cartographic research: should we train people to be better map readers, or should we train better map makers, since bad design hinders good and bad map readers alike? Phillips opts for the latter. He reports on investigations in progress toward this goal, but in general makes us aware that there is much to be done in this fairly new area of graphic language research.

On the basic assumption that production is the more difficult side of literacy, Foster and Waller feel that most of us as writers need all the help we can get. I think we would have to agree that as literate adults we are far better readers than writers. And, unfortunately, we cannot all send our rough drafts to Crouwel.

Foster discusses the more specific production technique for aiding a reader's organization and retention of material: visual cuing in continuous prose. He acknowledges the problem of the individual reader: the novice facing difficult material may appreciate considerable guidance, the expert may be incensed. There has been related research -- in newspaper reading, for example -- which indicates that the normal reader wants most to be left alone; bold-face subheads, italic paragraphs, and the like, may only provide convenient stopping points. And we are very soon into readability of text-- the author's own manipulation of paragraphs, phrases, and words to lead the reader through his ideas.

Waller is concerned that too little visible language research is pertinent to the production of educational materials. He questions the applicability of much theoretical research to "the real world" of reading and suggests that we begin to look more closely at the variety of strategies our writers and readers actually use, particularly in dealing with extended material such as a textbook. We might want to argue: first things first. But throughout this volume it is a moot point whether the psychologist analyzing our processing of individual letters, words, or even phrases is actually studying reading. And, indeed, if our eye movement strategies are modified as we approach words of different length and different importance -- as research here demonstrates -- then we can well ask how our reading strategies might be modified as we approach texts of different complexity and different format. For Waller, the reader must become an active participant in the communication process; his basic question, then, is how can we analyze and relate a writer's strategies to what we are learning about his prospective readers? This theme is presented too by Jansen, who discusses some relations of people to books, the physical properties of books that are likely to be read, and the conditions that affect choices by both children and adults. We need to know more about the writing process itself and how it is integrated with editing and design to provide a text or a book more accurately directed at its particular audience and function.

So, as I sit here producing visible language and you sit there processing it, I am exercising a faith that these pages of print can provide a meeting of minds. Despite all of our unanswered questions, visible language works because I want very much to be understood and you want to understand. These reports into graphic language research should help to reassure us, therefore, whether our major interests are in reading or in a unified theory of literacy.

A Schema for the Study of Graphic Language (Tutorial Paper)

Michael Twyman

This paper presents a schema that attempts to embrace all graphic language. The essence of the schema is shown in a matrix which presents a number of theoretical possibilities in terms of approaches to graphic language. One axis of the matrix describes the methods of configuration of graphic language, using such terms as pure linear, linear interrupted, list, linear branching, matrix, non-linear directed, non-linear open. The other axis describes the modes of symbolization of graphic language, using four somewhat crude categories: verbal/numerical, pictorial and verbal/numerical, pictorial, schematic. Numerous examples are shown to clarify terms and the underlying concepts they describe. It is emphasized that the matrix is a device for directing thinking, rather than a means of defining graphic language.

The paper is written from the standpoint of a practising graphic designer. The matrix is used to illustrate the wide range of approaches open to us in graphic language and the effect this is assumed to have on reading/viewing strategies and cognitive processes. It is suggested that the matrix is useful in focusing attention on two fundamental questions that ought always to be asked when deciding how a graphic message should be communicated: What should be the mode of symbolization and what should be the method of configuration? Legibility and related research is briefly reviewed in order to establish what light it throws on these questions; with a few notable exceptions it is found wanting. It is suggested that there is a need for more research that crosses the boundaries of the cells of the matrix.

This paper is not the culmination of a sustained programme of research and brings no firm evidence to bear on any aspect of graphic language. It is the contribution of a graphic designer who has had the opportunity of associating with research workers concerned with the evaluation of graphic language, and is written as a tutorial paper to stimulate thought and discussion. It is an attempt to define the scope of graphic language and to show relationships between different approaches to it that have been, and can be, used. Throughout the paper, the totality of graphic language and its specifically graphic variables are emphasized. Though the approach may appear to be somewhat theoretical, it is intended that it should have practical implications.

For the purpose of this paper "graphic designer" means someone who plans graphic language; "graphic" means drawn or otherwise made visible in response to conscious decisions, and "language" means a vehicle of communication. The graphic designer is usually seen as someone who operates between those with messages to transmit and those to whom they have to be communicated; in this respect he is the graphic equivalent of the radio producer. The graphic designer may not always be a professional however and, whether lay or professional, he may on occasions be the originator of the message. It should be stressed therefore that the term graphic designer is used here to refer to anyone who plans graphic language.

While all of us use graphic language as originators and consumers, very few of us are aware of how it should be planned so that it can be most effective. In this respect, as in many others, graphic language differs from oral language, which is either not consciously planned at all - as in most conversational situations - or is planned by those who engage in public speaking with a reasonable understanding of what they are doing. Our experience of planning graphic language - unless we have special problems, such as those presented by the preparation of a table for a scientific paper or a hand-made notice for a jumble sale - probably ended at school when we learned how to organize a letter, address an envelope, or set out a sum in mathematics. Most of those who use graphic means of communication professionally in everyday situations involving continuous prose merely pass on their problems to their typist who does the planning for them. In more complex areas of graphic communication, particularly when the message is non-linear, the originator has less control over the graphic presentation of his message and frequently relies on a specialist draughtsman, cartographer, or typographer. This is a situation that has few parallels in oral language.

Outline of Objectives
The principal objective of this paper is to demonstrate by means of a schema the wide range of approaches open to us in graphic language. The proposed schema, which is presented in the form of a matrix, draws attention to the different modes and configurations of graphic language and is firmly rooted in practical applications. It is relevant to consider a schema of this kind - though not necessarily the one proposed - for both practical and theoretical reasons. In practical terms it is important because a schema which presents graphic language as a whole has the value of drawing attention to the variety of approaches available when using graphic language and defines those areas where decisions have to be made. All this is made necessary because our training and experience, whether primarily verbal, numerical, or visual, tends

to predispose us towards particular approaches to graphic communication.
In more theoretical terms, the overall pattern presented by the schema
enables us to see points of connection between different areas of graphic
language that are normally seen as discrete and that our traditional attitudes
and terminology encourage us to keep separate.

The secondary objectives of this paper stem directly from the first. The
matrix will be used as a means of identifying, in a very general way, those
approaches to graphic language that are most commonly adopted. It will
also be used to consider the extent to which legibility and related research
has responded to the real needs of those making decisions about graphic
language.

The schema does not pretend to be watertight, and some of the boundaries
between the cells of the matrix are drawn subjectively. The fact that some
kinds of graphic language do not fit perfectly within the matrix serves only
to highlight the subtlety and flexibility of graphic language. This should not
invalidate the schema itself, which is intended as a device for directing our
thinking and not as an end in itself.

Fragmentation of the Study of Graphic Language
Over the last few years I have attempted to develop approaches to the description of graphic language. In this respect I have taken a leaf out of the book
of linguistic scientists, many of whom believe that description is a necessary
prelude to understanding. Certain aspects of graphic language have, of
course, been extremely well covered from a descriptive standpoint. The
characters of the Latin alphabet, for instance, have been minutely studied:
there are numerous classification systems designed to accommodate thousands
of different styles of letter forms (most of which are not even noticed by
the layman), and a precise language has been developed to describe the
various parts of letters and their related characters. All this can perhaps
be compared with phonetics as a branch of linguistics. There is also a vast
literature which focuses on the iconography of that part of graphic language
we call art, and traces subtle stylistic influences of one artist or school on
another. This activity might be seen, at least in some respects, as akin to
literary criticism.

These two aspects of graphic language have been chosen to highlight the
diversity of the field and of the activities of those who work within it. Those
who study letter forms in the manner described above are likely to be practising typographers or historians of printing; those who study the iconography
of paintings are likely to be art historians. Though related to one another
in that both are concerned with forms of graphic language, the two disciplines hardly interact. To a large degree the same must be said of other
fields of scholarship concerned with graphic language within a theoretical
framework, such as semiology, psychology, topology, anthropology, palaeo-
graphy, linguistic science, and cartography.

The Matrix
The proposed schema is based on the matrix (Figure 1) which presents a
number of theoretical possibilities in terms of approaches to graphic language.
The column headings describe what have been called methods of configuration, by which is meant the graphic organization or structure of a message

Method of configuration

	Pure linear	Linear interrupted	List	Linear branching	Matrix	Non-linear directed viewing	Non-linear most options open
Verbal/ numerical	1	2	3	4	5	6	7
Pictorial & verbal/ numerical	8	9	10	11	12	13	14
Pictorial	15	16	17	18	19	20	21
Schematic	22	23	24	25	26	27	28

Mode of symbolization

Figure 1. The matrix.

which influences and perhaps determines the "searching," "reading," and "looking" strategies adopted by the user. There is no accepted terminology in this field, apart from the headings "list," "linear branching," and "matrix," which will be readily understood. The division between the two headings to the extreme right of the matrix, "non-linear directed viewing" and "non-linear most options open" (shortened henceforth to "non-linear directed" and "non-linear open") is highly subjective and is therefore indicated by a dotted line. In reality the two categories, which are shown as discrete items in the matrix, form a continuum. There are elements of linear reading in some of the "nonlinear directed" categories, but the heading serves to emphasize that the principal searching strategy is non-linear. The most important general characteristic presented by the column headings is that they show a transition from pure linearity on the left to extreme non-linearity on the right.

Column headings have been limited to major categories since the main aim of this paper is to concentrate attention on a few central issues. It would not have been difficult to subdivide some of these major categories. For instance, the heading called "linear interrupted" could be further divided according to whether all reading was in the same direction (i.e., left to right, or right to left), or whether it was to be done boustrophedon (as the ox ploughs). Within each of these categories the interruption of the linear flow may be made on the following grounds:

1) semantically (with the lines broken only after linguistic units, the smallest such unit being the word)
2) quasi-semantically (with the lines broken only between words or within words according to etymology)
3) partially semantically (with the lines broken between words or within words either phonetically or arbitrarily)
4) mechanically (with words broken at the most convenient point, regardless of meaning).

Even within these four categories there are different ways in which these line endings may be achieved, and most of these can be found in everyday use. It is clear, however, that little is to be gained by producing a matrix of such complexity that it would be understood only by its originator or those prepared to spend an inordinate amount of time studying it.

The row headings describe the modes of symbolization. This is a fairly crude breakdown of modes, especially in relation to those sections that relate to pictorial language. The subject is one that has attracted considerable attention from semiologists over the last few decades, particularly in relation to iconic and symbolic images, but such issues are not central to the theme of this paper, which is more concerned with the relation between mode of symbolization and method of configuration. It should be said that it is more difficult to establish a distinction between pictorial and schematic modes than between the other categories on this axis; for this reason the division between them is indicated by a dotted line. A number of additional headings could also have been introduced on the axis of the matrix. A "numerical" mode might have been included as a separate category from "verbal/numerical"; in addition, it might have been valuable to introduce a combined "schematic and verbal/numerical" category and to distinguish between discrete pictorial symbols and unified synoptic pictures. However, it was felt that such additions

to the matrix would have blurred an important issue - the conflict in reading/-
viewing strategies that arises from the linearity of the verbal mode and the
non-linearity of both the pictorial and schematic modes.

In other respects, too, emphasis has been placed on ease of understanding.
Most obviously the matrix, as presented, takes no account of sequences in
time as seen in film and television; nor even of the interrupted sequences
in time presented by pages of a book or sets of slides. Such approaches could
have been accommodated by adding a third dimension to the matrix, but at
the expense of clarity. Similarly, a number of the graphic variables isolated
by Bertin (1967) - such as size, tone, texture, colour, and shape are not specifically catered for. These can, and should, be considered in relation to all
the combinations of modes of symbolization and methods of configuration
presented in the matrix.

The Cells of the Matrix
The cells of the matrix have been numbered for ease of reference, even
though this approach reinforces one particular reading strategy at the expense
of others. These numbers have been included in parentheses in the text of
this paper where relevant.

The examples chosen to fill the cells of the matrix are mainly from this
century and from those parts of the world using the roman alphabet. However, the matrix has validity in relation to other linguistic conventions and
other periods of time, and culturally and historically based approaches to
it would probably prove fruitful.

It is important to emphasize that each cell of the matrix offers a relatively wide range of graphic possibilities. The most effective way of presenting the essential characteristics of each cell would be to show numerous
examples, but clearly a printed paper does not lend itself to this approach.
There is the danger, in showing a single example, or even a limited number
of examples, that this might lead to the formulation of a narrow set of definitions for the cells. It should be said therefore that the prime reason for
presenting the matrix is neither to define nor confine graphic language. The
examples shown here should be considered with these comments in mind;
they are presented in list form in the numbered sequence of the cells of the
matrix, together with a brief commentary.

Cell 1.   These examples come as close to pure linearity as a limited two-dimensional format will allow. On the left is the Phaistos disc (Minoan, c.1700BC) and on the right a recent handwritten letter. Both examples read from the outside to the centre.

Cell 2.   In practice, linear flow of text is nearly always interrupted, as in the Codex Sinaiticus from the fourth century AD (left). The reasons for this practice are various (ergonomic, perceptual, practical) and apply throughout the world whether the direction of reading is left to right, right to left, or top to bottom (centre). Normally, line breaks do not relate to semantic units. Lines are usually more or less of the same length within a single passage of text, but linear interrupted text may take other forms (right). The methods used to make sequences of lines conform to predetermined arrays are too numerous to describe here.

Cell 3. Lists differ from 2 above in that the items presented on each line form discrete semantic units. On the left is the order of the coronation procession of George IV, 1821. On the right is a restaurant guide in which entries are distinguished from one another by occupying separate lines, though each entry consists of two parts which are distinguished from one another typographically.

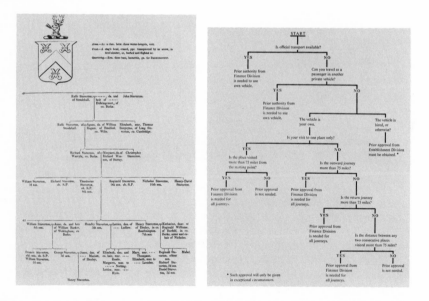

Cell 4. On the left is a traditional family tree of 1833, with many branches; on the right is an algorithm, which is binary.

		Home					Away				
	P	W	D	L	F	A	W	D	L	F A	Pts
Leeds	13	5	1	0	12	4	3	3	1	8 5	20
Arsenal	13	6	1	0	21	2	1	3	2	6 11	18
Man. C	12	3	3	0	12	4	3	2	1	5 4	17
Spurs	13	4	1	1	9	4	2	4	1	10 6	17
Cryst P	13	5	0	2	10	5	2	3	1	5 4	17
Chelsea	13	3	3	0	11	8	2	3	2	5 5	16
Wolves	13	3	1	2	12	13	4	1	2	14 14	16
L'pool	12	4	2	0	12	2	1	3	2	3 4	15
Stoke	13	4	3	0	13	7	0	2	4	5 15	13
Cov C	13	3	1	2	6	3	2	2	3	6 8	13
Newc U	13	1	4	1	6	6	3	1	3	9 10	13
S'hmptn	13	3	2	1	8	3	2	2	4	2 10	12
Everton	13	2	2	1	9	6	2	1	4	9 15	12
Derby	13	3	1	1	11	9	1	2	3	7 11	11
WBA	13	3	3	1	13	9	0	2	4	9 21	11
Man. U	13	2	3	2	6	4	1	2	3	7 14	11
Notts F	13	3	2	1	12	6	0	3	4	1 12	11
H'field	13	3	3	1	9	5	0	2	4	3 12	11
Ipswich	13	3	2	2	13	7	0	1	5	1 8	9
W Ham	13	1	4	2	9	10	0	3	3	6 11	9
B'pool	13	1	3	2	6	9	1	1	5	4 14	8
Burnley	13	0	2	5	4	12	0	2	4	2 10	4

Cell 5. Both these matrices would be described as tables: the football league table (left) is primarily numerical, the page from a company report (right) is primarily verbal.

Cell 6. The boundary between Cells 6 and 7 is subjectively drawn. "Non-linear directed" has traditionally been the language of advertising. Examples shown range from a consistent method of directing the viewing (left), where it is assumed that the bold headings will be scanned vertically as a first operation, to others (centre and right) where it is most unlikely that reading strategies will bear much relation to those adopted in relation to "linear interrupted" language.

Cell 7. In the "non-linear open" configuration, verbal language usually breaks down in terms of precise communication. In concrete poetry however it may take on other dimensions of meaning.

Cell 8. The Bayeux Tapestry is probably the nearest approach to a "pure linear" image in this mode that can be found. It is not purely linear, however, as the verbal image is divided into discrete units and the picture is not a continuous narrative.

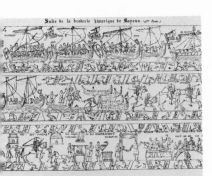

Cell 9. When presented in book form the Bayeux Tapestry (left) is usually divided into units of equal length as in traditional text setting. The broadsheet of the funeral procession of the Duke of Wellington in 1852 (centre) shows a division of pictorial and verbal information into hunks to form five columns. A well tried application of the linear interrupted configuration in this mode is the comic strip (right), where the interruptions to the story are usually made on the basis of what will fit into the line.

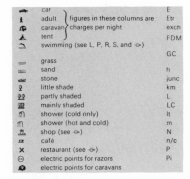

Cell 10. Combinations of pictures and words are found in list form in such things as keys to maps and guides (left) and travel regulations (right).

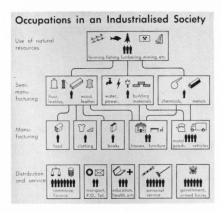

Cell 11. This is an unusual example of a multiple tree presented in the combined "pictorial & verbal/numerical" mode.

Cell 12. In the example on the left pictures are used as column and row headings to identify the numerical information in the cells of the matrix. In the example on the right, prepared for the Sunday Times, the actual content of the matrix is presented in pictorial terms and the user "reads off" the information by assessing the length of the miniskirts.

Cell 13. In the exhibition catalogue (left) the user's viewing is directed in a number of ways: horizontally along the row of pictures; horizontally from one column of text to another; and vertically so that each picture is read in conjunction with the passage of text beneath it. This scheme of organization is a rational one that has some of the characteristics of a matrix, whereas the directed viewing associated with advertising (centre) and popular journalism (right) is more intuitive and open to a wider range of reading/viewing strategies.

Cell 14. This early example of football reporting is probably as near as one can get to a graphic image in this mode, in which most options of viewing and reading are left open.

Cell 15. The story in relief sculpture spiralling up Trajan's Column of 112AD in Rome (left), and panoramic views of coastlines and rivers (right) are examples of the linear presentation of pictures.

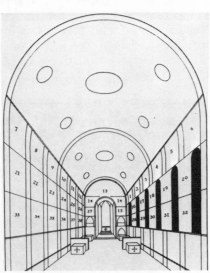

Cell 16. Wall paintings and mosaics have traditionally been presented in series of discrete scenes. The individual scenes of Giotto's fresco cycle in the Scrovegni Chapel, Padua (left and centre) of the early fourteenth century have been arranged, in so far as the structure of the building will allow, in much the same way as one reads text. A closer parallel with the "verbal/-numerical" mode is provided by the illustration of the funeral procession of Lord Nelson, 1806 (right) in which the rows of pictures have been "justified" by putting variable amounts of space between the pictorial units.

Cell 17. Amongst the simplest pictorial lists are arrays of symbols designed to facilitate international travel (left). A more complicated example is provided by the sequence of pictures (right), each of which represents a separate stage in the narrative.

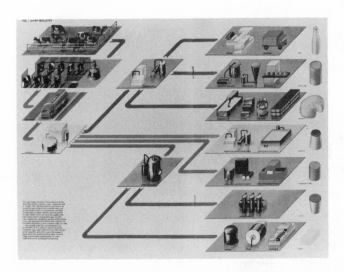

Cell 18. This pictorial tree from a recently published pictorial encyclopaedia illustrates the structure of the dairy industry. The original is colour coded.

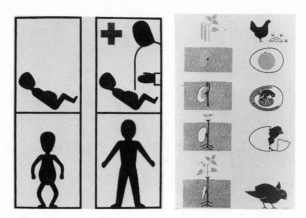

Cell 19. Matrices are rarely presented in the pictorial mode. In the example
on the left the viewer has to deduce the headings from the content of the
pictures (Column headings: no medical man / medical man. Row headings:
swollen stomach / after swollen stomach). The example on the right shows
the parallel life cycles of a bean and a chicken.

Cell 20. Most consciously-designed pictures fall into the category of "non-
linear directed," since it is usually the intention of an artist or photographer
to say something in visual terms. The difficulty lies in determining whether
viewers do respond to images in the intended manner. It has been assumed
that this perspective projection of the Great Exhibition building of 1851 provides a strong directive force in viewing.

Cell 21. For the reasons given in relation to cell 20, it is almost impossible to find an example of "non-linear open" in this mode. Even when a photograph is taken more or less at random there will be aspects in the organization of the image that influence our viewing. The example given is an aerial photograph.

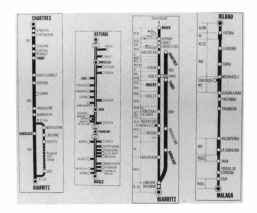

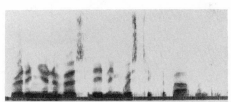

Cell 22. Route maps (left) and traces from graph plotters such as the spectrogram (right) provide well used examples of pure linear schematic language.

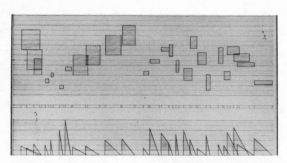

Cell 23. Traditional musical notation (left) and, more obviously, modern form: of notation (right) follow the "linear interrupted" method of configuration.

Cell 24. No example has yet been found for this cell.

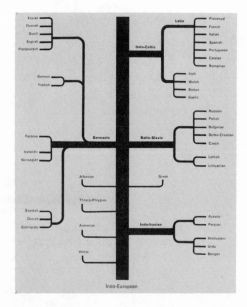

Cell 25. This schematic display of the relationship of the languages of the world follows a tree structure. The thickness of the lines relates to the evolutionary position of the languages shown.

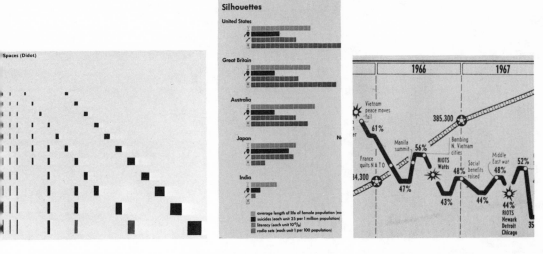

Cell 26. The example on the left presents the range of spacing units available in letterpress printing using the Didot system. As with the set of bar charts (centre) it requires the user to make searches about two axes. Line graphs (right) fall into this cell because they represent schematically the plotting of points on a matrix.

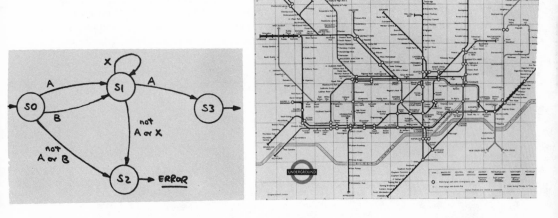

Cell 27. Most network diagrams fall into the "non-linear directed" category because only certain routes in them are regarded as legal. On the left is a network diagram by Wiseman and Linden (this volume). Some maps take the form of network diagrams: the London underground diagram, originally designed in 1933 (right), is perhaps the most influential network diagram ever produced.

Cell 28. Surface maps, such as this detail of a Canadian city, differ from
network diagrams in that they leave most options open to the user. Some
element of direction is provided for the user by such devices as colour coding
and categories of labelling.

The following items have been provided as a visual footnote to the examples
shown above in order to emphasize that the schema presented in this paper is a
device for directing thinking about graphic language rather than a schema for
the language itself. While there are many variants of graphic language that do
not fit precisely within a single cell of the matrix, most such variants can be
accommodated by it in that they combine the characteristics of a number of
cells.

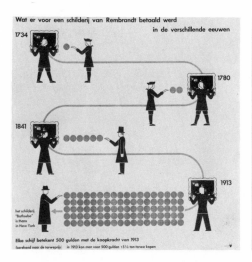

Display 29. This detail from a telephone directory shows a sequence of lines composed of three discrete items in terms of content (name, address, number). However, only two distinctions are made typographically (the number is distinguished from the other two items by space and by the fact that part of it appears in bold type). This is not a simple list, but further typographic distinctions would have to be made for it to be considered a matrix.

Displays 30 and 31. The pictorial chart (left) is particularly complex in its characteristics. It shows the growth in value of Rembrandt's paintings from top to bottom. In one sense it is purely linear in that viewing is directed in boustrophedon manner (as the ox ploughs) along a single drawn line; but there is a change in the orientation of the image on alternate rows as in some boustrophedon printing (right). Does this make it "purely linear" or "linear interrupted"? In any event, each row displays only one semantic unit, so that the chart has some of the characteristics of a list.

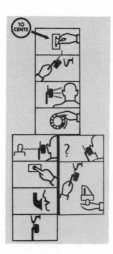

Display 32. This chart can be seen as a cross between a pictorial list and
a binary branching tree. It is a very simple example of its kind, but the possibilities for the development of this approach are obvious.

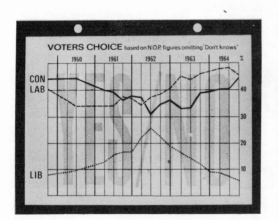 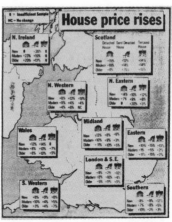

Displays 33 and 34. Many examples of everyday language we are presented
with combine different modes of symbolization and methods of configuration. The example on the left combines a simple statement in the verbal
mode with a more complex message stated schematically. The example on
the right is a map within which discrete units of information are presented
in matrix configurations.

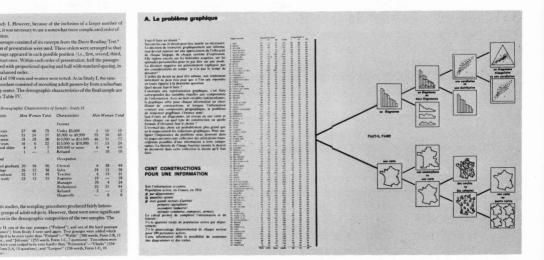

Displays 35 and 36. It is also common practice for a single sheet or other display of information to contain a variety of configurations such as tables with text (left), or text, tables, and trees (right). When other variables of graphic language are taken into account (such as size, tone, texture, colour, orientation, form, and projection) the range of graphic language becomes considerable.

What Does the Matrix Reveal?

A full discussion of the matrix and the way in which graphic language relates to it would clearly be a major undertaking, and beyond the scope of this paper. On a general level it seems valuable to approach each row, column, and cell of the matrix from the point of view of both the originator and consumer of graphic language. It scarcely needs stating that some of the cells of the matrix that are widely used by people when in the role of consumer are hardly used by them at all when in the role of originator. Few people produce pictures, though most make use of them. The matrix can also be approached from the standpoint of specialist and non-specialist users of graphic language (the term specialist here applies to anyone who in a particular situation adopts, or has to respond to, an approach to graphic language not held to be in general use). Clearly there are degrees of specialism and no clear line of demarcation exists between specialist and non-specialist users. Nevertheless, some cells of the matrix include approaches to graphic language that are frequently used by specialists, but hardly at all by non-specialists.

In a practical situation (that is, when a designer has to make decisions with regard to graphic language) it would be useful to consider the cells of the matrix in relation to such factors as ease and cost of production, user capabilities, interests, and training, and the effectiveness of various approaches in connection with specific learning tasks. In order to make valid decisions without running special tests, a designer would need to know what empirical research reveals about the effectiveness of different approaches to graphic language in various circumstances. The matrix might therefore be considered as a useful aid for reviewing empirical research in the field of graphic language.

Some of the approaches to the matrix mentioned above need to be considered in relation to one another; a few of them have been isolated for convenience and will be touched on in the following sections of this paper.

Specialist and Non-Specialist
A discussion of this topic should be based on a carefully controlled investigation. No such investigation has been undertaken and the comments made in this section are therefore highly subjective. All the same, it can be said with some confidence that the approaches to graphic language that fall into the "verbal/numerical, linear interrupted" cell (2) are the norm for both specialist and non-specialist adults; and this applies to the origination of a message as well as to its consumption. Such approaches have obvious advantages over most others in terms of ease and speed of production. What is more, teaching of graphic language is concentrated almost universally in cell 2 of the matrix. Approaches to graphic language that fall into this cell are so bounded by conventions that they are perhaps the only ones most originators feel they have more or less under their control from conception through to production. There is little to be gained from dwelling on these approaches to graphic language, except in order to compare them with approaches falling within other cells of the matrix.

Many approaches to graphic language appear to have been developed for special situations. Outside the "verbal/numerical, linear interrupted" cell (2) there is a much weaker relationship between the language of the specialist and the non-specialist on the one hand, and the originator and the consumer on the other. Thus algorithms (4) appear to be nearly always specialist in origination and mainly specialist in terms of consumption, but are used only rarely by non-specialists either as originators or consumers (even though research has shown that they can be highly effective under certain circumstances). Tables (5) and maps (27, 28) tend to be specialist in origination, though they are often intended for non-specialist consumption and in some cases, such as football league tables (where the nature of the information is usually understood), they appear to present few problems to the user. Even a casual survey of papers in particular branches of science and technology makes it clear that specialists in these fields frequently abandon both the "verbal/numerical" mode of symbolization and the "linear interrupted" method of configuration. At the other end of the complexity scale, stories for the entertainment of young children and poor readers frequently take the form of comic strips (9) which make use of the combined "pictorial and verbal/-numerical" mode of symbolization along with the "linear interrupted" method of configuration. The fact that there are common words in English for a approaches to graphic language which fall into some cells of the matrix, such

as family tree (4), table (5), strip cartoon (9), and map (27, 28) is in itself
testimony to the accepted use of such approaches in non-specialist situations.

It would also be of interest to consider the distribution within the matrix
of those cells of graphic language that are most commonly used. But how
does one determine common use? As a rough and ready way of doing so,
it is proposed that a further matrix might be considered within each cell
of the master matrix to record a positive or negative response according
to originator/consumer and specialist/non-specialist use (Figure 2). The
dotted line indicates that no clear line of demarcation exists between
specialist and non-specialist and, following the definition of specialist given
previously, it is possible to record the same response in both specialist and
non-specialist cells on the same axis.

	Specialist	Non-specialist
Originator		
Consumer		

Figure 2. Matrix according to use.

The writer's own subjective analysis of common use on this basis is included
in Figure 3 simply as a discussion point. Those cells marked ■ received
three or more positive responses; those marked □ received one or two.
Such an analysis reveals a clear clustering of commonly used cells at the
top left and bottom right of the matrix, and this reflects the association
of the verbal mode with linearity and the pictorial and schematic modes with
non-linearity.

It is perhaps surprising that the cells of the matrix that accommodate
those approaches to graphic language that can be described by common words
(family tree, table, strip cartoon, and map) are widely scattered in relation
to both axes of the matrix. One is forced to consider why this should be so
and, in particular, why some cells of the matrix appear to be used so much
less than others. Has there been a process of design gestation that has led
to the promotion and survival of appropriate combinations of mode of symbolization and method of configuration at the expense of others, or have
certain combinations never been seriously considered?

The Evolution of Graphic Language
This is not the place to consider the historical evolution of graphic language
in any serious way, but the matrix makes clear what many would claim is
self-evident: that language in the pictorial and schematic modes has tended

Method of configuration

Mode of symbolization

	Pure linear	Linear interrupted	List	Linear branching	Matrix	Non-linear directed viewing	Non-linear most options open
Verbal/ numerical	1	2 ■	3 ■	4 ■	5 ■	6 □	7
Pictorial & verbal/ numerical	8	9 □	10 ■	11	12 □	13 □	14 ■
Pictorial	15	16 □	17 □	18	19	20 ■	21 ■
Schematic	22 □	23 □	24	25	26 ■	27 ■	28 ■

Figure 3. Presumed common use of kinds of graphics.

to develop in non-linear ways, while language in the "verbal/numerical" mode has developed in linear ways. The relationship between oral and graphic verbal language accounts to a large degree for the linearity of the latter, but the technology of printing has undoubtedly helped to reinforce it. The ease of production of graphic language using the prefabricated and modular characters of printing type has been a powerful force in maintaining the dominance of the verbal mode and, consequently, graphic linearity. The constraints of ergonomics (book size), perception (line length), and the method of production have led to the linearity of graphic language being interrupted at regular, and usually non-semantically determined, points.

Nowadays it is largely the typewriter that determines the initial configuration of graphic language. One very reputable book published recently on the subject of typing for print (Westwood, 1976) even advises the originators of graphic language against the use of tables for simple information on the grounds that they are expensive to set. If production difficulties are to be a deterrent in such cases, when the organization of the language can be done on a machine using repeatable units, how much greater the production difficulties are going to be when the originator wishes to use modes of symbolization that involve purpose-made marks in addition to individual planning. It is hardly surprising that the approaches to graphic language most widely used are those involving the verbal mode of symbolization and linear methods of configuration.

Pictures almost certainly pre-date graphic verbal language as vehicles for graphic communication of ideas and information and, along with geometry and cartography, are major exceptions to the dominance of linearity in the early days of graphic communication. Tables too were in use before printing was invented, and so were scientific and concept diagrams. All the same, it was not until the work of Priestley and Playfair in the late eighteenth century that non-linear methods began to be widely used in relation to problems of communication in fields such as history and economics, which had hitherto been treated in predominantly linear ways. The movement towards non-linear pictorial or schematic modes of presenting information gained momentum in the nineteenth century, in the inter-war years of this century, and again in the 1960s. The general trend, taking a long-term view from the Renaissance, has been a shift from linear to non-linear methods of configuration.

The Teaching of Graphic Language

It makes little sense to consider the general issue of graphic design options and the evaluation of graphic language without some consideration of the teaching of graphic language, for the simple reason that nearly all language relies on the learning of conventions. Yet formal teaching of graphic language appears to be limited, at least in so far as general needs are concerned, to the "verbal/numerical" mode of symbolization and the "linear interrupted" method of configuration. In practice, literacy means the ability to write (originate) and read (consume) linear verbal language.

Children may be taught to draw simple maps (though rarely to originate them) and to read more complex ones; they may also be taught to organize such things as equations and calculations in non-linear ways. In recent years young children have been taught how to produce simple line graphs, bar charts, and pie charts from data they have acquired themselves. At a later

stage in their education, those specialising in certain fields may well learn
the particular approaches to graphic language that are held to be appropriate
to their speciality. On the whole, however, it is true to say that children
are not taught to read the wide range of graphic language they will be confronted with in later life. Still less of course are children taught to originate
information in anything like the range of approaches to graphic language
presented in the matrix. The issue of when to use one approach rather than
another hardly arises as far as the lay designer is concerned. What is more,
when it comes to a comparison of the effectiveness of different approaches
to the presentation of information, the long-term consequences of the dominance of one approach to graphic language cannot be calculated.

The Evaluation of Graphic Language
The graphic designer (both lay and professional) concerned with deciding
how to communicate a message effectively ought to ask himself two fundamental questions at the outset: What should be the mode of symbolization?
What should be the method of configuration? The answers to these questions
will not be arrived at easily and will be influenced by a number of factors:
the nature of the message to be communicated, the people to whom it is
directed, the effect it is intended to have, and practical considerations of
cost, time, and means of production. Though such matters are often crucial
in real situations, they are of interest in the context of this paper only in
so far that it has to be accepted that they have a bearing on the two fundamental questions concerning graphic language mentioned above. The wider
issue as to whether a communication problem should be solved by graphic
or non-graphic means, or by a combination of both, though important, falls
entirely outside the scope of this paper. The two axes of our matrix provide
the graphic designer with a synopsis of possible answers to the questions concerning mode of symbolization and method of configuration. But where does
he turn for help when making his decisions? It seems reasonable to look to
the findings of empirical research for guidance.

A review of research literature with our matrix in mind reveals two
interesting things. First, a large proportion of empirical research undertaken
in the field of graphic communication falls within two cells of the matrix
(2 and 20); second, other approaches to graphic language that have attracted
attention have, in the main, been confined to isolated cells of the matrix.
In other words, there has been little work that crosses cell boundaries either
horizontally or vertically in order to compare the effectiveness of different
modes of symbolization and different methods of configuration.

It was originally intended that this paper should include a survey of the
literature of graphic communication as it relates to some of the central
issues raised by the matrix. Since this paper was first planned, however,
two publications have appeared that make a survey somewhat superfluous.
An extensive bibliography of the subject has been compiled by Macdonald-
Ross and Smith (1977), which includes general observations on the field it
covers and perceptive comments on particular areas of research. The structure of the classification system adopted in the Macdonald-Ross and Smith
bibliography has points in common with the matrix presented in this paper
and the publication as a whole serves to underline the lack of research work
that crosses the boundaries of the cells of the matrix. Wright (1977) has

reviewed part of the field recently in a wide-ranging paper on the presentation of technical information which offers some guidelines based on research findings. Another useful contribution that relates to various cells of the matrix is a collection of some 600 abstracts of papers relating to social graphics prepared by Feinberg and Franklin (1975).

The match between the matrix and empirical research in the field of graphic language is a tidy one in the sense that the bulk of research seems to fall within two areas of the matrix - those already identified as areas of greatest use. The largest single body of research relates to the "verbal/-numerical" mode and the "liner interrupted" configuration (cell 2). Work in this field has been reviewed in general terms by Tinker (1965), Spencer (1968), and Foster (1971, 1972), by Watts and Nisbet (1974) as it relates to children, and by Plata (1974) as it relates to newspapers. The findings of research workers in this field are readily accessible and there is little point in stating more here than that empirical research over the last century relating to this cell of the matrix has, by and large, confirmed the "horse sense" of many practising typographic designers and printers. Considerable work has also been undertaken in relation to the pictorial mode, specifically in relation to cell 20 of the matrix. The general field has been reviewed by Kennedy (1974). Much of the most interesting applied work has been concerned with two specific target areas - children and the developing countries. Watts and Nisbet (1974) and Smith, Watkins, and MacManaway (1970) reviewed the field in relation to children, and Hudson (1967) in relation to the developing countries.

Some other cells of the matrix that have attracted empirical research should be mentioned in passing. A few papers relating to cell 3 appeared early in this century, but of particular relevance to designers are two recent papers relating to bibliographical lists by Spencer, Reynolds, and Coe (1973, 1974). In recent years important and influential work has been done in relation to cell 4 on algorithms by Wason (1968), Jones (1968), Wright (1971), and Wright and Reid (1973). Cell 5 includes tables which have attracted a fair amount of attention over the last fifty years from, amongst others, Washburne (1927), Carter (1947, 1948a, 1948b), Tinker (1954, 1960), Feliciano, Powers, and Kearl (1963), and Hartley, Young, and Burnhill (1975). The programme of work in this field undertaken over the last ten years by Wright (1968, 1971, 1977), Wright and Fox (1969, 1970, 1972), Wright and Barnard (1975) makes a particularly important contribution to the evaluation of such approaches to graphic language. Cell 6 raises the issue of typographic cuing (a term used for particular ways of directing viewing), and the literature on this subject is reviewed by Foster elsewhere in this volume. Cell 9 includes what are commonly known as comic strips. Though they have considerable literature of their own (see Macdonald-Ross & Smith, 1977), they do not appear to have attracted empirical research workers. However, Holmes (1963) found a series of pictures presented in a linear configuration more effective than only two pictures, in experiments run with Kenyans. Cell 13 would include the work done by Spencer (1973) on labelling, which points to the value of keeping labels separate from technical drawings when the material is complex. Cell 26 has probably attracted more empirical research than any other cell of the matrix, apart from cells 2 and 20. Charts, graphs, and diagrams, many of which fall into this cell, have been evaluated from various standpoints over the last fifty years, mainly in the USA. Research in this field has been reviewed by Feinberg and Franklin (1975) and Macdonald-Ross (1977). The findings of research workers in this area are somewhat conflicting, but work on one particular issue, a comparison of different kinds of charts and graphs, seems to be pointing to the superiority of bar charts, at least in certain circumstances. Cells 27 and 28 include network diagrams, maps, and plans. Research in the broad field of map design is not extensive and is reviewed by Phillips elsewhere in this volume.

Some, though very little, of the research referred to above crosses the boundaries of the cells of the matrix and thus helps to provide answers to our two fundamental questions: What should be the mode of symbolization and what should be the method of configuration? Research that specifically addresses itself to issues that cross the boundaries of the matrix is discussed in the following paragraphs.

As far as mode of symbolization is concerned, Dwyer (1972), Fuglesang (1973), and others have compared the effectiveness of different kinds of pictorial representations, such as photographs, masked out photographs, line drawings, shaded drawings, pictographs, and stick figures. But studies based on the rather crude differences between modes of symbolization as presented in our matrix have attracted little attention. Washburne (1972), in an experiment involving a comparison of fifteen approaches to the presentation of information which included different versions of text, tables, graphs, and charts, and Vernon (1946, 1950, 1952), in experiments involving a comparison of tables, graphs, and charts, studied, among other things, different modes of symbolization. Carter (1947, 1948a, 1948b) who compared the presentation of numerical data in tables and graphs, and Feliciano et al. (1962, 1963), who compared the effectiveness of text, tables, and graphs for statistical information, also crossed the boundaries of the cells of the matrix. The work of Walker, Nicolay, and Stearns (1965) on the responses of subjects to the largely verbal American road signs and symbolic signs similar to the international road signs, of Zeff (1965) and van Nes (1972) on digital and analogue time displays, and of Phillips, De Lucia, and Skelton (1975) in relation to digital and analogue presentation of relief on maps, are other examples of cross-modal research. More fundamental in this respect is the study by Magne and Parknäs (1963) in which the learning effect of pictorially and verbally presented information was assessed by running tests in different modes. Vernon (1951, 1952, 1953) and Smith and Watkins (1972) were concerned with establishing the part played by various kinds of illustrative matter (including pictures, graphs, and charts) when used with text; these experiments all included a comparison of illustrated and unillustrated material and in this respect can be regarded as cross-modal.

The question of method of configuration appears to have attracted even less attention from research workers than mode of symbolization, though it is a central one for typographic designers. The issue crops up incidentally in the work mentioned above on the comparative effectiveness of text and tables, both of which fall into the "verbal/numerical" mode but differ in their method of configuration. Papers by Coleman and Hahn (1966) and Carver (1970) on typographic "chunking" are also relevant to the issue of method of configuration.

The most interesting research in relation to method of configuration stems from work done in the 1960s more or less independently by P.C. Wason and B.N. Lewis, along with their colleagues, in developing ordinary language algorithms. Wason (1968) and Jones (1968) both provided evidence for the superiority of algorithms over certain kinds of prose. This line was followed up by Wright (1971) and Wright and Reid (1973), who compared the effectiveness of four different methods of presenting the same basic information. These methods are given below with the terminology of the matrix and the relevant cell number in parentheses:

Prose (linear interrupted, 2),
Short sentences (linear interrupted, 2),
Logical tree (linear branching, 4),
Table (matrix, 5).

It was found that prose was the least effective of the four in terms of both speed and accuracy, that the logical tree was the best when some uncertainty existed about the information presented, and that the table was the best when the user understood the problem beforehand. The conclusion was that the optimal configuration for verbal graphic language depends on the conditions of use. Such research, which was concerned with the effectiveness of different methods of configuration within the same mode of symbolization, closely matches the needs of graphic designers; yet it remains an isolated, or at least almost isolated, contribution of this kind.

It has to be said that the match between empirical research and those areas of graphic language that have been identified on a subjective basis as widely used, though described above as tidy, is not particularly helpful to the graphic designer. In practice there is a good chance that commonly used areas of graphic language work well, largely because they are commonly used (because of the craft design law - analogous to Darwinian theory - of the survival of the fittest). It is some of the less used areas of the matrix that call for the attention of research workers as far as the designer is concerned; and in particular there is a need for research that crosses the bundaries of the cells of the matrix.
boundaries of the cells of the matrix.

Conclusion

The matrix presented as the focal point of this paper reveals something of the scope and flexibility of graphic language. But how flexible is the human response to graphic language? The matrix invites us to ask how the reader/-viewer is expected to respond to the variety of graphic language he is bombarded with in everyday situations. Does he face up to images on a page or CRT in the same way that he responds to real-world situations with their multiplicity of visual stimuli? It is reasonable to assume that there is usually no great problem in identifying the mode of symbolization being used in graphic language; but how is the reader/viewer to determine the method of configuration of a graphic display of information? Various contributors to this volume have emphasized the importance of prediction in the reading process; but how does prediction apply when the rules of the game keep changing, or when there appear to be no rules? In any event, how does the reader/viewer develop an appropriate strategy for extracting information once he has identified the method of configuration? What problems are presented by the apparent conflict between the linearity of the verbal mode and the non-linearity of the pictorial mode? This is a particularly important question since the two modes are being combined more regularly now, and at all levels of language, than at any time since the Middle Ages. What are the consequences of switching from one mode to another and one configuration to another on both eye movements and cognitive processes? Are there essential differences between absorbing information and ideas through discrete verbal statements (words, clauses, sentences), discrete pictorial symbols (pictographs, arrays of pictographs), and unified, synoptic pictures? How do all these questions relate to training in basic skills and working methods? Questions of this kind appear to be fundamental in relation to the processing of visible language. They can be formulated relatively easily; but how are they to be answered?

I should like to acknowledge the help and encouragement I have received while preparing this paper from my colleague Ernest Hoch: a number of specific problems have been discussed with him and his suggestions have been most valuable.

Many of the illustrations used in this paper are, strictly speaking, protected by copyright. It would have been virtually impossible to trace the sources for some of the illustrations used and if, through oversight or other circumstances, material has been reproduced without appropriate acknowledgments apologies are presented here. Those to whom acknowledgments should be made include the Automobile Association, The British Steel Corporation, the Daily Mirror, Mouton Publishers, Her Majesty's Stationery Office, Isotype Institute Ltd, Kimberly-Clark Limited, KLM Royal Dutch Airlines, the Kynoch Press, London Transport Executive, Macdonald & Co (Publishers) Ltd, Marlborough Fine Art (London) Ltd, Marshall Cavendish Ltd, G.J. Matthews, Penguin Books Ltd, Phaidon Press Ltd, and The Sunday Times.

REFERENCES

Bertin, J. Sémiologie graphique: les diagrammes, les réseaux, les cartes (2nd ed.). Paris The Hague: Mouton and Gauthier-Villars, 1967.

Carter, L.F. An experiment on design of tables and graphs used for presenting numerical data. Journal of Applied Psychology, 1947, 31, 640-650.

Carter, L.F. Relative effectiveness of presenting numerical data by the use of tables and graphs. Washington, DC: U.S. Department of Commerce, 1948. (a)

Carter, L.F. Study of the best design of tables and graphs used for presenting numerical data. Washington, DC: U.S. Department of Commerce, 1948. (b)

Carver, R.P. Effect of a "chunked" typography on reading rate and comprehension. Journal of Applied Psychology, 1970, 54, 288-296.

Coleman, E.B., & Hahn, S.C. Failure to improve readability with a vertical typography. Journal of Applied Psychology, 1966, 50, 434-436.

Dwyer, F.M. A guide for improving visualized instruction. State College: Pennsylvania State University Learning Services Division, 1972.

Feinberg, B.M., & Franklin, C.A. Social graphics bibliography. Washington, D.C.: Bureau of Social Science Research, 1975.

Feliciano, G.D., Powers, R.D., & Kearl, B.E. Text, table or graphs for communicating statistical information. University of Wisconsin Agricultural Journalism Department, Bulletin 32, 1962.

Feliciano, G.F., Powers, R.D., & Kearl, B.E. The presentation of statistical information. AV Communication Review, 1963, 11, 32-39.

Foster, J.J. Legibility research abstracts 1970. London: Lund Humphries, 1971.

Foster, J.J. Legibility research abstracts 1971. London: Lund Humphries, 1972.

Foster, J.J. The use of visual cues in text. (This volume.)

Fuglesang, A. Applied communication in developing countries. Uppsala: The Dag Hammarskjöld Foundation, 1973.

Hartley, J., Young, M., & Burnhill, P. On the typing of tables. Applied Ergonomics, 1975, 6, 39-42.

Holmes, A.C. A study of understanding of visual symbols in Kenya. London: Overseas Visual Aids Centre, 1963.

Hudson, W. The study of the problem of pictorial perception among unacculturated groups. International Journal of Psychology, 1967, 2, 89-107.

Jones, S. Design of instruction. London: Her Majesty's Stationery Office, 1968.

Kennedy, J.M. A psychology of picture perception. San Francisco: Jossey-Bass, 1974.

Macdonald-Ross, M. How numbers are shown: A review of research on the presentation of quantitative data in text. AV Communication Review, 1977, 25, 359-409.

Macdonald-Ross, M., & Smith, E. Graphics in text: A bibliography. Milton Keynes: The Open University, Institute of Educational Technology, Monograph No. 6, 1977.

Magne, O. & Parknäs, L. The learning effects of pictures. British Journal of Educational Psychology, 1963, 33, 265-275.

van Nes, F.L. Determining temporal differences with analogue and digital time displays. Ergonomics, 1972, 15, 73-79.

Phillips, R.J. Making maps easy to read: A summary of research. (This volume).

Phillips, R.J., De Lucia, A., & Skelton, N. Some objective tests of the legibility of relief maps. Cartographic Journal, 1975, 12, 39-46.

Plata, W. A study of newspaper design: Analysis and synthesis of legibility research and its applications. Nairobi: Walter Plata, 1974.

Smith, J., & Watkins, H. An investigation into some aspects of the illustration of primary school books. University of Reading, Typography Unit, 1972.

Smith, J., Watkins, H., & MacManaway, R. A survey of research in connection with an investigation into some aspects of the illustration of primary school books. Unpublished report, University of Reading, Typography Unit, 1970.

Spencer, H. The visible word. London: Royal College of Art, 1968.

Spencer, H., Reynolds, L., & Coe, B. The relative effectiveness of ten alternative systems of typographic coding in bibliographical material. London: Royal College of Art, Readability of Print Research Unit, 1973.

Spencer, H., Reynolds, L., & Coe, B. The relative effectiveness of spatial and typographic coding systems within bibliographical entries. London: Royal College of Art, Readability of Print Research Unit, 1974.

Spencer, J. Presentation of information on engineering drawings. The visual presentation of technical data. University of Reading, Typography Unit, 1973, 24-27.

Tinker, M.A. Readability of mathematical tables. Journal of Applied Psycholog 1954, 38, 436-442.

Tinker, M.A. Legibility of mathematical tables. Journal of Applied Psychology 1960, 44, 83-87.

Tinker, M.A. Bases for effective reading. Minneapolis: University of Minnesot Press, 1965.

Vernon, M.D. Learning from graphical material. British Journal of Psychology, 1946, 36, 145-158.

Vernon, M.D. The visual presentation of factual data. British Journal of Educational Psychology, 1950, 20, 174-185.

Vernon, M.D. Learning and understanding. Quarterly Journal of Experimental Psychology, 1951, 3, 19-23.

Vernon, M.D. The use and value of graphical methods of presenting quantitative data. Occupational Psychology, 1952, 26, 22-34.

Vernon, M.D. The use and value of graphical material with a written text. Occupational Psychology, 1952, 26, 96-100.

Vernon, M.D. Presenting information in diagrams. AV Communication Review, 1953, 1, 147-158.

Walker, R.E., Nicolay, R.C., & Stearns, C.R. Comparative accuracy of recogniz American and international road signs. Journal of Applied Psychology, 1965, 49, 322-325.

Washburne, J.N. An experimental study of various graphic, tabular and textual methods of presenting quantitative material. Journal of Educational Psychology, 1927, 18, 361-376 & 465-476.

Wason, P.C. The drafting of rules. New Law Journal, 1968, 118, 548-549.

Watts, L., & Nisbet, J. Legibility in children's books: A review of research. London: National Foundation for Educational Research, 1974.

Westwood, J. Typing for print: A manual for typists and authors. London: Pitman, 1976.

Wiseman, N.E., & Linden, C.A. Non-serial language. (This volume)

Wright, P. Using tabulated information. Ergonomics, 1968, 11, 331-343.

Wright, P. Writing to be understood: Why use sentences? Applied Ergonomics, 1971, 2, 207-209.

Wright, P. Presenting technical information: A survey of research findings. Instructional Science, 1977, 6, 93-134.

Wright, P., Behavioural research and the technical communicator. The Communicator of Scientific and Technical Information, 1977, 32, 3-13.

Wright, P., & Barnard, P.J. Effects of "more than" and "less than" decisions on the use of numerical tables. Journal of Applied Psychology, 1975, 60, 606-611.

Wright, P. & Fox, K. Some studies of conversion tables. Report submitted to the Decimal Currency Board, 1969.

Wright, P., & Fox, K. Presenting information in tables. Applied Erogonomics, 1970, 1, 234-242.

Wright, P., & Fox, K. Explicit and implicit tabulation formats. Ergonomics, 1972, 15, 175-187.

Wright, P., & Reid, F. Written information: Some alternatives to prose for expressing the outcomes of complex contingencies. Journal of Applied Psychology, 1973, 57, 160-166.

Zeff, C. Comparison of conventional and digital time displays. Ergonomics, 1965, 8, 339-345.

Typography: A Technique of Making a Text 'Legible'

Wim Crouwel

Throughout the ages the influence of the designer on the visualization of written messages has been important. No matter what technical developments and functional considerations were involved, designers always managed to exert much influence with their personal tastes regarding form. This has been clearly visable in all periods of cultural history. The designer is, however, a child of his time; he works within the spirit of that time. The spheres of influence and currents of thought form the basis which both nurtures and restricts him.

Designers have always started from the idea that consistent conceptual unity was the highest attainable goal; they have taken for granted that texts would be interpreted as they had been intended. Not until the 1920s was it accepted that a text could be more comprehensible, and hence more functional, by means of deliberate emphasis on form. As a result of this development, the designer is often inclined to use a kind of "form overstatement" that overshadows the aims and functions of typography.

Today there is a constant search for new ideas and methods that will help us overcome the typical two-dimensional approach to typography and lead us to a more comprehensible "spatial" typography. Thinking of new, experimental, extra dimensional concepts fits logically into today's cultural pattern, but what about the public for whom the designer's work is intended? How do scientific researchers look at such experiments? Aren't the results of research in the field of perception, readability, and legibility contrary to the designer's ideas?

It is of the greatest importance that we, who are designers and researchers, pool our resources--that we cooperate.

151

Are we to expect that designers in the future will allow themselves to be
more directly guided by the outcome of research into functional demands,
or will rapid developments in the field of reproduction techniques force them
to subject themselves to this compelling technology?

Until today the influence of the designer has always been clearly discernible in the design of typefaces and in the typographical compositions fashioned
by those forms. The Gothic designer produced Gothic letters and typography;
the Renaissance had its own letters and typography, as did the Baroque, Classicist, Victorian, and Art-Nouveau periods. Movements in visual art and architecture and developments in typographical design go hand in hand. Letters and
typography can, like all forms of visual art and architecture, be accurately
dated on the basis of their form. I will restrict myself to letters and typographical designs, although occasional references to developments in other fields
of visual activity are inevitable.

In spite of the ostensible freedom claimed by the designer, he is a prisoner
of the framework imposed upon him by time. To give an example: writing
between traced lines, for the sake of regularity, constitutes the logical horizontal element of early books; vertical script, on the other hand, constitutes
the irrational, vertical element of Gothic style. In this way the Gothic framework emerged as a compelling pattern for the scribe and illuminator of the
early books. But the rigidity of the framework is never obvious; the basic
pattern appears to be adopted effortlessly, yielding individual results of the
highest order.

In the late Gothic period--that period of transition to a more humanistic
way of thinking and of the invention of the printing press --this framework
evolved towards that of the Renaissance. The verticalism disappears and
proportions increasingly tend toward the square, while the shapes of the letters become milder and rounder. The proportions are often those of the
Golden Section; the framework of the typeface is placed, on the basis of
these principles, in a specific relation to the composition of the page and
the marginal progression begins to play a more active visual role.

Then we see, in succession, the emergence of Baroque typography with
fuller forms and tighter formal schemes; Classicist typography with its strong
contrasts and sharply defined, shaded rules; Victorian typography in which
the forms become heavier and the letters start taking on the appearance
of the "egyptienne." Art Nouveau followed, with the organic line and the
first signs of asymmetrical elements in typography; Futurist and Constructivist typography made the clear break with traditional forms and launched
the concept of the integrated text and image. In the typographic designs
of the Functionalist and "Neue Sachlichkeit" movements, the printed image
is divested of all superfluous elements, resulting in a bare, pure form-language
in both letter and page make-up.

Designers have always started from the idea that consistent conceptual
unity was the highest attainable goal; they have taken for granted that the
text would be interpreted as they had intended. Not until the 1920s was the
idea accepted that a text could be even more comprehensible, and hence
more functional, by means of deliberate emphasis on form. But here again
this idea did not arise from a demand on the part of the public or from specific research findings; it emerged as a consequence of a general feeling for

Figure 1. Marinetti's Futurist manifesto, 1914.

pure, functional form-language--the same purism that manifests itself in
the abstracted application of glass, steel, and plain concrete in architecture
and in the application of elementary forms in general. Typography's reaction
to this was a form of purism of its own: a bare, constructed, objectivizing
form-language. In this respect, both feeling and intuition play a larger role
than reality.

Due to the discipline of the horizontal arrangement of letters imposed
by book-printing techniques, the system of horizontal lines has been adopted
as a compelling aid throughout the centuries. While the medieval scribe could
introduce some variation by italicizing, thickening, enlarging, and underlining
for emphasis, the book printer is forced to adhere to a much more rigid system.
The only way of introducing emphasis in a line of lead type is by using a heavier,
or italic, variant of the same typeface; the insertion of larger or smaller
type of sizes in a line entails complicated constructional adjustments. The
liveliness of the handwritten book was superseded by the hierarchic set of
rules which have governed typography to this day. Capitals followed by small
capitals, roman by italic, upper case by lower, and bold-face by light-face.
Symmetry continued to play a dominant role.

In spite of the rigidity of the typographic framework, designers in different
style periods of art and book printing succeeded, with ever-changing typefaces,

Figure 2. Poster of El Lissitzky, 1924.

in producing typographical designs which were both distinct and a reflection
of the time. Again and again subtle visual means were found by intuition,
with which it was possible to transcend dry uniformity.

Although the dictates of symmetry were abandoned by some Art Nouveau
artists at the end of the nineteenth centry, it was not until the beginning
of this century that the traditional typographical norms were seriously taken
to task. The first to do so were the Futurists; in 1914 the poet-propagandist
Marinetti published a Futurist manifesto which made convincing use of uncon-
ventional typographic means. The typefaces were chosen on the basis of
their semantic aspects, the horizontal rule was abandoned, while the phrases
followed and emphasized the meaning. The result was a vital image. Symmetry
was repudiated and denounced as a symbol of stagnation. The dynamism
of the time was expressed with all possible means.

The Constructivists continued in this direction, applying these principles
to architecture, visual art, and typography. The most important representative
was El Lissitzky, who produced very forceful typographic designs in which
text and illustration changed roles and the technique of photo-montage entered
the scene. In Holland it was Piet Zwart who made the most convincing visual
typographic designs in the twenties; they are advertisements, which must

Figure 3. Advertisement by Piet Zwart, 1930.

come across to the public even more directly than books.

We are led to ask: has the designer always had the greatest influence
on the way in which written messages are visualized? In the case of Piet
Zwart, for instance, was it his client's programme of requirements which
led to this constructivist typographic design; was it the demand of the public;
or was it Piet Zwart himself who ultimately chose the form, based on his
vision of international cultural developments?

Of course, it was Zwart. It is quite obvious that neither the general public
nor the majority of clients at that time were able or willing to follow these
developments as closely as he did. It required a great deal of conviction
to shake off the bonds of tradition. That technology did not play a decisive
role in Zwart's designs is demonstrated by the fact that in the days of Futurist and Constructivist experiments, book typography was still firmly controlled
by the compelling technique of "lead" printing. So in these experiments the
ultimate image was usually "constructed" by cutting out and pasting down,
and then reproduced by the printing block (a reproduction technique for illustration), or laborious lithographic techniques. The development of offset
printing greatly simplified reproduction of these composite images, but the
time-consuming procedure of montage remains the only basic means of reali-
zation.

In a very famous design of Piet Zwart's "Boek voor PTT"--a booklet for

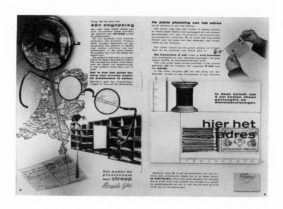

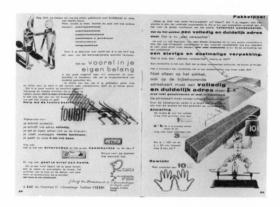

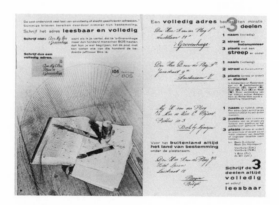

Figure 4. Double-spreads of Piet Zwart's "Boek voor PTT," 1938.

the postal services from the late thirties -- image and text merge to form
an integrated whole. The techniques he used clearly show how his early advertising experiments led to a plastic use of letters in all his work--for the sole
purpose of making the text easier to read and understand. Although the question of whether he was successful or not still remains, his work is not any
less important. Piet Zwart, with a few others, took the lead in the development of typography, and many valuable, innovative, extremely functional
forms are unthinkable without the research carried out by them.

In the same way, I believe that we should call visual artists and designers
who work progressively and experimentally "research workers." Just as in
scientific research, it may be some time before their work is proved to have
been truly fundamental. It is curious that designers are seldom, or never,
aware of the findings of research. By sheer intuition designers often reach
conclusions that are just as valid as the results of scientific research. But
the designer, with his awareness and appreciation for the contemporary cultural atmosphere, is inclined to use overstatement to emphasize his findings.

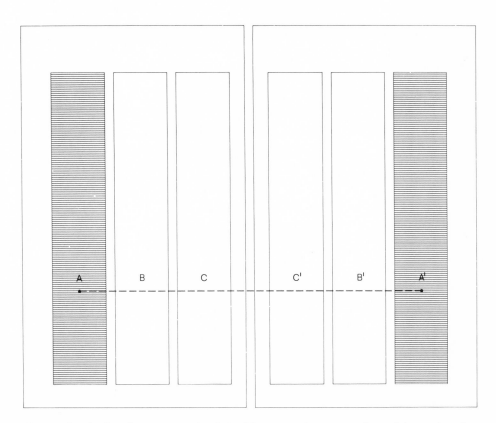

Figure 5. A classic symmetrical double-spread typography grid; a visual
column-to-column relation A-A', B-B', and C-C'.

In my opinion this is the case with "Boek voor PTT". The original idea
of design that aimed at improving legibility and comprehensibility is over-
shadowed by overstatement. But if this element of exaggeration had not
existed, the booklet would not have drawn so much attention, and would not
have fulfilled its pioneering role. It is a vicious circle -- what is more
important?

The experiments of the Futurists and Constructivists owe much of their
importance to their contribution to display typography, the kind of typography
that is used for short, quickly readable messages -- neon signs, advertisements,
posters. For longer texts -- brochures, magazines, books -- this influence
has continued to play an important role only with respect to covers and title
pages. The traditional, horizontalist pattern of lines is still of prime importance for books, brochures, and magazines; it is even more important in this
period which is characterized by a keen interest in systematization and principles of reordering, not only on the general level of culture but also among
free visual artists and architects.

The increasing complexity of typographical tasks, involving diverse kinds
of information in both text and illustrations, gave rise in the fifties to a need
for more detailed typographical grids; grids that are more than the straightforward page formats with simple column, line, and margin divisions. A more
spatial pattern of thinking requires more auxiliary lines to facilitate composing
pages in succession and to ensure that the arrangement of text and illustrative
material is both consistent and visually cohesive, not only per page, but also
from page to page throughout the entire work. The composition is no longer
determined exclusively by the image of two facing pages when the book is
opened out flat, but equally by the effect produced by quickly turning the
pages.

It is remarkable that in this case the need for more detailed typographical
grids arises in spite of the sophistication of all kinds of technical equipment
which gives us great freedom in the design of written information. Typesetting
with lead types has been almost completely replaced by photographic settings;
the dictates of the lines have thus, in principle, become obsolete. We have
even been liberated from our old, pre-Napoleonic typographical point system.
And photographic setting is now done by computer, which is capable of placing
all design elements in every desired way and in every desired position on
the page. Fixed, graded type sizes no longer exist. The italic letter with
its fixed angle has become flexible to any degree, the height/width proportions
of letters have changed from static to elastic, indentations and spacing can
even be used negatively. Yet the use of all these variations is restricted
to the aforementioned display purposes, and we tend to restrain ourselves
when it comes to made-up pages of reading matter. So here again there is
no parallel between technical development and design; in this case, technology
provides almost total freedom and the designer voluntarily adopts a straight-
jacket.

It is impossible as yet to predict which trend will persevere. The pioneers
have already experimented widely with the new technologies, and a kaleido-
scope of possibilities is before us. It is clear that the designer of today refuses

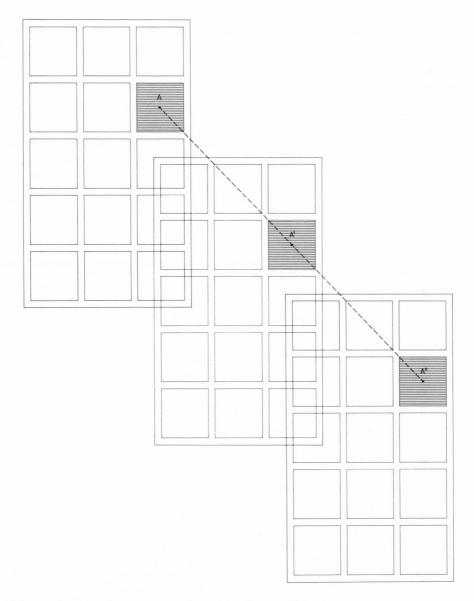

Figure 6. A modern typography grid; the possible visual unit-to-unit relation
A-A'-A"-etc. on a certain number of following pages.

to be dazzled by the wealth of possibilities; as we have seen, cultural atmosphere is a more decisive factor than technical developments. Use is sometimes made of the possibility of applying narrower or wider typefaces; the latest Dutch telephone directory is an example. The use of a slightly narrower version of the Universe face has resulted in a more practical, vertical column arrangement. The development of computer-guided composing techniques, the virtually unlimited possibilities of type size, and the new flexibility of letters have brought today's more spatial way of thinking closer to con-cretization.

We have, in fact, entered an era in which the characteristically two-dimensional approach to typography will be abandoned altogether. Even the twentieth-century experiments described above were largely based on the two-dimensional approach; under the influence of film, spatiality was sometimes suggested by means of perspective but no more than that. If we were to create a truly contemporary typographical grid, it would have to be a spatial grid in which every element can be more accurately positioned than in the past. Then we will have more than just horizontal and vertical directions and undulating or slanting movement across the plane; we will have a front and back also— in short, three-dimensional typography.

Three-dimensional grids may be represented on flat planes by means of perspective or axonometric projection techniques, depending on the desired effect. For all planes in such a grid it is possible to draw up typographical instructions for the flat typefaces in such a way that there is coherence between the planes. The texts on the various planes can be reproduced in a range of grey tones; the widely adopted offset technique ensures faultless reproduction

This concept is based on the idea that typography is concerned with static image-vehicles which -- unlike what the Futurists believed -- are not meant to suggest dynamism. When printed information is read, the dynamic element is provided by the reader, not by the printed image, unlike reading television and film screens or illuminated mosaic displays. Every medium has its own specific form-language; the Futurists dreamt of media that did not yet exist and had no choice but to suggest this via the static, familiar, printed image.

In the same way we now think in terms of concepts which have yet to be realized, such as the projection of our typefaces so that they may be viewed from different angles in space; they will thus literally have additional aspects. Aspects which may be conducive to better comprehension; a text can thus be approached from different sides. By means of holographic projection, typography then becomes a truly spatial event in which the viewer/reader can participate.

Today's designers, although dreaming of new concepts, should think of the public for whom their work is intended and at the same time should be aware of the outcome of recent research. They should, for instance, pay more attention to what is known about perception, readability and legibility. However a lot of designers think that too much knowledge of this type is detrimental to further creative development -- it could even lead to a complete standstill.

289

brandweer
alarmnummer, (02907) 55 55
37 07 96 bgg

32 41 41 brink's-gerlach, bv, liedewg 9, securitij serv
32 76 88 brons, b, liedewg 71
31 41 06 brouwer, b, penningsveer 4/ab, kermisadvis
32 77 81 duwel en zn, mw wed j, liedewg 23, schild bdr
31 53 65 frumau, g, penningsveer, ab zeepaard
32 78 84 gelderen, c j. van, liedewg 23, arts
32 76 86 geldorp, p. van, liedewg 25, aann
32 75 89 geldorp, j n. van, liedewg 40, firm fa p van geldorp en zn
31 63 47 geldorp, g. van, liedewg 45
31 75 19 geldrop-thorborg, c a m. van, liedewg 41
32 77 83 haverkort, e j a, liedewg 18
31 58 92 henkes, g, liedewg 25, dir drukk
32 78 48 jachtvereniging watervrienden, penningsveer
31 38 61 winterberging schoteroog, waarderwg 132
32 08 67 jansen, j, penningsveer, by 5, gross in vis
31 40 26 kemper, l j c, liedewg 61, veehoud
32 37 08 kerssans, j c m, dorpspln 3
31 27 98 kortekaas, h j c, dorpspln 2
31 46 47 kortekaas-rutte, e p m, liedewg 51
32 72 66 korthals, j j, dorpspln 10
32 77 82 kroon, j, liedewg 57
32 32 85 lemmers, a w m, dorpspln 6
32 78 81 lemmers, p, liedewg 5/a, rijksambt
32 01 36 lennep, jhr g. van, liedewg 21
32 78 88 leverink, j c. van, liedewg 31, verffabrik
32 78 87 loze, w th, liedewg 19
32 09 88 mens, j c m, penningsveer 7
32 77 88 molenaar, g j, liedewg 11
32 78 88 montalbetti, de, liedewg 31, j c van leverink
31 27 68 moolen, g p j. vd, liedewg 60
32 29 99 mulder, l p, dorpspln 4
32 78 85 mulder, a j l, liedewg 17

ongevallen
37 08 03 alarmnummer
bgg (02907) 45 93
bgg (02907) 44 54
bgg (02907) 48 20
bgg (02907) 44 05

33 22 23 oosterbaan, e e, liedewg, to 18, piano onderw
31 25 10 peeters, d, penningsveer, ab krikkemik
31 02 06 penningsveer, ab h914

politie
alarmnummer, (02907) 42 66

32 76 81 rabobank, liedewg 69
32 77 80 rooms kath pastorie h jacobus de meerdere, liedewg 30
32 07 79 rutte, a h m, dorpspln 11
32 68 43 rutte, c h, liedewg 28
32 41 34 rutte, k. van, liedewg 53
32 76 82 rutte, joh n, liedewg 56, veehoud
32 76 84 rutte, j a, liedewg 62
32 60 64 schie, h w p m. van, dorpspln 5
31 33 60 schie, j h d. van, liedewg 2, veeh
32 78 80 schie, d j. van, liedewg 10
33 21 77 schie, p d. van, liedewg 15, veeh
37 15 82 groenewg 8
31 58 49 schie, j p m. van, liedewg 34
32 35 01 schilte, c p m, liedewg 34/a

scholen (basisonderwijs)
32 01 35 franciscusschool, st, liedewg 79, hfd b h m harmes

32 68 39 schouten, c j m, liedewg 63
32 32 95 schouten, a, liedewg 67
32 36 82 sikkelerus, p j. van, dorpspln 7

32 04 62 slooten, j. van, dorpspln 8
33 16 69 spierings, a h, liedewg, to 17
32 07 62 stokman, h l, penningsveer 6
32 28 66 thorborg, j h, liedewg 15
31 73 65 vessem, d. van, liedewg 27
32 76 83 vries, w. de, liedewg 58, chef gar heeremans en zn
32 77 84 vriesekoop, h n a, liedewg 8
32 75 88 warmerdam, n h. van, liedewg 77, veehoud
32 76 89 weiden, drs w g. vd, liedewg 81
32 78 82 wempe, n, liedewg 7, assur medew rabobank
32 77 87 zoeren, e. van, liedewg 16

heemskerk

(02510)

alarmnummers
3 21 21 brandweer
2 55 55 ongevallen
3 91 11 politie
4 14 44 op nog te bepalen datum

3 26 51 a & o oosterwijk, maastr 5, buurthuis de lichtboei
3 14 69 aa, a a. vd, vd ploegstr 60
3 73 99 aafjes, j, verdistr 14
3 62 33 aalderen, w. van, j v polanenstr 48
3 57 85 aalsburg, h m. van, lessestr 93
3 44 56 aalst, f. van, d bakeln 68, gem pol
3 02 62 aalten, h c, j v rietwykstr 16
3 81 80 aannemersbedrijf g a van lith, g v assendelftstr 54, rep onderh
3 25 88 aannemersbedrijf j de bie nv, marquettein 2, dir j de bie
3 24 26 aannemersbedrijf g bakkum, rendorppk 21
3 68 46 aannemersbedrijf h j van kaam, gr willem 2 in 8
3 98 17 aannemingsbedrijf bv van tunen, strengwg 3/a
3 92 11 aar, c a j. vd, bachstr 32
3 95 72 aar, th. vd, daltonstr 29
3 94 93 aar, c m. vd, j ligthartstr 449/c
3 55 72 aar, j c. vd, v maerlantstr 31
3 22 39 aar, p f. vd, ryksstrwg 185, aann bdr
3 87 79 aar-kampkes, j. vd, westerheem 65
3 27 47 aardenburg, w a, rdr arnoudln 17
3 88 19 aardenburg, c a, ciewg 2, tuinder
3 74 41 aardenburg, g a, ciewg 6/a, tuinder
3 31 26 aardenburg, m h, hasebroekstr 5
3 20 35 aardenburg, g a, hondsbossewg 8
3 73 23 aardenburg, c g, luttik cie 38, tuinder boll kw
3 28 26 aardenburg, a n, oosterstreng 132
3 01 67 aardenburg-zonneveld, c m, rameaustr 31
3 96 35 aardenburg, c j, j vermeerstr 3
3 17 34 aardenburg-jacobs, a h, westerheem 55
3 56 48 aardenburg, r, woekeven 60
3 02 46 aardenburg, geber c en k, zuiderwentwg 19
3 94 23 aarlle, m. van, communicatiewg 18/v033, autosloper
3 81 37 aarsen, j l, m v heemskerckstr 162
3 43 17 aarts, a j, j v bergenstr 5, bdr l
3 33 86 abbenhuijs, l a, smalven 12
3 60 46 abbo, m, haasjesven 7
3 23 43 abc, maerein 4, kantoorboek- en speelgoedhdl
3 64 66 abeele bausch, m a. vd, westerheem 90/k428
3 69 56 abeelen, c h, bellinistr 58
3 59 44 aberkrom, j, mascagnistr 72
3 53 50 accountantskantoor koopman en bleeker bv, g v assendelftstr 44/a
3 29 47 accountantskantoor schuyt, rynstr 56, boekhoud belast adviezen
3 21 51 acker, a. van, p c hooftstr 5
3 50 03 acker, j. van, j ligthartstr 559
3 47 36 adams, j c f, j v scorelstr 28, won inr interieur verzorg
3 04 95 adema, f, bretagnestr 10
3 29 47 administratiekantoor bv elektro-efficiënt, rynstr 56

3 50 32 administratiemaatschappij h j reimes, maerein 198
3 96 82 admiraal, w j, d bakeln 108
4 03 58 admiraal, a, d bakeln 248
4 11 43 admiraal, m p, berliozstr 24
3 42 23 admiraal, a f, bonckenburchstr 36
3 10 57 admiraal, j, v govenstr 12
3 32 08 admiraal-de ruyter, th c, a morstr 4
3 02 97 admiraal, p j, valcooghstr 3
3 26 03 admiraal, p n, voorwg 1
3 04 56 admiraal, w j, gr willem 2 in 34
4 05 97 admiraal, t c, de zevenhoeven 55
3 26 70 admirals vleespaleis, dukasstr 2
3 59 51 ado-handbal, ryksstrwg 111, voorz c bakkum
3 73 71 secr l c koopman-zonneveld
3 96 20 secr c c m stolk-sinnige
3 34 26 ado 20, voetbalvereniging, yzerdraatwg 16, secr th vd fluit
3 59 77 adriaanse, s j, europapln 41
3 43 55 adrichem-henneman, mw a, st agnespints 1
3 24 83 adrichem, p, bonckenburchstr 20
3 23 51 adrichem, c, d vd ieckstr 15, melk- en zuivelhdl
3 27 87 adrichem, e th, luxemburgln 411
3 25 25 adrichem, j a, j maristr 19
3 71 09 adrichem, e, oosterwg 4/a
4 02 94 adrichem, q th, vd ploegstr 4
3 12 30 adrichem, j j, strengwg 3
3 39 59 adrichem, j, wentwg 9
3 72 82 adviesbureau toegepaste bdr interieurs, voor, deutzstr 8/a
3 18 09 aerts, j j, beethovenstr 111
3 09 17 aerts, f c j, p breughelstr 18
3 93 03 aerts, j n, luxemburgln 817
3 69 00 afwerkingsbedrijf vd heuvel, oosterstreng 116, graf prod enz
3 99 29 agerbeek, m e, bachstr 96
4 01 90 aguilera-ceballos, l m, hoogdorperwg 2/a
3 21 08 aken, n j. van, wagenaarstr 19
3 01 34 akker, j m. vd, bachstr 128, beh vennoot nobrak elektr
3 26 74 akker-akkerman, mw f. vd, c groenlandstr 23, heilgymnast mass
3 00 68 akkerboom, e j, w v velsenstr 37
3 38 93 akkerman, e, lombardyestr 30
3 83 12 akkerman, l h, mascagnistr 8
3 55 30 albers, l, f halsstr 7
3 63 39 albert heijn, kerkwg 85
3 63 39 alberto, drankenwinkel, kerkwg 85
3 03 30 idem
3 24 01 albregt, fa ton j, kerkwg 18, mode v mannen
3 50 07 alders, g w m, ten doesschatestr 269
4 03 20 alders, h j m, luxemburgln 5
4 09 81 alders, p j, monnetstr 224
3 96 58 aldershof, p a, maerein 270
3 75 97 alebregtse, h, ten doesschatestr 77
4 17 62 ales, j, j v rietwykstr 24
3 00 22 alessie, j th, rossinistr 458, ler mo lich opv
3 29 45 alexanderstichting, a verherrentstr 5, peuterspeelzaal
3 90 19 algemene bank nederland, nv, burg nielenpln 42
4 05 44 op nog te bepalen datum
3 00 07 algro, groothandel, toscanestr 30
3 86 30 ali, h e, luxemburgln 36
3 50 79 alleman, h h, ardennenstr 5
3 40 97 alofsen, j j, monnetstr 194
3 62 28 alphen-knijnenburg, p j. van, luxemburgln 869
3 05 36 alphen, j l. van, w v velsenstr 21
3 39 96 altena, w m, bilderdykstr 5
3 05 22 altena jr, h w. van, ruysdaelstr 132
3 10 81 altena, h h, spoelln 33
3 00 07 althoff, g j, toscanestr 30
3 00 93 alting, g, promenade 39, dir postkant
2 34 56 ambulancevervoer 3000, meerstr 41, beverwk
2 34 56 bgg
3 08 97 amersfoort, j. van, p breughelstr 72, bouwk
3 13 68 amiabel, a a, sambrestr 38
3 83 87 ammerlaan, j, deutzstr 10, dameskapp
3 54 52 amrobank, mv, g v assendelftstr 1
3 61 13 amsing, g h, toscanestr 43
3 84 39 amusementsbemidd bureau bema, deutzstr 13
3 70 11 andeweg, a, woekeven 9
3 89 04 andré, f c j a, abbenven 72, trainer

3 13 06 andrée wiltens, w j j, normandieln 2
3 31 68 andriesma, th w, c groenlandstr 15
3 59 00 andringe, d, abbenven 11
3 50 11 andringa, d, bizetstr 2
3 17 92 andringa, j, c geelvinckstr 30
3 52 62 andringa, m p, lessestr 89, soc cult w
3 76 65 andringa-stellingwerf, j, j ligthartstr 373
3 48 27 anema, p, rossinistr 15
3 50 12 angelen, j h g. van, chopinstr 92
3 74 62 anker, k, j ligthartstr 473/c
3 43 87 annmb, gounodstr 14, voorzitt afd heemskerk
3 97 79 anneese, f, luxemburgln 335
3 39 55 annink, b j, luxemburgln 164
3 68 59 ansink, g a, denemarkenstr 14, admin
3 79 39 antenbrink-wijers, c w a a, strauszstr 55
3 94 96 anthonisse, l w, montessoristr 3
3 08 50 anthonisse, j b j, oosterstreng 38
4 01 36 apeldoorn, b g, abbenven 9
3 36 27 apeldoorn, j, beneluxln 200
4 04 72 apeldoorn, c j, hoogdorperwg 33
3 21 34 apontowell, m c a, j ligthartstr 251
3 35 50 apotheek de heemskerkse, kerkwg 11, g w p linn
3 94 84 apotheek fortuna, maerein 93, apoth drs t h tan
3 28 59 aptroot, j, potgieterstr 28
3 27 67 aptroot, g a, w v velsenstr 11
4 01 95 arca miguez, j, ruysdaelstr 118
4 02 29 architectenbureau bv j kooij, c groenlandstr 20
3 50 16 ardesch, m, ten doesschatestr 257
3 38 18 arend, j. vd, j monnetstr 24
3 50 17 arends, j, elbestr 45
4 07 47 arends, w, mendelssohnstr 35, hfd uitv
4 06 66 arends, i f, oosterstreng 48
3 52 30 arends, a, toscanestr 14, leraar n v
3 98 38 arensen, j m p, maerein 98
3 15 53 arentshorst, a g, luxemburgin 705
3 35 79 arkel, t j. van, j v scorelstr 4
3 57 82 arling, m m, c franckstr 37
3 50 19 arp, j a, j ligthartstr 75
4 11 36 arts, h k, hobbemastr 10
3 04 66 arts, n, rhonestr 7
4 10 21 artsch, b, luxemburgln 3
3 15 95 as van schayk, w h. van, abbenven 22
3 04 21 aschmonelt, m, luxemburgln 415
3 30 23 asjes, ing e, f v alkemadestr 8, centr dir ptt
3 29 42 asjes jr, j, s v haerlemstr 182
3 99 11 asjes, d j, luxemburgln 785
3 09 78 asperen, p. van, mozartstr 43
3 30 95 asselman-van gijn, j f, j ligthartstr 561
3 68 45 asselt, mw h m. van, abbenven 48
3 11 40 assurantie fin kant l tijms, g v assendelftstr 8
3 55 29 assurantiekantoor noort, ardennenln 77, adv bur
3 53 53 assurantiekantoor p j huneker bv, g v assendelftstr 44/a
3 62 50 assurantiekantoor a n j brantjes, v coevenhovenstr 8
bgg d boon (02208) 24 80
3 24 68 assurantiekantoor l tijms, oosterwg 19
3 74 44 assurantiekantoor h scheerman, rendorppk 59
3 44 54 astma fonds, nederl, j v bergenstr 56, best lid h van winkel
3 81 82 asuni, a, wezerstr 14
3 55 96 atelier uniek, ryksstrwg 80/a
3 61 82 atjak, l m, beneluxln 409
3 32 28 attema, c, vd ploegstr 69
3 17 76 attema, j, ravelstr 21
3 58 93 atzei, s, vd ploegstr 12
3 09 85 atzema, ir s g, rendorppk 26
3 37 17 augustijn, c, handelstr 4
3 61 09 aukema, j, beneluxln 94
3 03 95 aukes, b, l homanstr 25
3 44 99 ausma, j, dordognestr 8
3 26 67 aust, g, luxemburgln 607, dilinger-stahlbau
3 37 00 auto service-station, kerkwg 152, g jongejans

Figure 7. The Dutch telephone directory.

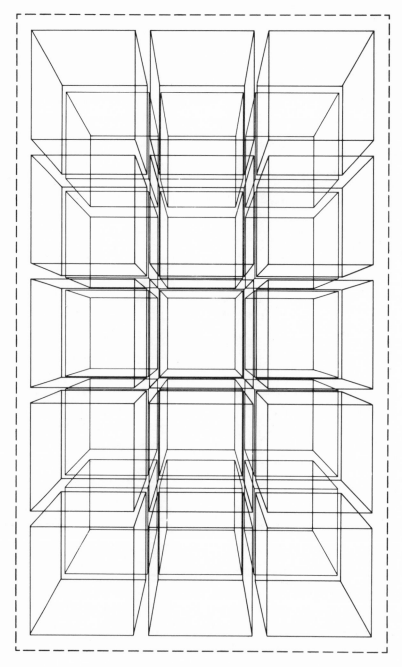

Figure 8. Experimental three-dimensional grid for complicated typographical problems.

Figure 9. Another experimental grid.

And will technology eventually succeed in constraining creativity? Already the decisions concerning design must be taken at ever earlier stages of production and entirely independently of the reproduction process. The machines roll on at great expense, and indecision on the part of the designer can be very expensive. The eternal question is the value that must be assigned to the well-developed (but as yet untested), innovative intuition. Is the proven point of departure eventually more important? At all events, it is of greatest importance that we should pool our resources; too little is known of each other's motives, and the circumstances under which we work are too isolated. We need to cooperate in favor of the visible language.

REFERENCES

Crouwel, W.H. Type design for the computer age. Delta, 1969, 12(1), 59-69.
Crouwel, W.H., Dirken, J.M., et alii. Alphanumeric symbols for mosaic printers and display tubes. Icographic, 1973, 6, 12-14.
Crouwel, W.H. A proposition for education in letterforms and handwriting. Visible Language, 1974, 3, 261-266.

Making Maps Easy to Read—A Summary of Research

Richard J. Phillips

*Poorly designed maps can seriously reduce the efficiency
of the map reader and lead to mistakes which are inconvenient, costly, or even dangerous. Experimental studies of
map legibility are beginning to provide the map designer
with objective information on topics such as colour coding,
relief portrayal, and lettering. Two research groups are
active in the United Kingdom and a number elsewhere, particularly in the United States. As testing methods improve,
there is a good possibility that designers may be persuaded
to use tests themselves to compare alternative map designs.*

In this paper I shall describe some experimental studies on making maps
easy to read, including some which I have conducted with R. J. Audley and
Liza Noyes at University College London. I should emphasize that this is
not a review of the literature, nor even a representative sample, but just
a personal choice. For further information, Board's (1976) bibliography and
Brandes's (1976) review are both useful.

There are two schools of thought on the question of making maps easy
to read: one holds that the deficiency is in the user. This view assumes that
maps, on the whole, are sufficiently legible and that people should be trained
to be better map readers. The other view blames the maps. Since poorly
designed maps hinder good and bad map readers alike, and because misreading
a map can be wasteful, inconvenient, or even dangerous, maps should be
designed to be as legible as possible. The view that the fault is in the user
is frequently held by those who teach geography (Balchin, 1972). But it is
also a view expressed by cartographers who are responsible for map design
(Wood, 1972).

Most people have little training in map reading, certainly very little in
comparison to training in reading words, but then the time spent reading
maps is very small in comparison to ordinary reading. The problem is that,

for most people, map reading is an important but relatively infrequent activity.
If training is to be worthwhile, it must be sustained by practice, but is this
possible when map reading occupies so little of the user's time?

There is a surprising degree of uniformity in the design of atlases and
topographic maps. This may of course mean we are all close to producing
the best possible map, but there could be other, less satisfactory reasons.
As Robinson (1952) points out, the map buying public is a conservative customer; map design is perhaps excessively influenced by the taste of school princi-
pals in purchasing atlases.

Cartographers and designers have written at length about the problems
of map design, often with great intelligence and imagination (Bertin, 1967).
But it is only recently that experimental research has entered the field.
Compared to the amount of research on the legibility of print, research on
map legibility is small, and includes a high proportion of studies of doubtful
experimental validity. Often a paper which purports to study the perception
of maps does no more than ask subjects to arrange alternative designs in
order of preference (Jenks & Knos, 1961; Crawford, 1976).

Search

When reading a map, a large amount of time is spent in searching. It is not
unusual for people to spend over a minute locating a name on a city street
map (Phillips & Noyes, 1977), and finding a feature on a map frequently takes
longer than interpreting it. A number of studies have shown that colour-coded
map symbols take less time to find than those coded by letter, number, or
shape (Hitt, 1961; Christner & Ray, 1961). The reason for this has been neatly
demonstrated in a series of experiments by L. G. Williams (1967, 1973).

Williams recorded the eye movements of subjects searching displays containing squares, circles, triangles, crosses, and semicircles of different colours and sizes. Subjects made a series of rapid eye fixations, nearly all of
which fell on or near one of the shapes. When they knew the colour of their
target, over half of their eye fixations fell on stimuli of the correct colour.
When they knew the size of the target, there was a weaker tendency to fixate
stimuli of the correct size. But when they knew the shape of the target,
the frequency of fixating stimuli of the correct shape was only a little above
the level expected by chance.

Peripheral vision plays an important part in the search process. While
a person is fixating on one stimulus he must decide, on the basis of information
available in peripheral vision, where to place his eyes next. Clearly, colour
codes are easy to distinguish in peripheral vision, size codes are more difficult,
and shape codes still more difficult.

Williams observed that the time taken to fixate a stimulus and make a
saccade remained fairly constant at about 300msec. Therefore the total
search time is simply dependent on the number of fixations made during the
search. From this, Williams developed a mathematical model which was
successful in predicting median search times from the type of target and
display.

For the map designer, it is clearly important to ensure that the more
important categories of map symbols can be discriminated in peripheral

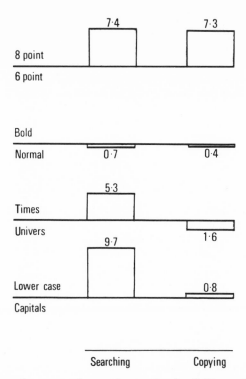

Figure 1. In an experiment to investigate the legibility of type on maps, subjects searched for and copied place names. The figure shows the effect of type style on performance as percentage differences. For example, searching was 7.4 per cent faster with 8 point type than with 6 point type.

vision. Colour coding is one way to achieve this, although too many colours can lead to confusion (Halsey & Chapanis, 1951). An example where search presents few problems to the map reader is Alice Coleman's series of British 1:25,000 Land Use maps which use colours to distinguish major types of land use (Arable, Transport, Industry) subdivided by texture patterns (Arable split into Cereals, Roots, Fodder).

It may not always be practical to code map symbols by colour, and in these cases data are needed on the discriminability of other codes in peripheral vision. Following Williams' methods, we are conducting some experiments on how to make the best of our rather poor discrimination of shape in peripheral vision.

Place Names
Search is an important consideration not only in the design of map symbols but also for place names. Bartz (1970) and Foster and Kirkland (1971) have shown that names are found more quickly when the type size or the colour

in which they appear is known. No doubt, as in Williams' experiments, most fixations are placed on names of the correct size or colour.

In an experiment using 256 geography undergraduates as subjects, a factorial design was employed to investigate the effect of type style on the speed of finding names on a map, and the speed and accuracy of copying them (Phillips, Noyes, & Audley, 1977). Typeface, size, weight, and case, as well as the complexity of the map and the pronounceability of the names was varied. Names set in lower case with an initial capital, although occupying less space on the map, were found 10 per cent more quickly than names in capitals. There was also some evidence for faster search with names set in Times rather than Univers, but this result was not statistically significant.

We have also investigated the eye movements used in searching for names on maps. A Polymetric V-1164-3 Eye Movement Recorder linked to a PDP-12 computer was used to record eye fixations using a corneal reflection monitored by a television camera. Subjects searched for names in map-like displays consisting of 20 typewritten names.

Our results were surprisingly different from the eye movements of people searching for symbols. In a series of experiments no evidence was found that subjects make a greater number of fixations on names resembling the target. We examined the first, second, and last letter of the name, the word shape, and the number of letters, but none of these showed an effect. When subjects move their eyes, they simply fixate one of the nearest names not fixated before, often following a search path characteristic of the individual. When we examined search times we found that these were not constant, but were consistently longer on names which resembled the target, for example, fixations on names with the same initial letter as the target were on average 97 msec longer than on names with a different initial.

Searching for names and searching for coloured symbols produce quite different eye movement data. In some ways, the data for names resemble the eye movements used in normal reading discussed by Levy-Schoen and O'Regan and others (this volume): the use of peripheral vision is very limited and fixation time reflects difficulty.

On maps, names are often placed close together. We have studied how this affects fixation times in a search task. Subjects were asked to search for horizontally placed names and ignore those vertically placed. When they fixated a horizontal name with a vertical name close to its initial letter, fixation times increased significantly, but there was no increase when the vertical name occurred at the end of a horizontal name. This suggests that when names are closely packed on a map the cartographer should try to keep the area surrounding the initial letter of a name free from other lettering.

Relief Maps
On a completely different topic, I will describe some work undertaken with Alan De Lucia and Nicholas Skelton (Phillips, De Lucia, & Skelton, 1975; described more fully in a report by Audley, Bickmore, & Phillips, 1974). We wanted to compare different ways in which a three-dimensional surface could be portrayed on a map. In a relief map this surface is the height of the land

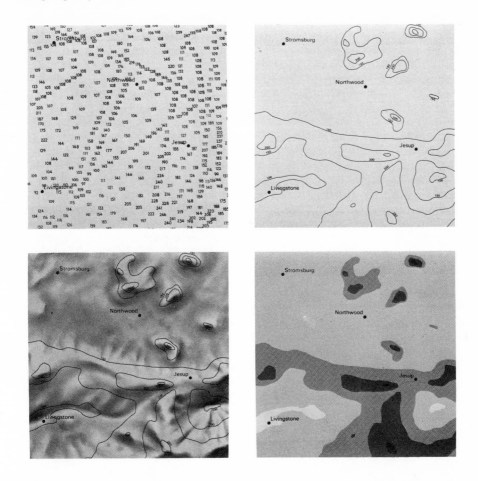

Figure 2. The four types of map used in the relief experiment: Digits (top left), Contours (top right), Shading (bottom left), and Tints (bottom right). The original maps were printed in black and brown.

across hills and valleys, but there are similar problems in depicting theoretical surfaces such as distribution of a mineral, annual rainfall, or degree of magnetic anomaly. Two areas from an oceanographic map were presented as a landscape to make it easy to ask questions about them. They were drawn in four different ways: contour lines, contour lines with hill shading, layer (or hypsometric) tints, and digits (a large number of spot heights resembling a nautical chart); see Figure 2.

A group of 179 police cadets were randomly assigned to one of the four
types of map and were given a series of timed map reading questions. In
one question short black lines were overprinted on the map and labelled alphabetically. The subjects were asked to work quickly and put a ring around
the end of each line which was on higher ground. The time limit was half
a minute and the score was the number of correct items completed.

In another question three profiles were printed at the bottom of the map
and subjects had to match these with three straight lines printed on the map.
Here there was less time pressure -- subjects had a minute and a half.

A third question involved the use of a plastic relief model. A number of
small areas of a map were cut out and mounted on separate pages of a booklet
and the subjects were asked to locate these areas on the model.

Although limited to what could be done with subjects sitting at desks,
we chose as wide a variety of questions as possible. When the results were
analyzed it was found that the 13 questions could be divided into four groups
on the basis of their scores, and this division was supported by a cluster
analysis.

The first group included a number of questions about relative height --
decide which end of a straight line was on higher ground and draw a river
which consistently flowed downhill. Figure 3 shows that for this type of
question the tint maps were best. In the second group there was a single
question on absolute height -- subjects simply had to estimate heights -- and
for this the digital maps were best. The third group consisted of questions
requiring subjects to visualize the landscape and included matching the map
to the plastic relief model, and a question on intervisibility (whether someone

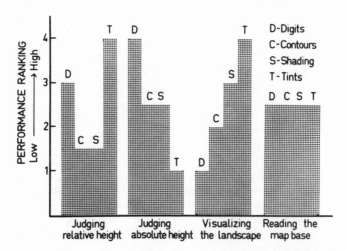

Figure 3. A summary of the results of an experiment to compare the legibility of relief maps using a number of map reading questions.

standing at one location could see a person standing somewhere else). For
this group the tint maps were best. The fourth group of questions was about
the map base, for example, searching for place names, but these failed to
show any significant differences.

Figure 3 illustrates the fact that one cannot talk of "map legibility" without reference to the way a map will be used. Previous experiments on relief
maps (Kempf & Poock, 1969; Shaw & MacLagan, 1972) have often compared
one map with another on the basis of just one or two questions -- estimating
heights was always one of them. Height estimation tasks are a misleading
way of evaluating relief maps. As Figure 3 shows, the rank order of maps
is nearly reversed when absolute height questions are compared with visualization questions.

We have replicated this experiment with geography undergraduates and
have completed a second experiment on computer generated methods of
depicting relief using the SYMAP and SYMVU programs. One further experiment is planned on relief representation. The two long term aims of this
research are to provide the map designer with objective data to help him
relate map design to map usage, and to encourage designers to test maps
themselves. We hope to make some recommendations on a series of relief
map tests which are easy to carry out, sensitive enough to show statistically
significant differences with small numbers of subjects, and representative
of most types of real life map reading.

Symbols for Woodland
R. M. Taylor and V. D. Hopkin of the RAF Institute of Aviation Medicine
at Farnborough have carried out a number of interesting studies of map legibility. Although all their work is on aeronautical charts for military use,
their results are often relevant to map design in general. Aeronautical charts
and other topographic maps at a scale of about 1:250,000 frequently show
woodland as a solid green area. This obscures other information on the map
making it impossible to show layer tints which portray the height of the land.
This problem is particularly serious on aeronautical charts where height
information is needed for safety and where the shape of woods and forests
is a useful navigational aid. Taylor (1975) has conducted some experiments
to compare the solid green woodland symbol with some alternatives such
as the use of a "vignette" where dark green on the edge of a wood fades into
a light green interior, or where the interior is marked with repeated tree
symbols.

Forty subjects were shown small areas of woodland printed in green against
a white background and asked to decide whether the woods were present
on specially printed test maps. Although this seems simple, it led to surprisingly
large differences between the alternative maps. When subjects used an experimental control map which showed nothing but woodland (also in solid green
on white), search times were about six seconds. With a realistic map using
a similar solid green symbol, search time was doubled. But with other types
of woodland symbols such as vignettes the search took roughly three times
as long.

Taylor discussed the problem of identifying woodland shapes in terms of segregating the visual field into areas of figure and ground. If woodlands were shaped like squares or triangles, there would be little difficulty in recognizing them. But they are usually irregular areas which lack "figural goodness." Even with a solid green woodland symbol, it is sometimes difficult to see the outline of a wood as a whole against the background clutter of the map. With other symbols such as vignettes, the separation of figure from ground becomes even more difficult.

Taylor's experiment is a good example of what the psychologist can offer the map designer. There is no simple solution, but alternatives which the designer should decide among on the basis of the psychologist's data. If aeronautical charts are to have woodland symbols, these must be areas of solid green, but this inevitably reduces the legibility of the rest of the map. A possible compromise is to depict only small areas of woodland which are useful as landmarks, and leave out large forests which obscure more than they inform. Vignettes are not a good compromise because they are difficult to use and obscure the map base as much as a solid green symbol does.

Repertory Grid Techniques

Most experiments on map legibility use performance tests: they measure the map reader's speed and accuracy. Although this is undoubtedly the right approach, other methods are also interesting. For example, Stringer (1973) was interested in comparing the efficacy of four types of map in communicating a number of different plans for the development of an area in south London. The plans affected an existing shopping centre and women living in the area were interviewed using a repertory grid technique. They looked at pairs of maps and suggested the implications for people living in the area. These "constructs" were then ranked for the alternative plans as well as for the present use of the land. Analysis of the data revealed the number of functionally distinct constructs elicited for each type of map. Using this and several other scores, Stringer assessed the merits of each type of map for this purpose.

This is an original approach to testing maps. It seems useful when maps are used in a divergent way, that is to say, where the user has no definite goal in using the map but is exploring possibilities, looking for ideas, and grasping implications. This can be contrasted with the convergent use of maps where specific information such as the shortest route home or the best place to bore for oil is sought. There is no doubt that maps are used in both convergent and divergent ways, although it can be argued that for the professional user -- the geologist or pilot -- convergent map reading is more frequent.

Conclusions

These examples illustrate current research on making maps easy to read. It has not been possible to describe other studies which are equally interesting, for example, Hill's (1974) work on orthophoto maps, or a large number of experiments on the perceived size of cartographic symbols (Williams, 1956; Clarke, 1959; Wright, 1967), or research on tactile maps for the blind (Leonard & Newman, 1970).

Map legibility resarch is too recent a phenomenon to assess its effect on map design. Cartographers' reactions to experimental data range from enthusiasm to scepticism. The sceptics may eventually be convinced by the size of effects found in map legibility experiments: differences of 50 or 100 per cent in speed or accuracy between one map and another are not uncommon, and it may be difficult to ignore the implications for real life map reading.

The preparation of this paper forms part of the United Kingdom Social Science Research Council project HR2917/1 awarded to R. J. Audley and R. J. Phillips. We gratefully acknowledge the Council's financial support.

REFERENCES

Audley, R.J., Bickmore, D.P., & Phillips, R.J. Legibility criteria for the efficient use of maps. Final report to the United Kingdom Social Science Research Council for project HR2167, 1974.

Balchin, W.G.V. Graphicacy. Geography, 1972, 57, 185-195.

Bartz, B.S. Experimental use of the search task in an analysis of type legibility in cartography. Cartographic Journal, 1970, 7, 103-112.

Bertin, J. Semiologie graphique. Paris: Mouton, 1967.

Board, C. Bibliography of works on cartographic communication. London: International Cartographic Association, 1976.

Brandes, D. The present state of perceptual research in cartography. Cartographic Journal, 1976, 13, 172-176.

Christner, C.A., & Ray, H.W. An evaluation of the effect of selected combinations of target and background coding on map-reading performance. Human Factors, 1961, 3, 131-146.

Clarke, J.I. Statistical map reading. Geography, 1959, 44, 96-104.

Crawford, P.V. Optimum spatial design for thematic maps. Cartographic Journal, 1976, 13, 134-144.

Foster, J.J., & Kirkland, W. Experimental studies of map typography. Bulletin of the Society of University Cartographers, 1971, 6, 40-45.

Halsey, R.M., & Chapanis, A. On the number of absolutely identifiable spectral hues. Journal of the Optical Society of America, 1951, 41, 1057-1058.

Hill, A.R. Cartographic performance: An evaluation of orthophoto maps. Final report to European Research Office, U. S. Army for contract DAJA37-70-C-2398, 1974.

Hitt, W.D. An evaluation of five different abstract coding methods. Human Factors, 1961, 3, 120-130.

Jenks, G.F., & Knos, D.S. The use of shading patterns in graded series. Annals of the Association of American Geographers, 1961, 51, 316-334.

Kempf, R.P., & Poock, G.K. Some effects of layer tinting on maps. Perceptual and Motor Skills, 1969, 29, 279-281.

Leonard, J.A., & Newman, R.C. Three types of 'maps' for blind travel. Ergonomics, 1970, 13, 165-179.

Levy-Schoen, A., & O'Regan, K. The control of eye movements in reading. (This volume.)

Phillips, R.J., De Lucia, A., & Skelton, N. Some objective tests of the legibility of relief maps. Cartographic Journal, 1975, 12, 39-46.

Phillips, R.J., & Noyes, L. Searching for names in two city street maps. Ergonomics, 1977, 8, 73-77.

Phillips, R.J., Noyes, L., & Audley, R.J. The legibility of type on maps. Ergonomics, 1977, 20, 671-682.

Robinson, A.H. The look of maps: An examination of cartographic design. Madison: University of Wisconsin Press, 1952.

Shaw, M.A., & MacLagan, M.J.R. Interpolating point information using contour maps. In M.A. Shaw (Ed.), Objective evaluation of graphic displays of information. Final report to the United Kingdom Social Science Research Council, 1972.

Stringer, P. Colour and base in urban planning maps. Cartographic Journal, 1973, 10, 89-94.

Taylor, R.M. Shape recognition on aeronautical charts: A study of woodland symbols. Paper read at the ICA International Symposium on Cartographic Communication, Royal Society, London, 1975.

Williams, L.G. The effects of target specification on objects fixated during visual search. Acta Psychologica, 1967, 27, 355-360.

Williams, L.G. Studies of extrafoveal discrimination and detection. Visual Search Symposium, National Academy of Sciences, Washington, D.C., 1973.

Williams, R.L. Statistical symbols for maps: Their design and relative value. New Haven: Yale University Map Laboratory, 1956.

Wood, M. Human factors in cartographic communication. Cartographic Journal, 1972, 9, 123-132.

Wright, R.D. Selection of line weights for solid, qualitative line symbols in a series on maps. Doctoral thesis, University of Kansas, 1967.

Typographic Access Structures for Educational Texts

Robert H.W. Waller

*The term "access structure" refers to the co-ordinated use
of typographically signalled structural cues that help students
to read texts using selective sampling strategies. In spite
of their prevalence, however, the research literature contains very few references to access devices which include
contents lists, headings, glossaries, and so on. This paper
suggests some reasons for this and proposes that for research
to be truly actionable it must be more firmly rooted in real-
world problems. Evidence for the significance of selective
reading is presented and some implications for research
strategies are discussed.*

If you were to compare an educational textbook and a novel, both in a language
you do not know, you would very probably be able to tell them apart just
by appearance. The novel will almost certainly consist solely of continuous
prose. The text of the educational book, though, may be surrounded by additional pedagogical components, such as contents, index, glossary, summaries
and so on. Why is the difference visible? It is not because the textbook has
a structure and the novel has none. It is because the structure of the textbook
has been typographically signalled, while the structure of the novel is signalled
by linguistic means alone. So, whereas the typography of plain text can be
evaluated by criteria of congeniality and legibility, the typography of textbooks
clearly involves additional factors.

Consider the readers' problem if the contents list or index of this publication were to be laid out as continuous prose. If we accept at face value the
conclusions of many studies in the field of reading, there would be few problems. The words would be legible, recognisable, comprehensible (by themselves),
and memorisable. Although the page might look attractive, it would never-

theless be completely unusable for its intended purpose. The problem would not be legibility so much as accessibility.

A contents list of index uses typographic layout and signalling to display structural (typically hierarchical) relations in its content. The structure of a complete book can be made accessible in a similar way. That is, typo-graphically signalled devices can be used to help readers overview the text and locate relevant parts efficiently. To the list of such devices in the first paragraph might be added headings, concept maps, questions, study notes, and learning objectives. Used together in a co-ordinated way they comprise the access structure of a text.

Typographic signalling is not, of course, an inherent characteristic of all these devices. Much of the information they convey might well be communi-cated in the main explanatory discourse. That they often are signalled repre-sents a prediction that publishers make about the purposes and strategies of readers. Whereas a continuous discourse assumes and perhaps enforces a relatively passive sequential reading strategy, a typographically structured text allows for more selective sampling. For example, when summarising paragraphs are embedded in the middle of a continuous text, they are useful only to the reader who is reading the book through in a sequential way. If the paragraphs are typographically signalled, they can be easily accessed and used for text selection, previewing the argument, reference, and revision.

It might be thought that the various components of an access structure, being so prevalent in modern textbooks, would have been the focus of reason-ably thorough experimentation. Instead, it is extraordinary that whereas innovative devices, such as the advance organiser or behavioural objectives, have been the subject of dozens of studies, there are only two or three papers that even mention headings as an aid to learners; and to my knowledge, no-one has yet looked at contents lists.

If it is accepted that there are circumstances in which readers may need to read selectively, then the models, theories, or methodologies used as the basis for empirical research should take this into account. This paper was prepared for a conference one of whose aims was to promote dialogue between psychologists and graphic designers interested in implementing research find-ings. It is therefore appropriate to examine why access devices have so rarely been featured in the research literature. Until they are, communications-media professionals will continue to complain with some justification that empirical research is not relevant to their needs.

What Practical Research has been done?

It would be a difficult task to classify all the research that has been published on texts. We are here primarily interested in studies that specifically aim to inform and evaluate the work of professional communicators. However, not only has a wide range of topics been identified for investigation but the purposes of researchers have differed greatly. Studies range from the highly theoretical to the pragmatic, from molecular issues to whole textbooks. Much of the research has investigated theories of memory, learning, or lan-guage processing and only incidentally the use of texts. Even research that is specifically concerned with text does not always aim at the same outcome. Frase (1973) has distinguished between three kinds of problem -- theoretical, methodological, and practical. He points out the danger of interpreting research which is primarily intended to solve theoretical or methodological problems as the source of advice about practical instructional situations.

Prescriptive research on text presentation ranges from studies of legibility, dominated by the work of Tinker (1963), to work on content sequence and structure (Posner & Strike, 1976). Readability research investigates language variables such as vocabulary, syntax, and abstractness. The main body of work was summarised by Klare (1963). "Adjunct learning aids" describe devices that researchers have examined for their effectiveness in encouraging the recall of prose. These include "pre-instructional strategies" such as advance-organisers and objectives (Hartley & Davies, 1976) and in-text aids, usually questions (Anderson & Biddle, 1975). Much, but not all, of this research has been done in the context of Rothkopf's theory of mathemagenics (1970). The word is coined from the Greek and means "giving birth to learning." Studies of adjunct aids attempt to manipulate the readers' learning set in order to improve recall. A recent overview of the area is by Faw and Waller (1976).

Why is the Research not Successful?
It would seem at first sight that text researchers are covering a wide range of factors. Most of these areas, though, are currently receiving substantial criticism not only from potential users but from within. Contradictory or inconclusive results have been reported in a number of recent reviews -- for example, Duchastel and Merrill (1973) on objectives, Barnes and Clawson (1975) on advance organisers, Rickards (1977) on questions -- and a number of criticisms have been made of research, particularly that which aims to be prescriptive rather than descriptive.

First, research has been criticised for its lack of a sound theoretical base (Hartley & Burnhill, 1977 on typography; Rickards, 1977 on questions). Even the most widely used frameworks fail to convince everybody (Carver, 1972 on mathemagenics; and reply by Rothkopf, 1974) or are misunderstood by those who use them -- Ausubel's "advance organiser" theory is particularly abused (Ausubel, 1963).

Second, methodology has been the focus of a great deal of criticism. The interpretation of results is made impossible by the wide variation among researchers in the variables they control and the experimental conditions that they report. In addition, a paper by Ladas (1973) demonstrates that different statistical techniques can be used to produce different results, using basically inconclusive data. Stokes (1978) presents evidence that questions the reliability of readability research.

Linked to problems of theory and methodology is the issue of representa-tiveness. Since many real-world factors are missing in laboratory experiments, research results are often unreliable as a basis for instructional practice. Molecular issues may be convenient to study in a controlled context, but in real life they will often be swamped by other, more dominant, aspects of the learning environment. For example, Faw and Waller (1976) remark that the effect of the continued use of the innovative mathemagenic aids used for experiments has never been studied; yet it would seem that experi-ence of using these devices would be an important determinant of their effect-iveness. Thorndyke (1975) makes a similar point in relation to psycholinguistic

research. He suggests that where experimental situations are too far removed
from normal experience, subjects may resort to special processing strategies.
Snow (1974) demonstrated that the enormous range of variables present in
a real-life instructional situation can never be completely replicated in a
laboratory. Macdonald-Ross and Waller (1975), in addition, point out that
the stimulus material used in many studies of typographic design fails to
meet basic standards of clarity achieved by most professional graphic designers.

As far as practical communicators are concerned, these sorts of criticism
imply that the outcomes of research are unactionable. Researchers have
too rarely addressed questions that those who write, edit, and design textbooks actually need answers to.

Research and the Real World
The problems of theory and methodology are linked to the question of how
representative the research on real world processes and events is. The relationship between research and the real world is discussed by Ravetz (1971),
who offers an analysis of what he terms "ineffective and immature disciplines."
His detailed comments echo the self-criticism heard in our own field of study.
Rothkopf (1973) has written, for example, "We, the practitioners of an infant
science, live in an age in which the elegant theoretical accomplishments
of the advanced physical sciences are taken as the model for all scientific
activity." He appeals for a return to the practical origins of science, saying
that "Highly abstract conceptions of learning and teaching have not served
the researcher's intuition well. They have distorted the sense of what ques-
ions are important and what results promise practicable contributions to
schooling. As a consequence many research endeavours appear sterile and
trivial."

As a solution, Rothkopf suggests that researchers need "cultural recon-
naissance" into the real world. Ravetz cites the historical development of
the now mature, positive sciences. He takes the view that immature disciplines
could benefit from the former distinction between "history," "philosophy,"
and "arts." "Philosophy" meant reflection and explanation of the real world
as described and classified by "history," while "arts" represented "the set
of principles defining the methods of any class of tasks."

Such a reorientation would result not in any major change in experimental
or statistical techniques, but in new research goals. Unlike the physical
scientist's goal -- the definition of universal general laws -- the concept of
"arts" would concentrate our efforts on identifying, refining, and testing
techniques and methods. The quality control of applied research would involve
the applicability of an idea to real-world situations in addition to laboratory
experiments. This view does not deny the validity of all experimentation.
The observation and classification that Ravetz calls "history" still needs
experimental investigation into the basis of, for example, perception and
cognition, but it does discourage what Anderson and Biddle (1976) call "mind-
less empiricism."

In Ravetz's view, knowledge in the immature disciplines is more realistically
embodied in the form of aphorisms than universal general laws. Aphorisms
are "where a craft knowledge finds verbal expression." They are not the
perfectly validated, scientific knowledge that researchers in our field have
failed to achieve. Where scientific knowledge claims to be generalisable

and value-free, aphorisms are unashamedly situation-specific and their values are openly admitted. Thus, according to the context of our problem, we are free to accept or reject them. They provide a framework in which to externalise and examine ideas and attitudes that would otherwise remain in the tacit domain.

In the field of typography the literature has always been aphoristic in nature --and the most interesting aspect of scientific research has often been its subjective element. The choice of issues is frequently more interesting than the actual results obtained. A compilation of typographic "commonsense" may be found in Zapf (1970) or Gerstner (1974). One may not agree with everything there, but will come away knowing a great deal more about typographic design. The role of empirical research is to monitor the effectiveness of the methods and techniques that aphoristic knowledge embodies, and provide an objective basis for observation of the real world of writers, books, and readers.

The Real World of Writers and Readers
What, then, are the characteristics of the real world on which research should be based? At present we are working with models that deal with only a fraction of its complexity, but which are relatively easy to investigate. For example, if we want to test the effectivensss of a particular text variable in improving learning, the criteria for successful learning (perhaps a high score in a comprehension test) will be determined by the experimenter. We could only extrapolate from such studies to situations where the achievement of predictable institutional goals was more important than the achievement of the students' personal goals. This, however, seems to deny the essence of the text medium: printed books are transportable and can be stored. That is, they can be used by people the author is not aware of and whose needs he cannot predict with any precision, and the reader is ultimately in control of the presentation sequence.

Studies of this sort seem to have a restricted view of the problems of textbook production and use. We may regain our perspective by looking at some of the other factors that in the real world of textbook publishing influence those whose job it is to oversee the production and evaluation process -- the editor, typographer, or educational adviser. The matrix in Figure 1 shows one way of representing their objectives. It is based on the assumption that all texts have a sponsor (author, publisher, etc.) and users. The ways in which these two groups influence the communicator's objectives are polarised in this diagram into positive purposes and negative constraints. The contents of the cells may, of course, vary. Although theorists and practitioners alike should ideally take account of factors appearing in all four cells, it is too often possible to identify a sort of professional tunnel-vision, that is not confined to applied psychologists. An example from the research literature is of the investigators who, often using incorrect terminology, have reported on the legibility of type without reference to particular typesetting systems. As Hartley and Burnhill (1977) point out, they have not addressed the questions typographers actually ask. They are thus quite firmly rooted in the user-constraints cell of the matrix. An example from the practitioners' side is of the many editorial house-styles that attempt to impose standard formats, presentation styles, and printing methods on publications without regard for

PURPOSES	CONSTRAINTS

Decide to/not to use
Search for particular item
Study in depth
Browse
USER Recap/review
Entertainment
etc.
	Physiological
	  (legibility, weight
	  of book)
	Psychological
	  (reading skills,
	  aptitude, previous
	  knowledge)
	Availability
	  (delivery, storage etc.)
	  etc.

Teach particular curriculum
Persuade
Enrich readers' outlook
SPONSOR Personal fulfilment
Sell books
etc.
	Production costs
	Legal factors
	  (libel, copyright etc.)
	Technology
	Standard procedures
	  (house-style, standard
	  forms, etc.)
	  etc.

Figure 1. The sources of textbook designers' objectives.

the nature of particular target readerships. The application of standards and rules that cannot be justified by reasons other than tradition alone places such house-styles in the sponsor-constraint cell.

This matrix demonstrates a significant omission in the advice that is available to producers of texts, either through research literature or the traditional practices of publishing. The issues raised by the user-purposes cell have not been dealt with. Information is available about most items in the constraints cells, while the sponsor-purposes cell has dominated instructional research with its stress on the achievement of institutional goals. However, the notion that users may approach texts for many different purposes has usually been overlooked in the reduction of the real world to theoretical models for controlled experiment. There is evidence, though, that although text is on the whole a linear sequential medium, it is likely to be read in a far from linear fashion.

Evidence of Selective Reading Strategies
The authors of some kinds of texts can make strong predictions about their readers. Novelists, for example, have a self-selecting readership who appreciate and understand their style. The authors of programmed-learning texts can, by entry tests, predict their readers' prior knowledge and ability. However, conventional textbooks are open to anyone, and authors know comparatively little about the abilities, purposes, opinions, prior knowledge, and circumstances of their readers. In fact, the only reading behaviour that they

can confidently predict is that their readers must read selectively. We can cite a number of factors as evidence for this assertion.

First, observation of reading styles and strategies by Pugh (1975) and Thomas (1976) shows that a straight-through linear strategy is not typical of efficient readers. Pugh links selectivity with reading efficiency. He lists five strategies of efficient readers (defined as those whose purpose is known and who achieve that purpose). Three of them are selective activities concerned with locating and making decisions about the content of a text. Indeed, writers on reading and study skills commonly recommend that students read in a selective fashion, previewing texts by scanning ahead and selecting particular areas for special attention.

Second, research on learning styles may be cited (Cronbach & Snow, 1976). If material is presented to suit a particular kind of learner, it may be unnecessarily difficult for those who adopt a different style. Mager (1961) found that instructional sequences planned by instructors were usually quite different from those elicited from learners. Indeed, the prevailing philosophy among educational theorists appears to have shifted from the highly directed, manipulative style of education exemplified by programmed learning, towards a more open facilitative approach. Increasingly, the emphasis is on enabling students to formulate and achieve their own objectives rather than those prescribed by institutionalised education. In addition to preferred learning styles, individuals study at different rates and, in courses overloaded with impossibly long reading lists, must adopt highly selective reading strategies.

Further evidence that readership is unpredictable is indicated in the way that textbooks are marketed. At the tertiary, and to some extent the secondary, level they are sold internationally. They are therefore likely to be read by people whose cultural background, even whose mother-tongue, is different from that of the author and his immediately perceived readership. Linked to this is the important growth of interdisciplinary studies which brings readers from widely differing educational backgrounds to the same texts.

Both the Pugh and the Thomas studies mentioned above arose from courses designed to help students read more efficiently. In both studies it was found that otherwise fluent readers often found difficulty in using books effectively as resources. It is interesting, though, to compare approaches to the teaching of reading skills at the middle and secondary school levels and at the tertiary level. At the lower levels, efforts at improving the text-reader interaction are often made on both sides; that is, texts are carefully selected, often with the aid of readability formulae, and students are given instruction in spelling, vocabulary, grammar, and so forth. At the higher level, students are assumed to be fluent readers and instruction centres around study skills. However, a corresponding selection of textbooks is rarely made at that level. While readability research deals with the same text-difficulty variables found among children in schools, there is a noticeable mismatch at the tertiary level between research on reading problems and research on text presentation.

Why has Selective Reading been Ignored?
There are probably several reasons for this apparent mismatch. Hartley and Davies (1976) suggest that the comparative absence of research on overviews in texts (which could aid selective readers) may be because their worth is

so obvious "that few people have felt any real need to subject the concept
to empirical investigation." However, that has not deterred researchers from
investigating other "obvious" ideas. Instead we may recall Frase (1973) who
was quoted earlier as saying that practical research on text has often arisen
out of theories on learning, or out of the development of existing methodologies and has been concerned with books and readers only incidentally.

Many examples of theory-driven research are found in the field of reading.
The size of the research effort on reading is out of proportion to the difficulty in either teaching or practising it, but it is full of issues that are
intriguing to the psychologist -- issues of perception, language, learning and
so on.

In the same review of learning from prose, Frase gives an example of
methodology-driven research. He notes that many of the research designs
prevented readers from reviewing the text they had read before answering
the test questions. Although this unnatural reading strategy allowed the
experimenter to attribute differences in performance to, say, question position, it would be difficult to extrapolate their findings for normal instructional purposes. In addition, experimenters make a tacit value-judgement
when they use retention as the sole criterion of success in the study of text,
whether the form is multi-choice questions or experimenter-marked free-
recall scripts. It is methodologically convenient to ignore other kinds of
reading outcome.

Appropriate Research Methods for Access Structures

What would truly practical "arts"-driven research, that access-structures
require, involve? It would probably be methodologically less neat; it would
also be based on theories that are imprecise about cognitive processes, but
which look at broader aspects of reading than has been customary.

Hatt (1976) reviewed some of the existing models of the reading process
and commented how many of them take the coming together of the reader
and the text as "given"; theorists have been almost solely concerned with
letter and word recognition issues. With the level of fluency expected from
textbook readers though, there are likely to be few such problems. Instead
it would be interesting to have a more comprehensive framework for discussing the reading process so that the effect of broader aspects of text, such
as the access structure, on reading behaviour might be predicted.

Hatt attempts such a framework, and it is deceptively simple. It is based
on three stages: a reader finds a text; he reads the text; he uses the message
(or not, as the case may be). As we have argued, many theorists confine
themselves to the cognitive processes that occur within the second stage,
though most now reject the early information-processing model (transmitter-
message-receiver) as casting the reader in an unduly passive role. Instead
we now see readers as not simply receiving information but as seeking and
finding it. Kintsch (1977) summarises the theory of selective attention.
Hatt extends these ideas by studying patterns of entry and patterns of exit
from the reading act.

For our purposes Hatt's framework appears unduly sequential. It may
be that aspects of all three of his behaviours can occur cyclically or simultaneously. So Hatt's stages may be termed "motivation," "strategy," and
"outcome." All three parts are "ongoing" rather than sequential. Thus reading

cannot continue satisfactorily if there is no motivation, no effective strategy, or no outcome perceived by the reader. Some factors that such a model would have to consider are listed in Figure 2.

Consider a reader-text mismatch in the readability level of the text. The syntax and vocabulary may be too difficult for a particular student who has done no full-time study previously, or for whom English is a second language. We can anticipate that this will demotivate him (he will not enjoy reading or feel he is achieving enough), it will slow him down (prevent him from skimming, perhaps), and may result in a less satisfactory learning outcome (he may miss subtleties, or not perceive the overall structure of the argument).

A mismatch in the access structure of the text would also affect all three aspects of reading behaviour. Since he cannot overview the content, it might be difficult for the student to see the relevance of the text to his needs. It will restrict his reading style because it assumes a passive linear strategy that he may not have enough time for. It will restrict learning since the text, having no surface structure, offers him no aids to memory.

Successful research on access devices would have to report on many of these factors. Only then could practical communicators determine the applicability of research observations to their own situations. There are indications that research strategies, broader in scope than those we have reviewed, are emerging.

```
MOTIVATION              STRATEGY            OUTCOME

Attention               Reading style       Goal achievement
  recommendation          browse              personal
  obligation              skim/preview        objectives
  attraction              search/scan
                          intense study       course
Selection                 review              assessment
  relevance to:
    course objectives   Purpose             Knowledge
    personal objectives   criticise           memory
  flavour                 memorise            insights
    context               revise              skills
    register              understand
                          assignment        Pleasure
Perseverance              make notes          amusement
  enjoyment                                   excitement
  achievement           Environment          fascination
                          home, library, etc.
                          distractions
                          lighting, health
                          comfort, etc.
```

Figure 2. Three aspects of the reading process.

Research, using appropriate measurements, should seek ways of observing reading behaviour, rather than simply measuring specific outcomes such as retention. A past problem has been that traditional eye-movement recording techniques, in addition to being expensive, elaborate to set up, and obtrusive to the reader, have been biassed towards micro-level reading. Recently, though, Whalley and Fleming (1975) and Pugh (this volume) have reported simple macro-level reading recorders which allow a relatively natural reading situation.

Behavioural records, of course, need sensitive interpretation. Whalley (1977) has proposed a research paradigm that calls for: the linking of reading records to formal structural analysis of text; subjective evaluation of text structure elicited from readers; and normal performance measures such as multi-choice texts, essays, and verbal protocols. Shebilske and Reid (this volume) have also reported studies of macro-level reading strategies related to structural analysis of text.

What Structure is to be Accessed?

The link between behavioural records of the reading process and the formal analysis of text structure makes this work of great practical interest. If the reader is, in fact, an active participant in the communication process, we are challenged to investigate ways of presenting texts that give readers a reliable basis for sensible sampling. If access is to be provided with headings, contents lists, and so on, they need to be related logically and consistently to the structure of the text and to each other.

This relationship is hard to define for some presentation devices that have been explored. Those based on research that obliges readers to adopt a linear sequential strategy -- adjunct questions or advance organisers, for example -- are essentially rhetorical devices; they are designed to influence the reader's concepts and facts as they are presented. In this sense they are conceptually indistinct from other aspects of argumentation that texts contain.

It is hoped that the rationale of access structures is more sound -- they are typographically signalled in order to be spotted by the skimming, searching, or browsing reader. Even so, how do these various graphic techniques relate to the transitional, organising, or signposting cues that are among the conventions of prose? While the mathemagenics-type research needs to know because in some ways it proposes a rival system, the designer of access devices needs to know what he is structuring. Linguistic cues are important because they may provide the key to such an analysis. In the field of cognitive psychology, a number of recent studies that employ story grammars to describe the structure of prose may be cited. There is no comprehensive review yet, but the studies by Thorndyke (1975) and Meyer (1975) are examples. This work is linked to the studies of linguists working at the inter-sentence level of text (Grimes, 1974). It is to be hoped that this effort will eventually lead to a workable system of text analysis for practical purposes. At present it is probably still too detailed to be used conveniently with large amounts of text.

When a usable macro-level system of text analysis is formulated, there will still be unanswered questions. What structures are appropriate for particular subject-areas, the teaching of particular skills, or for different educational levels? Indeed, is it even possible to arrive at such generalisations? A further question might be: how can the clarification, through headings, of a single overall structure help students with many different needs? An access structure cannot make a poor text good, nor can it ensure that an author perceives the various needs of his readership correctly. It does, though, help the reader make informed decisions about strategies for coping with texts that may not be directly aimed at him or her.

Each device in the access structure fills a need that cannot be met in another way: the contents page and headings give an overview of the text; glossaries provide definitions of terms; the index is the means of direct access to concepts appearing in the text; a list of objectives displays the anticipated purposes of the text; opening summaries give more detailed overviews of the arguments than simple headings; and final summaries present the conclusions. A less traditional device, the concept map, shows the structure of a subject area (not the same as the text-structure which is constrained by the linearity of the medium).

In conclusion it may be said that research on access structures is proposed in reaction to some of the problems encountered by other kinds of research on text. Methodological problems will not disappear but research on access for selective reading, by having different and in some ways less ambitious goals, may avoid some of the pitfalls. Instead of investigating the effect of particular aspects of texts on memory or the learning process, it may be more appropriate to ask conceptually less rigorous but practically based questions. What sort of presentation is found most acceptable by particular groups of readers, and in what circumstances? How are reading strategies influenced by particular text arrangements?

Our criterion of actionability calls for research on the writer as much as research on the reader. In other words, research on presentation should aim to offer usable methods of text construction as well as describe the effect on learners. That these devices, used correctly, are helpful to readers is hard to dispute -- empirical research on the issue would be self-fulfilling. But although the products of authors are being investigated, little is known about the writing process. How can authors be helped to produce coherent access structures? It is hoped that the effort to answer such questions will lead to useful research in the real world of writers, editors, designers, and readers of textbooks.

REFERENCES

Anderson, R.C., & Biddle, W.B. On asking people questions about what they are reading. In G. Bower (Ed.), Psychology of learning and motivation (Vol. 9). New York: Academic Press, 1975.

Ausubel, D.P. The psychology of meaningful verbal learning. New York: Grune and Stratton, 1963.

Barnes, B.R., & Clawson, E.U. Do advance organisers facilitate learning? Review of Educational Research, 1975, 45, 637-660.

Carver, R.P. A critical review of mathemagenic behaviours and the effect of questions upon the retention of prose materials. Journal of Reading Behavior, 1972, 4, 95-119.

Cronbach, L.J., & Snow, R.W. Aptitudes and instructional methods. New York: Irvington, 1976.

Duchastel, P.C., & Merrill, P.F. The effects of behavioural objectives on learning: A review of empirical studies. Review of Educational Research, 1973, 43, 53-70.

Faw, H.W., & Waller, T.G. Mathemagenic behaviours and efficiency in learning from prose. Review of Educational Research, 1976, 46, 691-720.

Frase, B.T. On learning from prose. Educational Psychologist (Vol. 10, No. 1), 1973.

Gerstner, K. Compendium for literates. Cambridge, MA: MIT Press, 1974.

Grimes, J.E. The thread of discourse. The Hague: Mouton, 1974.

Hartley, J., & Burnhill, P. Understanding instructional text: Typography, layout and design. In M.J.A. Howe (Ed.), Adult learning. London: John Wiley and Son, 1977.

Hartley, J., & Davies, I.K. Preinstructional strategies: The role of pretests, behavioural objectives, overviews, and advance organisers. Review of Educational Research, 1976, 46, 239-265.

Hatt, F. The reading process: A framework for analysis and description. London: Bingley, 1976.

Kintsch, W. Memory and cognition. New York: John Wiley and Sons, 1977.

Klare, G. The measurement of readability. Iowa State University Press, 1963.

Ladas, H. The mathemagenic effects of factual review questions on the learning of incidental information: A critical review. Review of Educational Research, 1973, 43, 71-82.

Macdonald-Ross, M., & Waller, R.H.W. Criticisms, alternatives and tests: A framework for improving typography. Programmed Learning and Educational Technology, 1975, 12, 75-83.

Mager, R.F. On the sequencing of instructional content. Psychological Reports, 1961, 9, 405-413.

Meyer, B.J.F. Identification of the structure of prose and its implications for the study of reading and memory. Journal of Reading Behavior, 1975, 7, 7-47.

Posner, G.J., & Strike, K.A. A categorization scheme for principles of sequencing content. Review of Educational Research, 1976, 46, 665-690.

Pugh, A.K. The development of silent reading. In W. Latham (Ed.), The road to effective reading. London: Ward Lock, 1975.

Pugh, A.K. Styles and strategies in adult silent reading. (This volume.)

Ravetz, J.R. Scientific knowledge and its social problems. Oxford University Press, 1971.

Rickards, J.P. On inserting questions before or after segments of text. Contemporary Educational Psychology, 1977, 2, 200-206.

Rothkopf, E.Z. The concept of mathemagenic activities. Review of Educational Research, 1970, 40, 325-336.

Rothkopf, E.Z. What are we trying to understand and improve? Educational research as Leerlaufreaktion, Educational Psychologist, 1973, 10, 58-66.

Rothkopf, E.Z. Barbarism and mathemagenic activities: Comments on criticism by Carver. Journal of Reading Behavior, 1974, 6, 3-8.

Shebilske, W., & Reid, L.S. Reading eye movements, macro-structure and goal-processing. (This volume.)

Snow, R.E. Representative and quasi-representative designs for research on teaching. Review of Educational Research, 1974, 44, 265-292.

Stokes, A.F. The reliabiilty of readability formulae. Journal of Research in Reading, 1978, 1, 21-34.

Thomas, L. The self-organised learner and the printed word. Centre for the Study of Human Learning, Brunel University, 1976.

Thorndyke, P. Cognitive structure in human story comprehension and memory. Ph.D. Thesis, Stanford University, 1975.

Tinker, M.A. The legibility of type. Iowa State University Press, 1963.

Whalley, P.C. Aspects of purposive reading: The analysis of reading records. Paper presented at the British Psychological Society conference, Exeter, 1977.

Whalley, P.C., & Fleming, R.W. An experiment with a simple recorder of reading behaviour. Programmed Learning and Educational Technology, 1975, 12, 120-124.

Zapf, H. Manuale typographica. Cambridge, MA: MIT Press, 1970.

The Use of Visual Cues in Text

Jeremy J. Foster

"Visual cues" are variations in the appearance of a graphic display which are intended to assist the reader in using the display more efficiently. Visual cues are frequently employed where the reader has to detect or discriminate target items, such as in maps or bibliographies, but are less frequently used in material read for comprehension.

The experimental literature on cuing, particularly in continuous prose, is surveyed. Two experiments are reported. One involved obtaining judgements of the key sentences in a 3,400-word text, and demonstrated the inconsistency of the judges; the second examined the effects of typographic cuing using a delayed free-recall test. The results indicated that cuing key material led readers to recall more of that key material.

Waller (personal communication) noted: "It seems promising...to explore ways of making the content and structure of textbooks accessible to the selective reader. It is proposed...that one way of achieving this effect could be through the use of typographically signalled structural cues...." The present paper is concerned with incorporating structural cues within the text itself by using typography to distinguish levels of content. The hypothesis is that this can facilitate effective reading of prose. It rests on the assumption that reading involves not only the comprehension of words but also an awareness of the underlying structure of prose, which can be signalled by typographic cues.

In visual search tasks, a target item can be located more rapidly if made visually dissimilar from the non-target items. Evidence for this comes from studies of maps (Phillips, this volume), bibliographies (Spencer, Reynolds, & Coe, 1974, 1975), tables (Wright & Fox, 1970), and labels (Dennis, 1975).

Supplementary Benefits are cash benefits payable if you are *not* in full-time work and your income (if any) from pension or other sources is not enough to meet your needs. You do not have to have paid any contributions. Benefit is paid as a right if your income is below the levels laid down by Parliament and if you satisfy certain conditions.

If you *are* in full-time work you are not entitled to supplementary benefit except in an emergency but if you have children you may be able to claim *family income supplement* (see leaflet FIS 1 from post-offices and Social Security offices).

There are two kinds of supplementary benefit: supplementary pension and supplementary allowance.

Supplementary pensions are paid to people over retirement age (65 for men, 60 for women), who are not in full-time work. For a married couple living together the pension is payable when the husband is over 65, whatever his wife's age.

Supplementary allowances are paid to people aged 16 and over, but under retirement age, who are not in full-time work. If you are physically fit you will normally have to sign on for work as a condition of receiving an allowance, unless you have the sole care of dependent children (for example if you are a widow or widower, an unmarried mother, or you are separated from your husband or wife) or you are needed full-time at home to care for a sick or aged relative.

If you are homeless and have no fixed address you may be able to get supplementary benefit if you need money urgently.

If you are unemployed, but fit and available for work, some of the information in this leaflet does not apply to you: you should get leaflet SL8 and make a claim on form B1 at the Unemployment Benefit office of the Department of Employment.

If you have a handicapped son or daughter aged 16 or over who is unable to do a full-time job because of mental or physical handicap, he or she may be entitled to a supplementary allowance. Normally people over 16 can claim in their own right but you can claim on the child's behalf if he or she is unable to do so.

How to claim

TO CLAIM SUPPLEMENTARY BENEFIT FILL IN THE SIMPLE FORM ON PAGE 7, TEAR IT OFF AND SEND IT TO THE LOCAL SOCIAL SECURITY OFFICE—YOU CAN GET THE ADDRESS AND A PREPAID ENVELOPE FROM THE POST OFFICE.

Figure 1. A real-life example of typographic cuing.

The results of an experiment by Poulton (1967) on scanning newspapers for headlines also demonstrate the value of visual cuing. Adding subsidiary headlines led to lower rates of target location if readers were not informed of the subsidiary headlines; this occurred even though the subsidiary headlines were typographically dissimilar from the main target ones. In other words, target location was retarded if additional distractor items were provided and the reader was not told beforehand that they were present or how they differed visually from the targets. Hartley and Burnhill (1976) have emphasised the value of cuing by spatial location: "We are particularly concerned to argue that space is the primary variable in typographic research, and that space can be manipulated to convey the structure of text." They demonstrated that respacing a document so that the spacing complemented the structure of the content led to faster location of specified items and fewer errors.

A prime feature of the tasks used in these experiments is that they all involved the reader searching for a previously specified target item among a set of targets and distractors. In extending cuing to text read for comprehension, one is asking whether it can be beneficial, when the reader is searching for a "target" not previously specified, except in very general terms.

Visual Cuing in Text

Figure 1 shows a British government pamphlet intended to inform the public about social security benefits (Leaflet SB1, issued by the Department of Health and Social Security, November 1976). It is apparent that the pamphlet designer believes that typographic cuing is useful for this type of material; on the single page shown, in addition to the heading, there are different cases, type sizes, interlinear spacings, and weights (bold, normal; and italicised). One presumes that the variations in visual features, by signing the reader toward relevant and important sections and away from non-relevant ones, are intended to help him identify the underlying structure of the information. It may well be, however, that the complexity of such a cuing system disrupts rather than facilitates comprehension.

Previous Research into Cuing in Text

Dearborn, Johnston, and Carmichael (1951) investigated a "peak stress" format which yielded higher comprehension scores and was preferred by 95% of people studied. Unfortunately no illustration and few details of this format are provided, but it was typewritten in two columns, single-spaced, and contained three forms of cuing. The one word in each sentence carrying peak stress in oral reading was typed in capitals, unspecified spatial arrangements "which break up the article for the reader into more comprehensible units of thought" were used, and sections deemed important were blackened by retyping over the original.

Klare, Mabry, and Gustafson (1955) compared two "patterning" formats with a control. "Patterning" consisted of underlining certain words in a 1,206-word lesson on engines: patterning lowered the scores of subjects with low aptitude and raised those of subjects with high aptitude on a multiple-choice post-test of lesson content. Format had a non-significant main effect, but did interact with the mechanical aptitude of the readers.

Christiansen and Stordahl (1955) used two texts, one of 2,600 words and one of 3,800 words, to study the effect of providing a summary, headings, and underlining of main points either singly or in combination. Thirty minutes was allowed for studying the passages and immediate and delayed (six days later) post-tests were administered. None of the organizational aids had a significant effect upon either post-test score.

Hershberger and Terry (1965) describe one of the major studies on typographic cuing in a report which contains the following justification for the practice: "Typographical cuing is intended to help the reader identify and distinguish various categories of lesson content, thereby allowing him to adjust his style of reading to the importance and difficulty of each." Their study used eighth-grade school pupils who were given either a programmed or a conventional text, and one of three typographic styles. The control style was in normal, lower-case black throughout. The two-category cue condition differentiated "core" from "enrichment" content by printing the former in red. Details of the procedure used in deciding what was core or enrichment content are not given. Core content consisted of new key words, familiar key words, key statements, basic core statements, key examples, and rephrasing of key statements. In the five-category condition, subdivisions of core content were made by using red capitals, lower case red underlined, lower case red, and lower case black with red underlining. Core content formed one-third of the total text, but the length is not stated by Hershberger and Terry. A multiple-choice and completion test was used to assess comprehension; this test was administered seven days before and one day after reading.

The data consisted of separate gain scores for core and enrichment sections of the text. There was a significant Format x Content interaction, due to the two-category format helping the reader to learn proportionately more of the core content as opposed to enrichment content. Hershberger and Terry conclude that "simple typographical cuing...significantly enhances the ratio of important to unimportant content learned without reducing the total amount learned." But "complex typographical cuing distinguishing five categories of lesson content does not appear to benefit the reader in the least." They suggest that the complex system may confuse the reader, a point made previously by Hershberger (1964).

Marks (1966) found that printing key words in bold or large type led more children to follow simple instructions. However, underlining the complete instructions led to poor performance, which Marks ascribes to its creating "an extremely crowded effect which militated against readability."

Cashen and Leicht (1970) gave students journal articles to study. In the experimental format five statements were underlined in red. The subsequent test included multiple-choice items on these statements and five adjacent ones. Experimental subjects were superior to subjects given the control-format texts on scores both for the items pertaining to the underlined items and for the items pertaining to adjacent statements.

In a 2,305-word passage, Kulhavy (1972) found that underlining testable items within it and telling subjects to pay attention to the underlined sections yielded higher scores on the post-test of both cued and incidental (non-cued) material. Crouse and Idstein (1972) found that underlining those parts of a text which were later tested did not lead to better post-test scores when the text and reading time were short (212 words, 2.5 or 5 minutes). But with a 6,000-word text and 25-minute reading period, underlining did lead to higher scores especially for faster readers.

Fowler and Barker (1974) compared performance on a post-test of subjects who had read text and cued it themselves during reading, read text cued by other readers, read texts cued by the experimenter, or read uncued text. The post-test was given seven days after reading following a brief review period. Subjects who had been given the text with cuing provided by the experimenter performed better on test-items related to the cued material than subjects given the uncued text. Since total scores did not differ, Fowler and Barker commented that retention of emphasised material may adversely affect the retention of the remainder.

Rickards and August (1975) examined the effects of active versus passive underlining on an 80-sentence passage, in which one sentence per paragraph (16 in all) was underlined by the reader (active condition) or presented with underlining. A free-recall test immediately followed the reading of the passage. Total recall scores for the group who actively underlined sentences of their own choosing were the only ones significantly higher than those of the control group. Scores on the test of non-underlined material showed that readers who underlined any sentence they chose recalled more incidental material than any other group. The group who were given underlining of high-importance material did not differ on this measure from the group given underlining of low-importance material.

Coles and Foster (1975) underlined 28 of 61 statements making up a 1050-word article and administered both a pretest and an immediate post-test on the cued material after a 3.5-minute reading. Cuing had no effect upon gain scores when readers were not informed that cuing would be provided (Experiment 1), nor when readers given cued material were simply told that the important points had been underlined. Cuing did yield greater gain scores when readers were instructed to use the SQ3R (Survey, Question, Read, Recall, Review) reading strategy. A subsequent experiment (Foster & Coles, 1977) used printed material, with cuing provided by bold or capital printing, and a post-test referring to both cued and noncued sections. SQ3R instructions were again given, but an additional variable of pretest condition was incorporated in the experiment. The pretest conditions complicated the results, but overall the results were interpreted as indicating that bold was a better format for cuing than capitals. One result which deserves mention is that in this experiment the readers given cued bold material did not perform less well than the controls on the post-test of noncued information: it did not appear that, for this group at least, the advantages of cuing on tests of cued material were bought at the expense of a decline in performance on a test of noncued material.

This literature on cuing indicates that although some negative findings have been reported there is considerable evidence that typographic cuing can benefit scores on a post-test, and that the effect has been demonstrated most frequently with immediate post-tests. There are numerous issues arising from this literature which might be considered more deeply, but two will be selected as these formed the basis for the experiments to be described.

What should be Cued?

There has been a marked lack of agreement about what material should be cued in prose. The earlier studies (Dearborn et al., 1951; Klare at al., 1955) cued single words, while more recent work has cued statements or sentences (Crouse & Idstein, 1972; Fowler & Barker, 1974). In some cases a restriction of one sentence per paragraph has been applied (Rickards & August, 1975), but many reports are vague about how the cued material is distributed within the passage. In some cases it is not clear what proportion of the total is cued, nor is it evident how it was decided which sections should be cued. If the intention is to cue the most important sections ("core" rather than "enrichment content" in Hershberger and Terry's terminology), one is faced with the problem of identifying the core content. The usual practice appears to have been for the research-worker to use his own judgement to distinguish core from enrichment content.

One immediate objection which demands comment is the argument that "core content" will vary for each individual reader, depending upon his familiarity with the text material. For the novice, a large amount of the text will be new and important; but for the expert, so much of the content and underlying concepts will be known that there will be only a small quantity of core material. One can accept these observations, but deny the conclusion that cuing of core content is thereby vitiated. First, authors write with a target-audience in mind, and attempt to moderate the complexity of their writing according to the expected features of this audience. Similarly, one should in principle be able to cue the material for a particular target-audience. The second counter-argument is that a cuing system which helps the novice will not necessarily obstruct the expert: it could still help him locate sections of the content and portray its structure. (One may doubt whether the converse is true, whether a cuing system for the expert would not obstruct the novice.)

A number of reports hint at the difficulties underlying the discrimination of core from enrichment content. Fowler and Barker (1974) had one condition in which subjects highlighted their own choice of content and they comment upon the large within-group variance that resulted. The amount of material highlighted varied from 4.2 to 32.1%. Rickards and August (1975) report that subjects instructed to underline sentences of high structural importance identified sentences which were significantly lower in importance than those underlined by Rickards and August, on the basis of normative ratings obtained from an independent sample of 43 subjects. Coles and Foster (1975), Bower (1976) and Meyer and McConkie (1973) all obtained ratings of the importance of sentences in prose passages but do not report variability data clearly.

A related issue concerns the amount of material that should be cued. It might be thought that if one could obtain reliable identification of the core content of a passage, this would determine what proportion of the total should be cued, since one could simply cue the core content. But this does not resolve the issue, since it is necessary to separate the two factors of core-versus-enrichment content and relative proportion of the cued material. Texts vary in the density of core content, some having more elaboration of the central issues than others. In a highly dense text, a large proportion may be rated as core. One could then have a situation in which the majority of the text would be cued; one might then obtain a kind of figure-ground reversal, so that the uncued material would be more visually distinctive and tend to attract attention. Such an effect would be contrary to the perceptual basis of visual cuing.

So far, there would seem to have been little consideration of this problem. Crouse and Idstein (1972) found underlining to be ineffective when the answers to 22 questions on a 210-word text were underlined, but beneficial when the answers to 30 questions in a 6,000-word text were underlined. Their argument that density of cued material will influence its effect is expressed as follows: "With fewer output items relative to the amount of text...encoding cues seem more likely to shift the subjects' effective study time to encoding information required by output that was not also encoded in the control condition." Although we may not disagree with such a view, it clearly leaves unanswered the basic questions of whether there is an optimal proportion of text material that should be cued, and whether this proportion should be measured relative to words or (as would seem more likely) relative to elements of thematic content.

Since the amount of cued material is not always specified, and is measured in different ways, the literature is unhelpful. Klare et al. (1975) underlined 199 and 129 words in their two experimental versions of a 1,206-word text. Cashen and Leicht (1970) underlined five statements from journal offprints of unspecified length. Kulhavy (1972) underlined 36 "testable units" from a 2,305-word text and had a criterion test of 72 units. Fowler and Barker (1974) highlighted 20% of their 8,000-word texts (Experiment 1). Rickards and August (1975) underlined 16 sentences out of 80. Foster and Coles (1977) cued 28 of 61 statements. (A misprint in the paper incorrectly states that 10 statements were cued.)

How should Comprehension be Tested?
The problem of measuring reading performance is fundamental to all reading research. As with any psychometric test, the aim is to obtain a valid and reliable measure. The controversy, summarised by Carroll (1972), is too complex to detail here, but broadly one can distinguish between measures by the way they attempt to assess comprehension (a validity question). There has been a trend to look for measures with high inter-judge reliability (such as multiple-choice tests).

All of the cuing experiments discussed above, with the exception of Rickards and August (1975), used some kind of multiple-choice or completion test. These tests were usually created for the particular experimental materials, and details are often sparse. The validity of such tests has been queried by Anderson (1972), who argues that a verbatim test item containing the same language included in the original instructional prose is not an adequate test of comprehension because "such a question can be answered by matching its elements with the surface orthographic or phonological features of the original communication." If one accepts Anderson's argument, it follows that many of the cuing experiments have used inadequate comprehension tests.

Anderson recommends recognition tests based on paraphrases. Carver (1975) was unable to devise such a test for a 100-word passage and suggests that the procedure may only be applicable to single sentences. Felker and Dapra (1975), on the other hand, report a successful attempt to apply Anderson's recommendations. We are trying to develop paraphrase tests for the text being used in our present experiments.

Rickards and August (1975) used a free-recall procedure, in which subjects were asked immediately after testing to recall as much as possible about the 80-sentence passage they had read. Since free recall is often what a reader is required to do in normal reading situations, this technique possesses high face validity and has been used in many recent studies of prose recall (Thorndyke, 1977; Meyer & McConkie, 1973; Mandler & Johnson, 1977).

Introduction to the Experiments

These considerations have prompted the following experiments. One is concerned with obtaining data on judgements of core content in a lengthy text, and the other attempts to assess the value of cuing using a free recall procedure.

Both experiments used an extract, approximately 3,400 words in length (172 sentences), from an introductory text on psychology. The extract discussed the difference between formal and informal psychology, the justification for basic as opposed to applied research, and the potential political threat posed by a successful psychology.

The text was prepared using a word processing computer phototypesetting system, and text material was formatted by the research software of my colleague Gordon Dixon. This software contains a number of unique features including an option by which the user may define which characters may end a line, and also attach to the alternative characters a hierarchy of precedence weightings. Line endings are additionally associated with discretionary hyphens which have their own precedence values. When text is transformed to an output format it may create and access macros, use logical hyphenation, construct multiple columns, format tabulations, switch to justification, instruct the system to accept part of the input text as is, or enter a variety of indentation phases.

The text was punched onto paper tape using a full character-set typewriter as input to an ICL 1906A computer, which transformed the text into two output driver-tapes. One of these could be used to produce a typewriter listing, the other drove an Addressograph-Multigraph AM725 phototypesetter. The output from the typesetter was a right-reading bromide substrate of 9pt Times. For the first experiment, a typewriter listing of the text was prepared and copies were circulated to the subjects.

Experiment 1

Twenty-six psychology students and lecturers were provided with a copy of the text and the following instructions: "I would like you to read through the whole passage, and then go through it again, underlining those sentencese which you feel are the most important ones for the passage as a whole. In other words, I would like you to underline those sentences which you think contain the key ideas that the author is trying to put over." Sentences were taken as the unit for identification, as our previous experiments using "idea-units" had led to some anomalies, with cuing being distributed within a sentence. Putting visual cues out of alignment with grammatical ones, we now feel, may disrupt semantic processing.

There were two conditions. In condition A, subjects were told not to underline more than 16 sentences, in condition B they were told not to underline more than eight. Subjects were assigned to conditions at random, with the restriction that three lecturers appeared in each group. The results of this experiment are contained in Table 1. In condition A, the 213 selections made were distributed across 80 sentences, with only nine sentences being selected by six or more judges. Condition B shows a similar pattern: the 102 selections were distributed over 52 sentences and only two were selected by six or more judges. In the two 2 conditions, 37 (17.4%) and 27 (26.5%) of the sentences selected were selected by only one judge. These data demonstrate the lack of agreement concerning key sentences even when the judges have a specified maximum number of selections to make. (Replications with shorter selections from the text yielded similar data.)

Two conclusions may be drawn: a) findings such as these pose considerable problems when an attempt is made to identify those sections of the text which should be cued, and b) the demonstrable lack of agreement among readers, given an unlimited time to identify the key sections, reinforces the suggestion that an external (typographic) aid to such identification may aid the reader who is trying to locate the key areas of a lengthy text in a restricted reading period. The problem raised by these data concerned the cuing that should be incorporated in the text for the second experiment. This was a study of the effects of cuing a text, using a delayed free-recall test as the measure of comprehension.

Procedure
Experiment 2

The "relevant-cue" version of the text was to contain 10% cuing, measured in terms of number of sentences. The frequencies of selection by the two groups of subjects from Experiment 1 were combined, and the 16 sentences selected by six or more subjects were chosen as the cued material. (These sentences are marked * in Table 1.) Due to a keying error, sentence 127 was also cued. A second "random-cue" version was also prepared; in this format cued sentences were selected by random number tables. Three of the randomly selected sentences (numbers 5, 158, and 146) also appeared cued in the relevant cue format. A third control version contained no cuing other than the headlines from the original text.

Because of administrative production difficulties, the cued material was printed in capitals. It has now been possible to obtain printings with the cued material set in bold, and these will be used in subsequent studies since there is evidence that bold is a better cuing format than capitals.

The three versions of the text were printed by the AMF photosetter in 9 and 10-point Times. The bromide outputs were then reproduced and stapled into five-page booklets (A4 size), printed both sides.

The experiment was performed in a single-group setting. Subjects were assigned at random to the three format conditions: relevant cue, random cue, control.

An estimate of reading speed was obtained by asking subjects to circle the last word they were reading at the end of the permitted 15 minutes, or to write "finished" if they had read the whole passage. Subjects were allowed to make notes on the text pages, if they wished. The texts were collected and one hour later (during which they listened to a lecture on psychometrics)

Table 1. Results of Experiment 1. Frequency with which Each Sentence was Identified as a Key Sentence for Conditions A and B.

Sentence	A	B	Sentence	A	B	Sentence	A	B
*1	6	4	53	3	1	117	1	1
4	2	3	*56	5	3	*120	6	3
*5	8	2	57	1	1	121	1	0
9	0	1	61	1	0	122	2	0
12	1	3	66	4	0	124	1	0
13	0	1	67	3	0	126	3	2
14	1	0	69	2	2	128	2	0
15	3	1	73	1	0	*129	5	3
17	1	0	74	1	0	*130	7	0
19	1	0	75	1	2	*131	4	3
21	1	1	76	2	2	132	0	1
22	1	1				*133	6	6
23	1	1	79	2	0	134	1	0
24	1	1	81	1	0	135	1	0
26	2	0	82	1	0	*138	6	2
27	1	0	86	0	1	*146	5	2
28	1	1	91	3	2	154	2	0
*30	12	11	93	3	0	155	4	1
31	0	1	94	3	0	156	3	0
32	3	0	*96	5	2	*161	4	2
33	1	1	97	1	4	*162	7	4
34	1	0	98	5	0	163	1	1
35	1	0	100	3	1	164	2	1
36	1	0	101	3	1	*165	8	2
39	1	0	102	1	0	168	3	0
40	1	0	104	2	1	169	4	1
41	1	0	106	0	2	*170	5	1
42	1	0	109	0	2	171	4	0
43	1	1	114	0	1	172	1	0
44	1	1	115	0	1			
50	1	0	116	0	2			

Maximum possible for each condition is 13.

____ Indicates a paragraph.

* Indicates that the sentence was cued in the Relevant Cue condition of Experiment 2.

subjects were asked to summarise as fully as possible the text they had read. Subjects were a group of trainee career officers whose ages varied from 21 to the mid-40's.

Results
Protocols were scored for the number of idea-units reproduced. Verbatim recall was rare, except for the text sub-headings. The response sheets from three subjects who recalled none of the core or enrichment content were discarded, leaving n = 8 for the control and relevant cue groups, n = 11 for the random cue group.

Estimates of reading speed, in terms of mean number of completed sentences read, were 146.4, 153.9, and 151.0 for the control, relevant cue, and random cue groups respectively. The number of subjects in each group reporting that they had read the complete text were 3, 4, and 4 respectively. Thus there was no evidence that cuing retarded reading.

Three scores were obtained for each subject: amount of core material recalled, amount of enrichment material recalled, and number of headlines reproduced. Table 2 shows the means for each group. Analyses of variance were performed on the core and enrichment scores. For enrichment content, $F = 0.60$, and for core content, $F(2,24) = 3.52$, $p < 0.05$). On a one-tailed test, the mean core score for the relevant cue group was superior to the mean scores of the control and random cue groups, which did not differ from each other.

Discussion
The results of this experiment provide further support for the hypothesis that typographic cuing can facilitate effective reading, insofar as this is identified with recall of core content. The present data indicate that the benefits of cuing can be observed with a delayed recall test (although it is admitted that the delay was only one hour), using a free-recall procedure. The greater proximity of these conditions to an extra-experimental study situation than has been the case in many previous experiments gives some grounds for believing that typographic cuing may have a general applicability in text as in more specific search-situations. To establish the replicability of these results, further experiments using the preferable bold type format are being planned.

The only comparable study is that of Rickards and August (1975), who used an immediate post-test and underlined material. They failed to observe that cuing facilitated recall of core content. There appear to be three main differences which may account for the discrepant outcomes between their experiment and the present one. First, they cued one sentence per paragraph, a procedure which may not reflect the underlying structure of a text; second, the relative effects of cuing may increase with time; third, their cuing mode (underlining) may have so disrupted reading as to militate against any positive effects being found. Clearly, further investigation is necessary to decide between these possibilities.

Contrary to our earlier studies, cuing with a free-recall procedure is apparently effective even when subjects are not requested to use the SQ3R reading strategy. Thus, there now seems to be considerable evidence that cuing can

Table 2. Results of Experiment 2.

Recall	Format		
	Relevant cue	Random cue	Control
Core	3.13	1.18	1.63
Enrichment	5.13	4.82	7.13
Headlines	1.00	0.91	1.50

promote effective reading under many conditions. As Foster and Coles (1977) pointed out, the poor cuing formats used in many of the experiments reported suggests that cuing may be more beneficial than the literature suggests.

Mention should be made of the possible influence of subjects' reading strategy upon the effects of cuing, and the probable need to train subjects to use cuing. Coles and Foster (1975) found that with a brief study time and immediate post-test, cuing only exerted a measurable influence upon performance when subjects were instructed to use the SQ3R (i.e., an active search) reading mode. The use of cuing in more strictly search-like situations, discussed in the introduction, prompts the suggestion that is likely to be most useful when text is also read so as to include a search operation. Many reading development courses attempt to teach variability in reading behaviour complementary to the variations in text content. Not only may cuing be most effective when search skills are applied to reading, but it could be that text cuing helps the reader to learn such skills by showing him when he should make the transition from one type of reading behaviour to another.

General Discussion

Cuing may be related to the contemporary interest in the semantic structure of prose. Psycholinguistic research using the concepts of transformational grammar has enjoyed considerable popularity over the last 20 years, but the application of these concepts and techniques to passages of prose is a comparatively recent development (Thorndyke, 1977; Mandler & Johnson, 1977). Simple, short stories have been the most frequent materials to which these grammars have been applied. Meyer and McConkie's (1973) paper reports an attempt to establish the semantic structure of scientific prose, but the longest passage was only 502 words. It is likely that as these techniques for identifying text structure become more sophisticated it will be possible to apply them to passages closer in length to a normal reading assignment. Potentially they would seem to have important implications for visual cuing. First, they will make possible the identification of key sections of the text with greater reliability. Second, answers might be provided to the question: How much cuing is optimal? If, as one may expect, cuing needs to be related to text density, more precise measures of this factor, applicable to any expository text, need to be obtained.

A major drawback to cuing research is that it is only loosely related to models of reading comprehension. It can be seen as a technique for influencing the mathemagenic behaviour which has been the subject of Rothkopf's research.

Rothkopf (1972) observed that, in his approach to learning from text, "What is being claimed is that the analysis of the structure of texts is not the most important source of prediction about learning. The analysis of the subjects' activities while he is exposed to the text is certainly at least as important." He summarises the research on mathemagenic behaviour: "The main tenor of the findings has been that manipulation, such as presenting questions, can produce general learning effects, i.e., that questions affect the acquisition of information other than that narrowly required to answer the adjunct questions."

Seen in the context of the mathemagenic hypothesis, typographic cuing may be a more economical form of influencing mathemagenic behaviour than the adjunct questions normally employed. If cuing operates by directing attention and prompting the subject to vary his reading style according to the level of content, then its effects can be seen as supporting the view, underlying Rothkopf's work, that effective reading depends upon an active, involved reading style.

Freedle and Carroll (1972) give the following summary of the reading process: "As we read, then, our knowledge structure (Image) is advanced by the organization of the discourse into paragraphs, topic sentences, and explanatory sentences....First, we grasp, and presumably entertain a belief of, the essential point that is asserted by the topic sentence. Then we go on to examine the sequence of explanatory sentences...." The rationale for typographic cuing in text rests upon a fundamental objection to Freedle and Carroll's model. The first stage is not grasping the essential point of the topic sentence; the first stage is identifying which sentence is the topic sentence.

I thank David Legge for permission to use material from his book "An Introduction to Psychological Science," and G. Dixon of the Institute of Advanced Studies, Manchester Polytechnic, for assistance with the computer typesetting of the text material.

REFERENCES

Anderson, R.C. How to construct achievement test to assess comprehension. Review of Educational Research, 1972, 42, 145-170.

Bower, G.H. Experiments on story understanding and recall. Quarterly Journal of Experimental Psychology, 1976, 28, 511-534.

Carroll, J.B. Defining language comprehension: Some speculations. In J.B. Carroll & R.O. Freedle (Eds.), Language comprehension and the acquisition of knowledge. Washington, DC: Winston, 1972.

Carver, R.P. Comparing the reading-storage test to the paraphrase test as measures of the primary effect in prose reading. Journal of Educational Psychology, 1975, 67, 274-284.

Cashen, V.M., & Leicht, K.L. Role of the isolation effect in a formal educational setting. Journal of Educational Psychology, 1970, 61, 484-486.

Christiansen, C.M., & Stordahl, K.E. The effect of organizational aids on comprehension and retention. Journal of Educational Psychology, 1955, 46, 65-74.

Coles, P., & Foster, J.J. Typographic cuing as an aid to learning from typewritten text. Programmed Learning and Educational Technology, 1975, 12, 102-108.

Crouse, J.H., & Idstein, P. Effects of encoding cues on prose learning. Journal of Educational Psychology, 1972, 63, 309-313.

Dearborn, W.F., Johnson, P.W., & Carmichael, L. Improving the readability of type-written manuscripts. Proceedings of the National Academy of Sciences, 1951, 37, 670-672.

Dennis, I. The design and experimental testing of a hospital drug labelling system. Programmed Learning and Educational Technology, 1975, 12, 88-94.

Felker, D.B., & Dapra, R.A. Effects of question type and question placement on problem-solving ability from prose material. Journal of Educational Psychology, 1975, 67, 380-384.

Foster, J.J., & Coles, P. An experimental study of typographic cuing in printed text. Ergonomics, 1977, 20, 57-66.

Fowler, R.L., & Barker, A.S. Effectiveness of highlighting for retention of text material. Journal of Applied Psychology, 1974, 59, 358-364.

Freedle, R.O., & Carroll, J.B. Language comprehension and the acquisition of knowledge: Some reflections. In J.B. Carroll and R.O. Freedle (Eds.), Language comprehension and the acquisition of knowledge. Washington, DC: Winston, 1972.

Hartley, J., & Burnhill, P. Explorations in space: A critique of the typography of BPS publications. Bulletin of the British Psychological Society, 1976, 29, 97-107.

Hershberger, W. Self-evaluational responding and typographical cuing. Journal of Educational Psychology, 1964, 55, 288-296.

Hershberger, W.A., & Terry, D.F. Typographical cuing in conventional and programmed texts. Journal of Applied Psychology, 1965, 49, 55-60.

Klare, G., Mabry, J.E., & Gustafson, L.M. Relationship of patterning (underlining) to immediate retention and to acceptability of technical material. Journal of Applied Psychology, 1955, 39, 40-42.

Kulhavy, R.W. Effects of embedding orienting stimuli in a prose passage. Psychonomic Science, 1972, 28, 213-214.

Mandler, J.M., & Johnson, N.S. Remembrance of things parsed: Story structure and recall. Cognitive Psychology, 1977, 9, 111-151.

Marks, M.B. Improve reading through better format. Journal of Educational Research, 1966, 60, 147-151.

Meyer, B.J.F., & McConkie, G.W. What is recalled after hearing a passage? Journal of Educational Psychology, 1973, 65, 109-117.

Phillips, R.J. Making maps easy to read: A summary of research. (This volume.)

Poulton, E.C. Searching for newspaper headlines printed in capitals or lower-case letters. Journal of Applied Psychology, 1967, 51, 417-425.

Rickards, J.P., & August G.J. Generative underlining strategies in prose recall. Journal of Educational Psychology, 1975, 67, 860-865.

Rothkopf, E.Z. Structural text features and the control of processes in learning from written materials. In J.B. Carroll & R.O. Freedle (Eds.), Language comprehension and the acquisition of knowledge. Washington, DC: Winston, 1972.

Spencer, H., Reynolds, L., & Coe, B. Typographic coding in lists and bibliographies. Applied Ergonomics, 1974, 5, 136-141.

Spencer, H., Reynolds, L., & Coe, B. Spatial and typographic coding within bibliographical entries. Programmed Learning and Educational Technology, 1975, 12, 95-101.

Thorndyke, P.W. Cognitive structures in comprehension and memory of narrative discourse. Cognitive Psychology, 1977, 9, 77-110.

Wright, P., & Fox, K. Presenting information in tables. Applied Ergonomics, 1970, 1, 234-242.

Relations between the Qualifications of Different Groups of Readers and Different Aspects of Text

Mogens Jansen

This paper surveys the several factors that contribute to the readability of a given text -- contents, linguistic appearance, and visual appearance. The reader's background and surroundings are also very important: an individual "reads, among other things, with his entire past".

Three (perhaps four) groups of readers are described in relation to the books they read, and their method of reading: rebus-readers, transition-readers, contents-readers, and the reading retarded.

Statistics are presented which indicate how children's and adults' use of libraries has developed during recent years, and an analysis is made of the types of books most frequently borrowed by children.

A survey of reading development, using the above criteria of evaluation (contents, linguistic appearance, and visual appearance), is presented and related to the groups of readers mentioned. Finally, some conceivable consequences of these observations are suggested.

General Survey

The road from printed type to a well-functioning reading ability might be schematically suggested as in Figure 1. It must be strongly emphasized that surroundings, directly and indirectly influence the individual reader's acquisition of texts. It is, of course, essential to take an interest in the basic visual processes; it is just as necessary to be interested in the entirety in which they function.

The road begins at the text, where certain questions must be asked: Is the language English or Dutch? And, if it is Dutch, what kind of Dutch? What are the contents of the text? What is the typography like? And,

incidentally, how is the linguistic presentation? Are there any illustrations?
What is the entire visual appearance? What is the reader's attitude to the
text? Visual perception, the second step, is what is seen by the eye. Here,
the interaction between the appearance of the text and the visual "entry"
may be observed.

In the third stage, brain processing, how does the brain (or perhaps better,
the person) process the stimuli received? This processing includes, for
instance, earlier experience, the intellectual capacity of the individual, and
linguistic factors. Within this field substantial differences in individual ability can be observed. Readers' emotional characteristics also contribute to
individual differences. Such differences are often quite pronounced, especially
during the first years of reading.

The fourth stage concerns the whole of the reading person. An individual
"reads with his entire past" -- this, as well as the immediate need, will contribute to the direction of the text acquisition. It also means that the entire
surroundings of the individual influence reading. Here surroundings mean
not only books, papers, and magazines, but also that part of the reader's surroundings not directly related to the printed texts. Naturally, libraries,
booksellers, and school play a special part in this connection, but home and
family, work and friends -- in other words the entire surrounding world --
are also important facts.

Groups of Readers Characterized by Choice of Books
In a series of research projects using the classroom observation method,
interviews, and analyses of educational materials, experienced teachers acted
as observers in grades one to seven (seven to fourteen year-old students).
(Danish grades are used throughout. As to students' ages, see Figure 2.)
During subsequent discussions, several teachers made the following
observation.

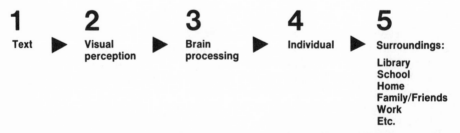

Figure 1. The road from printed type to a well-functioning reading ability,
schematically suggested.

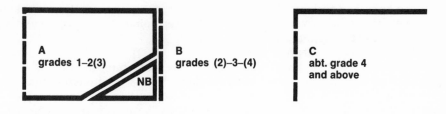

NB = reading retarded students

Student's age:

Grade	Age
1	7–8
2	8–9
3	9–10
4	10–11
above 4	11–16

Figure 2. Age and grade characteristics of students studied.

The students' reading could not possibly be described in exactly the same way in grades one through seven. At different grade levels there were distinct differences as to a) which books were accepted, b) which books were read, and c) how these books were read.

In grade two, of course, it was important whether the book was a comic strip or a primer, or whether it was an easy reader or a difficult professional book. However, when a, b, and c were related to each individual student, it was often noticed that comic strips were accepted in grade two but not read! The easy primer was barely accepted, but was read occasionally. However, this happened mostly when the student had no easy access to other reading material to which he or she was equal. The difficult professional books were not chosen, but the easy reader was chosen -- and read.

If one is interested in knowing whether library books are accepted and actually read -- not only borrowed -- it is not sufficient to characterize books by their placement within the library, nor by their appearance. It appears that factors such as the thickness of the books, the illustrations, the connection between text and pictures, and the presentation of the text, affected which texts were accepted and were actually read. But this still leaves the question, How were these texts read?

Very briefly it might be said that the books read by students at this level were characterized by the following factors:
1) the subject was of no particular importance (this caused much discussion, since contents are rarely unimportant to any reader; however, to these students the subject was definitely a secondary factor);
2) the pictures were often the decisive factor;

3) the book had to look like a book, and yet it must be easily read. However, if the book were actually read after being chosen, the deciding
   factors often appeared to be;
4) typography, layout, and so forth.

On several occasions it was obvious that the more familiar the visual
appearance of a book, the more easily readable it was for the students.
The following provides an example. In connection with a research project,
Icelandic students were observed when reading. These students had been
accustomed to Icelandic primers, which are relatively difficult, and they
often chose other books which looked like the ordinary Icelandic ones -- even
though these were objectively more difficult than other available books (Jansen, 1975). Thus what is considered easy may depend to some extent on
whether it looks familiar.

In addition, it looks as if at this level the success of the students' reading
was proportionate to the degree of interaction between pictures and text.
The picture must recount the text; it must, so to speak, contribute to "solving
the text of the book."

Incidentally, the books should also be linguistically comprehensible in
practice. This would rarely create problems in Denmark, since at this early
stage the students are, as a whole, confronted with (or choose for themselves)
only books which, at least to a certain degree, are adapted for them.

The Reading Retarded

More or less analogous factors manifested themselves in the reading retarded
group, even though they were much older. However, these students would
often choose "a thick book," maybe because it dealt with an interesting subject, or almost always as a matter of prestige. Here a massive pressure from
the surrounding world manifested itself, even in those cases where it was
not directly formulated or noticed by anyone but the reading retarded student. After having chosen "a big difficult book," these students would often
choose another, which they would be able to read.

Students Aged Nine to Eleven

However, by the age of nine, students appeared to have other criteria for
their choice of books. For them, the basic point was an interest in the
material, but it was also essential that the material must be readable as well.

It also appeared that at this level the readability of books was often dependent on the linguistic appearance. Admittedly, those writers producing easy
books, but in a patronizingly childish way, were rejected; but otherwise it
appeared that if the linguistic appearance was comprehensible in relation
to the subject, the books were accepted.

The professional books were readable only if unknown or only partly known
concepts were presented in a comprehensible way. And it was particularly
true of the professional books that the better the pictures functioned as a
support of the text, the more generally the books were accepted. At this
level it was not enough for the pictures to be merely eye-catching. Incidentally, it might be observed that the children now showed greater interest
in books with professionally marked contents -- a fact that was pointed out
by many teachers and librarians during the interviews.

Older Students

The primary criterion for the older students' choice of books was the individual student's interest in the book's subject and contents. It might as well be said that the contents of the book (interacting with the interest of the reader) decided which books were chosen.

A closer look at the question of whether these books were actually read indicated the presence of the same factors -- the contents of the text and the interest of the reader. Moreover, the factors mentioned in connection with the preceding level also played a part, although to varying degrees for different students.

Reading Characteristics of the Different Groups

Using the above observations made by teachers, it became possible to divide with great certainty the students into three different groups according to their reading habits.

Group A are rebus-readers. This group consists of students in the first few grades and reading retarded students. Their reading habits differ from the reading habits of students at other levels. Observation of these students' eye movements indicated that they made many regressions both along the lines and up the pages. This was so pronounced that it can be readily observed by the moderately experienced teacher. The teacher can also easily notice the quiet, oral reading of these students, their mumbling, lip movements, use of index finger, and so on.

These students' relation to what they read appears to differ from that of other pupils in other ways as well. If the rebus-readers were asked (after actually having read a text) what the contents were, they would have only a vague impression. And if they did know what the text contained, it would generally have been possible to observe them reading each part of the text at least a couple of times prior to the question. First the rebus-readers decipher the text (solve the rebus), then they work out the contents of the text, and finally they interpret it.

Unless confronted with reading matter that was very difficult, the reading behaviour of the older students -- contents-readers (Group C) -- could not be equated with that of rebus-readers. It was obvious that they had mastered the technique of reading so well that it had became a tool that allowed them to concentrate on the contents.

In some cases the oldest students were also capable of using different reading techniques, as when given assignments calling for skimming or scanning. Those who were unable to do so spontaneously could learn to rather easily, whereas making rebus-readers practice specific techniques would almost ruin their limited reading ability.

As students of many grades were observed, a third group of readers gradually emerged -- transition-readers. This group (B) seemed to be clearly situated somewhere between rebus-readers and contents-readers.

The reading skills of these students were markedly diminished when they read material from difficult professional fields. Considering their ability to read ordinary fictional texts, it was more difficult for them to read professional texts than it objectively "ought" to have been. It was also evident that a typography that was strange to these students damaged their reading ability.

There were exceptions to the above, but on the whole it appeared that it was possible to divide the groups of students according to their method of reading (see Figure 3).

In this connection, a series of observations on completely different groups of readers should be mentioned. In Denmark advanced reading instruction was introduced very pointedly during the 1960's by courses on the educational radio and television, especially for adults. This kind of instruction is now being integrated in to the oldest grades of elementary school (Jacobsen, 1978). Observation of this type of advanced methodical reading instruction for intelligent, skilled readers led to the following discoveries.

The more these students were exposed to pressure in concrete situations of training, the more their choice of books would be similar to that of the transition-readers. In stress situations, these extremely able and experienced readers would choose the same kind of books as many students in grade four. It must be emphasized that, in general, these students were fully educated at universities; they were doctors, librarians, teachers, and the like. Therefore, it is obvious that in stress situations an individual's reading level will decline.

These observations might be supplemented in various ways. For instance, it might be checked how many pages each individual student reads per week. See Figure 5 for the number of pages read weekly by students in the various grades.

What Did the Tests Show?

What is fascinating is that an extensive testing of large groups of students indicated an analogous reading development (Hansen & Søegård, 1977). A look at the latest statement (on a national basis) comparing students' present reading ability with that of 20-30 years ago, unquestionably indicates the same development. This, by the way, means that after six or seven years of schooling there are more good readers than previously; at the same time, however, there is now a small group that is lagging behind.

"It has been ascertained that generally students become just as competent in Danish, the mother tongue, during the first seven school years, as did students 10 or 20 years ago. But it can also be seen that a small group of

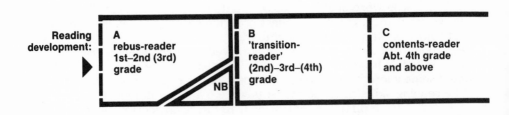

NB = reading retarded students

Figure 3. A comparison with quite a different group of readers.

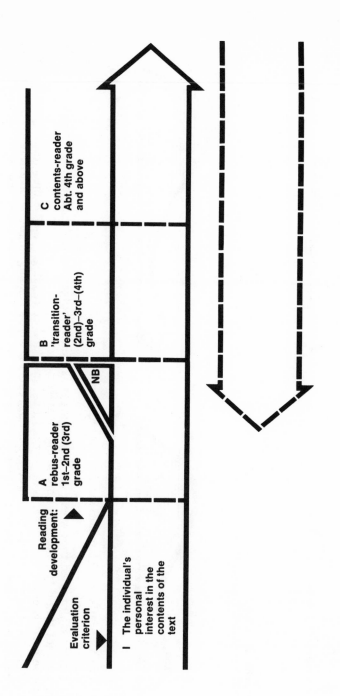

NB = reading retarded students

Figure 4. Some characteristics of evaluation.

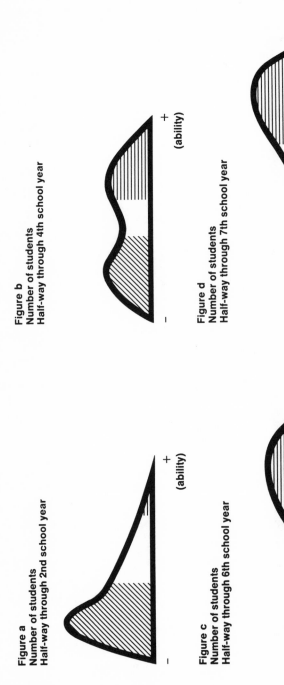

Figure a
Number of students
Half-way through 2nd school year

(ability)

Figure b
Number of students
Half-way through 4th school year

(ability)

Figure c
Number of students
Half-way through 6th school year

(ability)

Figure d
Number of students
Half-way through 7th school year

(ability)

Figure 5. Statistical distributions that create queries.

It is often maintained that whenever a grouping is as 'double-bulged' as is the case in this figure, it may be due to the fact that different things are being measured. Maybe what is being measured, is in fact not the same kind of 'reading.' Maybe these descriptions of reading courses could be related to the three groups of readers, whose reading might be characterized very roughly as three different kinds of reading? Does the diagonally hatched section represent the rebus-readers (Or: registration of rebus-reading), whereas the horizontally hatched section represents the contents-readers (registration of contents-reading)?

students fell behind in relation to fellow students ...(especially in spelling)...,
and that this group is larger than before. However, these analyses also show
that the best students are better than ever before, as well in reading as in
spelling" (Jansen & Glæsel, 1977).

The reason for more students falling behind might be that: "there are
fewer lessons in reading than 10 years ago" -- "today there are many more
handicapped students integrated in the normal classes than 10-20 years ago"
-- "many fewer students fail and are forced to repeat courses" (as a matter
of fact 30 years ago up to 30% failed once between grades two and seven
whereas today the figure is 2-3%) -- and perhaps "today most parents probably
have less time to help their children with their homework."

From this point of view, it is also evident that up through the grades it
is possible to find different groups of readers among the students. Do those
students who drop behind remain rebus-readers? And does the group which
makes early progress comprise the students who are already contents-readers?

How Much is Read?
In practice, a well-stocked school library is available at all Danish schools.
The national coverage of children's libraries is good, and bookmobiles have
become an integrated part of the itinerant library work.

It should also be added that within the instruction in Danish, especially
in grades two to five, a great deal of time is set aside for the students' individual reading. Such books probably make up about one-third of the library
lendings, although this cannot be ascertained through public statistics on
lending. Lending of handbooks is scarcely represented in Figure 6, and professional books are not included at all, although they appear in great numbers
at school. From Figure 6 which shows lendings from the public libraries to
adults and children during an 18-year period, it appears that a large increase
of book-lending has taken place (Bibliotekstilsynet, 1976).

The population of Denmark is about 5 million, and Danish children learn
to read relatively late (rarely before the age of eight). Thus, the group of
borrowers who are children must be reduced to the nine to sixteen year-olds,
at which time their reading material becomes adult literature (Jansen, 1973).
In 1960, of the 5 million inhabitants in Denmark, a million were children.
They borrowed a little more than 10 million books from the libraries, which
is more than twenty books a year per child (Elberling & Bruhn, 1967)! Today,
the same number of students take out about 50 million books -- equal to 100
books a year per student (and they still read most of the books).

The reading of the adults is shown by the dotted line. This does not
include books purchased from booksellers and bookclubs (Jansen, 1977). A
partial repetition of the study on spare-time habits made by the Danish
National Institute of Social Research in 1964, carried through in 1975, revealed
the following facts. In 1964, 27% of the persons asked were reading a book,
in 1974 the figure was 40%. In 1964, 25% used the libraries, in 1975, 37%.
The study covers the adult population only. In 1964 the age limit (downwards)
was 15 years; in 1975 it was 16 years.

Today Danish children read more than any previous group of children or
adults in the history of the nation. Children take out more books from the
libraries than adults do; and the reading ability is actually increasing. Books
are thinner than before, and a somewhat greater number of large comic strip

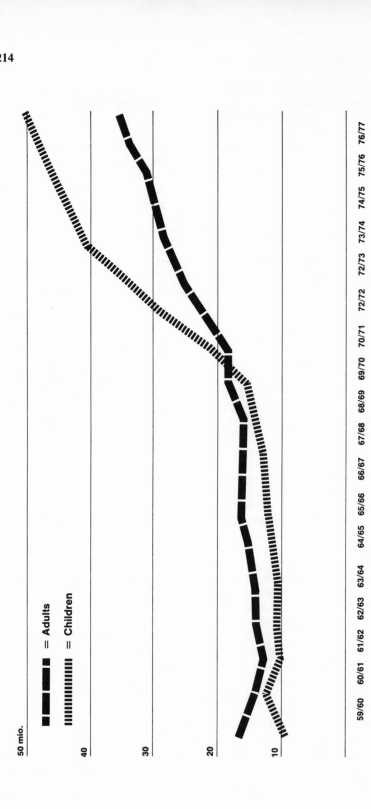

50 mio.

■ = Adults

▥ = Children

40

30

20

10

59/60 60/61 61/62 62/63 63/64 64/65 65/66 66/67 67/68 68/69 69/70 70/71 72/72 72/73 73/74 74/75 75/76 76/77

The total population, practically constant throughout the period. There is an extremely small increase in the number of children during the first 3 years after which the number of children is constant.

Figure 6. Lending of books from public libraries during the period 1959-1977.

books form part of the lendings. However, such factors alone do not explain the great increase in lendings.

The use of books at school and at home is becoming more professional. Handbooks are frequently used. The professional literature is advancing. Fiction is also read.

Until about 20 years ago it was generally known that a relatively few "bookworms" were responsible for most books borrowed from the Danish children's libraries. Those mass readers were boys as well as girls (more girls than boys), but were numerically few -- were they on the whole contents-readers?

Since then a gradual increase of the "average reader" group has taken place, and this group appears to comprise, as before, both girls and boys. The last decade has been characterized by a very strong increase of quite new groups of readers among children. These groups of "new readers" some-times seem to include a relatively large number of boys. They very often have a non-fiction outlook and form more consistent specialist groups than did the previous mass readers.

Many of the youngest students in elementary school have become more reading-minded than was the case earlier. The mass readers still exist. The readers of the previous middle group have become better readers. But in practice they have developed into "utility" readers. They have become iden-tical with the mass readers.

What Types of Books are Borrowed?

This question has not been thoroughly examined, although a non-systematic inquiry was carried out through visits to school libraries and children's libraries.

Interviews with librarians on library purchases, the use of books, the lending of books to children (and incidentally to adults), and an examination of the shelves of the libraries showed that two special types of books could be designated.

The first group is books that, somewhat unkindly, might be called "librar-ian's delight." They were purchased because they "ought" to be purchased. They represented the "right" opinion, the "right" literary attitude, etcetera, and they were taken out occasionally -- especially by parents accompanying their children or taking out books on behalf of their children. These books seemed to include classical and literarily valuable books (that is, books reviewed or evaluated as such), books of strong social criticism, and fre-quently rather incomprehensible children's books. To put it bluntly, these books appealed less to children than the librarians would have wished.

Another group of books looked much more worn. If these books could be said to display some common features, these would be that they were smaller in size, their linguistic appearance was more easily comprehensible, and they had more illustrations.

Of these books, some were originally written for reading retarded or for students less qualified in reading. In particular the easy readers were taken out relatively frequently.

Are students lazy or indolent? Do they prefer the easy books to the difficult ones? No. If anything, these realities should be related to the

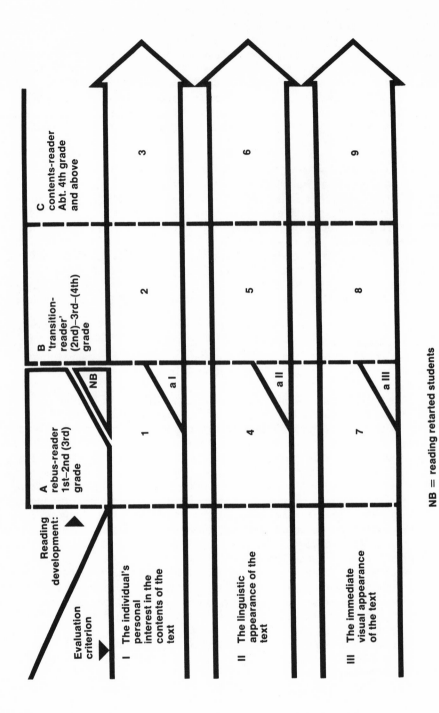

NB = reading retarted students

Figure 7. A survey of reading development related to three criteria of evaluation.

groups of readers mentioned previously, and above all to the B-group (and also to some degree, the C-group).

It is possible to relate the previously described reading development to a number of evaluation criteria applicable to books. Contents of course, is the critical factor. However, linguistic appearance, typography, layout, paper, and so forth, should all be taken into consideration. In Figure 7 the individual reading development is related to the above-mentioned criteria of evaluation.

The observations mentioned in this chapter of, for example, the concrete reading of students related to the three general criteria of evaluation seem to indicate that items 7, 5, and 3, in Figure 7 are essential to understanding the reading materials of the groups of readers concerned.

Considering especially the professional reading in grades three to six (and for some students at higher levels) item 5 should be noted. To the transition-reader the linguistic appearance of the text is absolutely decisive for whether he or she will be able to derive any benefit at all from the material. Many professional texts fail at this point. If the transition-reader cannot cope with the linguistic appearance of the text, his or her comprehension of concepts will fail. The influence of this factor probably reaches far beyond school and educational affairs; much public information obviously pays no attention to such matters.

Item 7 is quite decisive for the rebus-reader's ability to start reading at all. When the student does not realize that $R = r = r = R$, it is difficult to decipher a text! To the rebus-reader the immediate visual appearance of the text, including the typography, is simply the prior condition for his or her ability to work through the text. If the student cannot tell the difference between d and b, he will read "deer" for "beer," and if, for instance, the typography contains italics, where h and b are very much alike, the student will misread the text.

It is obvious that in most cases item 3 is by far the most important. This is the point referred to in all reviews and in general adult evaluation of a text.

Items 2, 4, 6 and 8, if not unessential, are at least far less important than the three items mentioned above. Items 1 and, especially, 9 seem quite secondary in most cases.

To the reading retarded students (in items aI, aII and aIII) all factors are essential -- which indicates how complex their problem is.

Some Conceivable Consequences

On this very slender basis no attempt will be made to draw any conclusions. However, with all possible caution, it might be suggested that if the relations outlined above are realistic, it would be relevant to consider possible consequences for the teaching of reading (and also for the selection of reading material).

It would probably also be advantageous to consider the concept "functional illiteracy" as being similar to the situation of the rebus-reader. The good readers are reliable contents-readers; however, item 7, which indicates that these readers, as well, occasionally function differently (and less well) is surely of importance.

Finally, it should be clear that reading is not learned once and for all;

even weak readers may obtain the ability to read many books, if the linguistic appearance of these books is adapted to the qualifications of their readers.

REFERENCES

Bibliotekstilsynet. Statistiske oplysninger. Folke-og skolebibliotekernes bogbestand, udlån og budgetter. Copenhagen: Bibliotekstilsynet, Beretning 1975-76, 32-37.

Bredsdorff, Aa. Library service to children in Denmark. In IFLA (International Federation of Library Associations and Institutions) Publications 12. Library service to children: An international survey. Munich: K.G. Sauer Verlag, 1978.

Elberling, B.V., & Bruhn, I. læste bøger. Voksnes læsning og biblioteksbenyttelse. 2nd rev. ed. Copenhagen: G.E.C. Gads Forlag, 1967. Danmarks Biblioteksskole.

Hansen, M., & Søegård, A. Læseudvikling og danskundervisning en beskrivelse af et praktisk forsøg med at sammenknytte læseprøveresultater med begynderundervisningen i dansk. Den gule serie. Pædagogiske forskningsrapporter, 5, 2nd ed. 1977.

Jacobsen, B. National television programs in reading instruction. In M. Jansen, B. Jacobsen, & P.E. Jensen (Eds.), The teaching of reading without really any method: An analysis of reading instruction in Denmark. Appendix D. Copenhagen: Munksgaard and New Jersey: Humanities Press, 1978.

Jansen, M. The languages of Denmark. In J. Downing (Ed.), Comparative reading: Cross-national studies of behavior and processes in reading and writing. New York: Macmillan, 1973.

Jansen, M. Aspects of literacy in changing societies. Paper presented at the First Regional European Study Conference on Reading, Beaumont-sur-Oise (Paris), April 1977.

Jansen, M., & Glæsel, B. Hvordan læser og staver eleverne? - en sammenlignende status. Læsepædagogen, 1977, 4, 193-204.

Jansen, M., Jacobsen, B., & Jensen, P.E. The teaching of reading without really any method: An analysis of reading instruction in Denmark. Copenhagen: Munksgaard and New Jersey: Humanities Press, 1978.

De læseretarderede og bibliotekerne. Copenhagen: Undervisningsministeriet (Ministry of Education) Bibliotekstilsynet and Bibleotekscentralen, 1978.

Word Perception and its Role in Reading

Introduction

H. Bouma

Printed text is composed of separate words and words are composed of letters. This seems to be the intuitive basis for the hypothesis that reading words (word recognition) is relevant to reading text and that letter recognition is relevant to word recognition. Since reading is a difficult process to study directly, one may decide to take word recognition or even letter recognition as a research topic instead. If relevance to reading is claimed, one has next to use the acquired insights into letter recognition to arrive at an understanding of word recognition, and use insights into word recognition to arrive at an understanding of reading. Let us trace some of the problems encountered along the way. We can use the notions of the recognition process as developed by Morton, although different views also exist.

Let us start with the recognition of a single letter. For research purposes, we consider explicit recognition as the triggering of an internalized concept of such a letter ("internal letter"), representing perceptual knowledge, by data from the senses representing perceptual information. Knowing that the configuration (shape, size) of a letter can be highly variable, we assume that less variable "features" act as an intermediate, and that combinations of features (feature sets) trigger the internal letter. If necessary, more than one level of features may be assumed (hierarchical structure of features). Since there are fewer letters than feature combinations, letters are overdetermined and only part of the feature set may be sufficient for correct recognition. The usually abundant information (its redundancy) is thought to increase perceptual certainty and to speed up the process of decision between alternative responses when feature sets overlap. If the eyes provide insufficient data, the few activated features may induce recognition as well, either correct or incorrect. The ease of eliciting incorrect responses makes confusion matrices a primary source for specifying features as related to stimulus configurations on the one hand and to internal letters on the other.

In this view, features are theoretical objects to be specified by subsequent research, and readers do not need to have any conscious intuition about them,

221

in contrast to single letters, which can be recognized and named explicitly. Research may then be directed within the framework of the theory at specifying for the various letters both features and feature sets or feature hierarchies, trigger thresholds, and also decision rules between alternatives. We need both qualitative and quantitative data, and we need to know the dynamics of the process, in order to compare the theory quantitatively with experimental data, at least, on correct and incorrect responses and on response latencies. As to the dynamics, feature activation and deactivation may well overlap in time with the activation of internal letters and with the decision process.

The same theoretical scheme is applicable to the recognition of single words and has in fact been developed for that purpose. Features may now be assumed to correspond with internal letters, and it follows that no explicit decision between alternative letters as such now has to be assumed. This latter point is of considerable importance: arguments against word recognition by means of letter recognition were based on the classic findings that words can be recognized even if some of their letters cannot, and that response latencies for letter recognition are not shorter than for words. Both findings can be accommodated once the necessity of a decision between alternative letters as part of the word recognition process is abandoned. This also opens the possibility of reconciling the seemingly opposite notions of "analytic features" (= letters) and "global features," which belong to the word as a whole rather than to one of its letters. Strictly speaking, letter position in a word is already a global feature.

So the scheme for the recognition of a single letter can be extended to the recognition of a single word. In fact, the papers in this session add the notion that certain letter sequences act as features, and that subjects use implicit knowledge about admissible letter sequences.

Nevertheless, word recognition is a more complex process in other respects. Whereas there are only some 26 letters, there are thousands of words, bringing in available word knowledge (or even knowledge of letter clusters) as an extra variable. Also, words have meanings and may induce "associations" of many types, appearing in experiments as an uncontrolled response bias. Sequential bias (repetition) certainly extends farther in time in word recognition than in letter recognition. So, in general, the decision process between alternatives will be rather complex to unravel.

Features make theory easier if they combine independently. If features have strong interactions among themselves, it is doubtful if they deserve separate treatment. For letters as features of single words, there can be no doubt of strong interactions. So why maintain letters as possible features? A pragmatic answer is: because theory is at present even more intractable without letters as features. A suitable route is then to specify the interactions first and next to see how the theory should be modified. Two main interactions are: 1) letters close together on the retina strongly interfere, even when quite close to the fixation point; the rules of lateral interference include position in the word and distance from the fovea as important parameters, and may be the source of the right visual field advantage for word recognition; 2) Adjacent letters in certain sequences may help each other's recognition, thus forming letter clusters. This causes certain non-words to be more word-like than others. Graphemic clusters may be traced back to different origins (phonemic and morphemic clusters). Present theory tries to deal with the two types of interaction by assuming that lateral interference is not letter-specific and is thus open to direct measurement from nonword letter strings, and that orthographically regular letter clusters have an internal representation of their own, intermediate between letters and words.

Here, gradually, the theoretical scheme changes from "passive" to "active" recognition, or from "stimulus analysis and projection upon existing perceptual knowledge" to "hypothesis in need of perceptual confirmation." In the future, the opposition will probably seem less clear-cut than it does today. Strong interactions between words could in principle eliminate the word as a useful theoretical unit for understanding reading, but it seems more likely that word clusters of several types will be added to the present levels of description. Also, morphemes capable of signifying relations between different words of a sentence will have to be accommodated.

Allport, in his review of present word recognition research, mentions recent doubts about whether overt responses by readers are representative indicators of recognition (even if they report "nothing seen," certain semantic influences of the stimulus word may be traced). There is, however, much cohesion in the body of overt word recognition experiments which Allport goes on to discuss. Errors made by patients with certain brain lesions point to two separate routes from stimulus to meaning: one through the visual lexicon, leading to incorrect response words, visually similar to the stimulus, and the other through phonological recoding leading to response words which sound similar to the stimulus. The increasing evidence from brain-injured patients makes it desirable to find out if their word recognition processes reflect processing routines or are only last resorts, available when the normal routines fail. A relevant observation might be, for example, to note whether their response speeds are anywhere near the normal range. Generally, "phonological recoding" (visual recognition based on speech sounds as features) has lost its status as an intermediary process in visual word recognition. This is consistent with Morton's logogen theory, although Allport proposes to refine its decision stage.

Morton reexamines his ten year old logogen theory, which stressed the independence for word recognition of activation from the senses, and expectation from the context through general knowledge. The time is ripe now for differentiation and quantitative elaboration of perceptual analysis and decision, followed by a better understanding of the magical "context" factor. Here, Morton splits the former single logogen into a visual, an auditory and a motor (speech) logogen, because of the sense-bound properties.

Bouwhuis further examines the quantitative relationship developed earlier between recognition of letters as such in non-words, and recognition of words composed of those letters. He restricts himself to words of three letters. The two interaction factors of letters in words, lateral interference and orthographic clustering, are taken into account implicitly. The precise theoretical predictions matched experimental values so closely that it became worthwhile to search for possible origins of the differences. This led to experiments on the differential accessibility of words out of context ("word knowledge") -- which turns out to be fairly independent of frequency counts. The results also indicate that subjects actually use orthographic factors in deciding whether letter strings are words or non-words.

Venezky delves deeply into the spelling regularities of English. Information theory teaches us that for optimal reading of words, the reader should use a perfect knowledge of transitional probabilities of letters (letter clusters) in his decoding. Therefore statistical descriptions of orthographic structure and redundancy may reflect the optimum adult reader. Position in the word turns out to be highly relevant to such cluster description. Orthographic clusters may relate back to visual, phonological (speech), and grammatical factors.

Pollatsek and Carr also discuss the role of letter clusters. They present two words or two non-words, which are either identical or differ in one or more letters. Subjects have to respond "same" or "different"; response latencies for two word stimuli are compared with latencies for two nonword stimuli. Subjects do just as well on orthographically regular non-words as on words, whereas other non-words require more time. This suggests that such decisions are made at some letter-cluster level and reflect perception of orthographic regularities.

Smith and Groat report on a letter monitoring task which is increasingly being used for finding relationships between letter and word recognition. Letters are more difficult to find in words than in orthographically irregular nonwords. Many factors mentioned earlier as possible factors in word recognition (including position in a word and phonemic and grammatical factors) seem to influence such scores, but there is no difference between pronounced and silent letters. The sensitivity of the task to so many factors makes it both potentially powerful in the long run, and difficult to interpret in the short run. Notice that explicit letter recognition is not a requirement for a theory which assumes letters as features for letter clusters or for words.

The papers in this section reveal a strong common theme in which "orthographically regular" letter clusters are defined as perceptually relevant concepts and such units are defined relative to their position in the word. The theme reminds one of research on speech perception, where phoneme sequences of about syllable size are among the units considered. A difficulty in working with letter clusters is that there are so many of them and that different ways of dividing words into letter clusters (including overlapping clusters) show great covariation. Since, moreover, different letter sequences will probably function as clusters "more or less" rather than "all or none," there is a need to work out the theoretical options quantitatively for a carefully chosen subset of (short) words. A transition from a confusion matrix for letter clusters to word confusions could then both be predicted and measured. There seems to be sufficient qualitative guidance available to make such a quantitative effort worthwhile.

Perhaps it should be added that the hypothesis of letter clusters as features of words does not require the subject to make explicit decisions between alternatives to such clusters. In experiments, however, such decisions may be required from subjects, and response latencies will then probably primarily reflect the difficulty of the decision process itself.

Laboratory situations designed for studying word recognition are often quite different from normal reading situations. They may have to be in order to produce useful answers to well-defined questions. For example, presentation durations are sometimes a few milliseconds only, presentations may be repeated many times with gradually increasing durations, and subjects

may be left with more than a second to quietly consider their answers. Those
interested in reading then have to consider whether the results can be generalized to the reading situation, where fixation durations are some 200 msec,
repeated presentations are at different retinal positions, and recognition
is quick and without much reflection. Of course, differences may concern
many more aspects of stimuli and tasks. This generalization is often difficult
to achieve, and if relevance to reading is pursued, one might consider designing the laboratory situation to approximate reading situations as closely as
possible. If so, the insight gained may also be applicable to related areas
such as the spelling of languages, learning foreign languages, or handwritten
text, to mention just a few of the many intriguing domains of actual reading.

In conclusion, word recognition is probably a key determiner of reading
and central to any theory of reading processes. The increase of qualitative
insight, in particular into letter clusters as a mediating processing level,
makes a quantitative theory of word recognition desirable. Such a theory
would have implications for assessing and improving the quality of written
communication.

Word Recognition in Reading (Tutorial Paper)

Alan Allport

This chapter offers a critical survey of evidence for functionally separable mechanisms in word recognition, and a theoretical framework for interpreting the contributions of linguistic, especially lexical, knowledge in both pre-attentive processing and conscious perception of written words.

Section 1 reviews evidence for independent parallel systems responsible for graphemic access to semantic and conceptual knowledge, and for conversion of alphabetic script into a phonological representation. The role of phonological coding in silent reading is discussed, including its role in interpreting certain syntactic components of text.

Section 2 discusses the effects of orthographic regularity and lexicality in the identification of words and letter strings. Evidence is summarized favouring an intermediate, tacit stage of letter identification. Contrasts between the recognition of words and of pictures are explored.

Section 3 introduces a procedural model for the mental lexicon, illustrated by means of the MARGIE system, in relation to both referential and syntagmatic word-meanings. It emphasizes the role in reading of pre-attentive expectations (contextual facilitation effects) generated by parallel, production-like mechanisms. Evidence of preattentive lexical access is surveyed.

In Section 4 theoretical issues concerning perceptual integration and its central place in the mechanism of word perception are raised. Some models of the integration process are also reviewed.

227

Some of the best camouflaged conceptual traps for psychologists lie in the way ordinary language is used to perform a quasi-technical role in the description of behaviour. "Word recognition" is full of such traps. "Recognition," like "perception," appears to refer both to the "discriminative uptake" of information from the senses and (in the adult human) to the ability to report or comment upon it, in answer to the question "What did you perceive?"
Yet there are many illustrations of the dissociation between these two abilities. One striking example is the phenomenon that Weiskrantz and colleagues have termed "blindsight" (Weiskrantz, Warrington, Sanders, & Marshall, 1974). Although subjectively blind in one quadrant of the visual field after surgical removal of a major portion of the calcarine visual cortex, one patient could reach with great accuracy to small visual objects and make crude shape-discriminations in the "blind" region. Throughout testing the patient remained convinced that he was guessing, and denied any awareness of "seeing" the stimuli.

In laboratory study of word recognition, a still popular form of experiment requires the subject to answer commentary questions such as "What do you see?" He is asked to pronounce or transcribe the names of words, letters, or nonsense-syllables, or to decide whether they are identical with other words or letters presented simultaneously or successively. These tasks are often investigated as though words were little more than arbitrarily familiar sequences of graphemes or phonemes, independent of any other functions of linguistic communication or understanding.

Yet there is abundant evidence that much linguistic or semantic processing of written words is independent of the ability to name them. Albert, Yamadori, Gardner, and Howes (1973) describe a brain-injured patient with well-preserved, fluent, spontaneous speech, who was however radically alexic. He was unable to read aloud written text, with the exception of 10% of short, high frequency words and single letters, and claimed to have "no idea" of the identity or meaning of the other words. Nevertheless, he could locate among a list of words the one relating to a given semantic field; thus, given orally the target specification "landscape," he could point out "mountain" in the visually presented set, "president, general, church, constitution, mountain, hydrant." Asked to read the word aloud, his response was, "That looks like company, c-o-m-u, c-o-m-p-a-n-y. I don't know." With non-alphabetic symbols he often indicated recognition orally, even when unable to name them. For example, he called 99% "not quite a hundred per cent."

A principal goal of current research in human information processing is to segment the mechanisms of behaviour into separable functional components. Until we are able to do so, the immense versatility of alternative "strategies," relying on different functional subsystems, is likely to defeat our efforts at understanding. The single most important contribution to our knowledge of the separable subsystems involved in word recognition has come from neuropsychological studies of dyslexic patients. Yet, until recently, there has been almost no contact between this research and laboratory studies of reading in normal subjects. Recent reviews of this literature can be found in Hécaen and Kremin (1976), Luria (1976), Marin, Saffran, and Schwartz (1976), and Marshall and Newcombe (1973).

READING AND PHONOLOGY

Phonemic Dyslexia
In processes related to word recognition and reading, the neuropsychological data suggest a sharp functional separation between mechanisms that enable some sort of rule-based translation from alphabetic strings to pronounceable sequences, and mechanisms of access to lexical and semantic knowledge. Between these two systems a "double dissociation" can be demonstrated (Marshall & Newcombe, 1973). Consider the case of loss of grapheme-phoneme encoding with preservation of some semantic access, known as phonemic (or "deep") dyslexia.

The primary characteristic of phonemic dyslexia is the inability to derive pronunciation of visually presented graphemes, except "post-lexically." A patient with phonemic dyslexia cannot read aloud nonsense syllables (Low, 1931; Patterson & Marcel, 1977); he cannot determine whether orthographically dissimilar words (hope-soap) rhyme; neither can he derive a lexical identity from homophonic misspellings such as "bote" (Saffran & Marin, 1977). On the other hand such patients can understand, and sometimes correctly name, a large vocabulary of written content-words, including words with complex orthography ("chrysanthemum") and low frequency of occurrence ("manikin"). Their errors in word naming are frequently semantically related to the stimulus word (crocus $\longrightarrow$ "tulip"; canal $\longrightarrow$ "small river"; liberty $\longrightarrow$ "freedom"), suggesting that the name produced has been generated from some non-linguistic conceptual base. A patient described by Luria (1960), attempting to read the word Holland, responded: "I know ... I know ... it's a country, not Europe ... no ... not Germany ... it's small ... it was captured ... Belgium! That's it, Belgium!" In the patient studied intensively by Marshall and Newcombe (1966), about 70% of all his errors in reading nouns were single word paralexias. Saffran, Schwartz, and Marin (1976) showed that the incidence of these paralexias could be substantially reduced if the same word was read as a proper name, or presented in the context of a familiar phrase.

In phonemic dyslexia the ability to name visually presented words is best preserved for words having a specific, concrete reference (the names of perceptible objects); it is much less intact for abstract nouns, or verbs, and is most impaired for grammatical function words (conjunctions, articles, demonstratives, or pronouns), that is, words that address syntagmatic procedures (Marshall & Newcombe, 1966; Shallice & Warrington, 1975; Richardson, 1975). One such patient who was unable to read "if" as a conjunction could read it as the title of a poem by Kipling (Morton, 1977b). Andreewsky and Seron (1975) have shown that a severely agrammatic dyslexic patient, who was unable to read aloud syntactic function words, could use them and other syntactic cues in a written sentence to assign syntactic class to other morphemes. Moreover a noun read easily in its normal sentential role was not read at all when it occurred in a position requiring a conjunction. Despite the selective inability of phonemic dyslexics to name written grammatical formatives, "lexical access" -- the ability to distinguish function words from orthographically similar nonword letter strings -- is essentially unimpaired (Patterson, in press).

One interesting conjecture is that word recognition by the phonemic dys-

lexic, with characteristically left-sided cerebral injury, depends on the availability of an intact lexicon for visually presented words in the right hemisphere (Coltheart, 1977a). On the basis of a variety of evidence in both dyslexic and normal readers, Marcel and Patterson (in press) suggest that communication between a visual input lexicon and an output lexicon may be m
mediated by the central conceptual system (which, I take it, includes the
system responsible for subjective imagery), rather than by any direct lexical-
lexical projection, and in contrast, presumably, to the connections between
the auditory input and the speech output lexicons. A diagram of functional
connections that reflects these observations is sketched in Figure 1. Discussion of the functional role of an input lexicon can be found in Section 3.
(There have been some important developments in the study of phonemic
dyslexia. See Coltheart, Marshall, & Patterson (in press), particularly the
chapter by Shallice and Warrington therein.)

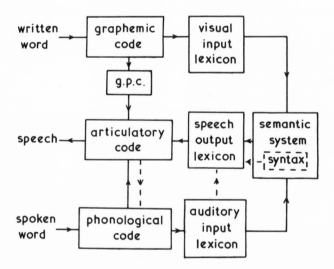

Figure 1. Diagram of suggested functional interconnections between components of the language system; g.p.c. = grapheme-phoneme conversion.

Surface Dyslexia

Marshall and Newcombe (1973) also describe the complementary syndrome, which they call "surface" dyslexia, as evidence of the double dissociation between access by graphemic stimuli respectively to phonological codes and to lexical morphology, or meaning.

The patient with surface dyslexia -- or pure verbal alexia in the terminology of Hécaen and Kremin (1976) -- assigns a semantic interpretation to individual words, if at all, entirely on the basis of a pre-lexical, phonological (possibly articulatory) coding, which he sounds out laboriously and often erroneously, one syllable at a time (island ⟶ "izland"; recent ⟶ "rikunt"). Success at identifying a word, in contrast with the phonemic dyslexic, appears to be independent of its grammatical category or lexical frequency (Hécaen & Kremin, 1976). For any letter-string that the pure verbal alexic is unable to pronounce, it is to be presumed that he will also be unable to decide whether it is a word or not, though I have found no direct observations on this.

Sasanuma (1975) and Marshall (1976) have reviewed the dissociations revealed by traumatic aphasias among readers of Japanese, where the ability to read one or other of the dual (syllabic or logographic) scripts can be impaired with preservation of the other. The logographic Kanji is normally used, in adult texts, to write contentives; the syllabic Kana is used for syntactic formatives and foreign loan-words. In normal readers, characters in the syllabic script, Kana, are more accurately reported from tachistoscopic presentation to the right visual field, as in the case of alphabetic scripts (Sasanuma, Itoh, Mori, & Kobayashi, 1977), whereas a superiority of report in the left visual field has been found for tachistoscopic identification of single, logographic, Kanji of both high and low frequency (Hatta, 1977). With frequency or familiarity controlled, there is evidence of superior recognition of Kanji which denote concrete objects (Hatta, Kitao, Ishida, Babazono, & Kondo, 1977).

Phonological Coding and Lexical Access

The evidence of phonemic dyslexia indicates unambiguously that grapheme-to-phoneme translation is not a necessary condition of lexical access for a written word, since inability to perform pre-lexical grapheme-phoneme encoding does not destroy the ability to understand or read aloud isolated words. Other considerations, not dependent on neuropsychological evidence, point to the same conclusion. Since several of the contributors to this volume have added evidence to the same end, discussion here will be kept to a minimum.

In English orthography there are many difficulties in determining the pronunciation of words, unless one knows the lexical identity of a word and thence its pronunciation (dough-cough, steak-sneak, fathom-fathead), or meaning (bow, lead, tear, wind, wound ...). Pronunciation commonly depends on "post-lexical" phonology, and if access to the lexicon in reading isolated words were mediated uniquely via a phonological coding, there would be no means of disambiguating homophone pairs such as sighed-side, heard-herd, or of distinguishing them from non-words like hurd. Even the most persistent protagonists of lexical access via pre-lexical phonological coding find it necessary to assume some sort of visual "spelling recheck" (Rubenstein, Lewis, & Rubenstein, 1971; Davelaar, Coltheart, Besner, & Jonasson, 1978).

In a critical review of the experimental literature Bradshaw (1975) concluded that there was no evidence favouring the necessity of phonological coding of single, visually presented, content-words as a precursor to lexical access and, in fact, there was considerable evidence to the contrary. I know of no more recent experimental evidence that might alter his conclusion. However, this does not rule out the possibility that phonological coding can play some role in silent reading. Not in question, of course, is the fact that normal readers can derive pronunciation for written nonsense words without the existence of a lexical entry. Coltheart (in press) cogently evaluates both mechanisms proposed, and the possible contributory or convergent role of phonological coding in lexical access.

Phonological and Articulatory Coding in Normal Reading

Given the functional separability of graphemic access respectively to phonological and lexical (or semantic) representations and procedures, what role may phonological coding play in normal reading?

One possibility worth further examination is that alphabetic texts are read somewhat like Japanese. That is, content words may be interpreted semantically without any phonological mediation, whereas syntactic morphemes (like Kana), if they are to be explicitly understood, depend on phonological coding. Except where syntax (or meaning) is obscure, the meaning of a sentence -- as in a telegram -- can generally be understood, and in rapid silent reading perhaps is understood, from the content words and word-order alone.

It is also suggested that phonological coding in reading provides additional temporary storage after lexical access, until the meaning of larger syntactic units, phrases and sentences, has been satisfactorily analyzed (Kleiman, 1975; Baron, 1976; Levy, in press; Baddeley, this volume). Kleiman's evidence in favour of this post-lexical, "working memory" hypothesis for phonological coding was based on the selective nature of the disruption of silent reading produced by a concurrent shadowing task. Continuous shadowing (oral repetition) of an auditory digit sequence significantly retarded sentential or syntagmatic acceptability judgments, as it did phonemic or rhyme judgments, relative to its effect on non-lexical graphemic decisions. By contrast, shadowing did not affect the speed of synonym or semantic category judgments for individual words. It should be noted, however, that concurrent shadowing affected only the speed, not the accuracy, of the sentence-acceptability judgments.

Baddeley (this volume) describes a variety of experiments that demonstrate that articulatory suppression impairs the recall of phonologically coded information in reading but not in listening. These results indicate that, while auditory speech can be retained in a phonological code not adversely affected by concurrent articulatory activity, visually presented letters or words can only be transformed into a phonological representation via the mechanisms responsible for the organization of articulatory motor acts. To restate this more directly, there appears to be no direct conversion from a graphemic to an auditory code, but only into a code of articulatory instructions. (Once formed, the implicit speech code may then be converted into auditory phonology without necessarily requiring overt articulation.) When beginning readers learn to "bark at print," what they acquire is the ability to translate from graphemes to articulatory acts. It has been frequently assumed that skilled readers also acquire the ability to translate directly from graphemic to auditory phonological form. The above evidence suggests that this may not be so.

Additional support for this view is gained from observations on the selective nature of reading disorders in Japanese. Sasanuma and Fujimura (1971) studied two groups of aphasic patients; both groups were equated in their ability to comprehend spoken speech. Group B differed from Group A in that patients in Group B also exhibited overt speech production disorder. Both groups were asked to identify words, written either in logographic or syllabic script, by matching each word to a picture of the object named. Patients in Group A, who had no articulatory disability, were slightly but equally impaired, relative to control subjects, in their understanding of both Kanji (logographic) and Kana (syllabic) script. Group B did not differ from them in their recognition of the logographic Kanji, but were selectively severely impaired in their understanding of Kana, particularly of words written in Hiragana (in adult texts normally written in Kanji). That is, comprehension of the phonologically based script was critically dependent on an intact articulatory output system, rather than on the auditory or input system.

An implicit articulatory code is evidently advantageous for recalling lists of written words or syllables in their original order. It may also be useful in silent reading, for holding syntactically complex sentences until satisfactorily understood, or wherever a heavy load is imposed on short-term memory. No clear evidence exists, however, that it is necessary for sentence comprehension in reading. One of the most critical results in this context is reported by Levy (in press). Articulatory suppression during reading impaired memory for the wording (and word order) of the sentences read, but had no effect on the ability to comprehend and remember the non-linguistic meaning of the text sentences.

There is some evidence that inhibition of implicit articulatory acts in silent reading can impair comprehension of "difficult" prose (Hardyck & Petrinovich, 1970). The performance of patients suffering from a "repetition deficit," a deficit apparent in conversion from either auditory or visual input into an articulatory code, suggests that the critical source of difficulty may lie in syntactic rather than conceptual complexity. These conduction aphasics, who are characteristically grossly impaired in reading aloud, have been reported able to read novels or medical textbooks silently "with apparently normal comprehension" (Benson & Geschwind, 1969). However, such patients are in fact selectively impaired in their auditory comprehension of syntactically complex word order, such as constructions containing embedded clauses or semantically reversible passives (Saffran & Marin, 1975). It is obviously important to know whether this is also true of the sentences that they read.

Silent reading comprehension is possible[1] for profoundly, congenitally deaf subjects who have no knowledge of auditory phonology and, as Conrad

---

[1]But we should be careful to note its limitations. See on this subject the Appendix in Gibson and Levin (1975).

(1972) has argued, no less so for those who do not use any concomitant articulatory coding. These deaf subjects demonstrate extensive textual comprehension when no phonology of any kind is involved. The contribution, if any, of substitute motor-linguistic representations such as implicit manual signing is as yet scarcely explored.

VISUAL PROCESSES IN WORD RECOGNITION

Words, Pseudo-Words and Letters

Since the nineteenth century it has been known that, for a given brief exposure, words -- and nonsense-syllables -- can be more accurately and more rapidly reported than arbitrary or unrelated letters, a finding that is nonetheless open to ambiguous interpretation. The revival of experimental interest in some of the associated issues dates from a small methodological development, intended to eliminate the contribution of guessing artefacts, introduced by Reicher (1969). This literature, up to 1975, has been reviewed with admirable astringency by Henderson (1977).

Reicher (1969) and Wheeler (1970) both demonstrated that, with a retrospective forced-choice probe of just one letter position in a pattern-masked display, subjects were still 10% more accurate, in respect of any given letter, in a four-letter word than when just a single letter was presented. After confirming this with a number of additional controls, Wheeler concluded that "word recognition cannot be analyzed into a set of independent letter recognition processes. There is an interaction among the letters such that the context of the other letters of a meaningful word improved recognition despite the control of letter redundancy" (Wheeler, 1970).

There was some question whether the effect was due to the presence of a meaningful word or to orthographic regularity or pronounceability alone. It is possible, for example, that the superiority of words relative to isolated letters may be due to the differential likelihood of articulatory coding of words versus letters. If subjects are instructed to vocalise all stimuli, prior to receiving the forced-choice alternatives, the word superiority can be eliminated or even reversed (Mezrich, 1973).[2] Baron and Thurston (1973) demonstrate a substantial superiority of pronounceable over "unpronounceable" nonsense words in the Reicher-Wheeler task, with no further advantage for their small and somewhat unusual set of words. They also found a comparable effect for regular over misspelled chemical formulae, arguing that pronounceability per se was therefore not a necessary condition.

Manelis (1974) and McClelland (1976) also obtained a small but consistent superiority (around 8%) of familiar words over orthographically regular nonwords, in carefully designed Reicher-Wheeler experiments. And in reaction-time measures in simultaneous visual comparisoe tasks, both Barron and Pittenger (1974) and Chambers and Forster (1975) obtained consistently faster matching times in response to words than to legal nonwords (CRAWN) equated with them for digram and trigram frequency, and in response to high-frequency

---

[2]Unfortunately, vocalization was confounded with probe delay; it would be desirable to repeat the experiment without this confound.

than to low-frequency words. In a similar matching task, Henderson (1974) reported a superiority for comparisons of familiar but "unspeakable" letter sequences, such as FBI, relative to meaningless ones like BFI, where orthographically rule-based regularity is not a distinguishing feature. The difference was abolished when the stimuli were presented in an unfamiliar format (fbi).

Some of these word superiority effects (WSE) can be eliminated by suitable manipulations of the subject's strategy. Neither in the Reicher-Wheeler task, nor in simultaneous visual matching, is there any necessity for lexical access. In spite of this, WSEs have been obtained under conditions of "physical" rather than "name" comparisons (Besner & Jackson, 1975; Pollatsek, Well, & Schindler, 1975). In line with Wheeler's (1970) hypothesis of "simultaneous constraints," Fisher (1977) found a non-independence in the accuracy of probed, non-adjacent letters for words but not for consonant strings; advance knowledge of the type of letter-string to be presented did not alter this. Also in the Reicher-Wheeler task the substantial superiority of words over irregular nonwords was undiminished over successive experimental sessions even when the alternative letters to be probed were known in advance (Carr, Lehmkuhle, Kottas, Astor-Stetson, & Arnold, 1976; Smith & Haviland, 1972). In contrast with this effect of regularity, the differential effect of word-frequency, at least in the lexical decision task, can be reduced or even eliminated after a single repetition (Scarborough, Cortese, & Scarborough, 1977). Pollatsek and Carr (this volume) have argued that the faster matching time for words over pronounceable nonwords in the comparison task reflects a response bias rather than faster recognition.

The significance of this research is not always clear. At the methodological level there was a basic question of whether performance in such experiments on isolated words was relevant to linguistic understanding in normal reading. Questioned at a theoretical level was the extent that word recognition, in the absence of a specific linguistic context, could be viewed as a "passive" process driven directly by the stimulus; or to what extent it demanded a more active contribution at all levels from the subject's prior knowledge.

The tidiest, most conservative approach is to suppose that the overt identification of written words is a product of successive stages of analysis, beginning with visual features, followed by identification of individual letters, possibly some intervening stage concerned with segmentation of morphemic units, and finally the recognition of words as lexical units. This atomistic, "bottom up" approach to word recognition has conceptual simplicity but suffers from certain drawbacks.

Visual Features
Despite the popularity of the general notion, there are no clearly motivated suggestions, still less agreement, about what the visual features used in alphabetic letter and word recognition might be. Townsend (1971) applied multidimensional scaling techniques to confusion matrices for the recognition of single letters, and obtained results suggesting four or five underlying stimulus dimensions; but he could find no appealling psychological dimensions corresponding to them. Those proposed by Gibson (1965), and Gibson and Levin (1975), are not based on an empirical evaluation of possible alternatives

(see Coltheart, 1977b). Of course, functional visual features are specified by the response properties in the visual system, and are not to be defined a priori.

Bouma (1970, 1973) demonstrated the increasingly radical effects of lateral interactions between adjacent letters with increasing retinal eccentricity. Of relevance to this finding is evidence that brief visual presentation selectively degrades local detail -- high spatial frequencies -- relative to lower spatial frequency -- more global information (Breitmeyer & Ganz, 1976). Broadbent and Broadbent (1977) have also shown how different methods of degrading stimulus information can have qualitatively differing effects on word recognition. Kolers (1974, 1975) demonstrated that skilled readers, in spite of the difficulties involved, can fluently read alphabetic texts geometrically transformed in various ways. If reading depends on the application of encoding procedures to elementary visual features, they must be capable of equivalent transformations and should not be thought of simply as local templates.

Individual Letters in Word Recognition

Suppose that word recognition is indeed dependent on prior identification of individual letters. It does not follow that the subject can make use of the letter identifications for any other purpose or commentary, least of all that he must therefore be able to name them. In auditory speech perception there is reason to believe that word recognition depends on identification of phonemes. Yet the latency of response indicating detection of a pre-specified word-initial phoneme depends on the transitional probability of the word in which it occurs (Morton & Long, 1976). That is, the phoneme detection response must be controlled by post-lexical processes. The equivalent problems in the analysis of visual word-recognition, in particular the problems of task-specific assumptions about "multiple read-off," are discussed by Henderson (1977).

In literal alexia, a patient may be able to read a word but be unable to name any of its letters (Hécaen, 1967). Letter recognition, in the sense of enabling explicit identification, is manifestly not a necessary condition for recognition or naming of words. Experimental approaches attempting to map the dependency between explicit identification of letters and of words therefore risk achieving relevance only to the kinds of laboratory transcription tasks in which the data are gathered, and not at all to the understanding of word meaning.

In looking for an explanation for the superiority of familiar over unfamiliar letter sequences in recognition or matching tasks, it is natural to appeal to the possible utilization of features spanning more than a single letter. (There is persuasive evidence that the visual system of the rhesus monkey, in many respects similar to man's, is capable of discriminating configurational cues in word-like compound stimuli (Gaffan, 1977), clearly without benefit of a verbal code.) Certainly, when a word is printed in alternating upper- and lower-case letters -- an operation presumed to disrupt most "transgraphemic" visual relationships -- recognition is impaired (Coltheart & Freeman, 1974; McClelland, 1976). However, in McClelland's study it was also found that case-alternation did not change the superiority of performance for real words over regular nonwords. Except where performance was masked by floor effects, no interaction between the manipulation of case-alternation and the superiority of regular over unrelated letter sequences was found. McClelland thus concluded that neither the recognition of supra-letter features, nor whole word patterns, could be responsible for these word-superiority or familiarity effects, but that, on the contrary, the identification of individual letters was the primary determinant. It is of interest that, as regards the capacity for explicit commentary, even when all letters of a four-letter word were correctly reported, the particular format in which they had appeared (all upper case, all lower case, or alternated in one of two ways) could be reported with only 52% accuracy.

Of some relevance to the functional separation between visual-graphic and abstract-graphemic-lexical levels of representation, it is worth recalling that the various lexical repetition effects described by Scarborough et al. (1977) and by Morton (this volume) are unaffected by change of case, or by change from handwritten to typewritten words, although they are apparently affected by a change of sensory modality.[3]

Are visually distorted (e.g. case-alternated) words read preferentially or exclusively by the phonological route, whereas the non-phonological route depends on holistic recognition of visual word-patterns? A pertinent observation on one phonemic dyslexic by Saffran and Marin (1977) opposes this conjecture. By ingenious and careful testing the patient was shown to be incapable of deriving phonological representations for pronounceable letter-sequences although possessing a reading vocabulary of more than 16,000 words. The presumption is strong, therefore, that her recognition performance was mediated entirely by the direct route. Yet, confronted with isolated words in which the internal spatial relations between letters had been disturbed by case-alternation (cAbiNeT), by vertical displacement ($l^e{}_t{}^t{}_e r$) or by interpolating plus signs between letters (n+i+g+h+t) she still read the words with apparently no difficulty, except in that 8/75 words tested elicited semantic paralexias. This result strongly supports the view that non-phonological access to lexical knowledge includes an intermediate level of abstract letter identification.

Reference : Words and Pictures

To what extent may words nevertheless be processed in ways similar to pictures? "Word and percept," as Miller and Johnson-Laird (1976) assert, "are 'associated' only in the sense that they can be alternative ways of gaining access to the same underlying procedures." Supporting their claim are a number of instructive parallels between the processing of individual words, and of pictures.

---

[3]McConkie (this volume) found that the substitution of one case-alternated text by another graphically quite different arrangement of the same text between successive fixation pauses is not even noticed by the reader. This is eloquent evidence that the integration of information over successive fixations occurs at or beyond the level of abstract letter identities.

For example, when a simple comparison is required between two types of object (e.g., "Which is larger?"), the response time varies inversely with the difference between the two objects on the relevant dimension -- the "distance effect" (Moyer, 1973). Such comparisons may be as much as 200-300msec faster when the objects compared are indicated by two pictures rather than when specified by their written names (Paivio, 1975). It is unlikely therefore that the picture comparisons depend on first accessing a name for each of the objects.[4] However, the size and character of the distance effect is identical for both word- and picture-based comparisons (Paivio, 1975), and remains so whether compared in terms of some physical property of the objects (e.g., size) or in terms of an abstract, or non-picturable property, such as intelligence (Banks & Flora, 1977).

By contrast the "size-congruity effect" -- where the larger of the two pictures yields a faster judgment that the real object depicted is in fact the larger -- is not observed when the objects compared are specified as words written in differing sizes (Paivio, 1975). It is interesting to note that a size congruity effect is obtained in comparisons of the numerical size of two simultaneously presented numerals, but not if the numbers compared are written as words (Besner, 1978). In this respect numerals function more like pictures than words. It is worth recalling the preservation of the ability to recognize, and name, numerals, even in severe cases of traumatic alexia (see Benson & Geschwind, 1969; Hécaen & Kremin, 1976, for summary reviews); and the indications of differential right hemisphere capability for recognition of digits, but not isolated letters (Teng & Sperry, 1973). We should perhaps be cautious, however, in concluding that numeral recognition is functionally identical with the recognition of other logograms. The ability to read and understand numerals is sometimes preserved, even with severe loss of the capacity to understand logographic Kanji (Sasanuma & Monoi, 1975), and the converse condition is also sometimes observed (Yamadori, 1975).

THE LEXICON

A question that has received inadequate attention in discussions of word recognition is "What is the nature of the mechanisms that are accessed, with access to the lexicon?" My theoretical bias is to think of words as evoking, or addressing, a variety of procedures for operating on other words, and for building conceptual representations of what it is that the speaker or writer intends to communicate (Davies & Isard, 1972). The recent book by Miller and Johnson-Laird (1976) is a monumental attempt to chart such an approach, in representing lexical meanings as cognitive procedures. If such procedures can be shown to be necessary for the understanding of text, they will not

---

[4]Overt naming of pictures is slower than the naming of written words (Fraisse, 1969), presumably reflecting the complex many-to-many mappings in the projection of a conceptual or semantic representation onto a unique name. When a word is to be named, on the other hand, by normal readers at least, the uncertainty inherent in this word-finding process can be constrained (and incorrect responses vetoed) by convergent information from grapheme-phoneme conversion (cf. Patterson & Marcel, 1977).

dissolve when the system is called on to process isolated words, and they may contribute critically to the subject's performance. Studies of word recog - nition which, on the contrary, set out to minimize the contribution of such mechanisms have questionable relevance for the understanding of normal reading.

It should not be imagined, however, that a well-developed theory of pro- cedural semantics already exists, and that all that is needed is to couple it with the existing knowledge of word recognition. Ignorance about lexical mechanisms is almost as great as it is on the subject of visual pattern and graphemic recognition. Linguistic theory does not seem to offer much help, in terms of mechanism, and the principal source of ideas at present springs from work in artificial intelligence (AI).

The following section attempts to illustrate a possible procedural approach to the role of the lexicon (Riesbeck, 1975), and to sketch some implications for the empirical study of word recognition.

The MARGIE System and Riesbeck's Conceptual Analyzer

MARGIE is a computational system, designed by Schank and his colleagues (Schank, 1975), which makes inferences and paraphrases from natural language text, by way of a language-independent conceptual representation of meaning. It is intended explicitly as a medium in which to develop a psychological theory of human language understanding.

Understanding in the MARGIE system is separated into two distinct stages: first, the translation of input sentences into a language-independent Concept- ual Dependency representation -- "conceptual analysis"; second, a potentially unlimited process of inference and filling in in respect of unspecified agents, causes, instruments, motives, consequences, and so forth. This separation of stages is not intended to reflect any fundamental theoretical distinction, and the "stages" could, with advantage, be merged. There is certainly no reason why all the memory inferences must wait until an initial, language- free representation of a sentence or larger text is complete. However, in relation to the more immediate implications for word recognition, I shall be concerned with that part of understanding that depends directly on proced- ures triggered by individual words addressing the lexicon, that is with the "conceptual analysis" process.

One of the most striking features of the MARGIE conceptual analysis program, written by Riesbeck (1975, 1978), is that almost all translating from natural language to Conceptual Dependency (CD) structures is done by procedures contained in the Dictionary, and evoked directly by individual words in the surface text. There is no separately identifiable syntactic com- ponent. For Riesbeck's analyzer, "words and not syntactic structures are the source of expectations in a sentence. This is because syntactic struc- tures, in so far as they can be said to exist in the analyzer, are themselves predictions" (Riesbeck, 1975). Indeed, the syntactic/semantic distinction is also completely unimportant for the system. Besides the Dictionary itself, there is only a relatively simple monitor program, which does the book-keep- ing necessary for implementing what is a parallel, production-like system (Davis & King, 1977) programmed on a sequential machine (see also Allport, 1978).

Each entry, for each word-form in the Dictionary, contains an unordered cluster of "requests." A request is a condition $\longrightarrow$ action rule, consisting of a procedure or action, coupled with a condition which the current state of analysis must satisfy before the procedure is executed. Procedures involve setting up or manipulating large or small fragments of CD graphs. The end product of the conceptual analysis process is the CD framework (if any) which has been put together by these procedures in working memory.

Some words in a text may be directly reflected in the resultant conceptual representation of the text meaning, while others (syntactic function words, many verbs, and abstract nouns) though essential in its construction will have nothing corresponding to them explicitly in the CD output.

Crucial to the operation of the analyzer are the conditions attached to each procedure. These act as expectations of words or conceptual structures that should be looked for next. They continue to monitor for their preferred pattern or event either until it is found, whereupon their associated action is executed, or until some other event triggers an action which inactivates them. (This might be the end of a sentence, or the successful evaluation of expectations set up by a different, homonymic word "sense" -- that is, a separate cluster of requests -- attached to the same word-form.) "Requests" are thus very similar mechanisms to Charniak's (1972, 1976) "Demons," used to help solve problems of anaphoric reference.

To take a relatively simple example, the article "a" activates a number of requests. A possible sequence of adjectives and nouns that will be collected into a noun phrase is expected. Another request looks for anything that would signal the end of the noun phrase (e.g., any word other than an adjective or noun). When this occurs complex actions are triggered that convert the collection of adjectives and nouns into a conceptual structure that is thereafter handled as a unit. The structure is also labelled as having been introduced by "a," a fact that will then be used by the "inference" mechanisms in finding a referent.

The Dictionary entries for some words, principally nouns, include semantic "features" such as # HUMAN or # LIQUID, which are important in satisfying expectations set up by other words. In the MARGIE system, as in other case-oriented approaches, the main responsibility for building a conceptual structure, and for setting up case-dependent expectations, is carried by the Verb. Thus the verb-sense "drink," which is translated into a conceptual action labelled *INGEST* -- i.e., the taking-of-substances-into-the-body-via-the-mouth -- includes an expectation of some conceptual entity having the feature # LIQUID. If found, the entity will be accepted as the preferred conceptual Object of INGESTing. "Drink" also activates other requests, looking for a # HUMAN (or # ANIMATE) Agent of the INGESTing, and so on.

Other thematic expectations, evoked by words in one sentence, can remain active over extended text passages, and affect the preferred sense of homonyms encountered later. Thus a different lexical sense of "beat" in "John beat Mary" will be accepted by Riesbeck's analyzer in the context of reference to a race or competition than that in the context of "anger."

This again raises the question of the interaction between lexical analysis and conceptual inference. Currently there is great interest in the role of large-scale structures of commonsense (non-linguistic) knowledge -- scripts, frames, macrostructures, schemata -- in the inference stage of understanding text (Charniak, 1976; Kuipers, 1975; Minsky, 1975; Schank & Abelson, 1977;

Wilks, 1977). An important question in computational models of text understanding is the extent to which whole frameworks of knowledge should be
activated, and inferences derived from them, beyond the immediate demands
of the text, or only when specifically needed. Some such option plausibly
corresponds to variation in the "depth of processing" in human linguistic
comprehension.

Little attention has been given either to the ways in which these large-
scale conceptual schemata might be accessed by lexical events (the problem,
in one sense, of extended lexical reference), or to the possible, directly lexical consequences of conceptual schema activation. Undoubtedly the referential functions of word-meaning must go beyond either the notions of "semantic
features" or the rather static pointing to images or concepts (where, at its
most vacuous, the meaning of "toy" is simply TOY 1), that are the stock-in-
trade of some treatments of meaning in word recognition.

Pre-attentive Processing and "Expectations" in Word Recognition

Riesbeck's analysis program is of course oriented specifically towards the
understanding of sentences and text. Several aspects of it are nonetheless
of direct relevance to consideration of lexical effects even in the reading
of single words.

The basic mechanisms of comprehension in the analyzer are the expectations, which are themselves activated by individual words in the text, through
the Dictionary. In particular they enable the assimilation of new linguistic
information into the conceptual structures already set up to represent the
meaning of that part of the text already read. The expectations are not
themselves directly reflected in the output of the program, but only indirectly
through the specific procedures that they trigger when satisfied.

These expectations suggest a very natural account of various phenomena
of contextual facilitation in reading. It is well known that contextual effects
can be observed even in the recognition of isolated words (Morton, 1964;
Tulving & Gold, 1963; Schuberth & Eimas, 1977), and can render contextually
associated words harder to ignore or suppress (Warren, 1972; Conrad, 1973).
Moreover, associative facilitation can also be produced by words presented
in isolation (Meyer, Schvaneveldt, & Ruddy, 1975). There is some empirical
disagreement about the extent to which contextual priming between pairs
of words can be magnified by experimental manipulations of the subject's
conscious expectations or strategy (Schmidt, 1976; Fischler, 1977; Tweedy,
Lapinsky, & Schvaneveldt, 1977), but the basic facilitation appears to develop
rapidly, and be independent of conscious control (Neely, 1977). Certainly
the basic effect is not contingent on expectancies open to explicit "commentary" by the subject.

The clearest demonstration of this appears in experiments by Marcel (Marcel,
1974 and in press; Marcel & Patterson, in press). In these experiments he
obtains associative "priming" consequent on the presentation of a word that
has been pattern-masked in such a way that the subject is unable to report
its identity. Indeed the criterion of masking is such that the subjects perform
at chance level in determining, on any trial, whether any letter-string had
been presented prior to the mask. Yet when a subsequent test word is presented for lexical decisions, without masking, the effect of semantic association
between prime and test word is of equal magnitude when the priming word

is masked, as it is when the prime is presented normally.

Rapidly repeated presentation of priming word and mask, up to around twelve successive presentations, increases the magnitude of the associative facilitation on the speed of lexical decision from 50 msec up to around 80 to 90 msec, without having any effect on the subject's ability to identify, or even detect the presence of, the masked word (Marcel & Patterson, in press).

I have reported elsewhere data of a similar nature (Allport, 1977), showing evidence of simultaneous, or parallel, lexical access on the part of several words in a pattern-masked array. In one of these experiments, the probability of correctly reporting a target word increases with the simultaneous presentation of a semantically related, pattern-masked word whose identity or even presence the subjects were unable to report. Since the results are contingent on the relation of meaning between the two words, it follows that both stimuli must have accessed some level of semantic knowledge. In other experiments, using multiple arrays of words presented symmetrically around a fixation point, but pattern masked such that, on average, only one could be explicitly identified from a given exposure, subjects were able selectively to report a word in a pre-specified semantic category. These results again suggest parallel lexical or semantic access for word stimuli prior to the stage at which perceptual selection occurred.

One of the clearest lessons from these experiments is that activation of lexical or semantic representations cannot, in itself, be a sufficient condition for perception of a word, or for the control of an explicit perceptual report.

It is of interest that apparently none of Marcel's effects are obtained when the priming word is peripherally masked by a bright post-stimulus-field, but only under central masking (Turvey, 1973) by a pattern of densely scattered letter fragments. A similar dissociation has been reported for the word superiority effect (Johnson & McClelland, 1973). It seems plausible in both cases that the pattern-mask selectively destroys information at the visual or graphemic level, but leaves unaffected information that has already reached a level of lexical or post-lexical representation. Hence the superiority, in the Reicher-Wheeler paradigm, of lexical over non-lexical stimuli.

The experimental literature on reading contains a number of cognate observations of indirect, semantically mediated effects of unattended words that the subject cannot explicitly repeat, but that nevertheless bias the interpretation of attended words (Bradshaw, 1974; Willows & McKinnon, 1973). There is also other evidence favouring the possibility of spatially-parallel symbolic classification of graphemic stimuli (Jonides & Gleitman, 1972, 1976; Egeth, Jonides, &Wall, 1972).

In unpublished experiments conducted in my laboratory, using Willows and McKinnon's (1973) selective-reading technique, it has been found that the meaning of unattended words, that elaborate on significant details left unspecified in the attended narrative are readily assimilated into a reader's memory for the attended text. Thus the words "water" (or "knife") occurring in an unattended line in the vicinity of the sentence "That night she killed herself" will bias the subject's subsequent acceptance in a recognition test of the sentence "That night she drowned (stabbed) herself." By contrast, synonyms, although equally strongly associated to the attended words (but that provide no new information) have no effect in subsequent recognition tests.

These sorts of results make good sense in terms of automatic access to the lexicon for both attended and unattended words, combined with a mechanism of active expectations and requests, which may be matched by information also from an "unattended" line of text. The results are certainly difficult to reconcile with current models of semantic interactions that depend simply on "spreading excitation" in an associative semantic network.

Expectations, Passive or Active?

The multiple expectations that can be concurrently active in a Production-like system such as Riesbeck's (1975) conceptual analyzer, should be clearly distinguished from a process of single-valued prediction, where failure of a hypothesis to be confirmed delays processing while an explanation for the failure is sought, or while the system backs up to form a new hypothesis. The latter is the type of sequential hypothesis testing model of reading suggested by Hochberg (1970), to which McConkie and Rayner (1976) take exception, on the grounds that the expected delays are not observed, at least in terms of an increased duration of fixations. In what may be a related observation, Neely (1977) finds no delay in lexical decision when the target word is preceded at short ISIs by an unrelated prime, although facilitation by a related prime is obtained, and although a delay or "inhibitory" effect -- possibily due to some consciously entertained prediction -- can be found at longer ISIs.

On the contrary, expectations in a Production-like system cause actions to be taken only when a condition for which they are looking is satisfied. Backup consequent on failure of some interpretations, though sometimes resorted to, is contrary to the spirit of the system. Expectations of disjunctive and often mutually exclusive events can be concurrently active, for example, when generated for different possible meanings of a lexically ambiguous word. Thus, in the MARGIE analyzer, the transitive verb-form "break" activates separate requests, one that looks for a physical object of the "breaking," and another that tests for an obligation (a promise, vow, rule, etc.) as the object of "breaking." Successful evaluation of either request results in the inactivation of the other, so that the unsuccessful interpretation will have no effect either on the temporal course of processing or on the conceptual representation that is constructed in working memory.

In the experimental literature on reading and listening, there is some evidence that ambiguous words activate multiple alternative expectations, as reflected in facilitation effects and intrusions found in different semantic fields (Conrad, 1973; Marcel, 1974; Warren &Warren, 1976), even where the homonym is disambiguated by a sentence-context and where the subject is not explicitly aware of any lexical ambiguity (Mackay, 1966).

Context and Word Frequency: Lexical or Post-lexical Facilitation?

In the MARGIE analyzer, expectations are set up predominantly at a post-lexical, semantic or conceptual level. For example "drink" sets up a test for the semantic feature # LIQUID rather than for specific words denoting objects of drinking. The principal exception to this is in requests for closed-class morphemes -- the prepositions to, by, etc., activated by verbs as potential cues to conceptual case-structure.

The psychological evidence, on the other hand, indicates much more interactive, heterarchical effects of semantic context, including processes that reflect specifically visual aspects of graphemic stimuli. For example, semantic priming interacts strongly with manipulations of the visual quality of the test word, becoming magnified by stimulus degradation, in lexical decision tasks (Meyer et al., 1975; Becker & Killion, 1977), thereby suggesting possibly direct facilitation of lexical word-detectors or logogens.

Given this marked interaction between relatively short-term, contextual priming effects and stimulus quality, one might expect similar interactions between stimulus quality and word frequency This might seem plausible in view of the way in which the effects of word frequency can be modified or even eliminated by the prior occurrence of a given word (Scarborough et al., 1977). However, a number of experiments have failed to find anything but a strictly additive relationship between stimulus degradation and long-term frequency (Stanners, Jastrzembski, & Westbrook, 1975; Becker & Killion, 1977). At the least, this result suggests that contextual facilitation effects do not operate through the same mechanism as that responsible for the effects of first-order word frequency. It seems unlikely, for example, that both could be mediated by threshold variations, respectively phasic or residual, on the same word detectors, as in the original logogen model (Morton, 1968). Compare also the absence of interaction between the word-nonword difference and stimulus degradation through case alternation (McClelland, 1976). It would be interesting to know whether case alternation interacts with associative priming.

Henderson and Chard (1976) reported that stimulus degradation does not appear to interact with whatever mechanism of logographic familiarity is responsible for the more rapid processing of FBI over IBF. Moreover Schuberth and Eimas (1977) failed to find any interaction, in a lexical decision task, between the effects of sentence-context and the frequency of the target word. As one further illustration of their dissociability, Meyer et al. (1975) obtained parallel effects of associative priming on both overt naming and on lexical decision time; whereas word frequency has a selectively greater effect on the latter (Forster & Chambers, 1973).

What of conjoint frequency, that is, the relative facility with which a category-member is produced (or recognised) as a member of a given class of objects? Is this a variable similar to unconditional, long-term word frequency, or is it essentially a form of priming, conditional on the activation of the category name or concept? The answer, so far, is that it depends on the experimental task being performed. Rosch (1975) found that latency of the decision, whether two visually presented words belonged to the same semantic category, varied systematically with their conjoint frequency in relation to a category prime. However, similar judgments in respect of two pictures exhibited an identical effect of conjoint frequency, and moreover were some 200-300 msec faster than the equivalent judgments in respect of words. This pattern of results appears to show that the effect of conjoint frequency depends on the organization of conceptual rather than of lexical memory, and that the relevant conceptual domain can be accessed more rapidly by simple line drawings than by written words. That is, in the processing or recognition of written words, the effect of conjoint frequency, like that apparently of first order or long-term frequency, is post-lexical. However, in an explicit naming task Sanford, Garrod, and Boyle (1977) found a strong interaction between the visual quality of the test word and its conjoint frequency relative to a category prime. In a semantic classification task, on the other hand, the effects of conjoint frequency and stimulus degradation were purely additive. This sort of result is a reminder of our inadequate understanding of the mechanisms of "context," either in the recognition of words or of anything else.

PERCEPTUAL INTEGRATION

The Logogen Model

Morton (1968, 1969, 1977a) proposed a basic theoretical framework that was particularly successful in accounting for the interactive effects of context in word recognition. His starting point was the assumption that each word (or free morpheme) in a subject's vocabulary was represented by an independent detector, or logogen, whose function was to collect evidence for the occurrence of that word. Evidence could be accumulated in parallel for each logogen, and additively both from sensory analyzers (visual analyzers, in reading) and from the semantic or cognitive system, though neither of these sources of evidence was specified in any functional detail. In addition, by the somewhat ad hoc assumption of different output thresholds on logogen units, respectively for output to the semantic system and to the mechanisms of speech production, Morton sought to account for the behavioural dissociation between certain semantically mediated consequences of exposure to a written word and the ability to name it correctly: the dissociation apparent, for example, in the paralexic errors made by phonemic dyslexics and, more recently, in some of the phenomena observed in normal readers under pattern-masking.

If evidence favouring a given logogen is assumed to accumulate more slowly when the visual stimulus is degraded, the logogen model can provide an attractively simple interpretation of the interactions between stimulus quality and priming. However, as referred to above, there is then some difficulty in also accounting for the effects of word frequency in terms of the same mechanism -- as a form of long-term priming -- given the absence of observable interactions between word frequency and stimulus quality.

Other variables, such as the rated imagibility of a word's referent, also affect the ease with which a word can be explicitly named from a tachistoscopic exposure, but do not affect lexical access as indexed by associative priming effects (Marcel & Patterson, in press). On the basis of somewhat similar partial dissociations, Morton (this volume), like Marcel and Patterson, now argues for the necessity of functionally distinct output logogens for word production, as well as for separate, modality-specific input logogens (cf. Figure 1).

Given the ability of subjects to organize sentential speech while listening (the speech output of a simultaneous interpreter typically overlaps in time as much as 75% with the input -- Gerver, 1974) there must also be considerable separation possible between the control structure of the cognitive or semantic systems in relation both to reception and production.

The Logogen Model and the Problem of Perceptual Integration

A number of other difficulties for the original logogen model could be enumerated, which might be accommodated by further theoretical elaboration. Seymour (1973) has suggested how the model might be extended in outline to deal with object or picture naming. To date, the logogen model does not include a mechanism for the pronunciation of written nonwords, though this may appear a less serious objection, in a model for reading, than Smith and Spoehr's (1974) approach to the perception of printed English, which lacks anything else.[5]

A more fundamental difficulty is the problem that arises for all attempts to characterize perceptual recognition, like Selfridge's Pandemonium, as essentially a process of categorizing, or "category filtering."

The output from a given logogen unit is always the same abstract category state, which conveys no further information about the non-lexical properties of the particular stimulus that excited it. Thus if two words are displayed simultaneously, each in a different colour or typeface, the system has no means of deciding which of the two potentially available logogen outputs relates to a particular location, colour, or appearance. In practice, however, there is little difficulty in knowing which is which and in selectively reporting one or other word, even in terms of sensory discriminanda specified only after the stimulus exposure. Even the previously discussed, severely alexic patient described by Albert et al. (1973), can readily point out the location of one word which relates to a different semantic field, among several simultaneously presented words, even though he does not know its name.

Similarly in the Stroop task, to which the logogen model has been explicitly addressed (Morton & Chambers, 1973), two logogen units supposedly will be excited, one in response to the stimulus orthography, one in response to its colour. No mechanism is proposed by which the system might distinguish which of the two specifies the correct name to be produced. Yet subjects perform the task correctly.

In a more general way, then, the logogen model lacks any machinery for perceptual integration, for putting together the results of processing from different domains (semantic, orthographic, spatial, lexical, phonological ...), each of which may be active in the encoding of a written word, so as to form an integrated representation of that specific perceptual episode, on which such decisions or perceptual reports might be based.

When subjects are able to name correctly one or more simultaneously presented pattern-masked words, they are also correct about 90% of the time in reporting its spatial location (Allport, 1977), but are less likely to report details of its typography (McClelland, 1976). See also Lawrence (1971) and Broadbent (1977) for striking evidence of temporal dissociations between

---

[5]Coltheart (in press) raises some fatal objections to Smith and Spoehr's (1974) proposals for pronunciation rules.

lexical and typographic category states. Clearly the processes of perceptual integration, like all other cerebral processes, are subject to processing limitations. Treisman, Sykes and Gelade (1977) describe some interesting results relevant to the perceptual integration of simple, non-linguistic stimulus attributes, suggesting a process performed sequentially over one object or spatial region at a time.

As already argued, lexical access is not in itself a sufficient condition for the conscious perception of a word. What is also needed is some "post lexical" integrative process that can interrelate information about lexical identity, spatial location, and other visual attributes. It is this further process that is a necessary condition of conscious perception and of the ability to report a word's identity. As suggested previously (Allport, 1977) it is also the mechanism responsible for the masking interval function, relating the number of symbolic items that can be named from a tachistoscopic display to the delay of onset of a pattern-mask The section that follows contains a brief discussion of some possible models for perceptual integration in relation to word recognition and reading. A more extended analysis can be found in Allport (1978).

Mechanisms of Perceptual Integration
One modification of the logogen model that might be proposed is that information specifying sensory or other non-lexical attributes of written words is somehow carried forward to label, temporarily, those logogen units that they are responsible for activating. However, it is not at all clear how such a proposal might be implemented, in particular, in respect to non-lexical properties that did not themselves play any role in addressing the logogen system. Any such system would radically alter the passive, autonomous nature of lexical access, which was a basic, and empirically desirable feature of the model.

A more promising alternative approach would be to reverse this latter suggestion: that is, to suggest that the lexical (and other) category states might be used to label items or perhaps locations in current visual or sensory memory. Several recent theoretical suggestions to this effect include Becker's verification model (Becker, 1976; Becker & Killion, 1977), the comparator model suggested by the author (Allport, 1977), and Rumelhart's (1977) interactive model of the reading process.

Becker and Killion's (1977) verification model starts from the assumption that the discriminative capacity of word-detectors (logogens) is insufficient to yield a unique logogen output in response to a visual stimulus. Each of the activated logogen units (candidate word-hypotheses) generates a corresponding structural description, which together comprise the verification set. The structural descriptions are then compared sequentially against a representation of the stimulus in visual memory, in order of long-term word frequency, until a successful match occurs. Priming establishes a verification set in advance of stimulus exposure. In this case the contents of the verification set are compared exhaustively against visual memory, somewhat autistically, even before any candidate word-hypotheses, generated by the stimulus itself, can be tested.

By no means are all details of the model clear. What happens, for example, if there is more than one word in visual memory, or if the words are in variable typeface, etc.? What determines the contents of a primed verification set? The primed set, ordered only by long-term word frequency, makes priming an all-or-nothing relationship. Even in its present form the model is vulnerable to a number of rather serious objections. Here are two:
1) Presumably the visual quality of the stimulus, clear or degraded, will be reflected in the quality of the representation in visual memory. If so, the effect of word frequency (that is, the relative disadvantage for low-frequency words) which, according to Becker's model, depends on the sequential ordering of word candidates for the comparison process, should also be amplified by stimulus degradation. That is, the effects of word frequency and stimulus quality should interact. But this interaction persistently fails to appear in the empirical data. On the other hand, if visual noise or degradation, present in the stimulus, is held not to be present in the visual record against which the lexical hypotheses are verified, the model must specify some non-lexical means whereby degraded graphemic stimuli can be disambiguated. Where the stimuli can only be disambiguated lexically, as typically in cursive handwriting, the model should presumabaly again predict that stimulus quality and lexical frequency will interact.
2) Through exhaustive comparison of the primed set, the effects of associative priming should be dissipated by the presentation of an unrelated word. Yet priming effects are known to persist over successive stimulus exposures (Meyer, Schvaneveldt, & Ruddy, 1972; Davelaar & Coltheart, 1975).

The "Blackboard" Model
Rumelhart's (1977) interactive model for reading is based on an analogy with the architecture of a very promising computational system for automatic speech recognition, known as HEARSAY (Fennell & Lesser, 1975; Reddy & Newell, 1975). The basic control structure of HEARSAY II is that of a more or less pure Production System (Davis & King, 1975). It can be compared to the similar, though much simpler organization of Riesbeck's (1975) conceptual analyzer. Both systems employ a globally accessible message centre, or working memory, in which an interpretation of the input text is constructed through the collaborative activity of numerous independent Knowledge Sources (KSs) or Production rules.

In HEARSAY II the centralized message centre, known as the "Blackboard," is a three-dimensional data structure, in which the dimensions are respectively time within the utterance being interpreted, levels of representation, and alternative possible readings. The lowest level contains a parametric (acoustic) representation of the speech utterance to be recognized, while others contain provisional hypotheses about the linguistic interpretation of particular temporal segments of that input, asserted at different linguistic levels from the segmental to phonetic, phonemic, lexical, syntactic, and conceptual. Different KSs, or clusters of production rules, are activated independently by patterns at different levels on the Blackboard. For example, one sort of lexical KS (logogen?) can be called by particular conditions at the phonetic and secondly at the syllabic level, and responds by asserting a new hypothesis at the lexical level to account for them. Another is activated by any new lexical hypothesis and responds by verifying expectations about possible surface-phonemic sequences that should be found if the lexical hypothesis is correct (cf. the preceding section). In each case a new link is also inserted in the working memory, connecting the data pattern that initially invoked the KS and the hypotheses at other linguistic levels that were asserted in consequence, and which it thereby supports.

Rumelhart's proposal is that a broadly similar organization provides a fruitful model of visual word recognition, but in which the centralized Blackboard would be organized along spatial dimensions, rather than (or as well as?) a temporal dimension. It is obvious that the reading of alphabetic print differs from the recognition of speech in many other respects, not least the relative absence of ambiguity and the clearly segmented word structure at the graphemic level, and the great complexity of the relations between this and certain other -- especially phonological -- domains or levels of representation.

HEARSAY II, and Rumelhart's adaptation of it to the reading task, are primarily concerned with the recogntion problem of identifying what was said (or written), while Riesbeck's conceptual analyzer is concerned only with the interpretation of what was meant. However, many of the Dictionary mechanisms in Riesbeck's analyzer would be usefully incorporated into a HEARSAY-based Blackboard model of reading. Notice that, in Riesbeck's system, as in HEARSAY, the process of interpretation -- of reading or recognition -- is not one of re-writing. The word is still present after the meaning has been assigned. "The word is not converted to a concept; but associated with one" (Riesbeck, 1975). One reason that memory for surface-lexical and syntactic detail in reading is shorter lasting than memory for gist may be that conceptual or meaning-structures span, and are supported by larger segments of the text. It is at the conceptual level, also, that the horizontal (within-level) support connections will be the richest.

Consciousness

What might the relationship be between data structures in the Blackboard, or working memory, and conscious awareness?

As a working hypothesis meriting further exploration, I wish to suggest the following outline. Consciously perceived physical objects or events (including written words) correspond to those representations -- hypotheses -- on the Blackboard which have obtained at least minimal, continuous chains of inferential support connecting them with the sensory input; hypotheses, that is, that have been successfully integrated between different levels of processing.

In rapid silent reading, on the other hand, it is presumably not necessary to verify the perceptual identity of each word. So long as hypotheses at the conceptual level can be constructed, with adequate horizontal support links within that level, and occasional vertical support from the lower levels of representation, the process of rapid reading as a form of "visually guided thinking" should continue. Overt naming of a written word, however, is controlled by hypotheses asserted in, and located by, the visual-spatial co-ordinates of the Blackboard, and not controlled directly by the logogen units.

Concluding Comments

The Production-system control structure in this interactive model is the anti-
thesis of the linear succession of processing stages, each one completed
before the next can begin, that has been the preferred experimental hypothesis
about the word-recognition process. Without the linear stages assumptions,
the interpretation of additive or interactive relationships between experimental variables becomes problematic, and many of the arguments based on these
relationships may need to be reassessed. Similarly, many of the traditional
questions addressed by experimental psychologists in relation to word recognition appear in a different light, if there is no fixed ordering of processing
stages, even within dual access models. Whether individual letter-identifica-
tion is a necessary precursor of lexical or semantic interpretation may depend
on the particular condition --action rules and the structures of support
connections associated with individual words, that they can build in working
memory.

Clearly the interactive Blackboard model for word recognition is as yet
little more than a potential framework for the control structure of the reading process. Essentially all of the detailed processes have yet to be specified.
Developing the model will present innumerable theoretical choices that will
challenge the ingenuity of experimentalists to resolve.

One final qualification. A central feature, indeed the central feature,
of Production System organization, as in the HEARSAY system, is that all
communication between the different, specialist, KSs is through the one centralized data-base. Here each specialist may read, and so act upon, the results
of actions made by any other, and no communications may be routed directly,
by private channels between individual pairs of specialists.

The neuropsychological evidence, in particular the great variety of disconnection syndromes both in reading and other tasks described by Geschwind
and others (Geschwind, 1965; Whitaker & Whitaker, 1976), on the contrary,
points toward a picture of specialized subsystems linked by individual, anatomically separable pathways. It is no doubt possible to interpret these patterns
of functional disconnection in terms of selective disablement of particular
categories of read and write actions, performed by different specialists within
an anatomically widely distributed Blackboard. A little reflection should
at least deter anyone from seeking a single anatomical site for the hypothetical working memory necessary for the integration of reading.

I thank Derek Besner, Max Coltheart, David Gaffan, and Eckart Scheerer
for valuable critical comments on a previous version of this chapter.

REFERENCES

Albert, M.L., Yamadori, A., Gardner, H., & Howes, D. Comprehension in
alexia. Brain, 1973, 96, 317-328.
Allport, D.A. On knowing the meaning of words we are unable to report:
The effects of visual masking. In S. Dornic (Ed.), Attention and per-
formance, VI. Hillsdale, NJ: Erlbaum, 1977.
Allport, D.A. Conscious and unconscious cognition: A computational metaphor

for the mechanism of attention and integration. In L.G. Nilsson (Ed.), Perspectives in memory research. Hillsdale, NJ: Erlbaum, 1978.

Andreewsky, E., & Seron, X. Implicit processing of grammatical rules in a classical case of agrammatism. Cortex, 1975, 11, 379-390.

Baddeley, A.D. Working memory and reading. (This volume.)

Banks, W.P., & Flora, J. Semantic and perceptual processes in symbolic comparisons. Journal of Experimental Psychology: Human Perception and Performance, 1977, 3, 278-290.

Baron, J. Mechanisms for pronouncing printed words: Use and acquisition. In D. LaBerge & S.J. Samuels (Eds.), Basic processes in reading: Perception and comprehension. Potomac, MD: Erlbaum, 1976.

Baron, J., & Thurston, I. An analysis of the word superiority effect. Cognitive Psychology, 1973, 4, 207-228.

Barron, R., & Pittinger, J.B. The effect of orthographic structure and lexical meaning on same-different judgments. Quarterly Journal of Experimental Psychology, 1974, 26, 566-581.

Becker, C.A. Allocation of attention during visual word recognition. Journal of Experimental Psychology: Human Perception and Performance, 1976, 2, 556-566.

Becker, C.A., & Killion, T.H. Interaction of visual and cognitive effects in word recognition. Journal of Experimental Psychology: Human Perception and Performance, 1977, 3, 389-401.

Benson, D.F., & Geschwind, N. The alexias. In P.K. Vinken & G.W. Bruyn (Eds.), Handbook of clinical neurology (Vol. 4). Amsterdam: North-Holland, 1969.

Besner, D. Mental looking. Paper presented to meeting of Experimental Psychology Society, Sussex, England, April 1978.

Besner, D., & Jackson, A. Same-different judgments with words and non-words: A word superiority/inferiority effect. Bulletin of the Psychonomic Society, 1975, 6, 578-580.

Bouma, H. Interaction effects in parafoveal letter recognition. Nature, 1970, 266, 177-178.

Bouma, H. Visual interference in the parafoveal recognition of initial and final letters of words. Vision Research, 1973, 13, 767-782.

Bradshaw, J.L. Peripherally presented and unreported words may bias the perceived meaning of a centrally fixated homograph. Journal of Experimental Psychology, 1974, 103, 1200-1202.

Bradshaw, J.L. Three interrelated problems in reading: A review. Memory and Cognition. 1975, 3, 123-134.

Breitmeyer, B.G., & Ganz, L. Implications of sustained and transient channels for theories of visual pattern masking, saccadic suppression, and information processing. Psychological Review, 1976, 83, 1-36.

Broadbent, D.E. The hidden preattentive processes. American Psychologist, 1977, 32, 109-118.

Broadbent, D.E., & Broadbent, M. General shape and local detail in word perception. In S. Dornic (Ed.), Attention and performance, VI. Hillsdale, NJ: Erlbaum, 1977.

Carr, T.H., Lehmkuhle, S.W., Astor-Stetson, E.C., & Arnold, D. Target position and practice in the identification of letters in varying contexts: A word superiority effect. Perception & Psychophysics, 1976, 19, 412-416.

Chambers, S.M., & Forster, K.I. Evidence for lexical access in a simultaneous matching task. Memory and Cognition, 1975, 3, 549-559.

Charniak, E. Toward a model of children's story comprehension. AI Memo TR-266. Cambridge, MA : MIT Press, 1972.

Charniak, E. Inference and knowledge II. In E. Charniak & Y. Wilks (Eds.), Computational semantics. Amsterdam: North-Holland, 1976.

Coltheart, M. Implications of acquired dyslexias for the study of normal reading. Paper presented to the International Neuropsychology Society, Oxford, August 1977. (a)

Coltheart, M. Critical notice of E.J. Gibson & H. Levin, The psychology of reading. Quarterly Journal of Experimental Psychology, 1977, 29, 157-167. (b)

Coltheart, M. Lexical access in simple reading tasks. In G. Underwood (Ed.), Strategies of information processing. London: Academic Press (in press).

Coltheart, M., & Freeman, R. Case alternation impairs word identification. Bulletin of the Psychonomic Society, 1974, 3, 102-104.

Coltheart, M., Marshall, J.C., & Patterson, K.E. (Eds.), Proceedings of the MRC conference on phonemic dyslexia. London: Routledge & Kegan Paul (in press).

Conrad, C. Context effects in sentence comprehension: A study of the subjective lexicon. Memory and Cognition, 1973, 2, 130-138.

Conrad, R. Speech and reading. In J.F. Kavanagh & I.G. Mattingly (Eds.), Language by eye and by ear. Cambridge, MA: MIT Press, 1972.

Davelaar, E., & Coltheart, M. Effects of interpolated items on the association effect in lexical decision tasks. Bulletin of the Psychonomic Society, 1975, 6, 269-272.

Davelaar, E., Coltheart, M., Besner, D., & Jonasson, J.T. Phonological recoding and lexical access. Memory & Cognition, 1978, 6, 391-402.

Davies, D.J.M., & Isard, S.D. Utterances as programs. In D. Michie (Eds.), Machine intelligence 7. Edinburgh: Edinburgh University Press, 1972.

Davis, R., & King, J. An overview of production systems. Reprinted in E.W. Elcock & D. Michie (Eds.), Machine intelligence 8. Chichester, Sussex: Ellis Horwood/Wiley, 1977.

Egeth, H., Jonides, J., & Wall, S. Parallel processing of multi-element displays. Cognitive Psychology, 1972, 3, 674-698.

Fennell, R.D., & Lesser, V.R. Parallelism in AI problem solving: A case study of Hearsay II. AI memo, Carnegie-Mellon University, Computer Science Department, October 1975.

Fischler, I.J. Associative facilitation without expectancy in a lexical decision task. Journal of Experimental Psychology: Human Perception and Performance, 1977, 3, 18-26.

Fisher, R. Perceptual units in word recognition. Unpublished MS, University of Toronto, 1977.

Forster, K.I., & Chambers, S.M. Lexical access and naming time. Journal of Verbal Learning and Verbal Behavior, 1973, 12, 627-635.

Fraisse, P. Why is naming longer than reading? Acta Psychologica, 1969, 30, 96-103.

Gaffan, D. Discrimination of word-like compound visual stimuli by monkeys. Quarterly Journal of Experimental Psychology, 1977, 29, 589-596.

Gerver, D. Simultaneous listening and speaking and retention of prose. Quarterly Journal of Experimental Psychology, 1974, 26, 337-341.

Geschwind, N. Disconnexion syndromes in animals and men. Brain, 1965, 88, 237-294; 585-644.

Gibson, E.J. Learning to read. Science, 1965, 148, 1066-1072.

Gibson, E.J., & Levin, H. The psychology of reading. Cambridge, MA: MIT Press, 1975.

Hardyck, C.D., & Petrinovich, L.F. Subvocal speech and comprehension level as a function of the difficulty level of reading material . Journal of Verbal Learning and Verbal Behavior, 1970, 9, 647-652.

Hatta, T. Recognition of Japanese Kanji in the left and right visual fields. Neuropsychologia, 1977, 15, 685-688.

Hatta, T., Kitao, N., Ishida, M., Babazono, Y., & Kondo, Y. Concreteness, hieroglyphicity and familiarity of Kanji. Japanese Journal of Psychology, 1977, 48, 105-111.

Hécaen, H. Aspects des troubles de la lecture (Alexies) au cours des lesions cerebrales en foyer. Word, 1967, 23, 265-287.

Hécaen, H., & Kremin, H. Neurolinguistic research on reading disorders resulting from left hemisphere lesions: Aphasic and "pure" alexias. In H. Whitaker & H.A. Whitaker (Eds.), Studies in neuro-linguistics (Vol. 2). New York: Academic Press, 1976.

Henderson, L. A word superiority effect without orthographic assistance. Quarterly Journal of Experimental Psychology, 1974, 26, 301-311.

Henderson, L. Word recognition. In N.S. Sutherland (Ed.), Tutorial essays in experimental psychology (Vol. 1). Potomac, MD: Erlbaum, 1977.

Henderson, L. Pandemonium and visual search. Perception , 1978, 7, 97-104.

Henderson, L., & Chard, J. On the nature of the facilitation of visual comparisons by lexical membership. Bulletin of the Psychonomic Society, 1977, 7, 432-434.

Hochberg, J. Components of literacy: Speculations and exploratory research. In H. Levin & J.P. Williams (Eds.), Basic studies on reading. NY: Basic Books, 1970.

Johnson, J.C., & McClelland, J.L. Visual factors in word perception. Perception and Psychophysics, 1973, 14, 365-370.

Jonides, J., & Gleitman, H. A conceptual category effect in visual search: O as letter or as digit. Perception and Psychophysics, 1972, 12, 457-460.

Jonides, J., & Gleitman, H. The benefit of categorization in visual search: Target location without identification. Perception and Psychophysics, 1976, 20, 289-298.

Kleiman, G.M. Speech recoding in reading. Journal of Verbal Learning and Verbal Behavior, 1975, 14, 323-339.

Kolers, P.A. Two kinds of recognition. Canadian Journal of Psychology, 1974, 28, 51-61.

Kolers, P.A. Memorial consequences of automatized encoding. Journal of Experimental Psychology: Human Learning and Memory, 1975, 1, 689-701.

Kuipers, B.J. A frame for frames: Representing knowledge for recognition. In D.G. Bobrow & A. Collins (Eds.), Representation and understanding: Studies in cognitive science. New York: Academic Press, 1975.

Lawrence, D.H. Two studies of visual search for word targets with controlled
rates of presentation. Perception and Psychophysics, 1971, 10, 85-89.

Levy, B.A. Reading: Speech and meaning processes. Journal of Verbal
Learning and Verbal Behavior, 1977, 16, 623-638.

Levy, B.A. Speech Processing during reading. NATO Conference on
Cognition and Instruction. Plenum Press (in press).

Low, A.A. A case of agrammatism in the English language. Archives of
Neurology and Psychiatry, 1931, 25, 556-597.

Luria, A.R. Traumatic aphasia. The Hague: Mouton, 1970.

Luria, A.R. Basic problems of neurolinguistics. The Hague: Mouton, 1976.

Mackay, D.G. To end ambiguous sentences. Perception and Psychophysics,
1966, 1, 426-436.

McClelland, J.L. Preliminary letter identification in the perception of words
and nonwords. Journal of Experimental Psychology: Human Perception
and Performance, 1976, 2, 80-91.

McConkie, G.W. On the role and control of eye movements in reading.
(This volume.)

McConkie, G.W., & Rayner, K. Identifying the span of the effective stimulus
in reading: Literature review and theories of reading. In H. Singer &
R.B. Ruddell (Eds.), Theoretical models and processes of reading (2nd
ed.). Newark, DE: International Reading Association, 1976.

Manelis, L. The effect of meaningfulness in tachistoscopic word perception.
Perception and Psychophysics, 1974, 16, 182-192.

Marcel, A.J. Perception with and without awareness. Paper presented to
meeting of Experimental Psychology Society, Stirling, July 1974.

Marcel, A.J. Conscious and unconscious reading: The effects of visual masking
on word perception. Cognitive Psychology (in press).

Marcel, T., & Patterson, K. Word recognition and production: Reciprocity in
clinical and normal studies. In J. Réquin (Ed.), Attention and
performance VII. Hillsdale, NJ: Erlbaum (in press).

Marin, O.S.M., Saffran, E.M., & Schwartz, M.F. Dissociations of language in
aphasia: Implications for normal function. Annals of the New York
Academy of Sciences, 1976, 280, 868-884.

Marshall, J.C. Neuropsychological aspects of orthographic representation.
In R.J. Wales & E. Walker (Eds.), New approaches to language mechanisms.
Amsterdam: North-Holland, 1976.

Marshall, J.C., & Newcombe, F. Syntactic and semantic mechanisms in
paralexia. Neuropsychologia, 1966, 4, 169-176.

Marshall, J.C., & Newcombe, F. Patterns of paralexia. Journal of Psycholinguistic Research, 1973, 2, 175-199.

Meyer, D.E., Schvaneveldt, R.W., & Ruddy, M.G. Activation of lexical memory.
Paper presented at meeting of the Psychonomic Society, St. Louis,
Missouri, November 1972.

Meyer, D.E. Schvaneveldt, R.W., & Ruddy, M.G. Loci of contextual effects
on visual word recognition. In P.M.A. Rabbitt and S. Dornic (Eds.),
Attention and performance V. London: Academic Press, 1975.

Mezrich, J.J. The word superiority effect in brief visual displays: Elimination
by vocalization. Perception and Psychophysics, 1973, 13, 45-48.

Miller, G.A., and Johnson-Laird, P.M. Language and perception. Cambridge: Cambridge Univeristy Press, 1976.

Minsky, M. A framework for representing knowledge. In P.H.Winston (Ed.), The psychology of computer vision. Cambridge, MA: MIT Press, 1975.

Morton, J. The effects of context on the visual duration threshold for words. British Journal of Psychology, 1964, 55, 165-180.

Morton, J. Consideration of grammar and computation in language behavior. In J.C. Catford (Ed.), Studies in language and language behavior. C.R.L.L.B. Progress Report No. VI, University of Michigan, 1968.

Morton, J. Interaction of information in word recognition. Psychological Review, 1969, 76, 165-178.

Morton, J. Word Recognition. In J. Morton & J.C. Marshall (Eds.), Psycholinguistics: Series II London: Elek Scientific Books, 1977. (a)

Morton, J. In-depth study of a phonemic dyslexic. Paper presented to meeting of Experimental Psychology Society, Oxford, July 1977. (b)

Morton, J. Facilitation in word recognition: Experience causing change in the logogen model. (This volume.)

Morton, J., & Chambers, S.M. Selective attention to words and colours. Quarterly Journal of Experimental Psychology, 1973, 25, 387-397.

Morton, J., & Long, J. Effect of word transitional probability on phoneme identification. Journal of Verbal Learning and Verbal Behavior, 1976, 15, 43-51.

Moyer, R.S. Comparing objects in memory: Evidence suggesting an internal psychophysics. Perception and Psychophysics, 1973, 13, 180-184.

Neely, J.H. Semantic priming and retrieval from lexical memory: Roles of inhibitionless spreading activation and limited-capacity attention. Journal of Experimental Psychology: General, 1977, 106, 226-254.

Paivio, A. Perceptual comparisons through the mind's eye. Memory and Cognition, 1975, 3, 635-647.

Patterson, K.E. What is right with "deep" dyslexic patients? Brain and Language (in press)

Patterson, K.E., & Marcel, A.J. Aphasia, dyslexia and the phonological coding of written words. Quarterly Journal of Expeimental Psychology, 1977, 29, 307-318.

Pollatsek, A., & Carr, T. Rule-governed and wholistic encoding processes in word perception. (This volume.)

Pollatsek, A., Well, A.D., & Schindler, R.M. Familiarity affects visual processing of words. Journal of Experimental Psychology: Human Perception and Performance, 1975, 1, 328-333.

Reddy, R., & Newell, A. Knowledge and its representation in a speech understanding system. In L.W.Gregg (Ed.), Knowledge and Cognition. Potomac, MD: Erlbaum, 1975.

Reicher, G.M. Perceptual recognition as a function of meaningfulness of stimulus material. Journal of Experimental Psychology, 1969, 81, 275-280.

Richardson, J.T.E. The effect of word imageability in acquired dyslexia. Neuropsychologia, 1975, 13, 281-288.

Riesbeck, C.K. Conceptual analysis. In R.C. Schank (Ed.), Conceptual information processing. Amsterdam: North-Holland, 1975.

Riesbeck, C.K. An expectation-driven production system for natural language understanding. In D.A. Waterman & F. Hayes-Roth (Eds.), Pattern-directed inference systems. New York: Academic Press, 1978.

Rosch, E. Cognitive represenations of semantic categories. Journal of Experimental Psychology: General, 1975, 104, 192-233.

Rubenstein, H., Lewis, S.S., & Rubenstein, M.A. Evidence for phonemic recoding in visual word recognition. Journal of Verbal Learning and Verbal Behavior, 1971, 10, 645-657.

Rumelhart, D.E. Toward an interactive model of reading. In S. Dornic (Ed.), Attention and performance VI. Hillsdale, NJ: Erlbaum, 1977.

Saffran, E.M., & Marin, O.S.M. Immediate memory for word lists and sentences in a patient with deficient auditory short term memory. Brain and Language, 1975, 2, 420-433.

Saffran, E.M., & Marin, O.S.M. Reading without phonology: Evidence from aphasia. Quarterly Journal of Experimental Psychology, 1977, 29, 515-525.

Saffran, E.M., Schwartz, M.F., & Marin, O.S.M. Semantic mechanisms in paralexia. Brain and Language, 1976, 3, 255-265.

Sanford, A.J., Garrod, S., & Boyle, J.M. An independence of mechanism in the origins of reading and classification-related semantic distance effects. Memory and Cognition, 1977, 5, 214-220.

Sasanuma, S. Kana and Kanji processing in Japanese aphasics. Brain and Language, 1975, 2, 369-383.

Sasunuma, S., & Fujimura, O. Selective impairment of phonetic and non-phonetic transcription of words in Japanese aphasic patients: Kana versus Kanji in visual recognition and writing. Cortex, 1971, 7, 1-18.

Sasunuma, S., Itoh, M., Mori, K., & Kobayashi, Y. Tachistoscopic recognition of Kana and Kanji words. Neurophychologia, 1977, 15, 547-553.

Sasanuma, S., & Monoi, H. The syndrome of Gogi (word-meaning) aphasia. Neurology, 1975, 25, 627-632.

Scarborough, D.L., Cortese, C., & Scarborough, H.S. Frequency and repetition effects in lexical memory. Journal of Experimental Psychology: Human Perception and Performance, 1977, 3, 1-17.

Schank, R.C. Conceptual information processing. Amsterdam: North-Holland, 1975.

Schank, R.C., & Abelson, R.P. Scripts, plans, goals and understanding. Hillsdale, NJ: Erlbaum, 1977.

Schmidt, R. Semantic expectancy effects on word access. Psychological Research, 1976, 39, 147-161.

Schuberth, R.E., & Eimas, P.D. Effects of context on the classification of words and nonwords. Journal of Experimental Psychology: Human Perception and Performance, 1977, 3, 27-36.

Seymour, P.J.K. A model for reading, naming and comparison. British Journal of Psychology, 1973, 64, 35-49.

Shallice, T., & Warrington, E.K. Word recognition in a phonemic dyslexic patient. Quarterly Journal of Experimental Psychology, 1975, 27, 187-199.

Smith, E.E., & Haviland, S.E. Why words are perceived more accurately than nonwords: Inference versus unitizaiton. Journal of Experimental Psychology, 1972, 92, 39-64.

Smith, E.E., & Spoehr, K.T. The perception of printed English: A theoretical perspective. In B.H. Kantowitz (Ed.), Human information processing: Tutorials in performance and cognition. Hillsdale, NJ: Erlbaum, 1974.

Stanners, R.F., Jastrzembski, J.E., & Westbrook, A. Frequency and visual quality in a word-nonword classification task. Journal of Verbal Learning and Verbal Behavior, 1975, 14, 259-264.

Teng, E.L., & Sperry, R.W. Interhemispheric interaction during simultaneous bilateral presentation of letters or digits in commissurotomized patients. Neuropsychologia, 1973, 11, 131-140.

Townsend, J.T. Alphabetic confusion: A test of models for individuals. Perception and Psychophysics, 1971, 9, 40-50.

Treisman, A.M., Sykes,M., & Gelade, G. Selective attention and stimulus integration. In S. Dornic (Ed.), Attention and performance, VI. Hillsdale,N.J.: Erlbaum, 1977.

Tulving, E., & Gold, C. Stimulus information and contextual information as determinants of tachistoscopic recognition of words. Journal of Experimental Psychology, 1963, 66, 319-327.

Turvey, M.T. On peripheral and central processes in vision: Inferences from an information-processing analysis of masking with patterned stimuli. Psychological Review, 1973, 80, 1-52.

Tweedy, J.R., Lapinsky, R.H., & Schvaneveldt, R.W. Semantic-context effects on word recognition: Influence of varying the proportion of items presented in an appropriate context. Memory and Cognition, 1977, 5, 84-89.

Warren, R.E. Stimulus encoding and memory. Journal of Experimental Psychology, 1972, 94, 90-100.

Warren, R.E., & Warren, N.T. Dual semantic encoding of homographs and homophones embedded in context. Memory and Cognition, 1976, 4, 586-592.

Weiskrantz, L., Warrington, E.K., Sanders, M.D., & Marshall, J. Visual capacity in the hemianopic field following a restricted occipital ablation. Brain, 1974, 97, 709-728.

Wheeler, D.D. Processes in word recognition. Cognitive Psychology, 1970, 1, 59-85.

Whitaker, H., & Whitaker, H.A. Studies in neurolinguistics (3 vols.). New York: Academic Press, 1976.

Wilks, Y. Knowledge structures and language boundaries. Proceedings of International Joint Conference on Artificial Intelligence. Cambridge, MA: MIT Press, 1977.

Willows, D.M., & MacKinnon, G.E. Selective reading: Attention to the "unattended" lines. Canadian Journal of Psychology, 1973, 27, 292-304.

Yamadori, A. Ideogram reading in alexia. Brain, 1975, 98, 231-238.

Facilitation in Word Recognition: Experiments Causing Change
in the Logogen Model

John Morton

The logogen has been defined as the unit which makes a
particular verbal response available from whatever source.
The simplest theoretical position has been that it was res-
ponsible for facilitation and the word frequency effect
through either the experience or the production of words.
Thus, producing a word in response to a picture should have
an effect equal to that of reading the word, on the subsequent
visual duration threshold of the word. An experiment by
Winnick and Daniel (1970) goes against this requirement.
This experiment has been replicated, and other experiments
indicate modality specificity in facilitation. These results
force the adaptation to the theory of two input logogens
and an output logogen to replace the original single structure.
Experiments on facilitation of picture recognition indicate
at least two relevant levels and a two-way independence
of picture and word recognition.

The logogen model (Morton, 1964, 1968, 1969, 1978) has been evolved to
account for (or in response to) a wide variety of phenomena in the area of
word recognition. The focal part of the model, the logogen system, is made
up of devices which are responsible for producing a phonological code whenever appropriate. The linguistic unit with which the logogen is concerned
is, roughly, a word. Thus, if the word "chair" is spoken, if the letter sequence
CHAIR is presented, if someone is asked to name the object or free associate
to "table," or if the word arises in spontaneous speech, the same logogen
is terminally responsible. Since it obviates the need for multiple representations of the phonological code for a word, this is clearly the most economical hypothesis.

The criterion of simplicity has been taken further. Not only is all output of a particular word the responsibility of the one element, but all inputs coincide on the same point (Figure 1). The Cognitive System subsumes all processing other than that specified in other parts of the model. Thus, given that a relevant context exists for understanding a stimulus word, the Cognitive System produces "semantic" information, which interacts positively in the Logogen System with the sensory information derived from the stimulus. In spontaneous speech all that is present is the semantic information which is sufficient to make a particular logogen produce its phonological output.

Differences in the recognisability of words are accounted for by saying that the logogens corresponding to common words require less information to make them produce an output; that is, they have lower criteria than uncommon words. These differences in criteria have been ascribed to logogen use. Thus it has been believed that words used a lot in spontaneous speech have lower visual duration thresholds (Daston, 1957). Also, experiments which mimic the word frequency effect by giving subjects differential experience of nonsense words and then testing the recognisability of these words show cross-modal transfer (Weissman & Crockett, 1957). In addition, the effects of such pretraining exert a strong influence on response production in the absence of any stimulus (Goldiamond & Hawkins, 1958).

All this information contributed to the logogen concept and is consistent with it. It is, then, a central part of the concept as it stood, that any use of the logogen will give rise to subsequent facilitation of its use. I have used this notion twice in evolving the model; once in its justification and once in extending it. The first use was of Neisser's (1954) experiment in which he pretrained subjects with either PHRASE or FRAYS and showed that the latter had no effect on the subsequent recognition of PHRASE. I interpreted this as showing that the definition of a logogen was not only the output code

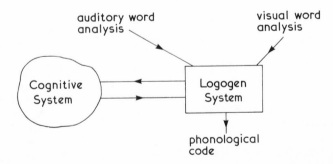

Figure 1. The essential parts of the original versions of the logogen model.

but also the visual or semantic codes that would be different for the two words. The second facilitation experiment was by Murrell and Morton (1974). In this study we showed that the subsequent recognition of BORED was affected by prior experience of BORING but not by more experience of BORN. The degree of visual and acoustic similarity between the practice and test words was equivalent; the difference was that BORING is morphologically related to BORED but BORN is not. Thus we concluded that logogens functioned at the level of the morpheme, not of the word as such. (It should be made clear that the morphemic identification is structural, not semantic. The logogen system is explicitly not a dictionary; I conceive semantic information as something to be discovered at a further stage when required.)

Winnick and Daniel (1970)

This position should have been badly weakened in 1970 when Winnick and Daniel published their paper. But somehow I managed to repress the implications of their study. In brief, they presented their subjects with a mixture of words, pictures of objects, and definitions of objects in which the object name did not occur. In all cases the subjects had to respond with the appropriate word. Later, all the words, plus controls with which no prior experience was associated, were presented for tachistoscopic recognition. The prediction from the logogen model is clear – the recognition of all the words should be facilitated with respect to the controls regardless of whether the words had previously been seen. In all three cases, within the existing logogen structure, if the response was made the logogen was used and so there must have been facilitation. In fact the mean tachistoscopic thresholds for the four groups of words are given in Table 1a. There were no differences apparent other than between the WORD group and the other groups. When I reread their paper last year, I realised I either had to find a flaw in their procedure or change my ideas. With this in mind I have participated in three series of experiments in the last year with Bob Clark, Clive Warren, and Anita Jackson. To anticipate the results, we replicated Winnick and Daniel's findings and extended the range of non-facilitation, and I have been forced to change the form of the model.

Facilitation of Visual Word Recognition

Experiment 1

In a pilot experiment Bob Clarke and I confirmed Winnick and Daniel's findings. The subjects were required to say words in response to the printed word, the picture, or a definition prior to a word threshold measurement. With very few subjects (n = 9) it became apparent that the basic results were being reproduced. The mean thresholds are given in Table 1b. The higher times are due to contrast, word size, and other factors which were different from those in Winnick and Daniel's study. It is clear that experience of neither pictures nor definitions had any effect on the subsequent recognition of the equivalent words. If just the pictures had given this result, it might have been argued that they were a special case, and that the phonological codes for object names were duplicated, once in the word system and once in the object recognition system. However, there is no such possibility in the case of definitions, for which no such special pleading is feasible.

Table 1(a). Winnick and Daniel (1970) Results.

Act like "dumb" words.

Type of Pretraining	Words	Pictures	Definitions	Controls
Mean Threshold (msec)	49.1	58.6	61.0	61.9

Table 1(b). Experiment 1, Winnick and Daniel Replication.

Pretraining	Words	Pictures	Definitions	Controls
Threshold (msec)	111	118	121.5	123.6

We seem to be forced into a position such as that illustrated in Figure 2. In this case the facilitation is the responsibility of the visual input system. When a word is presented, analysed information passes into this input system and the appropriate logogen is activated. The word can then be produced as a response either through a direct connection to the output system (if such a connection exists) or through the Cognitive System. The logogen in the input system then has a lower threshold in the second part of the experiment and the standard facilitation effect is found. The picture (of a butterfly, for example) will be processed in a separate system. After being classified, I assume, some semantic code is accessed in the Cognitive System. This code is then translated into a phonological code in the output system. The logogen for "butterfly" in the input system would not be affected by this sequence of events. Thus we would find no subsequent facilitation in visual word recognition. (Note that if the word were spoken out loud and fed back via the ears, and if this acoustic input affected the same system, then there would be effects. But see on.) Similarly, although a definition of "butterfly" would be processed through the language processing system, the input logogen for the word would not be affected. The information in the definition would be computed upon in the Cognitive System and the response would be produced via the output system only. Figure 2 is thus consistent with the data and, given certain presuppositions, seems to be entailed by it. The data also require that there is no facilitation in the input system over the time intervals found in this experiment.

The account given by Winnick and Daniel favoured facilitation by repetition of stimulus patterns. The result of Murrell and Morton mentioned above, where the morpheme was seen to be the base of the facilitation effect, argues against that. Experiment 2 was conducted to verify this.

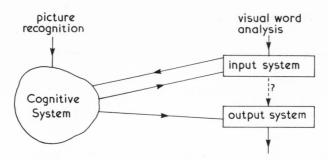

Figure 2. The minimum modification to Figure 1 forced by the results of Winnick and Daniel and Experiment 1. Only visual inputs are considered.

Experiment 2
The basic design was identical to the previous experiment. In this case the picture condition was dropped and a condition substituted in which the pretraining was a handwritten version of a word later to be seen in typewritten form. Care was taken to make the writing cursive so that although it could not be read letter for letter, it was still readable as a word. The other conditions were the typewritten word, the definition, and a control condition as before. This time the experimental procedure was more tightly controlled and the results were clear (Table 2).

The difference between typewritten and handwritten was not significant even at the 0.05 level. I am not going to argue that there is no difference there, simply that if there is one it is not at the level of the input logogen system. As before, the definitions had zero effect, the mean threshold being indistinguishable from that for the control group.

This result reinforces our belief in the correctness of the model in Figure 2. The facilitation effects are due to verbal inputs only. The next question is whether auditory and visual inputs affect the same system.

Table 2. Experiment 2 on Visual Recognition.

Pretraining	Typewritten	Handwritten	Definitions	Controls
Threshold (msec)	28.9	30.7	35.5	35.6

Table 3. Experiment 3 on Visual Recognition.

Pretraining	Visual repeat	Visual opposite	Auditory repeat	Auditory opposite	Control
	39.3	40.2	43.4	44.3	46.2

Experiment 3
In this experiment the pretraining was either visual or auditory. The recognition in the second part of the experiment was always visually based. A second variable, the nature of the response, was inserted into the pretraining. As each word was presented, the subject was instructed either to read or repeat the word (for visual and auditory presentation respectively), or to give the opposite. Stimuli were either polar adjectives like "hot" or "wide" or were nouns such as "queen" or "uncle," where the spontaneous opposite response always involved a gender change. This variable was introduced because we thought it possible that facilitation would only be found if the link posited tentatively between the input and output systems was used. If the subjects were required to give an opposite, this link would less likely be involved. (Of course this was a heavily contingent prediction - the negative result would prove nothing.)

From the data given in Table 3, it is clear that the nature of the response was immaterial. It is also clear that the modality of the pretraining did make a difference. There is no significant difference between the auditory conditions and the control, but we don't want to insist there is no difference. Suffice it here to say that we feel it necessary to talk in terms of two input logogens, one for each modality. Thus we have a model which in simplified form is shown in Figure 3. We can see now why no facilitation would be expected following feedback of someone naming a picture out loud. There are no connections between the two input systems, and any facilitation is restricted to the modality being tested. (This is the strongest form of the new model and is liable to falsification.)

Facilitation of Auditory Word Recognition
One alternative to Figure 3 is a model in which the visual input system feeds into the auditory input system, but not vice versa. This is demonstrated in an abbreviated form in Figure 4. This would be consistent with the previous data, but would give rise to the prediction that experience of visual words will facilitate subsequent recognition of auditorily presented words.

In this experiment Anita Jackson and I used a separate groups design where each subject received only one kind of pretraining. The pretraining consisted of the subjects making semantic judgments on a list of 100 words, which was

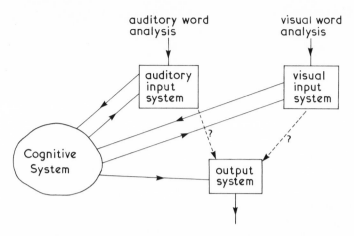

Figure 3. The elaboration of the model of Figure 2 to allow for auditory verbal stimuli.

presented twice. The subjects then heard a sequence of 200 words including the 100 which had been pretrained. These words were presented in white noise adjusted to give 40% correct identification with control subjects. There were four groups of interest for the present discussion, differing by the nature of the pretraining. One group had previously heard the test words spoken in the same clear female voice as that used in the recognition session. A second group had also heard the words previously, but in a male voice. The third group had seen the words, rather than heard them, and the fourth was a control group which went through the recognition session with no prior experience of the words. The results are given in Table 4. The figures represent the mean probability of correctly recognising a word in the pretraining set and the control set. The results are complicated by the fact that there are differences in performance for the untrained words between subject groups similar to the difference found between the pretrained words. When suitable

Table 4. The Effects of Different Prior Experience on Auditory Recognition.

Pretraining		Same voice	Different voice	Visual	Control
Prob. correct for:	Experimental words	.60	.51	.41	.33
	Control words	.49	.45	.44	.40

Table 5. Effects of Prior Experience on Picture Recognition--Experiment 1.

Pretraining	Same picture	Different picture	Words	Control
Threshold	35.7	40.9	43.6	43.8

adjustments are made, it is found that the effect of visual pretraining is just significantly different from the control group, but that the two groups with prior auditory experience, while not differing from each other, were very different from both the visual and control groups.

These results parallel those found with visual presentation. There is a small cross-modal effect and small differences within modality but the main thrust of the data favours the representation in Figure 3. Experience of a word affects the input logogen specific to the modality of presentation. Other effects and differences are smaller in magnitude and we expect to be able to attribute them to other causes.

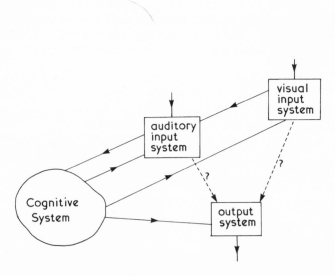

Figure 4. An alternative model consistent with the data from the first three experiments. The data presented in Table 4 force us to reject this alternative.

Facilitation of Picture Recognition

In a previous section I noted that Clark and Morton had replicated Winnick and Daniel's finding that naming pictures does not affect subsequent recognition of words. In this series of experiments by Clive Warren and me, the design was reversed and the question was posed as to the influences on picture recognition.

Experiment 1

There were two parts of interest. The first involved the subjects reading words or naming drawings of objects, and the second involved the tachistoscopic recognition of drawings. These drawings were of objects named by the words in the preceding session, or were drawings previously named, or different drawings of objects which had previously been named. Table 5 gives the mean thresholds of recognition.

It is clear that experience with the words has no effect on picture recognition. In light of the results already reported, this will come as no surprise. It is also apparent that experience of a specific drawing facilitates subsequent recognition of the same drawing. The question of transfer to a different picture of the same object is less clear. When questioned, a number of subjects revealed that they had been adopting the strategy of attempting literal recall of the pretraining drawings and matching them against the stimuli. This was possible because only eight drawings were used in the pretraining.

Experiment 2

Forty-four drawings were used in the pretraining - eight were later seen in the recognition session with eight different drawings of previously named drawings of objects, plus drawings for which there had been no relevant prior experience. The effect of these changes in procedure was a significant transfer from one picture of an object to another picture of the same object. The figures can be seen in Table 6.

Other evidence in this study has led us to believe that there are two sources of facilitation in picture recognition. The first is reactivation of a literal representation of a drawing; the second is a more abstract, idealised centre for each object type. This might be termed a "pictogen." The object recognition system, up to and including the pictogens, does not intersect the system

Table 6. Effects of Prior Experience on Picture Recognition--Experiment 2.

Pretraining	Same picture	Different picture	Control
Threshold	35.8	39.4	43.2

involved in word repetition.

Conclusions
The new form of the model has replaced the old logogen system with three elements: visual input logogens, auditory input logogens, and output logogens. The picture recognition system is completely separate. All the earlier results are still applicable to the model, usually to the input logogens. Apparent cases of cross-modal transfer are the exception (e.g., Weissman & Crockett, 1957). Such results would now be attributed to problem solving behaviour using information in the cognitive system (something like an episode related to the pretraining). The replacement of one construct by three others has added enormous power. The new formulation has something in common with recent proposals by Seymour (1975), Shallice (personal communication) and Marcel and Patterson (1978).

REFERENCES

Daston, P.G. Perception of idiosyncratically familiar words. Perceptual and Motor Skills, 1957, 7, 3-6.

Goldiamond, I., & Hawkins, W.F. Vexierversuch: the logarithmic relationship between word-frequency and recognition obtained in the absence of stimulus words. Journal of Experimental Psychology, 1958, 56, 457-463.

Marcel, A.J., & Patterson, K.E. Word recognition and production: Reciprocity in clinical and normal research. In J. Réquin (Ed.), Attention and performance VII, Hillsdale, NJ: Erlbaum, 1978.

Morton, J. A preliminary functional model for language behaviour. International Audiology, 1964, 3, 216-225. (Reprinted in R.C. Oldfield & J.C. Marshall (Eds.), Language. London: Penguin, 1968).

Morton, J. Grammar and computation in language behavior. In J.C. Catford (Ed.), Studies in language and language behavior. Center for Research in Language and Language Behavior Progress Report No. VI, University of Michigan, 1968.

Morton, J. The interaction of information in word recognition. Psychological Review, 1969, 76, 165-178.

Morton, J. Word recognition. In J. Morton and J.C. Marshall (Eds.), Psycholinguistics Series II, London: Elek Scientific Books, 1978.

Murrell, G.A., & Morton, J. Word recognition and morphemic structure. Journal of Experimental Psychology, 1974, 102, 963-968.

Neisser, U. An experimental distinction between perceptual process and verbal response. Journal of Experimental Psychology, 1954, 47, 399-402.

Seymour, P. H. K. A model for reading, naming, and comparison. British Journal of Psychology, 1973, 64, 35-49.

Weissman, S.L., & Crockett, W.H. Intersensory transfer of verbal material. American Journal of Psychology, 1957, 70, 283-285.

Winnick, W.A., & Daniel, S.A. Two kinds of response priming in tachistoscopic recognition. Journal of Experimental Psychology, 1970, 84, 74-81.

Word Knowledge and Letter Recognition as Determinants of Word Recognition

Don G. Bouwhuis

The recognition of words during reading implies not only that letters, or other constituent parts of words, are seen, but also that words are known. In a recognition model for words of three letters, developed by Bouma and Bouwhuis (1975), word perception is thought to be mediated both by recognition of the constituent letters in their position and by knowledge of the words. For reasons of simplicity it was assumed that subjects knew the same words, that the words were known equally well, and that frequency of occurrence did not influence response probability.

In the experiment reported here these assumptions were tested by presenting all Dutch words of three letters to 30 subjects and asking them if they knew them. Perceptually similar nonwords were also presented, making the task a lexical decision task. The most important result was that words varied considerably in familiarity, as indicated by both correct responses and response times. It also appeared that word knowledge was rather uniform over the 30 subjects. Frequency of word occurrence had only a minor effect and involved only the most rare, often unknown, words.

It is argued that incorporation of differential word familiarity into the vocabulary of a model could improve its predictions of word recognition.

When we read, new words move into our field of vision at the same time as others are being decoded, recognized, and a meaning attached to them. During this process expectations are formed concerning the words to come. The reader is usually able to guess words that might logically follow those he has just read. It is only through his knowledge of words that he can think of words that are suitable in a context. A word which is not part of the reader's word knowledge is not a word for that reader, while it may be perfectly acceptable to those who know it. It is not difficult to find such words and this observation merely stresses the fact that words are so numerous that they cannot all be known by any one individual. Words in a language range from common words of the vernacular to specialized jargon.

Word Recognition

Recognition of words involves both perceptual and linguistic processes. A general description of word recognition should therefore include a specification of word knowledge. However, one reader may know some words which another reader does not know; consequently, word knowledge would have, in addition to general components, substantial individual components, but to assess all those words which are individually known by any subject may be possible in principle, although not realistic. A description of word recognition is only feasible and productive when people have a major proportion of their word knowledge in common.

Word Counts

It is not uncommon to use word counts as an estimate of words which are known. Word counts have been published by Thorndike and Lorge (1944) and by Kučera and Francis (1967) for American English and by De la Court (Linschoten, 1963) and by Uit den Boogaart (1975) for Dutch. All these lists have been compiled from printed material in which word frequency varies. Several studies have shown that words which occur frequently are more easily identified (Broadbent, 1967). A possible explanation is that words which are regularly encountered by the reader are processed more efficiently. The frequency of occurrence might thus reflect how familiar they are to readers. Although it is not certain which words a particular reader has seen and how often he has seen them, word frequency lists might be considered to represent a fairly general body of word knowledge, but one in which fairly uncommon words, though perhaps widely known, are usually not represented.

Rumelhart and Siple (1974) used the three-letter words in the list of Kučera and Francis (1967) for their word recognition model. Word frequency was applied in such a way that infrequent words had a lower predicted probability of being responded to than frequent ones. The fact that their model was complicated and that their experiment took in so many words and strings (726), prevented the parameters of the model from being accurately estimated, thus precluding a clear idea of how important the incorporation of word frequency in the model was for the actual predictions. Nevertheless, examination of the experimental data suggests that frequency effects are small compared to the effects of the visual aspects of the words presented.

Thus, there appear to be two ways in which word frequency counts fall short of describing word knowledge. First, variations in the knowledge of words as expressed by their frequency has no basic impact on word recognition. Second, word counts include few of the most uncommon words. This fact was encountered during the development of a recognition model by Bouma and Bouwhuis (1975; Bouwhuis, 1978), a model also intended to describe recognition of three-letter words.

I will first describe how the reader's word knowledge was implemented in the model. The vocabularies adopted for testing the model influenced the model predictions in a specific manner which will be described below.

The shortcomings of the vocabularies used provided the motivation for investigating knowledge of words of three letters. The results shed light on the general situation with regard to word knowledge among readers and indeed indicate that the most important aspect of words is whether they are known or not!

Shaping A Vocabulary

The word recognition model of Bouma and Bouwhuis (Bouwhuis, 1978) describes the perception of a word as due to the perception of the constituent letters in their correct position. Letter perception is imperfect, however, because of parafoveal presentation, which impedes letter recognition. Thus a presented word may produce a large number of strings of three letters, perceptually similar to the word. Some of these strings form words and it is assumed that in his response the reader takes only those words into consideration. The decision rule which is assumed to operate is the constant ratio rule (Clarke, 1957); essentially, its application means that the probabilities that the word forms are present among the possibly perceived strings are normalized to add up to 1.0.

If such a model is to describe word recognition properly, it must employ the same lexicon as the general reader. In accordance with the principles outlined above, the appropriate words were taken from the most recent word count, that of Uit den Boogaart (1975). His list was compiled from 720,000 words of printed text and contained 1651 three-character sequences, including a number of actual words. All character sequences between two spaces were included in the count, so that the list also contained abbreviations (TUC, KLM, CIA); coding symbols (CO2, DC8, SO2); plural forms (A's, B's); numbers (3.6, 100, 010); and match scores (1-0, 3-4). Though these forms are interesting, they were not considered to be words and not admitted to the vocabulary used for the model. Both lists contained homographs. Some were lexically different while others were produced by verb conjugations ("arm" : body part, poor; "was" : (I,he) was, laundry, wash, growth, wax). Since words are presented in isolation in the word recognition experiment, no specific meaning can be inferred. These identical spelling forms need, therefore, appear only once in the vocabulary of the model; the assumption is that different meanings do not compete for recognition under the same spelling form since only one is functional at any one time (experimentally supported by Forster & Bednall, 1976). It may be noted here that homographs are more quickly identified than unique spelling forms (Rubenstein, Garfield, & Millikan, 1970; Forster & Bednall, 1976).

Thus revised, the list of Uit den Boogaart (1975) comprised 409 different words and was used as the word vocabulary of the model. It was soon obvious that this list was incomplete. Earlier in the recognition experiment by Bouma (1973), for which the recognition model predictions were intended, some words were reported that did not appear in the vocabulary adopted. It was therefore supplemented with the few words from Linschoten's compilation (1963) of the pre-war De la Court count which did not appear in the list of Uit den Boogaart. De la Court had counted some 1,000,000 words and among them

there were 329 different three-letter words. Finally, the vocabulary was
enlarged to include the results of questionnaires concerning three-letter
words, distributed among a group of readers to ensure that the words were
known. Thus a total of 541 words was compiled. In principle, the predictive
power of the model should have been increased by this expansion since more
responses could be accounted for.

Recognition and the Role of Knowledge

The recognition model was tested on recognition data collected by Bouma
(1973) with both vocabularies, the incomplete one with 409 entries and the
supplemented one comprising 541 entries. First, as was to be expected, the
model's prediction of erroneous responses was more accurate with the larger
vocabulary. Second, the probability of correct responses was underestimated
by 3% with the smaller vocabulary but by 8% with the larger one. This underestimation, especially with the large vocabulary, can be explained by the
nature of the decision rule applied. When there are more possible candidate
words for a presented word, the normalization of the constant ratio rule makes
the individual word response probabilities lower than when there are fewer
candidate words. There are simply more competitors for the response to
a word and this affects the correct responses most, since they are usually
the largest. Therefore it appears that both vocabularies have inadequacies:
the smaller one lacks accuracy, but the larger leads to greater underestimation of the predictions of correct responses. A reconsideration of the
all-or-none character of the fixed vocabulary seems to be called for.

What are the consequences for the recognition model of a vocabulary
in which the words are not equally well known? If the additional words in
the large vocabulary were less familiar they would, when activated by a
stimulus word, compete less with better known alternatives. After normalization of the word probabilities, the little known words would have a lower
probability of ever producing a response, and consequently the well-known
words would be more likely to produce a response.

Since the stimulus words in the study by Bouma (1973) were well known,
their predicted probabilities for correct identification would increase --
precisely the effect aimed at. Even the smaller vocabulary might contain
little known words. If this factor could be incorporated in the vocabulary,
the slight underestimation with the smaller vocabulary would also be offset.
Nonetheless, the larger vocabulary would appear preferable since it allows
predictions for a greater number of words and the responses to them. It would
even be possible to increase the number of words of the vocabulary for
greater generality. Since additions would probably be even less well known
than the words adopted, they would consequently have minor effects on the
response probabilities of the latter.

There is ample reason to study the degree to which words are known;
a task that is feasible in the case of words of three letters since these are
limited in number. That words vary in familiarity seems only logical.
Nevertheless, it is surprising to see to what extent word recognition can be
described on the assumption that words are equally well known (Bouma &
Bouwhuis, 1975).

EXPERIMENT

In contradistinction to a word-recognition test, words presented in a word-knowledge test should be perfectly readable since the operation of word knowledge must not be hampered by visual degradation. Since a subject can pretend to know the word presented, nonwords must be included so that the test becomes a lexical decision; in other words, the subject decides whether the string of letters presented forms a word or not. This type of task is not uncommon (Rubenstein, Garfield, & Millikan, 1970; Rubenstein, Lewis, & Rubenstein, 1971) but it rarely involves more than 200 words, and never a complete set like the present set of Dutch three-letter words.

Procedure

Material
All Dutch words consisting of three letters were taken from the largest up-to-date Dutch dictionary (Kruyskamp, 1970). Conjugated verb forms did not appear as such and were derived. In all, 713 three-letter words were found. Meaningless letter strings were selected on the basis of visual similarity to actual words. For this purpose we used the recognition model to predict the most probable but meaningless letter strings for real words. Most of these letter strings were easily pronounceable; as judged by two speakers, 250 had no normal Dutch pronunciation. The latter strings generally consisted of three consonants. The first type of meaningless strings will be called "regular nonwords," the latter type "irregular nonwords." Together they totalled 787.

Presentation
All words and strings were typed in lower-case Courier 10 typeface, and the visual field was 30 x 30 cm with a luminance of 150 cd/m^2, representative of normal reading situations. The reading distance was 60 cm, at which each letter space subtended a visual angle of 0.25 of a degree. Before each test the subject looked at a blurred fixation spot of a faint gray which did not interfere with the perception of the letters. The location of the spot corresponded to the middle letter of the string. Words and meaningless strings were presented in random order.

Subjects
Thirty subjects participated in the experiment. They responded by pressing one of two buttons corresponding to "word" and "nonword." They all saw each word and string only once. Before sessions started, they practised on lists of 100 words of four letters. They were instructed to respond as carefully as possible. Trials were completed in two sessions separated by an average of seven days.

Results
How do we measure word knowledge? One way is to list and count the number of words known by a subject. A word can also be considered to be less well known if it takes the subject longer to realize that it is a word. By this reasoning a word is well known when more subjects recognize it as such and

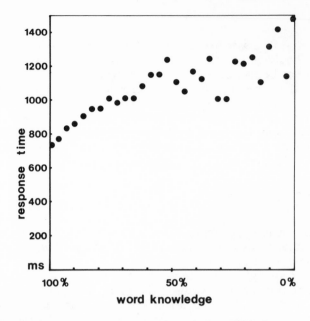

Figure 1. Response times for correct word classifications as a function of familiarity. Familiarity is the relative frequency of correct classifications by the 30 subjects.

when they do so quickly and efficiently. On average the subjects recognized 493 of the 713 words, with a standard deviation of 50. The subjects therefore seemed to form a reasonably homogeneous group. On average a subject knew 70% of all the words, while 37 words, or about 5%, were not known to any of them. On the other hand, only 163 words were known by all 30 subjects. Between these extremes were the words known to a varying number of subjects. The familiarity of these words can be defined as the proportion of subjects knowing them. This definition differs from other definitions of familiarity in the literature.

Response Times
In Figure 1 response times for correct word identification are plotted as a function of word familiarity. It can be seen that it took longer to recognize a word as such when it was less familiar. The average response time for the words known by all 30 subjects (familiarity 1.0) was 735 msec, that for the least well known (familiarity 0.033) 1479 msec, a one hundred percent increase. The standard deviation of these values rose from 70 msec for the best known words to 200 msec up to a familiarity value of 0.133, after which the standard deviation suddenly increased to about 550 msec, indicating much less homogeneity in this unfamiliar group of words.

Several of the nonwords were classified as words by the subjects. Yet

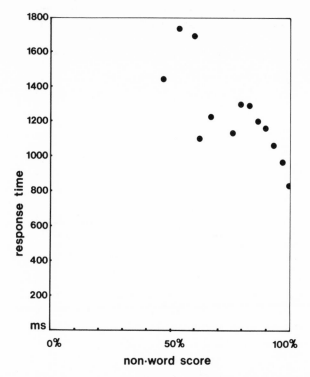

Figure 2. Response times for correctly classified nonwords as a function of the relative frequency with which they were classified by 30 subjects.

subjects were more sure about these; there were never more than 16 subjects who classified a nonword as a word. Of the 787 nonwords 542, or slightly less than 70%, were classified correctly by all 30 subjects, who on average had 770 nonwords or 98% correct as compared to the 70% for actual words. Response times for the various familiarity values are shown in Figure 2. The longest average time was 1735 msec, decreasing rapidly to 838 msec for the most definite nonwords, with standard deviations of about 150 msec. Consequently, the best known words were classified somewhat more quickly than a definite nonword. If the nonwords are divided into regular and irregular types, a different situation is found. The most definite irregular nonwords were classified in 715 msec, faster, but not appreciably, than the best known words.

Classification time as a function of word frequency is shown in Figure 3. Word frequency classes indicated in the figure are based on the 720,000 words counted by Uit den Boogaart (1975) in printed Dutch. Word frequency appears not to influence response times at all, except for the most uncommon words, which are classified 127 msec slower. These uncommon words include the words which do not appear in counts. Classifying irregular nonwords correctly took appreciably less time than for regular nonwords which resemble

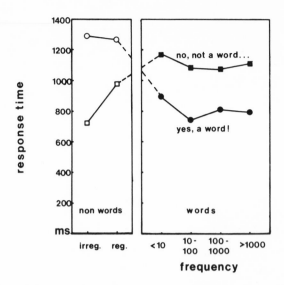

Figure 3. Left: response times for correct and incorrect responses to regular and irregular nonwords. Right: same for correct and incorrect responses to words as a function of word frequency. Round symbols refer to word responses, square symbols to nonword responses.

real words. The classification of irregular nonwords as words, however, took more time on average than all other responses. On average, erroneous responses take 300 msec longer than correct responses, except again in the case of irregular nonwords where the difference is almost twice as large.

In all these analyses geometric, rather than arithmetic, means have been calculated. Geometric means are less sensitive to the long response times which occasionally occur, a property which they share with the median (Noordman, 1977; Noordman-Vonk, 1977). Also their associated variances are more stable, but both measures of central tendency preclude the use of additive models. The differences discussed are maintained, or even increased if arithmetic means are used.

Accuracy Measurements
On the right in Figure 4 the percentage of word responses is shown as a function of word frequency. In this case, too, a frequency effect is only discernible for the most uncommon words — a drop from 0.95 to 0.62. On the left, the percentage of word responses to nonwords is shown. Of the regular nonwords 2.8% were called words while only 0.6% of the irregular nonwords were so designated. The rank order of accuracy measurements in Figure 4 is almost exactly the reverse of that for the word response times for words and nonwords in Figure 3.

If words and nonwords vary in familiarity, it is possible in principle to

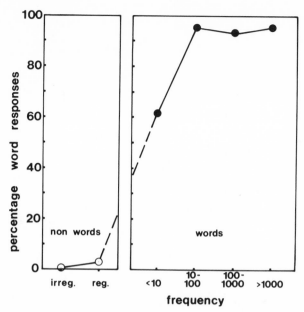

Figure 4. Left: relative frequency of word responses to regular and irregular nonwords. Right: relative frequency of word responses to words as a function of word frequency.

derive their familiarity distributions. If the familiarity distributions overlap (i.e., if some nonwords look more familiar than some words) the subject, who bases his response on subjective familiarity, is bound to make some errors. According to the theory of signal detectability (Green & Swets, 1966) the underlying distributions can be derived from the probabilities of correct word responses and incorrect nonword responses. Figure 5 shows these probabilities if both a word and a nonword are called words. (The points in Figure 5 were obtained by taking the cumulative proportions of numbers of words known and the cumulative proportions of numbers of nonwords classified as words by a varying number of subjects. The number of subjects is therefore used as the criterion in signal detectability: strict when all subjects agree, loose when the number of subjects knowing words decreases.) If this plot forms a straight line on normal probability axes, the distributions are normal. Since the plot in fact has a linear appearance, we used a regression procedure to estimate the distribution parameters. For the regular nonwords the accuracy of fit of a linear relation, expressed as a proportion of explained variance, is 0.991. For irregular nonwords there are only two observations since so few errors were made with them; a linear fit is therefore trivial. It can be clearly seen that a small shift in the familiarity of words corresponds to a large shift in the familiarity of both types of nonwords. This means that the familiarity of the nonwords must have a much narrower distribution than that of words. This can clearly be seen in Figure 6, where the distributions

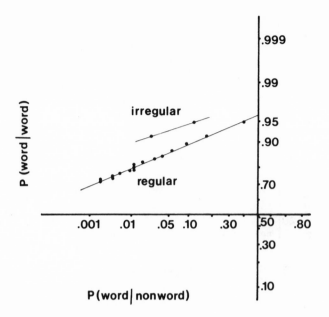

Figure 5. Probabilities of correct word responses plotted against probabilities of word responses to regular and irregular nonwords. The units of both axes are normal deviates.

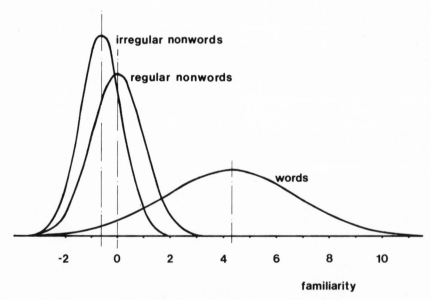

Figure 6. Theoretical familiarity distributions of irregular nonwords, regular nonwords, and words derived from the data points in Figure 5. The unit is the standard deviation of the regular nonwords.

are shown for irregular nonwords, regular nonwords, and words. Compared to nonwords, words appear to have greater spread in familiarity. Though there is little confidence about the irregular nonwords, whatever there is indicates that their familiarity is still lower and less variable than that of regular nonwords.

Discussion

The principal objective of this study was to assess which three-letter words subjects knew and thus to improve the vocabulary of the recognition model developed (Bouwhuis, 1978). In the word recognition model the vocabulary was limited to 541 words of three letters, all considered equally accessible. The present study reveals that subjects effectively know 493 words and that the words known vary substantially in accessibility. Though the words known vary from one subject to another, any two subjects know, on average, 426 words in common. It can be seen in Figure 1 that if words are less well known, they are responded to more slowly. But these response times are for subjects who knew the words at the time of presentation. Accessibility therefore seems fairly uniform for the subjects; on the whole, subjects know the same words well; and they all have difficulties with little-known words. It can be concluded from the above findings that the number of words adopted in the large vocabulary was slightly on the high side. Any lower number would reduce the underestimation of the predicted correct responses.

However, although the nominal number should be lower, the actual number of accessible words might be greater because not all words are equally accessible. Since some words come quickly and others are difficult to evoke, a gradation of accessibility seems to be called for. This could be achieved by weighting each word with its familiarity value. The number of possible alternatives increases, allowing greater precision, while the unfamiliar words figure less prominently in the alternatives, thus counterbalancing the underestimation in the predictions. The familiarity values are therefore based on experimental data other than word recognition as predicted by the model. Since letter perception as defined in the model was also based on separate experiments, the recognition model would need no parameter estimation from word recognition data, which it is meant to describe.

Orthographic Structure

In this volume Pollatsek and Carr argue that abstract orthographic rules facilitate word perception. They conclude this from a range of "same-different" experiments in which subjects decide more quickly that two words are the same than that two nonwords are the same. The ability to decide more readily that words are identical is called the word superiority effect, which Pollatsek and Carr associate with orthographic regularity.

In our experiment it appeared that the familiarity of words in particular was responsible for variation of word-identification response time. This indicates that accessing operations in the reader's lexicon account for most of the time (Figure 1). For the present argument it may be assumed that orthographic regularity does not differ systematically for familiar and unfamiliar words. Then, if orthography were a major factor, unfamiliar words with a normal spelling pattern would have been correctly classified in about the same time as more familiar words. But Figure 3 shows familiarity to have the largest effect of all, for words of the same degree of regularity. However, orthographic regularity does play an important role in the nonword classifications. Irregular nonwords are classified fastest and display the fewest errors (left half of Figures 3 and 4). Regular nonwords, however, retaining orthographic regularity, are classified more slowly and with more errors. In view of its many influences, orthographic regularity (Venezky, this volume, for example) should be related to a process model for word recognition; its role would then probably be greater in the recognition of words in running text.

Word Frequency
It is interesting to note that, except for relatively unfamiliar words, no frequency effect is found in the response times or errors. Instead, response times vary as a function of familiarity. Frequency and familiarity seem to be distinct properties: the first objective, the latter dependent on the subject's experience, but an experience which seems to be fairly general. Other lexical decision experiments have yielded results showing some word-frequency effects (Rubenstein et al., 1970; Rubenstein et al., 1971; Forster & Chambers, 1973; Stanners, Jastrzemski, & Westbrook, 1975). These effects are an increase of at most some 150 ms in the response time for infrequent but still well-known words; the number of words presented is small and subjects are usually instructed to respond as soon as possible. The similar frequency effect in the present experiment is 127 ms for words of a much lower frequency than usually employed in the literature (except in the study by Forster & Chambers, 1973). There is no apparent effect for the higher frequencies. Its absence may have been caused by the lenient instruction. In difficult perceptual situations the frequency effect is more prone to occur (Richards, 1973). Word length is another factor which might influence decision speed.

To summarize, it would appear that the most important factor identified in this experiment is the widely varying familiarity of words when presented in isolation. Thus the original assumption of a limited word vocabulary of equally important words for the recognition model of Bouma and Bouwhuis (1975) is certainly too restricted. The vocabulary would have to be extended and the accessibility of its entries modified. That context may facilitate the perception of unfamiliar words seems logical, but it implies the existence of very efficient accessing rules. As previously mentioned (Bouwhuis, 1978), the word-recognition model in its present form applies only to words of three letters. In longer words constituent letters are not as clearly discerned and even word length is misperceived. These observations may also be suggestive regarding the lack of a word frequency effect: there are fewer three-letter words in the language than longer words and grammatically they tend to be restricted to the functors (prepositions, conjunctions, etc.). These characteristics of three-letter words suggest that it would be desirable to try to extend the model to longer words.

REFERENCES

Bouma, H. Visual interference in the parafoveal recognition of initial and
     final letters of words. Vision Research, 1973, 13, 767-782.
Bouma, H., & Bouwhuis, D.G. Word recognition and letter recognition.

Annual Progress Report No. 10, Institute for Perception Research, Eindhoven, 1975, 53-59.

Bouwhuis, D.G. A model for the visual recognition of words of three letters. In J. Réquin (Ed.), Attention and performance VII. Hillsdale, NJ: Erlbaum 1978.

Broadbent, D.E. Word frequency effect and response bias. Psychological Review, 1967, 74, 1-15.

Chambers, S.M., & Forster, K.I. Evidence for lexical access in a simultaneous matching task. Memory & Cognition, 1975, 3, 549-560.

Clarke, F.R. Constant ratio rule for confusion matrices in speech communication. Journal of the Acoustical Society of America, 1957, 29, 715-720.

Forster, K.I., & Chambers, S.M. Lexical access and naming time. Journal of Verbal Learning and Verbal Behavior, 1973, 12, 627-635.

Forster, K.I., & Bednall, E.S. Terminating and exhaustive search in lexical access. Memory & Cognition, 1976, 4, 53-61.

Green, D.M., & Swets, J.A. Signal detection theory and psychophysics. New York: Wiley, 1966.

Kruyskamp, C. Van Dale groot woordenboek der Nederlandse taal. The Hague: Martinus Nijhof, 1970.

Kučera, H., & Francis, W.N. Computational analysis of present-day English. Providence: Brown University Press, 1967.

Linschoten, J. De la Court's frequentietelling van Nederlandse woorden. Report no. 6301, Psychological Laboratory, University of Utrecht, 1963.

Noordman, L.G.M. Inferring from language. Unpublished doctoral dissertation, University of Groningen, 1977.

Noordman-Vonk, W. Retrieval from semantic memory. Unpublished doctoral dissertation, University of Groningen, 1977.

Pollatsek, A., & Carr, T. Wholistic and rule governed encoding processes in word perception. (This volume.)

Richards, L.G. "Vexierversuch" revisited: A reexamination of Goldiamond and Hawkins' experiment. American Journal of Psychology, 1973, 86, 707-715.

Rubenstein, H., Garfield, L., & Millikan, J. Homographic entries in the internal lexicon. Journal of Verbal Learning and Verbal Behavior, 1970, 9, 487-494.

Rubenstein, H., Lewis, S.S., & Rubenstein, M.A. Homographic entries in the internal lexicon: Effects of systematicity and relative frequency of meanings. Journal of Verbal Learning and Verbal Behavior, 1971, 10, 57-62.

Rumelhart, D.E., & Siple, P. Process of recognizing tachistoscopically presented words. Psychological Review, 1974, 81, 99-118.

Stanners, R.F., Jastrzemski, J.E., & Westbrook, A. Frequency and visual quality in a word-nonword classification task. Journal of Verbal Learning and Verbal Behavior, 1975, 14, 259-264.

Thorndike, E.L., & Lorge, I. The teacher's wordbook of 30,000 words. New York: Bureau of Publications, Teacher's College, 1944.

Uit den Boogaart, P.C. Woordfrequenties in gesproken en geschreven Nederlands. Utrecht: Oosthoek/Scheltema en Holkema, 1975.

Venezky, R.L. Orthographic regularities in English words. (This volume.)

Orthographic Regularities in English Words

Richard L. Venezky

The feature that most clearly distinguishes present day investigation of visual word recognition from studies of the same phenomenon done at the turn of the century is the current emphasis on within-word familiarity. Beginning with the sequential probability notions formalized by Claude Shannon in the late 1940s, a variety of different and often contradictory descriptions of within-word familiarity have been utilized in psychological studies. All such descriptions can be divided into two major classes: a statistical redundancy class which consists of quantitative approximations based on random samples of text words (word tokens), and a rule-governed regularity class consisting of rulebased approximations generalized from dictionary lists (word types). In the redundancy class are sequential probabilities, single-letter positional frequencies, and bigram and trigram counts. In the structure class are letter-sound rules and orthographic structure rules. Analysis of the differences within and across descriptions, especially as they relate to the generation of pseudowords, yields testable hypotheses for building information processing models of visual word recognition.

Included in the purview of the paper will be those descriptions of English regularity which are based on the identity, as opposed to the graphic shape, of letters or letter sequences. This excludes, for example, descriptions based on word shape or on the graphic forms of particular letters. What remains will be labeled orthographic regularity, a phrase which is etymologically suited to the subject, but nevertheless ambiguous in its present day applications. Central to all descriptions of orthographic regularity is the assumption that through repeated exposure to printed words, readers acquire

283

expectations for letters or letter sequences which normally occur at different word positions. Descriptions differ in the manner in which these expectations are defined, and often, by implication, the role they play in word recognition.

Statistical Redundancy Measures

Ordered Approximations. Ordered approximations to English, based on algorithms proposed by Shannon (1948), were the first descriptions of orthographic regularity utilized by psychologists. In Shannon (1948), a zero order approximation to English was created by drawing letters with replacement from an unweighted pool of the letters of the alphabet. If this same procedure is employed with symbols that are weighted according to their frequencies of occurrence in texts, first order approximations result.

An i-th order approximation is produced by first selecting an initial string of length i-1 (not including the initial space). This forms the initial part of the new string. A text is then scanned for the first non-final occurrence of this initial string. When found, the next letter after the target sequence is added to the string being generated, and a new search string constructed by dropping the first letter of the last search string and adding the letter just located. This procedure is then repeated until a desired length is achieved. (This description has been modified to describe how strings of a desired length can be generated. If length is not fixed, then zero order approximations are drawn from a pool of 27 symbols--the 26 letters plus space. First order approximations, as originally suggested by Shannon, could be done by using a random number table to select letters (or spaces) from a text, thus ensuring letter frequency distributions comparable to those in natural (written) use. Higher order approximations would be done as described here, but without the requirement that the unit being searched for be non-final (word non-final, that is).) Miller, Bruner, and Postman (1954) used this technique to generate eight-letter pseudowords for a full-report task. Their fourth order approximations include items like mossiant, oneticul, preveral, and favorial, all quite English-like. Wallach (1963), on the other hand, truncated two letters from each string used by Miller et al., thus occasionally producing a non-English beginning or ending (e.g., iorial, mossia). Although Miller et al. used ordered approximations to control for the information which each letter conveyed in a recognition (and memory) task, their application differs little in principle from the use of this measure in more recent experiments (Lefton, Spragins, & Byrnes, 1973) in classifying orthographic regularity.

One major deficiency in this approach is that only left-to-right sequential redundancy is allowed. Thus, the ability of readers to fill in more accurately the missing letter in _ld (old) and _ypes (types) than in _ore (more, core, etc.) or _ord (cord, ford, etc.) cannot be predicted by an ordered approximation description. There is no a priori reason to assume that in a word recognition task a subject will reject certain available information in attempting to resolve the identity of a visually degraded letter. If, for example, a subject had resolved #b_mp# and were expecting words or orthographically regular pseudowords, he would almost certainly assume a vowel letter for the missing item. A second order approximation strategy, on the other hand, might yield a vowel letter, but could also give r or l since br, rm, bl, and lm all occur in English words.

A second shortcoming of ordered approximation descriptions is their insensitivity to frequency. Although any large group of stimuli generated by this technique will approximate the frequencies of occurrence of English letter sequences, there is no metric incorporated into the method for assessing the relative familiarity of strings within order classes.

n-grams. To overcome this difficulty, summed bigram and trigram counts have been proposed. Underwood and Schulz (1960) tabulated the bigrams and trigrams in 2,080 words sampled from Thorndike and Lorge (1944). Since each sample word was weighted by its frequency of occurrence in texts, token based bigram and trigram counts resulted.

By summing the frequencies of all the bigrams or trigrams within a pseudo-word, a familiarity index can be derived. Such a procedure was used by Anisfeld (1964), for example, in reanalyzing the Gibson, Pick, Osser, and Hammond (1962) results. According to Anisfeld, the Gibson et al. results could be accounted for as easily by differences in summed bigram counts as they could by the units advocated by Gibson et al. (spelling units, see below). Gibson (1964) showed, however, that correlations with subject responses of summed bigram and summed trigram counts were non-significant. In addition, Gibson, Shurcliff, and Yonas (1970) found that neither summed bigram nor summed trigram counts was an adequate predictor of recognition scores on pronounceable and unpronounceable pseudowords.

The Underwood and Schulz (1960) tables provide a means for differentiating familiar and unfamiliar strings within approximation classes, but suffer from lack of attention to word length or position of letter string within a word. A common suffix like _ies would heavily weight a trigram count for a pseudoword whether in initial or final position, according to these tables, yet in English words this sequence never occurs initially. Although strong evidence is lacking for demonstrating letter position within a word as a psychologically relevant variable, the Underwood and Schulz (1960) tables could not be used for exploring this factor.

This shortcoming has been overcome in Mayzner and Tresselt (1965) and Mayzner, Tresselt, and Wolin (1965a, b), which give bigram and trigram counts by word position and by word length for words from three to seven characters in length. Mayzner and Tresselt (1965) also gives single-letter positional frequencies, which have been used by M. Mason (1975) to explore differences between good and poor readers in a target search task. Although Mason (1975) confounds rule-governed orthographic structure (see below) with positional frequency, a small but significant positional frequency effect remains when these variables are separated (Massaro, Venezky, & Taylor, 1977).

The relationships among single-letter positional frequency, bigram frequency, and trigram frequency have yet to be explored. Experimenters who use single-letter or bigram frequencies tend not to control for differences in the next higher order unit, thus confounding cannot be ruled out. It is possible, however, to generate pseudowords that covary summed single-letter positional frequency and summed bigram count, and with some straining, the same can be done for summed bigram and summed trigram counts. For example, nachim has (according to Mayzner et al., 1965a, b), legal bigrams but no legal trigrams. Nather, on the other hand, has legal bigrams and trigrams. (That is, all of the bigrams and all of the trigrams occur with frequencies above zero in the Mayzner et al. tables.) New tables based on larger corpuses like the Kučera and Francis (1967) million-word list are required, however, to allow good resolution of trigram frequencies.

Whatever such an untangling might show, the psychological role of these units would remain to be resolved. If summed frequency is psychologically relevant, then the utilization of bigram frequency requires a maximizing process. Consider the task of resolving a pseudoword where the visual information allows an acceptable resolution of all letters except one; for example, $L_1 L_2 - L_4 L_5$. Assume further that no visual information were available for L_3. If the subject were expecting English-like words, a bigram strategy requires that L_3 be selected to maximize the sum of the bigram frequencies $L_2 L_3$ and $L_3 L_4$, selecting L_3 from a pool of all 26 letters. If some visual information were available for L_3, then the pool of allowable letters would be restricted to those which were graphically acceptable, but otherwise the strategy would be the same.

For a trigram strategy, a similar process could be argued, but with maximizing of the frequencies for $L_1 L_2 L_3 + L_2 L_3 L_4 + L_3 L_4 L_5$. Besides the complexity of the maximizing function, both of these strategies suffer from a limitation similar to that stated for ordered approximations, namely, the inability to use all available information in predicting a missing letter from a real word.

Rule-governed Regularity Measures

Phonologically-based Measures

Statistical schemes, even when position and word length are observed, can generate pseudowords which are intuitively non-English like. For example, bipon, slevy, and dufip are pronounceable pseudowords which are low in summed bigram counts while thrsm, sthse, and whrst are unpronounceable pseudowords which have relatively high summed bigram counts. This problem can be avoided, for the most part, by using position sensitive, fourth order approximations which are also high in summed trigram counts.

An alternative is to use pronounceability as a defining metric. Gibson et al. (1962) found that pronounceable pseudowords were more easily recalled in a brief exposure paradigm than were unpronounceable pseudowords (e.g., dink versus nkid). The authors hypothesized that the operative unit in word perception was not the letter (or whole word), but a sequence of letters which had an invariant letter-sound relationship. However, Gibson et al. (1970) obtained the same results with congenitally deaf subjects, thereby demonstrating that orthographic structure alone could account for the response differences. Letter-sound regularity has also been utilized in word recognition models by Rubenstein, Lewis, and Rubenstein (1971) and by Smith and Spoehr (1974). However, the assumed use of letter-sound relationships in the latter two studies differed from that assumed in Gibson et al. (1962).

Both Rubenstein et al. (1971) and Smith and Spoehr (1974) assumed that letter recognition occurs on the basis of letter features; then sounds (at a subauditory level) are attached to letters or letter sequences and lexical access made on the basis of the resulting phonological unit. Gibson et al. (1962) assumed that word recognition occurred on the basis of higher order visual units which the reader formed through experience with letter-sound translation. The viability of any of these hypotheses, when viewed in relation to the complexities of letter-sound correspondences, is questionable (Venezky, 1970; Massaro 1975).

Orthographic Structure Measures
Orthographic structure, as opposed to letter-sound regularity, refers to the sequences of letters which occur or could occur in English words, regardless of the regularity of their pronunciations. Rules for describing this structure are quite complex, depending upon both scribal and phonological influences. To understand these rules, it is necessary to examine both the manner in which spelling relates to sound, and the scribal constraints which have evolved independently of sound, for unlike the orthographies of other major languages, modern English spelling preserves clear evidence of nearly 1300 years of sound change, scribal tampering, and foreign intrusions. There is an underlying pattern to this orthography, as described in Venezky (1970), but there is also a substantial marginal mess which can only in part be organized into sub-patterns or justified by appeal to such principles as the orthographic separation of homophones (e.g., bell - belle). Nevertheless, permeating the entire spelling system from organized core to the most disjoint outer fringes is an interaction between phonological and visual forces which ranges from productive counterpoint, as in such spellings as cone - conic, to the dissonance of such mots noirs as women.

Since no language academy ever imposed a grand design on English spelling, what general principles there are result from the confluence of various scribal traditions with the periodic ravages of sound change unaccompanied by spelling change. Yet, a principle of sorts does emerge from the current system: "Accede to all visual interests up to but not beyond the point where passage from spelling to sound is impaired." How this principle is realized in English spelling and its implications for psychological studies is the subject of the next few sections.

The Phonological Base. Phonological representation is vested, for English, in a series of functional units, which are further divided into "relational units" and "markers." A relational unit is a string of one or more letters (graphemes) which relates ultimately to sound (which might be silence), and whose behavior cannot be predicted by the behaviors of its sub-components. By this definition, all single letters are relational units by default, but so are th, sh, and tch, for example. On the other hand, bb is not, nor is st. Markers serve primarily to indicate the correspondences of relational units or to preserve graphotactical or morphological patterns. These latter functions comprise a major part of the structure in English spelling and will be expanded upon shortly. Examples of markers for correspondences of relational units are the e in race, which marks the pronunciation of both a and c; the u in guest, which marks the pronunciation of g; and the k in picknicking, which marks the pronunciation of c (picnic). We might treat the h in initial gh as a marker for preserving the hard sound of g, especially since in spellings like ghost the h is a Caxton-inspired intrusion. But the pronunciation of medial and final gh (might, high) makes this classification difficult and the criterion of simplicity makes it undesirable.

With this armory of functional units, plus a few general rules, the majority of English spelling-to-sound relationships can be accounted for. The most important rule directs the pronunciations of the single-letter vowel spellings a, e, i, y, o, and u. When one of these occurs before a functionally simple consonant spelling, followed by a vowel spelling, its pronunciation is free (long); otherwise, checked (short). A functionally simple consonant spelling is one that represents, at a morphophonemic level, a single segmental unit. This pattern can be understood without delving completely into the morphophonemic interpretation by classing x, tch, dg, wh, and ck as compound and all the other consonant units as simple.

By this rule the first vowels in anal, robe, and bathe have their free pronunciations, but the first vowels in annals, rob, bridge, and axe have their checked pronunciations. This same rule dictates the doubling of final consonants before adding suffixes starting with vowels to words like run and swim.

For the secondary vowel spellings (e.g., ai/ay, au/aw, ea), no such rule holds. These spellings tend to have a single major pronunciation each, and since they originated as free vowel spellings, they do not (with rare exception) occur before doubled consonant spellings. Therefore, from a standpoint of orthographic structure, a spelling like couff would be scribally irregular for English.

The consonant spellings c and g have, like the primary vowel spellings, two environmentally conditioned pronunciations. Each has its soft pronunciation before e, i, or y and its hard pronunciation otherwise. For c, the rule is almost without exception, although complicated somewhat in medial position by palatalization (e.g., ocean, social). For g, however, a heavy influx of Scandinavian loan words like girl, get, and gear has obscured the pattern considerably.

Given these practices, plus several others not mentioned here, the phonological component of modern English spelling can be accounted for. However, to go beyond what exists to predict what could be, requires delineation of one further phonological constraint, that of the allowable sound sequences for English. For example, initial clusters of the form STOP+LATERAL (/r/ or /l/) are legal if, and only if, the place of articulation of the two components is not identical. This allows clusters like /pl/, /dr/, /tr/, and /gl/, but eliminates /tl/ and /dl/, which occur in many American Indian languages, but not in English. On the other hand, final clusters of the form NASAL+STOP are legal only for articulation of the two components in the same place. This produces all of the legal clusters and two that were legal several centuries ago, but no longer are so (/mb/ and /ŋg/).

A complete set of rules for generating orthographically regular letter strings would have to account not only for consonant clusters before and after juncture, but also for those which occur intervocalically. Approaches to describing the phonological component can be found in Whorf (1956), who developed rules for describing phonological clusters in monosyllabic words, and Chomsky and Halle (1968).

Scribal Components.   The scribal components of English orthography function on two levels: graphemic, that is, the constraints on letter sequences;
and morphemic, that is, constraints on morphemic or lexical units. Graphic
constraints, although of obvious interest to typographers and psychologists,
are not a concern here. For those interested in the topic, Spencer (1969)
presents a well illustrated review of the research on legibility with an extensive bibliography.

Graphemic Features.   Graphemic constraints regulate primarily the distribution of 1) geminated (doubled) letters, 2) u-v-w, and 3) i - y. First, unlike
Spanish, English resists doubled letters in word-initial position, especially
consonants. Only a handful of exceptions to this exist, primarily involving
the form oo (oodles, ooze, aardvark). In other positions only 16 letters can
double; those that don't are a,h, i, j, k, u, v, w, x, y. (A few exceptions exist;
for example trekked, savvy, navvy.) But there are further restrictions. With
few exceptions, doubled consonants do not occur after secondary vowels,
and in final position only ff, ll, and ss are common. (Rr and tt occur in about
a half-dozen words each; on ebb, add, odd, egg and inn, see below.) Finally,
the digraph units are not allowed to double. For one, ch, a pseudogeminate
(tch) was adopted in early Modern English, at about the same time that dg
was adopted to represent doubled g when it represented /ǰ/ and ck was invented for doubled k, which now occurs only in inflected forms of trek (trekking).
    A second set of graphemic constraints regulate the distribution of u -v - w
and i - y. From the Middle English period up to about the middle of the 17th
century, u and v were used indiscriminately to represent /u/ and /v/, although
v tended to be used initially and u elsewhere. (According to Pyles (1964),
v was also preferred in the vicinity of m and n.) Digraphs like ou, when written before a vowel, might be mistaken for ov; therefore u was doubled, and
eventually written w. In time u (vocalic) in final position was replaced by
w, giving the present-day alternations au/aw, eu/ew, and ou/ow. In general,
the w variant occurs before vowels and in final position; the u variant occurs
elsewhere. There are numerous exceptions to this distribution, however,
especially for ow (e.g., own, owl).
    To reduce further the ambiguity of u - v spellings, v was also eliminated
from final position. But since no simple replacement was available as was
for u, an e was added after the letter, thus giving present-day spellings like
dove, love, and have where the final e does not mark a free vowel pronunciation.
    Similarly, i - y now alternate as second elements of digraph vowels, exactly
as u and w do. Thus, maid but may; oil but boy; and either but grey.

Morphemic Features

Morphemic Identity. The retention of morphemic identity as in pairs like
cone - conic is a natural consequence of conditioned sound change unaccompanied by a corresponding spelling change, and not the result of overt scribal
intention. For the most part, however, retention of morphemic identity is
limited to vowels and those consonant letters which are silent in one form
but pronounced in a related one. In the first category are alternations of
the form sane - sanity and telegraph - telegraphy; in the latter are pairs akin
to sign - signal, bomb - bombard, and hymn - hymnal. Where no single spelling

can stand for a pair of sounds, consistant spelling of allomorphs which differ by those sounds is not possible. Thus, collide - collision must utilize different spellings for /d/ and /z/.

In bound morphemes, similar processes can be seen as exemplified by the noun plural (and 3rd singular) s and the past tense marker ed.

Separation of Homophones. Partly by accident and partly by overt attention, English spelling has tended to differentiate homophones wherever phonological license would allow. Pairs like sea - see, blue - blew, and right - write belong to the accident category, but foul - fowl, plain - plane, and sun - son result from overt scribal practice (Vachek, 1959, 1973. On the orthographic distinctiveness of homophones, see Olson & Kausler, 1971.)

The Two-letter Word Ban. Since at least the time of Noah Webster and probably before, English lexicographers have avoided extending the repertoire of two-letter words beyond a small group of function words (e.g., in, of, up, on, if). Two mechanisms were adopted for lengthening two-letter words which didn't qualify for inclusion in this group: doubling the final consonant (ebb, add, odd, egg, and inn), or adding a final e (e.g., doe, hoe, dye, lye). The former mechanism has created unique final consonant clusters in that b, d, g, and n do not double in final position in any other English words.

Recognition Processes

Most readers are probably not aware as they read words like belle or love what the purposes of the final e's are, nor do they attend overtly to the retention of o in both cone and conic. Yet many of these features may be utilized to facilitate reading processes. We might, for example, hypothesize a special role for two-letter words, in that even without full resolution of their component letters, the reader can assume he is encountering a function word.

We might also speculate on whether or not the scribal and phonological elements are separated psychologically. Are for example, irregular strings like clav and cklib processed differently from an illegal string like tprif? All are illegal and non-occurring, yet they differ in type of illegality. Tprif contains an intitial consonant cluster that is phonologically illegal and also scribally non-occurring. Kn in knife also represents an illegal phonological sequence, but the spelling occurs, nevertheless. Srp- could, by analogy with kn-, be a legal phonological cluster if we assumed that any one of the three consonants was silent. Clav and cklib are both phonologically acceptable, but contain scribally outlawed features (final v in clav and initial ck in cklib). In, for example, a lexical decision task, do subjects reject phonologically illegal strings before scribally illegal ones? If so, must we then postulate two different mechanisms for the lexical decision task, a phonological mediation process, á la Rubenstein, Lewis, and Rubenstein (1971), and a scribal process for pre- or post-screening? There is already some evidence for different processes operating in the lexical decision task (J. Mason, 1976), although support for phonological mediation as one of them is questionable. The lexical decision task seems especially well suited for exploring this problem, although alternative tasks are desirable for covergence.

Orthographic structure descriptions differ from other definitions of orthographic regularity in two aspects. First, in the utilization of word types rather than word tokens, and second, in classing as regular, spellings which do not occur in English words, and classing as irregular some that do. The first difference is not essential to the definition of orthographic structure, but is probably more a reflection of the differing epistemologies of linguists and psychologists. (On the use of word types to generate bigram counts, see Solso and King, 1976.) The second difference, however, is central to the concept of orthographic structure and requires further explication.

The primary assumption behind the orthographic structure rules presented here is that readers abstract from their experiences with printed words those spellings which are productive in present-day English, and use these to facilitate recognition. For example, silent initial letters, regardless of the frequency of occurrence of the words in which they occur, are classed as irregular since it is unlikely that new words brought into the English language would ever be spelled with them. (Spelling analogies might present an exception to this assumption and cannot be ignored. However, it is unlikely that silent initial spellings would ever be widely extended.)

On the other hand, the initial sequences voa- and woa- and the final sequences -eng, -erl, and -ofe do not occur in the first 20,000 words in the Thorndike and Lorge (1944) list, yet they are classed as orthographically regular since they do not violate any phonological or scribal pattern. Thus, pseudowords like voam, woach, treng, and strofe are pronounceable and structurally regular, even though they contain trigrams which do not occur in English words.

Similarly, spellings like initial kl- and kr- (which occur only in proper nouns) violate an extremely low level rule that distributes k, c, ck, and q as spellings for /k/. Although kl- would not be classed as regular, it would also not be placed in the same irregularity class as tl- which violates a high level phonological rule.

How orthographic structure might aid in word recognition has rarely been discussed. One prediction that could be made on the basis of the discussion presented here is that frequently occurring but illegal spellings (e.g., initial wr-) would not facilitate recognition tasks as much as regular spellings would. Results reported by Baron and Strawson (1976) tend to support this hypothesis, although the task used in this study, reading words aloud from a list, involves both articulation and parallel processing, and therefore may not provide a strong test of recognition differences.

In contrast to the sequential probability approaches, the definition of orthographic structure given here does not rule out the utilization of variable size units in recognition. Thus, to resolve a letter for which insufficient graphic information is available, the reader might attempt to use the immediately adjacent letters to eliminate structurally irregular alternatives. If a unique choice cannot then be made, additional letters might be considered. This leaves open the possibility of using all available letters in the missing first letter example presented above.

One criticism which might be made of the orthographic structure approach is its lack of attention to frequency. By the definitions given here a nonoccurring ending like -eng and a frequently occurring ending like -ing would be weighted equally in facilitating recognition. Although there are no empirical data which show that these should be treated differently, the issue deserves to be investigated.

Conclusions

Most, if not all, of the differing descriptions of orthographic regularity are subject to empirical investigation. The statistical redundancy approaches can be compared, as discussed earlier and, in addition, type and token comparisons can be made within each description. In a similar manner, descriptions based upon different sets of abstracted rules for letters and letter sequences could be compared, as could rules based on type and token counts. A great number of years might be spent doing such comparisons, with perhaps some gain in our understanding of within-word familiarity. What seems to be lacking, however, are well articulated hypotheses about the processes by which orthographic regularity facilitates word recognition. Without better insight into the recognition processes, testing of different descriptions will continue to be a hit-or-miss procedure.

REFERENCES

Anisfeld, M.A. Comment on "The role of grapheme-phoneme correspondence in the perception of words." American Journal of Psychology, 1964, 77, 320-326.

Baron, J.M & Strawson, C. Use of orthographic and word specific knowledge in reading words aloud. Journal of Experimental Psychology: Human Perception and Performance, 1976, 2, 386-393.

Chomsky, N., & Halle, M. The sound pattern of English. New York: Harper & Row, 1968.

Gibson, E.J. On the perception of words. American Journal of Psychology, 1964, 77, 667-669.

Gibson, E.J., Pick A., Osser, H., & Hammond, M. The role of grapheme-phoneme correspondence in the perception of words. American Journal of Psychology, 1962, 75, 554-570.

Gibson, E.J., Shurcliff, A., & Yonas, A. Utilization of spelling patterns by deaf and hearing subjects. In H. Levin and J.P. Williams (Eds.), Basic studies on reading. New York: Basic Books, 1970.

Kučera, H., & Francis, N.W. Computational analysis of present-day American English. Providence: Brown University Press, 1967.

Lefton, L.A., Spragins, A.B., & Byrnes, J. English orthography: Relation to reading experience. Bulletin of the Psychonomic Society, 1973, 2, 281-282.

Mason, J.M. The roles of orthographic, phonological, and word frequency variables on word-nonword decisions. American Educational Research Journal, 1976, 13, 199-206.

Mason, M. Reading ability and letter search time: Effects of orthographic structure defined by single-letter positional frequency. Journal of Experimental Psychology: General, 1975, 104, 146-166.

Massaro, D.W. Primary and secondary recognition in reading. In D.W. Massaro (Ed.), Understanding language: An information processing analysis of speech perception, reading, and psycholinguistics. New York: Academic Press, 1975.

Massaro, D.W., Venezky, R.L., & Taylor, G.A. Orthographic regularity, positional frequency, and visual processing of letter strings. Technical

Report No. 413. Wisconsin Research and Development Center for Cognitive Learning, Madison, Wisconsin, 1977.

Mayzner, M.S., & Tresselt, M.E. Tables of single-letter and digram frequency counts for various word-length and letter-position combinations. Psychonomic Monograph Supplements, 1965, 1 (Whole No. 2).

Mayzner, M.S., Tresselt, M.E., & Wolin, B.R. Tables of trigram frequency counts for various word-length and letter-position combinations. Psychonomic Monograph Supplements, 1965, 1 (3, whole No 3), 33-78. (a)

Mayzner, M.S., Tresselt, M.E., & Wolin, B.R. Tables of tetragram frequency counts for various word-length and letter-position combinations. Psychonomic Monograph Supplements, 1965, 1 (4, whole No. 4), 79-143. (b)

Miller, G.A., Bruner, J.S., & Postman, L. Familiarity of letter sequences and tachistoscopic identification. Journal of General Psychology, 1954, 50, 129-139.

Olson, G.A., & Kausler, D.H. Orthographic distinctiveness of homonyms. Behavior Research Methods and Instrumentation, 1971, 3, 298-299.

Pyles, T. The origins and development of the English language. New York: Harcourt, Brace & World, 1964.

Rubenstein, H., Lewis, S.S., & Rubenstein, M.A. Evidence for phonemic recoding in visual word recognition. Journal of Verbal Learning and Verbal Behavior, 1971, 10, 645-657.

Shannon, C.E. A mathematical theory of communication. Bell System Technical Journal, 1948, 27, 379-423, 622-656.

Smith, E.E. & Spoehr, K.T. The perception of printed English: A theoretical perspective. In B.H. Kantowitz (Ed.), Human information processing: Tutorials in performance and cognition. Potomac, MD: Erlbaum, 1974.

Solso, R.L., & King, J.F. Frequency and versatility of letters in the English language. Behavior Research Methods and Instrumentation, 1976, 8, 283-286.

Spencer, H. The visible word (2nd ed.). New York: Hastings House, 1969.

Thorndike, E.L., & Lorge, I. The teacher's word book of 30,000 words. New York: Teachers College, 1944.

Underwood, B.J., & Schulz, R.W. Meaningfulness and verbal learning. New York: Lippincott, 1960.

Vachek, J. Two chapters on written English. Brno Studies in English, 1959, 1, 7-38.

Vachek, J. Written language. The Hague: Mouton, 1973.

Venezky, R. The structure of English orthography. The Hague: Mouton, 1970.

Wallach, M.A. Perceptual recognition of approximations to English in relation to spelling achievement. Journal of Educational Psychology, 1963, 54, 57-62.

Whorf, B.L. Language, thought, and reality. Cambridge, MA: MIT Press, 1956.

Rule-governed and Wholistic Encoding Processes in Word Perception

Alexander Pollatsek and Thomas H. Carr

*It has been claimed that both rule-governed and wholistic
encoding processes occur in the visual system during word
perception. These claims are based on various effects of
orthography and familiarity found in perceptual decision
tasks such as same-different matching. It is argued in the
present paper that strings of letters which are orthographically regular (i.e., consist of legal sequences of letters) have
been shown to be processed more rapidly and accurately in
visual tasks than orthographically irregular strings. However,
there is no completely convincing demonstration that familiarity of the letter sequence produces any additional processing advantage attributable to visual events. When familiarity effects are found in visual tasks, they seem to involve
response biases rather than increases in the efficiency of
information accrual. Furthermore, orthographic regularity
still speeds processing in situations where letter sequences
are in unusual configurations or orientations, and where the
characters are somewhat unusual in shape. The absence of
perceptual consequences, due to either familiarity of the
entire letter sequence or aspects of its spatial arrangement,
argues that the visual processing advantage of words over
strings of unrelated letters is due almost completely to the
fact that the word is a legal or well-structured letter sequence.
We therefore conclude from the currently available evidence
that orthographic structure operates in the visual system
during word perception, but familiarity probably does not.
This evidence supports rule-governed encoding operations,
but tends to rule out wholistic encoding operations as medi-
ators of visual word processing.*

The original experiments on what is now called the word superiority effect required people to report all they could from a briefly exposed display of letters (Cattell, 1886; Huey, 1908). Because more letters could be identified from words than from random arrays, psychologists were tempted to believe that prior experience affects events which occur quite early in the visual processing of language. However, the results of these experiments may only mean that words are easier to remember than strings of unrelated letters and that people can more accurately guess letters they have not actually seen when the letters are parts of words. Although memory and inference are clearly important components of reading, it would be desirable to know whether the initial formation and manipulation of visual codes representing printed letters is in fact more efficient for words than for random letter strings. If visual code formation were affected, it would be useful to know the mechanism by which this influence of past experience with words occurs. Such knowledge would have implications for both the psychology of human information processing and the pedagogy of reading.

Several more recently developed experimental techniques have uncovered word superiority effects (or WSEs) which are harder to explain on the basis of non-visual or post-perceptual events. In the present discussion, we will focus on results first obtained in a visual matching paradigm (Eichelman, 1970) in which subjects were shown two strings of letters, one on top of the other as in Table 1, and were asked to judge whether the two strings were identical. Reaction times (RTs) and error rates in this task were reliably lower for words than for strings of unrelated letters. Memory requirements were minimal because of the simultaneous presentation and spatial contiguity of the stimuli to be compared, and guessing strategies were minimized by randomizing the location of differing letters in words and nonwords.

One might argue that because subjects can pronounce and assign meaning more readily to words than to nonwords, the comparison of non-visual codes redundant to the visual information was responsible for this WSE. However, Barron and Henderson (1977) have shown that meaning has no influence in

Table 1. Sample Stimulus Displays Ordinarily Used in "Same-Different" Visual Matching.

Stimulus		Response
Words	Nonwords	
W O R D	O R W D	Same
W O R D	O R W D	
W O R D	O R W D	Different
W O R K	O R W K	

the matching task. Further, an experiment by Pollatsek, Well, and Schindler (1975) found that detecting a difference in case between an otherwise identical pair of letter strings was faster for words than for unrelated letter strings. In addition, the size of the word advantage for letter strings differing only in case (WORD versus WORd) was not significantly different from the advantage found for strings differing in a letter (WORD versus WORK), for which differences in names and meaning could potentially aid the decision. Furthermore, Pollatsek et al. replicated Baron's results (1975) in showing that different responses to pairs of homophonic words (CITE versus SITE) were no slower than those to pairs of non-homophonic words (COLD versus SOLD), indicating that name codes play no role in these decision processes.

Thus the simultaneous matching task has uncovered a word superiority effect that may be quite important to the psychology of reading. It occurs in the visual system, it is not likely to be due to the properties of short-term memory, it is not likely to be explained by guessing strategies, and it can be observed in processing that is approximately as rapid as that which occurs during fluent reading. Response times in matching tasks which show word advantages typically range from 400 to 900 msec.

Possible Mechanisms for Superior Word Perception
A large number of mechanisms have been proposed to account for a visual word superiority effect. They can be divided into three main classes. The first might be called "whole-unit" mechanisms, in which the word, as a familiar gestalt, mediates the WSE by means of a visual template, image, or integrated feature set. The second class, which might be called "part-unit" mechanisms, claims that portions of words, such as spelling patterns or syllables, become unitized. This facilitates word processing by reducing the number of units to be identified relative to random strings, which can only be processed as individual letters. In contrast to these two notions of unitization, the third class of explanation posits some "rule-governed" process in which the structure of the stimulus is used to form expectations that increase the efficiency with which component letters are identified. Examples of theories that use the predictability of word structure to reduce uncertainty during perceptual identification are analysis by synthesis (Neisser, 1967) and Spoehr and Smith's (1973) vocalic center-group parsing scheme. In analysis by synthesis, spelling rules are applied from left to right to predict what letters are likely to be found. In Spoehr and Smith's model, expectations based on word structure are implemented in a more complex parallel fashion. The ability to utilize stimulus predictability is regarded as a property of the visual encoding system in the above rule-governed theories. We should make clear that these orthographic rules are distinct from the rules of lettertosound correspondence, although they may be related to them.

There are two major distinctions to be made among these three classes of explanation. The first is whether codes representing words in the visual system are activated as gestalts or put together from component parts. This issue separates whole-unit from part-unit and rule-governed mechanisms. Both part-unit and rule-governed mechanisms predict that stimuli which have never been encountered in their entirety before may be processed just as efficiently as familiar stimuli because of the parts from which they are constructed. Whole-unit mechanisms, however, predict that an advantage should accrue to familiar stimuli even when the unfamiliar comparison stimuli are composed of parts with which the perceiver is completely familiar.

The second issue is whether the WSE is due to the direct activation of familiar whole-word or part-word visual codes, or whether it is due to the application of more abstract orthographic rules that are learned during exposure to words. If supraletter visual codes were the important factor, then the structure of the stimulus should matter less than its visual familiarity, but if the learning of orthographic rules were the important factor, then the familiarity of the stimulus should not matter as long as the stimulus is regular (conforms to the orthographic rules).

Testing these predictions would allow us to assess the relative contribution to visual word processing of the three classes of facilitation mechanism. Empirically, the predictions correspond to ways of evaluating the WSE which are already well-established in the literature. One of these involves dividing the WSE into a comparison between words and pseudowords, which are orthographically regular but unfamiliar strings of letters, and another comparison between pseudowords and unrelated letter strings, which are usually constructed by permuting the letters in words so that the string is as orthographically irregular and unpronounceable as possible.

Below we will argue that in the matching task there is a reliable difference in performance between pseudowords and unrelated letter strings, which we will call an orthography effect. We will argue further that a processing advantage based on familiarity or meaning has yet to be convincingly demonstrated. In the literature, there is no sound evidence either for an advantage of words over pseudowords or of familiar but orthographically irregular acronyms (FBI, ESP, JFK, BBC) over unrelated letter strings. These results seem to rule out whole-unit mechanisms of encoding in the visual system.

Another body of evidence shows that the WSE is surprisingly durable in the face of spatial transformations such as vertical rather than horizontal stimulus presentation, stimulus rotations, and irregular spacing of letters. Coupled with the absence of facilitation for three-letter acronyms, which are about the same size as the spelling patterns usually proposed, this durability argues against part-unit mechanisms. To our minds, then, the most satisfying explanation of the available data on the visual word superiority effect is provided by a mechanism in which a rule-governed system sensitive to orthographic structure facilitates the processing of orthographically legal strings. There appears to be no substantial evidence at this time that directly activatable, multi-letter units influence the efficiency of word perception in the visual system.

The Case against Whole-Unit Mechanisms

Turning to the data on which we base these claims, an orthography effect is found universally in the matching task whenever there is also a reliable WSE (as well as in the visual search paradigm and, with few exceptions, in tachistoscopic forced-choice recognition). Response times are faster and, when they are reported, error rates are lower, for both Same and Different responses to pseudowords than to nonwords in experiments by Baron (1975); Carr, Posner, Pollatsek, and Snyder (in press); Chambers and Forster (1975); Peterson and LaBerge (1977); and Taylor, Miller, and Juola (1977). As far as we know, only Hershenson (1972), who did not include words for comparison, has failed to obtain an overall orthography advantage. Barron and Pittenger (1974) failed to obtain differences of any kind among words, pseudowords, and nonwords for Different responses, although Same responses showed the usual orthography effect. In Hershenson's experiment, times were fast and error rates high relative to other studies employing strings of similar length, and in both studies Different pairs were different in almost all positions. Both null results may therefore reflect the superficiality of processing required to achieve the performance levels accepted in the experiments.

In contrast, data concerning differences between words and pseudowords are quite variable. Part of the variability is due to difficulty in gaining proper control over stimulus materials. A major problem facing experimenters attempting to demonstrate a whole-unit effect via word-pseudoword differences is to balance the words and pseudowords with respect to various part-unit and sequential constraints. Often, this has been done casually, for example, by constructing anagrams of words that look regular and seem pronounceable. Sometimes balancing has been done more formally, for example, by equating the sets of words and pseudowords for average bigram frequency, trigram frequency, or positional redundancy. While one could always quibble over the balancing procedure, a word-pseudoword difference would be reasonably convincing if a) word and pseudowords were both equally wordlike on an intuitive basis and balanced on at least some of the formal measures of word structure; b) the difference held up when analyzed with stimuli as a random variable, given that stimulus selection procedures warranted such an analysis; c) word advantages for Same decisions were not offset by word disadvantages for Different decisions (or vice versa), which would be evidence for criterion-shifting rather than differences in the efficiency of information accrual; and d) word advantages in response times were not offset by word disadvantages in error rates, which would be evidence for speed-accuracy tradeoff rather than for greater efficiency in processing words. Unfortunately, there is currently no study in the simultaneous matching literature that satisfies all of these criteria.

One consideration is that several studies fail to use convincingly wordlike pseudowords. Examples taken from Taylor et al. (1977) are SNEPD, MHEET, and HUWARD, and from Barron and Pittenger (1976) are SPAHE, TRUIF, and VEROC. It is worth commenting that even though Barron and Pittenger's pseudowords were matched to their words on average bigram and trigram frequency, the pseudoword set still contained such odd stimuli. Hence it would seem that if formal measures of structure are to be used, they should include positional probabilities of occurrence as well as bigram and trigram cluster frequencies (Gibson, Pick, Osser, & Hammond, 1962).

While there are no matching studies available which simultaneously control all three of these measures, there are some which control cluster frequencies and whose pseudowords seem acceptable on intuitive grounds as well. The data from these studies, however, are far from conclusive in supporting whole-word processing. The problem is that these experiments uniformly report an advantage of words over pseudowords for Same displays in both RT and error measures, but they report either no difference or a small familiarity disadvantage for Different RTs and error rates. One or the other of these patterns characterizes the results of Barron and Henderson (1977), Chambers and Forster's (1975) Experiment I, and the first experiment reported by Carr et al. (in press). Chambers and Forster (1975) did obtain in their second experiment a small advantage of words over pseudowords, averaged across all Different response times. However, error rates, crucial for the evaluation of their data, were not reported.

The pattern of results observed in these studies suggests a mechanism of criterion shifting, in which familiarity biases subjects toward responding Same and against responding Different, rather than an improvement in the overall efficiency of performance. It is interesting to note that all of these experiments presented words and pseudowords randomly in the same block of trials. When Carr et al. (in press) presented words and pseudowords in pure blocks (Experiment II), eliminating differential effects of familiarity across trials, evidence for criterion shifting disappeared. In the absence of response bias, no familiarity effects of any kind were found in either decision latencies or error rates.

A second class of studies which might be thought to demonstrate a whole-unit familiarity effect has compared matching performance on acronyms with performance on unrelated letter strings. The same problem of equating stimuli for structural regularity must be addressed here as well, since differences in tachistoscopic whole report have been found even for zero order versus first order approximations to English (Miller, Bruner, & Postman, 1954), even though neither approximation seems at all word-like when casually examined. That problem aside, these studies have produced results almost identical to those comparing words and pseudowords.

Henderson and Chard (1976) found an advantage for acronyms in Same decisions but a disadvantage for Different decisions. Henderson (1974), on the other hand, obtained advantages for acronyms in both Same and Different decisions, but he presented stimuli side by side and fairly far apart, maximizing the role of memory. Since codes at many levels can be utilized to make a stimulus more memorable, Henderson's result is not diagnostic with respect to visual processing. The most widely cited experiment of this kind (Egeth & Blecker, 1971) factorially varied familiarity and orthography, presenting words, pseudowords, acronyms, and unrelated letter strings at random in mixed blocks. While Egeth and Blecker obtained no latency difference between words and pseudowords, they did find an advantage in Same latencies for acronyms over unrelated letter strings. However, they did not report either Different latencies or error rates, making it difficult to interpret their results. In a replication of this experiment, already mentioned briefly in discussing word-pseudoword differences, Carr et al. (in press) found a pattern of results identical to Egeth and Blecker's in Same latencies and error rates (Experiment I), but no effect of orthography and a disadvantage of familiarity in Different latencies. In addition, subjects made more mistakes on Different displays containing orthographically regular strings than on those containing irregular strings, and more mistakes on familiar strings than on unfamiliar strings. When stimuli were presented in pure blocks (Experiment II), a robust advantage of orthography occurred in latencies and error rates for both decision types, but familiarity produced no differences.

In these acronym studies, the letter strings were short and subjects' past histories of exposure to the strings were highly variable. Another way to assess the effect of whole-stimulus familiarity in the absence of orthographic regularity is to induce familiarity under controlled conditions through laboratory

training. Carr et al. (in press) have done that, (Experiment III) and found
only a small and statistically insignificant (p > .20) difference of 20 msec
in a matching task between four-letter stimuli that had never been seen and
stimuli that had been seen sixteen times a day for eight days. Furthermore,
this difference was offset by a small increase in errors for the familiar
stimuli. Since these letter strings have been actively processed more times
than most people have seen most acronyms, we found the negative result
impressive. This caused us to re-examine previous experiments in which
matching facilitation was obtained from laboratory exposure to strings of
unrelated letters. In a study by Kidd, Pollatsek, and Well (1977), the familiar
set of consonant strings was highly structured because of counterbalancing
procedures used in stimulus generation. Therefore, subjects may have learned
what amounted to a new orthography for the set of familiar stimuli rather
than learning whole-unit representations for individual stimuli. Spatial redundancy, bigram and trigram cluster frequencies, and sequential constraints
all differed between familiar and unfamiliar stimuli, though none of the
differences corresponded to English orthography.

In an earlier experiment by Schindler, Well, and Pollatsek (1976), frequencies of occurrence and positional constraints for single letters and bigrams
were approximately equated among familiar and unfamiliar consonant strings,
but higher-order structural differences were not controlled, so that learning
of part-units or spelling sequences cannot be dismissed. Furthermore, the
study produced clear evidence that some kind of transferable part-learning
actually had occurred, leaving open the possibility that constraints on recur-
rent letter sequences, rather than independent familiarity with individual
strings, was in fact responsible for the observed facilitation. For example,
transfer tests showed that if the string BCDFGH had been seen during training,
subjects were able to match the string BCDXYZ faster than XYZBCD, and
that both of these strings were matched faster than completely unfamiliar
strings. A study by Baron (1974) showed that matching was improved by
learning sequential constraints on bigrams, and that the necessary learning
occurred within the first hour of practice. Thus the learning of higher-order
structural characteristics in the sixteen days of practice given by Schindler
et al. does not seem implausible.

To summarize, while the evidence for advantages of pseudowords over
nonwords in the visual matching task is quite clear, the evidence for additional advantages due to whole-stimulus familiarity is not very good. If we
accept for the moment the assertion that there is no whole-word unit mediating the WSE, we can go on to consider whether the direct activation of
visual chunks larger than single letters but smaller than whole words could
account for the word superiority effect.

The Case against Part-Unit Mechanisms

While most of the data cited above are not inconsistent with this view, there
are several pieces of evidence which argue against the visual chunk hypothesis. One is that most of the facilitation effects reported above were obtained
with words constructed entirely from uppercase letters--a relatively unfamiliar visual stimulus--and many used computer-generated displays, which often
use unfamiliar looking characters. One might try to save the visual subunit
hypothesis by postulating that supraletter chunks are defined by sets of

features which are invariant across case and typeface (F. Smith, 1971). However, one finding argues strongly against that idea: the WSE can still be obtained in the matching task, though reduced somewhat in magnitude, with vertically arranged strings (Well, Pollatsek, & Schindler, 1975). Let us assume for a moment that TH (or some set of features of it) is a visual unit that facilitates processing for strings that contain TH as opposed to a less frequent combination such as HT. If those features are preserved in vertical presentation (where the T would be above the H), then there is no reason to believe that they would not also be present for the combination HT, and thus there would be no reason to expect any orthography advantage in the first place. Therefore this finding would seem to rule out part-unit mechanisms at least as the sole source of the WSE. Further, an undiminished WSE can be obtained with large gaps between some of the letters as well as with strings of letters rotated 180 deg (Schindler, Well, & Pollatsek, 1974; Well et al., 1975). Thus it is quite difficult to think of directly-activatable visual units, even units smaller than the whole word, as mediating the WSE in its entirety.

Because some visual manipulations do decrease the size of the word advantage, though, one might want to maintain visual part-word units or higher-order features as responsible for a portion of the word advantage (Taylor et al., 1977). This is true of vertical stimulus presentation, as mentioned above, and it is also true of mixing letter cases within stimulus strings (McClelland, 1976; Pollatsek et al., 1975; Taylor et al., 1977). While such decrements could be explained by the disruption of visual part-units, they could also be handled by a theory of the visual word advantage which relies only on a rule-governed mechanism. The latter kind of theory could explain all the other data discussed so far, as well. Since it would seem more profitable to have a unified conception of the WSE if one were possible, we will opt for a rule-governed mechanism as the only source of visual facilitation, at least for the present.

Characteristics of a Rule-Governed Mechanism of Visual Encoding
Thus, visual processing of words appears to be facilitated chiefly by the application of rules defining legal letter sequences in the English language. The questions of what these rules are and how they might be used in a plausible mechanism of rapid visual processing are both important and complex. As mentioned previously, attempts to explain the rules in terms of crude statistical descriptions of the written language (bigram and trigram frequencies) appear to be inadequate. A more promising approach to describing the structure of English spelling patterns is in terms of a system of co-occurrence rules derived from constraints imposed by the spoken language and arbitrary conventions such as scribal practices (Venezky, 1970; Venezky, this volume). While Venezky's system appears to correspond in many respects to our intuitive ideas of orthographic regularity, it needs further development. Unfortunately, the rules are capable of generating a number of strings that do not seem particularly word-like (see Massaro, Taylor, and Venezky, in press) and as yet, it is not easy to see how such a formal system should be embodied in the operation of a mechanism capable of actually encoding a sequence of printed letters.

Whatever the ultimate character of the rules, the evidence is strong that constraints which might be described quite abstractly are not applied to print at an equally abstract level, but are translated into expectations about visual features to be sought out and identified (Becker, 1976; Becker & Killion, 1977; McLean, in press; Neisser, 1967). Therefore, orthographic parsing models which do not allow rules to operate all the way down to the level of feature extraction and visual code formation do not seem sufficient. In Spoehr and Smith's (1973) model, for example, word perception is regarded as a sequence of stages. Abstract letter identities, independent of case and typeface, are the output of the first stage. The WSE is thought to arise in a subsequent analysis which constructs vocalic center groups or syllabic units from the abstract letter identities. Such a model would have difficulty explaining how judgments of case differences could be facilitated in words (Pollatsek et al., 1975). Moreover, the model is indifferent to case transitions at levels of processing where word advantages could occur, and therefore cannot explain why increasing the number of case transitions in the word tends to decrease the magnitude of the WSE.

If expectations based on orthographic structure were implemented at the level of visual features, however, both of these effects would be at least qualitatively understandable. An expectation for any given letter or letter sequence could be expressed specifically enough to include features that would discriminate upper-case from lower-case letters, allowing even the detection of differences defined by case to be facilitated. However, if case changes occur between adjacent letters of a word, then the expectations will not be fulfilled if we assume that subjects generally expect letters to be in the same case as surrounding letters which have already been identified. The more case transitions occurring between adjacent letters, the more this expectation will prove counterproductive. Thus if the degree to which orthographic expectations are met accounts for the WSE, one can see how case alternation might reduce the WSE, or even eliminate it.

More about the content of orthographic expectations is implied by the reduction in the WSE caused by vertical stimulus presentation. Apparently they include the prediction that letters in the same word will occur to the right and left of one another rather than in some other organization. A long history of reading horizontally-arrayed words could make this a very deeply ingrained expectation, associated with highly automated or habitualized scanning patterns. Some flexibility in patterned scanning is apparently possible, however, and if flexibility can be achieved, the WSE ceases to be disrupted. In Well, Pollatsek, and Schindler's (1975) study of stimulus rotation, the majority of subjects showed evidence of scanning rotated words from right to left, and these subjects showed word advantages equivalent to normal presentation. Subjects who scanned rotated words from left to right showed little facilitation. While these data might be taken to imply that under ordinary circumstances expectations are implemented in serial processing from left to right, they need not be. Letters may well be processed in parallel by the visual system, with information obtained from early-finishing letters (often but not necessarily the leftmost) feeding back to the processing of remaining letters anywhere in the string. Unlike vertical presentation or rotation, however, irregular spacing of letters apparently does not interfere in any substantial way with the generation of expectations and utilization of feedback, at least as long as subjects know in advance that words are to be presented (Schindler et al., 1974). Thus the details of spacing, which commonly vary from display to display, do not figure as centrally in the orthographic mechanism's operation as more universal attributes of text, such as horizontal organization of upright words in standardized case formats.

To summarize, the expectation model seems to be a fairly parsimonious and useful framework within which to view the WSE. While it does not in any real sense explain the data, it seems to capture both the fixed and the flexible characteristics of word (and pseudoword) perception in the human visual system. It also seems to provide a useful language in which to pose unanswered questions (why are sequential constraints harder to employ in vertical presentation than in 180 deg rotation?). Furthermore, when the WSE is looked at from this perspective, current arguments over the size of the unit in word processing (Massaro, 1975; Smith & Spoehr, 1974; Taylor et al., 1977) seem less important. There may be situations in which information such as whether the stimulus is actually a word or not can be brought to bear in visual processing. Since we know that orthographically regular stimuli can be identified as words or nonwords in 500-700 msec (Meyer, Schvaneveldt, & Ruddy, 1975), some contact must be made with the lexicon or semantic memory in less than 0.5 sec. Several studies have reported evidence that semantic expectations, at least if formed well enough in advance, can feed back into the visual processing necessary for these decisions (Becker & Killion, 1977; Meyer et al., 1975). On the other hand, in visual matching experiments, where expectations have both less time to form and less time to operate, the effect of lexical contact appears to be solely one of biasing the subject to respond Same, indicating that lexical information was not available sufficiently early to affect encoding.

Carr et al. (in press) have collected some direct evidence concerning the time required for orthographic versus lexical information to build up in the processing system. (Experiment IV). One part of their experiment required subjects to decide whether a string of letters was a word. Subjects took no longer to reject acronyms than unrelated letter strings (439 and 437 msec, respectively), but were much slower to accept words (504 msec) and to reject pseudowords (515 msec) when all four kinds of stimuli were mixed randomly in a block of trials. Thus subjects were apparently able to make a quick classification based on orthographic structure. When the classification was negative, they could decide immediately that the string was not a word, but if the classification was positive, they needed to wait for lexical or semantic information. While it cannot be argued from this result that orthographic processing must be completed before a search of semantic memory is begun, it is clear that orthographic information is available before the semantic search is finished and that meaning, when irrelevant, does not interfere with decisions made on the basis of structure. James (1975) and Shulman and Davison (1977) have reported data consistent with this conclusion: various semantic effects ordinarily found in lexical decision are attenuated or eliminated when the nonwords are all orthographically irregular.

The experiments of Carr et al., however, used three-letter strings and response times were quite fast. It is possible that when visual processing requires more time (for example, in matching tasks with long strings such as in Chambers and Forster, 1975), lexical information could begin to feed back into visual code formation. The point which remains, however, is that because it appears to take considerably more time for lexicality, as opposed to orthographic regularity, to affect processing efficiency, there is nothing magic about the whole word as a visual unit.

The major conclusion of this paper, then, is that most of the facilitation in visual code formation observed in the matching task is produced by the application of relatively abstract rules extracted from past experience with the written language. It is worth noting that the accuracy of forced-choice recognition when words, pseudowords, and unrelated letter strings are presented tachistoscopically is quite similar to the pattern of results obtained in the matching paradigm, at least when subjects know what kinds of stimuli can potentially occur. Pseudowords are consistently identified more accurately than unrelated letter strings, while words may (Manelis, 1974; McClelland, 1976) or may not (Carr, Davidson, & Hawkins, 1978; Baron & Thurston, 1973; McClelland & Johnston, 1977) be identified any more accurately than pseudowords. To the extent that these word perception tasks share encoding processes with various modes of ordinary reading, the results suggest that one should make every attempt to define the rules of orthography precisely and construct situations in which they can be learned most efficiently. Unfortunately we have at the present time a poor grasp of the optimal way to learn rules even in tasks with much simpler and better-defined stimulus structure than reading (Brooks, 1977; Brooks & Miller, this volume). One also has to deal with the question of whether a strong emphasis on rules might adversely affect the initial learning of words that may have regular sequences of letters but have irregular grapheme-to-phoneme correspondences, since many of these words with irregular pronunciations are quite common, at least in English. Perhaps the best course to follow at this point is to try to get an idea of what kinds of structures can be learned, and at what levels of processing various structures can have an influence. Brooks and Miller have made an excellent start in this direction, showing that orthographic structure corresponding to that of English can be extracted and used to facilitate the naming of "words" printed in an artificial alphabet. Their data indicate that early in learning, facilitation is greater when words are learned as wholes through paired-associate training, but that longer-term facilitation is greater when words are taught through spelling-to-sound correspondence rules. In addition, their experiments nicely distinguish between learning rules of letter sequencing and rules of letter-to-sound translation. Even when the pairing of letter patterns and sound patterns was arbitrary, subjects learned something about the visual structure of the stimulus set, since they were later able to separate "regular" from "irregular" new stimuli at better than chance rates. Further, Singer and Carr (1975) and Singer and Lappin (1977) have shown in other training studies using artificial materials, that subjects can learn and profit from implicit visual structure through visual practice alone, without any kind of support from phonetic or semantic task activity. These studies indicate that orthography may in fact make two independent contributions to word identification, one through visual structure and another through spelling-to-sound translation. Experimentation of this kind would seem to be a valuable way of studying the nature of orthography and the psychological mechanisms by which orthographic structure is put to use during reading.

This work was supported by NSF Grant No. BMS 73-00963 to Michael I. Posner at the Univeristy of Oregon and NIH Postdoctoral Fellowship No. 1-F32-HD05157 from NICHHD to the second author under his sponsorship. We thank Denise Frieder Carr for help in collecting data, and Charles Clifton, Jr., Robert Lorch, Michael I. Posner, and Lee Brooks for conversation, comments, and criticism during preparation of the manuscript.

REFERENCES

Baron, J. Facilitation of perception by spelling constraints. Canadian Journal of Psychology, 1974, 28, 37-50.

Baron, J. Successive stages in word recognition. In P.M.A. Rabbitt & S. Dornic (Eds.), Attention and performance V. London: Academic Press, 1975.

Baron, J., & Thurston, I. An analysis of the word superiority effect. Cognitive Psychology, 1973, 4, 207-228.

Barron, R.W., & Henderson, L. The effects of lexical and semantic information on same-different visual comparison of words. Memory & Cognition, 1977, 5, 566-579.

Barron, R.W., & Pittenger, J.B. The effect of orthographic structure and lexical meaning on "same"-"different" judgments. Quarterly Journal of Experimental Psychology, 1974, 26, 566-581.

Becker, C.A. Allocation of attention during visual word recognition. Journal of Experimental Psychology: Human Perception and Performance, 1976, 2, 556-566.

Becker, C.A., & Killion, T.H. Interaction of visual and cognitive effects in word recognition. Journal of Experimental Psychology: Human Perception and Performance, 1977, 3, 389-401.

Brooks, L. Visual pattern in fluent word identification. In A.S. Reber & D. L. Scarborough (Eds.), Toward a psychology of reading. Hillsdale, NJ: Erlbaum, 1977.

Brooks, L., & Miller, A. A comparison of explicit and implicit knowledge about an alphabet. (This volume.)

Carr, T.H., Posner, M.I., Pollatsek, A., & Snyder, C.R.R. Orthography and familiarity effects in word perception. Journal of Experimental Psychology: General (in press).

Carr, T.H., Davidson, B.J., & Hawkins, H.L. Perceptual flexibility in word recognition: Strategies affect orthographic computation but not lexical access. Journal of Experimental Psychology: Human Perception and Performance, 1978, 4, 674-690.

Cattell, J.M. The time taken up by cerebral operations. Mind, 1886, 11, 277-292, 524-538.

Chambers, S.M. & Forster, K.I. Evidence for lexical access in a simultaneous matching task. Memory & Cognition, 1975, 3, 549-560.

Egeth, H., & Blecker, D. Differential effects of familiartiy on judgments of sameness and difference. Perception & Psychophysics, 1971, 9, 321-326.

Eichelman, W. H. Familiarity effects in the simultaneous matching task. Journal of Experimental Psychology, 1970, 86, 275-282.

Gibson, E.J., Pick, A.D., Osser, H., & Hammond, M. The role of grapheme-phoneme correspondence in the perception of words. American Journal of Psychology, 1962, 75, 554-570.

Henderson, L. A word superiority effect without orthographic assistance. Quarterly Journal of Experimental Psychology, 1974, 20, 301-311.

Henderson, L., & Chard, J. On the nature of the facilitation of visual comparisons by lexical membership. Bulletin of the Psychonomic Society, 1976, 7, 432-434.

Hershenson, M. Verbal report and visual matching latency as a function of the pronounceability of letter arrays. Journal of Experimental Psychology, 1972, 96, 104-109.

Huey, E.B. The psychology and pedagogy of reading. New York: Macmillan, 1908. Reprinted, Cambridge, MA: MIT Press, 1968.

James, C.T. The role of semantic information in lexical decisions. Journal of Experimental Psychology: Human Perception and Performance, 1975, 1, 130-136.

Kidd, G.R., Pollatsek, A., & Well, A.D. Two types of induced familiarity in the matching of letter strings. Bulletin of the Psychonomic Society, 1977, 10, 179-182.

Manelis, L. The effect of meaningfulness in tachistoscopic word perception. Perception & Psychophysics, 1974, 16, 182-192.

Massaro, D. Primary and secondary recognition in reading. In D. Massaro (Ed.), Understanding language. New York: Academic Press, 1975.

Massaro, D., Taylor, G.A., & Venezky, R. Orthographic regularity, positional frequency, and visual processing of letter strings. Journal of Experimental Psychology: General (in press).

McClelland, J. Preliminary letter identification in the perception of words and nonwords. Journal of Experimental Psychology: Human Perception and Performance, 1976, 2, 80-91.

McClelland, J.L., & Johnston, J.C. The role of familiar units in perception of words and nonwords. Perception & Psychophysics, 1977, 22, 249-261.

McLean, J.P. On the construction of expectancies. Quarterly Journal of Experimental Psychology (in press).

Meyer, D., Schvaneveldt, R., & Ruddy, M. Loci of contextual effects on visual word recognition. In P.M.A. Rabbitt & S. Dornic (Eds.), Attention and performance V. London: Academic Press, 1975.

Miller, G.A., Bruner, J.S., & Postman, L. Familiarity of letter sequences and tachistoscopic identification. Journal of General Psychology, 1954, 50, 129-139.

Neisser, U. Cognitive psychology. New York: Appleton-Century-Crofts, 1967.

Petersen, R., & LaBerge, D. Contextual control of letter perception. Memory & Cognition, 1977, 5, 205-213.

Pollatsek, A., Well, A.D., & Schindler, R.M. Familiarity affects visual processing of words. Journal of Experimental Psychology: Human Perception and Performance, 1975, 1, 328-333.

Schindler, R.M., Well, A.D., & Pollatsek, A. Effects of segmentation and expectancy on matching times for words and nonwords. Journal of Experimental Psychology, 1974, 103, 107-111.

Schindler, R.M., Well, A.D., & Pollatsek, A. Inducing the familiarity effect. Perception & Psychophysics, 1976, 19, 425-432.

Shulman, H.G., & Davison, T.C.B. Control properties of semantic coding on a lexical decision task. Journal of Verbal Learning and Verbal Behavior, 1977, 16, 91-98.

Singer, M.H., & Carr, T.H. Unpublished data, Department of Psychology, Vanderbilt University, 1976.

Singer, M.A., & Lappin, J.S. The use of visual and phonetic information in the analysis of letter strings: An experiment with artificial letters. Paper presented at the annual meeting of the Psychonomic Society, Washington, DC, November 1977.

Smith, E.E., & Spoehr, K.T. The perception of printed English: A theoretical perspective. In B. Kantowitz (Ed.), Human information processing: Tutorials in performance and cognition. Hillsdale, NJ: Erlbaum, 1974.

Smith, F. Understanding reading. New York: Holt, 1971.

Spoehr, K.T., & Smith, E.E. The role of syllables in perceptual processing. Cognitive Psychology, 1973, 5, 71-89.

Taylor, G.A., Miller, T.J., & Juola, J.F. Isolating visual units in the perception of words and nonwords. Perception & Psychophysics, 1977, 21, 377-386.

Venezky, R. The structure of English orthography. The Hague: Mouton, 1970.

Venezky, R. Orthographic regularities in English words. (This volume.)

Well, A.D., Pollatsek, A., & Schindler, R.M. Facilitation of both "same" and "different" judgments of letter strings by familiarity of letter sequence. Perception & Psychophysics, 1975, 17, 511-520.

Spelling Patterns, Letter Cancellation and the Processing of Text

Philip T. Smith and Anne Groat

*Two experiments are reported in which an attempt is made
to identify those parts of words and sentences that readers
pay particular attention to during fluent silent reading. Using
a technique first reported by Corcoran (1966), we asked university students to cross out all the letter e's appearing in
a text they read. In the first experiment the nature of the
text was systematically varied (there were various degrees
of difficult, easy, and nonsensical texts); in the second experiment the instructions to subjects were varied (to pay attention to or ignore meaning).*

*The primary results are 1) contrary to Corcoran's (1966)
findings, there is not an acoustic factor in this task (i.e.,
silent e's are as readily detected as pronounced e's); 2) there
is a strong tendency, even with the most nonsensical texts,
to miss a greater proportion of e's at the end of words;
3) e's in unstressed syllables are more likely to be missed
than e's in stressed syllables; 4) there are several grammatical and lexical effects (i.e., the linguistic function of the
e to a large extent determines the probability that it will
be missed); and 5) the position of a word within a sentence
and its position on each line of text also contribute substantially to the probability that any e's in the word will be
missed. The implications of the above results for a theory
of reading are discussed.*

This paper has two aims: to attack the idea that acoustic factors play a significant role in fluent silent reading, and to demonstrate that one of the
methods that has been used to investigate acoustic factors is in fact a sensitive tool for studying the micro-structure of the reading process.

A skilled reader of English is able to carry out many operations on written text: he can read the text aloud (produce a phonetic version of the text), he can tell the meaning of isolated words (produce lexical information), and he is able to comprehend sentences and paragraphs (extract semantic information), among others. Many researchers have claimed that the extraction of phonetic information is an essential part of the reading process, and may facilitate or disrupt the extraction of lexical and semantic information. This is what is meant by an "acoustic" factor in reading. It is our contention that this claim is misguided since there is no reliable empirical evidence to support it, at least for university students reading coherent text.

Massaro (1975) has thoroughly reviewed the work on acoustic factors in reading (what he calls phonological mediation) and we shall not repeat it here. Our principal objection to this work is that where acoustic factors have been shown to disrupt performance, the task involves the subject making judgments about differences between isolated words and pseudo-words (Rubenstein, Lewis, & Rubenstein, 1971; Meyer & Ruddy, 1973), or judging whether an isolated sentence is anomalous (Kleiman, 1975; Baddeley, 1976). Neither of these tasks is closely related to normal comprehension processes, where a reader rarely needs to question whether he is reading English or whether the sentences make sense.

One technique that escapes these criticisms was reported by Corcoran (1966). He required subjects to read a coherent piece of prose and to cancel every letter e that they noticed. Corcoran's major finding was that silent e's were cancelled less often than pronounced e's, and he concluded that this was because the material was being stored in an acoustic short-term memory, where pronounced e's, but not silent e's, would be directly represented.

Several aspects of Corcoran's study are not completely satisfactory. First, his subjects were naval ratings, and the material was a passage from the magazine Punch. Since this material would likely be unfamiliar to the subjects, atypical reading performances might be produced. Second, subjects were not told whether they should pay any attention to meaning, yet it seems reasonable to expect different results if subjects were attending to meaning rather than ignoring it. Third, as will be seen in the following experiments, the efficiency with which e's are cancelled varies as a complicated function of many linguistic factors, not all of which are properly controlled for in Corcoran's analyses.

In this paper we report studies where Corcoran's technique has been applied to a variety of texts and with several different sets of instructions to subjects. Our results show conclusively that when allowance is made for certain artifacts which Corcoran did not take account of, there is no acoustic factor in this task. Our main reason for undertaking the study, however, was not to prove that Corcoran was wrong; rather, we were looking for a task which allowed us to observe some of the micro-structure of the reading process and which at the same time would give us some insight into how subjects integrate information simultaneously from several different linguistic levels. A priori the e cancellation experiment would seem to be a promising candidate for this task. If a subject fails to cancel an e in a particular word, it may be because he has not attended to the word, or that the word was not retained in short-term store for sufficient time, or that the part of the word in which the e occurs has not received detailed analysis. In any of these cases an uncancelled e indicates that this part of the text has not received sufficient processing (not sufficient, that is, to identify the e as a separate unit, though possibly quite sufficient to understand the text). If this hypothesis is correct, and in view of the high frequency of e in the English language, this technique will allow us to estimate many times in each sentence the amount of processing that is taking place within words and groups of words, without seriously disrupting the fluency of the reader's performance. As such, this approach is not dissimilar to that of eye-movement studies: whereas eye-movement recording tells us which parts of a text have been looked at, the e-cancellation task tells us which parts (of a sub-set of the entire text) have received particular attention. O'Regan's and Shebilske and Reid's papers (this volume) have an approach similar to ours. The advantage of our approach is that it is technologically so much simpler, being (literally) only a pencil and paper task.

The other attractive feature of the e-cancellation task is that the letter e is used in English orthography to indicate a wide range of linguistic distinctions. If we confine our attention to silent e's at the end of words, we can distinguish four broad categories: (I) Graphemic, (II) Phonemic, (III) Lexical, (IV) Etymological. Graphemic e has no direct linguistic function, and is present because it is conventional for a final e to follow certain consonants (especially v and z) (give, have, freeze). Phonemic e modifies the pronunciation of a previous consonant or vowel (bare, fine, huge, in contrast with bar, fin, hug). Lexical e provides information about the lexical category to which a word belongs (please is not the plural of plea), and there is a substantial class of function words ending in -ere and -ore (there, where, more, before). The Etymological category refers to words that cannot be assigned to the other classes (programme, definite). We speculated that if a reader uses various spelling patterns to help him read the text, the extent to which he pays attention to a particular e will vary as a function of the linguistic role played by the e in the text, and that as we varied instructions to subjects (whether to pay attention to or ignore the meaning), the extent to which he paid attention to e's fulfilling different linguistic roles might be expected to change differentially. It is possible then that e cancellation could give us information not only about the absolute amount of attention being paid to different parts of a word, but also the relative amounts of processing going on at different linguistic levels.

Method

Passages of two different types were used: difficult: selections from Hilgard and Bower's Theories of Learning; easy: selections from thrillers by Morris West.

Texts were constructed as follows. Normal text was about 750 words of one of the two types of passage. Scrambled words was identical to the normal text except that the order of words was altered to render the passage meaningless; words containing e occupied the same position in this text as they did in normal text. Scrambled letters was identical to normal text except the letters in each word were rearranged to make the word as nearly as possible unpronounceable, with the sole restriction that each letter e occupied the same position in each scrambled word as it did in the normal text.

For example: Normal text   The psychology of reading
                Scrambled words   The of psychology reading
                Scrambled letters   hte lpcyyhsgoo fo iegarda

The scrambled texts then preserved gross features of English, such as
the frequency and position of the letter e, but critical linguistic features,
particularly meaning and pronounceability, were absent or attenuated.

Texts were typed, with 1½ spaces between lines.

Subjects

One hundred first-year students of psychology at Stirling University took
part in the experiment as part of a course requirement. Mean age was
twenty years; there were equal numbers of males and females.

Procedure

Each subject received two texts, separated by a brief rest.

Experiment 1. The subject was given no specific instructions, beyond the
requirement that he should read through each text and cross out all the e's
as he did so. Each subject received one difficult passage and one easy passage, and each passage could appear as normal text, scrambled words, or
scrambled letters. An individual subject did not receive the same text condition for the two texts. (If he received the scrambled words condition for
the first text, he received the normal text or the scrambled letters condition
for the second text.) Across subjects, order of presentation of passages and
text conditions was counterbalanced. Sixty subjects took part.

Experiment 2. Only normal texts were used in this experiment. Again, each
subject received one easy passage and one difficult passage (order counterbalanced across subjects). Half the subjects were told to cancel e's, but at
the same time to pay particular attention to meaning since they would be
asked questions about the passage later. Half the subjects were told to cancel
e's but to ignore meaning since, said the experimenter, this would help them
with the cancellation task. After each subject had cancelled e's in both passages he was given a comprehension test, consisting of a recognition memory
test for words in the passage and a series of questions designed to tap comprehension ("Who was responsible for the reintroduction of the concept of
insight into American psychology?" "What was the potential danger in crawl-
ing through the dead leaves?"). Forty subjects took part.

Results

One problem in the analysis is lack of a satisfactory definition of a silent
e. Indeed the term silent could be misleading since it might imply that the
e in question had no influence on the sound of the word at all. We prefer
to talk about syllabic and non-syllabic e's, defined as follows: a syllabic e
is closely associated with a syllable; where several vowels uninterrupted by
a consonant are associated with a syllable, all the vowels are said to be syllabic. Thus the e's in be, been and toe are all syllabic. Non-syllabic e's are
those that appear in words such as lovely, give, huge. There are a few difficult borderline cases: we treat as non-syllabic a final e following an l or r

that is preceded by a consonant (capable, ochre), arguing that the e is merely an indicator of the preceding syllabic liquid but is not a syllable itself; the e in toes is treated as syllabic, since the word is related to toe which, according to our definition, contains a syllabic e, whereas the e in goes is non-syllabic, since the e is part of an orthographic convention for forming the third-person singular form of the verb. Other investigators might prefer different analyses, but fortunately our borderline cases are few in number and not in any way crucial to our argument. Essentially the same results would be obtained if these cases were excluded or reassigned to different categories.

Excluded from our analyses are double e's (see, trees, speech, etc.). Preliminary analysis suggested these e's to be much more readily detected than e's in any other class of words (even than similar sounding words). For example, double e's are missed (fail to be cancelled) overall on 0.9% of occasions, whereas similar sounding monosyllables not containing a double e (he, these, each, etc.) are missed on 3.5% of occasions. The effect of double e is not influenced by instructions, by type of text, or by the frequency or part of speech of the word; it is presumably purely visual, and will not be discussed further.

General Results
Corcoran found, and we readily confirmed, that e's were most often missed in final and penultimate position in a word, and that the e in "the" was very frequently missed. Also, in our particular sample, no non-syllabic e's occurred more than six letters from the end of the word. Accordingly, we computed separately the percentage of e's missed in the word the, the percentage of e's missed in final position, in penultimate position, and between three and six letters from the end of the word ("early" in the word). These distinctions were made so that syllabic and non-syllabic e's would be compared in similar positions within the word. In addition we computed separately the e's missed in the affix -ed (in words such as missed, treated, etc.) and whether the e was in a syllable that received primary stress within the word (the e's in "be, mental, instead" are part of primary stressed syllables, the e's in "higher, react" are not part of primary stressed syllables). The gross results, averaged over all subjects and conditions, are shown in Figure 1.

Figure 1 clearly shows that e's in final position and in -ed words are omitted most often. While detailed analysis will be carried out later in this paper to establish the point more carefully, inspection of Figure 1 shows there are only small and inconsistent differences between syllabic and non-syllabic e's. In early positions non-syllabic e is in fact more often missed than unstressed syllabic e's; in penultimate position, once the possible artifact of -ed words is controlled for, syllabic e's again are missed slightly more often than non-syllabic e's (-ed words contain a high proportion of non-syllabic e's and could artifactually give the impression that penultimate non-syllabic e is in general more easily missed); in final position, once words ending in double e have been excluded, there is no significant difference between syllabic and non-syllabic e's, though in this case the trend is the same as that predicted by Corcoran's "acoustic" explanation. In summary, Figure 1 shows us that there is no major acoustic effect in the data, but suggests that there are other variances worth investigating. These additional variances are examined in turn.

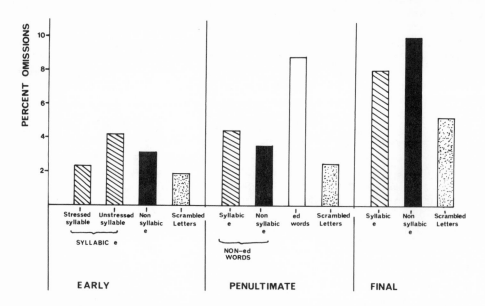

Figure 1. Omission rate for e. The results are averaged over all subjects and conditions, except for the scrambled letters condition which was analysed separately.

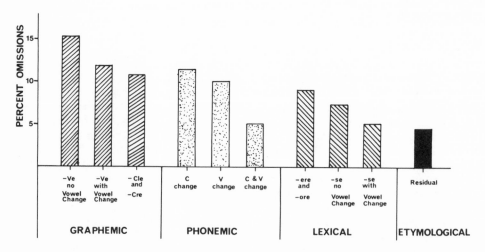

Figure 2. Omission rates for final non-syllabic e's. The results are averaged over all subjects in the normal and scrambled words text conditions.

Table 1. Classification of Final Non-Syllabic e's Used in Our Analyses.

		Class	Spelling	Example
I	1.	Graphemic	-ve, no vowel change	have
	2.	Graphemic/Phonemic	-ve, with vowel change	gave
	3.	Graphemic/Phonemic	-le or -re following a consonant	able, centre
II	4.	Phonemic	consonant change	large, since
	5.	Phonemic	vowel change	time
	6.	Phonemic	consonant and vowel change	place, change
III	7.	Lexical	-ere, -ore	there, more
	8.	Lexical	-se, no vowel change	sense
	9.	Lexical/Phonemic	-se with vowel change	these
IV	10.	Etymological	anything not covered above	examine

Final Position
High frequency words (Thorndike-Lorge frequency A or higher) and low frequency words (less than Thorndike-Lorge frequency A) were analysed separately. For final e's there are no significant effects of syllabic versus non-
syllabic e (mean amount of variance accounted for = 0.2%) and no effects
of frequency (variance accounted for = 0.7%). However, in line with the
distinctions made earlier about the linguistic functions of e, we divide words
ending in non-syllabic e into 10 classes (see Table 1).

The results of computing e omissions for these different classes are shown in Figure 2. Analysis of variance of each of the passages separately shows comfortably significant effects of word class in each case. Consistency across passages however is not very high, but there are two reliable results. First, Lexical e's are less frequently missed than Graphemic and Phonemic e's and, second, when an e serves two functions (classes 2, 6, 9 in Table 1) it is less likely to be missed than when it serves only one function; for example, an e that changes both consonant and vowel (price) is less likely to be missed than an e that changes only the consonant (prince) or only the vowel (prime).

There are no consistent differences across texts or instructions. Both these results suggest that it is the function of e that is important in this task: the more functions an e serves, the more likely it is to be detected, and Lexical functions, which are probably more related to the processes of comprehension, lead to better detection rates than Graphemic and Phonemic functions, which are concerned with relatively superficial aspects of spelling and pronunciation.

Penultimate Position
Results are shown in Figure 3. There are no reliable effects of frequency (0.1% of the variance accounted for) nor of syllabic versus non-syllabic e (0.7% of the variance). The major effect is that if words end in the affix -ed, the e is much more likely to be missed than otherwise (7.5% of the variance accounted for). This effect is due to the affix nature of -ed and not to some peculiar masking effect of the d: words ending in -ed where the -ed is not an affix (led, hundred, sacred, naked) show an omission rate of 2.8%, comparable to the rate for penultimate e in words not ending in d (4.0%) and substantially less than in words where -ed is an affix (9.4%). There is

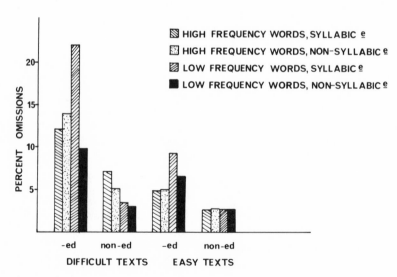

Figure 3. Omission rate for penultimate e's.

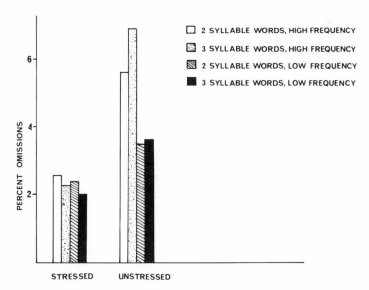

Figure 4. Omission rate for e's in stressed and unstressed syllables.

an effect of passage difficulty, with difficult passages in their normal text versions resulting in more omissions than in the other passages. There is one awkward result: as can be seen from Figure 3, syllabic e in low frequency words with an -ed affix more often fails to be cancelled than any other class of words ending in an -ed affix. The best we can suggest for this result is that there are only a small number of low frequency words (Thorndike-Lorge frequency A or less in this particular analysis) which have a syllabic e in the affix -ed (treated, shunted, etc.), and so this effect may be the chance result of two or three of these words showing fortuitously high omission rates.

Effects of Stress
Figure 1 shows that in the early positions of words, syllabic e's in unstressed syllables are more likely to be missed than those in stressed syllables. This in fact is a robust and very general effect, it is not confined merely to the early parts of words, and it applies to words of all lengths. Systematic statistical analysis is easiest with two and three syllable words, of which there are sufficient numbers to give reliable results. The results of this analysis are shown in Figure 4.

An analysis of variance was carried out in which the factors were texts, frequency, word length (two or three syllables) and whether the syllabic e was stressed or unstressed. There is a frequency effect, which is due to high frequency words suffering more omissions; there is a stress effect with unstressed e's being more often missed. Although there are differences between passages, there are no differences with respect to type of text (normal text or scrambled words) or with respect to instructions (pay attention to meaning or ignore meaning). There is an interaction between frequency and stress that is due to a larger omission rate difference between stressed and unstressed e's for high frequency words. Overall, 10.3% of the variance is accounted for by frequency and the stressed/unstressed e distinction.

The Definite Article
Corcoran found that the e in "the" was very often missed in the cancellation task. This effect we readily confirmed. As shown in Figure 5, the type of text influences omission rate in "the." Difficult texts without special instructions or with instructions to attend to meaning have the highest omission rate, this being significantly greater than the omission rate for the corresponding easy texts.

Easy texts have themselves a higher omission rate than scrambled words texts and normal texts (both difficult and easy) where the subject has been told to ignore meaning. Scrambled texts and the "ignore meaning" texts do not differ significantly. Healy (1976) has obtained similar results, using the equivalent of our easy texts and scrambled words texts, but she did not manipulate instructions to subjects.

Position Effects
Despite the high significance levels of many of the effects described, they account for a relatively small amount of variance (about 10%). In contrast, if we look at the same e occurring in the same word in the same text in different conditions, about 50% of the variance is accounted for. That is, there are consistent effects in these experiments which cannot be ascribed to the distinctions made so far. Most of these additional effects can be identified. First, there are small practice effects, particularly with "the" and -ed, whereby a subject improves steadily as he proceeds through the passage. A much larger effect is obtained if we examine the position of the e on each line of text. Each line was divided into 13 positions. Positions 1 to 6 consisted of the first six words on the line, positions 8 to 13 consisted of the last six words, and position 7 covered any remaining words. The results are

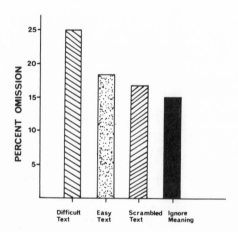

Figure 5. Omission rates for the e in "the."

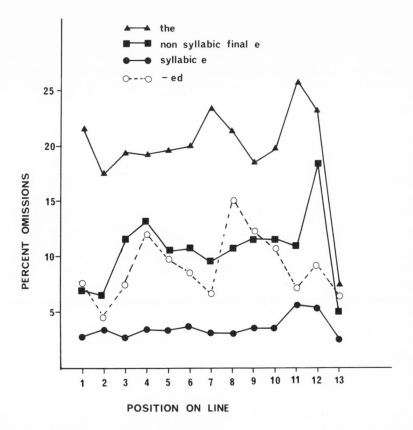

Figure 6. Omission rate as a function of position on each line of text. The data are pooled over all the normal texts.

shown in Figure 6. There is a position effect that is characterised by a large rise in omissions in positions 11 or 12, and a sharp drop in omissions in position 13 (the last word of the line). This effect is present for non-syllabic final e's, for syllabic e's, and for "the"; however, there is no position effect for -ed words.

Figure 7 shows differences between normal texts and scrambled words texts. The scrambled words texts show uneven position effects that are barely significant, whereas normal texts show the penultimate peak and final fall with great regularity. The two serial position curves are similar only in that minimum omission rate occurs on the last word of the line for both of them.

In summary, in normal texts certain classes of word containing e show regular serial position effects which might be explained with reference to some sort of model of peripheral visual memory; however, the fact that not all types of word containing e show the same effect, and the fact that scrambled words texts also show a different effect, emphasises that linguistic factors are also involved. The same pattern of results emerged when each of the positions on the line is analysed separately; so, for example, we cannot identify position 13 as reflecting "visual memory" performance and positions 11 and 12 as reflecting "linguistic memory," since the pattern of errors in both cases shows the same linguistic effects.

There are also substantial position effects within sentences. Again, we divided the material into 13 positions, with positions 1 to 6 occupied by the first six words of the sentence, positions 8 to 13 occupied by the last six words, and the remainder assigned to position 7 (with short sentences, only the extreme positions were used, so that a six-word sentence would have words in positions 1, 2, 3, 11, 12, 13). The results are shown in Figure 8. There are position effects for the, -ed and non-syllabic final e, but not for syllabic e. Since our texts were not selected to allow a systematic comparison of different sentence structures, we postpone detailed analysis of sentence position effects for future work. The point we wish to emphasise here is that position effects are different for different types of word: -ed and non-syllabic final e are similar and are plotted together in Figure 8; "the" is quite different. This rules out explanations based on momentary processing load within each sentence, since if load were high at a certain position, we would expect all types of e to show increased omissions. Rather it seems that we are witnessing the effects of subjects' expectancies for different classes of words, these expectancies changing in different ways in the course of the sentence.

Discussion

Homogeneity of Data

In all our analyses we have averaged over subjects in each condition. The danger of this type of analysis is that we are missing important differences

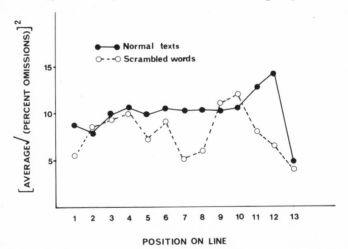

Figure 7. Omission rate as a function of position on line, for normal and scrambled words texts. The data are averaged over syllable e's, non-syllable final e's, and "the."

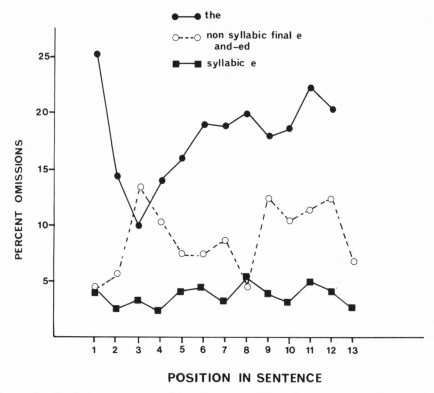

Figure 8. Omission rate as a function of position in sentence. The data are pooled over all of the normal texts.

between subjects, and that the average data do not accurately reflect the performance of individual subjects. It seems unlikely that this is the case with the present experiment. Subjects took an average of 10 minutes to read each text (77% of the subjects took between 8 and 12 minutes). Surprisingly, neither type of text (normal, scrambled words, scrambled letters) nor instructions (no instruction, attend to meaning, ignore meaning) influenced reading time. Subjects did vary in the number of omissions made (0% for the best subject, 36% for the worst subject), but the same gross trends (difficulty with "the" and e's in final position) were present in almost all subjects. Sex differences were insignificant compared with individual variations: this contrasts with the results of Coltheart, Hull, and Slater (1975) who found substantial differences on a similar task. Coltheart et al.'s largest effect was for the cancellation of h in "the," where females made about 27% errors and males about 15% errors; in contrast, in cancelling e in "the," our males made 17.7% errors and our females 19.5% errors. Even this small trend is not consistent across conditions, and is reversed in conditions not requiring semantic analysis. One important difference between Coltheart's procedure and our own is that he required a high reading rate (2 minutes per page), which is about 3 or 4 times faster than our unpaced subjects preferred to read.

Does the Subject's Performance in this Task Bear any Resemblance to Performance during Normal Reading?
One of the jobs of an experimental psychologist is to ensure that his experiments extract significant information about the procedures his subjects use outside the laboratory. One of our principal objections to much reading research is that subjects are often required to make unusual decisions (word/non-word) about isolated words or artificial sentences: the strategies induced by such tasks may not disclose anything relevant about normal reading. This type of objection can of course be made to the present experiment also, and there is no fully satisfactory reply. On the negative side, reading rate is only 75 words per minute, much slower than normal, and subjects find the task quite taxing, which suggests they are doing more than normal reading. On the positive side, we can point to the use of coherent text, the variety of linguistically relevant variables influencing the task, and to the fact that subjects are able to respond to instructions and make a reasonable show of comprehending the texts when so instructed. (The mean proportion of questions about the text correctly answered when subjects were instructed to attend to meaning was 54%, compared with 28% in the "ignore meaning" condition.) This suggests that our task has something in common with normal reading, and if this suggestion is far from conclusive, at least we are in a better position to claim our task reflects normal processes than many other experiments in this area.

Summary and Conclusion
We have identified the following effects:
1) a stressed versus unstressed syllable effect that interacts with frequency, but is uninfluenced by type of passage or text.
2) a word class effect for final non-syllabic e's (Lexical e's being easier to detect than Graphemic or Phonemic e's); this effect does not interact with frequency, nor is it influenced by type of passage or text.
3) an affix effect: the e in -ed is often not cancelled; there is no interaction with frequency, but the effect is more marked for difficult passages.
4) a definite article effect: the e in "the" is often missed, and type of passage (difficult or easy), type of text (normal or scrambled), and instructions to subjects (pay attention to meaning or ignore meaning) all influence performance.
     Our interpretation of these effects is in terms of the linguistic representations a subject computes when reading a text. We assume that the reader is capable of constructing various visual, phonetic, phonemic, morphemic, syntactic, and semantic representations of the text: this is the sum total of his knowledge about the text. We suppose he uses these representations to identify e's in the cancellation task. This leads to unexceptionable interpretations of many of our effects: low level representations, operating at roughly the level of individual words, are associated with the effects of stress and the superiority of Lexical e's over Graphemic and Phonemic e's. These can be seen as word level effects partly because the stress effect, at least, is influenced by frequency, and frequency is known to affect the identification

of isolated words but not words in a substantial context; also because higher level manipulations (scrambling of the text, instructions to attend to meaning) have no effect. Low level representations then emphasise word stress and those aspects of a word that are relevant to its lexical class. In contrast, the -ed and "the" effects have components which are associated with syntactic and semantic representations, because of their sensitivity to those very manipulations which do not influence the stress effect or the lexical e effect. Presumably -ed and "the" are stored as unanalyzed units, or even deleted, in a syntactic or semantic analysis of the sentence.

There are several difficulties associated with this type of interpretation. First, there is the problem of why there should be a stress effect. At first consideration, stress is a very "acoustic" feature, yet the stress effect is occurring in experiments in which we have taken pains to show that acoustic effects do not occur. Subsidiary investigations confirm this point: requiring the subject to articulate (repeat series of digits) while cancelling e's does not effect the magnitude of the stress effect, yet such articulation is a reliable way of interfering with acoustic processing (Baddeley, 1976), and acoustic features of the e (whether it is long (be), short (bet) or reduced (torrent)) do not have a separate influence in addition to the effects of stress. We are thus studying a level of representation in which stress figures prominently, but where the level of representation is not phonetic. This suggests stress plays a key role at some more abstract level, possibly in lexical identification.

Uta Frith (this volume) is right to point out the correlation between predictability and stress. In a subsidiary experiment we examined the predictability of various classes of words by compiling lists of words and deleting critical syllables from them. We classified words by word length (two or three syllables), whether the word was high frequency or low frequency, and whether the missing syllable was stressed or unstressed. We found a correlation of +0.52 between the average accuracy with which subjects could restore a missing syllable in a word belonging to a particular class, and the corresponding average omission rate of e's in words in this class in the main experiment. However, there are important differences between the two experiments. When we look at e omission rates, the differences between stressed and unstressed syllables are larger for high frequency words than for low frequency words, but there is no interaction between stress and frequency in the predictability experiment; on the other hand, it is easier to predict the missing syllable in a three-syllable word than in a two-syllable word, but the e omission rates for two- and three-syllable words are roughly the same. This suggests that predictability can account for only part of the stress effects in our main experiments.

Another problem is created by position effects: scrambled texts and -ed words show no reliable effects of the position in which they appear in each line of text; all the other analyses do show strong position effects, and the effects are all similar to each other. This suggests that linguistic representations are constructed in at least two ways, one way consisting of an ordered (serial?) form of processing (leading to regular position effects), the second way showing no such orderly effects. Why -ed words, of all the classes of words we have looked at, should be unique in showing no position effects is not clear. Certainly -ed words occupy a special position in our data: no

other affix is associated with such a high omission rate, with the sole exception of -en (written, fallen: average omisssion rate 10.8%), and -en has a
similar linguistic function to -ed.

Reading is not a simple linear process, but rather a set of procedures
which allows the reader to construct a rich array of linguistic information.
Psycholinguistic theories and methods that ignore this truism are suspect.
The e cancellation task, by the diversity of the data it provides, suggests
that relatively simple techniques can still be developed that will give us
genuine insights into reading.

This research was supported by the Social Science Research Council. We
thank Uta Frith and D. C. Mitchell for criticisms of an earlier draft.

REFERENCES

Baddeley, A.D. The psychology of memory. New York: Basic Books, 1976.
Coltheart, M., Hull, E., & Slater, D. Sex differences in imagery and reading.
    Nature, 1975, 253, 438-440.
Corcoran, D.W.J. An acoustic factor in letter cancellation. Nature, 1966,
    210, 658.
Frith, U. Reading by eye and writing by ear. (This volume.)
Healy, A.F. Detection errors on the word the: Evidence for reading units
    larger than letters. Journal of Experimental Psychology: Human Per-
    ception and Performance, 1976, 2, 235-242.
Kleiman, G.M. Speech recoding in reading. Journal of Verbal Learning and
    Verbal Behavior, 1975, 14, 323-339.
Massaro, D.W. Understanding language. New York: Academic Press, 1975.
Meyer, D.E., & Ruddy, M.G. Lexical-memory retrieval based on graphemic
    and phonemic representations of printed words. Paper presented at
    Psychonomic Society meeting, St. Louis, 1973.
O'Regan, K. Moment-to-moment control of eye saccades as a function of
    textual parameters in reading. (This volume.)
Rubenstein, H., Lewis, S.S., & Rubenstein, M.A. Evidence for phonemic
    recoding in visual word recognition. Journal of Verbal Learning and
    Verbal Behavior, 1971, 10, 645-657.
Shebilske, W., & Reid, L.S. Reading eye movements, macro-structure,
    and comprehension processes. (This volume.)

Perceiving and Producing

Introduction

P.A. Kolers

Research topics often run to themes, many investigators approaching the same question or theme from slightly different directions. Some themes are large and inclusive, others are more refined and particular. Two of the large themes that have motivated considerable debate historically regarding reading and listening and still exercise some appeal are the relations among the four activities of reading and listening, speaking and writing. A second theme of historical and contemporary interest is the role of speech in reading and writing. These two topics underlie the studies in the first part of this section.

Some students find it heuristically useful to draw close parallels between the productive processes of speaking and writing, and the receptive processes of listening and reading. Others dispute the parallelism on two counts; first, that reading is quite different from listening, and writing different from speaking, and second, that the notions of receptive and productive constitute an ill-conceived dichotomy, for both reading and listening -- the receptive activities -- have productive aspects associated with them. Holders of such a view of active processing would find it difficult to square interpretation of performance with any strictly inflow model; but such views often unwittingly compromise themselves by failing to establish bounds on the activities that they believe characterize the active processing. An unconstrained constructivism may be as unsound as an unconstrained inflow model.

Almost to test the limits, Massaro presents in his tutorial paper a clear description of an inflow model, based on hypothetical stages during which various operations are carried out on signals. The model is a sort of capstone of such efforts -- a particularly clear and carefully thought-through version of the kind of stage-wise theory that has reached an apogee of popularity during the past decade. It is useful to have such a model whether one agrees with it or not, for it is so clearly set out that one knows at least what it is that one agrees or disagrees with.

Central to Massaro's notions are conversion or translation processes that transform the visible signal into a speech-based form. The speech-based nature of literacy has been one of the long-term debates in its investigation. The argument is whether written language and reading are parasitic upon spoken language, whether writing is really only silent speech and reading is visual listening. There are few more confirmed introspections than that some sort of implicit speech accompanies reading; what the nature, source, and function are of that occasionally enlivened but usually dull monotone, sometimes heard when one reads, has been debated long and furiously.

The principal query concerns the degree of the visual system's intelligence. One view is that the visual system's intelligence is so limited as to enable it only to acquire the printed marks and hold them for that interval of time required by a language mechanism to translate them into a speech-based form. The codification and interpretation of the written signals then goes forward, so the argument has it, as it would for the more "natural" process of listening. An alternate view is that the visual system is capable of interpreting the visible marks in their own terms, or in what is sometimes referred to as a visual code. Does one recognize a chair by transforming its appearance into its name which is recognized, or can one recognize a chair from its appearance alone? Does one recognize a word by transforming its appearance into its implicitly sounded name which is recognized, or can one recognize a word from its appearance alone? The argument has gone on for a long time.

Baddeley reviews a number of experiments that firmly face the introspective evidence of interior monologue during reading and reaches a modest but interesting conclusion: transformation to sound may but does not need to accompany reading; it is an optional not an obligatory transformation of the printed word. If the text is difficult, its processing may be supplemented or aided by subvocal speech; if the text is easy, little subvocal speech accompanies the reading. (The reading may in fact be accompanied by a general tensing of musculature, but the question whether subvocal speech is merely an artifact of that greater state of tension has not been addressed.) Although these conclusions have been reached before, one of the interesting aspects of Baddeley's research is that there they were reached in the course of other concerns; his interest was more in the function of memory than in reading itself.

Directly concerned with the issues of phonological representation were the papers of Frith and of Reich and Cherry. Using the well-known Stroop effect in which a stimulus is presented in such a way that it elicits incompatible and conflicting encodings -- the normally more salient response usually required to be inhibited in favor of the less salient -- Reich and Cherry argue for direct visual access, for the visual system's ability to interpret the configurations presented to it without dependence upon the speech system. Frith, in turn, examines the role of speech in the two processes of reading and writing. Pursuing the same line of investigation as Smith and Groat in their study of the invisibility of the letter e, Frith concluded that reading may under many circumstances be carried out in terms of the visual processing of the visible symbols without recourse to their transformation to speech; writing, on the other hand, may require activating the speech system. The latter claim may be premature, however; it seems to rule out the automatized writing that Gertrude Stein long ago studied, the writing of one's signature, and other well-practiced forms. Perhaps the contrast can be related to that that Baddeley brought out: reading unfamiliar and difficult text may be aided by speech, whereas the familiar may not require it; perhaps unfamiliar and difficult writing equally may be aided by speech, the familiar or automatized not requiring it. The role of automatization and the "silent work" of the cognitive machinery in reading have not been sufficiently studied. It is at this point that Brooks and Miller's paper comes to mind, for they have interested themselves in just that contrast between implicit and explicit learning that theory seems unable to handle. Under what circumstances can one teach a skill directly by description, and under what circumstances must it be learned by inculcation or practice; and how does explicit teaching modify implicit learning? Brooks and Miller establish some issues to be debated around these points at the level of perception of characters and words.

The remaining papers in this section are concerned with some of these latter issues, the way that readers organize and infer the structure and content of prose, usually using techniques or strategies they would be hard pressed to identify, let alone describe. The way that meaning is obtained from text seems not yet to have been well worked out. On the standard serial inflow view, the meaning is "extracted" from the text -- "meaning" treated as an independent variable, independent both of the words that embody it and of the writer and reader using the words. On an alternate view, meaning is attributed to or projected upon text, the words on the page constituting the occasion for the projection. On still a third view, the meaning of the text is derived by hard cognitive work from the structure of the materials on the page, especially the linguistic and thematic structure, and from the skills and strategies of the reader, operating on that structure. Chapman is concerned with structure in the more thematic sense; Wright and Wilcox study cognitive structure as a function of sentential structure; and Pugh reveals some of the labors the reader engages in. The minimum conclusion one can reach is that more goes into understanding a text than psycholinguistics accommodates.

If we knew what we meant by "meaning," and understood what was removed in its "extraction," we would indeed know much about reading. But perhaps one way of looking at the articles in this section is that they raise the question whether such metaphors may not only be limited, they may even be perverse, for they may hide the processes that underlie an intelligent reader's interaction with symbols.

Reading and Listening (Tutorial Paper)

Dominic W. Massaro

Reading text and listening to speech involve a sequence of processing stages that take the language user from the spoken or written message to meaning. This paper describes each stage in an information processing model. At each stage of the model there are storage and process components: the storage component defines the type of information available at the stage of processing; the process component specifies the procedures that operate on the information held in the corresponding storage component. The model is used heuristically to incorporate data and theory from a variety of approaches to reading and speech perception. Some relevant issues are the properties of the various storage structures, the dynamics of the functional processes, and the active utilization of the various sources of knowledge available to the language receiver. One central assumption is that analogous structures and processes occur in speech perception and reading. It is valuable, therefore, to ask similar experimental questions in both areas, and to attempt to develop a unitary model of both reading and speech perception.

A session on Reading and Listening must be motivated by the belief that these two skills are not unrelated. And, in fact, it has been commonly believed by many that reading is somehow a skill parasitic to listening: that is, all that is necessary in order to read is to translate the written word into its spoken counterpart, and then to listen to the message. Since most literate people learn to listen long before they learn to read, it seems natural that reading instruction should exploit what the child knows about listening. Faced with a new word in written text, the child is encouraged to decode it (sound it out) on the assumption that the spoken rendering will more likely be recognized. The primacy of speech has been one motivating influence on theories of reading that view reading as a process of going from print to some speech code enroute to the meaning (Gough, 1972). Since it is a common belief that man spoke and listened long before he wrote and read, one could also argue that language learning recapitulates the development of spoken and written language. However Wrolstad (1976), in a stimulating and fascinating manifesto, argues the reverse.

This author rejects the idea that speech is primary and that reading is subservient to or dependent on listening. Reading and listening can be viewed as independent but analogous processes, the goal of which is to derive the meaning of a message. One argument for these being analogous processes can be formulated in terms of convergent evolution: Two independent processes may develop similar solutions to a problem of survival. As an example, the eye of the octopus (a cephalopod) and the eye of man (a mammal) evolved completely independently of one another. But, as Blakemore (1977) observed, the eyes evolved to be very similar to one another. Both organisms developed functionally similar solutions to the problem of seeing. Following this logic, the assumption that reading and listening can be viewed as similar processes does not necessitate an assumption of a common phylogenetic or ontogenetic evolution. Given that reading and listening solve the same problem, it is not unreasonable to assume that they are analogous rather than hierarchical solutions to the problem.

Analogous solutions to language understanding would not be limited to reading and listening. Consider the recent proliferation of research on the processing of manual-visual languages such as American Sign Language (ASL). Remarkable parallels have been found between understanding signs and understanding speech. Lane, Boyes-Braem, and Bellugi (1976) found that perceptual confusions among signs can be described utilizing a distinctive feature system, analogous to systems developed for perceptual confusions in speech. Tweney, Heiman, and Hoemann (1977) demonstrated that grammatical structure in sign language plays the same functional role that it does in spoken language. These results support the claim that grammatical processes of language are relatively general and abstract—not tied uniquely to the input modality. Although this paper is limited to reading and listening, the work on ASL encourages the belief that there are similar and analogous processes in all forms of language understanding.

A Stage Model of Language Processing
Reading can be defined as the abstraction of meaning from printed text; listening as the abstraction of meaning from speech. Deriving meaning from a spoken or written message requires a series of transformations of the energy signal after it arrives at the appropriate receptors. Language processing can be studied as a sequence of processing stages or operations that occur between the energy stimulus and the meaning. In this framework, language processing can be understood only to the extent that each of these processing stages is described. In a previous effort, a general information-processing model was utilized for a theoretical analysis of speech perception, reading, and psycholinguistics (Massaro, 1975a). The model was used heuristically to incorporate data and theory from a wide variety of approaches in the study

of language processing. The model should be seen as an organizational structure for the state of the art in language processing. In this paper, I will present a general overview of the information-processing model, and use the model to describe and incorporate recent research.

Figure 1 presents a flow chart of the temporal course of reading and listening. At each stage the system contains storage and process components. The storage component defines the information available to a particular stage of processing. The process component specifies the procedures and processes that operate on the information held in the corresponding storage component. The model distinguishes four process components: feature detection, primary recognition, secondary recognition, and rehearsal-recoding. The model will be described in more detail below, and contrasted with other models of language processing.

The primary assumption of a stage model is that, at some level, the stages are necessarily successive. The feature-detection process transforms the energy pattern created by the language stimulus and transduced by the appropriate receptor system into a set of features held in preperceptual storage (PS). Primary recognition which evaluates and integrates the features in PS into a synthesized percept must necessarily follow feature detection. However, not all of the features must be detected before primary recognition begins. Given that different features require different detection times, not

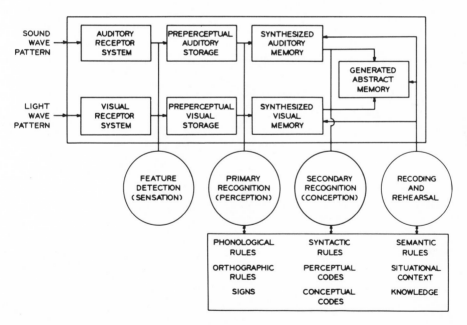

Figure 1. A flow diagram of the temporal course of reading and listening.

all of the features will enter PS simultaneously. Primary recognition could, therefore, evaluate, integrate, and continually update its analysis of the contents of PS while feature detection goes to completion. As can be seen in this example, a basic assumption is that the successive processes necessarily over-lap in time. Although this assumption complicates the traditional serial nonoverlapping-stages model, the model continues to have predictive and descriptive power. The serial model is necessary, in the present view, because later stages of processing do not have access to early, low levels of informa-tion at early stages. As an example, rehearsal-recoding does not appear to have direct access to the features that are detected and held in preperceptual storage.

Criticisms of Stage Models
The model under discussion here can be classified in a successive-stage informa-tion-processing framework; it therefore has some similarities to the stage models developed by Estes (1975), Gough (1972), and LaBerge and Samuels (1974). Rumelhart (1977) justly criticizes Gough's and LaBerge and Samuels' models because of the assumption that "no higher level can in any way modify or change the analysis at a lower level". As evidence against this assumption, he mentions the well-known finding that the perception of a letter can be influenced by the letters that surround it. A letter that is part of a word or a pseudoword is more accurately perceived than the same letter presented in a nonword context. In this case, then, it appears that higher-order knowledge of letter groups or words influences the perception of individual letters. In Rumelhart's opinion and also that of Allport (1977), this result cannot be easily handled by serial models. I would like to stress, however, that not only is this result easily described by the present serial model, but the model was also instrumental in generating hypotheses and experiments on exactly this phenomenon (Massaro, 1973, 1975a; Massaro, Venezky, & Taylor, in press; Thompson & Massaro, 1973). In our model two sources of information are available at the primary recognition stage in reading: (1) the featural informa-tion in perceptual visual storage (PVS) and 2) knowledge about the orthographic structure of English spelling stored in long-term memory (LTM). Both of these sources of information contribute to the perception of individual letters in a letter string. (See Massaro, 1975a; and Venezky & Massaro, in press, for a more detailed description).

Although it is clear that the present model allows orthographic structure to influence letter perception, the influence of syntactic/semantic constraints may not be immediately obvious. It seems obvious that the same visual infor-mation can be interpreted differently in different syntactic/semantic con-texts (Nash-Weber, 1975). Figure 2 shows that, faced with the same visual configuration, the preceding context supports the recognition of cast in one case and east in the other. In our model, knowledge obtained at the level of generated abstract memory (GAM) would be combined with the featural information in PVS. Given the same featural information, different contexts can lead to different outcomes of primary recognition. Although this possibi-lity was acknowledged in our earlier work, very few data were available and, therefore, the influence of semantic/syntactic constraints at primary recognition was not made explicit (however, see Massaro, 1975a, pp. 258-259). More recently, Marslen-Wilson and Welsh (1978) have found that the message

It was an old film with a east of thousands.

The tourist took a train going east.

Figure 2. The same visual configuration can be interpreted differently in different syntactic/semantic contexts.

being understood at the level of GAM can influence the recognition of the message. I will extend the model by developing a quantitative formulation of how syntactic/semantic constraints and acoustic information are combined and integrated at the recognition stage of processing (see the section on Secondary Recognition).

Parallel Interactive Models
In two recent schemata of reading systems, Allport (1977) and Rumelhart (1977) have drawn heavily from contemporary work in artificial intelligence (AI). The distinctive feature of Rumelhart's system is a set of independent knowledge sources, each of which applies specialized knowledge about some aspect of reading. More specifically, each knowledge source generates hypotheses about the input and relays these to a message center which maintains a running list of all incoming hypotheses. The knowledge sources evaluate their current hypotheses and generate new ones until some decision can be reached. In this model, all levels of knowledge interact, and each contributes independent evidence for the final interpretation.

Although this view has some appeal, there are a number of deficiencies when it is evaluated in terms of a psychologically real description of reading. The primary problem arises because the model is a direct application of a nonhuman system. In this case, the system HEARSAY II was developed for automatic speech understanding (Lesser, Fennell, Erman, & Reddy, 1975). Although the system proved effective in understanding speech, it had to perform in a manner that was clearly different from the way humans understand speech.

The specific advantage that HEARSAY II has over its human counterpart is that it has a high resolution memory. In HEARSAY II, the parametric level holds the most basic representation of the utterance in terms of fine-grained acoustic parameters. These low-level decisions are not final since the original parameters can be processed and evaluated continuously throughout the understanding process. By failing to make final, low-level decisions, the number of hypotheses and amount of data that have to be maintained would far exceed the capacity of human memory structures. We know that preperceptual auditory storage holds featural information for roughly a quarter of a second, less than the time required to hold a complete sentence until it is finally interpreted (Massaro, 1975a).

This observation is not meant as a criticism of automatic speech recognition, but rather as a caveat for those who seek psychological models in that arena. Although HEARSAY II is a very successful system, it does not make any final decisions about the first part of a sentence until all of the sentence has been processed. Humans recognize speech while it is being spoken, if not before. My criterion for the application of AI theories to humans is not that machines perform as well as humans, but that machines perform like humans.

Allowing low-level data to be continuously available may be more compatible with reading than with speech perception, since the reader can always make a regressive eye movement to refresh the image. In this case, the low-level information in reading can be maintained indefinitely as it is in automatic speech recognition. Considering the number of hypotheses that might have to be checked at this level, however, the number of regressive eye movements would be enormous and the reader would never finish the passage. The small number of regressions in normal reading infirms the idea that low level information in reading is continually rechecked until a decision is made. Although some concepts developed in AI understanding systems have obvious relevance to psychological theory, current AI schemes are not good models of what is known about how humans process language.

Summary
The model presented here was developed in the genre of a serial stage and information processing framework. A number of recent statements have pointed out limitations to this approach, and have argued for a system based on parallel and interactive channels (Allport, 1977; Rumelhart, 1977). In the serial stage model, each stage has contact with only the information available to that stage and some neighboring stages, and with the appropriate information in long-term memory. For example, the secondary recognition operation in our model has contact with synthesized memory but not with preperceptual storage. Accordingly, the information that was lost during the primary recognition transformation cannot influence secondary recognition. In an interactive model, the featural information at preperceptual storage would influence very late and high-level processing stages. This assumption is unreasonable because the early low-level information does not remain intact long enough to contribute to later stages of processing. For example, an eye movement in reading erases and replaces the featural information derived in the earlier fixation. It is only the transformed information, then, that can contribute to later processing. The temporal limitations on retention of the various information sources is the primary motivation for utilizing a serial model, and in this regard the parallel interactive models are not good psychological models. The stage model will now be developed in more detail by tracing the flow of information processed in reading and listening. By reviewing relevant issues and research, it is hoped that the heuristic value of the model will become apparent.

Feature Detection

The feature detection process transforms the energy pattern into features in preperceptual storage. The features for reading and listening are described as visual and acoustic, respectively, since it is assumed that there is a direct relationship between the nature of the energy signal and the information in preperceptual storage. There are a number of prominent characteristics in speech and reading stimuli that are potential candidates for features. A characteristic is called a feature only when it is psychologically functional, that is, when it is used to distinguish between different speech sounds or written symbols (Massaro, 1975a).

Audible Features

The study of features in speech perception has had a long history. A good portion of the work was influenced by linguistic descriptions of binary all-or-none distinctive features (Jakobson, Fant, & Halle, 1961). One of the goals of distinctive feature theory was to minimize the number of distinctive features of the language. Distinctive features were designed to be general rather than specific: if a distinctive-feature difference distinguished two phonemes in the language, that same distinction was assumed to distinguish several other phoneme pairs. Given the distinctive feature of voicing, for example, the distinction of voiced versus voiceless could account for the differences between /z/ and /s/, /v/ and /f/, and so on.

In contrast to the linguistic description of binary all-or-none features, the features held in preperceptual auditory storage (PAS) are assumed to be continuous, so that a feature indicates the degree to which the quality is present in the speech sound. This assumption is similar to the more recent treatment of distinctive features provided by Chomsky and Halle (1968) and Ladefoged (1975). Chomsky and Halle distinguish between the classificatory and phonetic function of distinctive features. The features are assumed to be binary in their classificatory function, but multivalued in their phonetic or descriptive function. Ladefoged distinguishes between the phonetic and phonemic level of feature description. A feature describing the phonetic quality of a sound has a value along a continuous scale whereas a feature classifying the phonemic composition is given a discrete value.

In the present model an acoustic feature in PAS is expressed as a continuous value. That is to say, the listener will be able to hear the degree of presence or absence of a particular feature, even though his judgment in a forced choice task will be discrete. Thus, Oden and Massaro (1978) have described acoustic features as fuzzy predicates which may be more or less true rather than only absolutely true or false (Zadeh, 1971). In addition to being concerned with the acoustic features in preperceptual storage, this analysis of the feature evaluation process makes apparent that an important question in speech perception research is how the various continuous features are integrated into a synthesized percept.

The integration of features has not been extensively studied in speech perception research for two main reasons. If distinctive features are binary, the integration of information from two or more features would be a trivial problem. Given binary features representing voicing and place of articulation, for example, the integration would be a simple logical conjunction. If the consonant /b/ is represented as voiced and labial, a voiced labial sound would be identified as /b/ whereas a voiceless labial sound or a voiced non-labial sound would not be identified as /b/.

A second reason for the neglect of the integration problem is methodological. The primary method of study involved experiments in which the speech sound was varied along a single relevant dimension. For example, in a study of voicing, all voicing cues were made neutral except one, such as voice onset time, and then this dimension was varied through the relevant values. Very few experiments independently varied two cues. Therefore, no information was available about how two or more cues were integrated into a synthesized percept.

More recently, Massaro and Cohen (1976) and Oden and Massaro (1978) have utilized factorial designs and functional measurement techniques (Anderson, 1974) to study the integration of acoustic features in speech perception. The work has illuminated how fuzzy features are integrated into a synthesized percept. The methods allow the investigator to determine which acoustic characteristics in the signal are perceptually functional, the relative weight that each feature carries in the integration process, and the exact combinatorial algorithm that is used.

Visible Features

One of the oldest areas of reading-related research is the study of the functional cues in recognizing printed characters. Much of this work was performed by typographers and artists concerned with good design and legibility of type faces. Although many of the early conclusions appear to be still valid (see Spencer, 1969, for a summary), they are almost totally ignored in the contemporary study of letter recognition. One influence in current studies has been the well-known neurophysiological findings of an amazing stimulus-selectivity in the responses of cells in the visual cortex (Hubel & Wiesel, 1962). There appear to be specialized detectors in the visual system for lines of specific size and orientation (for intelligible reviews of this work see Blakemore, 1973; Lindsay & Norman, 1977).

As in speech, psychological descriptions have centered around binary all-or-none features. Feature sets usually consist of the presence or absence of horizontal, vertical, or oblique lines, curves, intersections, angles, and so on. The feature sets are typically derived from and tested against the recognition confusions of capital letters (see Massaro, 1975a, Chapter 6, for a review). In contrast to the idea of binary all-or-none features, however, visible features, like audible features, may be fuzzy. Rather than a feature being present or absent, the information in preperceptual visual storage (PVS) could represent the degree to which a given feature is present in the signal. Given this conceptualization, it is necessary to develop a methodological and theoretical study of visible features that parallels the work on audible features.

Recently, Blesser and his colleagues have developed and studied ambiguous characters (Blesser, Shillman, Kuklinski, Cox, Eden, & Ventura, 1974; Shillman, Cox, Kuklinski, Ventura, Blesser, & Eden, 1974). Figure 3 presents a matrix of ambiguous characters having one or more functional attributes in transition between two letters. A completely ambiguous character is one that would

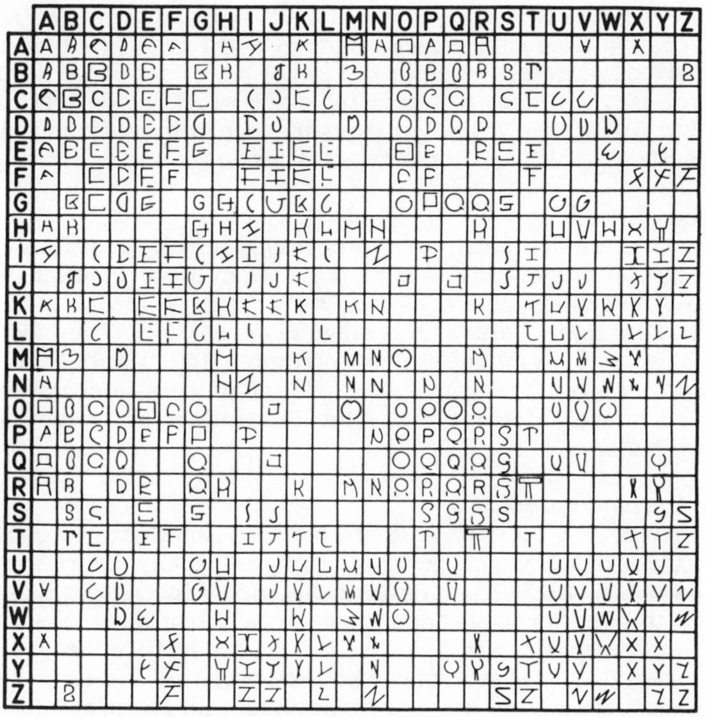

Figure 3. A matrix of ambiguous characters having one or more functional attributes in transition between two letters. (After Naus & Shillman, 1976).

be assigned to either letter class with equal probability. As an example, a v can be gradually transformed into a y by continuously increasing the right oblique line below the intersection (Naus & Shillman, 1976). Analogous to the recent work in speech perception, the theoretical notion of fuzzy information and the experimental methods of factorial designs and functional measurement techniques should advance the study of visible features in reading.

Given that most of the contemporary research on features is carried out with uppercase letters, it is important to know to what extent these features may generalize to perception of lowercase. Bouma (1971) showed that the visual confusions in the recognition of lowercase letters were better described in terms of the overall shape or envelope of the letter rather than the commonly assumed component features. The envelope of the letter is defined as the smallest enclosing polygon without indentations. The envelope for e would be circular, whereas v would be enclosed by an inverted triangle.

That the overall envelope of a letter may be resolved before details of its component features is consistent with Fourier-analysis studies. There is good evidence that low spatial frequency information is processed faster than high frequencies (Breitmeyer & Ganz, 1976; Broadbent, 1977). Either limited processing time or a reduced figure-ground contrast could allow envelope resolution without corresponding resolution of letter detail. In terms of the present analysis, the reader will have to decide which letter best fits the perceived but fuzzy envelope. For example, recognition of a circular envelope would limit the alternatives to the three letters e, c, and o.

Primary Recognition

In the framework of the information processing model, the primary recognition process integrates the featural integration held in preperceptual storage into a percept in synthesized memory. One question relevant to the model concerns the functional units at this stage of processing. The functional units are called perceptual units; they correspond to units that are described in long-term memory. The primary recognition process finds the best match between the featural information and the descriptions of perceptual units in long-term memory.

Perceptual Units in Speech

Sound patterns of V, CV, or VC size are the best candidates for perceptual units since these patterns can be described by relatively invariant acoustic features (Fujimura, 1975). Smaller patterns such as phonemes lack invariance, and, in fact, this lack of invariance has been a central focus of speech perception theory (cf. Liberman, Cooper, Shankweiler, & Studdert-Kennedy, 1967). Although perceptual units of larger size have also been proposed, research has demonstrated that preperceptual auditory storage cannot maintain featural information for a greater period than roughly one quarter of a second (Massaro, 1975a, Chapter 4). It follows that clauses, phrases, or even words are inappropriate perceptual units at the primary recognition stage of processing. (For further discussion see Massaro, 1975a, Chapter 4).

Target Search in Listening

If syllables are perceptual units in speech processing, they should be accessed before the phonemes that make them up. One test of this idea has been to study the reaction times to syllable and phoneme targets in speech processing. Savin and Bever (1970) asked listeners to release a telegraph key as soon as they heard a specified target in a sequence of nonsense consonant-vowel-consonant syllables (CVCs). Listeners were slower in responding to initial consonant phoneme targets such as /b/ or /s/ than in responding to a CVC target such as /bæb/ or /sæb/. Savin and Bever interpreted the differences in reaction time (RTs) as directly reflecting differences in the time required to perceive the phoneme and syllable targets and concluded that phonemes must be perceived only by an analysis of already perceived syllables. Warren (1971) reached similar conclusions from a target-search task through spoken sentences.

Foss and Swinney (1973) objected to the conclusion that phoneme perception must follow syllable perception. They used search lists of two-syllable words and asked subjects to search for an initial phoneme, initial syllable, or a complete word. Reaction times were actually somewhat shorter for word than for syllable targets, although phoneme targets were responded to slowest of all. In terms of the logic of the target search task, their results would argue that words are accessed before the syllables that make them up. Burying the logic of the target search task even deeper, McNeill and Lindig (1973) included sentence targets and lists in a complete factorial design of phoneme, syllable, word, and sentence targets crossed with the same four kinds of lists. In general, RTs were slowed when the linguistic level of the target differed from that of the search list.

The latter studies have been used to support the thesis that the target-search task is inappropriate for a study of perceptual units in speech processing. This conclusion may be premature, however, given the inappropriate design of the experiments. The critical confounding was that appropriate test foils were not included in the experiments. For example, Foss and Swinney's (1973) results indicated that subjects were not faster in responding to syllable versus word targets. However, the foils were chosen in such a way that subjects could have based their decision on the first syllable of the word in both the target syllable and target word conditions. Given either the syllable target "can" or the word target "candy," subjects could have selected a reliable response after processing just the first syllable, since the test foils never began with "can." Apparently, this is the strategy that was used since the RT averaged about 350 msec, much less than the 500 msec duration of the test words. Similarly, McNeill and Lindig's subjects responded in less than 1/3 sec, showing that a response was initiated long before a word or sentence could have been processed. Therefore the target search task should be reconsidered as an appropriate paradigm, but it should be structured to account for both perceptual and comparison processes (see Ball, Wood, & Smith, 1975; Massaro & Klitzke, 1977; Sloboda, 1977).

Perceptual Units in Reading
In contrast to the acoustic structure of phonemes, printed letters of a given face are invariantly defined with respect to their visual characteristics. It follows that units as small as letters are reasonable candidates for perceptual units at the primary recognition stage in reading. Units of larger size have been proposed, however. Spelling patterns, pronunciation units, words, and even phrases have been proposed as perceptual units at the stage of processing responsible for the integration of visual features into a synthesized percept (Massaro, 1975a). If letters are basic perceptual units in primary recognition, words must be perceived by the letters that make them up. This hypothesis addresses the old and familiar question of whether word recognition can be described in terms of component letter recognition, or whether a word is recognized on the basis of supraletter features without reference to the letters that make it up.

Target Search in Reading
The target search task has also been used to address the issue of whether word recognition is mediated by letter perception. In an experiment carried out by Johnson (1975), subjects indicated whether or not a test item was the same as a target item. Response latencies did not depend on whether the target and test items were both single letters or both whole words. These results led Johnson to reject the idea that word recognition is mediated by letter recognition. However, Johnson's results are not necessarily incompatible

with preliminary letter recognition if the letters in a word are processed in parallel.

Massaro and Klitzke (1977) observed that the population of words of a given length may be more dissimilar from one another than are a set of single letters. If this is the case, a subject could perform with a less stringent criterion for accepting a match in the word condition than in the letter condition. Johnson (1975) made no attempt to control for the similarity of the test foils to the target items, thereby producing test foils that were naturally more dissimilar on word than on letter trials. Increasing the similarity between the target and test foils should decrease the advantages of parallel processing on word trials and, therefore, produce a letter advantage because of reduced figure-ground contrast (lateral masking) in processing word strings.

Massaro and Klitzke (1977) replicated Johnson's experiment while simultaneously investigating the role of similarity in the identification of words and letters. Half of the test foils were highly similar to the target and half were dissimilar. The manipulation of similarity was effective in that responses to similar test foils required 40 msec more than responses to dissimilar nontargets. In contrast to Johnson's finding of no difference, reaction times were 8 % (43 msec) faster for letter stimuli than word stimuli. The letter advantage was significant even when the analysis was restricted to target and dissimilar test foil trials. By including similar test foils, subjects could not maintain a lax criterion of sameness because a test foil word could be very similar to the target word. In this case, subjects could not select and execute a positive response as quickly as they might have with a more lax criterion of sameness. Massaro and Klitzke interpret the results as suggesting that perceptual processing and comparison are continuous and overlapping processes in the target search task. A subject does not first perceive the test item and then compare it to the target item in memory but rather the reader is able to make comparisons as partial information about the test item is resolved. Notice that this interpretation is consistent with the general idea of successive but overlapping stages in language processing. Therefore, the normal dissimilarity advantage of word strings over single letters can work to neutralize the word's disadvantage of lateral masking. Another important advantage for words is orthographic structure. But in both cases, the word advantage is not incompatible with the idea of letter units mediating word recognition (Sloboda, 1976, 1977).

Secondary Recognition

Secondary recognition transforms synthesized percepts into meaningful forms in generated abstract memory. In speech perception, it is assumed that the input is analyzed syllable by syllable for meaning. In reading, letter sequences are closed off in word units. In both cases, the secondary recognition process makes the transformation from percept to meaning by finding the best match between the perceptual information and the lexicon in long-term memory. Each word in the lexicon contains both perceptual and conceptual information. The concept recognized is a function of two independent sources of information: the perceptual information in synthesized memory and the syntactic/semantic context in the message.

Perceptual and Contextual Contributions to Listening
Abstracting meaning is a joint function of the independent contributions of
the perceptual and contextual information available. In one experiment, Cole
(1973) asked subjects to push a button every time they heard a mispronunciation in a spoken rendering of Lewis Carroll's "Through-the-Looking-Glass."
A mispronunciation involved changing a phoneme by 1, 2, or 4 distinctive
features (for example, "confusion" mispronounced as "gunfusion," "bunfusion,"
and "sunfusion," respectively). The probability of recognizing a mispronunciation increased from 30 to 75% with increases in the number of feature changes,
making apparent the contribution of the perceptual information passed on by
the primary recognition process. The contribution of contextual information
should work against the recognition of a mispronunciation since context would
support a correct rendering of the mispronounced word. In support of this
idea, all mispronunciations were correctly recognized when the syllables
were isolated and removed from the passage.

Cole and Jakimik (1977) extended Cole's (1973) mispronunciation task to
evaluate how higher-order contextual information can influence sentence
processing. To the extent that a word is predicted by its preceding context,
the listener should be faster at detecting a mispronunciation. This follows
from the idea that the quickest way to detect a mispronunciation is first to
determine what the intended word is and then notice a mismatch with what
was said. Given the sentences, "He sat reading a (book/bill) until it was time
to go home for his tea," mispronouncing the /b/ in "book" as /v/ should be
detected faster than the same mispronunciation of "bill." In fact, listeners
were 150 msec faster detecting mispronunciations in highly predictable words
than in unpredictable words.

Marslen-Wilson (1973) asked subjects to shadow (repeat back) prose as
quickly as they heard it. Some individuals were able to shadow the speech at
extremely close delays with lags of 250 msec, about the duration of a syllable
or so. One might argue that the shadowing response was simply a sound-to-
sound mapping without any higher order semantic-syntactic analyses. When
subjects make errors in shadowing, however, the errors are syntactically and
semantically appropriate given the preceding context. For example, given the
sentence "He had heard at the Brigade," some subjects repeated "He had heard
that the Brigade." The nature of the errors did not vary with their latency; the
shadowing errors were always well-formed given the preceding context.

Marslen-Wilson and Welsh (1978) asked observers to shadow spoken passages
from a popular novel. At random throughout the passage, common three-
syllable words were mispronounced. When the words were mispronounced, only
a single consonant phoneme was changed to a new consonant phoneme. The
new phoneme differed from the original by one or three distinctive features,
based on Keyser and Halle's (1968) classification system. Independently of the
degree of feature change, the changes could occur in the first or third syllable
of the three-syllable word. Finally, the mispronounced words were either
highly predictable or unpredictable given the preceding portion of the passage.
Subjects were not told that words could be mispronounced although they probably became aware of this early in the experiment. All subjects shadowed
at relatively long delays greater than 600 msec. The primary dependent measure in the task was the percentage of fluent restorations, that is, the proportion of times the shadowers repeated what should have been said rather than
what was said. About half of the mispronounced words were restored, the

restorations were made on-line with an average latency, and the shadowing was not disrupted. (When the mispronunciation was not restored, shadowing was disrupted and response times increased).

The change in the percentage of restorations as a function of the three independent variables in Marslen-Wilson and Welsh's study can illuminate how the listener integrates acoustic information and higher-order context. Figure 4 presents the observed results in terms of the percentage of fluent restorations. All three variables influenced the likelihood of a restoration. Shadowers were more likely to restore a one-feature than a three-feature change, a change in the third than in the first syllable, and a change in a highly predictable than in an unpredictable word.

The serial processing model can be quantified to predict the results of this experiment. The central assumption of the model is that the information passed on by feature detection does not change with changes in semantic/ syntactic constraints. In terms of the model, the listener should be more likely to restore a single-feature change than a three-feature change. Substituting /f/ for /v/ should give the subject more acoustic information for /v/ than substituting /n/ for /v/. Letting A_i represent the acoustic information available for the original sound, then A_1 for a one-feature change should be larger than A_3 for a three-feature change. Mispronouncing the word in the first or third syllable should also influence the likelihood of a restoration. I have argued previously that speech is processed syllable by syllable (Massaro, 1975a), and the listener attempts to make lexical access at each syllable boundary. We might expect that lexical access of an upcoming word is usually not possible before some of the word is heard. This means that the lexical information available for the mispronounced word should be much higher at the time of the third than the first syllable. Accordingly, a subject should be much more likely to restore a mispronunciation in the third than the first syllable. Letting L_i equal the amount of lexical information that is available, L_3 should be much larger than L_1, where 1 and 3 refer to a mispronunciation in the first and third syllables, respectively. Finally, highly constrained context should make a restoration much more likely than unconstrained context. Therefore, letting S_c and S_u represent the amount of preceding sentential information under constrained and unconstrained contexts, we would expect S_c to be much larger than S_u.

The critical feature of our analysis is that the three sources of information— acoustic, lexical, and sentential—are assumed to have independent influences on a restoration. That is to say, in contrast to some top-down processing models, highly constrained context does not change low-level perceptual analyses. In this model, the values of A_1 and A_3 do not change as a function of the amount of preceding sentential context. This assumption is similar to Morton's (1969) idea that the stimulus information available to the Logogen System does not vary with the amount of context information. Similarly, low-level perceptual processes do not override higher-order constraints: the values of S_c and S_u do not change as a function of the acoustic information that is available.

Figure 4 also presents the predicted results based on a quantification of this model (Massaro, 1977). In addition to the good fit of the model, the parameter estimates confirm our analysis. The value of A for a single-feature change was .76 whereas it was only .24 for a three-feature change. The value of L representing the degree of lexical constraint was .44 when the first syllable was mispronounced and .56 when the third syllable was mispronounced.

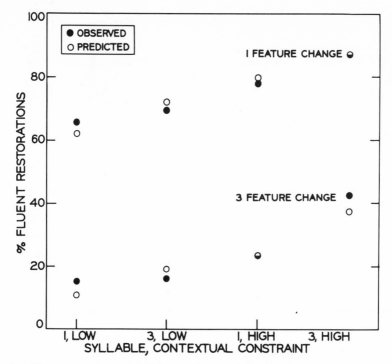

Figure 4. The percentage of fluent restorations as a function of the amount of acoustic change, the syllable changed, and the predictability of the changed word.

Finally, the degree of sentential constraint was .60 with highly predictable words and only .38 with a word nonpredictable from the preceding context.

These results support the common belief that both low-level perceptual information and high-level contextual information contribute to speech processing (and reading). What remains to be discovered is exactly how these two sources of information are combined in the abstraction of the meaning of the message. Empirically, this calls for the independent variation of the two sources of information. On the theoretical level, it is necessary to develop and test quantitative models of how the sources of information are integrated into meaning. It seems likely that many of the upcoming generation of language experiments will address this issue.

Phonetic Mediation in Reading
One persistent question in reading-related research is the extent to which the speech code is necessary for the derivation of meaning. (Phonetic, phonological, and speech codes are used synonymously to mean a code based on sound and/or articulation.) Figure 5 presents two extreme answers to the phonetic mediation question. In the first model, letters are identified and mapped into a speech code using spelling-to-sound rules, and meaning is

determined on the basis of the derived speech code. In the second model, meaning is determined from letter resolution and a speech code is not made available until after meaning has been accessed. In an earlier review, I concluded that, "although phonological mediation can be rejected in word recognition, it may play a significant role in later processing stages such as rehearsal and recoding in generated abstract memory" (Massaro, 1975a). Although a relatively large amount of research has been added to the data base, the story does not require any modification.

Gough and Cosky (1976) believe that they have some new data in support of the phonological-mediation view of Gough (1972). Subjects were asked to read aloud as rapidly as possible words that violated or obeyed spelling-to-sound rules. If phonological mediation occurs, regular words which conform to spelling-to-sound rules should be converted to a speech code faster than exception words which violate the rules. Accordingly, the time required to comprehend the word and name it aloud should take longer for words that violate spelling-to-sound rules. In support of their hypothesis, the pronuncia-

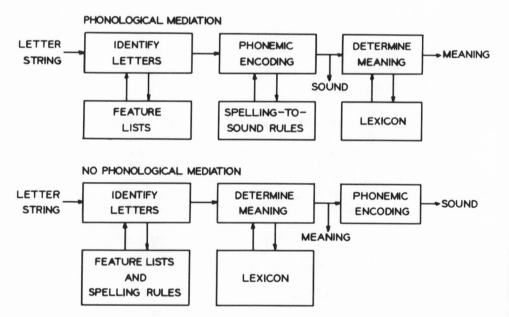

Figure 5. Two stage models of the locus of phonological mediation in reading.

tion times for exception words averaged 27 msec longer than the pronunciation times for regular words. However, there is no assurance that differences
in pronunciation time result from differences in word recognition time. The
differences in reaction time could also have resulted from differences in
the time for response selection and programming after the word had already
been identified (see Massaro, 1975a; Massaro, 1977).

Green and Shallice (1976) asked subjects to judge whether two words
rhymed or whether they belonged to the same broad semantic category (animate or inanimate). On half of the trials, the words were misspelled to give
homophonic pseudowords ("wise" would be spelled "wize"). Misspelling the
words produced a much larger decrement in the semantic than the rhyming
task. If lexical access occurs via phonological coding, there is no reason
that the semantic task should have been slowed more by misspelling than
the rhyming task was. Spelling-to-sound rules would have been sufficient
to perform the rhyming task and misspelling should have very little effect
on this process. In support of this, misspelling the words increased reaction
times by only 11% in the rhyming task. Lexical access should be drastically
influenced by misspelling, however, if it occurs via a visual code. Reaction
times were slowed by 58 percent in the semantic task, arguing against the
idea of phonological or speech recoding in lexical access and derivation of
meaning. The results support other findings that demonstrate that phonemic
encoding is not necessary in processing written language for meaning (see
Massaro, 1975a; Massaro, 1977).

Rehearsal and Recoding
In this model, the same abstract structure stores the meaning of both listening
and reading. Generated abstract memory (GAM) in the model corresponds
to the working memory of contemporary information processing theory.
Rehearsal and recoding processes operate at this stage to maintain and build
semantic/syntactic structures. There is good evidence that this memory
has a limited capacity, holding about 5 ± 2 chunks of information. For a more
detailed discussion of processing at this stage, see Massaro (1975b, Chapter 27).

Generated Abstract Memory
Although generated abstract memory (GAM) is assumed to hold abstract information relative to the earlier auditory and visual memories, the nature of the
information appears to be tied to the surface structure of the language.
Some relevant research comes from experiments carried out with bilingual
subjects (Dornic, 1975). Recall from immediate memory (supposedly tapping
GAM) does not differ for unilingual and bilingual lists, whereas recall of items
assumed to be no longer in GAM was poorer in bilingual than unilingual lists
(Tulving & Colotla, 1970). Similarly, Kintsch and Kintsch (1969) showed that
the semantic relationship between the words in different languages did not
influence immediate memory, but did affect recall of items no longer active
in GAM. Saegert, Hamayan and Ahmar (1975) showed that multilingual subjects
remembered the specific language of words in a mixed-language list of unrelated
words, but this information was forgotten when the words were presented
in sentence contexts. Dornic (1975) points out that surface structure and
item information are integrally related in immediate memory; subjects seldom

report translations for the words. If the items are remembered, so are the appropriate surface structure forms.

Not only is GAM tied to the surface structure of the language, it appears to be closely tied to a speech code. Given an alphabetic writing system, it may not be surprising that memory would contain a speech-code dimension since the written language has a fairly direct mapping to the spoken language. However, there is now good evidence that memory for non-alphabetic material also exploits a speech code. Chinese logograms and Japanese Kanji are non-phonetic symbols and map into speech at the level of words rather than at the level of letters or spelling patterns. It is more difficult to remember an auditory presentation of a group of letters that are phonemically similar than a group of letters that are phonemically dissimilar (Wickelgren, 1965). If a person remembers the letters in terms of a speech code, it is not surprising that similar sounding letters will be more difficult to remember. Given this result, it becomes important to ask whether similarity effects will also occur in memory for visual presentations of nonalphabetic characters.

Erickson, Mattingly, and Turvey (1972) present some evidence that GAM for Japanese Kanji is based on a speech code. Their Japanese subjects had more difficulty in immediate memory for phonetically similar or homophonic words than for semantically similar or unrelated words. Given the short-term memory requirements, it appears that the phonetic coding of the Kanji was a better medium for retention than the corresponding meaning from which the phonetic reading may have been derived.

Tzeng, Hung, and Wang (1977) asked Chinese subjects to remember lists of phonetically similar or phonetically dissimilar Chinese characters. Phonetic similarity was defined in terms of the number of characters that had the same consonant or vowel sounds in their spoken rendering. Subjects were given a list of four characters followed by 15 sec of shadowing before a serial recall of the test list. Recall was significantly poorer for the similar than for the dissimilar lists. In a second task, subjects judged whether or not a sentence was grammatical and meaningful. The judgment times were longer for the sentences composed of phonetically similar characters. The results of Erickson et al. and Tzeng et al. show that a speech code is a critical dimension in GAM for nonalphabetic characters. Given that meaning was probably accessed before or simultaneously with the speech code, it is important to note that a speech code in GAM does not imply that the meaning of written characters is derived by their sound (see Phonetic Mediation in Reading).

Memory Codes in Reading
Although phonological encoding is not necessary to derive meaning from print, there is growing evidence that visual information in reading must be transformed into another code very quickly after it is viewed. Observers in tachistoscopic tasks appear to remember very little about the visual properties of a short display presentation. Thompson and Massaro (1973) and Juola, Choe, and Leavitt (1974) varied the similarity of the two forced-choice alternatives in the Reicher (1969) task. Subjects saw a word or letter followed by two letter alternatives and reported which letter was present in the display. Performance did not differ for confusable and distinctive letter alternatives. This result indicates that observers did not maintain partial visual featural

information to aid in their choice between the letter alternatives. The subjects must have recoded the information into whole letters or words or an abstract code, preventing the utilization of partial visual information in this task (Massaro, 1975a).

McClelland (1976) presented words and letter strings in upper, lower, or mixed cases. In addition to reporting the letters themselves, McClelland asked the subjects to indicate whether the letter strings were upper, lower, or mixed case. Subjects averaged only 39% correct where chance would be 33%. Even when subjects were able to report all of the four letters in the string in a whole report, they were able to identify the appropriate case only half of the time.

More recently, Hawkins, Reicher, Rogers, and Peterson (1976) evaluated the degree to which subjects are dependent on a phonetic code in the Reicher paradigm. On word trials, the two alternatives were either homophones (cent, sent) or phonetically different (sold, cold). Observers were given either a large or small proportion of word trials that had homophone alternatives. Single-letter trials were also interspersed throughout the session. In the condition with a high proportion of homophones, Hawkins et al. found the same 15% word advantage over single letters for trials with homophone alternatives as for trials with nonhomophone alternatives. Accordingly, a phonetic code did not improve performance in this task either because subjects did not use it or because it did not contribute more information than that given by other (semantic or visual) codes. In the condition with a low proportion of trials with homophone alternatives, however, the word advantage was only 6% with homophone alternatives and 20% with nonhomophone alternatives. The phonetic code in this condition improved performance 14% relative to information given by other codes.

Why might a phonetic code have been more successful than the visual or semantic code in the Hawkins et al. study? One reason is that subjects may have had both the phonetic and semantic codes available but they were more likely to discard or forget the semantic code, especially when the phonetic code was usually successful in the low-homophone condition. A second reason might be that subjects were unlikely to recognize the whole word in the task. If correct recognition of a single letter was .7, then recognition of all four letters would be $.7^4$ or about one time in four. Given partial information about the letter string and the fragility of a visual representation, subjects might be likely to utilize a speech code. Given a phonetic code in the low-homophone condition, they would be more likely to be correct when the word alternatives were phonetically different. The fact that homophone alternatives do not disrupt performance in the high-homophone condition shows that other codes besides a phonetic code are available.

Kleiman (1975) has recently presented a nice series of experiments showing that although speech recoding is not necessary in deriving meaning from print, it is a critical determinant of storage in working memory. The work centers on the idea that the disruptive effect of concurrent shadowing in different tasks reveals the degree to which speech recoding occurs in each of the tasks. Subjects performed each of three tasks in the first experiment. Subjects saw two words side by side and had to indicate whether the words were graphemically similar, phonemically similar, or semantically similar. For example, the subject in the phonemic task would respond true to tickle-pickle but false to lemon-demon since the former rhyme but the latter do not. A "false" response in the graphemic task was made if the words differed by more than a single letter. Each of the three tasks was performed with and without the shadowing task. It is unlikely that the graphemic task requires speech decoding, and the interference caused by shadowing should provide an index of the general disruptive effects of shadowing. The additional interference caused by shadowing in the phonemic task, which requires speech decoding, indexes the direct interference of shadowing on speech decoding. Given these measures, the degree of interference caused by shadowing on the semantic task should reveal the degree that speech decoding is present in this task. The results showed that the interference caused by shadowing was equivalent in the graphemic and semantic tasks and significantly greater in the phonemic task. This means that the amount of phonemic encoding was equivalent in the graphemic and semantic tasks and signficantly greater in the phonemic task. In a second experiment Kleiman showed that phonemic similarity did not disrupt the graphemic task. This result shows that no phonemic encoding occurred in the graphemic task. Therefore, phonemic encoding did not occur in the semantic task either, since shadowing had equivalent effects in the graphemic and semantic tasks.

In a third experiment, observers were given five-word sentences in two different tasks with and without shadowing. In the category task, subjects were given a category name and asked to indicate whether or not the following sentence contained a member of that category. In the acceptability task, the subject indicated whether or not the word string was a semantically acceptable sentence. Shadowing increased reaction time 78 msec in the category task and 394 msec in the acceptability task. Given that the category task could be performed without much working memory load whereas the acceptability task could not, the author concludes that speech recoding is important to storage in working memory but not to initial processing for meaning.

Conclusion

It seems valuable to attack reading and listening with similar methodological and theoretical forces in the framework of an information-processing model. Our concern is with how the reader and listener perform, and with the dynamics of this performance. Although the surface structures of written text and speech present unique questions to each skill, the apparent similarities in deep structure offer the hope of a single framework for understanding both reading and listening.

The author's research is supported by grants from the Public Health Service, the National Institute of Education, and the Wisconsin Alumni Research Foundation. The substantive contributions of Michael M. Cohen, David Klitzke, Gregg C. Oden, Glen A. Taylor, and Richard L. Venezky are gratefully acknowledged. Herman Bouma and Glen Taylor provided very helpful reviews of an earlier version of the paper.

REFERENCES

Allport, D.A. On knowing the meaning of words we are unable to report: The effects of visual masking. In S. Dornic (Ed.), Attention and Performance VI. Hillsdale, NJ: Erlbaum, 1977.

Anderson, N.H. Information integration theory: A brief survey. In D.H. Krantz, R.C. Atkinson, R.D. Luce, & P. Suppes (Eds.), Contemporary developments in mathematical psychology (Vol. 2). San Francisco: W.H. Freeman, 1974.

Ball, F., Wood, C., & Smith, E.E. When are semantic targets detected faster than visual or acoustic ones? Perception & Psychophysics, 1975, 7, 1-8.

Blakemore, C. The baffled brain. In R.L. Gregory & E.H. Gombrich (Eds.), Illusion in nature and art. London: Duckworth, 1973.

Blakemore, C. Mechanics of the mind. New York: Cambridge University Press, 1977.

Blesser, B., Shillman, R., Kuklinski, T., Cox, C., Eden, M., & Ventura, J. A theoretical approach for character recognition based on phenomenological attributes. International Journal of Man-Machine Studies, 1974, 6, 701-714.

Bouma, H. Visual recognition of isolated lower-case letters. Vision Research, 1971, 11, 459-474.

Breitmeyer, B.G., & Ganz, L. Implications of sustained and transient channels for theories of visual pattern masking, saccadic suppression, and information processing. Psychological Review, 1976, 83, 1-36.

Broadbent, D.A. The hidden preattentive processes. American Psychologist, 1977, 32, 109-118.

Chomsky, N., & Halle, M. The sound pattern of English. New York: Harper & Row, 1968.

Cole, R.A. Listening for mispronunciations: A measure of what we hear during speech. Perception & Psychophysics, 1973, 13, 153-156.

Cole, R.A., & Jakimik, J. Understanding speech: How words are heard. Technical report, Department of Psychology, Carnegie-Mellon Univeristy, 1977.

Dornic, S. Human information processing and bilingualism. Report from the Institute of Applied Psychology. The University of Stockholm, No. 67, 1975.

Erickson, D., Mattingly, I.G., & Turvey, M.T. Phonetic coding of Kanji. Paper presented at the 83rd meeting of the Acoustical Society of America, Buffalo, New York, 1972.

Estes, W.K. The locus of inferential and perceptual processes in letter identification. Journal of Experimental Psychology: General, 1975, 104, 122-145.

Foss, D.J., & Swinney, D.A. On the psychological reality of the phoneme: Perception, identification, and consciousness. Journal of Verbal Learning and Verbal Behavior, 1973, 12, 246-257.

Fujimura, O. Syllable as a unit of speech perception. IEEE Transactions on acoustics, speech, and signal processing, 1975, ASSP-23, 82-86.

Gough, P.B. One second of reading. In J.F. Kavanagh & I. G. Mattingly (Eds.), Language by ear and by eye. Cambridge, MA: MIT Press, 1972.

Gough, P.B., & Cosky, M.J. One second of reading again. In N.J. Castellan, Jr., D.B. Pisoni, & G.R. Potts (Eds.), Cognitive theory (Vol. 2). Hillsdale, NJ: Erlbaum, 1976.

Green, D.W., & Shallice, T. Direct visual access in reading for meaning. Memory & Cognition, 1976, 4, 753-758.

Hawkins, H .L., Reicher, G.M., Rogers, M., & Peterson, L. Flexible coding in word recognition. Journal of Experimental Psychology: Human Perception and Performance, 1976, 2, 380-385.

Hubel, D.N., & Wiesel, T.N. Receptive fields, binocular interaction, and functional architecture in the cat's visual cortex. Journal of Physiology, 1962, 160, 106-154.

Jakobson, R., Fant, C.G.M., & Halle, M. Preliminaries to speech analysis: The distinctive features and their correlates. Cambridge, MA: MIT Press, 1961.

Johnson, N.F. On the function of letters in word identification: Some data and a preliminary model. Journal of Verbal Learning and Verbal Behavior, 1975, 14, 17-29.

Juola, J.F., Choe, C.S., & Leavitt, D.D. A reanalysis of the word-superiority effect. Paper presented at the Psychonomic Society, Boston, MA, November, 1974.

Keyser, S.J., & Halle, M. What we do when we speak. In P.A. Kolers & M. Eden (Eds.), Recognizing patterns. Cambridge, MA: MIT Press, 1968.

Kintsch, W., & Kintsch, E. Interlingual interference and memory processes. Journal of Verbal Learning and Verbal Behavior, 1969, 8, 16-19.

Kleiman, G.M. Speech recoding in reading. Journal of Verbal Learning and Verbal Behavior, 1975, 14, 323-340.

Ladefoged, P. A course in phonetics. New York: Harcourt, Brace, & Jovanovich, 1975.

LaBerge, D., & Samuels, S.J. Toward a theory of automatic information processing in reading. Cognitive Psychology, 1974, 6, 293-323.

Lane, H., Boyes-Braem, P., & Bellugi, U. Preliminaries to a distinctive feature analysis of handshapes in American sign language. Cognitive Psychology, 1976, 8, 263-289.

Lesser, V.R., Fennell, R.D., Erman, L.D., & Reddy, D.J. Organization of the Hearsay II Speech Understanding System. IEEE Transactions on Acoustics, Speech, and Signal Processing, 1975, ASSP-23, 11-23.

Liberman, A.M., Cooper, F.S., Shankweiler, D.P., & Studdert-Kennedy, M. Perception of the speech code. Psychological Review, 1967, 74, 431-461.

Lindsay, P.H., & Norman, D.A. Human information processing. New York: Academic Press, 1977.

Marslen-Wilson, W.D. Linguistic structure and speech shadowing at very short latencies. Nature, 1973, 244, 522-523.

Marslen-Wilson, W.D., & Welsh, A. Processing interactions and lexical access during word recognition in continuous speech. Cognitive Psychology, 1978, 10, 29-63.

Massaro, D.W. Perception of letters, words, and nonwords. Journal of Experimental Psychology, 1973, 100, 349-353.

Massaro, D.W. Understanidng language: An information processing model of speech perception, reading, and psycholinguistics. New York: Academic Press, 1975. (a)

Massaro, D.W. Experimental psychology and information processing. Chicago: Rand-McNally, 1975. (b)

Massaro, D.W. Reading and listening. Technical Report, Wisconsin Research and Development Center for Cognitive Learning. University of Wisconsin, Madison, Wisconsin, 1977.

Massaro, D.W., & Cohen, M.M. The contribution of fundamental frequency and voice onset time to the /zi/-/si/ distinction. Journal of the Acoustical Society of America, 1976, 60, 704-717.

Massaro, D.W., & Klitzke, D. Letters are functional in word identification. Memory & Cognition, 1977, 5, 292-298.

Massaro, D.W., Venezky, R.L., & Taylor, G.A. Orthographic regularity, positional frequency, and visual processing of letter strings. Journal of Experimental Psychology: General, in press.

McClelland, J.L. Preliminary letter identification in the perception of words and nonwords. Journal of Experimental Psychology: Human Perception and Performance, 1976, 2, 80-91.

McNeill, D., & Lindig, K. The perceptual reality of phonemes, syllables, words, and sentences. Journal of Verbal Learning and Verbal Behavior, 1973, 12, 419-430.

Morton, J. Interaction of information in word recognition. Psychological Review, 1969, 76, 165-178.

Nash-Weber, B. The role of semantics in automatic speech understanding. In D.G. Bobrow & A. Collins (Eds.), Representation and understanding. New York: Academic Press, 1975.

Naus, M.J., & Shillman, R.J. Why a Y is not a V: A new look at the distinctive features of letters. Journal of Experimental Psychology: Human Perception and Performance, 1976, 2, 394-400.

Oden, G.C., & Massaro, D.W. Integration of featural information in speech perception. Psychological Review, 1978, 85, 172-191.

Reicher, G.M. Perceptual recognition as a function of meaningfulness of stimulus material. Journal of Experimental Psychology, 1969, 81, 275-280.

Rumelhart, D.E. Toward an interactive model of reading. In S. Dornic (Ed.), Attention and performance VI. Hillsdale, NJ: Erlbaum, 1977.

Saegert, J., Hamayan, E., & Ahmar, H. Memory for language input in polyglots. Journal of Experimental Psychology: Human Learning and Memory, 1975, 1, 607-613.

Savin, H.B., & Bever, T.G. The nonperceptual reality of the phoneme. Journal of Verbal Learning and Verbal Behavior, 1970, 9, 295-302.

Shillman, R.J., Cox, C., Kuklinski, T., Ventura, J., Blesser, B., & Eden, M. A bibliography in character recognition. Techniques for describing characters. Visible Language, 1974, 8, 151-166.

Sloboda, J.A. Decision times for word and letter search: A holistic word identification model examined. Journal of Verbal Learning and Verbal Behavior, 1976, 15, 93-101.

Sloboda, J.A. The locus of the word-priority effect in a target-detection task. Memory & Cognition, 1977, 5, 371-376.

Spencer, H. The visible word. New York: Hastings, 1968.

Thompson, M.C., & Massaro, D.W. The role of visual information and redundancy in reading. Journal of Experimental Psychology, 1973, 98, 49-54.

Tulving, E., & Colotla, V.A. Free recall of trilingual lists. Cognitive Psychology, 1970, 1, 86-98.

Tweney, R.D., Heiman, G.W., & Hoemann, H.W. Psychological processing of sign language: Effects of visual description on sign intelligibility. Journal of Experimental Psychology: General, 1977, 106, 255-268.

Tzeng, O.J.L., Hung,D.L., & Wang, W.S-Y. Speech recoding in reading Chinese characters. Journal of Experimental Psychology: Human Learning and Memory, 1977, 3, 621-630.

Venezky, R.L., & Massaro, D.W. The role of orthographic regularity in word recognition. In L. Resnick & P. Weaver (Eds.), Theory and practice of early reading. Hillsdale, NJ: Erlbaum, in press.

Warren, R.M. Identification times for phonemic components of graded complexity and for spelling of speech. Perception & Psychophysics, 1971, 9, 345-349.

Wickelgren, W.A. Short-term memory for phonemically similar lists. American Journal of Psychology, 1965, 78, 567-574.

Wrolstad, M.E. A manifesto for visible language. Visible Language, 1976, 10, 4-40.

Zadeh, L.A. Quantitative fuzzy semantics. Information Sciences, 1971, 3, 159-176.

Working Memory and Reading

A. D. Baddeley

The possible role of short-term or working memory in reading is discussed. A distinction is drawn between two hypothetical components of working memory -- a central executive that is responsible for information processing and decision taking, and an articulatory loop which acts as a slave system, enabling verbal material to be maintained sub-vocally. On the basis of existing evidence, it is argued that the articulatory loop plays an important role in learning to read, but is less essential for fluent reading. Experiments are presented which show that subjects may read and comprehend statements without utilisation of the articulatory loop. Conditions under which the loop will be utilised are discussed. It is suggested that these include situations where 1) judgments of phonological similarity are required; 2) retention of the surface structure of the passage is required; 3) strict word order is crucial to comprehension, and possibly 4) the rate of input of material exceeds the rate of semantic processing.

My primary research interest is in human memory, and my interest in reading stems from this. A few years ago Graham Hitch and I began a series of experiments aimed at exploring the role of short-term memory in a number of information-processing tasks. This resulted in a substantial change in our concept of the nature of short-term memory, and the resulting hypothetical system, which we term working memory, seemed to suggest some interesting hypotheses about the nature of reading. In the present chapter, I want to discuss these hypotheses and describe some experiments stemming from them.

We carried out a series of experiments which explored the role of short-term memory in tasks such as verbal reasoning, verbal memory, and comprehension (Baddeley & Hitch, 1974). On the basis of the results, we produced

355

a modified version of the dichotomous model of memory in which the short-
term store was further split into two components -- a central executive
system, and an articulatory loop used for sub-vocal rehearsal of material.
Although we have explored this in much less detail, an analogous spatial
rehearsal system probably also occurs (Baddeley, Grant, Wight, & Thomson,
1975). The central executive system was assumed to be responsible for information processing and decision taking as well as storage. As Hitch and
Baddeley (1976) subsequently pointed out, it is unclear whether this central
processor should be viewed as a pool of processing capacity which may be
devoted to either storage or processing, or whether one should separate out
distinct storage and processing components.

The articulatory loop seems to offer a more easily explored concept than
the central executive, and we have made more progress in delineating the
characteristics of this hypothetical system. It is assumed that the loop is
responsible for the speech-based characteristics of STM as measured by the
memory span procedure, in which the subject is presented with a string of
items and required to repeat them in the same order. Conrad (1964) showed
that in a memory span task, when subjects are required to repeat sequences
of consonants, the errors made are phonemically similar to the correct item.
Thus, if the subject forgets the letter B, he is more likely to misremember
it as V than F, even though the material was presented visually. Similarly,
subjects find it more difficult to repeat a string of phonemically similar consonants (G T V D B) than a sequence of letters that differ from each other
in sound or articulation (F K Y N R). A comparable effect occurs in the
immediate memory for sequences of unrelated words, with phonemically
similar items being harder to repeat than dissimilar sequences. Similarity
of meaning is unimportant in this situation, although in long-term learning
meaning is important and phonemic factors are relatively unimportant
(Baddeley 1966a, b).

Further evidence for the role of phonemic coding in memory span comes
from a series of experiments by Baddeley, Thomson, and Buchanan (1975)
on the role of word length. They showed a clear relationship between memory
span and word length, with spans for long words being substantially shorter
than for short words. Spoken duration rather than the number of syllables
appears to be the crucial variable, and their data suggest that memory span
is approximately equivalent to the number of words which can be read in
1½ secs.

Both the phonemic similarity and the word length effects can be abolished
if material is presented visually, and the subject prevented from sub-vocal
rehearsal by requiring him to articulate some irrelevant sound such as "the"
or to count from one to six repeatedly. Under these conditions of articulatory suppression, performance is impaired, but subjects can still perform
the memory span task, implying that sub-vocal articulation is useful, but
not essential for retaining sequences of items.

These results are consistent with the concept of an articulatory loop which
functions rather as a tape loop of limited duration. It can be used to supplement the central executive component of the working memory system,
thereby freeing some of the central space for processing or further storage
if necessary. The rehearsal loop appears to be based on articulation, since
blocking articulation by means of irrelevant vocalization not only impairs

performance but also abolishes the phonemic similarity and word length effects.

In this study, I shall talk about the articulatory loop as if it functioned like a simple tape loop. However, it is worth bearing in mind that this is certainly an oversimplification, and may turn out to be an inappropriate analogy. The reason for this caution stems from experiments in which articulatory suppression is used, but material is presented auditorily. When this occurs, both phonemic similarity and word length effects remain. If such effects are dependent on the subject articulating the material, then they should disappear even though presentation is auditory. The current best guess therefore is that phonemic similarity and word length effects reflect the operation of a system, perhaps involving motor speech programmes, which can be primed either by articulation, or by hearing a particular sequence of speech sounds. On this view, sub-vocal articulation is a means of priming the system, but it is not the sub-vocalisation itself that holds the phonemic information. However, I shall continue to use the term articulatory loop since, for the purpose of this present discussion, the detailed underlying mechanism is probably not crucial.

We assume, then, a short-term memory system comprising a central executive capable of both storage and control, somewhat analogous to an attentional system or perhaps to consciousness. This is aided by one or more slave systems, the most important of which for the present purposes is the articulatory sub-vocal loop. What are the implications of such a system for the understanding of reading? The most obvious link is with the classic question of the role of sub-vocalisation in reading. In discussing this, I shall distinguish between the role of sub-vocalisation in learning to read and its function in the performance of the fluent reader.

Working Memory and Learning to Read

In a paper concerned with the possible relationship between memory and reading, R. Conrad (1972) described a series of experiments in which children were required to remember a sequence of pictures of easily nameable objects. In one condition, the objects had names that were phonemically similar (hat, bat, rat), whereas in the other the items were dissimilar phonemically (girl, bus, spoon). Very young children showed no difference in performance between the two sets, but by the age of five or six an effect was beginning to appear, and by eight there was a clear advantage to the dissimilar set. Conrad suggests that this difference reflects the subject's use of a phonological short-term store, and points out that it appears to become common just at the point at which British children are learning to read. He suggests that the relationship between phonemic coding and learning to read may be important.

Why should this be? One possible interpretation (not necessarily that held by Conrad) might be the following. When a child learns to read, he is usually taught more than a simple visual association between a pattern of letters and the sound of a given word. He is taught "word attack skills" in which he is encouraged to break up words into their constituent syllables, and syllables into their individual letters. He must then decode the individual letters, and blend them into the speech sounds that they represent. Take a very simple word like "mad"; if the child simply reads off the sound made by each individual letter he is likely to come up with something sounding

like "muh," "a," "duh," which strung together sound something like "muaduh."
Getting from this to "mad" is a far from trivial problem. In fact, of course,
most words are much less straightforward than this; simply changing the
word "mad" to "made" clearly introduces further problems.

Suppose we look at this problem from the viewpoint of our simple working
memory model. The central executive part of the system is presumably
involved both in translating the individual speech sounds, and in getting from
a sequence of unrelated sounds to a real English word. It can also presumably
be used to hold the decoded speech sounds during this process, but probably
the greater the memory load imposed on the central executive, the less processing space will remain for decoding and blending. Suppose then that the
articulatory loop is used as a supplementary way of storing sequences of
sounds. As each sound is decoded it can be stored in the loop, thereby leaving
the central executive free to decode the next item and hypothesise about
what the final target word is likely to be. When two or three speech sounds
have been loaded into the loop, they can presumably be blended into a single
syllable. This briefer, more integrated articulation can then be returned
to the loop pending the decoding of further letters, which in turn can be
blended with the initial syllable. This can be contrasted with the strategy
of using the central executive for both storage and general processing; each
letter decoded will use up "space" in the central executive, leaving progressively less capacity for letter analysis, blending, and word-finding. Therefore, a child who is able to utilise the articulatory loop will be at a substantial advantage in decoding unfamiliar words in contrast with a child who
attempts to carry out the whole procedure via the central executive
component.

What evidence is there for such a hypothesis? Liberman, Shankweiler,
Liberman, Fowler, and Fischer (1977) have shown that children have difficulty both in blending and in breaking up words into their constituent syllables and phonemes. An analysis of errors made by beginning readers showed
more errors on final than on initial consonants, a finding which is consistent
with the working memory hypothesis if one assumes that the child is using
up his available central processing space as he works through the word. In
a series of experiments in which good and poor readers were required to
remember sequences of consonants, Liberman et al. (1977) observed that
poor readers showed a much weaker phonemic similarity effect than good
readers. It will be recalled that the working memory model attributes the
phonemic similarity effect to the sub-vocal articulatory loop; this result
is therefore consistent with the hypothesis that poor readers make inadequate
use of the loop.

There is a good deal of other evidence to suggest that dyslexic children
do not make full use of the articulatory loop. It will be recalled that the
loop is regarded as an important component in memory span. Naidoo (1970)
and Miles and Wheeler (1974) have both pointed out that one of the most
striking features of dyslexic children is their impaired digit span, and their
even more greatly impaired backward digit span. It would be interesting
to ascertain whether the backward digit span is particularly susceptible to
disruption by articulatory suppression in normal subjects as one would predict
if it were very heavily dependent on the articulatory loop. In a similar vein,
Bakker (1972) has shown that dyslexics have great difficulty in performing

tasks which involve the retention of order information, again a component of short-term memory which appears to rely heavily on the articulatory loop. Finally, an unpublished experiment carried out at the Cambridge University Institute of Education by Jean Hull, a teacher of subnormal children, suggests that their ability to learn to read may be crucially dependent on whether or not they have use of an articulatory loop system. She had noticed that in attempting to teach children to read, their digit span provided a good predictor of success. In an unpublished study, she showed a clear relationship between performance on a test of phonic blending and digit span, with general intelligence partialled out. She also found training using vocal rehearsal significantly improved performance on the phonic blending test.

Therefore, although I have not worked directly with dyslexic children or with beginning readers, I would like to suggest that the concept of working memory does provide some potentially fruitful hypotheses. That is not of course to say that adequate use of the articulatory loop is the only problem in learning to read, or indeed the most important. It seems probable that a skill as complex as reading will involve many subcomponents, and that a breakdown in any of these may lead to dyslexia. Nonetheless, the evidence seems to suggest that inadequate use of the articulatory loop may be one important cause of reading difficulty. If this is so, then it suggests a further question as to whether the failure to use the articulatory loop stems from a structural inadequacy -- the system has simply not developed -- or from a failure to appreciate a strategy. If the latter is the case, then the further question arises of whether such a strategy can be taught.

Working Memory and Fluent Reading
Our interest in reading stemmed from a more general concern with the problem of language comprehension. One of the problems which stimulated our interest in the role of working memory in comprehension was raised by the patient K.F. (Shallice & Warrington, 1970) who had a grossly impaired STM, as measured by digit span, but who had no difficulty in comprehending language, at least under normal conversational conditions. We therefore decided to explore the role of working memory in the comprehension of spoken prose, using a concurrent digit load technique. We found that requiring our subjects to hold six digits while listening to prose impaired comprehension, whether this was measured by questions on the meaning of the passage or by the Cloze procedure in which the subject was subsequently given the passage, with every fifth word deleted, and required to write in as many words as possible (Baddeley & Hitch, 1974).

A further experiment explored the influence of phonemic similarity on comprehension. It may be recalled that the working memory model attributes phonemic similarity effects to the articulatory loop; hence the presence of an effect on comprehension would seem to implicate the articulatory rehearsal loop. In order to avoid any complication due to the mishearing of the phonemically similar material, we moved from auditory comprehension to visual presentation. Subjects were given short sentences and required to decide whether the sentence was sensible or nonsense. The nonsense sentences were created by permuting the order of two words. Given the phonemically similar sentence "Red headed Ned said Ted fed in bed," the nonsense version might read "Red headed Ned Ted said fed in bed." Each phonemically similar

Table 1. Mean Time Taken to Verify or Read Aloud Sentences Varying in Inter-Word Phonemic Similarity.*

Sentence type	Mean RT for judgment of "possibility" (sec)			Mean reading time (sec)		
	Possible version	Impossible version	Average	Possible version	Impossible version	Average
Phonemically dissimilar	2.84	2.64	2.73	2.93	3.18	3.06
Phonemically similar	3.03	2.83	2.93	2.96	3.19	3.08

*Data from Baddeley and Hitch, 1974.

sentence was matched with a dissimilar version which resembled it as closely as possible semantically ("Dark skinned Ian thought Harry ate in bed" and "Dark skinned Ian Harry thought ate in bed"). Although the constraints of creating sentences out of phonemically similar words produced some semantically unusual English prose, subjects nevertheless had no difficulty in distinguishing the possible from the impossible.

The mean decision times for sentences of each type are shown in Table 1, together with the time taken for subjects subsequently to read each sentence aloud with no comprehension required. There was a pronounced tendency ($p < .01$) for phonemic similarity to increase judgment times for both possible and impossible sentences. Since this does not apply in the reading aloud task, the effect is presumably on comprehension rather than on the translation of printed words into spoken form. Note also that whereas the impossible version takes slightly longer to read than the possible version, the pattern is reversed in the case of judgment time. This suggests that subjects were deciding that a sentence was impossible as soon as they reached the non-permissible pair of words, and hence did not need to finish reading the sentence. It would clearly be unwise to generalise too much from this somewhat curious task, but it does suggest that the articulatory loop may play a role in the comprehension of written material.

The Articulatory Loop and Fluent Reading

The question of what role, if any, is played in fluent reading by sub-vocalisation or inner speech has concerned reading theorists for many years. In his classic book on reading, Huey (1908) comments "The carrying range of inner speech is considerably larger than that of vision.... The initial sub-vocalisation seems to help hold the word in consciousness until enough others are given to combine with it in touching off the unitary utterance of the sentence which they form.... It is of the greatest service to the reader or listener that at at each moment a considerable amount of what is being read should hang suspended in the primary memory of the inner speech. It is doubtless true that without something of this there could be no comprehension of speech at all."

There have been several recent reviews of the evidence for speech recoding in reading (Baron, 1976; R. Conrad, 1972; Levy, 1977, 1978, in press). In general, the evidence seems to suggest that in the case of individual words, meaning may be accessed without the need for phonological coding. When subjects are required to make judgments about the phonemic characteristics of a word, the articulatory loop appears to enhance performance (Kleiman, 1975). Similarly, in performing a lexical decision task in which the subject is required to decide whether a string of letters constitutes an English word or not, sequences that are phonemically similar to an English word (Brane) take longer to reject than sequences that are phonologically less similar (Brone) (Rubenstein, Lewis, & Rubenstein, 1971). However, n neither of these tasks can be regarded as necessarily typical of normal fluent reading. Furthermore, meaning can apparently be extracted from individual words without phonemic coding by both normal subjects (Kleiman, 1975; Marcel & Patterson, 1978; Green & Shallice, 1976) and phonemic dyslexic patients (Marshall & Newcombe, 1973; Patterson & Marcel, 1977; Shallice & Warrington, 1975).

In the case of phrases and sentences, the picture is less clear. Baron (1973) argues that the phonemic stage is not necessary for reading. He bases this conclusion on an experiment in which subjects were required to categorise phrases as meaningful or nonsense. Nonsense phrases that were phonemically identical to meaningful phrases (Tie the not, and Tie the knot) took no longer to reject than phrases which were visually similar, but phonemically distinct (I am kill, and I am ill). Unfortunately, however, there was a significant increase in errors on phonologically similar phrases which suggested that there was indeed an effect, although not on reaction time.

Levy (1977) investigated the role of speech recoding in reading by means of the articulatory suppression technique. In a series of experiments her subjects were presented either visually or auditorally with a sequence of sentences. On half the trials subjects were required to count rapidly from one to ten (the articulatory suppression condition); on the remainder they were left free to sub-vocalise if they wished. Performance was then tested by presenting the subject with one of the sentences either in identical form, or with a minor change of wording which the subject was instructed to detect. The changes were either lexical or semantic. Lexical changes involved a semantically equivalent word being substituted for the subject or object (The busy policeman ignored an approaching child, for The busy officer ignored an approaching child). Semantic changes were produced by permuting the subject and object of the sentences, all of which were selected so as to be reversible (The busy child ignored an approaching policeman).

With visual presentation suppression impaired performance on both types of test item, while no such decrement occurred with auditory presentation. Levy interpreted this as evidence for the role of articulation in reading (visual presentation), but not in comprehension (listening). Unfortunately however, as she pointed out, her results demonstrated that articulatory suppression impairs memory but not necessarily reading or comprehension. Furthermore, the particular tests of memory involved may be atypical in requiring retention of the surface characteristic of words selected to be semantically equivalent, or in the "semantic change" condition being crucially dependent on order information. It is arguable that the articulatory loop is particularly well adapted to handling both these types of test although such demands may be highly atypical of normal reading.

Evidence in favour of such an interpretation comes from a subsequent study (Levy, 1978) in which retention of meaning was tested independently of either the surface characteristic of the words or their syntactic order. Subjects were required to detect paraphrases of sentences which had previously occurred. Hence the sentence "The solemn physician distressed the anxious mother" might be tested by a correct paraphrase -- "The solemn doctor upset the anxious mother" -- or an incorrect paraphrase -- "The solemn officer helped the anxious mother". Once again, subjects were presented with a series of such sentences and were required to suppress articulation by counting, or were free to sub-vocalise. Under these conditions no suppression effect occurred, suggesting that suppression does not impair either the comprehension of sentences read, or the retention of their meaning when tested in this way.

The articulatory suppression technique was also used by Kleiman (1975) in a study which attempted to use the concept of working memory to understand reading. Articulation was suppressed by requiring the subject to repeat a stream of random digits while reading material of various types. He found that digit shadowing impaired a subject's ability to detect a rhyme within a sentence, e.g. Is there a word rhyming with "cream" in the sentence "He awakened from the dream?" (Yes). Is there a word rhyming with "soul" in "The referee called a foul?" (No). On the other hand, digit repetition had a much smaller effect on judgments of graphemic similarity (Is there a word graphemically similar to "bury" in the sentence "Yesterday the Grand Jury adjourned?") and on category judgments (Is a game mentioned in the sentence "Everyone at home played Monopoly?"). Note however that in all these conditions, subjects processed only one word at a time -- a situation very different from normal reading. Kleiman therefore included a fourth condition in which subjects were required to judge the semantic acceptability of sentences such as "Noisy parties disturb sleeping neighbours" (Yes) or "Pizzas have been eating Jerry" (No). This condition, which Kleiman claimed required the processing of the sentence as a whole, was impaired by articulatory suppression.

On the basis of these results, Kleiman argued for a working memory model containing both a visual and an articulatory store. Provided the visual store is not overloaded, no articulatory coding need occur. However, when input to the visual store exceeds the rate of semantic processing, the articulatory store is used as a supplementary backup system. The suggestion that subvocal articulation may be important in reading difficult but not easy material is intuitively plausible; it is also consistent with the results of Hardyck and Petrinovich (1970), who used electromyographic measures of subvocalisation. They trained their subjects to suppress EMG activity while reading, and found that this was possible for simple texts, but not for difficult material.

Kleiman's results however are not unequivocal. His use of shadowing as a suppression technique is unfortunate since it is a demanding information processing task that seems likely to take up some of the central executive or decision making component of working memory as well as occupying the articulatory loop. Such a view is supported by the fact that performance is impaired on both the graphemic and category decision tasks, although the impairment is substantially less than that observed for either the phonemic or semantic acceptability condition. The possibility arises therefore that the impairment in performance on the semantic acceptability judgement may stem from its greater sensitivity to the demands placed on the central executive. A second problem is raised by the nature of the semantically anomalous sentences. In some, though not all, cases, order information is crucial (Pizza has been eating Jerry), and it may have been the case that subjects were forced into a strategy of routinely processing order information much more precisely than is normal in reading.

Our concern with this problem stemmed from an attempt to extend our previous work on the role of working memory and comprehension. It will be recalled that our previous studies involved reading passages of prose to subjects who were concurrently holding sequences of digits. Comprehension of the material was then tested indirectly by the subject's memory for either the surface characteristics of the material, as measured by the Cloze Test, or their retention of the gist, as measured by subsequent test questions. In order to avoid such reliance on memory for the material presented, Hitch and I adapted a procedure popularised by Collins and Quillian (1969) where subjects were required to answer questions based on general knowledge.

Sentences presented in our first study all involved statements about the properties of well-known items. As in the Collins and Quillian study, such statements could either be about a characteristic that was peculiar to the item in question (Wasps have stings), or they could be characteristic of the category from which the item was taken. In this case the category would be insect and the statement might be of the form "Wasps have legs." Negatives were created by attaching a property which clearly did not apply (Wasps have oars). Collins and Quillian observed that it took longer to verify statements about the superordinate category than it did to verify statements about the item itself, an effect they attributed to the structure of the semantic memory system.

In order to examine the role of working memory in performing this task, we presented our subjects with a sequence of six random digits. The subject listened to these and then repeated them. As he repeated the third of the six digits, a flap was raised exposing a card on which one of the sentences was typed. The subject was required to continue repeating the digits until he had decided whether the sentence was true or false, and pressed a button accordingly. The second condition involved articulatory suppression, with the subject required to count repeatedly from one to six. Again as he articulated the third digit, the sentence was exposed and he was required to go on articulating until he had made his response. A third condition acted as a control, with no memory load or articulation required. Eighteen university undergraduates were tested in a Latin square design in which the concurrent load conditions were blocked. The results are shown in Table 2.

Analysis of variance indicated significant effects of sentence type, $F(2,34) = 13.7$, $p < .001$, and of load, $F(2,34) = 3.55$, $p < .05$. The sentence type effect is clearly due to the slower performance on false items; the difference between item attributes and superordinate attributes predicted by the Collins and Quillian model was not observed. It is clear from Table 2 that the difference between conditions is entirely due to the concurrent digit load task, with articulatory suppression having no effect on performance.

These results are consistent with our earlier comprehension studies in suggesting that the concurrent load of six items impairs performance. However, they deviate from our study in which phonemic similarity was manipulated in suggesting that the articulatory loop is not necessary for comprehension. Our data failed to replicate the difference between sentences reported by Collins and Quillian, however, and we were concerned that injudicious selection of material may have invalidated our result. Vivien Lewis and I therefore decided to repeat the study using somewhat longer sentences, selected carefully with a view to optimizing the chance of obtaining the Collins and Quillian effect. The material had been selected by Neil Thomson and myself with a view to creating a semantic processing test for use as an indicator of performance decrement under stress. It was based on Battig and Montague's (1969) category norms, and involved a hierarchy of nested and balanced categories which produced a total of 1250 sentences of which half were positive and half were negative. The positives were true statements about category membership (Sharks are fish, or Sharks are living creatures), while the false items were created by mismatching

Table 2. Mean Verification Time for Sentences as a Function of Articulatory Suppression and Memory Load.*

Working Memory and Mean Sentence
Verification Time (secs)

	Sentence Type			
Condition	Same Level	Hierarchical	False	Mean
Control	1.22	1.27	1.40	1.30
Suppression	1.23	1.25	1.34	1.27
6-Digit Load	1.39	1.41	1.43	1.41
Mean	1.28	1.31	1.39	

*Data from an unpublished study by Hitch and Baddeley.

a true item and its category (Desks are fruit, or Desks are living creatures). Similarly, we had statements about the properties of items at various hierarchical levels (Robins have red breasts, or Robins move around searching for food); again, negatives were produced by mismatching properties (Generals have red breasts, Screwdrivers move around searching for food). The test procedure was as before, except that the 18 subjects were members of the Applied Psychology Unit Subject Panel, principally men.

The results are shown in Table 3. We again found a clear effect of concurrent memory load on performance, but no consistent influence of suppression. Again, we failed to replicate the hierarchical effects obtained by Collins and Quillian, at least in the case of properties, although we obtained differences in the predicted direction for statements about category membership. In this respect, our results are consistent with those of Carol Conrad (1972), who suggested that the hierarchical effect obtained by Collins and Quillian in their study was attributable largely to differences in associative frequency across their examples. When this was controlled, she failed to obtain a hierarchical effect for properties but, as in our study, continued to observe a category membership effect.

Our results therefore suggest that the articulatory loop is not necessary for either reading or comprehending simple sentences. It might however be argued that the type of sentence used is so simple as to be atypical of most reading. This is not true of a series of unpublished experiments carried out by Davina Simmonds at the Applied Psychology Unit. She has

Table 3. Mean Verification Time (Sec) as a Function of Sentence Type and Concurrent Load.*

				Sentence Type			
		A	B	C	D	E	Mean
	Control	1.20	1.22	1.18	1.12	1.16	1.18
TRUE SENTENCES	Suppression	1.37	1.28	1.17	1.08	1.14	1.21
	Memory Load	1.39	1.45	1.30	1.22	1.31	1.33
	Mean	1.32	1.32	1.22	1.14	1.20	
	Control	1.26	1.25	1.18	1.15	1.20	1.21
FALSE SENTENCES	Suppression	1.28	1.26	1.23	1.18	1.22	1.23
	Memory Load	1.46	1.34	1.29	1.28	1.30	1.33
	Mean	1.33	1.25	1.23	1.20	1.34	

	Examples	
	Positive	Negative
A = Exemplar Attribute	Robins have red breasts	Screwdrivers have red breasts
B = Sub-category Attribute	Birds have wings	Screwdrivers have wings
C = Category Attribute	Birds move around looking for food	Screwdrivers move around looking for food
D = Sub-category	Robins are birds	Screwdrivers are birds
E = Category	Robins are living things	Screwdrivers are living things

*Data from an unpublished study by Baddeley and Lewis.

studied the role of articulatory suppression in the reading of a wide range of passages. Performance is measured by reading speed and ability to answer questions about the material. Apart from a tendency for suppression to increase reading speed in some conditions, there was no effect on performance; subjects appeared to have no difficulty in comprehending and indeed retaining the information acquired under articulatory suppression.

Taken as a whole then, the evidence suggests that the articulatory loop is not essential for normal reading and comprehension. There do, however, appear to be conditions under which it is employed. These probably include 1) phonemic comparisons; suppression appears to slow down, but not prevent, the process of making rhyme decisions (Kleiman, 1975; Folkard, personal communication). The fact that the judgment is not prevented implies that the articulatory loop is not essential, but merely facilitates the judgment, presumably by allowing the subject to hold one of the comparison words in the loop while performing the comparison. This of course implies that phonological information may be stored elsewhere in the system. 2) Certain "difficult" material appears to benefit from the use of the articulatory loop. This raises the crucial issue of what determines the difficulty of such material. As argued previously, it seems likely that order information is one characteristic; the articulatory loop seems to be particularly adapted to maintaining verbal material in specific order, and hence would presumably be helpful in detecting word order reversals such as those used in the phonemically similar sentence experiment. A second example is found when the material is semantically very similar, and differs primarily in its phonological characteristics; to take an example from Levy's work, the terms Air Hostess and Air Stewardess are sufficiently semantically similar to confuse most of us, so that if a distinction must be made, the phonological difference between the two becomes crucial. It seems reasonable to assume that the articulatory loop will help emphasise the phonological features of such material and hence presumably enhance their retention.

Are there other types of difficulty which induce the utilisation of the articulatory loop? The evidence on this point is sparse, but it seems possible that any condition in which the information comes into the system more rapidly than it can be semantically processed may cause the subject to use his articulatory loop as a back-up store (Kleiman, 1975). A possible example of this type of material occurs from the Token Test, in which subjects are required to respond to complex instructions such as, Touch the small green circle with the large red triangle. An instruction of this type can be obeyed by a normal subject, but not by patients such as Shallice and Warrington's (1970) patient K.F. who has a grossly defective digit span. Performance on the Token Test relies, of course, on order information; it would be interesting to see if a source of difficult material which did not rely on order information would present the same problem for such patients.

It is very clear to me that when I read, my reading is accompanied by something akin to an auditory or articulatory image of the words being processed. This occurs with or without articulatory suppression. Both Kleiman (1975) and Folkard (personal communication) have presented evidence indicating that subjects can make phonemic comparisons while suppressing. It therefore seems likely that there is some form of phonemic, articulatory, or auditory code that is independent of the articulatory loop. Presumably the loop itself must be linked with long-term memory by some system which can operate or trigger speech-motor programmes. It may well be this system rather than the articulatory loop that is responsible for the internal monologue which often appears to accompany reading and which was termed by Huey (1908) "the primary memory of inner speech."

The Central Executive and Fluent Reading

Levy (1978, in press) has justifiably criticised the working memory approach to reading on the grounds that it attributes many of the most crucial components of the reading process to the central executive, while leaving no detailed specification as to how they are performed. It is certainly true that working memory does not present a comprehensive model of reading, or indeed of memory: what it does provide is a framework within which to conceptualise a range of information processing tasks of which reading is one. The framework however is still extremely vague about the nature of the all-important central executive.

The central executive presents a much more difficult problem to tackle than the articulatory loop. It raises interesting questions which, unfortunately, are difficult to pose experimentally. For example, how does one empirically investigate the storage-processing distinction? What is the relationship between attention and short-term memory? What are the implications of showing that two tasks interact when performed simultaneously? How does one get from this to the underlying processes? Although I think these are difficult questions, such difficulties are probably inevitable, given the problem of understanding working memory, attention, and consciousness. Some progress in understanding the role of the central executive is being made, but results are too preliminary to justify discussion.

Conclusion

Reading could be regarded as the process whereby a semantic interpretation is derived from a visual graphemic stimulus. Since the working memory model discussed here has said nothing about vision, graphemes, or semantics, I need hardly point out that it does not claim to be a model of reading. As mentioned initially, my interest is in memory and I have used reading as a phenomenon which allows me to test and develop the concept or working memory. I believe that the problem of reading is proving useful in such development; I can only hope that the concept of working memory will prove equally useful in understanding the complex and challenging process of reading.

I am grateful to Betty Ann Levy and Graham Hitch for some very useful discussions, and to Vivien Lewis who ran and analysed the final experiment.

REFERENCES

Baddeley, A.D. The influence of acoustic and semantic similarity on long-term memory for word sequences. Quarterly Journal of Experimental Psychology, 1966, 18, 302-309. (a)

Baddeley, A.D. Short-term memory for word sequences as a function of acoustic, semantic and formal similarity. Quarterly Journal of Experimental Psychology, 1966. 18, 362-365. (b)

Baddeley, A.D., Grant, S., Wight, E., & Thomson, N. Imagery and visual working memory. In P.M. Rabbitt & S. Dornic (Eds.), Attention and performance V. London: Academic Press, 1975.

Baddeley, A.D., & Hitch, G. Working memory. In G.A. Bower (Ed.), The psychology of learning and motivation. Vol. 8. New York: Academic Press, 1974.

Baddeley, A.D. Thomson, N., & Buchanan, M. Word length and the structure of short-term memory. Journal of Verbal Learning and Verbal Behavior, 1975, 14, 575-589.

Bakker, D.J. Temporal order in disturbed reading. Rotterdam: Rotterdam University Press, 1972.

Baron, J. Phonemic stage not necessary for reading. Quarterly Journal of Experimental Psychology, 1973, 25, 241-246.

Baron, J. Mechanisms for pronouncing printed words: Use and acquisition. In D. La Berge & S.J. Samuels (Eds.), Basic processes in reading. Hillsdale, NJ: Erlbaum, 1976.

Battig, W.F., & Montague, W.E. Category norms for verbal items in 56 categories: A replication and extension of the Connecticut category norms. Journal of Experimental Psychology Monograph, 1969, 80, 3, Pt. II.

Conrad, C. Cognitive economy in semantic memory. Journal of Experimental Psychology, 1972, 92, 149-154.

Conrad, R. Acoustic confusion in immediate memory. British Journal of Psychology, 1964, 55, 75-84.

Conrad, R. The developmental role of vocalizing in short-term memory. Journal of Verbal Learning and Verbal Behavior, 1972, 11, 521-533.

Collins, A.M., & Qullian, M.R. Retrieval time from semantic memory. Journal of Verbal Learning and Verbal Behavior, 1969, 8, 240-247.

Green, D.W., & Shallice, T.   Direct visual access in reading for meaning. Memory & Cognition, 1976, 4, 753-758.

Hardyck, C.D., & Petrinovitch, L.R. Subvocal speech and comprehension level as a function of the difficulty level of reading material. Journal of Verbal Learning and Verbal Behavior, 1970, 9, 647-652.

Hitch, G.J., & Baddeley, A.D. Verbal reasoning and working memory. Quarterly Journal of Experimental Psychology, 1976, 28, 603-621.

Huey, E.B., The psychology and pedagogy of reading. New York: Macmillan, 1908. Reprinted, Cambridge, MA: MIT Press, 1968.

Kleiman, G.M. Speech recoding in reading. Journal of Verbal Learning and Verbal Behavior, 1975, 24, 323-339.

Levy, B.A. Reading: Speech and meaning processes. Journal of Verbal Learning and Verbal Behavior, 1977, 16, 623-638.

Levy, B.A. Speech analysis during sentence processing: Reading versus listening. Visible Language, 1978, 12, 81-101.

Levy, B.A. Speech processing during reading. To appear in A.M. Lesgold, J.W. Pellegrino, J.W. Fokkema, & R. Glaser (Eds.), Cognitive psychology and instruction. New York: Plenum, in press.

Liberman, I.Y., Shankweiler, D., Liberman, A.M., Fowler, C., & Fischer, F.W. Phonetic segmentation and recoding in the beginning reader. In

A.S. Reber & D. Scarborough (Eds.), Towards a psychology of reading. Hillsdale, NJ: Erlbaum, 1977.

Marcel, A.J., & Patterson, K.E. Word recognition and production: Reciprocity in clinical and normal studies. In J. Réquin (Ed.), Attention and performance VII. Hillsdale, NJ: Erlbaum, 1978.

Marshall, J.C., & Newcombe, F. Patterns of paralexia: A psycholinguistic approach. Journal of Psycholiguistic Research, 1973, 2, 175-199.

Miles, T.R., & Wheeler, T.J. Toward a new theory of dyslexia. Dyslexia Review, 1974, 11, 9-11.

Naidoo, S. The assessment of dyslexic children. In A.W. Franklin & S. Naidoo (Eds.), Assessment and teaching of dyslexic children. London: Invalid Children's Aid Association, 1970.

Patterson, K.E., & Marcel, A.J. Aphasia, dyslexia and the phonological coding of written words. Quarterly Journal of Experimental Psychology, 1977, 29, 307-318.

Rubenstein, H., Lewis, S.S., & Rubenstein, M.A. Homographic entries in the internal lexicon: Effects of systemacity and relative frequency meanings. Journal of Verbal Learning and Verbal Behavior, 1971, 10, 57-62.

Shallice, T., & Warrington, E.K. Independent functioning of verbal memory stores: A neuropsychological study. Quarterly Journal of Experimental Psychology, 1970, 22, 261-273.

Shallice, T., & Warrington, E.K. Word recognition in a phonemic dyslexic patient. Quarterly Journal of Experimental Psychology, 1975, 27, 187-199.

A Direct Access from Graphics to Meaning: A Study of the Stroop
Effect in Sentences

Shulamit S. Reich and Colin Cherry

*The present experiment was designed to investigate the
effect of nonlinguistic cues on comprehension of printed
sentences. In particular, the effect of change in the size
of words was examined in a picture-sentence verification
task. The size of nouns or adjectives was varied in a manner
that was either congruent or incongruent with the meaning
of the word in the sentence. Irrespective of the locus of
the size change, congruent sentences were evaluated more
rapidly than incongruent sentences. Thus, unlike the traditional Stroop paradigms that have used single words as
stimuli, the present demonstration of the Stroop effect
extends to units as large as sentences. Implications of the
data for models of lexical access in reading are discussed.*

Recent research on reading has been conducted in the context of traditional
orthography; few experiments have investigated the possibilities of change
in the style or layout of the text. However, some studies have departed from
this trend and have examined the effects of factors such as change of case
(Henderson, Coltheart, & Woodhouse, 1973; Fisher, 1975; Coltheart & Freeman, 1974), typeface (Spencer, Reynolds, & Coe, 1973; Poulton, 1972), and
spacing (Shaw & Weigel, 1973; Spragins, Lefton, & Fisher, 1976). Most of
these studies have been confined to tasks involving semantic, lexical, or
readability decisions. In the present study, we examine the effect of typographic variations on comprehension.

The paucity of recent research in this field may be due partially to the
current preoccupation with the phonemic encoding controversy. This debate
concerns the decoding route that is pursued by visual linguistic stimuli undergoing semantic analysis. Some researchers argue that visual stimuli must
be converted into a phonemic code before they can be analysed for meaning

(Rubenstein, Lewis, & Rubenstein, 1971). Others maintain that there is a direct link between the visual graphemic information and the semantic analyzers, which short circuits the need for a phonemic analysis (Bower, 1970; Kolers, 1972). The two systems are illustrated in Figure 1.

If visual stimuli undergo a phonemic transformation before they are understood, graphic changes in the nature of the text would not be expected to exert a major influence on comprehension. However, such changes would be regarded as more critical in a model that postulates a direct route from the graphemic input to the semantic analyzers. Nevertheless, current research has attempted to disprove the phonemic decoding hypothesis rather than to explore the possibilities raised by the direct access model.

Despite this trend, recent explorations of the Stroop paradigm have suggested new directions for research. Stroop (1935) reported that the presence of a colour word interfered with the naming of the ink colour in which the word was printed. This finding has been extended to examinations of the effects of other irrelevant words on the speed of classifying and naming words, objects, and colours (Dyer, 1973; Morton, 1969; Shor, 1970; Seymour, 1977; Flowers & Dutch, 1976). The primary concern of these studies was to demonstrate the effect of words on the naming or classifying of colours, direction or orientation. More recently, an analogous effect of congruence has been demonstrated on the performance of nonlinguistic perceptual tasks. Congruity effects were obtained in paradigms involving judgements of animal pictures (Paivio, 1975), digits (Banks, Fujii, & Kayra Stuart, 1976), and direction (Clark & Brownell, 1975). In these studies, both the targets and the irrelevant stimuli were nonverbal in character. In this context, "irrelevant" refers to the relationship between the stimuli and the task requirements, while "congruity" refers to the relationship (match or mismatch) between the various attributes of the stimulus array.

The congruity effect in its original form (Stroop, 1935) is not, therefore, exclusive to a situation where a perceptual task is set in a context of

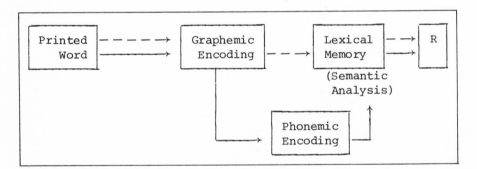

Figure 1. Possible stages in visual word recognition. Dashed and solid lines indicate the sequence of operations according to the graphemic and phonemic encoding hypotheses respectively. (After Meyer, Schvaneveldt, & Ruddy, 1974). Items in parentheses are present authors'.

1.	JOHN	is	taller	than	Sue	
2.	John	is	TALLER	than	Sue	Congruent
3.	John	is	taller	than	Sue	
4.	John	is	taller	than	Sue	
5.	John	is	taller	than	Sue	Incongruent
6.	John	is	taller	than	SUE	

Figure 2. Congruent and incongruent size changes in sentences.

neighbouring and irrelevant verbal stimuli. It appears to be a more general phenomenon where the presence of irrelevant visual or linguistic stimuli can influence performance on verbal or nonverbal judgements.

There has been little research into the effect of irrelevant changes in the size or colour of words on the performance of linguistic tasks. A single study failed to obtain any effect of word size on a size judgement task involving comparison of animal names (Paivio, 1975). Furthermore, there have been no known attempts to extend these findings to performance in reading sentences. The present experiment was designed to rectify this situation, and examined the effect of changes in letter size on comprehension.

The task involved comparisons of size in a picture-sentence verification task. This paradigm has been extensively employed in recent psycholinguistic literature to provide insight into the linguistic aspects of the coding strategies involved in sentence processing (Clark & Chase, 1972; Carpenter, 1974). In our experiment, sentences of the type "Sue is taller than John" were evaluated against pictures of a boy and a girl. The relative sizes of the boy and girl were varied, and the size of critical words was varied in a manner either congruent or incongruent with the meaning. Examples of both types of sentence are shown in Figure 2. According to the theory of phonemically mediated encoding, there would be few systematic effects of such graphic changes. But according to the direct access model of word processing, the present manipulations would likely exert a significant effect on performance. Our hypothesis was that sentences containing words with a congruent size change would be easier to evaluate than those with incongruent size changes.

Method
The subjects in this experiment were six right-handed male undergraduates. Sentences of the type "John is smaller than Sue" were prepared using one of the four adjectives "shorter, smaller, taller, larger." Each sentence was printed once in this form and once with the order of the subject and object nouns reversed, as in "Sue is smaller than John." As shown in Figure 2, the critical word in each sentence was printed in larger (18 pt.) or smaller (10 pt.) type than the rest of the sentence (14 pt.). Six copies of the eight sentences

were produced with variations in the size of either subject noun, object noun, or adjective. Each sentence was mounted on a 6" x 4" card. The two pictures consisted of Letraset figures of a boy and a girl mounted on 6" x 4" cards. In one picture, the boy was larger than the girl, with the boy on the left and the girl on the right. In the other picture, the size and position relationships were reversed.

Procedure
A test trial consisted of a 5 sec exposure of the picture, followed by a sentence. The subject's response terminated the exposure of the sentence, which was replaced by the fixation card for 10 sec.

Subjects were instructed to look at the picture, then read the sentence and press the "true" or "false" key. They were advised to respond as accurately and as quickly as possible. Response latencies were measured from sentence onset to the key press.

In order to counterbalance the effects of type of response (true are faster than false) and handedness (right faster than left) subjects were instructed to press the true key with their left hand and the false with their right (Sloboda, 1976).

Results and Discussion
As predicted, the data indicated that congruent sentences were evaluated more rapidly than incongruent (F $(1, 5)$ = 6.93, p < .025). The mean difference between congruent and incongruent responses was 100 msec, and was significant for each of the three sentence locations as shown in Table 1. There was a suggestion of a greater effect of congruence at the adjective than at either of the noun locations, but this effect was not significant (F $(2, 10)$ = 3.84). True responses were 60 msec faster than false, but this effect was not significant (F $(2, 10)$ = 0.61).

The magnitude of the present difference between congruent and incongruent sentences is comparable to that obtained by Paivio (1975) in his study of size comparisons using pictures of animals (110 msec). Furthermore, the congruity effect cannot be explained in terms of a main effect of letter size.

Table 1. The Effect of Locus of Size Change on Reactions to Congruity in a Picture Sentence Verification Task (sec).

	Subject Noun	Adjective	Object Noun
Congruent	1.43	1.45	1.32
Incongruent	1.49	1.59	1.43

Table 2. The Effect of Adjective Type on Reactions to Congruity in a Picture Sentence Verification Task (sec).

	Congruent	Incongruent
Larger	1.33	1.58
Smaller	1.47	1.44

Such an effect would have been indicated by an interaction between type of adjective and congruence. Adjectives such as "smaller" should have benefitted more from the incongruent (large print) condition, whereas adjectives such as "larger" should have been evaluated more rapidly in the congruent condition (large print). Table 2 indicates that sentences containing the adjective "larger" are evaluated more rapidly when the print is large while sentences containing the adjective smaller are unaffected by changes in print size.

It is not easy to reconcile these findings with a model of mediated verbal encoding. In such a model (Rubenstein et al., 1971), the obligatory phonemic encoding would tend to reduce and possibly even eliminate differences originating from the visual/graphic level. By the time that the stimuli reached the level of semantic analysis, the congruent and incongruent sentences would probably be indistinguishable from one another.

Conceivably, one could postulate a separate, language-free storage system for visual features such as letter size, but it is difficult to see how the traces of these features would endure sufficiently to interact with the propositional information in the present sentences. Furthermore, conventional models of mediated verbal encoding do not provide for the persistence and influence of nonverbal information in verbal tasks. Instead, the data would appear to be more consistent with the direct access model of lexical processing (Bower, 1970). Since the linguistic and phonemic aspects of sentences in the congruent and incongruent conditions were identical, the congruity effect must be due to the influence of the graphic features of the stimuli on the semantic coding of the sentence. This strongly suggests the presence of a direct route from the graphic characteristics of the stimuli to meaning.

Although the demonstration of a congruity effect for comprehension is interesting, the particular significance of the results is in the extent of the effect. Previous reports of the congruity effect have been confined to the word or attribute that is directly related to the irrelevant dimension. Thus, the word "red" facilitates naming ink colour (Dyer, 1973), a season name facilitates naming the season associated with the colour in which the name is printed (Seymour, 1977), and a northerly direction within a rectangle affects the naming of an arrow pointing in an upward direction (Clark &

Brownell, 1975). A word-by-word examination of the sentences in the present experiment reveals that the adjective is the only term referring to size. Thus, the adjective "taller" signifies a size relationship, whereas the nouns "John" and "Sue" do not. On that basis, the present congruity effect should have been confined to the adjective. However, the results indicate that the congruity effect was obtained for changes in the size of the adjective or in either of the nouns. This suggests that sentences were not analyzed on a word-by-word basis. Instead, it is likely that the words in each sentence were combined to form a unitary proposition or image. Thus the sentence "John is taller than Sue" might have been decoded as "tall John" or "small Sue." In this way, the nouns "John" and "Sue" become as closely associated with the concept of size as the adjectives "taller" and "smaller." This would account for the fact that subject and object nouns were as sensitive to changes in letter size as adjectives.

In conclusion, the data indicate the potential of nonlinguistic cues for the performance of verbal tasks. The adherence to conventional typography in printed texts should not mislead one into thinking that it is necessarily the most appropriate form of presentation. The derivation of meaning from a text is a complex task which can benefit from graphic as well as purely linguistic information.

REFERENCES

Banks, W.P., Fujii, M., & Kayra Stuart, F. Semantic congruity effects in comparative judgements of the magnitude of digits. Journal of Experimental Psychology, 1976, 2, 435-447.

Bower, T.G.R. Reading by eye. In H. Levin and J.P. Williams (Eds.), Basic studies on reading. N.Y.: Basic Books, 1970.

Carpenter, P.A. On the comprehension, storage and retrieval of comparative sentences. Journal of Verbal Learning and Verbal Behavior, 1974, 13, 401-411.

Clark, H.H., & Brownell, H.H. Judging up and down. Journal of Experimental Psychology, 1975, 1, 339-352.

Clark, H.H., & Chase, W.G. On the process of comparing sentences against pictures. Cognitive Psychology, 1972, 3, 472-517.

Coltheart, M., & Freeman, R. Case alternation impairs word identification. Bulletin of the Psychonomic Society, 1974, 3, 102-104.

Dyer, F.N. The Stroop phenomenon and its use in the study of perceptual, cognitive and response processes. Memory & Cognition, 1973, 1, 106-120.

Fisher, D.F. Reading and visual search. Memory & Cognition, 1975, 3, 188-196.

Flowers, J.H., & Dutch, S. The use of visual and name codes in scanning and classifying colours. Memory & Cognition, 1976, 4, 384-390.

Henderson, L., Coltheart, M., & Woodhouse, D. Failure to find a syllabic effect in number naming. Memory & Cognition, 1973, 1, 304-306.

Kolers, P.A. Experiments in reading. Scientific American, 1972, 227, 84-91.

Meyer, D.E., Schvaneveldt, R.W., & Ruddy, M.G. Functions of graphemic and phonemic codes in visual word recognition. Memory & Cognition, 1974, 2, 309-321.

Morton, J. Categories of interference: Verbal mediation and conflict in card sorting. British Journal of Psychology, 1969, 60, 329-346.

Paivio, A. Perceptual comparisons through the mind's eye. Memory & Cognition, 1975, 3, 635-647.

Poulton, E.C. Size, style and vertical spacing in the legibility of small typefaces. Journal of Applied Psychology, 1972, 56, 156-161.

Rubenstein, H., Lewis, S.S., & Rubenstein, M.A. Evidence for phonemic recoding in visual word recognition. Journal of Verbal Learning and Verbal Behavior, 1971, 10, 645-657.

Seymour, P.H.K. Conceptual encoding and the locus of the Stroop effect. Quarterly Journal of Experimental Psychology, 1977, 29, 245-265.

Shaw, P., & Weigel, G.A. Effects of bars and blanks on recognition of words and nonwords embedded in a row of letters. Perception & Psychophysics, 1973, 14, 117-124.

Shor, R.F. The processing of the conceptual information on spatial directions from pictorial and linguistic symbols. Acta Psychologica, 1970, 32, 346-365.

Sloboda, J.A. Decision times for word and letter search: A wholistic word identification model examined. Journal of Verbal Learning and Verbal Behavior, 1976, 15, 93-101.

Spencer, H., Reynolds, L., & Coe, B. A comparison of the effectiveness of selected typographic variations. London: Royal College of Art, 1973, Research report.

Spragins, A.B., Lefton, L.A., & Fisher, D.F. Eye movements while reading and searching spatially transformed text: A developmental examination. Memory & Cognition, 1976, 4, 36-42.

Stroop, V.R. Studies of interference in serial verbal reactions. Journal of Experimental Psychology, 1935, 18, 643-662.

Reading by Eye and Writing by Ear

Uta Frith

*The role of sound in reading is far from clear. Results from
letter-cancellation tasks have been used as evidence for
immediate translation of visible language into sound. An
experiment reported here suggests that this view is not ten-
able and that, on the contrary, the results provide evidence
for immediate lexical identification. Another experiment
on reading misspelled and graphically distorted text also provides evidence against prior phonological encoding. It was
more difficult to read text that preserved only the sound
than text that preserved only the visual outline of the original words. This was true even for very young readers.   It
is likely that sound in reading plays a secondary role.*

*The role of sound in writing, however, appears to be primary
and dominant. Most spelling errors and unintentional slips
of the pen show letter patterns that sound like the target
word. Some experiments are discussed that show that the
same person may read "by eye" and write "by ear." In particular there is a group of people who are good readers and
poor spellers and are unable to coordinate these two strategies. Hence, it is necessary to consider language reception,
as in reading, and language production, as in writing, to be
two separate, specialised skills.*

How closely can we equate spoken and written language? Is reading just
a form of listening and writing just a form of speaking? It would be simpler
to understand both language systems in terms of the same processes. Also,
it seems likely that handling visible language would benefit from the well
rehearsed processes that have been established previously for handling spoken
language. Given this rationale, it is plausible to assume that the way we

recognise written words is first to translate them into sound, then to treat the resulting sounds as if they were heard speech. However, rather than assuming that reading is parasitic on listening, it might be assumed that listening to speech and silently reading prose share the same process for understanding.

Thus, I want to argue for a common process underlying both reading and listening. However, I also want to argue for totally separate processes for language input and language output. I would like to suggest that processes used for reading are different, to the point of incompatibility, from those used for writing. By analogy, processes underlying listening could be different from those used for speaking.

The Role of Sound in Reading

There is an interesting controversy about the extent to which reading is a grapheme-to-phoneme translation task. This may seem odd if one considers reading nonsense words, like "multh." Of course, in this case there must be grapheme-to-phoneme translation. However, with words, a translation into sound may not be a prerequisite for deriving meaning. Thus the question can be asked: Are words translated first into sound and then into meaning, or are words first understood and then sounded out?

Coltheart, Davelaar, Jonasson, and Besner (1977) have reviewed a number of authors who are divided on this question. I shall select and discuss two experiments, each of which has been used as strong support for the two opposing points of view.

One argument in favour of implicit and involuntary translation to sound during silent reading is Corcoran's (1966) letter-cancellation task. In this task subjects had to scan text and cancel the letter "e" whenever it occurred. This experiment suggested that words had been translated into sound because silent e's were missed more often than sounded e's.

One criticism of the cancellation task is that little control was exerted over the kinds of e's that occurred in the texts. One major finding was that the letter "e" when it occurred in the word "the" was missed frequently, and this applied in general to e's as the last letter of a word. However, in English, e as the last letter is almost always silent. Thus a position effect might simply account for apparently more silent e's being missed than any other e's. If this was the case, the result would provide no evidence for phonological coding.

In order to control the position of pronounced and unpronounced e's, I compiled a list of words which contained as many stressed as unstressed syllables with the letter "e", the e occurring equally often at the beginning, middle, or end of the word. Table 1 shows examples of each of these categories. The contrast between stressed and unstressed e (e.g. dimension, compensation) was chosen, as there could not have been control for position with silent e's. Thus e's never occurred as the last letter of a word.

Other controls were also taken with this word list. Half the words in each category contained only one e, half contained two e's. Double e's were excluded, as they attract special attention. The frequency and length (6 to 10 characters) of the words was roughly matched. There were 30 e's in each condition, as shown in Table 1. There were also 30 words that did not contain an e. All words were randomly typed all in lower case, and then again, in a different random order. Both lists, containing the same words, were then

Table 1. e-Cancellation Task: Percentage of Letters Missed. (Based on 30 Words in Each Condition.) Adult Sample (n = 10).

	Stressed e			Unstressed e		
	Beginning	Middle	End	Beginning	Middle	End
	CENTURY	PROFESSOR	SUCCESS	DELIGHT	LIBERTY	INNOCENT
X̄	3.50	1.90	3.80	3.40	1.80	10.40
(SD)	(4.22)	(1.52)	(3.01)	(4.40)	(2.09)	(5.83)

Table 2. e-Cancellation Task: Effect of Letter Position.

Position of Letter in Word		Number of Subjects (out of 10) Who Missed More	
		Stressed e	Unstressed e
Beginning	(CENTURY)	6	3
Middle	(PROFESSOR)	3	2
End	(INNOCENT)	0	10

presented to ten skilled readers.   They were asked to cancel all e's as fast
as possible. The missed e's were then scored and compared between the six
conditions. This method differs from that used by Smith and Groat (this volume,
who used connected prose. Nevertheless, the results are in substantial agreement, with one exception which at present can only be attributed to the differences in method. As Table 1 shows, there was no difference between
stressed and unstressed e's at beginning and middle positions of a word, but
there was a very strong effect in the end position. Table 2 shows that 10
out of 10 people missed more unstressed e's than stressed e's in this particular
position. If only the total numbers of stressed and unstressed e's were compared regardless of position, a significant effect of sound would have appeared.
However, the separation of the positions clearly shows that this is not a general
effect. Thus, because stressed and unstressed e's were missed equally often,
except at the end position, it is unlikely that phonological encoding need
be invoked. In order to retain the phonological encoding hypothesis, one would
have to believe that people only encode the ends of words into sound.

However, even if only in the end position of a word, why were unstressed
e's missed more often than stressed e's? What can account for this very clear-
cut effect? One explanation is as follows: while scanning, people identify
the meaning of the words. They do this involuntarily, even though it is not
required and is even disadvantageous to the task. Identifying the meaning
of a word is compulsive for skilled readers. This is supported by the Stroop
phenomenon in which the meaning of a word, say "green," is recognised and
interferes with the naming of the ink colour the word is printed in, say red.

The explanation requires further that people can often get the meaning
of a word they are looking at, before their scanning has reached the end of
the word. As soon as they have identified the meaning on the basis of beginning and middle of a word, they stop looking at it. Hence e's are likely to
be missed at the end of words.

Why then should unstressed e's be missed more often? It might simply
be because endings containing unstressed e's are more predictable and hence
not necessary for the identification of a word, while endings with stressed
e's are. Conversely, it would be reasonable if syllables that are less predictable would also receive stress. Thus it should follow that words ending with
stressed e are less easy to predict and hence more difficult to identify from
the beginning and middle than words ending with unstressed e. In consequence,
the last syllable would have to be looked at and the e it contains would be
noticed.

The hypothesis that people identified the words ending in a syllable with
unstressed e before and without looking at the ending - and hence missed
the e - was tested as follows. The 60 words used for the condition with stressed
and unstressed e in their last syllable were partially typed, up to the letter
just preceding the critical e (incorr-, conc-, suffic-, appar-). Eight people
were asked to complete them with the first word that came to mind. It was
predicted that the unstressed e words would more likely be completed to
the original word used. In contrast, the stressed e words would be less likely
to be completed to the original form.

This was in fact the result obtained. For the unstressed e list 25 out
of 30 words were completed to the original word; for the stressed list it
was only 19 out of 30. Since all eight subjects obtained higher scores for

e list, this difference is highly significant. It means that when reading parts of words such as conc-, resp-, refr-, the ending cannot be guessed readily. On the other hand, when reading parts of words such as helm-, answ-, evid-, the ending can be guessed. This is probably the same as saying that there were more alternative endings available for stressed list words than for unstressed list words.

The finding of the cancellation task--that more unstressed e's than stressed e's were missed in the last syllable--cannot be explained by phonological coding, unless one made the eccentric claim that such coding only applies to word endings. However, the effect can be explained by assuming fast word identification without sound: word endings that are predictable are skipped. It so happens that these predictable endings often contain unstressed e's. It is possible to extend this explanation to e's in other positions in a word. Thus, it could also partially account for Smith and Groat's (this volume) results that showed an effect of stress regardless of position.

There must still be some doubt whether this explanation is specific to the present word list, which had been made up without any intention to show a difference in predictability in a completion task. It would be possible to test the predictability hypothesis more directly with carefully selected words, where stress was kept constant, and where predictable and unpredictable syllables were contrasted. In any case we must conclude that the evidence provided by Corcoran's (1966) cancellation task for prior phonological encoding is dubious. The same conclusion has also been drawn by Smith and Groat on the basis of their experiments on letter cancellation.

A strong argument against the assumption of involuntary prior translation to sound is provided by an experiment by Bower (1970). He showed that reading was disrupted by graphically altered but phonetically correct text. If understanding text was based entirely on the sound of the text, which has first to be derived from the graphic symbols, then the correct sound should be all that matters, and reading phonetically rendered text should be easy.

However, altered text might well slow down reading just because spelling rules are broken or because the words look unfamiliar. Reading may be further retarded by the necessity to check derived sound with the conventional spelling patterns. Hence, a more critical test of the hypothesis would be to use two different kinds of alterations, one leaving sound intact, the other changing sound. One could then see whether reading was still more disrupted in the condition where sound was altered.

Since it is often assumed that the most likely instance of grapheme-to-phoneme translation should be found at the early stages of reading acquisition (Gibson & Levin, 1975), very young readers (7- year-olds) were used as subjects, in an experiment on reading altered text, and were compared with highly skilled adult readers.

The texts used were stories of 26 words based on the 7- year level of the Neale Analysis of Reading material. Each story was prepared in four different versions, and each subject had to read aloud all four stories, in a different random order. The time taken to read was a measure for the comparison. In addition, subsequent questions checked that the subjects read for meaning.

The four conditions were as follows:

1) Normal text. This provided a baseline. All children could read this version without errors and with perfect comprehension.
2) Each letter in a different script. This distortion removed any cues based on visual familiarity with the outline of words, but left spelling patterns intact.
3) Letters substituted by those that were visually similar. This distortion removed sound cues (e.g. "bock" for "book"), but left visual outline intact.
4) Graphemes substituted by those that were phonologically similar. This distortion removed visual outline cues (e.g. "taibl" for "table"), but left sound intact.

Some attempt was made to equate the degree of distortion between these last two conditions. This was done by having 20 people judge the extent of the alteration for each word, and using those that obtained similar ratings. Hence it was justified to make the crucial comparison between the visually similar and the phonologically similar text. In both conditions spelling patterns were altered. Any slowing down due to unfamiliarity should therefore

Table 3. Reading Distorted Text: Average Reading Times (sec) for a Paragraph of 26 Words.

	Children (n = 13)		Adults (n = 8)	
	Mean	(SD)	Mean	(SD)
Normal text	11.7	(3.4)	5.9	(1.4)
Distorted text				
Spelling preserved[1]	16.7	(5.6)	6.4	(1.2)
Look preserved[2]	25.3	(13.0)	7.5	(2.2)
Sound preserved[3]	30.9	(11.7)	10.1	(2.3)

1. *A rObiN ꓘopPeD*

2. A robln hoppeb up to my windcw

3. A robbin hoppt up to my winndo

be similar for both. However, with prior phonological encoding one would predict that it should be easier to read the distortion that preserved sound. Table 3 shows the results, which do not support this prediction. Unskilled and skilled readers were alike in the pattern of performance, and this pattern is clearly counter to the phonological encoding hypothesis. Both groups found text that only sounded correct harder to read than text that only looked correct ($t(7) = 3.33$, $p < .05$ for the adults; $t(12) = 2.32$, $p < .05$ for the children). Hence, it is likely that reading for meaning even at an early stage of acquisition is "by eye," rather than "by ear."

Another result was that text in multiple script was surprisingly easy to read. Presumably, the correct spelling pattern, which was preserved in this condition, was sufficient for word recognition. Reading "by eye" therefore does not imply making use of purely graphic outline cues. Orthographic structure, even if represented in severe graphic distortion, can be extracted and used to understand meaning.

What then can be concluded, on the basis of the evidence given here, about the role of sound in reading? The hypothesis of phonological encoding is unchallenged for explaining how nonsense and unfamiliar words are read. However, it is severely challenged and, indeed, appears untenable for explaining how meaningful reading matter is read, even if this is full of graphic distortions or misspellings, even at very early stages of reading skill.

It seems likely that, in normal reading, sound does not play the role of a conveyor of meaning. However, it undoubtedly does play a role in other aspects of reading. There is more to reading than getting the meaning. Written poetry and indeed most works of literature cannot be fully appreciated unless we take account of their sound qualities. We also want to remember what we read. Conrad (1972) has argued convincingly that it is advantageous in terms of how memory works to translate visible language into an acoustic code. Thus, sound must be considered to be frequently involved in reading, but only after meaning has been arrived at, or when meaning could not be arrived at.

What happens before meaning is arrived at? I would like to suggest that even in listening to speech, we do not listen to sounds that are then analysed and perceived as words. Rather, we listen to words, which we construct from a combination of cues, visual, auditory, semantic, cognitive, etcetera.

I would like to emphasise that this hypothesis applies to both listening and reading and that it applies to meaningful language input only. Both language reception systems, for visible and for spoken language, may largely rely on a common process that we know little about, but that is likely to be quite unspecific to modality.

The Role of Sound in Writing
Psychologists have taken an extraordinary interest in reading, but they have strangely neglected writing or spelling. Thus, I can appear to be entirely uncontroversial in my statements, based as they are on a very limited amount of data. The experiments I shall briefly describe were all carried out on a small sample of 12- year- old school children.

The hypothesis put forward is that the role of sound is of overriding importance in writing or written spelling. There are two sources of evidence for this hypothesis: frequent spelling errors and unintentional writing errors (i.e., slips of the pen).

It has been frequently observed that most spelling errors are phonetic, that is, they sound similar to the target word but do not have the correct letter pattern (Simon, 1976). Hotopf (in press) in an analysis of slips of the pen has found that a high proportion, about 20%, can be attributed unambiguously to confusions between similar sounds ("their" for "there"). In contrast, there are hardly any slips that can be unambiguously attributed to visual confusions, such as "these" for "there" -- even though they may look very similar in handwriting. Hotopf suggests that words are retrieved as they are heard , not as they are seen.

An interesting problem now arises. Having dismissed phonological coding for reading, I now propose phonological coding for writing. This implies that word recognition processes, as in reading, and word production processes, as in writing, are handled by totally different systems. If there were little sharing of processes between recognition and production systems, the following prediction could be made. There should be people who possess excellent skill in one process, and at the same time have poor skill in the other.

In view of the fact that people with such a discrepancy in reading and spelling skills have not been described or investigated, it was surprisingly easy to find them. Out of about 200 12-year-olds, 10 children with average intelligence and average reading ability, were seriously below average in spelling ability. Table 4 shows their (Group B) reading and spelling scores expressed as a quotient with a supposed average of 100. There were two comparison groups, also shown in the table, also of average intelligence, who were either good at both reading and spelling (Group A) or poor at both (Group C).

The number of spelling errors was the same for Group B and Group C and much higher in both than in Group A. A qualitative analysis of the type of error made was carried out regardless of the absolute number of errors. Three results are of interest. First, the analysis confirmed that for good readers at least, most spelling errors were phonetic, that is they preserved the sound of the target word. Thus, it seems likely that the misspellings were often produced from their sound, not from their visual forms. Second, for poor readers who are also poor spellers, spelling errors were as often phonetic as not. The simplest interpretation of this result is that these children did not know sound-letter correspondence rules very well. Only in half their errors did they apply such rules with any success. Third, for good readers who are poor spellers, just as for good spellers, most errors preserved the sound of the target word. Thus, we can conclude that these poor spellers were able to use phoneme-to-grapheme rules very well, as opposed to the other group of poor spellers. Their problem may well be that they rely too much on such rules. English orthography is only partially guided by straightforward sound-letter correspondence rules. Moreover, even in very regular words there are often a large number of graphemes to choose from for the same phoneme. It would seem to be unwise as well as misleading to rely primarily on sound-letter rules for spelling.

Thus, from the analysis of spelling errors there can be little doubt about the important role of sound in writing. This is the more convincing as a sound-based strategy is not generally advantageous.

Table 4. Spelling Error Analysis of the Three Groups.*

Percentage of Spelling Errors	Group A (n = 10)		Group B (n = 10)		Group C (n = 9)	
	Mean	(SD)	Mean	(SD)	Mean	(SD)
Sound is not preserved (e.g., lowet, agian)	19.1	(15.6)	29.6	(9.6)	49.8	(15.9)
Sound is preserved (e.g., lowist, agane)	76.1	(20.3)	67.2	(11.2)	44.7	(11.9)
Schonell Spelling Quotient	109	(6.1)	89	(9.8)	82	(9.4)
Schonell Reading Quotient	105	(5.6)	100	(9.0)	80	(9.9)

*Based on Schonell graded spelling test performance of 12-year-olds.

Group A = good readers, good spellers; Group B = good readers, poor spellers;
Group C = poor readers, poor spellers.

Table 5. Ability to Read One's Own Spelling Errors. Percentage of Words Read Correctly and Without Hesitation (Based on 20 Words). 12-Year-Old Sample.

Groups		Own Correct Spellings		Own Incorrect Spellings	
		Mean	(SD)	Mean	(SD)
Good spellers (also good readers)	A	96.1	(6.3)	90.8	(12.7)
Poor spellers (but good readers)	B	93.5	(6.8)	78.3	(14.4)
Poor spellers (also poor readers)	C	92.8	(6.8)	64.9	(23.1)

A very strong prediction could now be made for the group of children who showed a discrepancy in reading and spelling. If reading proceeds by eye and spelling in this group proceeds by ear, then the same person should have some difficulty in reading his own misspellings.

This prediction was tested by presenting the typewritten versions of the children's own misspellings mixed with words that they had spelled correctly. Table 5 shows the results. As expected, there was a low rate of errors or hesitations. Nevertheless, it was found that both groups B and C experienced a significant increase in difficulty when reading their own errors ($t(9) = 3.01$, $p < .02$ for B; $t(8) = 3.73$, $p < .01$ for C). For Group C this result is difficult to interpret, as half of their errors did preserve sound and half did not. For Group B however, we could say, that the "inner eye" did not see what the "inner ear" wrote.

There might be some doubt whether Group B, which apparently strongly depends on sound in writing, would not after all also depend on sound in reading. Several experiments, of which I shall describe just one, showed that this was unlikely.

This experiment used a rhyming task. For the appreciation of rhyme, sound is essential, even in silent reading. Hence, if Group B did normally prefer sound-based strategies in reading, then presumably they would be at an advantage, or at least not at a disadvantage, when asked to say whether two words rhymed or not. All three groups of children were given such a task. They were given a long list of word- pairs, such as soap-rope or peat-pear, and they had to go through this list silently, ticking each rhyming pair and crossing each non-rhyming one. They had to go as fast as possible and the number of pairs correctly judged in 60 sec was the score. It was found that Group B was significantly less proficient than Group A ($t(18) = 2.36$, $p < .05$), and at about the same level as Group C, who had of course also been much poorer on the Schonell reading test. Thus, sound is unlikely to be a preferred reading strategy for Group B. This is also confirmed by the finding that Group B found phonetically rendered text more difficult to read than text that bore strong visual similarity to the original. Therefore we may safely assume that the predominant use of sound for producing written words cannot be accounted for by a predominant use of sound for recognising written words.

Can we again draw an analogy between writing and speaking? Is there a contrast between these two language output systems, and the input systems of reading and listening?

Dodd (1975) found that very young children, listening to their own imperfectly rendered speech, do not understand their own phonological forms if they deviate markedly from the correct phonological form. This result is directly analogous to poor spellers not being able to read their own misspellings. A contrast between input and output in listening and speech can also be observed in young infants who are able to discriminate many sounds that they cannot produce. The same phenomenon is observed when learning a foreign language.

The following hypothesis is therefore quite general for visible and spoken language: the quality of perceptual input discrimination is independent of the quality of output. A "good ear" or a "good eye" does not entail automatically good speech or spelling. Conversely, we can postulate that poor auditory or poor visual discrimination is no explanation for poor speech or spelling.

The theory that this set of experiments would support states that word recognition and word production have to be considered as separate processes.

Table 6. Rhyming Task. 12-Year-Old Sample.

Groups		Number of Pairs Judged Correctly in 60 Sec	
		X̄	(SD)
Good spellers (also good readers)	A	36.5	(5.1)
Poor spellers (but good readers)	B	29.1	(8.4)
Poor spellers (also poor readers)	C	23.6	(3.4)

Examples: soap-rope, third-word, fine-lane, peat-pear.

However, ideally, there should be cross-connections, so that the inner eye and inner ear are able to communicate. That the cross-connections can be very poor is suggested by the existence of people who are good readers but very poor spellers.

The potential incompatibility of reading and writing might be further investigated in terms of a difference in site of brain control or in terms of a difference in preferred modality. Alternatively, and more directly, it could be investigated in terms of differences in input and output systems in general. At this stage, it seems likely that one needs to go beyond looking and listening, if one really wants to understand more about visible and audible language.

I thank Ms Jocelyn Robson and Ms Maggie Snowling for their substantial help in carrying out the experiments reported.

REFERENCES

Bower, T. G. R. Reading by eye. In H. Levin & J. P. Williams (Eds.), Basic studies on reading. New York: Basic Books, 1970.

Coltheart, M., Davelaar, E., Jonasson, J. T., & Besner, D. Access to the internal lexicon. In S. Dornic & P. M. A. Rabbitt (Eds.), Attention and performance VI. Hillsdale, NJ: Erlbaum, 1977.

Conrad, R. The relationship between speech and reading. In J. F. Kavanagh & I. G. Mattingly (Eds.), Language by ear and by eye. Cambridge, MA: MIT Press, 1972.

Corcoran, D. W. J. An acoustic factor in letter cancellation. Nature, 1966, 210, 658.

Dodd, B. Children's understanding of their own phonological forms. Quarterly Journal of Experimental Psychology, 1975, 27, 165-172.

Gibson, E. J., & Levin, H. The psychology of reading. Cambridge, MA: MIT Press, 1975.

Hotopf, N. Slips of the pen and slips of the tongue. In U. Frith (Ed.), Cognitive processes in spelling. London: Academic Press, in press.

Simon, D. P. Spelling--a task analysis. Instructional Science, 1976, 5, 277-302.

Smith, P.T., & Groat, A. Spelling patterns, letter cancellation, and the processing of text. (This volume.)

A Comparison of Explicit and Implicit Knowledge of an Alphabet

Lee Brooks and Amina Miller

*Several instances are reported in which an adult who is
learning to fluently pronounce a set of artifical words persistently performs more slowly after he is taught the underlying alphabet than when he either does not know the alphabet
or the alphabet does not exist. We suggest that this does
not result from the subject slowly applying unfamiliar general
rules; rather, the effect seems to be some word-specific
after-effect of what at first was decoding by general rules.
For example, the reader might attend only to cues that are
relevant for an initial decoding of a word and omit cues,
such as overall form, that would be useful for identification
of that word later in practice. Or, the application of the
rules to a particular word might become such a specific,
routine process that little of the practice with that word
generalizes to the decoding of new words.*

When a person pronounces a familiar word written in an alphabetic writing
system, there are, in principle, two radically different ways he could accom-
plish this. At one extreme, he could use the visual cues or letter identities
to look up the specific word in memory and find stored there the instructions
for producing the correct pronunciation. In the traditional view this process
is completely "rote" since there is no influence of the spelling-to-sound correspondences and little generalization to learning other items. Instead, the
reader simply has to learn which features distinguish this word from any
others appropriate to the context. At the other extreme, the reader could
apply general spelling-to-sound rules very rapidly with the result that any
legal word could be pronounced, and any word in the spoken vocabulary could
be accessed for meaning with something like phonological cues.

Although these mechanisms sound quite different in principle, when an attempt is made to specify them and use them to account for a set of data, they do not have clearly different consequences. We would like to document this point by discussing data collected from adults who were learning to pronounce a small set of words written in artificial letters. Artificial material was used in order to produce or eliminate spelling-to-sound correspondences and to study their effect on the identification of words printed in these letters. Adults were tested since it was assumed that they were capable of using an alphabet for the purposes it is normally used.

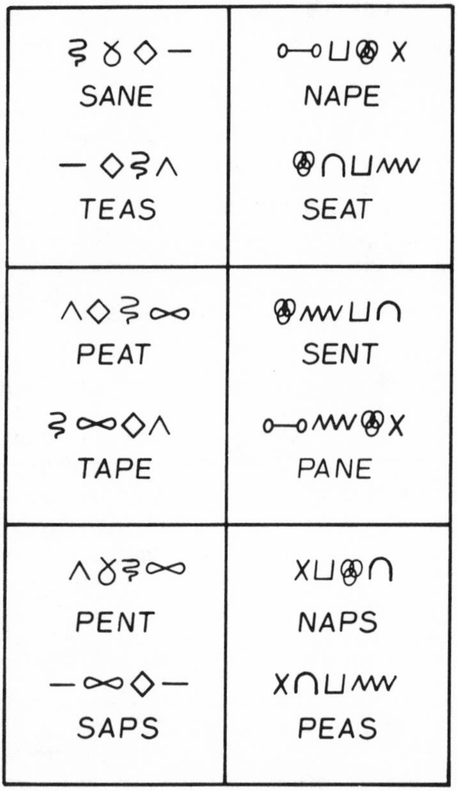

Figure 1. A sample set of material. For the list of words on the right there is no systematic correspondence between the symbols and the letters or sounds of the associated response. For the words in the left column there is an alphabetic relation if the symbols are decoded from right to left. The words were introduced to the subjects in mixed sets of four, with the top four being mastered before the next four were introduced, and these eight mastered before the bottom four were introduced.

A Study of the Effect of Alphabetic Knowledge

For this study two lists of twelve words were used, one of which is shown
in Figure 1. Six of the words in each list were written with one set of symbols
and the other six with a different set. In order to keep the existence of an
alphabet from being obvious, the words were spelled with the artificial letters
ordered from right to left. For one of the symbol sets, the six responses
were reassigned to different symbol strings so that there were no consistent
spelling-to-sound correspondences in that set. The set of words that remained
alphabetic and the set that had the responses reassigned were counterbalanced
across subjects. The overall effect was to produce two conditions, balanced
on the average for stimulus and response characteristics; in one there was
a set of non-obvious spelling-to-sound correspondences, and in the other there
were no correspondences.

One of the groups of eight McMaster undergraduates that we tested was
told that they would be working with an artificial alphabet and was given
a preliminary period to study the associations between the relevant six artificial symbols and the six corresponding English letters. When they were able
to identify the symbols with the name of the associated English letter at
the rate of at least 30 symbols in 45 seconds, they were told that some of
the words that they were about to see would be spelled from right to left
with these symbols, and the other words would be made up of a different
set of symbols for which no alphabet existed. In either case they were to
learn the correct responses and eventually produce them as rapidly as possible.

Throughout the subsequent word training and testing procedure we were
careful to treat the two types of words equally. For reasons that will become
clear, we chose a training method that could easily be construed as a whole
word method. In the preliminary word training phase a subject was shown
a set of four words one at a time, two words coming from each condition
(for example, the top four words in Figure 1), and was told the response for
that word. The four words were then presented in a different order, and
the subject was asked to identify each one. When the subject had gone
through these words twice correctly, another two alphabetic and another
two non-correspondence words (for example, the middle four words in Figure 1)
were mixed in. Again the subject was shown the words one at a time, was
asked to identify the old words, and was immediately given the correct response for the new words. When the subject had correctly identified each
word on two successive passes through the eight words, the remaining four
words were included and the subject was taken through the same process
on the entire list of twelve. Notice that throughout this procedure the two
types of words were mixed together, and the subjects were never asked to
explicitly decode the alphabetic words although, of course, they could if they
so chose. Our procedure of introducing the words in small sets minimized
the number of errors and was intended to increase the chances that both
types of words could be practiced with a minimum of decoding or prompting
from the experimenter.

Immediately following this training phase, the speed of the subjects' responses was measured during eighty additional trials on each condition. On
a given trial the six cards from one condition were spread out in random
sequence in front of the subject (approximately 12 cm between items that
themselves were 2.5 to 3.5 cm wide) and the subject was asked to identify

all six of them as rapidly as possible. A single response time was taken for all six items, and correction was given for the very infrequent errors. Five trials were given in one condition followed by five in the other, alternating up to a total of eighty trials for each condition.

In order to be certain that any effects obtained were not due solely to the procedure of testing the words in groups of six, responses to the twelve items were individually timed in a single randomly ordered list after ten group trials on each condition, up to the end of the seventieth trial. To insure accurate timing on these trials, the stimuli were shown for 5 sec in a tachistoscope with a timer that started automatically with the presentation of an item; the onset of the subject's response in a voice key stopped the clock.

At this point the subjects were transfered to a very similar list of twelve new words (sate, past, span, nets, pans, stem; pats, nest, tans, step, snap, pate) with one six-word set written in the now familiar alphabetic symbols and the other six-word set in the non-alphabetic symbols. All details of the training and testing procedure were the same except that only thirty group timing trials were carried out for each condition (again, in alternating five trial blocks), with one individually timed trial after each ten trials on each of the conditions.

The Effect of Explicit Alphabetic Knowledge
For both kinds of timed trials and for both lists the words for which the underlying alphabet were known were identified significantly less rapidly than were the non-alphabetic words (see group A in Figure 2). This effect and its persistence are remarkable for several reasons. First is the strictly technical reason that the lists were carefully matched and exactly the same stimuli and responses were used across subjects in the two conditions. Second, the experiment was carried out within subjects, and since all of the subjects reported noticing that they performed faster on the non-alphabetic conditions, this might have prompted them to adopt a more efficient strategy for the alphabetic items. Third, the training procedure would have allowed the subjects to treat both sets of words identically, which might not have been the case if large numbers of words had been used or if we had ever required the subjects to decode the alphabetic words. We first found an effect like this in a pair of collaborative experiments done with Jon Baron (Baron, 1977; Brooks, 1977). But in that experiment, since our interest was with asymptotic performance (which will be commented upon in a moment), we did not treat the alphabetic and non-alphabetic items identically at the beginning of the procedure as was done in the present experiment. Finally, the effect continues into a second list, at which point one might have expected either increasing facility with the alphabet or a shift in strategy to have markedly attenuated the disadvantage of the alphabetic items.

A reasonable first guess about the source of this disadvantage for the explicit alphabet might be that the subjects were persistently applying the rather unfamiliar symbol-to-letter or to-sound correspondences that they had just learned. There is a sense in which this might be true, but first we must notice that a reasonable portion of the improvement in identification speed for the alphabetic items is specific to the list; when a new set of items using the same letters is introduced, times for the alphabetic items go up at least as much as for the non-correspondence items. If correspondence

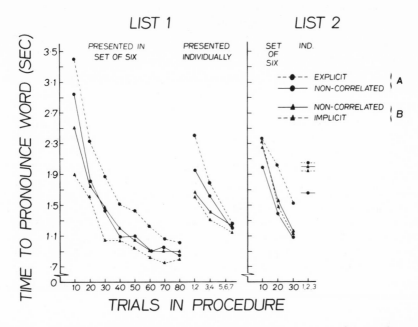

Figure 2. Results of the timed trials. Subjects in group A (circles) explicitly knew that one of the lists was made up of words that were spelled alphabetically and that in the other list there were no symbol-to-sound correspondences. Subjects in group B (triangles) were not told and apparently did not discover the alphabetic relationships. The plotted times are either one-sixth of the time taken to identify all six words in a condition or times taken from interspersed trials in which the words were timed individually.

rules were still being applied just before transfer, the rules would have become so conditional or the method of application so routine that very little of the practice with these words would have generalized to new words even though they were composed of the same letters and many of the same letter combinations. As Kolers (1973, 1975) has pointed out, it may still be useful to conceive of memory for items as a set of operations rather than a list of encoded aspects, but the word-specific operations necessary to account for the present data are clearly different from the general application of rules usually referred to in discussions of alphabetic decoding. As a possible analogy, imagine that a subject were given a multiplication problem to work mentally. The first time that he went through it he might in fact be brushing up on his general multiplication skills, but if he persisted in going through each of the steps on subsequent presentations of the same problem, the nature of the operations would change, particularly if the presentations were massed (see Jacoby, in press). So, even if the steps were run off they would no longer constitute practice on general rules.

Another way of looking at the biasing effect of explicit knowledge of the alphabet is to focus on the unused information in the printed word. In order to apply general pronunciation rules, the learner has to attend to particular information in the word. Having once organized his encoding around that information he might perform subsequent trials using only that information and organization, even though more distinctive information might be available.

A striking example of this is given by an experiment first described in Brooks (1977). The artificial letters in that experiment were either arranged in normal left-to-right order as discrete strings of symbols, or they were arranged from top to bottom in the form of connected glyphs (Figure 3.) The subjects learned 24 words printed in one of these forms to a criterion of correctly naming them at the rate of one per sec. They then learned a list of 24 new words printed with the same symbols but arranged in the other form (i.e., first glyphic, then discrete, or for other subjects vice-versa). This procedure was repeated for another two lists of new words. Finally, the 48 glyphic words were combined into a single list and practiced again to the one-per-sec rate as were the 48 discrete words (again in balanced order across subjects). For the group of subjects who were first taught the alphabet, there was not much difference between the glyphic and discrete forms (Table 1) until they had to combine them later. For the subjects in the non-correspondence condition (produced by reassociation of stimuli and responses,

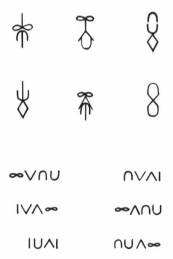

Figure 3. Two ways of arranging the artificial letters. Both the glyphic form, to be scanned from top to bottom, and the discrete form, to be scanned from left to right, are composed of the same artificial letters and consequently have the same potential for signalling phonological values. The intention in arranging the letters in the glyphic form was to increase the overall distinctiveness of the words.

as in the present paper) the difference was striking. Apparently a visual difference as robust as the one shown in Figure 3 was not exploited by the explicit alphabet subjects until after considerable practice.

While the persistent nature of the encoding disadvantage has been stressed, we already possess data that indicate that it is overcome with enough practice. In the collaborative experiments with Baron, after approximately 180 practice trials on each of two six-word lists similar to the ones used in the present experiment, performance on the alphabetic list became significantly faster than on the non-correspondence list. One of these experiments also included alphabetic and non-alphabetic lists printed in the glyphic format. Performance on the glyphic alphabetic list became faster than on the discrete alphabetic list after about 60 trials and faster than on the glyphic no-correspondence list after 200 trials, indicating that the advantage of distinctive visual form did gradually become effective. However, considering that there were only six words in any one of these lists, these numbers of trials are high. Unfortunately, we did not transfer the subjects in either of these two experiments to a new list, so we cannot comment on whether such intensive practice on a single list would have led to more general transfer than was obtained in the present experiment. However, the study referred to in Table 1 (as well as another study reported in Brooks, 1977) involved at least as many total exposures to artificial words as did the Baron and Brooks studies, and the word-specific effect of practice remained substantially more impressive than the general transferable effect. Finally, since in all of the studies mentioned in this paragraph the explicit alphabet items were printed in the normal left-to-right order, we know that the disadvantage of the explicit alphabet condition in the present study was not due to the backward order of the printing.

We obviously cannot specify the circumstances under which the restrictive effects of initial alphabetic decoding will be this persistent. However, if a major condition is that the learner is under too much pressure for speed

Table 1.   Trials to a Criterion of One Identification Per Sec. D_1 and D_2 Refer to Two Lists of 24 Words Each Printed in the Discrete Format. G_1 and G_2 Refer to Two 24-Word Lists in the Glyphic Format.

Lists:		Mean Trials to Criterion				
	D_1	G_1	D_2	G_2	D_{1+2}	G_{1+2}
Explicit alphabet group	79.6	83.8	50.2	45.4	37.6	23.4
No-correspondence group	81.5	26.0	42.0	27.0	28.5	24.0

or from competing aspects of the reading process to devote attention to amending the basis of encoding, then such circumstances could be fairly widespread and could interact with methods of teaching reading. At the very least we must be cautious in assuming that learners will very rapidly rely on or even include the most efficient cues for distinguishing the words in a given context.

The Implicit Effect of an Alphabet

Another group of eight subjects was trained and tested on the material shown in Figure 1 with the one difference that they were not told of the existence of the right-to-left alphabet. The idea of using the right-to-left scan to hide the existence of an alphabet was originated by Baron and Hodge (1978). Despite the fact that most of their subjects reported that they had no idea that an alphabet existed, performance was faster and more accurate on the implicit alphabetic items than on the matched no-correspondence items. This same result was subsequently found by Brooks (1978b) with materials similar to those in Figure 1. The general result was again replicated in the group timed trials for the first list of the present experiment (see group B in Figure 2), although the best that can be said for the other measures is that they were generally in the right direction. We obviously need to discuss the strength and consistency of the effect, but for the moment we will assert that there are at least some circumstances in which an advantage can be found for an alphabet of whose existence the subjects profess complete ignorance.

There are two general ways of interpreting this outcome. One is to say that in fact the subjects had to some degree learned the correspondences between parts of the stimulus and parts of the response. However, while we can all think of many everyday instances in which we show behavioural evidence for rules that we cannot consciously report, this is an explanation that is badly strained in the present circumstances. Our subjects were articulate adults who reported looking for possible correspondences and giving up. Since we were not trying to interview them on learning accomplished earlier, we do not have to contend with the extremely poor memory conditions that normally affect our everyday reports. Yet despite this our subjects were unable after the experiment to match the six artificial symbols with a list of the six English letters at above-chance accuracy. Further, they expressed surprise at the idea that there had been the backward right-to-left ordering in the material they had just learned and instead reported using the selective, semantic type of mnemonics commonly reported in the non-correspondence conditions.

The other interpretation of the advantage for an implicit alphabet is that it is a result of general similarity relations. One of the consequences of an alphabetic system is that, on average, words that look alike sound alike. As a result of this, mechanisms such as stimulus or response generalization could produce transfer effects without the subjects knowing the component correspondences (see Baron and Hodge, 1978, and Brooks, 1978b, for discussions of these possibilities; Reber and Allen, 1978, and Brooks, 1978a, debate similar points for the implicit learning of concepts and artificial grammars). The curious thing is that in the reading literature the process of rote whole word-learning usually has the reputation of producing either no interword transfer or only negative transfer. But both the associative study of memory and the cognitive study of retrieval structures have suggested many sources of positive transfer without using the correspondences between parts of the stimulus and parts of the response that exist in an explicit use of the alphabet. That is, the fact that words that look alike also sound alike might be an important retrieval cue, independent of knowledge about which symbols went with which component sounds.

Having convinced ourselves of the likelihood of a positive effect of an implicit alphabet, we now have to acknowledge that we do not have the empirical control of the phenomenon to be able to evaluate its importance. Figure 2 shows the typical, frustrating, results obtained on several recent studies. We had hoped for several reasons that the effect might be stronger after transfer to a new list, but the rather strange results for the group B no-correspondence condition on list 2 do not give us confidence that we even have a clear negative effect.

Regardless of the interpretation of these results, there are two final comments that should be made. One is that the effect of an implicit alphabet is consistently in the opposite direction from that of an explicit alphabet. The implicit condition thus acts as a control to assure us that the disadvantage of the explicit condition is due to the knowledge and use of the alphabet, not solely to the effect of its existence on similarity relations among items. The final comment is that we have no difficulty getting robust signs of implicit learning of the orthography (the legal symbol sequences in the stimuli) for our artificial words. After the experiment shown in Table 1 was complete, the no-correspondence subjects were given a new set of items half of which spelled legal words and half of which were random strings made from the same letters. Recall that the no-correspondence condition was produced by spelling words in one of the artificial alphabets and then re-associating stimuli and responses within the list. This means that the stimuli retained their within-item structure, that is, their orthography. But, since the spelling-to-sound correspondences had been destroyed, the subjects could not make decisions about the orthographic regularity of an item by sounding it out. Despite their inability to give orthographic rules that even remotely accounted for their performance (a typical statement was that the illegal strings "looked funny"), these subjects were able to sort over 75% of the items correctly.

Mechanisms for Producing Pronunciations
In the introduction, two extreme mechanisms for producing pronunciations were outlined. Although extreme, they contain a common assumption of which we need to be quite wary: that generalizable knowledge is equivalent to usable general rules. One connotation of the word rule is that it is a powerful, generally applicable procedure that has at least the potential for being verbally communicated. This of course is a legitimate use in the context of talking about methods of instruction. The problem is that there are important forms of generalizable knowledge that bear little resemblance to the general rules that are useful in explicit teaching.

The most extreme form of non-rule-like generalizable knowledge is in the use of analogy. In analogy a person uses one or more specific instances to guide his response to a different instance. Baron (1977) and Glushko and

Rumelhart (1977) have produced evidence that strongly implicates something as specific as analogy in the pronunciation of pseudowords. In the Glushko and Rumelhart study, pseudowords like BINT were pronounced more slowly than pseudowords like BINK, presumably because of the availability of the exception word PINT for the former pseudoword and the absence of such an exception for the latter. Note that this explanation assumes that one, and possibly more, visually similar, real words are elicited by the pseudoword and influence its pronunciation. This type of mechanism could also partly explain the fact that both Baron and Strawson (1976) and Glushko and Rumelhart found that regular real words are pronounced more rapidly than exception words; regular words then would be words that have consistent analogies and exception words are words that have not. A comparable explanation could be given for the effect of the implicit alphabet in the present study, and possibly also the eventual superiority of the explicit alphabetic condition reported in Brooks (1977) and Baron (1977). That is, because of the similarity relations that are a consequence of the alphabet, the responses that are evoked by the similar alphabetic items are more compatible than those evoked by the non-alphabetic items. In this case of the implicit alphabet, we have a special reason for using this kind of explanation, unless we are willing to assume that the subjects had within a few trials induced letter-to-sound correspondences in such an unconscious fashion as to be unaware even of the principle of the backward scanning order.

The relevance of this to pronunciation mechanisms is that generalizable knowledge is assumed to come from the elicitation of individual instances. Such an explanation underlines the perverseness of the results of this study. The condition that started with the apparent application of general rules resulted in a relatively inefficient word-specific access procedure. The condition that started with learning specific associations to stimulus items can plausibly be interpreted as having resulted in more productive generalization between items. We do not believe that these results are as whimsical as they might seem. Many methods of teaching reading start with general rules because the general rules are relatively easy to communicate. However, we suspect that when a person attains the ability to respond rapidly he is using a combination of word-specific access and generalizable knowledge that, in the main, is specific to the point of including analogies. The processes by which general rules influence the development of specific associations, as well as the processes by which the general rules become the highly conditional rules and analogies that probably carry much of the load in rapid responding, are ones that undoubtedly should repay study.

The research in this paper was supported by a grant from the National Research Council of Canada. We thank Larry Jacoby for valuable discussions on this topic.·

REFERENCES

Baron, J. Mechanisms for pronouncing printed words: Use and acquisition. In D. LaBerge and S.J. Samuels (Eds.), Basic processes in reading: Perception and comprehension. Hillsdale, NJ: Erlbaum, 1977.

Baron, J., & Hodge, J. Using spelling-sound correspondences without trying to learn them. Visible Language, 1978, 12, 55-70.

Baron, J. & Strawson, C. Use of orthographic and word-specific knowledge in reading words aloud. Journal of Experimental Psychology: Human Perception and Performance, 1976, 2, 386-393.

Brooks, L.R. Visual pattern in fluent word identification. In A.S. Reber & D. Scarborough (Eds.), Toward a psychology of reading. Hillsdale, NJ: Erlbaum, 1977.

Brooks, L.R. Non-analytic concept formation and memory for instances. In E. Rosch and B. Lloyd (Eds.), Cognition and categorization. Hillsdale, NJ: Erlbaum, 1978. (a)

Brooks, L.R. Non-analytic correspondences and pattern in word identification. In J. Réquin (Ed.), Attention and performance VII. Hillsdale, NJ: Erlbaum, 1978. (b).

Glushko, R.J., & Rumelhart, D.E. Orthographically regular and irregular words: Pronunciation by analogy. Manuscript of a talk presented at Psychonomic Society meeting, November, 1977.

Jacoby, L.L. On interpreting the effects of repetition: Solving a problem versus remembering a solution. Journal of Verbal Learning and Verbal Behavior, in press.

Kolers, P.A. Remembering operations. Memory & Cognition, 1973, 1, 347-355.

Kolers, P.A. Memorial consequences of automatized encoding. Journal of Experimental Psychology: Human Learning and Memory, 1975, 1, 689-701.

Reber, A.S. & Allen, R. Analogic and abstraction strategies in synthetic grammar learning: A functionalist interpretation. Cognition, 1978, 6, 189-221.

The Perception of Language Cohesion during Fluent Reading

L. J. Chapman

One of the significant distinguishing features between the performance of 74 eight-year-old fluent and non-fluent readers was the ability to integrate anaphoric relationships in reading continuous texts. This was demonstrated by using the semantic field of pronouns as an experimental variable. It was found that the fluent readers could more frequently supply the missing pronouns than the non-fluent readers. It was also found that although the general level of perform- ance improved when the missing words were supplied, the non-fluent readers improved very little.

It is suggested that these findings support the proposition that the perception of cohesive ties, by providing cues for textual integration and the recovery of meaning, is a major determinant of reading fluency.

Much has been written during the last decade about the process of learning to read and its relationship to the spoken language ability of children. It has often been pointed out that the child has acquired his language naturally and that by the time reading instruction begins the process of learning is virtually complete (Smith, 1972). However, in any class of children it can be observed that some rapidly become fluent readers— some even prior to schooling (Clark, 1976) — while others do not. In this paper it is suggested that, when some children are faced with the difficulties of reading continuous text, underlying language competence may not be sufficiently established for fluency to develop successfully, even though spoken language ability appears to be fully operational.

A great deal of the research in reading has been concerned with the minutiae of the reading process. This emphasis probably stems from inves- tigations concerned with the initial stages of children's learning to read (e.g., the processing of small units like the perception of letters and the recognition of words). However, while the value of such work is acknowledged, children are not thought to be reading until a degree of fluency has been established. And fluency, by definition, requires texts that are larger units than letters or words. In addition, in the real world, as opposed to laboratory situations, the vast majority of readers are faced with continuous texts of various types.

It is important, therefore, that attempts be made to explore some of those features that characterise texts that are more than one sentence long. Some recent proposals by linguists on the characteristics of texts seem apposite. Halliday and Hasan (1976), for example, have suggested that it is the potential for cohesion that distinguishes a text from a non-text or haphazard collection of words. Various elements are specified as creating cohesion -- that continuity that exists between one part of a text and another. At each stage of the discourse, cohesive elements give points of contact with what has preceded; these elements or points of contact have been termed cohesive ties.

The functioning of these cohesive ties, it is suggested, give a text semantic unity so that the reader, when recovering the meaning of the passage, must perceive them swiftly and accurately. The reader will also be cued by them to supply other linkages to those exophoric elements that are not actually in the text, but that relate it to outside features required for its comprehension. These features have been described as "all those components of the picture which are not present in the text but are necessary to its interpretation." (Halliday & Hasan, 1976).

The nature of text cohesion can be illustrated by simply splitting related pairs of sentences. When presented with the second sentence of a pair in isolation, a fluent reader will explore the various cohesive ties to recover as much of the meaning as possible. Thus, for example, when presented with (a) "Two rolled off it and stopped, as though arrested by a witch's wand, at Mrs. Oliver's feet," the reader recognises at once that it is an incomplete message. Notice how the reader's attention centres on certain words like "Two" and "it." Two what are being referred to, and what is the antecedent of it? The reader continually seeks semantic integration. If sentence (a) is preceded by (a') "Joyce, a sturdy thirteen year old, seized a bowl of apples", the earlier unrelated "two" is immediately linked with apples, and similarly "it" with bowl. The previous problem of incomplete meaning is resolved by tying the cohesive elements.

As will be readily appreciated, these cohesive elements have considerable variety, as the following selection from Halliday and Hasan's collection of everyday texts demonstrates. In each case, a pair of sentences is split, the second being given first.

b) This is a one with animals too, animals that go in water.
c) Administration spokesmen were prompt to say it should not be considered any such thing.
d) You could see them coming on him, before your very eyes.
e) I expect you will get this but I'll send it if you want.
f) It was the morning caught for ever.
g) So he proposed having his discovery copied before parting with it.

The first sentences completing the pairs are:

b') This mobile's got fishes, yours has animals.

c') During the hearing on Wednesday, Inouye said the questions furnished
by Buzhardt 'should serve as a substitute, admittedly not the very best,
but a substitute for cross-examination of Mr. Dean by the President of
the United States'.

d') Spots. All over his face and hands -

e') Nothing else has come for you except Staff Bulletin no. 2.

f') There on the rough thick paper, reduced to their simplest possible terms,
were the stream, glittering and dimpling, the stone arch of the bridge
flushed in morning sunlight, the moor and the hills.

g') The nobleman, it appeared, had by this time become rather fond of Nanna
and Pippa. He liked, it might be said, the way they comported themselves.

When the cohesive ties are broken in this very simple way the skilled reader
searches for cues that will help him complete the ties and resolve the problems surrounding incomplete meanings.

Various categories of cohesion have been cited in linguistic papers; the
more important are Reference, Substitution, Ellipsis, Conjunction and Lexical
Cohesion.

It seems obvious that the perception of these linguistically defined cohesive elements requires further investigation as they have considerable implications for the development of fluent reading. From a psychological point
of view, for instance, if texts display these properties, what psychological
mechanisms are involved in their perception? How are readers cued to respond to these abstract cohesive elements? If there are various categories
of cohesive ties, are some more powerful (cohesive) than others? Are associative factors involved in lexical cohesion, and so on? Investigation of such
questions would contribute much to our understanding of some of the complex
factors involved in the development of reading fluency and have implications
for pedagogy.

As the linguistic description and categorisation of cohesive ties is fairly
recent, it is not surprising that little research can be found into the processes
involved. There are, however, a few pertinent studies. Two papers by Garrod
and Sanford (1977, 1978) throw some light on one of the major features
involved in the processing of cohesion — that of anaphora. This process, in
its normal form, presupposes that something has gone before, whether in
the preceding sentence or not. Occasionally the presupposed element is in
the following sentence, but in the great majority of cases the process is one
of referring back to an antecedent.

In the first of these papers Garrod and Sanford (1977) confirmed by experiments that interpreting anaphoric relations poses problems for the reader,
who first has to identify the antecedent to the anaphoric phrase, and then
represent the information that is currently being dealt with in terms of the
previous text. In a set of related experiments with adult subjects, the authors
demonstrate that it is possible to isolate the identification of a component
in text comprehension. They also show how semantic comparison between
anaphor and antecedent is involved.

In the second paper Garrod and Sanford (1978) provide further experimental
evidence concerning anaphoric processes. They point out that textual material

requires integration during reading, and show that the time taken to read
the second sentence of an anaphorically related pair is in part determined
by the semantic distance between the two items to be integrated. For
example, they stated that to fully understand the pair of sentences, "A bus
came roaring round the corner. The vehicle narrowly missed the pedestrians",
the reader has to deduce that the vehicle in question is a bus that came roaring round the corner. They found that the reading time for the second sentence is in part determined by the semantic distance between the two items
to be integrated (vehicle and bus in this case). The semantic distance between
the two words is indicated by comparing conjoint frequencies, so "vehicle
and bus" for instance is of a high conjoint frequency while "vehicle and tank"
would be of a lower conjoint frequency.

From these experiments it follows that the notion of semantic integration
during adult reading has psychological reality, and that it makes demands
on central processing systems. If we transfer these findings to children who
are learning to read, it seems very probable that the perception and processing of cohesive ties will also have a significant bearing on the development
of their reading fluency. Confirmation of this has come in a recent report
by Richek (1976-77), who showed that third grade children's mastery of anaphora was incomplete when they were required to read sentences in a variety
of linguistic contexts. In the study, three anaphoric forms were investigated
together with the effect of contextual variation. The three anaphoric forms
used were noun, pronoun, and null as exemplified in the following sentences:
1   Noun. John saw Mary and John said hello to Mary.
2   Pronoun. John saw Mary and he said hello to her.
3   Null. John saw Mary and said hello to her.
The noun form, as expected, was easiest to comprehend, the pronoun next
and the null form least comprehensible. It was also suggested in this work
that the complexity of the sentence affects comprehension of the structure
of that sentence.

What little evidence there is indicates that the perception and processing
of anaphoric elements of continuous texts is important in adult reading.
Further to this, the small amount of available data on children's reading
points to the importance of the mastery of processes like anaphora for fluent
reading.

Experimentation

An investigation examined the ability of eight-year-old children to perceive
and process cohesive elements in simple continuous texts. It was decided
to concentrate on the semantic field of pronouns in the first instance. This
was done for three reasons; pronouns are commonly used in reading primers,
they are featured in Richek's research and, finally, some data on their order
of acquisition and functioning was available (Chapman, 1975). In the latter
research it was found that children's ability to judge the semantic distance
between pronouns depended upon the way in which the children perceived
the dimensions of that semantic field's organisation. The research also showed
that meaning relationships between pronouns only develop slowly with age
and, contrary to expectation, are still unstable at nine years of age.

Subjects

The 74 subjects chosen for the study were from a first school in a new town. Nearly all of the 340 children attending the school came from three newly-built housing estates. There is a mixture of socio-economic groupings in the school catchment area, and the Headteacher states that there is a wide range of ability represented in the school. No children in the experimental groups were physically or mentally handicapped. The mean chronological age (CA) of the subjects was 101.69 and the mean Reading Age (RA) was 103.70 (Schonell Graded Word Reading Test, revised scoring, Young & Stirton, 1971).

The children were allocated to two groups by the Head and Class teacher so that Group A contained fluent readers and Group B contained non-fluent readers. The rating of the teachers was confirmed by the results of the Reading Age test mentioned above. Those scoring between 96 and 146 (mean RA 114.77) were placed in Group A, while those scoring between 94 and 105 (mean RA 90.22) were in Group B. These two groups were sub-divided into two further groups so that there was equivalent reading ability in each sub-group. These groups are called Group A1, A2, B1, B2.

Experimental Material

Seven test stories were written by a teacher especially for the study and to the following specifications:
1) To encourage motivation and provide context, each of the seven texts were in story form and resembled stories found in children's primers.
2) The target pronouns to be investigated were incorporated into the text in such a way as to preserve the flow of language.
3) The position of the target pronouns was varied in order to eliminate positional effects within sentences and paragraphs.
4) Each story involved a sub-set of related pronouns taken from a grammatical model provided by Gleason (1969), so that:
   the target pronouns in: Story 1 were I, me, my, mine; in Story 2 they were our, ours, us, we; in Story 3 they were his, him, he; in Story 4 were yours, your, you; in Story 5 were them, their, theirs, they; in Story 6 were she, hers, her; in Story 7 they were its, it.
5) The target pronouns were deleted systematically story by story, a seventh word deletion operating in almost every instance. Each story had a run-in paragraph of three or four sentences before deleting commenced. Each story was printed on a separate sheet and the seven were bound together to make small individual booklets.
6) The experimental procedure required that the children produce the correct pronoun and then write it in. This demanded more than a strict reading task when the word was actually present on the page awaiting recognition. This was judged to make extra demands of young children so it was decided to include a further control. Half the booklets, Book 1, contained the seven stories with a list of the deleted pronouns under each story (words +). The other half, Book 2, contained the seven stories without the list of pronouns (words -).

Table 1. Composition of Groups A and B by Chronological Age (CA).

		CA (in months)	
Group	N	Mean	S.D.
A	39	103.56	2.94
B	35	99.49	3.61

Table 2. Composition of Groups A and B by Reading Age (RA).

		Reading Ages	
Group	N	Mean	S.D.
A	39	114.7	16.15
B	35	90.22	9.7

Table 3. Correlations Between CA and RA, and CA and Mean Story Scores (All Subjects).

N	CA/RA	Sig. Level	CA/Mean Story Score	Sig. Level
74	$r = 0.54$	0.001	$r = 0.307$	> 0.05

Procedure
Each child received a booklet, Book 1 or 2, according to the group to which he or she had been allocated, so that sub-groups A1 and B1 received Book 1 and sub-groups A2 and B2 received Book 2. A set of instructions was then given, and after a practice run the children filled in the deletions. A time limit of 30 minutes was set, as speed is an important factor in reading fluency.

Care was taken in the design of this investigation, both in the composition of the materials and in procedural matters, to keep the tasks as close to the normal classroom reading experience of the children as possible. In order to remove any adverse effects that might occur in test-like situations, as well as to establish a familiar continuous linguistic context for the anaphoric processes, the stories were specially written to resemble children's stories, and the investigation was conducted by a teacher known to the children.

Results
The two main groupings of children are described by Chronological Age (CA) and Reading Age (RA). Table 1 gives the mean chronological ages and standard deviations for the two groups.

Table 2 gives the details of the two groups by Reading Ages. It will be seen that Group A, the fluent readers, were older than Group B but not significantly so.

Although there was some overlap of Reading Ages, there was a considerable difference between the two groups. Table 3 gives the correlations between Chronological Age and Reading Age, and between Chronological Age and Mean score on the seven stories.

When the whole sample was looked at, Chronological Age was found to be significantly related both to Reading Age and to overall performance on the seven stories. In order to determine the relationship of fluency to the differences in performance on the seven stories between the two groups when the missing words were either present (words +) or not (words -), the data were submitted to a two-way analysis of variance. The first factor involved was fluency and the second was concerned with the words given condition.

A two-way analysis of variance was used to analyse the data, and because there were one or two missing figures, due to the illness of one of the subjects, a design with unequal cell frequencies was used (Nie, Hull, Jenkins, Steinbrenner, & Brent, 1970). The criterion variable (the mean scores on the seven stories) was significant and so were the fluency and word condition variables. The joint additive effect of fluency and the word condition was significant. Interaction effects were not significant.

Discussion of Results
Given the setting for the investigation and the grouping of the children, the main purpose of the study was to explore the characteristics of continuous texts that provide a passage with cohesion, and to explore children's perception of some of the linguistically significant elements. If, as has been proposed, the perception of anaphoric elements (such as the relationship between pronoun and antecedent) is a major function in fluent reading, it follows that it should be one of the major distinguishing factors between the performance of fluent and non-fluent readers. This is exactly what was found.

Table 4. Two-Way Analysis of Variance to Determine the Fluency and Word Effects.

	Sum of Squares	DF	Mean Squares	F	Sig. Level
Main Effects	6612.227	2	3306.113	47.68	0.001
Fluency/ Non-Fluency	4209.477	1	4209.477	60.712	0.001
Words (+) or (-)	2761.545	1	2761.545	39.829	0.001

It should be recalled that, although all subjects were required to read and fill in the blanks in the same seven stories, two different conditions were presented to the sub-groups. In the first condition (words +), sub-groups A1 and B1 were given a list of the missing words at the foot of their stories; in the other condition (words -), sub-groups A2 and B2 were not provided with the missing words.

It is important at this stage to clarify what is required of the subjects by these tasks. In order to supply a missing word to complete a deletion (condition words +) a series of sub-routines is almost certainly involved during reading of the texts, such that

1) the subject is cued to the use of pronouns from the general context during the reading of the introductory (or run-in) paragraph;
2) the subject is cued to a specific anaphoric relation by a particular cohesive tie. (The reader's awareness will have been heightened by the deletion in these particular texts);
3) the subject searches for the specific pronoun from within the array of pronouns stored in long term memory, while holding the anaphoric relationship in working memory until a match is located;
4) in condition word +, the subject searches, or checks, the list for the correct pronoun to confirm the results of routine 3, or provide a further prompt using word recognition cues;
5) the subject writes in the selected word (if found).

Although mis-cuing or failure could occur during any of these sub-routines, for two important reasons the most demanding stage for the immature fluent reader is the third. First, the array of pronouns in memory and their inter-relationships may, at this age, still be unstable (Chapman, 1975). Second, the demands being made on central processing systems when nearing the span of working memory may affect the subject's ability to hold the relation together while actively searching for a match (Baddeley & Hitch, 1976). (It is worth recalling that the immediate memory span of children is very limited and only increases slowly with age.) The direction of the relationship appears particularly crucial in these tasks. For example, when a deletion occurs at the beginning of a sentence, it is necessary for the child to read ahead to discover the extent of the anaphoric relationship, although the missing pronoun is also related to part of the previous text.

The data provided by the study give some credence to the proposal that texts, because they are texts, have abstract cohesive features, and that the perception of these features plays a large part in reading fluency.

Only one part of one of the elements — pronouns in reference situations — has been looked at, but there are indications that it is a major factor in reading performance. The work raises many questions and introduces a perspective of reading development that has not had much detailed study.

REFERENCES

Baddeley, A.D., & Hitch, G. Working memory. In G.H. Bower (Ed.), The psychology of learning and motivation, New York: Academic Press, 1976.

Chapman, L.J. An investigation of a structuring model for the acquisition of semantic structures by young children. Unpublished Ph.D. Thesis, University of Aston in Birmingham, 1975.

Clark, M.M. Young fluent readers. London: Heinemann Educational, 1976.

Garrod, S., & Sanford, A. Interpreting anaphoric relations: The integration of semantic information while reading. Journal of Verbal Learning and Verbal Behavior, 1977, 16 (1), 77-90.

Garrod, S., & Sanford, A. Anaphora: A problem in text comprehension. In R. Campbell & P.T. Smith (Eds.), Recent advances in the psychology of language, Vol. 2. New York: Plenum, 1978.

Gleason, H.A. An introduction to descriptive linguistics. (Revised Edition.) Bournemouth: Holt, Rinehart and Winston, 1969.

Halliday, M.A.K., & Hasan, R. Cohesion in English. London: Longmans, 1976.

Nie, N.H., Hull, C.H., Jenkins, J.E., Steinbrenner, K., & Brent, D.H. Statistical package for the social sciences (2nd ed.). New York: McGraw-Hill, 1970.

Richek, M.A. Reading comprehension of anaphoric forms in varying linguistic contexts. Reading Research Quarterly, 1976-1977, 2, 145-165.

Smith, F. The learner and his language. In R. Hodges & E.H. Rodorf (Eds.), Language and learning to read. Boston: Houghton Mifflin, 1972.

Young, D., & Stirton, M.E. G.W.R. test equivalences and reading ages. Remedial Education, 1971, 6 (3), 7-8.

When Two No's Nearly Make a Yes: A Study of Conditional Imperatives

P. Wright and P. Wilcox

Performance was monitored in various tasks, in all of which people carried out instructions to respond appropriately to specified events. The tasks varied in presentation modality and in the temporal interval between the instruction and the event requiring a response.

Types of instruction were compared, having either zero, one, or two negative elements. When there was only one negative in an instruction, it occurred either as the element "not" in the main clause or as the connective "unless" introducing the subordinate clause. The instructions with double negatives included both "not" and "unless."

It was found that, in some tasks, performance with instructions having double negatives was better than with instructions having only one negative. However, the instructions showed no consistent rank order of difficulty across tasks. It is suggested that psycholinguistic models of comprehension need to incorporate situational factors explicitly. Generalisability across task and contextual variables can be as important as generalisability across subjects and specific sentence contents.

Negative imperatives are commonplace (Do not touch, No Parking, No admittance). At times, the importance of correctly understanding such instructions can be critical (Do not remove cover unless power is disconnected). Nevertheless, relatively little of the empirical work on negation has been done with imperatives. Clark and Lucy (1975) introduced negative elements into conversational imperatives (Will you close the door?). They found that performance was determined more by the negativity of the conveyed meaning than by the negativity of the surface structure. Consequently a sentence having

413

two negative elements ("sad" and "unless") and a positive conveyed meaning
(I'll be very sad unless you make the circle blue) showed a pattern of response
latencies that was typical of affirmative sentences ("True" responses were
always faster than "False" responses). Clark and Lucy interpreted this as
suggesting that subjects recoded the double negative into some affirmative
internal representation prior to responding. The binary stimulus set they
used may have facilitated such recoding. In the test, subjects could be sure
that "not blue" meant "pink." Such recoding may not occur, indeed may
not even be possible, in other situations (No smoking).

The Clark and Lucy study also showed that performance with sentences
containing two negatives (sad, unless) was neither slower nor more error-prone
than with sentences containing only one (happy, unless). However, questions
about the generality of these findings arise because they contrast with those
of Sherman (1976), who found that increasing the number of negative elements
in a sentence increased both response latency and error rate. His experimental
task was different, however. He asked people about the semantic reasonable-
ness of sentences such as "Because he usually worked for 10 min at a time
no one believed he was not capable of sustained effort." He also used a variety
of negative elements (no one, doubted, not, un-). Presumably, both the task
and the materials contributed to the divergence of the results from those
obtained by Clark and Lucy.

Certainly, there are no grounds for assuming that all negative elements
are of equivalent difficulty. In an earlier study, Sherman (1973) had shown
that negative prefixes (un-, in-, etc.) were easier to comprehend than the
negative particle "not." Moreover, in the 1976 study Sherman found that
performance with "no one doubted" was actually faster and more accurate
than with the verb "doubted" alone. This finding did not occur for the other
five combinations of negation which he examined. Perhaps people treated
the phrase "no one doubted" as if it were "everyone believed." If so, the
question again arises as to when people will choose to recode sentences with
negative elements so as to represent the meaning in a fully affirmative form.

Since many negative instructions cannot be recoded, expectancies may
be generated that dissuade people from attempting to use such a strategy
when dealing with instructions. Certainly there is evidence that people may
not recode an instruction even when it would be advantageous to do so. Jones
(1966a, b) presented people with a series of items drawn from a set of eight.
Subjects were instructed either to "Respond to four items" or "Respond to
all except four items." Fourteen of the thirty-two subjects (44%) who were
given the instructions containing "except" recoded the instruction into the
fully affirmative form (Jones, 1966b). The other 56% responded more slowly
and with many more false positive errors, responding to the items mentioned
in the instructions instead of to the non-excluded items.

Again, there are a number of differences between the studies of Jones
and those of Sherman and of Clark and Lucy discussed above. As previously
mentioned, recoding may be more likely when there is a binary stimulus set,
rather than a set of eight items as used by Jones. There may also be effects
arising from the size of the response set. Clark and Lucy used a binary response set, which meant that people could recode "Do not respond True if
blue" as "Response False if blue." Jones was using a Go/No Go response
situation where responses were either made or withheld. In this situation

there is no opportunity to recode only the response component, just as there is no alternative wording for Do not touch.

Recoding may also be influenced by at least two other factors - presentation modality and temporal contiguity. Visual presentation of instructions may facilitate recoding operations because the original instruction is constantly available for reference. All the studies mentioned so far have used visual presentation. However, when instructions are presented auditorily, the original has to be stored in memory. The processes of storage may be deleterious to subsequent recoding operations, or they may introduce extra-linguistic sources of error (Wright & Kahneman, 1971).

In addition, temporal variation can exist between instructions and the time an appropriate response must be made. Such variation may affect both the encoding and the retention of the instructions. If subjects know that the stimulus requiring a response is a blue circle, they may recode the instruction so that the encoded item is also a blue circle. Without such knowledge, recoding options might be determined by other priorities, such as removing the negative element from the main verb or from the subordinate clause.

In order to understand how people deal with negative instructions, it therefore seems necessary to examine performance across a range of situations that vary in the size of the stimulus and response sets, in the presentation modality used, and in the simultaneity of the instruction and the context for a response. The instructions to be used are derived from the form of the prohibition included in the British Highway Code: "Do not park on the hard shoulder of a motorway except in an emergency." Such an instruction has negative elements in both the main and subordinate clauses. The results of the Clark and Lucy study suggested that negation in the subordinate clause was the major cause of difficulty. The generality of this finding will be examined across a range of contexts. Comparisons will be be made of performance with instructions having zero negative elements, or having one negative either in the main or subordinate clause, or having two negative elements.

The following hypotheses can be put forward concerning the relative difficulty of the instructions having double negatives: performance will be poorest with the double negative in tasks that do not facilitate recoding (Sherman), and performance with double negatives may not differ from that with instructions containing only a single negative in tasks that do facilitate recoding (Clark and Lucy).

Method, Series 1
Series 1 tasks required Go/No Go responses. Presentation conditions were visual concurrent, visual sequential, and auditory sequential.

Materials and Procedure
Subjects were given a thumb operated push-button and were presented with a sequence of 48 instructions compiled from the four types of instruction shown in Table 1.

Each instruction was either followed or accompanied by the visual presentation of a single letter projected onto a screen. The letter presented was either that mentioned in the instruction or an acoustically similar letter. Six such letter pairs were used (p-b, s-x, d-t, m-n, c-e, a-k). The order of

Table 1. The Four Types of Instruction Used in Series 1.

(++)   Only press if the letter is P

(-+)   Do not press if the letter is P

(+-)   Press unless the letter is P

(--)   Do not press unless the letter is P

---

the instructions was scrambled, and half the subjects had the sequence reversed to counterbalance any practice effects.

All subjects were given examples of the four types of instruction and were told that when appropriate they should respond as quickly as possible. It was emphasized that they should always respond unless the instruction expressly prohibited it. Consequently a (-+) instruction such as "Do not press if the letter is P" implied that they should respond to any letter other than P.

The latency of subjects' responses was recorded by a special purpose digital tape-recorder. This apparatus made it possible to test groups of subjects simultaneously. The three presentation conditions were treated as separate experiments.

For the visual concurrent task, the instruction was written in lower case typescript in two horizontal rows across the top of the slide, with the top line terminating at the clause boundary. A single letter, also in lower case, appeared in the centre of the slide underneath the instruction. Slides changed every 7 sec and the response latency was measured from this slide change.

In the visual sequential task, the letters underneath each instruction were masked, and identical letters were presented for 7 sec after each slide. The instruction slide also remained on for 7 sec. Response latency was measured from the onset of the letter slide.

For the auditory sequential task, the instructions were tape-recorded. In order to ensure that the letters were heard accurately, a tag phrase such as "P for Peter" was used with each letter. These tag phrases and their purpose were explained to subjects at the start of the experiment.

Each auditory instruction was followed by a visually presented letter which remained visible for 7 sec. Response latency was measured, as above, from the onset of the letter slide. During the auditory instruction the screen was blank.

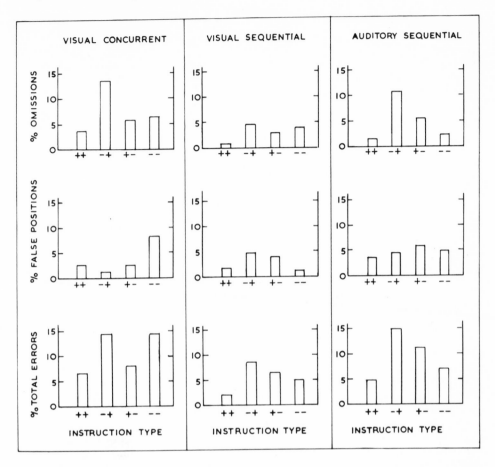

Figure 1. The distribution of errors, both omissions and false positives, across the four instructions for each presentation condition in Series 1. (All figures are given as a percentage of the number of times that such instruction was presented, i.e., maximum cell value is 100%.)

Subjects
All subjects were adult volunteers from the subject panel of the Applied Psychology Unit. The numbers in each presentation condition are shown below. Each subject took part in only one experiment.

Visual Concurrent: 62 subjects were tested in two groups of 13 and two groups of 18 subjects.

Visual Sequential: 50 subjects were tested in two groups of 10 and two groups of 15 subjects.

Auditory Sequential: 52 subjects were tested in four groups of 13 subjects.

Results, Series 1
The overall error rates in the three presentation conditions were: visual concurrent 10.8%, visual sequential 5.4%, and auditory sequential 9.5%. Statistical analysis using chi square tests on the frequency of subjects making
either zero or more than three errors showed that the difference between
the two visual presentation conditions was significant ($\chi^2 = 8.4$, $p < 0.01$;
all significance levels are two-tailed unless otherwise stated). So too was
the difference between the sequential conditions ($\chi^2 = 3.4$, $p < 0.05$, one-
tailed test).

Two kinds of errors were possible. Subjects could omit responses that
should have been made, or respond when this was inappropriate. Figure 1
shows how such errors were distributed in the three presentation conditions.

Statistical analysis of the omission errors showed that it was not the
double negative but the single negative (-+) (Do not press if) which was the
most error-inducing instruction. In all presentation conditions, significantly
more responses were omitted with (-+) than with (++) instructions (Wilcoxon
tests, $p < 0.05$). The (-+) instructions produced significantly more omission
errors than any other instruction except the visual sequential presentation
condition, where there was no difference between the two single negatives
(-+) and (+-). In all presentation conditions, omission errors were no more
frequent with the double negative than with the fully affirmative instruction
(++). Thus, the typical pattern of omission errors was (++) = (+-) = (--) < (-+).

The pattern of false positive errors was rather different, particularly
when presentation was visual concurrent; significantly more false positive
responses were made with (--) than with any of the other instructions
($p < 0.05$, sign tests). However, this was not the case with the other two
presentation conditions. With visual sequential presentation, the double
negative produced significantly fewer false positives than either of the single
negative instructions ($p = 0.02$, sign tests). With auditory sequential presentation, there were no statistically reliable differences among the instructions.

For the sake of comparison with studies reported in the literature, where
the types of error are not always separately identified, Figure 1 shows the
total error rate for each type of instruction. Statistical analysis of these
totals suggested that a similar error pattern obtained in the two sequential
presentation conditions. Fewer errors were made with those instructions
having a positive conveyed meaning, (++) and (--), than with the negative
instructions, (-+) and (+-). However, when presentation was visual concurrent, the negativity of the first clause seemed to be the critical element,
since (++) and (+-) instructions produced significantly fewer total errors than
(-+) and (--). Yet, as we have seen, this discrepancy among the presentation
conditions is mainly attributable to differences in the frequency of false
positive errors. The implications of this will be considered in the discussion
of the results from the Series 2 experiments. One of the important points
to notice from these patterns of total errors is the variation in the relative
difficulty among these four instructions. Presentation factors contribute
to the determination of the relative difficulty of following verbal instructions. By implication, such factors also contribute to determining the information processing underlying "comprehension."

Given the differences in error rates, caution is needed in interpreting the
latency data. The times taken to make a correct response are shown in Table 2.

Statistical analysis indicated that there was a similar pattern of latencies when presentation was visual concurrent and auditory sequential. In these conditions latencies fell into three bands, with the double negative instructions being in the middle band, that is (++) < (+-) = (--) < (-+) (all differences significant at $p < 0.05$, sign tests). When presentation was visual sequential, a different pattern of relative speeds was found. There were now only two latency bands: (++) = (--) < (-+) = ($p < 0.05$ for all significant differences). Thus again, as with the error data, presentation factors interact with linguistic factors in determining the relative speeds of carrying out the different instructions. There is no unique and generalisable rank order of difficulty for these four types of instruction.

Discussion, Series 1

We shall first discuss the relative difficulty of these instructions. The data indicate that there are circumstances where people have considerable success in handling double negatives. Only when presentation was visual concurrent was there an appreciable number of errors with (--). These errors were predominantly false positive responses (responses to the item not mentioned in the instruction itself). This could be taken as evidence for incomplete recoding of the instruction and will be considered in more detail after the next series of experiments.

The responses to (--) instructions were significantly faster than to (-+) in all three experiments. These findings appear consistent with those of Clark and Lucy (1975) in suggesting that a double negative need be no more difficult than a single negative. However, unlike Clark and Lucy, who found that a single negative element impaired performance most when it occurred in the subordinate clause, the present experiments find that performance is poorer when the single negative element occurs in the main clause. One reason for the discrepancy is that the type of negative element is very different

Table 2. Latencies of Correct Responses in Series 1.

	Visual Concurrent	Visual Sequential	Auditory Sequential
++	3.51	2.22	2.17
-+	4.67	2.57	2.56
+-	4.27	2.54	2.43
--	4.28	2.30	2.30

in the two studies. Sherman (1973, 1976) has shown that the particle "not" is often more difficult to comprehend than other negative elements. The present study used "not" in the main clause, whereas the study of Clark and Lucy used the negative prefix un (unhappy). Conclusions about the location of the negative element are therefore premature.

We turn now to the effects of temporal factors. The pattern within the latency data suggests that auditory sequential presentation encouraged similar processing to that with visual concurrent presentation. In both these conditions there were three performance bands, with (-+) being slower than (+-). In contrast, with visual sequential presentation there were two performance bands with no difference between (-+) and (+-). This similarity between visual concurrent and auditory sequential implies that subjects may not have had a long enough time between hearing the end of the sentence and the presentation of the letter to carry out recoding operations that might otherwise have taken place. Yet, it must be remembered that the task was not hurried. Table 2 shows that subjects chose to use, on average, only 2.5 sec of the available 7 sec response interval. There was certainly ample time for subjects to complete any recoding they might have desired. Perhaps the occurrence of the cue to respond changed the processing strategy from one which would have led to recoding to one that did not. A longer delay between the end of the instruction and the occurrence of the letter slide might have given results comparable to those found with visual sequential presentation.

Recoding of the double negative does take place when the temporal parameters of the task encourage it. This is shown by the pattern of response latencies with visual sequential presentation. Here no latency differences were found between the two instructions with a positive conveyed meaning (++) and (--), nor between the two instructions with a negative conveyed meaning (+-) and (-+). As expected, the instructions with positive conveyed meanings had shorter response latencies than the other instructions.

The relative performance on the instructions having a single negative was also influenced by the temporal interval between the instruction itself and the event referred to in that instruction. When the cue for responding is not known (visual sequential), the speed of responding is the same for (+-) and (-+). This suggests that instructions having a single negative element are recoded into a common form. In contrast, when the cue for responding is available simultaneously with the instruction, then responses to (+-) instructions are faster than to (-+) instructions. This suggests that these instructions are represented differently even though their meaning is the same. This point will be discussed further after Series 2.

The size of the set from which the stimuli and responses were drawn is investigated in the experiments of Series 2. In the interest of economy of effort, both the stimulus and the response factors in Series 2 will be changed from those of Series 1 because if these conjointly do not affect the response pattern there is no need to examine the effect of each separately.

With the presentation rates used here, auditory sequential presentation gives results that are very similar to those obtained with visual concurrent presentation. Therefore, the auditory modality will be dropped from the comparison series and only the visual sequential and visual concurrent presentation conditions will be retained.

Method, Series 2

Series 2 tasks required binary responses to binary stimuli. Presentation conditions were treated as separate experiments. Each experiment used a within-subject design, in which the four kinds of instruction were encountered in a scrambled order. Half the subjects in each experiment had the presentation order reversed, as a rough control for practice/boredom effects. As in Series 1, the dependent variables were latency and errors when carrying out the instructions. In the visual-sequential experiment it was possible to separate sentence coding time from the time needed to execute the response.

The changes from Series 1 were as follows. The wording of the instructions now specified whether a left- or right-hand button was to be pressed. The referential event was also changed to be either a circle or a square. The instructions were of the same four syntactic forms as in Series 1 and were typed on two lines with the first line terminating at the clause boundary; for example,

> Do not press the right hand button
> unless the picture is a square.

A sequence of 64 instruction slides was prepared, 16 for each of the four instructions. These sets of 16 were devised so that the right and left buttons were mentioned and pressed equally often. Thus, in half the instructions the picture mentioned in the instruction matched that shown either underneath or subsequently, and in half there was a mismatch. The buttons were thumb-operated.

Subjects were told that they would be shown slides telling them which of the two buttons to press. It was emphasised that they would always have to press one of the buttons and the example was given of an instruction which said "Press the right-hand button if the picture is a circle." It was pointed out that when such an instruction was accompanied by a picture of a square they would be expected to press the left-hand button. Examples of all four types of instruction were given. Subjects were told to respond as quickly and as accurately as possible, but that if they pressed the wrong button they could subsequently press the correct one when they realised their mistake. They were also told that if they had not responded to one instruction by the time the next instruction occurred, it would be too late and they should turn their attention to the new instruction. The trial began with eight practice slides, two from each instruction, and these were followed without interruption by the experimental sequence.

In the visual concurrent task, the instruction slides were presented for 14 sec and were followed by the picture slide for 7 sec. Subjects were told that during the instruction slide they should press both buttons simultaneously when they felt they had understood the instruction. This enabled separate measures analogous to sentence coding and picture verification times to be obtained (Clark, 1971).

Subjects

Forty-one volunteers from the APU subject panel took part, twenty-one in the visual concurrent study, and twenty in the visual sequential study.

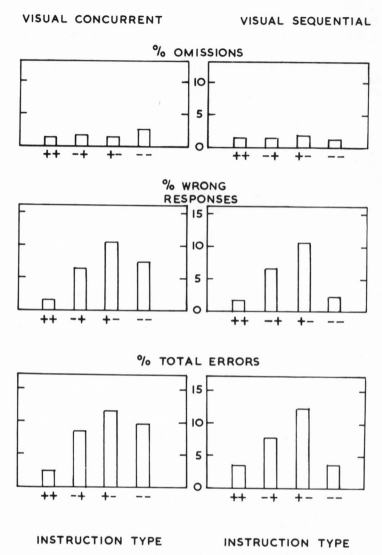

Figure 2. The distribution of errors, both omissions and wrong responses, across the four instructions for each presentation condition in Series 2. (All figures are given as a percentage of the number of times that each instruction was presented, i.e., maximum cell value is 100%.)

Results, Series 2

First, as to errors, subjects could make two kinds. They could either press the wrong button or fail to make any response at all. Pooling across both classes of error, the mean rates were: visual concurrent 8.1%, visual sequential 6.7%. The distribution of these errors across sentence types is shown in Figure 2. It can be seen that omission errors were too few for statistical analysis. Pressing the wrong button was the more common mistake with all four instructions.

Wrong responses can be analysed in a number of ways. In Figure 3 the data are subdivided on the basis of whether the picture shown was the one mentioned in the instruction or not. The results of Clark and Lucy (1975) suggest that fewer wrong responses are made when the picture is mentioned in the instructions.

Figure 3 shows that most wrong responses occurred when there was a mismatch between the picture mentioned in the instruction and that actually illustrated. Pooling across all four types of instruction, this difference was statistically significant for visual concurrent (sign test, $p < 0.01$) although not for visual sequential presentation.

Figure 3 also shows that the relative difficulty of the instructions interacts with the match-mismatch factor for visual concurrent but not for visual sequential presentation. When the instruction and picture matched, (+-) was the only instruction more error inducing than (++) (visual concurrent $p < 0.06$; visual sequential $p < 0.04$). However, when the picture was not the one mentioned in the sentence, both instructions having a single negative were more error-inducing than the fully affirmative instruction (visual concurrent, (-+) $p < 0.01$, (+-) $p < 0.01$; visual sequential (-+) $p < 0.04$; (+-) $p < 0.02$). The apparently high error rate with the double negative for visual concurrent presentation was not statistically reliable (seven subjects made more errors with (--) than (++) but two subjects made more errors with the affirmative, $p = 0.18$). This non-significant finding contrasts with the significantly high

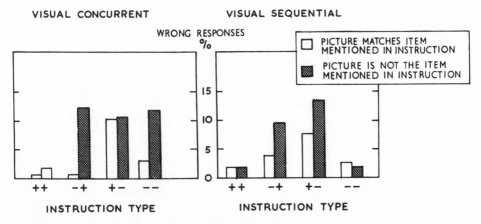

Figure 3. The distribution of wrong responses as a function of whether the picture shown was mentioned in the instruction. (All figures are given as a percentage of the number of times the particular instruction-plus-picture combination occurred, i.e., the means of these values give the values shown in Figure 2.)

Table 3. Latencies of Correct Responses with Visual Concurrent
Presentation in Series 2.

Instruction	Visual Concurrent		Clark & Lucy	
	Match	Mismatch	Match	Mismatch
++	3.89	4.65	1.78	2.10
-+	4.48	6.30	1.88	2.36
+-	5.11	5.61	2.32	2.69
--	5.01	6.55	2.36	2.80

false positive response rate for double negatives found in Series 1 for visual
concurrent presentation.

Perhaps the most important difference between the error data found in
Series 2 and Series 1 is the relative difficulty of the two instructions which
had only a single negative element. In Series 1 (-+) was more error-inducing;
in Series 2 (+-) was more influential.

Consider now latency in the visual concurrent task. Because the error-
rates are different when instruction and picture match rather than mismatch,
it seems advisable to retain this distinction when analyzing the latencies.
Table 3 shows the latency data obtained when presentation was visual concurrent. The data from Clark and Lucy (1975) are included for comparison.
Statistical analysis confirmed that for each of the four instructions, responses
were faster when the picture matched that mentioned in the instruction (for
instruction (+-) $p < 0.03$, for all other instructions $p < 0.01$).

Statistical analysis of performance with matching items showed that
(++) < (-+) < (+-) = (--), for all comparisons $p < 0.01$. Analysis of performance
with mismatching items showed that (++) < (+-) < (-+) = (--). The (++) advantage was statistically significant at $p < 0.01$, and (+-) advantage at $p < 0.05$.

Table 3 shows that, as with the error data, the relative difficulty of instructions containing a single negative interacted with the match-mismatch
variable. The McNemar test for a significant change confirmed that this
interaction was statistically significant ($\chi^2 = 6.67$, $p < 0.01$).

In the visual sequential task, performance was operationally split into
a time to encode the instruction and a time to respond to the subsequent
picture. These latencies are shown in Table 4. When direct comparisons
were made within each type of instruction, there were no differences in
coding times between the match and mismatch conditions. This was as e
expected because until the picture has been presented there is nothing to
match. Consequently, the data were pooled across the match-mismatch
factor for analysis of relative performance with each type of instruction.

This analysis showed that the latencies divided into three significantly different bands (++) < (+-) < (-+) = (--) with p < 0.05 between bands.

Statistical analysis showed that the match-mismatch variable was a significant factor only for those instructions having a positive conveyed meaning (i.e., (++) and (--), p < 0.05). When the picture was not that mentioned in the instruction, there were no reliable differences in times to respond to different instructions. However, when the picture matched that mentioned in the instruction, responses were significantly faster to instructions having a positive conveyed meaning (i.e. (++) = (--) < (+-) = (-+), for all differences p < 0.01). This pattern of verification times corresponds to the pattern of latencies found in Series 1 with visual sequential presentation.

Discussion, Series 2

The binary response task has made it possible to show that a major determinant of performance is the relation between the picture shown and that mentioned in the instruction. For visual concurrent presentation performance is worse when these mismatch. In Series 1 the responses to (++) and (--) involved matched events, whereas the responses to (+-) and (-+) involved mismatch events. So, there is a sense in which the earlier apparent ease in handling the double negative was spurious, an artefact of the response requirements of the task. When the mapping between what is mentioned in the instruction and what must be responded to is comparable across instructions, the expected greater difficulty of the double negative is reflected in slower response latencies, although not in more errors. This not only suggests limitations to the generality of the Series 1 findings, but also has implications for notions about the underlying processes which mediate comprehension.

One way to illustrate these implications is by reference to a simple-minded, three-component model of the recoding operations that people might undertake when carrying out these instructions. Such a model might simply postulate

Table 4. Latencies of Correct Responses with Visual Sequential Presentation in Series 2.

Instruction	Coding Times		Verification Times	
	Match	Mismatch	Match	Mismatch
++	3.36	3.35	1.82	1.94
-+	3.67	3.80	2.05	2.03
+-	3.52	3.49	2.02	2.02
--	3.87	3.92	1.84	1.99

Table 5. A Simple Model of the Processes Underlying Performance in Series 2. All Instruction Types Mention Right (R) and Circle (C) (the Alternatives are Left (L) and Square (S)).

	Assumed Initial Internal Representation			
	+	-	+	-
	+	+	-	-
Assumed recoding processes	(R) (C)	(-R) (C)	(R) (-C)	(-R) (-C)
a) Remove negative from subordinate clause.	....	....	→ (R) (S)	→ (-R) (S)
b) Remove negative from main clause.	....	→ (L) (C)	....	→ (L) (S)
c) Does picture match noun in internal representation?	If No recode → (L) (S)	If No recode → (R) (S)	If No recode → (L) (C)	If No recode → (R) (S)
Predictions				
1) a. Number of recoding operations if picture is a circle.	0	1	2	3
b. Number of recoding questions if picture is a square.	1	2	1	2
2) Effect on latency of match between picture and noun mentioned in instruction.	C < S	C < S	S < C	S < C

the removal of all negative elements from the internal representation of the instruction, and a subsequent comparison of this internal representation with the picture presented. Table 5 shows the consequences of the application of these three processes to the four types of instruction. It will be noted that prediction 1b of this model makes the wrong predictions about the effect of the match-mismatch variable on performance with double negatives. However, it correctly accounts for the ordering $(++) < (+-) < (-+)$ which was found in Series 1. So perhaps the double negatives are a special case.

Within Series 2, the instructions most influenced by presentation conditions appear to be the double negatives. There is a much higher incidence of wrong responses to $(--)$ with visual concurrent presentation than with visual sequential presentation. A comparable increase in the false positive errors has also been noted in Series 1. Perhaps under time pressure subjects recode only one instead of both negative elements. The question, then, is which one? It has been noted that wrong responses are more prevalent when there is a picture mismatch than when there is a match. This might suggest that subjects usually recode the subordinate clause, but sometimes ignore the negative particle in the main clause. For example, "Do not press right unless circle" might be treated as Right if square. The alternative assumption, that subjects sometimes recode only the main clause (giving: Left if circle), generates the prediction that most wrong button responses would occur when the picture matched that mentioned in the sentence. This is not the error pattern shown in Figure 3.

There is other evidence consistent with this suggestion that recoding of the subordinate clause is completed before that of the main clause. Consider the coding times obtained with visual sequential presentation. Of the two instructions having only one negative element, coding times are shorter when the negative element occurs in the subordinate clause $(+-)$ than when it is in the main clause $(-+)$. The recoding of the two clauses need not be sequential operations, they might occur in parallel. But the present data suggest that, after a finite period of time, a recoded representation is more likely to be available for the subordinate clause than for the main clause. The generality of this finding cannot be established from the present experiments, since the categories subordinate clause and main clause are confounded both with serial order within the sentence and with the type of negative element used (not, unless). Further studies are being undertaken to separate these factors.

Analysis of the verification times from visual sequential presentation shows that the match-mismatch difference remained only for $(++)$ and $(--)$. This would be consistent with the suggestion implicit in Table 5 that subjects internally represent only one of the contingency relationships conveyed by the instruction. Furthermore, the relationship represented appears to be determined by the shape mentioned in the instruction. It is almost as if people read an instruction which mentions a circle and then ask themselves, "What do I do if it is a circle?" The lack of any such effects for $(+-)$ and $(-+)$ is difficult to account for, particularly since these were both as slow as the mismatched performance with $(++)$ and $(--)$ instructions.

The general conclusions to be drawn from these two series of experiments are as follows:

1. Performance is always better with fully affirmative instructions than with double negatives having the same conveyed meaning. Nevertheless

2. Performance with instructions having two negatives is not necessarily worse and may even be significantly better than performance with instructions having only one negative element.

3. Double negatives appear to be difficult in binary response situations but not in Go/No Go response situations. This is because

4. Responses are more easily made to the event explicitly mentioned in the instruction than to events referenced implicitly.

5. The relative difficulty of negative instructions depends on the temporal relation between the instruction and the event which occasions a response.

General Discussion

The variation in relative difficulty of the four instructions raises serious doubts about relating the findings from psycholinguistic experiments to practical problems of written communication. When is it realistic to generalise from the findings of a single experiment? There seem to be two major constraints. One is the variety of language processing strategies that are available to people (Aaronson, 1976). Experimenters working on the problems of communication are increasingly recognising that just as learning proved not to be a unitary variable, neither is comprehension. Consequently, the linguistic form of an utterance is only one of several factors that conjointly determine which of several processing operations will take place. Successful application of psycholinguistic findings therefore requires the development of theories of language processing which specify when particular strategies will be selected (Wright, 1978).

The term comprehension as used throughout this paper is different from its uses in other contexts. The present usage includes components which some theorists would prefer to keep separate from, because they see them as subsequent to, processes of lexical access. Consequently, in analysing the performance of aphasic patients it seems more convenient to say that the patient who reads "chair" as "seat" has understood the item presented, but has made an output error. However, the semantic access of discrete lexical items is only a small part of the problem faced by someone who wants to understand a sentence. For example, consider the difficulties in answering the question, "Is it true that a minute is not longer than a second?" Confining the term comprehension to just the processing of individual word meanings is not satisfactory to many psychologists interested in larger units of language processing. Demonstrating that a question can be accurately answered is in many areas an acceptable yardstick of comprehension. Demonstrating that an instruction can be carried out is a straightforward extension of this procedure.

A concluding comment concerns method. The present experiments have illustrated how important contextual variables can be in determining the relative difficulty of particular linguistic forms. There have been several attempts to systematize the way in which contextual constraints may operate.

Notions derived from the Craik and Lockhart (1972) suggestions of variations in "depth" of processing were one move in this direction — Glucksberg, Trabasso, and Wald (1973) accounted for some of the effects of sentence reversibility by this means. Nevertheless, there is a lack of any clear theoretical statement about how deeply a message will be processed. Indeed, the present tasks illustrate how difficult it can be to apply a depth of processing metric. Are instructions that must be remembered until an appropriate item is presented, processed to a deeper level than those which can be executed without delay? Or does the similarity of the response to be made mean that the comprehension processes will be the same in the delayed and non-delayed conditions? Would either answer predict the differences found?

A concern for the generalisability of psycholinguistic findings was expressed by Clark (1973). He saw the problem as one of generalising across the experimental materials to sentences having other content items, and he proposed a statistical solution. The problems raised here cannot be dealt with so easily; yet it is possible that increasing use of factorial designs, and perhaps in particular of treatment "x" levels experimental designs, would be a step in the right direction. In such designs, the same experimental comparisons are made at different "levels" of context, task, etcetera. The levels which might be examined include individual differences (differences in reading ability or use of imagery), environmental differences (the availability of information or the constraints of the task), and information processing differences (the involvement of retention processes or decision making strategies). In tasks other than following instructions, variables such as reading purpose are likely to be an important factor which has consequences for the generality of the experimental findings.

Such experimental designs are inevitably larger, involve more work, and take more time than conventional single level studies. Nevertheless, for purposes of successfully applying experimental results there are no alternatives. The present system of waiting for an apparent failure to replicate and then trying to determine just where the critical differences lie between separate experiments is even more time consuming. Indeed, such a procedure is wasteful because the appropriate treatment "x" levels analysis has eventually to be undertaken in order to reconcile the apparent conflict. At some stage the critical parameters must be manipulated in a controlled environment where it is known that they alone are the only variables affecting performance.

In the strict statistical sense, the present series of experiments have not used a treatment "x" levels design since the difficulties of precisely equating the measures of performance across the various presentation conditions made such a design seem inappropriate. However, by examining performance in a range of instructional environments the spirit underlying such an analysis is honoured.

The value of incorporating into experimental designs the replication of treatment effects at different levels lies not only in the greater opportunity doing so affords for successful generalisation of the results, but also in the highlighting of multiple determinants of linguistic performance. This may offset the risks of preoccupation with a single experimental paradigm, a preoccupation which may generate apparently powerful models of sentence comprehension that have neither generality nor relevance to the practical problems of written communication.

The present experiments have not produced a definitive model of the comprehension processes that enable people to respond correctly to verbal instructions containing one or two negatives. This is partially because these experiments are part of the initial stages of a broader investigation into conditional imperatives. It therefore seems premature to present detailed notions about such processing. Just how premature, can be seen by looking at some of the other findings. From the data accumulated so far, it looks as though reversing the order of clauses affects only one of the four instructions. Yet there is nothing in the present study which would indicate either which instruction is affected or in which direction (better or worse). Thus, there is a readily apparent need to explore performance across a range of situations before developing theories about the processes mediating comprehension.

The authors thank Mr. Raymond Bloomfield, who designed and built the apparatus which enabled the latency data to be collected.

REFERENCES

Aaronson, D. Performance theories for sentence coding: Some qualitative evidence. Journal of Experimental Psychology: Human Perception and Performance, 1976, 2, 42-55.

Clark, H.H. The chronometric study of meaning components. Paper presented at the CRNS Colloque International sur les Problemes Actuels de Psycholinguistique, Paris, 1971.

Clark, H.H. The language-as-a-fixed-effect-fallacy: A critique of language statistics in psychological research. Journal of Verbal Learning and Verbal Behavior, 1973, 12, 335-339.

Clark, H.H., & Lucy, P. Understanding what is meant from what is said: A study of conversationally conveyed requests. Journal of Verbal Learning and Verbal Behavior, 1975, 14, 56-72.

Craik, F.I.M., & Lockhart, R.S. Levels of processing: A framework for memory research. Journal of Verbal Learning and Verbal Behavior, 1972, 11, 671-684.

Glucksberg, S., Trabasso, T., & Wald, J. Linguistic structures and mental operations. Cognitive Psychology, 1973, 5, 338-470.

Jones, S. The effect of a negative qualifier in an instruction. Journal of Verbal Learning and Verbal Behavior, 1966, 5, 497-501. (a)

Jones, S. Decoding a deceptive instruction. Journal of Verbal Learning and Behavior, 1966, 57, 405-411. (b)

Sherman, M.A. Bound to be easier? The negative prefix and sentence comprehension. Journal of Verbal Learning and Verbal Behavior, 1973, 12, 76-84.

Sherman, M.A. Adjectival negation and the comprehension of multiply negated sentences. Journal of Verbal Learning and Verbal Behavior, 1976, 15, 143-157.

Wright, P. Feeding the information eaters: Suggestions for integrating pure and applied research on language comprehension. Instructional Science, 1978, 7, 249-312.

Wright, P., & Kahneman, D. Evidence for alternative strategies of sentence retention. Quarterly Journal of Experimental Psychology, 1971, 23, 197-213.

Styles and Strategies in Silent Reading

A. K. Pugh

*Most of the research into reading eye movements has been
concerned with making accurate observations of readers
carrying out unusual tasks under restrictive conditions.
However, the applicability of such findings to normal reading
is limited, and has precluded investigation of strategies
employed by skilled silent readers, which recent emphasis
on flexibility in reading necessitate.*

*This paper describes apparatus devised by the writer for
studying styles and strategies used by skilled readers under
normal conditions. It also reviews three studies where the
method was used to investigate location of information in
books. In addition, a correlational analysis is given that
relates performance on this task to scores on several tests.*

*It is concluded that more work needs to be done in obser-
ving readers' purposeful use of texts, and that the neglect
of this area may be due not only to methodological problems,
but also to lack of knowledge about how adults read.*

Early studies of eye movements in reading appear to have been motivated
by the belief that this topic provided an opportunity to observe the less accessible mental behaviour which is part of reading and thinking. "To completely
analyse what we do when we read would almost be the acme of a psychologist's achievements, for it would be to describe very many of the most intricate
workings of the human mind...." said Huey (1908, p. 6) in reviewing the early
work. Reviews by later writers (Vernon, 1931; Carmichael & Dearborn, 1948;
Tinker, 1965) show that eye movement research has also concerned itself
with applied fields, notably legibility, but an attempt to "understand what
we do when we read" has nevertheless continued. Some important work in
eye movement research (Yarbus, 1967; Ditchburn, 1973) has avoided reading

as a topic, however, and it appears that our knowledge of the processes involved in reading has not increased markedly, despite the research. For example,
Geyer (1972) concluded from his review of 48 models of the reading process,
that we have insufficient understanding to be able to apply most of the models
to normal reading.

Research has tended to concentrate upon extremely accurate measurements
of eye behaviour (Mackworth, 1976), but in doing so, investigators have made
it difficult to use their findings to make inferences about normal reading
(Pugh, 1977). Levy-Schoen and O'Regan (this volume) have noted that most
eye movement research relates to the sensory-motor adjustment aspect of
reading, rather than to higher level control. Shebilske and Reid, elsewhere
in this volume, argue for more concern with normal reading situations. They
particularly examine the undue emphasis on recognition and the neglect of
comprehension processes. Studies such as these make it apparent that it
is not only the imposition of physical restraints upon the reader which restrict
the validity of eye movement studies, but also the limited view of reading
which some investigators have adopted.

The question of stages in reading development is contentious, as is the
role of speech in reading. Nevertheless, if one can accept that there are
broadly three stages in the development of reading proficiency (Goodman,
1968), designated elsewhere the oral, aural, and silent stages (Pugh, 1975),
then it is the aural stage which is most commonly the subject of investigation.
It is designated the aural stage because it involves the sequential following
of a text, and is in a sense heard by the reader (Neville & Pugh, 1975a).

Not only has the type of reading appropriate to the oral and aural stages
received most attention in eye movement studies, but it also appears to be
stressed most in formal education. Perry (1959), reporting on Harvard students,
suggests that they were in general unable to read strategically, but followed
a test which simulated a study task with "obedient purposelessness." It is
questionable whether the students were quite as naive as the report suggests.
They may have read in this way because they thought that a test demanded
sequential reading, but this interpretation would also support the view that
formal education underemphasises strategic reading. (Sequential, rapid,
reading is encouraged in adults by the test passages in speed reading courses,
and it is interesting that Perry also reported a decline in the use of speed
reading films at Harvard. These films, devised by Dearborn and Anderson
(1937), modified by Perry (Perry & Whitlock, 1948), and subsequently disowned
by all of them (Anderson & Dearborn, 1952; Perry, 1959), were an indirect
result of early research into eye movements.)

General discrediting, even among the researchers themselves, of the
application to training of eye movement research (Tinker, 1965; Vernon, 1969)
has led to uncertainty about what can be done to enable readers to read more
effectively. Recently, however, there has been growing emphasis on flexibility and the use of strategy in reading. Factors such as the purpose in
reading and the difficulty of the text have been examined. Flexibility, as
Rankin (1974) indicates, is difficult to measure, but so is speed (Farr, 1969),
and gains on speed reading courses may be little more than an artefact of
the test situation (Maxwell, 1965; Pugh, 1976). Even if speed of reading were
readily measurable, it would nevertheless be important to emphasise the
variety of reading styles used by adults. This was done in the context of

Table 1. Mean Scores and Times Obtained by the Two Groups
in the Information Location Tasks.

	Control group		Experimental group		Both groups compared	
	Mean	S.D.	Mean	S.D.	F	t
"Memory" time (sec)	455.7	155.5	504.3	330.3	4.50	0.59
Accuracy	4.286	1.145	4.857	1.196	1.09	1.54
"Victorian Cities" Time (sec)	602.4	288.8	477.6	182.6	2.50	1.63
Accuracy	2.429	0.675	2.762	0.436	2.39	1.85

courses at the University of Leeds intended to help students (and some staff members) improve their ability to use reading for study. In order to evaluate the courses, studies were made of the strategic use of styles to locate information. The studies were extended to include sixth-form school children and, later, middle-school children. Other aspects of measured reading skill were considered and scores on certain other measures were taken in an attempt to find the correlates of ability to use a book.

Apparatus used for Studying Reading Behaviour

The apparatus devised for studying styles of reading and their strategic use in locating information consists of a video-camera, recorder and monitor, together with a specially made reading stand. The stand, which is placed on a table, is made of wood and specialised glass. The glass (Pilkington Solar-shield 15/23) forms the upper part of the stand. Since its reflective qualities are fairly high (light reflection 37%, absorption 48%, transmission 15%), it is possible to obtain a reflected image of the subject's head while he/she reads a book placed on the stand. By lighting the underside of the glass and by adjusting the angle of the camera, a good image can be obtained without the subject being distracted by his own reflection.

The video-camera placed unobtrusively about 1.7 meters above the subject's head receives, therefore, a direct image of the book on the stand and a reflected image of the subject's head from the glass. The image is transmitted to an adjoining room for recording and monitoring. During monitoring, notes are taken on strategies and styles employed and on the time taken to obtain information. The tape can, of course, be played back in the presence of the subject for clarification of his actions or intentions.

The advantage of the apparatus is that it permits reading of ordinary

text under near normal conditions. The main constraint on the subject is
that he must keep the book on the stand. A disadvantage of the apparatus
is that it does not permit accurate observation of eye movements, but that
is not very important here. A more serious disadvantage is the need for a
skilled human observer, since the analysis of the data requires judgement,
and the form in which they are recorded does not lend itself to easy analysis.
Nevertheless, this apparatus, suggested by some equipment devised by Karslake (1940), does permit observation of some of the important things that
a reader does when he reads. Apart from some work originating at Brunel
University, which used different equipment and had different aims (Thomas
& Harri-Augustein, 1976; Whalley & Fleming, 1975), there has been little
examination of the macro-behaviour of reading.

The Information Location Tasks

The ability to locate information in books was chosen for studies of normal
reading, since it is difficult to assess what is achieved from reading unles
the reader's intentions are clear both to himself and to the investigator.
There are problems enough in taking into account both rate of work and
quality of work (Farr, 1969) without introducing the further factor of the
reader's intention. Consequently, subjects were given a book and some questions on it. The questions (which varied, as did the books, from group to
group), were explained as far as deemed necessary, and subjects were told
that they were being recorded. They were not told that they were being
monitored, however, and in no case did the situation (as opposed to the task)
appear to put stress on the subjects.

The questions were devised so that they would elicit different styles of
reading, although one strategy was usually more efficient than another. For
example, one question might be answered using the index and then turning
to the relevant page and looking for a particular word, whereas another might
best be answered by turning to a certain chapter and then using search reading
or skimming.

Styles Used In Silent Reading

Delineation of the styles used in silent reading was necessary in order to
provide students with a conceptual framework for thinking about their reading
and also to permit the devising of exercises where students were to choose
the style appropriate to a particular reading purpose. Of course, it was also
necessary to have a list of styles in order to analyse and discuss the behaviour
in the information location tasks. Since there appeared to be confusion over
terms in the literature, and lack of a comprehensive list which took the
reader's purpose into account, introspection, discussion, and observation were
used to produce a list which distinguished five styles. (The term style is preferred to the term skill since style implies some degree of choice.) The
styles identified were scanning, search reading, skimming, receptive reading,
and responsive reading. Scanning and search reading used when the reader
knows what he is looking for, receptive reading is used to find out what an
author has to say, and responsive reading is used not only to find out what
he has to say, but also to use this information as a prompt for various types
of thinking. Skimming is primarily a process operation that enables the reader
to decide whether to use the text and, if so, in what way. (Fuller descriptions

of these styles are given in Pugh, 1975, 1978.)

Studies of Information Location
Four studies have been made using the apparatus. Of these, the report of
the study of undergraduates has not been published elsewhere, but is given
in my thesis (Pugh, 1975); the study of sixth-formers is reported in Pugh
(1976); and the joint work with Mary Neville on middle-school children is
reported in Neville and Pugh (1975b, 1977).

Undergraduate
The main purpose of this study was to test the hypothesis that a course in
reading efficiency would help students to locate information more rapidly
or, accurately, than a control group would. The subjects (N = 21, mainly men)
were matched, as far as possible, for age, sex, faculty, and type of course.
Tests of intelligence (AH4, Heim, 1970), sentence completion, and reading
comprehension (Reading Test B, Warden, 1956) were administered; the groups
did not differ significantly on these variables. Motivation was also controlled,
since it could be argued that those who volunteer for reading efficiency
courses differ from those who do not (Francis, Collins, & Cassel, 1973). Consequently the control group consisted of students who had applied to take
a course, but had not yet done so. Apart from the comparison between groups
necessary to contribute to the evaluation of the course, information was
also sought within groups as to what relationships might exist between score
on the test of intelligence, score on the sentence completion test, speed of
reading a passage of 1,000 words, performance in answering questions on this
passage, and performance on the information location tasks. The reading
passage test was one or both of two tests I devised, with known (though not
high) reliabilities. For the book task there were three questions from
"Victorian Cities" (Briggs, 1968) and four on "Memory" (Hunter, 1964), one
of which was scored out of three.

    Analysis of the results indicated that the experimental group, in general,
did not differ significantly with regard to time or accuracy from the control
group (see Table 1). However, the difference in time spent on the task based
on "Memory" is significant (p < .02). The other values of F are not significant.
Since a one-tailed test was used, in line with the original hypothesis, the
value of t for accuracy on "Victorian Cities" is significant (p < .05).

    It was also found, using a 2 x 2 table to compare totals of correct and
incorrect responses to all seven questions, that the experimental group was
superior overall at answering the questions (χ^2 = 6.182, p < .02). The correlational aspect of the study suggests that, with homogeneous groups such
as these, there is little relationship between performance on the various
tests, including the tasks of information location. It had been expected that
performance on these might be similar, although evidence in Table 1 suggests
otherwise, and since the questions had been designed to elicit various styles
of reading, the low correlations between performance on the two books does
not necessarily indicate that the tests had low validity. It certainly does
not seem that these, or other, low correlations are due to features in the
test situation, since there was a check on this possibility in the AH4 test,
which was administered and marked in two parts. Correlations between total
scores and score on either of the two parts were as high as, or higher than,

those required in the manual. The high correlations shown in the tables are generally between measures which are not independent of each other, but which are obtained by calculation from those to which they relate (see Tables 2 and 3).

Sixth-Formers
Subjects (N = 32, 11 boys and 21 girls, mean chronological age 17 yrs. 3 months) were volunteers from among those in their penultimate year in school who intended to proceed to higher education. The aim was to examine the behaviour displayed in the book tasks and to correlate performance on various tests. The correlations obtained (Table 4) are similar to those in the case of the undergraduates, although it will be noted that only one book was used here. The information on styles used, and their employment as part of a strategy, does not lend itself to analysis as readily as do the scores on tests. However, with both the sixth-formers and the undergraduates there was evidence that many of these relatively highly-skilled readers had difficulty in doing what appeared to be a straightforward task. Some of the problems may have resulted from the test situation, although subsequent discussion with the subjects suggested that this was rarely (and never markedly) the case. The sixth-form girl who spent the whole session reading the book through from the beginning was exceptional, but a great many failed to use the book's index until they had exhausted other possibilities. Search reading to locate information, and skimming to find out quickly the gist of a passage, also seemed to be more rarely employed than one might expect.

Comparison of the three correlation matrices suggests that, with the groups and test used here, there was no consistent and clear relationship between ability to use a book, measured intelligence, speed at which one chooses to read, and so on. These findings shed light on a number of long standing debates about silent reading, such as the relationship between intelligence and the speed at which one chooses to read, and the relevance of rapid reading to using books efficiently. They also leave a number of questions unanswered. The most important question is the extent to which the ability to use books can be usefully taught. The apparent independence of ability to use a book may be construed as either support for the view that teaching could be very effective, or it can suggest that what teaching has already taken place has been relatively ineffective. The question is also raised (as it is by Phillips in this volume, with regard to map reading), about to what extent inefficiency is due to the reader, or to the design of what he is reading. Waller, also in this volume advocates changes in the textual design to aid users, and Foster, in the same section, also examines the possibility of cuing readers more effectively.

Middle School Children
The teaching of strategies for locating information in books was the main concern in the studies of middle-school children. Here again, however, some attempt was made to discover what factors related to ability to use a book, although in these studies only scores on standardised reading tests were taken into account (intelligence, reading speed, and the like were not considered). The book used with these subjects was "Rats and Mice" (Silverstein & Silverstein, 1968), chosen because its topic seemed relatively neutral and because

Table 2. Matrix Showing Spearman Rank Order Correlation Coefficients between Scores on Certain Tasks: Untrained 1st year Undergraduates (n = 24).

	Sentence completion (Test B)	Reading speed (Food)	Recall comprehension (Food)	Efficiency (Food: comprehension x speed)	Intelligence (AH4 total)	Book task: time ("Memory")	Book task: time ("Victorian Cities")	Book task: accuracy ("Memory")	Book task: accuracy ("Victorian Cities")	Book task: rate of work ("Memory")	Book task: rate of work ("Victorian Cities")
Sentence completion (Test B)	–	.27	.25	.43*	.21	.14	.17	.43*	.10	.44*	.09
Reading speed (Food)	.27	–	.24	.77**	.16	.38*	.34	.11	.50	.35*	.49**
Recall comprehension (Food)	.25	.24	–	.75**	−.19	.05	−.27	.33	.01	.25	−.24
Efficiency (Food: Comprehension x speed)	.43*	.77**	.75**	–	−.23	.39*	.24	.34*	.26	.40*	.17
Intelligence (AH4 total)	.21	−.16	−.19	−.23	–	.08	.22	−.15	−.04	.04	.08
Book task time ("Memory")	.14	−.38*	.05	.39*	.08	–	.33	.21	.17	.73**	.47*
Book task: time ("Victorian Cities")	.17	.34	−.27	.24	.22	.33	–	.19	.10	.14	.88**
Book task: accuracy ("Memory")	.43*	.11	.33	.34*	−.15	.21	−.19	–	−.04	.74**	−.28
Book task: accuracy ("Victorian Cities")	.10	.50**	.01	.26	−.04	.17	.10	−.04	–	.14	.63**
Book task: rate of work ("Memory")	.44*	.35*	.25	.40*	.04	.73**	.15	.74**	.14	–	.10
Book task: rate of work ("Victorian Cities")	.89	.49**	−.24	.17	.08	.47*	.88**	−.28	.63**	.10	–

† Scores for all of the sample from which the control group of 21 was chosen are considered.
* p < 0.05; ** p < 0.01.

Table 3. Matrix Showing Spearman Rank Order Correlation Coefficients between Scores on Certain Tests: 1st year University Undergraduates (n = 19) who had taken a Reading Efficiency Course.

	Test B	Pre-test speed	Pre-test comprehension	Pre-test efficiency	Post-test speed	Post-test comprehension	Post-test efficiency	AH4	"Memory" time	"Victorian Cities" time	"Memory" accuracy	"Victorian Cities" accuracy	"Memory" rate of work	"Victorian Cities" rate of work
Test B	-	-25	.41*	.14	.15	.35	.37	-03	.30	.42*	-03	.07	.20	.34
Pre-test speed	-25	-	-33	.38	-18	.06	-08	.11	.01	.00	.16	.29	.01	-03
Pre-test comprehension	.41	-33	-	.65**	.30	.53**	.58**	.36	.20	.24	.05	.38	.07	.38
Pre-test efficiency	.14	.38	.65**	-	.24	.49*	.56**	.31	.13	.32	-04	.30	-03	.46*
Post-test speed	.15	-18	.30	.24	-	-15	.79**	.24	.21	.49**	-07	.26	.09	.64**
Post-test comprehension	.35	.06	.53*	.49*	-15	-	.36	-11	.09	.20	.32	.46*	.10	.35
Post-test efficiency	.37	-08	.58**	.56**	.79**	.36	-	.15	.07	.64**	-15	.39*	-08	.87**
AH4	-03	.11	.36	.31	.24	-11	.15	-	.38	.16	-04	.28	.29	.08
"Memory" time	.30	.01	.20	.13	.21	.09	.07	.38	-	-03	.29	.12	.93**	-11
"Victorian Cities" time	.42	.00	.24	.32	.49*	.20	.64**	.16	-03	-	-06	.03	-05	.84**
"Memory" accuracy	-03	.16	.05	-04	-07	.32	-15	-04	.29	-06	-	.14	.57**	-14
"Victorian Cities" accuracy	.07	.29	.38	.30	.26	.46*	.39*	.28	.12	.03	.14	-	.03	.38
"Memory" rate of work	.20	.01	.07	-03	.09	.10	-08	.29	.93**	.05	.57**	.03	-	-23
"Victorian Cities" rate of work	.34	-03	.38	.46*	.64**	.35	.87**	.08	-11	.84**	-14	.38	-23	-

† Data for 2 subjects in the experimental group were incomplete.
* $p < 0.05$; ** $p < 0.01$.

Table 4. Matrix Showing Spearman Rank Order Correlation Coefficients between Scores on Certain Tests: Sixth Form Pupils (n = 32).

	Test B	Speed	Comp.	Effic-iency	AH4	Accuracy ("Memory")	Rate of work ("Memory")
Sentence completion (Test B)	-	.32	.32	.47**	.32	.28	.39*
Reading speed (Food)	.32	-	-.10	.80**	.21	.12	.16
Recall comprehension (Food)	.32	-.10	-	.45**	.26	.47**	.36*
Efficiency (Food: Comprehension x speed)	.47**	.80**	.45**	-	.34	.42*	.39*
Intelligence (AH4 total)	.32	.21	.26	.34	-	.14	.10
Book task: accuracy ("Memory")	.28	.12	.47**	.42*	.14	-	.84**
Book task: rate of work ("Memory")	.39*	.16	.36*	.39*	.10	.84**	-

* $p < 0.05$; ** $p < 0.01$.

it contained an index. Three questions were prepared, and the children's teachers were consulted to ensure that the task appeared to be similar to tasks the children would need to do in project work. (It was noted, of course, that children would often generate their own questions in the realistic situation, whereas the questions asked in the study were not the children's own and, furthermore, the answers were closed in the sense that they would not lead to further reading.) The apparatus and procedure were, in all important respects, as described earlier. However, an attempt was made in analysing and presenting the results to give a clearer indication than in the earlier studies of what strategies children used.

For the first study (Neville & Pugh, 1975b), subjects were 30 children (18 girls and 12 boys), chosen from all first year children considered by the school to be capable of reading independently. In effect, this meant that about 40% of the children of the year group were excluded. Each school class in the year group was equally represented. Ages ranged from 9 years 4 months to 10 years 6 months.

Since performance of children in the first study appeared to the investigators to be unsatisfactory, and their teachers on viewing video-recordings felt so too, an attempt was made by the teachers in the following year to pay particular attention to the skills needed for information location. The investigators did not set down methods for the teachers to follow in doing

Table 5. Frequencies of Subjects Using Different Methods of Locating Information.*

| | | Method | | | | |
Study No.	Table of Contents	Index	Index & Table of Contents	Table of Contents & Chap. Heads	No Apparent Method	Total
All subjects attempting questions						
1	11	2	8	3	6	30
2	14	1	10	2	3	30

*Based on Neville and Pugh, 1977

Table 6. Middle School Children's Use of Books. Frequencies According to Number of Questions Correct and Appropriateness of Strategy.*

| No. of questions correct | Strategy | | | | | | | |
| | Appropriate | | Partially Appropriate | | Inappropriate | | N | |
	Study 1	Study 2	Study 1	Study 2	Study 1	Study 2	Study 1	Study 2
None	1	–	6	5	6	8	13	13
One	2	4	4	5	–	1	6	10
Two	3	3	–	2	–	–	3	5
Three	8	2	–	–	–	–	8	2
N	14	9	10	12	6	9	30	30

*Based on Neville and Pugh, 1977

this, but discussed the problem and left the teachers to devise solutions. Subjects on this occasion (Neville & Pugh, 1977) were a similar group of children to those studied in the previous year. Hence, the findings in Tables 5 and 6 are for comparable samples. Table 5 shows the methods used and, for each year, the number of children using a particular method. There appears to be a slight improvement here, but this is balanced by a decline in those using strategies deemed to be inappropriate (Table 6).

A follow-up study of the children in the first group was made four years later. The data are not yet fully analysed, but it appears that some of these children still have difficulty with this task. However, these are not the poorest readers as judged by standardised tests of reading. As with the studies of undergraduates and of sixth-formers, correlational analysis revealed no consistent patterns of relationship between reading ability, as measured here by a sentence completion test (N.F.E.R., 1970) and a cloze test (McLeod & Unwin, 1970), and ability to use a book, considered as accuracy of answers or appropriateness of strategy.

Conclusions

Due to the method of observation and to the need to specify a task for the subjects, the studies described here have serious limitations. However, as argued earlier, accuracy of recording may be misleading if unusual constraints on the subject render the task of doubtful validity. The emphasis here has been to record behaviour in realistic reading situations, while sacrificing accuracy of recording. For future work, however, it would be useful to refine the strategies used, although this may naturally arise from more experience of observation of readers. In other words, the problem could be less that of research technique than of knowledge about the area being studied.

Implications for teaching are considerable, for there appears to have been little attention paid to how to use books to locate information. More broadly, there have been few attempts to teach the uses of silent reading, beyond speed reading courses which have already been criticised for their misleading model of what is involved in reading. The hints on reading strategies given in courses on study skills indicate that there is a concern with strategy in reading, but they appear to be based almost entirely on the introspection of those who propose them.

Methods described by Shebilske and Reid (this volume) for studying reader's perceptions of the macro-structure of texts may cast light on the strategies used in certain types of reading. Nevertheless, if our understanding of the styles and strategies used in silent reading is to increase, and the teaching of them is to develop, much more evidence is needed about, to use Huey's phrase, "what we do when we read." Approaches described here can, it is suggested, help obtain this evidence.

REFERENCES

Anderson, I.H., & Dearborn, W.F.   The psychology of teaching reading. New
    York: Ronald Press, 1952.
Briggs, A. Victorian cities (Revised ed.). Harmondsworth: Penguin Books, 1968.

Carmichael, L., & Dearborn, W.F. Reading and visual fatigue. London: Harrap, 1948.

Dearborn, W.F., & Anderson, I.H. A new method for teaching phrasing and for increasing the size of reading fixations. Psychological Record, 1973, 1, 459-475.

Ditchburn, R.W. Eye-movements and visual perception. Oxford: Clarendon Press, 1973.

Farr, R. Reading: What can be measured? Newark, Del.: International Reading Association, 1969.

Foster, J. The use of visual cues in text. (This volume.)

Francis, R.D., Collins, J.K., & Cassel, A.J. The effect of reading tuition on academic achievement: Volunteering and method of tuition. British Journal of Educational Psychology, 1973, 43, 298-300.

Geyer, J.J. Comprehensive and partial models related to the reading process. Reading Research Quarterly, 1972, 7(4), 541-587.

Goodman, K.S. The psycholinguistic nature of the reading process. In K.S. Goodman (Ed.), The psycholinguistic nature of the reading process. Detroit: Wayne State University Press, 1968, 13-26.

Heim, Alice W. AH4 group test of general intelligence. (Test and revised manual). Windsor: National Foundation for Educational Research, 1970.

Huey, E.B. The psychology and pedagogy of reading. New York: Macmillan, 1908. Reprinted, Cambridge, MA: MIT Press, 1968.

Hunter, I.M.L. Memory. (Revised ed.). Harmondsworth: Penguin Books, 1964.

Karslake, J.S. The Purdue eye-camera: A practical apparatus for studying the attention value of advertisements. Journal of Applied Psychology, 1940, 24, 417-440.

Levy-Schoen, A. & O'Regan, K. The control of eye movements in reading. (This volume.)

McLeod, J., & Unwin, D. Gap reading comprehension test. London: Heinemann, 1970.

Mackworth, N.H. Ways of recording line of sight. In R.A. Monty & J.W. Senders (Eds.), Eye movements and psychological processes. Hillsdale, NJ: Erlbaum, 1976.

Maxwell, Martha J. An experimental investigation of the effect of instructional set and information on reading rate. In E.L. Thurston & L.E. Hafner (Eds.), Philosophical and sociological bases of recording. Milwaukee, Wisconsin: National Reading conference, 1965, 181-187.

Neville, M.H., & Pugh, A.K. An exploratory study of the application of time-compressed and time-expanded speech in the development of the English language proficiency of foreign students. English Language Teaching Journal, 1975, 29 (4), 320-329. (a)

Neville, M.H., & Pugh, A.K. Reading ability and ability to use a book: a study of middle school children. Reading, 1975, 9 (3), 23-31. (b)

Neville, M.H., & Pugh, A.K. Ability to use a book: The effect of teaching. Reading, 1977, 11(3), 13-22.

National Foundation for Educational Research. Reading test AD. Slough: National Foundation for Educational Research, 1970.

Perry, W.G. Students' uses and misuses of reading skills. Harvard Educational Review, 1959, 29 (3), 193-200. In A. Melnik & J. Merritt (Eds.), Reading: Today and tomorrow. London: University of London Press, 1972.

Perry, W.G., & Whitlock, C.P. Harvard University Reading Films, Series Two. Cambridge, MA: Harvard University Press, 1948.

Pugh, A.K. The design and evaluation of reading efficiency courses. Unpublished M.Phil. thesis: University of Leeds, School of Education, 1974.

Pugh, A.K. The development of silent reading. In W. Latham (Ed.), The road to effective reading. London: Ward Lock, 1975.

Pugh, A.K. Implications of problems of language testing for the validity of speed reading courses. System, 1976, 4 (1), 29-39.

Pugh, A.K. Methods of studying silent reading behaviour. Research Intelligence, 1977, 3 (1), 42-43.

Pugh, A.K. The study and teaching of silent reading. London: Heinemann, 1978.

Rankin, E.F. The measurement of reading flexibility. Newark, DE: International Reading Association, 1974.

Shebilske, W., & Reid, L.S. Reading eye movements, macro structure and comprehension processes. (This volume.)

Silverstein, A. & Silverstein, V. Rats and mice: Friends and foes of man. Glasgow: Blackie, 1968.

Thomas, L.F., & Harri-Augustein, E. S. The self-organised learner and the printed word. A report to the Social Science Research Council. Uxbridge: Brunel University Centre for the Study of Human Learning, 1976.

Tinker, M.A. Bases for effective reading. Minneapolis: University of Minnesota Press, 1965.

Vernon, M.D. The experimental study of reading. Cambridge: Cambridge University Press, 1931.

Vernon, M.D. Review of G.R. Wainwright: Towards efficiency in reading. Reading, 1969, 3 (2), 33-34.

Waller, R.H.W. Typographic access structures for educational texts. (This volume.)

Warden, V.B. Construction and standardisation of a reading test. University of London: unpublished M.A. thesis, 1956.

Whalley, P.C., & Fleming, R.W. An experiment with a simple recorder of reading behaviour. Programmed Learning and Educational Technology, 1975, 12 (2), 120-123.

Yarbus, A.L. Eye movements and vision. (Translated by B. Haigh.) New York: Plenum Press, 1967.

Technological Media Designed for Visual Presentation

Introduction

H. Bouma

One of the reasons for organizing our symposium was a feeling of concern
about the rapidly increasing use of technological media for the presentation
of visible language. Reflection on the use of such media now and in the near
future can lead to:
1) better insight into the dynamics of reading and visual search;
2) understanding of how humans adapt to new ways of presenting visual
   information;
3) optimal designs of such media;
4) The development or modification of visible languages and sign systems,
   optimally adapted to the human user.
Properties of such technological media are therefore of both theoretical
and practical concern. If the study of human information processing concerns
the types of processing actually occurring in everyday life, it follows that
new information media have an impact on such research. As yet, psychological literature hardly reflects the developments in technological media,
thus leaving the first two purposes underdeveloped. On the practical side,
engineers designing displays and display systems tend to concentrate on technical and economic questions and to take human information processing into
account only on an intuitive basis. Graphic designers, skilled in applying
their creative intuition, have always adapted to the technology involved,
but the rapid rate of technological development has restricted the designer's
role in the shaping of the visible information on displays. The organizers
of the symposium think that psychologists, graphic designers, and display
engineers should cooperate closely in studying man in his technological
environment and in optimizing the situation for the display of visual
information.

All technological displays have properties that differ from normally
printed text -- the most common way of presenting information. These properties may be of a limiting character, such as brightness, contrast, or

447

resolution, the amount of information simultaneously available, the lay-out, and the type of visual information to which the medium is limited. For example, in the 7-segment digits used in displays, several pairs differ in one segment only. Cathode ray tubes usually have low contrast, display white on black, and are restricted to some 1000 characters for the full screen. Moreover they are vulnerable to illumination from outside, which may produce specular reflections and disturbing contrasts with the environment. As another example, printed computer output often contains far more information than users can adequately handle, so that overview is easily lost. Display medium and user are often poorly adapted to each other, making it difficult for people to take sufficient advantage of the possibilities that technology offers, especially those that go beyond paper and books, such as the interactive options that the computer allows.

Since human information processing is flexible and adaptive, users can learn to handle many different types of displayed information. Such flexibility has probably led to a neglect of the extra difficulties caused by non-optimal links between display and user, a neglect that has often resulted in speed and error rates that are far from optimum and that often put users under too much stress, particularly after prolonged interaction with a device. The reasons for the stress may be intuitively clear, but cannot be really understood in terms of disturbances in processes of reading and search. It is only fair to the users to take their processing abilities into account when designing such displays. However, insights into relevant human processing abilities are weak, and well designed laboratory studies are necessary for a real understanding of the processing dynamics. That understanding should be supplied by more direct, "real time" studies that examine performance where such displays are actually in use for long periods of time. A few relevant questions to be examined in this field might be: How does the eye control system operate? How much more time and effort are required to recognize closely spaced visual items in low contrast, foveally and parafoveally? Can size and contrast compensate for each other? What influence does poor legibility have on the amount of information momentarily available to the user in his "working memory" or on the amount of rehearsal required? The section on Technological Media is therefore central to the theme of the volume, and it is hoped that the issues examined will lead to an increase in research directed toward such questions and to a continuous exchange of information between display engineers, reading researchers, and graphic designers. From the papers of this session, it is apparent that the distinction between dedicated users and general users is relevant. Whereas dedicated users may be assumed to have had a considerable amount of training, general users in their home environment are on their own. For them, shortcomings in the displayed information lead immediately to difficulties which feed back only slowly to the designers.

Rosenthal's paper bears witness to the fact that even for professional users there are problems to be solved and, fortunately for them, inadequate solutions lead to direct financial consequences which speed up the feedback cycle. The system described by Rosenthal is an interactive display system for guiding operators to optimize the functioning of the telephone network in the U.S.A. The relevance of his description and his findings is not confined to this particular system since many of the points he raises can be applied to the semi-professional or general user.

Hoekstra describes the semi-professional use of visual display systems in the office of the near future. One of the problems involved is the overview which users require of the information stored in the electronic archives and of the options open to them at any particular moment. Even such an apparently simple question as the form of the display, long side vertical (as in standard paper for letters and books) or horizontal (as in electronic displays, borrowed from regular TV) cannot satisfactorily be answered. Maybe the issue does not matter, maybe it does. It seems at least somewhat odd, that electronic text systems have been introduced on a large scale without being preceded or accompanied by studies concerned with usage and the user. Hoekstra is anxious to remedy the situation and raises questions which should be solved before mass production overtakes the options for control.

Jackson describes preliminary experiences with an experimental network that provides the home user with general information on a great many subjects. The information is received on a television screen either by television broadcast or via telephone lines from a local memory. The many problems he mentions are unlikely to be solved before the general introduction of the medium, but his awareness of the type of problems (normal techniques for search and scanning, as developed for books and newspapers, do not necessarily apply) and his presentation may help psychologists and graphic designers to deal more effectively with display problems.

The other papers in this section concern special instances of the problems at hand. Wiseman and Linden recommend in their paper an increased use of certain network structures as a possible language suited both for the computer and for the human user. Marcel and Barnard have actually translated a practical situation into a laboratory task in which a number of general aspects of man-machine interaction can be studied. Eger puts to advantage limitations of certain computer displays for the design of pictograms. Such results are encouraging in that they can be generalized to many more situations than the one actually studied.

The Design of Technological Displays (Tutorial Paper)

Robert I. Rosenthal

A technological display is the interface between the human and technological systems. This tutorial is concerned with computer-based systems and displays that enable humans to interact with computers, and most of the examples are taken from real-time systems. It is with these systems that display design becomes most critical, since the human must respond accurately under speed stress. The displays must help the human comprehend complex and rapidly changing system events. Due to limitations in display size, the data are often highly coded and difficult to interpret. The learnability and memorability of displays are therefore important aspects of display design.

The field of technological displays can be described in terms of certain broad categories. From a presentation point of view, displays can be classified as either alphanumeric or graphic. Within the field of alphanumeric CRT displays, a further distinction occurs between the conversational mode, where input is limited to a specific CRT location, and the formatted display that allows entry at pre-specified locations anywhere on a fixed mask. These types of displays are illustrated with examples from real-time telephone traffic management systems.

The fundamental display design process consists of eight major steps that carry the designer from the initial analysis of the operating system to the detailed formatting of each display. At each stage the designer makes decisions based on adequate knowledge of human needs and limitations. Specific areas for additional psychological research are pointed out.

In its broadest sense, the technological display is any presentation of data associated with an engineering or scientific discipline. To narrow things somewhat, it is necessary to distinguish between real-time displays and non-real-time displays. The distinction has more to do with the intended mode of use by the human than with the data or their method of generation. A display is an aid to the performance of some task. The user of the real-time display is involved in tasks that force him to decode and encode information within a rapidly changing environment. The speedometer in a car is an example. It is updated frequently and the driver needs to obtain information in a brief glance. If the display lags behind the speed of the auto or if it is difficult to determine quickly the current reading, the display is poorly designed. Thus, in general, real-time displays have the advantage that they can be objectively evaluated by the criteria of speed and accuracy of use.

Nonreal-time displays, like the weather forecast in the newspaper, are meant to be studied leisurely. The criteria for good design are more difficult to define, and the merit of any particular display is more difficult to determine. Thus, the psychological factor places less constraint on the display designer. Since one purpose of this tutorial is to define areas where psychological research is needed in the field of technological displays, I shall focus on real-time display as the field of greater interest. For additional discussion of both real-time and nonreal-time displays, see Biberman (1973), Dodwell (1970), Howard (1963), Handler and Weizenbaum (1972), Kelley (1972), Meister (1976), Stewart (1976).

Since World War 2 the history of technological systems, both military and industrial, has been that the role of the human has become less important as computers have become more sophisticated and more readily available. This has caused fundamental changes in display design. First, the human task is less strictly determined; often, the human does whatever is left to be done when the programmer runs out of time or budget. Second, and even more important, there has been a significant increase in the data available to be displayed. Usually the computer can afford to generate many more measurements than were cost-justifiable with hardware instrumentation. Thus the designer has more options, while the definition of the human's role has become more elusive.

The term that best describes the human role in the modern computerized system is "management." This discussion will draw its examples from the field of real-time computer-based management displays. This does not significantly limit the discussion, since this field is broad enough to amply illustrate all the human factors considerations found in other display applications. Furthermore, since management is such a new field, the right kind of psychological research can have enormous impact on current design practice.

This paper is organized into three parts. I will describe the real-time management system in functional terms, using as illustration the system designed by Bell Laboratories for the management of telephone traffic. Within this context, I will describe the major types of display options available, and, finally, the display design process itself will be discussed. Certain critical areas where psychological research can provide an important input to design decision will be examined.

Real-Time Management Systems

Let us consider an operating system and try to understand why it needs real-time management. Since I am with Bell Laboratories, I have chosen the telephone network for consideration. This network consists of thousands of switching machines and the connections between them that are called trunk groups. Figure 1 shows a simplified example of how a call might be routed through a telephone network. Suppose customer 1 in Albuquerque, New Mexico, wishes to call customer 2 in Oklahoma. He dials ten digits into a switching machine called a central office. This office contains equipment that can determine that no connection exists to the central office in Oklahoma. Therefore, the call is sent to a sectional center in Albuquerque which does have a trunk group to Oklahoma City. If there is an idle circuit in this trunk group, the call will be established and the talking path will involve just those four switching offices. In the majority of cases that is what happens. However, suppose that due to heavy traffic there are no idle circuits in the trunk group from Albuquerque to Oklahoma City; the Albuquerque office would then use its trunk group to the Denver regional center to establish a path through Denver and Dallas, thus involving six offices.

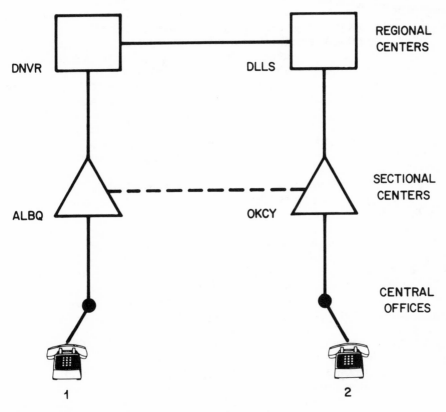

Figure 1. Example of telephone traffic routing.

In the majority of cases customer 1's call will be successfully switched to customer 2. However, under unusual circumstances such as abnormal traffic loads, hurricanes, unavoidable equipment failures, etc., calls may not be completed. It is such circumstances that make a network management system necessary. The manager is provided with tools that can preserve service when conditions would otherwise cause service degradation.

The telephone network has been liberally sized so that call failures should rarely occur. This sizing is based on two factors: predicted customer calling patterns and predicted equipment reliabilities. If the equipment functions are reliable and the customer calling patterns are as predicted, then obviously the system will work. However, in the real world customers do not always behave as expected and the equipment does not always function perfectly. A natural disaster such as a hurricane may damage telephone facilities for hundreds of miles. When the news is nationally televised, thousands of calls per hour may reach the disaster area. The switching capacity of the machines may be overwhelmed causing sender delay, and ultimately affecting the switching of calls throughout the United States. If sender delay spreads unchecked, service will be disrupted even between points quite distant from the hurricane site.

To deal with such problems the Bell System established a network of management centers to monitor and control the telephone system. Each center manages the traffic in a particular geographical area. Data about switching machines and trunk groups in the area are fed by means of telemetry into a computer located in the network management center. This center is responsible for the four basic functions of real-time management: surveillance, analysis, control, and evaluation. The surveillance function consists of a continuous automatic monitoring of the incoming data to quickly detect real or potential problems. Once a problem has been identified, then an analysis must be undertaken to determine the best course of management action. Traffic may be rerouted from one path to another; some of the alternate routes normally available may be temporarily closed to prevent further network overload; or customers may be routed to special announcements in an attempt to influence their calling behavior. In determining the best course of action, the manager interrogates the data base using interactive displays, and often calls on specially designed decision algorithms that can recommend courses of action.

Once analysis is complete, the manager may wish to implement control. The display system makes available a variety of means to format control messages that will be sent by the computer to the switching offices for execution. In a final step, the manager evaluates his control to see whether it is in fact helping the situation. I will return frequently to these four basic management functions -- surveillance, analysis, control, and evaluation since they constitute the core activities that must be supported by the display system.

There are three major types of display hardware in the network management center: a wall display composed of alphanumeric labels and binary indicators, receive-only printers, and five interactive cathode ray tube (CRT) terminals. The basic operation of the center is as follows. The surveillance function is accomplished by the joint activity of the computer and the human. The first step, the responsibility of the computer, is the detection of conditions

that might indicate overflow or delay problems. The computer executes
thousands of calculations each 5 minutes and compares the results to preset
thresholds. If a threshold is exceeded, the associated indicator on the wall-
mounted exception display is turned on, and in preselected critical cases,
the exception will cause an audible alarm. At the same time, a message
is printed stating the details of the exception.

Many exceptions are not really problems, they are simply statistical fluctu-
ations of the traffic that produce random symptoms but not persistent conditions calling for control. Therefore, the next step is to investigate the exception to determine its seriousness and likely persistence. To do this the manager uses his interactive cathode ray tube (CRT) display -- the primary display
tool in the center. He interrogates the data base asking to see trend information about trunk group and office exceptions, and examines the recent history
of each exception to identify persistent conditions.

Once the existence of a problem has been verified, the manager must
make an analysis in order to select the appropriate network control. Here
again, he will use the CRT as his basic tool for accessing the data base. If
he decides to control, input of that control is again a CRT function.

The entry of a control signals the beginning of evaluation. This is one
of the most important display functions, and the one most often neglected.
The key to evaluation is that the human should at all times be able to see
an overview of the relation of controls to problems throughout the entire
system. In a telephone network, the controls that reroute or otherwise affect
traffic must be highly visible in relation to the existing network situation.
This function is performed by the wall display which shows control status
in direct relation to known exceptions. In addition, special programs automatically monitor the controls to make sure they are effective. The results of
this monitoring are displayed by printed messages and special indications
on the wall display.

I have described the operation of the network management center with
respect to the four basic real-time management functions and the displays
that support these functions. Some of these are receive-only displays -- print-
outs and visual indicators generated by the computer when reporting exceptions. On the other hand, we may have input-only displays such as control
panels, teletypewriters, or keyboards. Of course, the most powerful and
widely used displays are interactive, performing both send and receive functions. We have seen that the CRT is the basic tool for interactions between
human and the computer. Some typical examples of interactive CRT displays
follow.

Interactive CRT Displays

Interactive displays may be divided into two basic types: alphanumeric and
graphic. Each type can be further subdivided into conversational and formatted
varieties. In conversational entry, the human and the computer exchange
information by typing. In formatted displays the computer presents a prepared
background, called a page, that allows entry windows at many locations.
The human can now enter symbols specifying a complex data search all at
once, rather than serially. It is important to recognize that these four basic
types of displays are functionally equivalent from an information-flow point
of view. Any given data, supporting any given task, can be communicated

by any of the four methods.

I shall now examine factors that should influence the designer in the selection of the display type and offer some comments about design guide-lines within each type. Discussed, in historical order, are the conversational alphanumeric display, the formatted alphanumeric display, and finally the graphic display.

Conversational Alphanumeric Displays

The alphanumeric CRT typically uses the standard typewriter keyboard as an input device and the CRT screen as the output device. The interaction, called a dialogue, can be initiated either by the human or by the system. A large number of dialogues have been written in the past 15 years and there is a lucid and thorough review of this field by James Martin (1973).

```
SELECT AN OPTION
0 = EXIT
1 = SPECIFIC OFFICE
2 = ALL OFFICES IN SPECIFIC REGION
3 = ALL OFFICES IN ALL REGIONS

***** 2

SC      SN      DN      DL

ST      NR      RC      PI

WA      WH      MT      RE

SELECT REGION(S)

***** NR

ENTER SEARCH LIMITS

***** ALL
```

OFFICE	%MFD	%OVSD	%COD	%MC1	%MC2	%IMA	%PSC
1 NRWY IL NO 41T	0			0	0	28 *	
2 LSLL IL LS 07T	3			0	0	36 *	
3 SPFD IL SF 06T	2			0	0	23 *	
4 CHMP IL TC ADO	5 *			0	0	40 *	
5 DAVL IL DA 07T	3			0	0	31 *	
6 DCTR IL DC 01T	1			0	0	18 *	
7 PEOR IL 03 6AT	5 *			0	0	33 *	
8 RCIS IL RI 01T	11 *			0	0	56 *	
9 BLTN IL XD 06T	2			0	0	21 *	
10 CHCG IL EG 43T	96 *			100 *	100 *	1	
11 CHHG IL CH 07T	7 *			0	0	64 *	
12 HGPK IL HP 07T	2			0	0	42 *	

Figure 2. Example of a conversational alphanumeric display.

The sample dialogue discussed is shown in Figure 2. The computer asks the human the number of offices in the data base he wishes to investigate. The defining characteristic of a conversational format is that the human's response must be typed in at a single specific location, wherever the computer has placed the cursor. Since the user is not allowed to enter data at random locations on the display surface, the designer must find a way to instruct the user as to possible entry options. In some cases, he can depend on the user's memory. If not, a frequently used device is to index each possible user option. At the beginning of this dialogue four options were provided. He is given a standard indication, five asterisks, to let him know he can now type in his answer. He inputs a 2, indicating an interest in one specific region, and the program returns a list of all regions in standard two character form. The user selects the Norway region, and the computer next asks for specific search limits. The dialogue, at this point, could have used an index method to display the possible search limits. However, lengthy dialogue can be costly, especially if the computer is remote from the terminal. Since this particular item appears in many dialogues in this system, the designer felt he could assume the user would know his optional search limits -- whether he wants all offices, or offices of a particular class. The user in this case specifies all, and the computer now produces data for all offices in the Norway region. To enable the operator to correlate this display with the binary indicators on the wall display, asterisks are used to indicate where exception thresholds are exceeded.

This example is typical of interactive CRT displays of the conversational type. The method can be used in a wide variety of ways, some good, some bad, but, in general, there is a tradeoff between the amount of labeling and the cost of transmission. Some early designers strove for English language inputs as well as outputs. It is now recognized that the objective for input should be brevity rather than natural language. The use of indexing to reduce the number of symbols that must be entered is generally recommended (Ma (Martin, 1973).

Formatted Alphanumeric Displays
Several drawbacks to conversational format may be obvious. The conversation can become quite lengthy: six interactions were required before the search could be made. Clearly, all of these possibilities could have been enumerated in a single multiple-choice format, and the user could have entered his entire selection in one interaction.

A second important characteristic of conversation is its inherent linearity. This is of course a great advantage from the point of view of programming simplicity. The computer has limited the human to a very small number of possible input alternatives. But suppose the search becomes more complicated; suppose we wish to allow the human to branch extensively. As the number of possible options to be selected at each decision point increases, the need for some more flexible means of input becomes clear. One wants to use the display surface as an external memory that will continuously keep him aware of exactly where he is in the investigation. The formatted display is therefore the preferred method when the data base and nature of the analysis becomes sufficiently complex.

EX 51   MACHINE EXCEPTIONS   OFFICE (   )   CL

SC SN DN DL ST NR RC PI WA WH MT RE ALL   R   S   PT ALL
( ) ( ) ( ) ( ) ( ) (S) ( ) ( ) ( ) ( ) ( ) ( ) ( )   ( ) ( ) ( ) (S)

| | | | | | | | | | DISCRETE | CB | HTR | TG |
OFFICE	%MFD	%OVSD	%COD	%MC1	%MC2	%IMA	%PSC	CS	MC	CC	TO	A	M	X	C
RCIS IL RI 01T ( )	11 *			0	0	56 ˙									
BLTN IL 06T ( )	2			0	0	21 ˙									
CHCG IL EG 43T ( )	96 *			100 *	100 *	1									
CHHG IL CH 07T ( )	7 *			0	0	64 ˙									
HGPK IL HP 07T ( )	2			0	0	42 ˙									
MILW WI 48 01T ( )	8 *			0	0	34 ˙									
WKSH WI 02 41T ( )	0			0	0	17 ˙									

	%MFD	%OVSD	%COD	%MC1	%MC2	%IMA	%PSC								
EXPANSION NEW								CSOV	CSMF	CSCC		MC1	MC2	MC3		PSC LKF LKC TLKF TLKC
2ND															
3RD															
4TH															

PART (2) OF 3   FRWD ( )   BKWD ( )   DATA FOR   TRANSFER TO

NO-PROB ( )   INTRA: 0 ( )   AS-IS ( )   ALL ( )   INTER: 0 ( )   AS-IS ( )   ALL ( )   P( )   TGX ( )

Figure 3.   Example of a formatted alphanumeric display.

To illustrate the formatted display concept, I have taken the simple dialogue shown in Figure 2 and presented it as a formatted display in Figure 3. Remember that the initial appearance of the conversational format asked whether the user was interested in a single office, a single region, or all offices in the data base. The formatted display gives these options on the top two lines. The user can type in an office of interest, designate a region of interest, or ask for all offices. The "S" symbol indicates he will obtain all as the default if he designates nothing. Likewise, the search limits are specified on the second line, with "all" given as the default. Having designated the Norway region, he strikes the SEND key and with this single input obtains the search that, in conversational method, he needed three inputs to obtain.

Graphics Displays
Alphanumeric display has several important disadvantages. First, it places heavy emphasis on the presentation of detailed lists, at the expense of pattern overview. Second, the cursor interaction is relatively clumsy due to hardware limitations, and the speed of painting the CRT can also be slow. Graphics provide capabilities to meet these kinds of limitations. Pattern overview can be enhanced by pictorial methods, using either black and white or color. Interactions with light pen or joystick cursor are typically faster than alphanumeric displays. A simple graphical equivalent of CRT page EX51 has been developed. Although it is not a sophisticated demonstration of graphical capability, it does make the point that the same task can be encoded into any of the basic types of formats, and that the final decision must really be made on the basis of engineering considerations, human factors considerations, and cost.

One purpose of graphical display is to show complete network pattern overview. A background format was therefore developed that would show in a standard way all office locations in all regions. Figure 4 shows what this might look like. The rectangles represent a quasi-geographical organization of the 12 United States and Canadian regions. The symbols indicate offices in sender delay. The symbols are standard network management symbols for the type of office, and the symbol locations are roughly equivalent to the geographical location of the office. The size of the symbol encodes the degree of sender delay, while the arrow indicates whether the trend is increasing or decreasing over the preceding 20 minutes. Thus, the display allows the manager to see at a glance that he has many delay problems in the Norway region and few or no problems elsewhere. The most serious is the Chicago sectional center because it is an important machine (a triangle denotes a sectonal center), its size is large, indicating heavy delay, and its trend is increasing.

Although this display gives overview pattern, it provides little detail. The user would, at this point, be interested in seeing the actual offices that are control candidates, so this is shown on the graphics detail display (Figure 5). Since congestion tends to spread between offices that have close routing relationships, this display shows these particular offices connected to the Chicago sectional center by solid lines. Cursor designation of any office would allow the manager to obtain alphanumeric detail about the office. He can also request a printout on an associated receive-only printer that gives listing-type information.

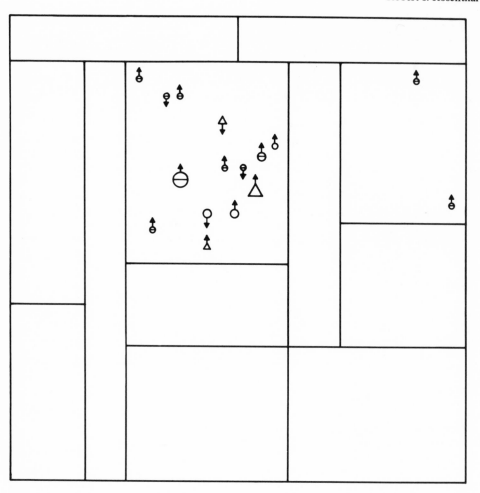

Figure 4. Example of a graphics overview display.

To summarize, the graphical display provides a kind of overview and immediate patterning of significant events that is impossible with a straight listing.
Clearly, the modern control center has need for all three types of display.
Each has its strengths and weaknesses, and the art of display design is to
employ each as it suits the task and data interactions.

The Process of Display Design
The display system has been defined as the interface between the human
and technological system. Let us now examine more closely the process
by which a display system is designed, keeping in mind those aspects that
seem to depend on psychological factors. An overview of the design process
is shown in Figure 6. The first step is an analysis of the operating system

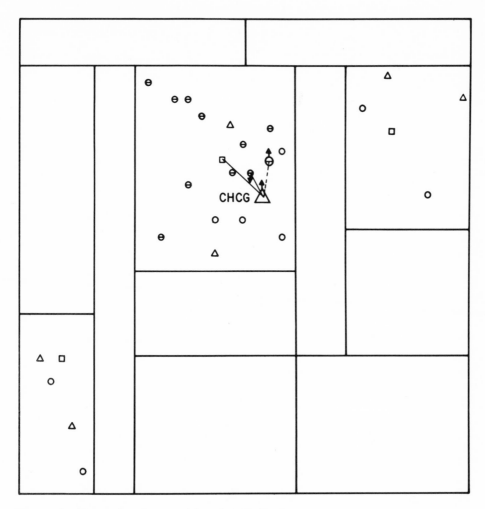

Figure 5. Example of a graphics detail display.

to identify and describe the management functions that need to be performed. Next, these functions are divided between software and human within the managing system. The result of this allocation of resources is to make possible an explicit organization of the displays needed to support the human's piece of the action.

The third box indicates a task analysis that results in a flow diagram presentation blocking out the major interactions between the human and the display system. The steps in the task flow can now be assigned to specific areas of a two-dimensional formatted display, or specific interactions of a sequential dialogue. This is done in the process referred to as formatting. Once the overall format of the display is determined, the design proceeds to the detailed encoding of each part.

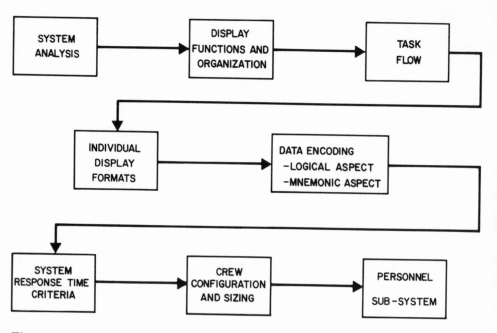

Figure 6. Functional view of the display design process.

The encoding has two principal aspects. In the logical aspect, the human must decode data in accordance with a specific rule. He must know that, if A and B, then I do C, whereas if not A or not B, then I am not justified in doing C. This logic is ultimately related to the original system analysis that specified the relationship between conditions in the operating system and measures in the data base.

The second aspect the designer must consider is mnemonic. The human must be able to recognize the labels, even though they are necessarily abbreviated. He must have a mental model of the system that enables him to recall the rules. Often, this model will be quite complicated, and the issue of comprehension is ever present in complex display systems.

The output of this detailed design step is a display that may now be programmed and tested. The final three steps shown in the flow diagram involve additional information that must be generated by the designer to guide systems development. Response time is the delay imposed by the system on the human-computer interaction; the computer must be fast enough to adequately support the human. The other side of this coin, how fast can the human respond, becomes an issue in the next step -- crew configuration and crew sizing. Here the designer attempts to specify how many humans and display interfaces are needed to meet the dynamics of the operating system. Finally, there is the entire question of the personnel subsystem. This includes the development of technical documentation, training, and other kinds of personnel support.

The following discussion will describe in more detail the specific steps in display design. To make each step more meaningful, I have taken an example from a display system recently completed. It will be seen that each step in the process leads naturally to the next, and itself depends on information generated by the previous step.

The reader will recall the example of customer 1 in Albuquerque, New Mexico, attempting to call customer 2 in Oklahoma. If the call overflowed the high usage group between Albuquerque and Oklahoma City, it was offered to a final path, Albuquerque-to-Denver-to-Dallas-to-Oklahoma City. If this final path were to overflow, calls would begin to fail. A system analysis has shown that in order to detect and solve this type of final overflow problem, data need to be collected and displayed at a network management center that can monitor trunk groups across the entire North American continent.

FUNCTION	COMPUTER	HUMAN
1. DETECT OVERFLOW PROBLEM	X	
2. PRELIMINARY SCREENING	X	
3. SELECTION OF NEXT PROBLEM TO BE ANALYZED		X
4. ANALYTIC DETERMINATION OF BEST REROUTE CANDIDATES	X	
5. FINAL SELECTION		X
6. IMPLEMENTATION OF REROUTE		X
7. MONITORING OF REROUTES-IN-EFFECT	X	
8. REMOVAL OF POORLY PERFORMING REROUTES		X

Figure 7. Allocation of functions to human and computer in traffic reroute selection.

The system analysis phase of this particular study took many months. It resulted in the development of a computerized decision algorithm that examines all the possible traffic reroutes and presents real-time recommendations. The human, knowing certain information not available to the algorithm, makes the final selection. Figure 7 shows the sequence of functions and their allocation to human and computer in the final system design. The display system must provide support to all these functions. Figure 8 shows how the display system was organized.

Two CRTs were used for the following reasons. First, the job seemed to break down naturally into two separate parts: tasks related to the selection of new reroutes, versus tasks related to monitoring existing reroutes. Second, the program developers showed a marked preference for segregating the receive-only display functions involved in reroute monitoring from the interactive display functions involved in reroute selection, since that considerably simplified the hardware interfaces.

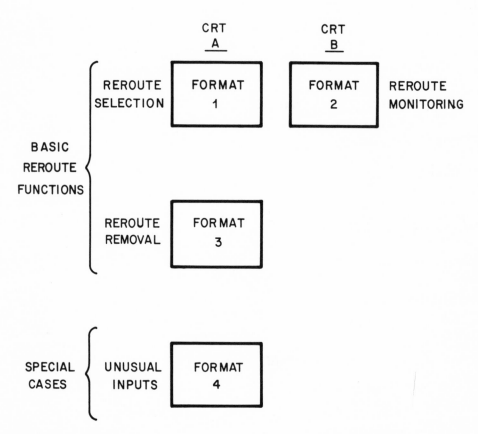

Figure 8. CRT display organization to support reroute functions.

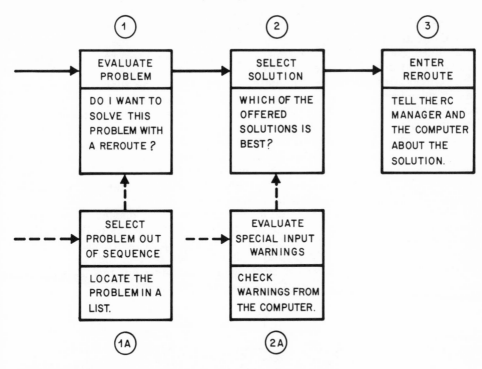

Figure 9. Task flow for the reroute selection function.

Thus there were two CRTs, one to be used for interactions, the other for receive-only monitoring displays. Interactive functions were further broken down into three categories: those associated with reroute selection, those associated with reroute removal, and some specific interactions that occurred on a more infrequent basis. A separate alphanumeric format was found to be necessary for each one.

The next step in display design is the definition of the task sequence for each individual display format. I shall take Format 1, which supports the reroute selection function, as the basis for working out the example.

Figure 9 shows a simplified portion of the task flow for Format 1. The manager can enter this Reroute Selection display in one of two ways. He can either ask to examine that particular overflow problem that the computer has determined is of highest priority (Task 1), or he can select some other overflow (Task 1A). Providing these alternate capabilities goes back to the original system analysis. There it was determined that ordinarily the manager will want to work on the most severe problem -- the problem that has resulted in the most lost calls. However, sometimes he gets special requests from regional centers and would like the ability to select a problem out of sequence -- a problem lower in the priority list. Accordingly, the task flow must recognize both entry points.

Completion of the task analysis illustrated in this figure allows the designer to begin the next stage, the formatting of the CRT display. Ordinarily this involves allocating space on the surface of the display to each of the tasks called out in the flow diagram (Figure 10). The CRT surface itself consists of 24 lines, each of which is 80 characters long. Space was reserved at the bottom and top of the page for certain functions not relevant to this discussion. The central 20-line area was allocated to the five tasks called out in the task flow diagram. The first decision that had to be made concerned the number of problems that could simultaneously be present. A review of records and discussion with operators indicated that 25 was probably an adequate number. Accordingly, the lower half of the display surface was allocated to the display of up to 25 AB problems. Beside each is an input window where the manager can place a designate symbol. Transmitting this designate to the computer by depressing a key on the control keyboard tells the computer which "out-of-sequence" problem to analyse.

The analysis itself is presented in the top half of the display. Ordinarily, this would be the analysis of the problem the computer takes to be of highest priority. To obtain this highest priority analysis requires only a simple one-stroke keyboard action. The display of information follows the rule that a task sequence should generally be shown in a left-to-right top-to-bottom

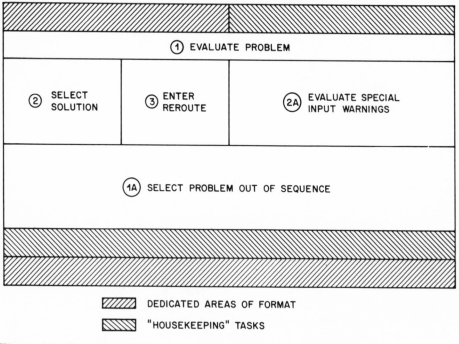

Figure 10. Reroute selection tasks mapped onto CRT format.

flow. Thus, Task 1 appears at the top, Tasks 2 and 3 follow a left-to-right pattern, and Task 2A, performed only rarely, has the less prominent location at the right.

The display organization shown in this figure completes the gross formatting of the page. The next step, the encoding step, is to do the detailed layout of each individual area. It has two essential aspects, logical and mnemonic. The logic of the presentation is closely tied to a technological theory and universe of discourse shared by the engineer, the traffic theorist, the display designer, the training specialist, and the human operator. This theory can be reduced to a rule, or truth table, that relates the measures to the human decision.

I have noted the logical aspect of this display in order to stress an important factor unique to technological displays -- the user is in fact a technician, an expert, and the appropriateness of the encoded information can only be evaluated in relation to the technical field itself. Likewise, the memorability of the labels, their ease of recognition, and the user's ability to correctly apply the decoding rule, depend on how widely current this learning is within the general technical field, in this case the field of network management.

This factor -- the relationship between the necessarily abbreviated presentation of information on the CRT display and the technical knowledge that makes this brief presentation meaningful -- is left out of most current psychological research on encoding problems. Yet the precise form of the encoding is an important factor in performance (for example, Hayes, 1973).

Before assessing the next display design function, that of specifying required system response times, I wish to deal with the issue of encoding. In my experience research in this area could be of significant help. Intuitively it is felt that the display should serve as what Newell and Simon (1972) call an "external memory." Since the display surface is very small, we often end up with abbreviations such as ABOCCH and rarely have room to provide specific aids to the recall of the decoding rule itself. The training burden is therefore increased, but precise information about necessary additional training is lacking. Studies that developed such a relationship would force an earlier consideration of human factors limitations in the display design process. Right now most designers feel the human can learn to do any task as long as the rules are logical and the data are all there. But it is surely a fact that overly compact presentation may force more expensive initial and on-site training. Research that quantified such a relationship could have a significant impact on current design practice. (For additional readings on the subjects of system task analysis, response time, and the man/computer interface, see Bailey (1972), De Greene (1970), Harris and Chaney (1969), Kirk (1973), Mashour (1974).)

System Response Time Criteria
From the overview diagram, it can be seen that once the display surface is completely designed, the next step is the specification of allowable system response times. Because of its inherently quantitative nature, this is an important research area. First, I should like to present the response time analysis done for our own system. I will then identify certain common assumptions -- many of them originated in an important article by R. B. Miller (1968). His assumptions are very much in need of research evaluation.

Any interactive display system can be described in terms of its basic interactive capabilities. Obviously a graphic CRT will have different interactions from an alphanumeric CRT. For the alphanumeric CRT used in our network management center, all interactions are based on a common sequence. First, the human enters information in various locations on the fixed format. Next he strikes a key marked SEND on the control keyboard. The system reads the information and starts a flashing single word message in a window referred to as the feedback window. This continues while the system is processing the command, to assure the user that his input is being worked on. When processing is complete, the system writes the data in the appropriate output windows. The time from striking the SEND key to the start of system output is called system response time. It is the interval for which specification is required. As one might imagine, requiring too fast a system response can significantly increase system cost. On the other hand, a slow system will be much less acceptable to the customer. The exact numerical value of the response time objective is therefore a topic of lively discussion between the human factors specialist and the system development engineer.

The analysis of system response times must begin with an identification of basic response categories. Syntactic responses are those system responses that maintain the dialogue but do not yet provide the full answer to the user's question. The system output that provides the data necessary to solve the problem is called a semantic response. In our system we have required syntactic response times on the order of 2 to 4 seconds, while allowing semantic response times to stretch to thirty seconds in some very large searches.

The notion of syntactic interaction leans heavily on the analogy with human conversation. Early papers by Simon and others (Carbonell, Elkind, & Nickerson, 1963; Miller, 1968; Parsons, 1970; Simon, 1966) proposed this analogy as a model for the design of human/computer dialogues, and it has been the basis of much design practice. The theory, if I may try to paraphrase it, goes something like this. Any conversation, whether between two humans or between human and computer, depends on a fairly rapid exchange of signals. Delays threaten the integrity of the conversation, and if excessive, will cause the human to become annoyed. Annoyance can be measured by rating scales and other methods of subjective measurement. When so measured it will be found that specific syntactic functions require slightly different response times. For example, immediate feedback should occur in response to any request for the system's attention. The delay (according to Miller) should be less than 2 seconds. On the other hand Miller allows error messages to take as long as 4 seconds, and claims they may be an annoyance if they occur too rapidly (Miller, 1968).

There have come to be fairly precise limits about what delays it is thought the human will tolerate in this area of syntactic interaction. Yet the experimental basis for these practices is all too slim. Ultimately the justification goes back to some notion like perceptual immediacy. Woodrow's summary (1951) is quoted by Miller (1968) to justify placing the perceived moment at somewhere between .75 and 3.4 seconds. Yet in the same article Woodrow mentions that some investigations have found a sense of immediacy as long as 12 seconds. Recent experiments at IBM (Williams, 1973) have suggested that humans will easily tolerate delays of four and perhaps even eight seconds. Little is known about the so-called integrity of a conversation, whether between humans or between human and computer. Unreasonably severe response time objectives can increase system costs purposelessly. Research aimed at finding the bounds of tolerance for system delay, and -- even more importantly --helping us understand what psychological variables influence those bounds, could have great influence on design practice.

Most human/computer interactions in real-time systems are serial in nature. For example, inputting a complex request may be a multistage operation. At each stage the computer responds with a list of options, one of which is selected by the human. These would be considered syntactic interactions. However, even at the semantic level there are often serial operations. Several items of a list may be investigated one at a time, with the human designating each in turn and reviewing the detail on that item in an expansion window. Considering such series tasks, Miller proposes a theory that has important implications for the question of response times. He supposes a phenomenon that he calls closure. The notion is that in any hierarchical activity high-level tasks organize more detailed subtasks. Subtasks are separated by breaks that bring little psychological closure. At a higher level are tasks that are separated by more substantial closures. Miller proposes that the human will be more tolerant of delay at the task level, since he has completed a more meaningful chunk of behavior. However, this same delay at the subtask level would be very annoying. Miller's idea, if true, would be an important tool for task analysis. An experimental verification of this hypothesis would be of great interest theoretically, and could also provide the display designer with a firmer basis on which to analyze the response times in his own system.

I have talked about research into syntactic interactions and into serial operations. Let us now look at the issue of semantic interactions. Here the human is asking the computer to search its data base and perform often quite complicated calculations and algorithms. The specification of response time objectives is on very shaky ground indeed. Four areas of controversy or uncertainty are worth mentioning.

1) It can be argued that the size or complexity of the computer's search will have no effect on the human's annoyance. The user needs data when he needs it, and if it is not returned at that point he becomes increasingly annoyed. On the other hand, it could be that the human has, or can be made to have, an appreciation for the computer's problem. Thus he would have some idea as to when he is asking for a small amount of processing versus a large amount, and he would be less annoyed at a given delay in the latter case.

2) Somewhat related is the claim by some (Cohen, 1977) that the tolerance for delay is partly a function of the duration of the prior and subsequent human activities. If the human has taken longer to set up the request, and if he takes a longer time to review the output because of its volume, he will be more tolerant of delay. The other point of view is that these factors have no measurable influence.

3) It is sometimes claimed (Simon, 1966) that the annoyance engendered by any particular delay is a function of the delay distribution for that display. The deviation from the expected delay is thus the critical factor, and efforts should be directed at reducing the variance, even at the cost of some increase in the mean. Although one often hears about the importance of the variance,

I know of no solid experimental evidence on this point. Obviously it is very reasonable to consider that reduced operator uncertainty must increase operator satisfaction. However, that by itself is not helpful. Some variance is inevitable in these systems, since each human is time-sharing the facility with other humans and with automatically scheduled operations. What we really need to know is quantitatively how does annoyance vary as a function of delay variance.

4) Finally, I should mention the issue of magic numbers. We all love magic numbers because they are so easy to remember. Miller (1968) has proposed that 15 seconds is a magic number. A delay greater than 15 seconds is supposed to make the human feel like a slave to the machine. This is presumed to cause annoyance, and even lead the user to abandon the terminal. On the other side of this coin are some studies that show contrary facts. Problem-solving behavior is often unaffected by delays even as long as 30 seconds (Morfield, Wiesen, Grossberg, & Yntema, 1969). For many tasks the human has useful work he must finish before he is prepared to process the output. If the output comes too soon he may in fact not be able to use it efficiently (Williams, Swenson, Hegarty, & Tullis, 1977; see also, Seven, Boehm & Watson, 1974).

These are but a few of the controversial questions in the system response time area. Research into the effects of delay in problem-solving performance, and on the more subtle question of human annoyance, would provide an important antidote for the fear and superstition that currently abounds in this field.

The final two steps in the design process deal with issues of crew configuration, crew sizing, and the development of personnel subsystem products such as training course materials, technical documentation, etc. These areas are beyond the scope of the present discussion. They offer many interesting and important opportunities for research in their own right. However, they typically have less direct influence on the design process than the factors mentioned.

In summary, I have reviewed the field of real-time displays and described the process by which the fundamental design decisions are made. Several areas for research emphasis have been identified, and one of them, system response time, has been discussed at some length. If I have stimulated interest in this broad and rapidly growing field, then my purpose has been achieved.

REFERENCES

Bailey, R.W. An example of task analysis in a computer-based business information system. Proceedings of the Conference on Uses of Task Analysis in the Bell System, Hopewell, NJ: 1972.

Biberman, L.M. Perception of displayed information. New York: Plenum, 1973.

Carbonell, J.R., Elkind, J.I., & Nickerson, R.S. On the psychological importance of time in a time-sharing system. Human Factors, 1963, 10, 135-142.

Cohen, H.S. Effects of conversation time on grade of service ratings. Bell Laboratory Technical Memorandum, 77-3433-3, May 1977.

DeGreene, K.B. Man-computer interrelationship. In K.B. DeGreene (Ed.),
    Systems psychology. New York: McGraw-Hill, 1970.
Dodwell, P.C. Visual pattern recognition. New York: Holt, Rinehart and
    Winston, 1970.
Handler, W., & Weizenbaum, J. (Ed.), Display use for man-machine dialogue.
    New York: Crane, Russak, 1972.
Harris, D.G., & Chaney, F.B. Human factors in quality assurance. New York:
    Wiley, 1969.
Hayes, J.R. On the function of visual imagery in elementary mathematics.
    In W.G. Chase, Visual information processing. New York: Academic
    Press, 1973.
Howard, J.R. (Ed.), Electronic information display systems. Washington, DC:
    Spartan Books, 1963.
Kelley, C.R. Display layout. In K.P. Gartner (Ed.), Displays and controls.
    Amsterdam: Swets and Zertlinger, 1972.
Kirk, F.G. Total system development for information systems. New York:
    Wiley, 1973.
Martin, J. Design of man-computer dialogues. Englewood-Cliffs, NJ:
    Prentice-Hall, 1973.
Mashour, M. Human factors in signaling systems. New York: Wiley, 1974.
Miller, R.B. Response time in man-computer conversational transactions.
    AFIPS Conference Proceedings (Fall Joint Computer Conference, 1968),
    Washington, DC: Thompson, 1968.
Meister, D. Behaviorial foundations of system development. New York:
    Wiley, 1976.
Morfield, M.A., Wiesen, R.A., Grassberg, M., & Yntema, D.B. Initial experi-
    ments on the effects of system delay on on-line problem-solving. MIT
    Lincoln Labs Technical Notes 1969-5, June 1969.
Newell, A., & Simon, H.A. Human problem solving. New York: Prentice-
    Hall, 1972.
Parsons, H.M. The scope of human factors in computer-based data proces-
    sing systems, Human Factors, 1970, 12, 165-175.
Rosenthal, R.I. A TORC-ASSIST computer for long lines network operations
    center. Proceedings of the Seventh International Symposium on Human
    Factors in Telecommunications, Montreal, 1974.
Rosenthal, R.I. Human factors aspects of display design. SID International
    Symposium: Digest of Technical Papers, Los Angeles, 1976.
Seven, M.J., Boehm, B.W., &Watson, R.A. A study of user behavior in
    problem-solving with an interactive computer. Rand Report R-513-NASA,
    April, 1974.
Simon, H.K. Reflections on time-sharing from a user's point of view. Com-
    puter Science Research Review, Pittsburgh, PA: Carnegie-Mellon
    Institute, 1966, 43-51.
Stewart, T.F.M. Displays and the software interface. Applied Ergonomics,
    1976, 7.3, 136-146.
Williams, C.M. System response time: A study of user's tolerance. IBM
    Technical Report 17-272, July 1973.
Williams, J.D., Swenson, J.S., Hegarty, J.A., & Tullis, T.S. The effects of

mean CSS response time and task type on operators performance in an interactive computer system. Bell Laboratory Technical Memorandum, 77-9131-1, February 1977.

Woodrow, H. Time Perception. In S.S. Stevens, Handbook of experimental psychology. New York: Wiley, 1951.

Electronic Paperwork Processing in the Office of the Future

W. Hoekstra

A possible evolution of the electronic office is outlined and areas in which investigation of non-technical disciplines is required are specifically pointed out.

Image quality is considered a major subject, as is man-machine interaction, since user convenience is regarded as the main factor in the acceptance of electronic paperwork-processing equipment. Compatibility between present-day paperwork and future processing is felt to be crucial.

Information-processing in offices is executed by human beings, with the assistance of machines. The type and amount of such processing depends on the function of the office, as does also the type of paperwork. For example, the life-cycle of a bank cheque will differ completely from that of a patient's medical record. I shall restrict myself in this discussion to the paperwork (such as correspondence) done in a general office by secretarial staff.

Paperwork-processing can be most appropriately described as the work to be performed during document generation at the addresser's end, together with the work to be done at the adressee's end. In the first case, activities such as dictating, stenography, typing, drawing of figures, correcting, duplicating, and addressing are involved; in the second, interpretation of contents, the addition of remarks, and indexing for storage and retrieval purposes are encompassed. But operations between the two (e.g., transport) must not be neglected.

In practice, matters can become complicated because an office worker acts as both an addresser and an addressee. One document can be distributed to several receivers, and each receiver may in turn redistribute the document, with or without comments, or create a new document. All these possibilities are expressed in Figure 1.

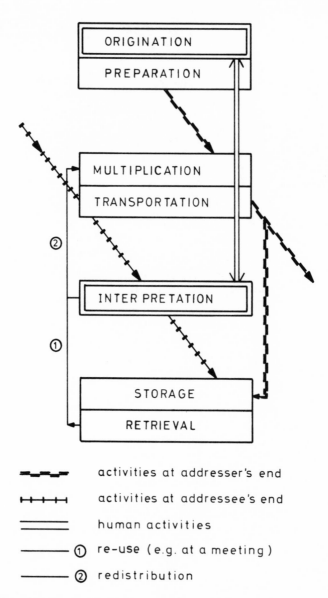

Figure 1. Paperwork processing in a general office.

Document Characteristics

The preparation process can be facilitated by using an electronic typewriter with a display and a memory for temporary storage of text (Wohl, 1977). These word-processors are expensive and consequently only typing pools possess them. It can however be predicted that, in the near future, the price of such typewriters will drop considerably and they will therefore be readily available to every office worker.

At that time, additional functions will be demanded of this keyboard-display apparatus (Burns, 1977). From Figure 1 it can be deduced that these functions will include electronic mailing (Kaiser, 1976; Potter, 1977), electronic filing, and an integration of word-processing and data-processing.

However, not all paperwork can be easily dealt with using present-day data equipment: images, for example, cannot be produced by means of a word-processor. To ensure a competitive, compatible evolution of a mixed system of electronic paperwork and the present method of handling, there will have to be a good interface between these two. The principal aspects of this interfacing are indicated in Figure 2.

The evolution will start with electronic mailing and filing of "home-made" text. Mailing, however, will only be possible to addressees possessing similar equipment. Consequently, paper will still be transported.

Text received on paper will generally not have been produced by an OCR character font, and it will therefore have to be handled like images. As soon as electronic paperwork processing is extended beyond the text preparation phase, the need for handling images via the same channels will grow rapidly.

Images can be transported by fascimile, but with the drawback of a long transmission time due to the small bandwidth of the telephone lines. The storage of images has an equivalent drawback (see Figure 2). In connection with filing, an additional argument has to be taken into account. As can be seen in Figure 1, both received and originated documents are filed. In a general office there can be a close relationship between these documents (e.g. correspondence) resulting from the activities, in contrast to literature where only loose relationships exist due to similarities in content (Hoekstra & Evers, 1977). Storing documents in different media will reduce the ease with which causally related documents can be handled. In practice the user likes to have related documents stored near each other to enable him to "browse."

It is not just the interface between the traditional paper world and the new electronic world, which I have been discussing, that is relevant. The interface between the new equipment and the user is also decisive, and the two interface areas are by no means independent of each other. I will return to this point later.

Human Convenience

The most obvious aspect of the future office that will necessitate convenient human interfacing is the display. This interface has to achieve two objectives: it must provide a soft copy of each page, and it has to participate in the man-machine dialogue. With regard to the first objective, the size now in use (with a width-height ratio of 4:3) is inadequate for displaying a full paper page (requiring $1:\sqrt{2}$). But the document display must also be able to produce a high-resolution picture, while maintaining attractive contrast

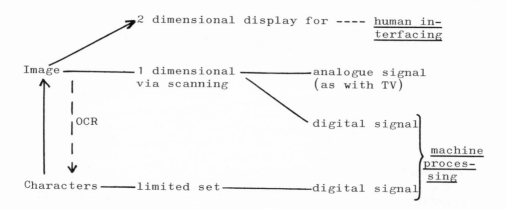

Figure 2. An A4 page (8½" x 11") contains at most 5000 characters; 8 bits per character results in 4.10^4 bits. The same page scanned with a resolution of 8 lines per millimeter gives 4.10^6 picture elements, equivalent to 4.10^6 bits if the only distinction is between black and white. This quantity can be reduced, by a factor of 10 on average, via coding techniques.

and good luminance. Data-processing companies, neglecting image require-ments in their eagerness to expand markets, may ignore that fact to the extent that even paper documents in the future may consist of pages with 24 rows of 80 characters.

In general, however, it has to be recognized that two types of activities are performed by office workers: reading documents and issuing instructions either on a document-related basis (indexing, routing) or on a contents-related basis (short memoranda for various purposes). The data terminal of today seems best suited for these control purposes, thus leading to the idea of a separate document-reading display. This data terminal might be expanded to permit not only man-machine dialogue but also face-to-face dialogue (video telephone), while the reading display might even be integrated with an electric writing tablet. Attention would then have to be paid to the layout of the office worker's desk.

This brings us to the dialogue itself. A multi-task keyboard will evolve from the electronic typewriter keyboard. Until recently, only professional people in the data-processing field used keyboard display combinations in their daily work. Nowadays, however, this situation has extended to people who know nothing about computers. Two user categories can be distinguished here. First, there are those who are still engaged in a dedicated task (typing) and, second, there are general users, subdvided into those who perform a broad range of tasks at a terminal, and those who are only incidently con-fronted with such a machine ("naive" users) (Zimmermann, 1977).

In designing an interface for all these last-mentioned users it has to be borne in mind that: mnemonics are not natural, and it can be inconvenient to have too many function keys; and the system structure has to be clear, enabling the user to know at all times where he is, and what further steps he can take. No obvious solutions to these problems have emerged.

But the man-machine interface is not the only vital subject in the future office. The overall organization will change. Managers will acquire greater alertness (Hoekstra & Evers, 1977), and secretaries will develop into administrative specialists (R.B. White, 1977; Puchhase, 1976).

Progress

Two forces are promoting the present office evolution. First, there is the office world itself. Productivity remains practically static and wages are increasing, while the need for paperwork processing is expanding as a result of the "information explosion." Second, as already mentioned, the data-processing companies are in search of new markets now that the market for large computers is showing signs of saturation and such new markets can be opened up using micro-processors.

It has been predicted that within the next couple of decades there will be an office revolution comparable with the industrial revolution. It therefore seems vitally important that psychologists and graphic designers should join forces to attack some major problems. If they do not, inadequate equipment may be introduced, creating "stress" in office workers.

In the area of image quality, images will be scanned by an electronic copier (facsimile used as a present-day copier) and reproduced as hard or soft copy. Variable dot density may be used for grey-level pictures, while spatial filtering techniques may be used inside the display to obtain a flicker-free image. Shurtleff (1974) and T.W. White (1977) have made a start in this area.

Second, there is the man-computer interaction. Further investigation is required in all the application areas mentioned in the preceding paragraph. Is a manual-input visual-output interaction always the best approach? Since the telephone is certain to be integrated into the office system, as described above, speech input and output will also have to be taken into account.

For what reason did the A4 (8½" x 11") format evolve? (For zooming versus overview versus browsing reasons?) What is the human process that occurs during the use of a dictation machine? (No visual feedback!) A lot of questions have not even been identified. Many of these questions will only arise inside the future office, but a basic consideration is that most of these questions cannot be solved by technologists on their own.

REFERENCES

Burns, J.C. The evolution of office information systems. Datamation, 1977, 60-64.

Hoekstra, W., & Evers, V.H.C. Automated microfiche filing system for personal use. IEEE Transactions on Professional Communications, 1977, 20-6, 228-233.

Kaiser, W. Zukünftige Telekommunikation in der Bundesrepublik Deutschland, Ergebnisse der KtK-beratungen. Nachrichtentechnische Zeitschrift, 1976, 29, 190-197.

Potter, R.J. Electronic mail. Science, 1977, 195, 1160-1164.

Puchhase, A. Office of the future. SRI Business Intelligence Program.
    No. 1001, 1976.
Shurtleff, D.A. Legibility research. Proceedings of the Society of Information
    Displays, 1974, 15, 41-47.
White, R.B. A prototype for the automated office. Datamation, 1977, 83-90.
White, T.W. Subjective assessment of interline flicker in television displays.
    Proceedings of the Congress on Human Factors in Telecommunications,
    1977, 45-51.
Wohl, A.D. What's happening in word processing. Datamation, 1977, 65-74.
Zimmerman, R. Dialoge zwischen ungeübten Benutzern und rechnergesteuerten
    Informationssystemen. Nachrichtentechnische Zeitschrift, 1977,
    30, 632-641.

Television Text: First Experience with a New Medium

Richard Jackson

*New information services are becoming available for home
users. These use the broadcast television channels--as in
Teletext--and the public telephone network--as in Viewdata--
to make information in the form of text and diagrams available on the screens of domestic television receivers. The
viewer has a keyboard so that he or she can choose what
to see and when to see it. Such services are expected to
grow, and further sources of information will become available which use similar display facilities. The main features
of these new systems are outlined and an experimental home
terminal equipment that has been used to explore development
in this field is described.*

*The displayed text pages are currently limited to a maxi-
mum of 960 alphanumeric characters or to simple diagrams.
This represents a very small window with which to observe
what may be a very large amount of information. Normal
search and scanning techniques developed for books and
newspapers do not necessarily apply. The paper outlines
the methods currently used and their limitations, and describes possible further technological development which may
be helpful. Other features of the display, such as the restricted paragraph size and the free availability of coloured
text, are also commented upon. It is concluded that television text is an attractive medium that will play an important role in future communications.*

479

In recent years a new technology in electronics, known as Very Large Scale Integration (VLSI) has been introduced. Using this technology, it becomes possible to manufacture complex circuits involving hundreds or even thousands of devices which occupy only a minute space and can be mass-produced cheaply. As a result, the electronic storage and processing of information is easier than ever before, and the cost of the circuits is within reach of the ordinary person. The electronic calculator is perhaps the best known example of this phenomenon. However, hard on the heels of the home calculator, we now have the home information system.

Rainger and Anderson (1974) have described one form of information service now available via the broadcast television channels. Information in the form of text and diagrams is transmitted using spare capacity in existing channels. This information gives no disturbance to the normal picture material, but can be detected by a special receiver and displayed instead of the t.v. program. The choice of material displayed (and when) is in the hands of the viewer. This system is known as Teletext.

Fedida (1977) has described a complementary system which makes available a virtually unlimited number of data pages--again having text and diagrams--from a computer-operated data base (store). In this case the public telephone network is used for transmission of the signal. In this system, known as Viewdata, the information is again displayed on a television screen.

At the U.K. Philips Research Laboratories we have been studying these systems and also looking forward to the future possibilities suggested by such techniques. During the course of our work we have built an experimental equipment which represents an early form of home computer. It is able to transmit and receive information to and from the outside world (e.g. by telephone). It can also operate independently of all outside services for local, private information filing, retrieval, and processing. It can act as the mentor in a variety of word and number games, serve as a home Telex machine, electronic typewriter, electronic book, and so on. All of these functions depend on the presentation of alphanumeric text and diagrams. Although it will eventually be possible to present the output as traditional ink-on-paper printed copy, it is expected that the bulk of the material will be viewed on a t.v. screen.

The method of presentation of all these systems imposes certain limitations on the text, such as the size and capacity of a page, the minimum character size, and the method of selecting a new page. However, it also opens new opportunities. Colour is more readily available than with other media, special fonts can easily be programmed for headings, portions of text can be flashed on and off, and it is even possible (although not necessarily desirable) to give a measure of control of the observed text characteristics to the reader. This paper presents the current status of t.v. text display, mentions some future possibilities, and discusses two aspects of the new system which seem particularly relevant to the subject of processing visible language. These are the techniques used for searching for material and organising its presentation, and the factors affecting the comprehension of the text.

Systems and Possibilities

Teletext
Home electronic data services arose from the experimental broadcast Teletext services in the U.K., mentioned above. Data have been broadcast experimentally over the u.h.f. television network since 1974. By 1976 the British receiver industry had agreed standards with the broadcasting authorities and this led to the transmission of regularly updated "magazines" by both the BBC (called Ceefax) and the IBA (called Oracle). Several other European countries are also experimenting with this system, and in France a similar technique, known as Antiope, is being examined.

Many of the technical details of the broadcast Teletext system are not relevant to this paper, but a brief description may be helpful. The data signals are transmitted in spare space in the normal t.v. transmission--in effect, between successive pictures. Since this space is limited, it takes time to transmit a full page of text in this way--about 1/4 sec for a page of 960 characters. As the system is one-way, the whole range of material has to be transmitted, and the reader makes his/her selection of the material at the receiver.

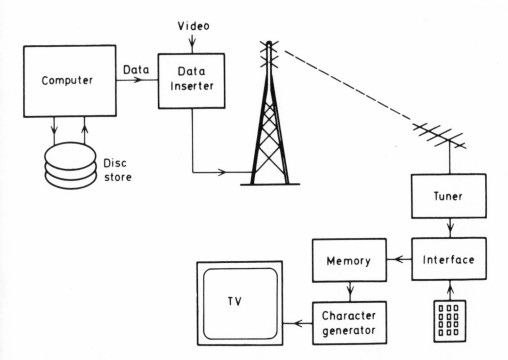

Figure 1. Broadcast Teletext System. Data signals are transmitted to a normal t.v. tuner and converted by special circuits for display on a television receiver.

A magazine of (say) 100 pages is transmitted repeatedly, each transmission taking 24 sec. The pages have number labels and the viewer is able to select the required page number using a keyboard (Figure 1). When that page arrives, it is stored locally and displayed on the t.v. screen. One page number is permanently reserved as an index which indicates the contents of the other pages. In order to minimise costs, receivers currently available on the market have storage capacity for only one page. Thus every request for a new page will occasion a delay of up to 24 sec while the stored material is being replaced. Further details of this system can be found in Rainger and Anderson (1974) and in the published specification (1976).

Viewdata

At an early stage in the Teletext experiments, it was realised that other electronic sources of data could be used besides broadcast channels. For example, computer organised data bases could be contacted via telephone. The U.K. Post Office pioneered the field for a Telephone Data service and in 1975 proposed the "Viewdata" telephone-to-t.v. system.

The telephone system provides a two-way communication link so the reader can use the keyboard to request particular information from a remote source. When the request is received, that specific information is sent to his individual receiver, where it is stored for display (Figure 2). With proper system design the delay in answering the request can be negligible, and the text begins to appear immediately. However, as telephone lines have a much lower signal handling capacity than t.v. channels, it takes a few seconds to write the text on the screen. (A completely filled page would take 8 sec). Since a very large choice of data is available, defining the required page calls for a special search procedure. This is described in detail below.

The Viewdata system is currently undergoing technical trials in England with perhaps a few tens of receivers in use by electronic research laboratories, market research organisations, and would-be information originators. A public service trial is planned to commence in 1978 with about 1,000 receivers in ordinary homes. Full public service might follow in 1979/80. Further details are given in Fedida (1977).

Home Terminal

Given the availability of a digital page memory and circuits for translating the content of the memory into text on a t.v. screen, a wide range of new applications may be foreseen. Many of these have been described by Sharpless and Clark (1977) and by Sharpless, Penna, and Turner (1977). It is useful to give a resume of these to set the scene for consideration of the text requirements.

For example if an alphanumeric keyboard is provided, this can be used to enter information directly into the memory and thence on to the t.v. display screen. We thus have the elements of an electronic typewriter. One application for this, with which our laboratory is experimenting, is in sending messages. The message is composed by typing it on to the t.v. screen. When completed, the message can then be transmitted to another t.v. receiver by telephone. If the recipient is not available, the message can be left in the store at the remote receiver and displayed later. We call this function the Home Telex.

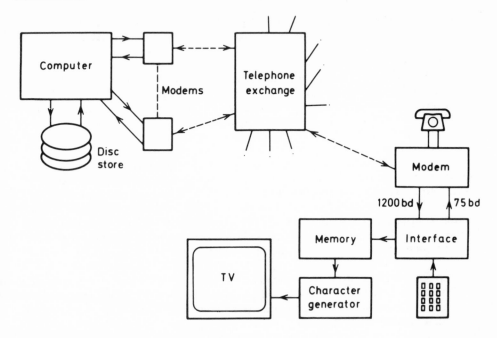

Figure 2. Telephone to TV Information System. Viewdata: Data signals are transmitted to and from a computer by telephone.

Another application is the keeping of private records by electronic means. In this case there needs to be a local store for much more than a single page. A cheap store of large capacity can be provided using magnetic tape. Sharpless et al. (1977) have described and demonstrated the use of standard audio cassettes for this purpose. A C60 size audio cassette can store about 300 pages of the t.v. display size. The cassette can be used to store either text produced locally on the keyboard or text obtained from external sources, and can thus form the basis for a Home Archive system. Alternatively, pre-recorded tapes can be played to produce pages of information as a sort of Electronic Book.

Clearly, some way of identifying what material is stored on which part of a cassette tape is required. In our experiments we have built the cassette player into a multi-function apparatus, known as the "Home Terminal," and have arranged that the record/replay function is under control of the user via the keyboard. The terminal has its own built-in microcomputer which controls the tape recorder, and all locations on the tape are numbered and may be called up by keying the number required. The tape is then automatically fast wound to the appropriate point.

The inclusion of the microprocessor in the unit opens further possibilities for interactive use. For example, the viewer can play word or number games using the t.v. screen as the gameboard and the microprocessor as the opponent. An example is a well known game in which the player must guess which four digits have been chosen and in what order, out of a possible six digits. The microprocessor can be programmed to perform other functions, such as calculations, and there are clearly educational uses for such a system.

User Characteristics

Thus far I have dealt mainly with hardware and technical system aspects of this subject. The major interest for the study of processing visible language, however, is more in the message than in the medium. What are the text characteristics and how is the message handled by the reader?

Display Features

All the systems mentioned above group the data into information pages for display on the screen of a standard colour t.v. receiver. A careful balance has had to be struck between having sufficient characters on the screen to convey a useful message and the insurance of good legibility. Facilities to provide simple diagrams and to vary the characters are used to enhance the display and assist legibility. Figure 3 shows a monochrome photograph of the text format which has the following features:

1)   A page consists of up to 24 rows of up to 40 alphanumeric characters. The basic character set is based on a matrix of 6 x 10 dots used in various combinations to provide upper and lower case letters, numerals, and a variety of symbols.
2)   The basic character set may be extended so that double height characters are displayed--up to 12 rows of such characters on a page. The characters can also be produced in red, green, blue, cyan, magenta, yellow or white. They may also be caused to flash on and off.
3)   A simple graphical presentation based on a grid of 80 points horizontally by 72 vertically is also available. This graphical information may be coloured in the same way as text.

The exact appearance of the characters on the screen is dependent on the individual receiver design. A typical approach is to divide the television screen conceptually into 960 adjacent areas, 40 horizontally by 24 vertically. Each area is 6 resolution elements (dots) wide x 10 dots deep. Upper case letters each occupy a space 7 dots high x 5 dots wide so that the inter-line spacing is 3 dots and the minimum inter-symbol spacing for adjacent letters is one dot. Any number of whole symbol spaces may be arranged between words of a message and, of course, whole lines may be omitted to increase the vertical spacing. Lower case letters are formed on the same basic grid, but in these the descenders or "tails" of the letters can fall two dots below the 7x 5 area so that the effective matrix becomes 7 x 9 dot elements for such letters as j and y.

In these respects the teletex system is similar to many computer displays and the actual character shapes used conform to a well established code developed for computers (ISO-7). However, in television text systems a useful electronic trick is employed to improve the character shape. Television scanning is interlaced so that the spot traces every other line on the screen in one sweep and then returns to trace the inter-leaving lines. The character dot pattern is repeated during this second sweep so that the observed characters actually occupy 20 lines on the screen. Figure 4(a) shows a typical upper

Figure 3. Example of a Television Text Display.

case letter presented by this method. By use of a special processing circuit
the character shapes can be "rounded" so that they then appear as shown
in Figure 4(b). This greatly improves their appearance compared with normal,
un-rounded, dot matrix characters.

     Further comment needs to be made on the size and shape of the charac-
ters. If the text is displayed on a normal (European) domestic television
receiver having, say, a 66 cm diagonal screen, the text will occupy up to
83% of the height of the screen. This is because it will occupy 480 lines out
of an available 575 (a nominal 625 line television receiver "loses" 50 lines
of picture due to the need for unseen technical processes). The height of
an upper case character will thus be approximately 10mm and the minimum
pitch of the lines of the text (from the bottom of one line to the bottom of
the next) will be approximately 14mm. Twyman (personal communication)
has commented that this spacing is closer than desirable from the point of
view of the readability of continuous text. It is, for example, closer than
normal typewriter text spacing. The author has observed that a full page
of text at the maximum possible density can have a somewhat unpleasing
appearance and present some difficulties. However, a similar effect was
encountered during experiments at our laboratory some years ago using television text that was based on typewritten source material where the inter-
line spacing was larger than in Teletext. During experiments in which television

was used to present programmed-instruction material to students, Johnson (1968) noted that the full capacity of the screen was never used by the editors. A factor of about 3:1 was typical for the ratio of page capacity to the actual displayed characters.

The width of the characters in Teletext depends on the electronic circuit and can, in principle, be varied. However, in practice, a compromise has to be made between a number of conflicting technical problems. Thus it is usual to fix the text line width at about 77% of screen width, giving a character width of about 8.5mm for the screen referred to above. A slightly "square" character appearance results, but there is no evidence that this affects the legibility of the characters.

At normal television viewing distance (about 2.5m) the standard Teletext character will subtend an angle of between 14 and 20 minutes of arc to the eye. Since the characters will be bright (170 cd/m^2) and the contrast against their background will be good (50:1), they are normally readily legible. However, for purposes of emphasis, an option is included in the specification to double the height of the character so that it occupies a matrix area 20 dots high by 6 dots wide. These double height characters thus have a more upright appearance.

The graphics presentation on both Teletext and Viewdata is related to the text presentation in that the screen is again seen conceptually as divided into the same 40 x 24 areas. In the graphics case, however, each area is subdivided into 6 large dots: 2 horizontally and 3 vertically. Thus a graphics grid of 80 x 72 elements is available. The technical reasons for this and the possibilities for a more refined graphics display are beyond the scope of this paper. What is of interest is the use to which the graphics capability has been put by the information providers. Apart from the obvious use for simple

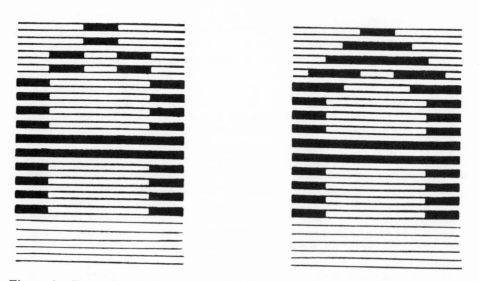

Figure 4. Examples of characters. (a) Typical upper case letter without character rounding; (b) same character rounded to improve appearance.

bar charts, diagrams, and the like, a major use has been for the composition of special character fonts for headlines. An example of this is shown in the photograph (Figure 3).

Finding the Information

This page capacity represents a very small window with which to observe, say, a computer data base running into many millions of words. Since the pages "turn" rather slowly--taking seconds to transmit and receive--it is not possible to flick rapidly through them as in a book. Nor can one glance around as in a newspaper. Thus the search technique currently in use is based on indexes. However, the page capacity similarly limits the size of an individual index so that in practice a multi-level index is needed.

In Viewdata the procedure follows a tree of indices. On contacting the computer--and thereafter by use of a special key sequence--a main index is displayed giving major subject headings. Each subject has a number and pressing that number key will call up a further index. The new index will have headings which refine the request (from "Entertainment" to "Concerts") and give numbers for selecting the next level of index and so on until the actual required data are found. Typically, the actual information may be obtained at from four to ten levels down such a tree.

As far as I am aware, no rigorous test of the efficacy of the tree access has yet been published. On first impression the procedure seems to work very well for completely uninitiated viewers; it requires only a simple numeric keyboard and it is easy to follow. However it does have disadvantages. It can be tedious, and the successive key operations and delays can be irritating to the initiated, particularly if the desired information is not in fact available at the end of the search!

Several features can be included to alleviate this. In the Viewdata system the successive numbers keyed combine to make the final page number. If that number is known, the exact page can be located directly by keying the entire number. The problem then is that of remembering a ten digit number to retrieve the information. Recently, an alphabetic index has been added to Viewdata. This index is itself interrogated by a number tree so that the route to the information is not necessarily shortened. However, the alphabetic index is helpful in identifying information in categories not immediately obvious from the main index.

With our data base we have tried two alternatives, both of which need a more complex alphanumeric keyboard. First, viewers were asked to key a simple two-letter mnemonic rather than numeral. These mnemonics could also be strung together to locate a page directly. For example EN CO PR would take one directly to the index for Promenade Concerts in London (Entertainment, Concerts, Proms). The method was attractive in the initial stages when little information was available, but has not proved successful for the extended system since the choice of "obvious" mnemonics is extremely difficult.

The second alternative was the use of keywords to identify certain strategic pages: when the user types a keyword such as "Concerts," he or she obtains direct access to the relevant part of the data base. The keyword system has certainly proved helpful so far as our initial trials--almost entirely with engineers--have gone. It not only cuts down the access time for an individual page but also facilitates jumps from one part of the tree to another in the event that one changes one's mind (e.g. to look up data about a play instead of a concert).

This brings me to a second feature we have observed. In a book or newspaper or even a telephone directory, the reader usually "knows where he is"; he has some idea of the relationship between the text he is actually reading and the rest of the contents of the volume. Although able to ascertain this to some extent when, in the early stages, we were familiar with the small fixed amount of data available, it was never as apparent as in printed text and became increasingly more difficult with a large amount of data. One feels the need of a "map" of the data territory.

To improve the sense of relationships, it would be possible, for example, to provide for storage of a block of data in the receiver--one chapter of the material rather than one page. Having acquired this, electronic means to scan the material could then be provided so that rapid familiarisation should be possible. However the electronics required to do this would be costly. Rosenthal (this volume) also comments on the need for an overview map as well as presentation of local data in visual display systems and describes the use of two display screens for this purpose. Again this would be a costly solution for the home. Thus further work is needed to clarify the extent to which the need for an overview is fundamental and, if so, to suggest economic solutions.

For a stable central data base, of course, a simple way out is to keep, so far as possible, the location of the material static and issue a printed directory. However, if we are thinking of the individual house archiving system of the future, this is not appropriate. Also to an electronic engineer it feels like cheating.

Comprehension

In a strictly technical sense this new method of text presentation clearly "works." Albeit without rigorous tests, there seems little doubt as to the legibility of the text and comments of the general public seem favourable. Indeed the variable font and colour facilities offered make Teletext and Viewdata an important step forward in the presentation of text on screens. As for the level of readability or comprehension so far achieved, the position is less certain. Again, as far as the author is aware no controlled experiments of this have yet been published. Nor has there been sufficient experience to give a good indication of aspects such as fatigue. As with any new medium, a learning phase must be completed before either the originators of the information or the recipients can make best use of the facilities offered. An important engineering concern is how the technical receiver design can best be optimised to achieve an acceptable result for the user. There are many factors involved in this, of which two are included here.

Italics and Colour

First, the use of colour. When used for headings, colour can be extremely effective. However a new use is arising which is both interesting and puzzling. The various character fonts available do not include an italic version. In normal English language texts, italics are commonly used for emphasis; without unduly intruding on text or affecting readability. In t.v. text it is possible to use colour as an alternative to italics so that one gets a coloured word or phrase in the middle of an otherwise monochrome paragraph. The author has noticed that this practice disturbs his normal reading pattern. The eye is drawn to the coloured word and, as it were, "forgets" to read the paragraph properly so that several attempts at scanning are made before the sense of the wording comes through. Question: Is this fundamental or is it again simply a matter of experience? Italic is not the only form of emphasis normal use. For example, underlining also occurs and in some texts from continental Europe double letter spacing is employed. This has a similar effect as colour on the author, but presumably it is acceptable to those familiar with that form of emphasis.

Broken Paragraphs
A second feature is the effect of breaking the text so that it appears on two or more pages. Since the text capacity of a page is small, this can happen quite frequently. As in the earlier case cited, the problem is that one cannot glance rapidly ahead to see where a paragraph or section of text ends. This creates some uncertainty in the reading which may (or may not) affect comprehension.

To improve the comprehension we have incorporated a feature in the Philips experimental home terminal which does seem to help. Instead of a single page memory, we have included three pages of fast random access memory for this purpose. It is then possible to store two other pages besides the one actually on the screen. It is also possible to view these extra stored pages virtually instantaneously. Each time a "new page" button is pressed, the display screen contents are changed within a fraction of a second. (This is in contrast with the magnetic cassette memory which takes seconds to replace a page.) It is thus possible to "flip" through the pages to assess their contents. Another feature which could be helpful would be the use of "roll up" as is commonly employed in computer displays. The contents of two or more pages may be caused to slide vertically so that the screen is effectively used as a window open to a scroll of text.

As commented before: such features cost money. Are they really necessary?

Conclusion
This paper has outlined the many possibilities opening up for the visual display of text and diagrams on home television receivers. From the perceptual point of view, this is a new and largely uncharted area. Very little work has yet been done on factors such as the readability of television text, and the level of comprehension to be expected. Studies of the social implications of the new medium are also limited. Thus, in many instances, I have only been able to report my first impressions and those of a few colleagues.

An objective of the paper has been to encourage interest in the medium and, better still, to stimulate new studies which will show how to make the best use of the technology. In particular, work leading to a "code of good practice" for the use of coloured text, and studies of the human factors involved in electronic information retrieval could benefit information providers and users alike.

REFERENCES

British Radio Equipment Manufacturers Association et al. (publishers). Specification of standards for broadcast teletext signals 1976.

Fedida, S. Viewdata: A computer-based visual information and communication system with interactive capabilities. Eurocon 77 Conference Proceedings on Communications, 1977, Section 2.11.21. to 2.11.28.

Johnson K.E. Experimental use of MASTER for programmed instruction. Mullard Research Laboratories, Technical Note 980, 1968.

Rainger, P., & Anderson, W.N. Domestic information display by television: - A review. International Broadcasting Convention, 1974, Institution of Electrical Engineers Conference Publication, 119 295-304.

Rosenthal, R.I. The design of technological displays. (This volume.)

Sharpless, G.T., & Clark, D.G. Interactive data communication using an intelligent home terminal. Eurocon 77 Conference Proceedings, 1977, 211.1.1bis to 2.11.2.6bis.

Sharpless, G.T., Penna, D., & Turner, S.R. An advanced home terminal for interactive data communication. International Communications Conference Record, 1977, 2, 47-50.

Non-serial Language

N.E. Wiseman and C.A. Linden

The paper introduces a technique being developed for the processing of non-serial constructions by computer. The elementary components are topological patterns and their rules of composition form a grammar. We are interested in the ways in which such grammars can be represented and interpreted by computer programs.

The particular method reported here is based on the use of transition networks. Transition networks are of general value in language processing research, and their use for serial constructions is widely reported in the literature. They are also applicable for non-linear structures but the first results are only just emerging. In this paper, it is the latter use which is emphasised.

Suppose you are asked to describe a walk through the streets of a small town. At each junction, a decision must be taken about which way to turn, and your description will reflect the chosen route. On another occasion, walking the streets of the same town, you might make different decisions at the junctions. Although referring to the same streets in the same town, the two descriptions will not look much alike. The reason is that an unnatural serialization has arisen (from the single thread which your route followed), and this has made it difficult to compare the two descriptions and see that they clearly refer to the same thing. The streets form a topological pattern (a graph) which is non-linear, and the structure is obscured by any attempt to describe it serially.

A map would have been a better basis for comparison, and even though badly drawn and out of scale, the similarities between two maps of the town would have been easily seen. Maps preserve the topological structure of streets. Unfortunately, a verbal description of a map will re-introduce the

problem that the map is intended to solve! Perhaps the map is the description we are seeking, and perhaps its representation has a formal basis as
disciplined as that of the verbal one which is failing us on this occasion.
In that case, we should see the map as a "sentence" (or possibly several) that
obeys some rules of composition--a "grammar"--by which its elementary
components may be assembled into the whole. However, whereas in every
serial language each such component (letter, word, noun-phrase, etc.) has
exactly two attachment points--a beginning and an end--and relates to other
components by juxtaposition, in the case of our map we should need components, such as T-junctions and roundabouts, which have more than two attachment points. This is, of course, why the map is more expressive of the street
pattern and why we speak of a non-serial language. It is a language for drawing and seeing, not for speaking and hearing.

Computer science is a subject much concerned with formal language.
Communication with machines, and between people about machines, is dominated by a need for language. We want languages that are expressive, powerful, and compact and that obey a rigid discipline so that computers may
process them without ambiguity or error. The study of formal languages
in computer science is reaching the point where many things which we know
how to do by computer can be expressed in some available language (and
then done). Non-serial languages are included in this work, but progress is
slower, and simplicity and elegance more elusive. Nevertheless, the need
for such languages exists in areas such as the design of computer programs
in which concurrency must be expressed, picture processing in which features
in two or three dimensional images must be extracted and recognised, interactive graphics such as map and schematic processing and shape design where
the designer needs the discipline of a language to guide his hand and mind,
and data bases in which the control of internally stored structure and the
maintenance of its consistency in a changing environment is necessary.

The problem in general terms is this: given a requirement for non-serial
structures in the computer-modelling of some problem, find a grammar which
the structures must obey; find a means for interpreting the grammar so that
the computer can process and make structures. Computations are, of course,
normally expressed in the form of serially executed algorithms, whether the
data they process is arranged serially or not. Thus we are interested in finding methods for imposing discipline on an otherwise conventional calcula-
tion--in the way that a disciplined walk through the town (following the same
rules on each occasion) would have solved the earlier problem.

Several approaches to non-serial language theory are being investigated.
At Cambridge, experiments with transition network grammars are being
undertaken, and the indications are very promising, at least for certain kinds
of non-serial language processing (Linden 1977, 1978). The basic ideas will
be presented in the paper and some examples given to indicate the scope
and power of the method.

Transition Networks

A transition network is a labelled directed graph whose nodes represent states
and whose arcs represent the permissible transitions between states. The
network can be seen as an abstract model of some discrete system having
as many states as the network has nodes, and can be used to answer certain

questions about the operation of the system. For example, a formal language may have its grammar modelled by such a network and it can then be deduced, simply by tracing paths through the network, which sentences are legal with respect to that grammar. As will become clear later, the network can be used for generation or analysis. As a simple example, consider the transition network of Figure 1. The symbol on each arc is that which must be present at the next position on the input pattern for the arc to be enabled and the corresponding state transition effected. The analysis of an input pattern proceeds as follows. The analyser starts in state S0 and examines the exit arcs from that state to find one which is enabled (there will, in this example, always be exactly one such arc for each state in which the analyser can be). The enabled arc is followed, moving the analyser to a new state and stepping along the input pattern at the same time to reveal the next input symbol. This action is repeated until

a)   The analyser reaches state S3. The input pattern up to the current position is then deemed a legal construction with respect to the grammar represented by the transition network.

b)   The analyser reaches state S2. The input pattern in this case does not conform to the grammar.

c)   The input pattern is exhausted. The analyser stops in an intermediate state at which no exit arcs are enabled. This situation may be accepted as pathological or it can be avoided by adding new arcs to the network at appropriate places carrying a test for null input symbol.

The example defines a grammar for which the legal constructions are:

    AA, AXA, AXXA, AXXXA ----------
    BA, BXA, BXXA, BXXXA ----------

Grammars of this sort are very restrictive and cannot help much with the search for new languages such as those which are the subject of this paper. However, a small enhancement of the idea can make a radical difference. The enhancement required is to add conditions to the arcs and to allow an action on following an arc. The conditions and actions refer to

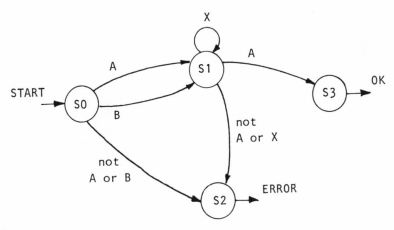

Figure 1. A simple transition network.

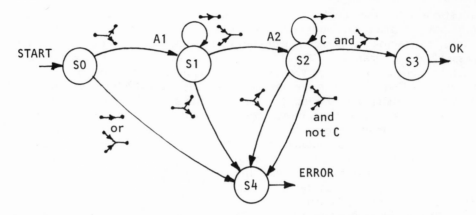

Figure 2. Actions and conditions. The Actions are A1 = save bottom exit, move to top exit; A2 = mark symbol, move to saved exit. The Condition is C = if symbol is marked.

testing and setting certain values held by the analyser while traversing the network. These values can refer to the context of the current input symbol or to steering information for finding the next input symbol, and it is this latter feature that is of particular interest here. Consider, for example, the network shown in Figure 2. This grammar refers to patterns of symbols of the following sort:

and the ability to describe parallel constructions is immediately apparent.

The variables held by the analyser, to which the conditions and actions refer, amount to an augmentation of the environment in which the transition network operates. The input pattern is also, of course, a part of this environment and the behaviour of the analyser is enriched because of the ability provided by the actions to change the environment. Thus the analyser is able to record a particular fact and refer to it again later when the selection of an arc leaving some particular state requires it.

We are now able to construct networks representing finite automata having full computing power and therefore, in principle at least, we can find one for the analysis of any formal language (whether serial or not). The analysis is, in every case, achieved by a single thread of activity through the transition network, so we are able to investigate non-serial constructions with a strictly serial algorithm. Of course the traversal of the pattern itself, though serial, is not in general contiguous. The example above exhibits this at the point where the strand being scanned reaches the final symbol for

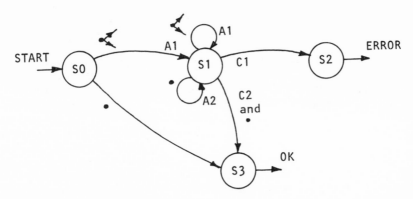

Figure 3. A network describing binary trees. C1 = if symbol is marked;
C2 = if stack is empty; A1 = stack top exit, mark symbol and move to bottom exit; A2 = mark symbol and unstack next position.

the first time--there is an abrupt jump to another point in the pattern before
scanning resumes.
    Another example having more complex jumps is shown in Figure 3. This
network represents the grammar for all binary trees:

    Transition network grammars (TNGs) are known for many interesting
patterns and can be used either to test whether some pattern belongs to a
certain class, or to generate patterns which do. They can also be used to
guide a search for some feature within a pattern, or to control the manner
in which large patterns may be assembled from simpler ones.
    So far our examples have illustrated only a simple parsing action, in which
a pattern is offered to the grammar and its validity with respect to that grammar is deduced by whether the OK or ERROR state in the transition network
is reached. More, however, can be done. During the passage of the analyser
over the TNG it is evident that arrivals in particular states correspond to
the recognition of certain substructures in the input pattern. If the analyser
is to control the emission of responses to the input pattern, some of the information needed to do it can be gathered from these intermediate transitions,
and the actions will then include operations that are able to dispense more
than the one bit of classification so far discussed (OK or ERROR). We can,
for example, arrange that the path taken by the analyser over the TNG generates a response which describes the input pattern in detail (this, of course,
is the usual product of syntax analysis). This description is built incrementally
and hence may be of value in an interactive system where a dialogue is used

to negotiate details of the input pattern while it is still in construction. An architectural designer may, for example, use a TNG running in his computer to verify, as he draws, that certain constraints of a unit building system are being observed. When not, he is told immediately and must repair the mistake before drawing is allowed to continue. There are many interesting possibilities (and unsolved problems) in the use of TNGs in design systems of this kind. Note that, since the pattern is being built with the assistance of a TNG, something more than analysis appears to be occurring. Is the TNG generating the pattern? Evidently any grammar can be seen both as a means of analysing constructions for legality, and as a generator of legal constructions. Some care is needed, however, to ensure that the grammar defines the same language in both cases. If the architect is generating patterns and the TNG is used to analyse his results, it is possible that we get a different effect from that where the analyser catches him up and TNG is used to direct his actions. This apparently odd state of affairs is best explained with an example.

Figure 4 shows a network with two arcs which lead from state SO carrying non-exclusive tests: that is, one arc is followed if a certain pattern occurs in the input and the other if a condition C is true. It is the behaviour when both arcs are enabled which concerns us here. In analysis we can avoid any difficulty by testing the arcs in some specified order and always accepting the first one which is enabled. In generation, however, the user has to furnish a decision about which path to take and, unless he is constrained in some way, he can stimulate an arc which the analyser would not take (even though the arc is enabled). Thus, although the same TNG is used to control analyser and generator, the language it defines may differ in the two cases. The difficulty emerges when the transition network is a faulty analogue of the finite automaton which the analyser or generator purports to be. It is forbidden for an automaton to have multiply enabled arcs leading from its current state, and once the transition network is similarly constrained the problem described vanishes. The conversion of some network into another for which this condition obtains may lead, however, to increased complication and hence slower computation.

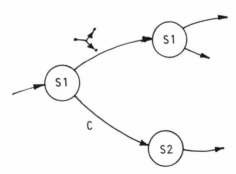

Figure 4. Multiple enabling.

Analysis and generation can also be merged to provide an editing facility. A TNG is used to pilot the editing program to a selected area of a pattern and then to check that changes proposed are legal with respect to the grammar before incorporation in the pattern. Some general purpose editing programs can be made to adopt an application-specific discipline (defined by its TNG) and react helpfully to users in their own notation. Though little has been reported yet, this is a powerful concept worthy of study.

In the above examples we have used TNGs with only two types of arc. A MATCH arc tests part of the input pattern and a JUMP arc does not. Each can carry conditions and actions. In the simple use of a TNG described first, the result, OK or ERROR, refers to whether the input pattern is a member of a certain class of patterns. It is obvious that when the class has exactly one member, its TNG is a recogniser for that specific pattern. It thus performs a MATCH function for that pattern and we could use it in place of a MATCH arc in another TNG which needed such an arc. This gives the facility for hierarchical grammars in which the constructions at one level make the terminal symbols for the next. The replacement operation is indicated by a new arc type, PUSH, which saves the state of the analyser and re-enters it with an appropriate TNG to carry out the required matching function. Another arc type, POP, is also required; it restores the saved state of the analyser when resuming processing at the higher level, with the result that the matching function is delivered to the higher level.

Suppose the TNG of Figure 2 is modified slightly so that it can be called recursively in states S1 and S2 (see Figure 5). This refers to constructions of the following sort,

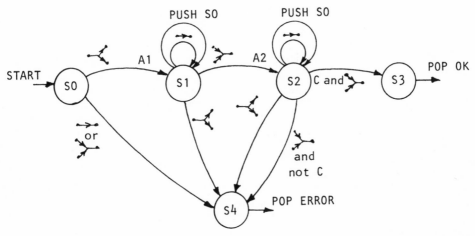

with the simple proviso that the mark put on a symbol is unique to each level of activation of the analyser.

Figure 5. Network with recursion.

Using the four arc types JUMP, MATCH, PUSH and POP, and a set of conditions and actions specific to the problem, transition networks provide a compact and flexible means to model the problem. The specification of a TNG in a form suitable for input to a computer can be done with a simple compiler which accepts a description of the following sort:

```
NETWORK
ENTRYSTATE  SO //  FORK EXPECTED
    MATCH  FORK  TO  Sl DO Al
STATE  Sl  //  JOIN EXPECTED
    MATCH  LINE  TO  Sl DO MOVE.ALONG.LINE
    MATCH  JOIN  TO  S2 DO A2
    .  .  .
    .  .  .
    .  .  .
ENDNETWORK
GRAPH
    FORK  -----  //  FORK LOOKS LIKE
    LINE  -----  //  LINE LOOKS LIKE
    JOIN  -----  //   JOIN LOOKS LIKE
END
```

Using computer graphics equipment it is also possible to prepare the TNG in the machine, working from a pictorial form similar to those used in this paper (Gibbons, 1977).

The networks correspond with finite automata which can have full computing power, and although we have interpreted them here as a model of certain formal grammars, it will be clear that there are many other areas in which they may be used. Multiply enabled transitions, mentioned earlier in connection with a possible inconsistency, can also be turned to advantage. Suppose that the interpretation of some symbol in the input pattern depends on its context. Some of this, call it its past context, is known by the analyser when the symbol is encountered. The remainder of the context information is only revealed as the analyser continues to examine the input, and a conclusive interpretation of the current symbol may require any or all of this "future context." Such context sensitivity can be represented by multiply enabled paths in the network. (Note that the network is then not a direct analogue of a finite automaton.) Enabled paths emanating from some state are tried in turn to evaluate the current symbol with respect to its different possible future contexts. Each failure to resolve the symbol causes the state of the analyser to backtrack and another enabled path to be explored.

Woods (1970) used transition networks to model context sensitivity in this way for the study of natural language. Note that such behaviour is introduced as a matter of convenience only; it is always possible to eliminate backtracking by examining enough future context to resolve the symbol before moving on to the next. With non-serial constructions it will in fact be common to encounter a given symbol several times (arriving on different attachment points or via different paths) and on each arrival more of the context of the symbol is removed from "future" to "past." Thus, symbols, whether recognised or not, are not discarded when encountered, and there is no analogy with the LR parsing of string grammars.

Returning to the opening theme of this paper, we could find a TNG which could be used to discipline a walk through the streets of the town so that the decisions made at junctions were not arbitrary and the description written down followed precise rules. That would make the comparison between two descriptions trivial. We could also use a TNG to verify that certain features of the street layout were sensible; for example, that each street in a one-way system could be reached. When supplemented by programs for analysis of delay time, flow rate, etcetera, TNGs could help with the design of urban highway systems.

It has been the purpose of this paper to point out the application of TNGs to non-serial constructions of this sort. As the theory emerges, we should expect to find wide application of these methods (e.g., Levelt & Flores d'Arcais, 1978, chaps. 1 & 8). There have been several attempts to develop picture grammars in which a geometrical arrangement of symbols is described in two or three dimensions (Gotlieb & Furtado, 1974; Pfaltz, 1972). Our intention has been to deal with topological structures and we have not sought picture grammars specifically. Line diagrams and wire frame pictures of two or three dimensional objects can, however, be handled quite naturally.

The use of TNGs for serial language research, though not the subject of this paper, should also be mentioned. The ability to control both fine detail and gross construction (through the proper use of hierarchy) and the ease with which grammars can be developed for a new problem requirement make them of quite general usefulness.

We acknowledge the work of our colleagues on the RAINBOW research project in which TNGs are being applied. Our work is done in association with a project on the computer support of design data supported by the Science Research Council on grant number B/RG/96169.

REFERENCES

Gibbons, J.J. TINGES: Transition network grammar editing system. Diploma Dissertation, University of Cambridge, 1977.

Gotlieb, C.C. & Furtado, A.L. Data schemata based on directed graphs. University of Toronto, Department of Computer Science, Technical report No. 70, 1974.

Levelt, W.J.M., & Flores d'Arcais, G.B. Studies in the perception of language. New York: Wiley, 1978.

Linden, C.A. Manipulation of design data. 14th Design Automation Conference, Association for Computing Machinery/Institute of Electrical and Electronic Engineers; New Orleans, June 1977.

Linden, C.A. Grammars which describe large bodies of data. Computer Aided Design, 1978, 10(1).

Pfaltz, J.L. Web grammars and picture description. Computer Graphics
    and Image Processing, 1972, 1(2), 193-220.
Woods, W.A. Transition network grammars for natural language analysis.
    Communications of the Association for Computing Machinery, 1970,
    13(10), 591-606.

Paragraphs of Pictographs: The Use of Non-verbal Instructions for Equipment

Tony Marcel and Philip Barnard

This paper is concerned with pictorial means of communicating instructions for the use of equipment. The problems differ from those involved in development of discrete symbols, in that instructions require representations of states, actions, and conditional relations comparable to those represented in natural language. Accordingly, our approach concentrates on analogues of linguistic factors and pictorial aspects of sequence and context.

Two tasks were used involving interpretation of sequences of pictorial instructions for an apparatus. In one task subjects gave a verbal interpretation of pictorial instructions; in the other task they used the same instructions to operate the device, which simulated the operation of an English payphone. Comprehension was affected by how much of the apparatus was depicted in each picture, segmentations of the picture sequence, and the use of insets. The effects of graphic variables and the error patterns implicate cognitive structures underlying comprehension of pictorial instructions (especially relations between actions and states). Amongst other comparisons with natural language, the inferential nature of interpretation is emphasised. Differences between the two tasks indicate people's strategies in using instructions to operate equipment. Indeed, the effect of graphic variables can only be understood in the context of users' strategies and their preconceptions about particular equipment.

There has been surprisingly little research on pictorial instructions for the operation of equipment. Obvious applications include international usage and user populations of limited literacy or with impaired language. Even literate native speakers of a language often find written instructions difficult to follow. Not only might pictorial instructions serve as an alternative to verbal texts, but they might also aid comprehension when the two are presented together.

Discrete graphic symbols are in widespread use and have received some attention in human factors research (Easterby, 1970; Cahill, 1975). However, their function is restricted to denotational reference or single unconditional commands. For most equipment whose operation requires a paragraph of instructional text, actions and their preconditional or resultant states must be represented. If these are to be structured into an unambiguous message, it would be desirable to parallel the use of logical connectives as well as various linguistic devices that influence interprepretation (e.g., sentence structure and punctuation). If direct functional analogues for these variables are not to be found, then one needs either to teach a new, international visual language or to find other means to guide the user's interpretations.

The approach to visual language taken by Premack (1971) with primates is to attempt to replace virtually all lexical items or morphemes with logograms or discrete symbols. To a large extent, the representation of relationships and most function words is arbitrary. Indeed, this approach has not proved a clear success with aphasic patients (Gardner, 1977). Bearing this in mind, we decided to use "comic strips," where representational pictures, corresponding to phrases or clauses, individually have fairly unambiguous semantics (conceptual reference), but whose sequential relationships provide a problem of inference. Recent ventures by designers into the use of such structured pictorial sequences have been restricted to meeting specific equipment needs, such as the telephone (Ericsson, 1972; Hadler, 1972; Design, 1975), and the research has a characteristically ad hoc approach. Almost a decade ago Kolers (1969) pointed out that "we need to study the kinds of instructions that can be represented pictorially, the characteristics of such pictures, and the rules useful in their successful concatenation – the syntax of picture writing." While information on a wide range of topics is available to the designer of verbal instructions and information (Broadbent, 1977; Wright, 1977; Wright & Barnard, 1975), there appears to be little published work examining more general issues associated with the comprehension and use of pictorial instructions.

Even individual pictures are not necessarily understood "directly." Conventions underlie the reading not only of deliberately symbolic art (e.g., Egyptian wall paintings or Botticelli's "Primavera"), as delineated by art historians (Gombrich, 1950, 1972; Goodman, 1968), but also of simple line drawings or any representational depiction (Arnheim, 1974; Deregowski, 1977). However, sequences of pictures present the additional problems of the logical and semantic links between pictures. Although we have some speculative notions about spontaneous interpretations of smoothly changing visual sequences (Michotte, 1963), little is known about juxtapositions of static or noncontinuous images. Cinematic montage is an example of such juxtapositions for which people have a visual sophistication. Mascelli (1965) has articulated some of the cinematic rules, but the only investigation relating them to human cognition is that of Frith and Robson (1975), who showed that children could reconstruct a film sequence better if it obeyed inter-shot rules of directional continuity. They related this finding to the influence of the rules of sentence and text grammars on comprehension and recall of verbal narratives (see Bower, 1976, for discussion). But this raises an important point. Are the rules for comprehension rooted more strongly in the structures of the communication language itself or in the perceiver's preconceptions about the topic of discourse and the pragmatics of communication? Thus in the case of comprehension of pictorial instructions for equipment, how important are general rules of depiction and syntax per se, as opposed to people's beliefs about the equipment and task? Indeed, Winograd (1972) and Wason and Johnson-Laird (1972, pp. 190-193) have already illustrated different ways in which natural language comprehension may ultimately rely on inferences from situation-specific knowledge.

This study attempts to tackle the problems outlined above. Our inital objectives were to find parallels of linguistic variables within and between individual frames of a picture sequence, and to explore the effects of graphic variables themselves. We hoped that this would provide an approach to rules for picture sequences equivalent to those of sentence and text grammars. Indeed, this paper is partly concerned with evaluating specific pictorial variables. However, there are certain aspects of our results that not only qualify the adequacy of our approach, but without reference to which the effect of the graphic variables cannot be understood. Hence the other purpose of this paper is to discuss those characteristics of behaviour which have fundamental implications for the way people comprehend and use pictorial instructions in general.

Method

Our method is based on an artificial piece of equipment and instructions for its use. In the long term, our intended variables are instructional factors, users' knowledge of equipment function and pictorial conventions, and user populations. In addition, the subjects either have to render the instructions in words or operate the equipment. So far we have varied some instructional factors and used both tasks. There were two reasons for using artificial equipment. First, we feared that with pre-existing equipment, performance would reflect general knowledge rather than comprehension of the instructions. Second, we wished to be able to modify the logic of the equipment functioning. The instructional variables reflect our concern with pictorial rendering of "if..., then..." relationships between actions and states, and the effects of topic-comment division in language. This is because in instructions, temporal and causal relations, presuppositions, and the focussing of attention are particularly important. In addition, the problems of what to do, when to do it, and what will happen become acute when some state-changes are user-caused but others are not. The use of the two tasks is addressed to two issues: Do verbal and performance measures of comprehension reflect different underlying cognitive representations? Does the presence and operation of equipment significantly affect comprehension, either positively by limiting interpretations of graphic ambiguities, or negatively by directing attention away from the instructions? The following description of the equipment, experimental procedure, and results is necessarily summarized.

For more detailed presentation, see Barnard and Marcel (1977).

The Experimental Equipment
Our applied starting point was the English coin-operated telephone, whose operation requires a simple but contingent sequence of actions and outcomes. Therefore the required actions and resultant or preconditional states at the interface of our equipment functionally paralleled those of the pay-phone. The experimental equipment is shown in Figure 1. Table 1 illustrates its required operation and the logical parallels with the telephone.

Instructional Sequences
For the initial study, instructions did not depict all possible outcomes of each action. Only the desired sequence of actions and outcomes were shown. Thus, those outcomes marked with a double asterisk in Table 1 were not shown. Eight pictographic sequences were designed, differing in representation of the equipment and organization of the sequence of picture frames (Figure 2). The variables chosen reflected options open to and used by graphic designers and were also guided by factors known to influence verbal messages.

Part versus Whole Representation of Equipment. Designers sometimes represent the entire equipment in each frame and sometimes only those parts relevant to the current action or state of affairs (e.g., only the telephone

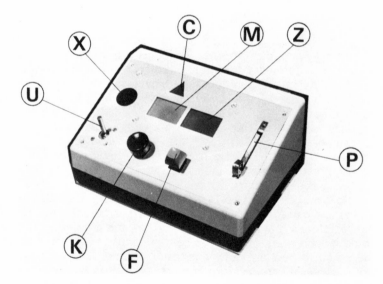

Figure 1. The Experimental Equipment. Subjects in the verbal description task were shown this photograph. The letters were for their use to refer unambiguously to equipment components.

Table 1. The Parallel Operation of the Experimental Equipment
and a Coin Operated Telephone.

Action		Contingent results	
Telephone	Experimental Equipment	Telephone	Experimental Equipment
Lift handset	Move switch U down	(a) dial tone (b) no dial tone*	X lights up X does not light up**
Dial number	Press button K	(a) ringing tone followed by connection & rapid pips (b) ringing tone but no answer* (c) engaged tone* (d) number unobtainable	M lights up followed after 3 sec by M going off and Z lighting up M lights up and stays on - Z does not light up** C lights up** M does not light up**
Insert money	Press button F	rapid pips cease	Z goes off
Speak	Insert card in slot P	(a) called party available (b) called party not available	card goes in card entry blocked**
Replace handset	Move switch U up	terminates call	X goes off

* for any of these contingencies terminate call by replacing receiver
** for any of these contingencies terminate by moving switch U up

dial is shown in Ericsson, 1972). The assumption underlying representation of only the relevant portions of the equipment fascia is that this directs attention and reduces visual search of each frame. The alternative of maintaining full representation throughout might provide more explicit reference and reduce visual search of the equipment. The two pictographic sequences exemplifying this distinction are shown in Figures 2(a) and 2(b). Apart from the representational difference, the sequence structure is the same. Individual frames depict either an action to be performed or a state of the equipment: both sequences start and end with a state frame. These instructions will be referred to as Part or P-S/A and Whole or W-S/A.

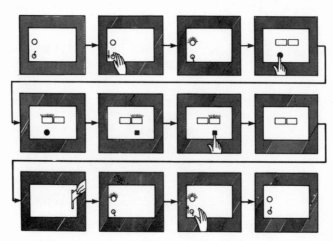

Figure 2. Pictographic instructions. (a) Part (P-S/A).

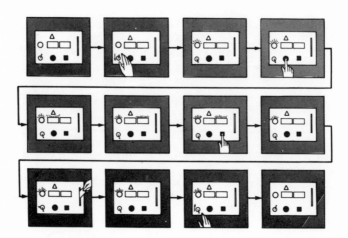

Figure 2 (b). Whole (W-S/A).

Order of State and Action within Sequence Segments. In the context of a sequence, desired states of the equipment can be viewed both as the outcome of the last action and as the precondition for the next action. If a sequence such as that in Figure 2(b) is partitioned into single-action segments (analogous to sentences), the action can precede a state or follow one-- (S_0, A_1, S_1, A_2, S_2 can become A_1S_1, A_2S_2, or S_0A_1, S_1A_2. Such segmentations might be interpreted in terms of states as results of actions, as opposed to preconditions for, actions. Further, they might vary in their compatibility with either perceptual parsing tendencies or peoples' control strategies in using equipment. Figures 2(c) and 2(d) show the first few frames for the Action-State (A-S) and State-Action (S-A) orderings. In these and the remaining instructions the entire equipment is shown in each frame.

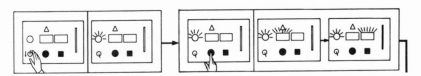

Figure 2(c). Action-State (A-S).

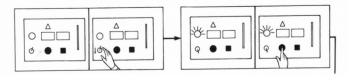

Figure 2(d). State-Action (S-A).

Use of Insets. Insetting a subframe within a larger frame is frequently used to focus attention or provide supportive information. Four pictographic sequences systematically varied relationships between mainframe and subframe information. One factor varied was the assignment of action and state information. Either an action was depicted in the mainframe with the appropriate state in the inset, or vice-versa. The second factor was the position of the inset --either in the top-left or top-right corner of the mainframe.

Figures 2(e) and 2(f). ACTION-state (A-s), left; action-STATE (a-S), right.

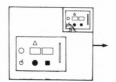 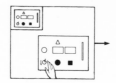

Figures 2(g) and 2(h). STATE-action (S-a), left; state-ACTION (s-A), right.

This of course depended on whether the frame was action-state or state-action. Single frame examples of the four combinations of inset content and location are presented in Figures 2(e), (f), (g) and (h). The abbreviated titles refer to mainframe content in upper case type and inset content in lower case. The order of the two letters indicates whether the inset was at top-left or top-right of the mainframe.

The Two Tasks

Verbal Description. A slide of Figure 1 was displayed to the subjects. Each subject was given one of the eight types of instructions and asked to write a detailed description of what they thought the instructions meant. They were not told precise functions of the equipment, but were informed that the components were switches, buttons, lights, and a slot. They were asked to refer to these components with the letter codes shown on the slide (Figure 1). They were also told that anyone using the device would have some plastic cards, not shown on the slide. They were asked to be sufficiently explicit to enable someone at the other end of a telephone to operate the equipment, and were advised to include both actions to be performed and what happened on the equipment. Twenty women described each instructional sequence.

The Performance Task. The conditions evaluated to date in this task are those which contrast Part versus Whole representation and the order of representing State and Action in sequence segments (Figure 2, sequences (a) to (d)).

After initial briefing by the experimenter, subjects were asked to operate the equipment on the basis of the pictorial instructions alone. The equipment worked as shown in Table 1. The instructions could be consulted on a back-projection device for as long as a special button was depressed; the same instructions were redisplayed at each press. Subjects were required to use their preferred hand both to display the instructions and to carry them out. This permitted recording of when and for how long subjects consulted the instructions.

The equipment was described as a device for carrying out a series of checks (such as those required for entry to a nuclear reactor area). Subjects were told that they could consult the instructions whenever and for as long as they wished. They were told that the instructions showed only the desired sequence of operations and states of the equipment. If at any stage there was a departure from this sequence, which there would be, they were to terminate without proceeding further, by carrying out the terminal action shown in the instructions (moving switch U up).

Since this was an investigation of understanding instructions, there were neither practice trials nor previews of the instructions. There were ten experimental trials and for five of these the equipment was preset to permit completion of the sequence of actions ("GO" trials). There were five different "NO GO" trials, where the equipment failed in each of the ways indicated by double asterisks in Table 1. The first, second, and tenth trials were always GO trials. The order of the intervening seven trials was randomized.

A digital tape recorder registered the time of each action and the start and end of each consultation of the instructions. After the ten trials the instruction slide was switched on permanently and the subject was asked to give a verbal description of what she thought the instructions said, pointing to the picture frames. The whole session was video-recorded. Four groups of fifteen women used each of the instructions.

Results and Discussion
The results can be divided into the more planned and quantitative aspects of the data, and the less planned more qualitative aspects. The former bear upon the evaluation of instructional variables, while the latter, arising from differences between the two tasks, relate more to methodological questions and how subjects use instructions and equipment.

Differences between the Instructional Sequences

Verbal Description. The subjects' descriptions were analyzed by two judges from the viewpoint of whether they would lead to successful operation of the equipment. All misinterpretations and errors were noted. Errors fell into three main classes. 1) Misinterpretations of the graphic representations of components, e.g., calling a switch a button or describing a light illuminating as something emitting a sound. These errors, although of interest, were treated separately since they either arose from our own graphics or would have been disambiguated by the presence of the equipment. 2) Errors of omission, i.e., where what is represented by one or more picture frames is left out. Without exception what was omitted was mention of a state or change of state constituting a precondition or result of an action. 3) Explicit relational misinterpretations, where there was an erroneous sequencing of, or relationship between, actions and contingent states of the equipment. The number of errors appears in Table 2.

In order to classify descriptions as leading to success or failure in operation, two criteria were used. The strict criterion required a faultless description of the sequences of actions and states. Of course graphic misinterpretations were ignored. The lenient criterion was designed to accept those protocols in which potential ambiguities of interpretation would have been resolved correctly by the presence or operation of the equipment, or where certain types of added or omitted information would not have led directly to failure. For example, a subject who omitted that M went off when Z came on (see Figure 1 and Table 1) would have passed the lenient criterion. The percentages of subjects passing the strict and lenient criteria are also presented in Table 2.

The results concerning particular types of errors will be left until later. Since there was substantial agreement in relative success between the strict and lenient criteria, particular points will be discussed later. Concerning the overall effects of type of instructions on success rate, there are three

Table 2. The Number of Omission and Relational Errors and the Percentage of the Subjects Passing the Strict and Lenient Criteria in Verbal Descriptions of the Eight Types of Instructions.

	Instruction Type (see Figure 2)							
	P-S/A	W-S/A	A-S	S-A	s-A	a-S	A-s	S-a
Omission Errors	18	2	7	9	25	16	11	10
Relational Misinterpretations	22	12 ·	6	7	17	8	13	20
Percentage successful (strict)	5	60	65	55	5	40	20	25
Percentage successful (lenient)	55	75	95	70	15	55	35	45

main points. 1) Representing the entire equipment fascia in each frame
led to greater success than showing only the currently relevant parts.
2) Action-State ordering of segments was not reliably better than State-
Action. However when taken together with the orderings in the inset conditions, the Action-State ordering yielded a consistently greater proportion
of success (i.e., AS > SA; As > sA; aS > Sa). 3) Although aS was better than
sA, there were no other reliable differences among the inset sequences.
Therefore those with the same ordering of action and state were combined
(aS and As; sA and Sa) and contrasted with the appropriate non-inset sequences
(A-S; S-A). In both instances the instructions with insets gave rise to less
accurate interpretations. It is also worth nothing that when states were presented in the mainframe, people did better and made fewer omission errors
than when states were presented in the inset.

The Performance Task. The first comparison from the performance data
is the percentage of occasions on which subjects successfully carried out
the instructions. Table 3 shows the overall percentages for the five GO and
five NO GO trials. Also shown are the three fixed GO trials. These permit
comparison both on the first attempt and after nine trials. On NO GO trials
subjects were allowed to repeat the unsuccessful action before terminating.
If they continued or did anything else they were deemed to have failed. It
should be remembered that subjects could err prior to the NO GO point.
Therefore differences in the figures presented here are conservative estimates. NO GO trials are plausibly a more sensitive index of comprehension,
since they reflect the extent to which subjects base each action on the appropriate result of the prior action.

   The largest differences were between instructions showing only parts
of the equipment and those showing the whole fascia in each frame. The
differences are largest on the first trial and on the NO GO trials. Among

Table 3. Percentage of Trials on which Instructions were Successfully
Executed.

Instruction Type	GO TRIALS				NO GO TRIALS
	Trial 1	Trial 2	Trial 10	Across 5 trials	Across 5 trials
P–S/A	20	53	60	47	55
W–S/A	67	73	80	76	83
A–S	73	73	87	77	77
S–A	73	67	87	81	87

Table 4. Mean Duration (sec) of Instruction Inspection prior to First Action.

Instruction Type	Trial	1	2	10
P–S/A		36.0	11.6	5.8
W–S/A		22.0	7.4	3.6
A–S		26.3	6.1	2.5
S–A		25.0	6.6	3.2

those instructions showing the whole fascia, the differences in percentage correct were small. If anything, State-Action had a consistent but nonsignificant advantage.

Table 4 shows the length of time subjects looked at the instructions prior to performing any action on trials 1, 2, and 10. By trial 10 the pre-trial inspection time probably reflects only a check on how to start. The same gross pattern of results as above is apparent in these data. "Part" instructions seem to need more inspection than "Whole." If anything, people initially spend more time looking at the segmented sequences, but finish by looking at them for less time. The first pre-trial inspection times probably consist of people examining the instructions fairly fully. They therefore plausibly reflect differences in the apparentness of the graphic conventions and the ease of following the sequence. On later trials initial inspection is probably confined to confirmation of the nature of the first action to be performed, and therefore is an index more of differences in ease of locating particular significant points which are searched for. If so, it is noteworthy that the least cluttered sequence still demands inspection time at the tenth trial.

Subjects' performance was also analyzed in terms of the time taken from the first to the last action of each trial (Time on Task), which of course includes instruction inspection time. Correctly executed GO trials are the only type of trial which can be compared fairly on this measure. The mean Time on Task in seconds for the four conditions was as follows: Part - 35.3; Whole - 34.3; Action-State - 39.6; State-Action - 33.8. There were no reliable differences found in these data. This may indicate that the instructions are primarily read prior to initial action and in the course of GO trials are referred to only as reminders. The more telling comparison would be between inspection times following specific failures on NO GO trials, since it is then that subjects are forced to question their understanding. However, since these comparisons depend on the relative success rate for each NO GO case, the results with the present numbers of subjects would be inconclusive.

Discussion of the Instructional Variables. To summarize the performance measures, representation of only the relevant parts led to less successful operation of the equipment and longer pre-trial inspection times, particularly on the initial trials. This confirms and extends the results of the Verbal Description task. Among those instructions depicting the whole equipment, segmentation had little effect by itself. The State-Action ordering was slightly more advantageous, the reverse of the order of success in Verbal Descriptions.

The main result of both tasks is that those instructions which show only the relevant parts are more difficult to comprehend and carry out. Although reference to Figures 2(a) and (b) probably yields an impression that Part instructions would be harder to use, it is not easy to say why. Certainly the essential information relevant to each stage of the task is given. There are three possible factors contributing to the Part-Whole difference. First, the visual frame of reference in the Part instructions may be inadequate, making it difficult to identify individual components. Indeed, in the Performance task it was only with these instructions that the error occurred on the first trial of trying to star with button K instead of switch U. However, this will not account for continued errors in performance after the first couple of trials. A second possibility is that depiction of the entire equipment enables people to grasp better the relationship between parts of the equipment and stages of the task. That is, giving the whole frame of reference, in Minsky's (1975) sense of frame, helps people to keep track of where they are in the sequence. This suggestion is supported by the fact that subjects coped more readily on trials involving departures from the instructional sequence when the entire equipment was shown (NO GO trials in Table 3). A third possible factor is that in certain cases ambiguities leading to false inferences were reduced by visual context. In the Verbal Description task an error which appeared frequently (55% of subjects) in the Part instructions, but nowhere else, was saying that card insertion switched on light X. Interestingly, subjects who said this had already said that light X had come on, but had not said (quite correctly) that it had gone off. This error was not made in descriptions of other sequences, which show light X on throughout, nor in the Performance task where likewise the equipment shows X remaining on. Thus frame 10, which was intended to represent a precondition for the action of frame 11 and a contrast with its result shown in frame 12, tends to be interpreted as a result of the prior action in frame 9, unless contextual information prevents the inference.

It is also of note, in this context, that the main effect of the lenient criterion was on the Part instructions, suggesting that these instructions, more than others, have ambiguities which would be resolved by the presence of the equipment.

Finally, it is important to bear in mind that differences in effectiveness of the instructions could well be due to the particular format of the sequences used here. There are other ways of focussing attention than showing only the relevant parts, such as depicting the whole apparatus lightly, but the relevant parts more boldly. Again, omitting frame 10 altogether from the Part sequence might reduce the number of errors. Therefore these results cannot be generalized without adequate testing of other alternatives.

The second variable was that of segmentation and the ordering of Action and State. Although segmentation had little effect overall, there was a tendency for Action-State instructions to yield superior verbal descriptions, a difference which, if anything, was in the opposite direction in the performance task. The smallness of the difference between the results from the two sequences may well be due to the already high level of comprehension produced by representing the entire equipment. The disparities in comprehension are clarified by the errors causing failure in the two tasks. In the Performance task errors due to ignoring the relevant states (i.e., omission errors) were proportionately much more frequent than in the Description task. There was a tendency to "shoot first and ask question later," i.e., to pay more attention to actions than states. This is plausibly curbed by placing State frames on the left, as in State-Action sequences, where subjects encounter them first, in each left-to-right scan for the next action. The "shoot-first" tendency may well reflect a tendency to parse into cause-and-effect. This is substantiated by examination of the post-experiment verbal protocols. A-S sequences resulted overwhelmingly in descriptions of the form "If you press x, then y should happen," while S-A sequences produced more descriptions of the form "Do x. When y occurs, do z." In the unsegmented sequences, providing an unbiased control (which incidentally started with a State frame), 75% of descriptions had sentences of cause-effect (action-state) form. Thus it is arguable that one type of segmentation maps more readily onto a predominant parsing tendency. When people do not have the opportunity to carry out the actions, as in the Verbal Description task, then the greater compatibility of A-S instructions with their cognitive structuring leads to greater accuracy of comprehension.

Although the Inset sequences have not yet been tested in the performance task, two aspects of their verbal description are worth nothing, the differential success of individual sequences, and their poor overall comprehensibility. The superiority of action-state orderings is consistent with the results of the non-inset segmented sequences and may be explained in the same way. The superiority of sequences with states in the main frame is also most probably due to the tendency to ignore states and concentrate on actions. States are more difficult to ignore when they are larger, just as when they are encountered first in segmented sequences. The poor overall performance could be due to the absolute smallness of the insets making it difficult to discern what was depicted within them. But this is unlikely to be the principal reason. Inset sequences produced more relational errors than non-inset sequences, especially reversing the sequence of light F and button Z. This implies that the inset had at least beeen accurately perceived. More probably two other factors are responsible. First, each inset is always one of the logical parts of a contingency. If relative size encourages less attention to be paid to insets, this would result in the contingencies being grasped less well. Second, the left-right relationship of mainframe and inset may not be understood as sequential, since it is not linear and lacks arrows. Indeed, many subjects commented that they could not see the point of the inset frames. Since designers use insets, attention should be paid to the clarity of each use of insets.

In the case of the Verbal Description task, it may well be that relative compatibilities of the structural variables are parallel to effects found in natural language understanding. Thus sentences are easier to understand when the order of their consitituent clauses mirrors the actual order of events (Clark & Clark, 1968). Hence the sentence "When the blue light comes on, turn the knob" would be easier than the sentence "Turn the knob when the blue light comes on." Similarly, one effect of insets within mainframes may be to parallel the way subordinate and main clauses determine the relative importance of sentence parts. Experiments on natural language show that less important constituents may be overlooked in comprehension (Hornby, 1974) and that they are less easy to remember (Johnson, 1970).

How People do the Task

The Level of Representation. The suggestion that people tend to parse pictorial instructions as cause and effect is supported by the most frequent and interesting of all errors, but one which did not occur at all in Verbal Descriptions of the A-S sequence. This error was to reverse the order of light Z coming on and button F being pushed. Frames 4 to 8 show K being pushed, M lit up, M off and Z lit up, F being pushed, Z off. Subjects said that after M comes on, F should be pushed, which illuminates Z. This is especially noteworthy since all subjects followed the convention of left-to-right order denoting temporal sequence. The reason was revealed in the verbal descriptions following the performance task. Subjects said that they thought that something could only happen on the equipment when action was taken. Their assumption was therefore overriding what they saw. This has important implications. The automatic replacement of light M by light Z at the level of the equipment interface was meant to parallel the change from ringing tone to rapid pips on the English pay-phone. However, the rapid pips are usually understood not just as a cue for insertion of money (pressing F here), but as signifying that someone has lifted the handset at the dialed location. Thus in the real world the equivalent of Z is caused by an action, though of someone else. In general, our understanding is not at the level of the proximal or physical stimulus, but at the level of its meaning or function. Winograd (1972) has pointed out that comprehension requires inferences from real-world knowledge and Wason and Johnson-Laird (1972) have shown that people are poor at drawing inferences about terms which lack concrete real-world referents. Concerning the design of instructions, this implies that we need to know our goal and how to get to it, not only at the level of the interface components but also at the level of their function.

Differences between the Tasks. The two task situations seem to have different advantages and disadvantages. When actually using the equipment, people do better in the sense that potential ambiguities in the instructions are resolved by the observable constraints. Relational misinterpretations were proportionately less frequent in performance. For example, no one appeared to understand card insertion as causing light X to illuminate with the Part instructions in performance, since it was visibly alight throughout. This example can be viewed in terms of Olson's (1977) point that written text usually has to be more explicit than utterances because utterances occur in social, conversational, and environmental contexts. It is in this sense that comprehension of surface messages is a context-dependent inferential process, and it is for this reason that it is invalid to assess intelligibility of instructions out of the appropriate context.

On the other hand, when using equipment, people tend to exhibit the "shoot first" tendency described above. Asking people to give a verbal description reduces the preponderance of omission errors and seems to force them to look more carefully at the instructions. But this implies that instructions which are comprehendible when assessed by verbalization are not necessarily useable when people attempt to operate equipment. When using equipment for the first time, people do not necessarily read pictorial instructions in the sense of deriving a consistent semantic representation before acting, which can be referred to on each trial. They often prefer to interact with equipment in a problem-solving manner, interpreting the instructions in the light of their interactions. (Indeed this is Evans' (1968) prescription for successful comprehension and solution of analogy problems.) This account is consistent with some striking observations regarding the Performance task. In many cases people operated the equipment incorrectly, but in almost all cases were correct in their post-performance verbal descriptions, some not even noticing this difference. What is more, many subjects appeared to utilize one principle on one trial, and another on a subsequent trial. The percentage of subjects showing this inconsistency, irrespective of correctness, for each of the instruction types was: Part - 60; Whole - 46; Action-State - 46; State-Action - 40. (This does not reflect learning, since these figures only include correct followed by incorrect interpretation.) It is interesting that some subjects, when asked to describe the instructions after the ten trials, paused and expressed surprise at understanding the instructions for the first time. Others, giving a correct description, did not realise any inconsistency, either within their performance or between their performance and their verbalizations. Subjects thus seem to behave in two distinct modes — one when attempting to carry out instructions, the other when attempting to render the instructions verbally. Possibly the reason is as follows. As with telling a story, verbal description involves a connected output, presumably based on propositional representation. The necessary linking, not only of surface structures but also of underlying semantics, demands systematic monitoring of the sequence of propositions. This will tend to produce internal consistency. Indeed, while written description leaves a record, the verbal representational form itself in speech probably involves a short-term memory, which enables monitoring. When performing actions without verbalization, subjects are freer to behave in a piecemeal fashion. That is, at any moment in the task, all that is logically necessary for the subject is to know the current state of the equipment and the appropriate action. More importantly, when someone is operating equipment, what they seem to do is ask questions of the instructions relevant to each problem as they encounter it, updating their representation of the equipment's operation from trial to trial. "When all else fails, read the instructions" should not be taken as a failure of the user, but as a failure of designers to understand how people perform. The implication is that it is inadequate to approach instruction design from the a priori structure of the task alone. One must find out if there is a consistent set of questions that users have for particular purposes rather than particular pieces of equipment. Instructions should then be designed to meet the questions arising out of the interactions between peoples' representations of their purpose and the particular equipment. We intend to pursue this issue in two ways: first, by giving subjects a richer functional representation of the purpose of the equipment and its components; second, by finding out what questions subjects ask when confronted by equipment for the first time. We hope that not only a truer, but a more effective maxim than that above can be arrived at: "Interactions with instructions guide deductions."

Concluding Comments

It appears that certain graphic variables do have effects on comprehension. These appear to be related to ambiguity of the picture sequence, cognitive predispositions such as notions of cause and effect, and the explicitness of the conventions underlying the sequence structure. However, it is not clear to what extent the results obtained depend on the particular pictorial formats used in this study. Nor is it clear to what extent they are independent of users' beliefs about equipment and its purpose or their strategies of interaction. The effects of graphic variables may only be interpretable in the light of such factors. In answer to an issue raised in the introduction, while the syntax of natural language can be partially divorced from semantics, since parsing can be driven at least in part by bound morphemes and function words, their absence in pictures severely limits picture syntax in the absence of referential knowledge. While the picture components did have reference to the equipment components, what was missing was an understanding of the underlying function of the task which would permit appropriate inferences. The design of pictorial instructions, even more than verbal instructions, needs to be driven by users' existing knowledge of the task. Where they have no such understanding it must be given to them.

We would like to acknowledge the help Patricia Wright has given us in thinking about and writing this paper.

REFERENCES

Arnheim, R. Art and visual perception, Revised edition. Berkeley: University of California Press, 1974.

Barnard, P.J., & Marcel, A.J. A preliminary investigation of factors influencing the interpretation of pictorial instructions for the use of apparatus. In D. Anderson (Ed.), Proceedings of the 8th International Symposium on Human Factors in Telecommunications. Harlow, Essex: Standard Telecommunications Laboratories, Ltd., 1977.

Bower, G.H. Experiments on story understanding and recall. Quarterly Journal of Experimental Psychology, 1976, 28, 511-534.

Broadbent, D.E. Language and ergonomics. Applied Ergonomics, 1977, 8, 15-18.

Cahill, M. Interpretability of graphic symbols as a function of context and experience factors. Journal of Applied Psychology, 1975, 60, 376-380.

Clark, H., & Clark, E. Semantic distinctions and memory for complex sentences. Quarterly Journal of Experimental Psychology, 1968, 20, 129-138.

Deregowski, J. Perception. In H.C. Triandis, W. Lonner, & A. Heron (Eds.), Handbook of cross-cultural psychology, Vol. II: Basic processes. Boston: Allyn and Bacon, 1977.

Design. I've rediscovered hieroglyphics. Editorial article, Design, 1975, 323, November 1975, 48-51.

Easterby, R.S. Perception of symbols for machine displays. Ergonomics, 1970, 13, 149-158.

Ericsson, E.A. Use of pictograms in instructions. In, Proceedings of 6th International Symposium on Human Factors in Telecommunications. Paper VII.2. Swedish Telecommunications Administration, 1972.

Evans, T.G. A program for the solution of a class of geometric analogy intelligence-test questions. In M. Minsky (Ed.), Semantic information processing. Cambridge, MA: M.I.T. Press, 1968.

Frith, U., & Robson, J.E. Perceiving the language of films. Perception, 1975, 4, 97-103.

Gardner, H. The processing of non-linguistic symbols by aphasics. In Proceedings of International Neuropsychology Society European Conference, Oxford, August, 1977.

Gombrich, E.H. The story of art. London: Phaidon, 1950.

Gombrich, E.H. Symbolic images. London: Phaidon, 1972.

Goodman, N. Languages of art: An approach to a theory of symbols. Indianapolis: Bobbs-Merrill, 1968.

Hadler, U. Instructions for use by means of symbols. In Proceedings of 6th International Symposium on Human Factors in Telecommunications. Paper VII.1. Swedish Telecommunications Administration, 1972.

Hornby, P.A. Surface structure and presupposition. Journal of Verbal Learning and Verbal Behavior, 1974, 13, 530-538.

Johnson, R.E. Recall of prose as a function of the structural importance of linguistic units. Journal of Verbal Learning and Verbal Behavior, 1970, 9, 12-20.

Kolers, P.A. Some formal characteristics of pictograms. American Scientist, 1969, 57(3), 348-363.

Mascelli, J. The five C's of cinematography. Hollywood: Cinegrafic Publications, 1965.

Michotte, A. The perception of causality. (Translated by T.R. Miles & E. Miles). London: Methuen, 1963.

Minsky, M. A framework for representing knowledge. In P. Winston (Ed.), The psychology of computer vision. New York: McGraw-Hill, 1975.

Olson, D.R. From utterance to text: The bias of language in speech and writing. Harvard Educational Review, 1977, 47(3), 257-281.

Premack, D. Language in chimpanzees? Science, 1971, 172, 808-822.

Wason, P.C., & Johnson-Laird, P.N. Psychology of reasoning: Structure and content. London: Batsford, 1972.

Winograd, T. Understanding natural language. Cognitive Pyschology, 1972 3, 1-191.

Wright, P. Presenting technical information: A survey of research findings. Instructional Science, 1977, 6, 93-134.

Wright, P., & Barnard, P.J. "Just fill in this form" - A review for designers. Applied Ergonomics, 1975, 6.4, 213-220.

Computer Aided Design of Graphic Symbols

Arthur O. Eger

Using the example of an alphabet, we have tried to develop graphic symbols such that every image looks different, but in fact belongs to the same visual system defined by a specific grid. Symbols were designed for the following referents: direction, telephone, helicopter, tram, bus, man, woman, smoking, post office, telegram, restaurant, currency exchange, gasoline station, and elevator. The design of the graphic symbols is based on the design brief proposed by the International Organization for Standardization.

The ISO proposals are set up according to various principles. The abstract concept "direction" is represented by a conventional symbol (a symbol based on an agreement that must be learned), in this case, an arrow. The concrete concepts are represented by the entire object (a helicopter); part of the object (a telephone receiver representing a telephone); a symbolic representation (a letter representing a post-office).

One wonders if so many principles should be used at the same time. A few examples make the necessity quite clear, however. Neither post offices nor restaurants possess well-known standard forms. Nor do the buildings of gasoline stations all look alike. Therefore, one cannot use a depiction of the entire object in these cases.

We aimed therefore to design graphic symbols:

1) that cannot be wrongly interpreted,

2) that cannot lead to confusion between symbols. For this, not only the difference in form can be used but also the difference in position of the graphic symbol within the framework (Bertin, 1972; Eger, 1973-1975); e.g., the helicopter was placed in the upper part of the design but the tram and bus were placed in the lower part.

3) that are easily seen to be related to each other, or fall into a recognizable family like the characters of an alphabet. We tried to achieve this by basing the graphic symbols on a grid.

4) that are not influenced by fashion, or can be modified if they cannot

519

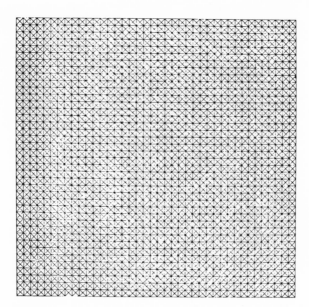

Figure 1. The grid.

meet this requirement. This modification could be achieved by changing
or deleting small details, using the grid as a basis for such modifications.

5) that are very legible. We aimed to do this by accentuating the unique
details of particular referents, giving the symbols taut external forms, avoiding blurred images by abandoning small details.

We do not propose to design "the" system of graphic symbols: we believe
that a number of such systems should be designed, based on the design brief.
We do not believe that standard graphic symbols will ever be in common use.
New techniques will need new graphic symbols and fashion will influence
the symbols.

Design
We decided to utilize a computer for two reasons, first, to allow rapid variation (in form and dimensions) of the graphic symbols, and second, to survey
the consequences of form variations tested in one symbol and to be used in
all the symbols. The grid is depicted in Figure 1. Within the grid a number
of basic elements were programmed. If these basic elements are linked,
they can form both lines and planes.

Figure 2. The basic lines and elements.

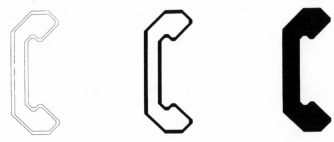

Figure 3. Three forms of a telephone symbol, in outline (left), bold (centre), and filled (right).

Aided by the lines, complicated drawings can be generated, drawings that would not be possible if they were shaded. It is possible to bring these pictures back - shaded - on a different screen (storage display) that does not need memory for drawing. Figure 3 shows examples. The telephone receiver symbol on the left in Figure 3 can be stored on disk or tape, and then brought back as in the centre. With a further small step the symbol on the right can be generated.

The Programs
Using the software of the Graphics Group of the computer center of Delft University of Technology, two design programs were developed to work with the different elements. GRID works with the basic elements, while RASTER works with the basic lines. Both programs work on a refresh display. The only difference between GRID and RASTER is that in RASTER instead of ARCEER the subroutine OUTLYN (outline) is called.

The subroutines ARCEER and OUTLYN are for drawing. They make use of a lightpen, tracking cross, and function keyboard. With the aid of the lightpen the tracking cross can be moved over the screen. The program receives the coordinates of the center of the tracking cross. After the tracking cross is positioned, a programmed action can be carried out, for example, generating a picture segment, shading a rectangle or a triangle, deleting a picture segment.

With the program VORM (form), pictures, designed with GRID or RASTER, can be reproduced or transformed. This program works on a storage display. With a function keyboard or an alphanumeric keyboard, form and size of the grid can be fixed.

Results
Two series of graphic symbols were developed, one using lines alone and one using a combination of lines and planes (Figure 4). Using the grid has a number of consequences. The thickness of the lines in the horizontal and vertical directions differs from that of the slanting lines. It is not possible to use curved lines or lines that slant at an angle other than 45 deg. We tried to exploit the properties of the grid in the designs by accentuating certain forms

and by creating tension in the forms. The differences in the thickness of the lines are shown best in the line version of the graphic symbols. The filled-in version seems to be preferable with respect to legibility and ease of recognition.

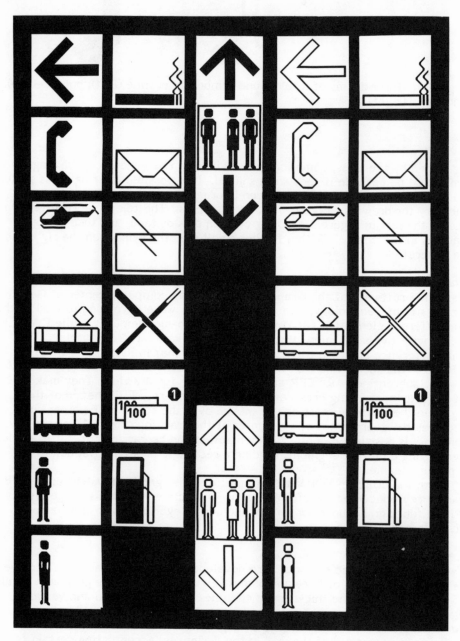

Figure 4. The two series of graphic symbols.

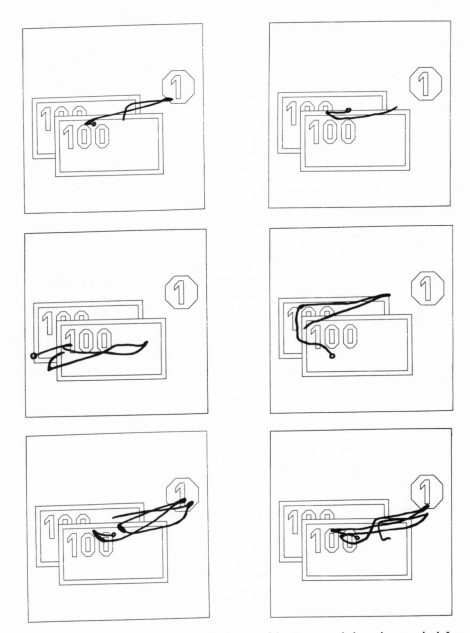

Figure 5. The eye movements of three subjects examining the symbol for currency exchange. The "o" indicates the starting point.

To test the ease of recognition of the graphic symbols and to determine the relative importance of the details, the following experiment was set up. Ten subjects were asked to name the referents of the graphic symbols while their eye movements were measured. Half of the subjects first saw the line version, the other half first saw the filled-in version. It was predicted that the filled-in version of the graphic symbols would be more easily recognizable, with the exception of the symbol for smoking. We also decided that for a small number of subjects such as this, 90% correct answers would define a good graphic symbol.

It was found that, with the exception of the symbol for restaurant, the filled version did not prove to be better than the line version; the line version of the symbol for smoking seems to be better than the filled-in version. Ten symbols can be described as "good," achieving 90-100% correct responses. Two symbols proved very difficult to recognize, those for telegram and elevator. The symbols for gasoline station and money-exchange proved somewhat easier to recognize, but still needed improvement.

For some referents the subjects needed only a quick look, one or two fixations, e.g., for direction, telephone, bus, postoffice. Only the more complicated graphic symbols showed a search pattern. In Figure 5 the eye movements of three subjects with the graphic symbol for currency exchange are compared: a subject who answered correctly twice, a subject who answered incorrectly twice, and a subject who answered correctly - though with hesitation - the first time but incorrectly the second time the symbol was shown.

This illustrates that the search pattern of the subjects did not depend on what sort of answer was given. After an unsuccessful search over the symbol (not resulting in an answer), the subjects often repeated the same search. There often seemed to be a correlation between search pattern and graphic symbol but not between search pattern and the given answer.

We also found that the eye is attracted to striking details (the contact-bow of the tram) rather than always following a systematic search (left to right). If there were no such striking details, the subjects tended to look from top to bottom and from left to right, probably due to reading practice.

REFERENCES

Bertin, J. Semiologie graphique. The Hague: Mouton, 1972.
Eger, A.O. Verkeerssignalering I-VI, Rapporten TH Delft. Tussenafdeling Industriele Vormgeving, Delft, 1973-1975.

Name Index

525

Subject Index

Access Structures, 175, 184
  effect on reading behaviour, 183
  infrequent use of, 176
Acoustic Factors
  in reading, 310, 313
  in spelling patterns, 309
  and stress effect, 323
Algorithms, 124, 248
  specialists' use of, 140
  as substitutes for prose, 147
Alphabetic knowledge
  explicit, 394, 395-397
  implicit, 398-399
Analogies, 399-400
Apparatus, 501
  colour as, 165-167, 479, 488
  computers as, 158, 160, 467, 469, 491, 494
  pictorial instructions and, 501, 502, 508, 515-516
  real time systems in, 451, 452, 454
  See also Display; Equipment
Articulation, 363
  articulatory loop, 355-359, 361, 363, 365
  articulatory suppression, 356, 362, 364
Attention, during a fixation, 38, 39, 42
  See also Fixations
Automaticity, 77, 86, 87

Boek voor PTT, 155, 157
Books, 155
  book lending, 205, 207, 213, 214
  book printing, 153, 157

Cartography, 115, 162-172
  See also Maps; Relief Maps
Cathode Ray Tube, 451, 454-457, 459, 460, 464-465,
    467, 468
  See also Apparatus (computers); Display
Coding: and double negatives, 414, 415, 419-420, 427
  of scrambled instructions, 421
  and a single negative, 424
Cognitive Search Guidance (CSG), 23, 84, 86, 87, 91
Cognitive Structures, 501
Cohesion, of language, 403-406 passim, 409, 410
  See also Language
Constant Ratio Rule, 271, 272
Contents - readers, 205, 213, 215
Context, 19, 501
  and constraint, 344
  information gained from, 343, 345

Cues, 189, 190
  and design 436, 440
  'random-cue', 198
  'relevant-cue', 198
  underlining and, 193, 197
  See also Type

Data Bases, 480, 487-488, 492
  See also Apparatus (computers)
Design, and graphic language, 114, 117, 118
  and computers, 519, 521
  decisive factors in, 139-140
  historical use of, 152
  research in, 156-163
  symbolization in, 144-147
  symmetry in, 153-154
  See also Type
Display, technological: alphanumeric, 459-6
  Cathode Ray Tube, 454-469 passim
  difficulty for user, 448
  and telephone traffic, 452-454
  and Teletext, 479-489 passim
  and Viewdata, 480, 482, 486-488
  See also Apparatus; Cathode Ray Tube
Dyslexia, 16, 228, 229-234
  children with, 358-359

Equipment, use of: communicating instructions for,
    501-517 passim
Eye movement: cognitive processes and, 37-38, 68
  comprehension and, 97-107 passim
  drifts and glissades, 8
  and integration, 67, 72
  progressive and regressive, 12, 19
  and scanning, 23
  in skilled readers, 431
  with spaces in text, 52
  techniques of recording, 184
  triangulated loops in, 81, 86, 87
  and word length, 52
  See also Saccades; Words

Features: audible, 337, 338
  in a distinguishing system, 332, 337-338, 343
  fuzzy, 337
  as a process of detection, 333
  visible, 338
  See also Visibility

535